The C
Struggle f
19

MW01259169

41

The Czecho-Slovak Struggle for Independence, 1914–1920

BRENT MUEGGENBERG

OCT 1 5 2014

OAK LAWN LIBRARY

McFarland & Company, Inc., Publishers
Jefferson, North Carolina

All photographs courtesy of the Czech Legion Project.

LIBRARY OF CONGRESS CATALOGUING-IN-PUBLICATION DATA

Mueggenberg, Brent, 1980–
The Czecho-Slovak struggle for independence, 1914–1920 / Brent
Mueggenberg.
p.   cm.
Includes bibliographical references and index.

ISBN 978-0-7864-9625-9 (softcover : acid free paper) ∞
ISBN 978-1-4766-1762-6 (ebook)

1. Czechoslovakia—History—Autonomy and independence movements.
2. Czechoslovakia—Politics and government—20th century.
3. National liberation movements—Czechoslovakia—History—20th century.
4. Nationalism—Czechoslovakia—History—20th century.
5. World War, 1914–1918—Czechoslovakia.
6. World War, 1914–1918—Influence.   I. Title.
DB2178.7.M84 2014   943.7'024—dc23   2014027045

BRITISH LIBRARY CATALOGUING DATA ARE AVAILABLE

© 2014 Brent Mueggenberg. All rights reserved

*No part of this book may be reproduced or transmitted in any form
or by any means, electronic or mechanical, including photocopying
or recording, or by any information storage and retrieval system,
without permission in writing from the publisher.*

On the cover: With the stars and stripes unfurled above them,
Americans show their support for the Czechoslovak cause in a parade,
in an undated photograph (courtesy of the Czech Legion Project)

Printed in the United States of America

*McFarland & Company, Inc., Publishers
Box 611, Jefferson, North Carolina 28640
www.mcfarlandpub.com*

Acknowledgments

The author would like to express gratitude to the following persons and institutions without whom this book could never have been written: to the excellent staff at the libraries of Iowa State University and Buena Vista University; to John Smith for helping me locate various research materials; to David Nieland for providing me generous access to his private book collection; and to the wonderful staff at McFarland & Company who spent countless hours refining my manuscript. I would also like to extend my appreciation to the men and women serving on the board of The Czech Legion Project, particularly Bruce Bendinger, for permission to reprint the photographs which appear in this book. Last but not least, my mother, Nancy Mueggenberg, deserves special mention for providing me with the encouragement to embark on and finish this project.

Table of Contents

Preface

Nearly a century has passed since an independent Czechoslovak state sprouted into existence during the autumn of 1918. At the time, the news that the Czech and Slovak peoples had finally achieved self-determination, though overshadowed by headlines celebrating the Armistice in France, was greeted with applause throughout the world. The general publics in Western Europe and North America had read in newspapers of how Czecho-Slovak émigrés and prisoners of war fought with their brothers and sons against the Central Powers in France, Italy and Russia, forming "the army without a country." They had been most impressed by the operations of the Czecho-Slovak legionaries in Russia who swept Bolshevik power from Siberia that summer and for a time controlled the strategically-important Trans-Siberian Railway. Among Allied statesmen, the three main Czecho-Slovak exile leaders—Tomáš Masaryk, Edvard Beneš and Milan Štefánik—were held in high esteem as brilliant, trustworthy gentlemen who lacked the eccentric and pretentious baggage typically carried by most nationalist exiles. They also knew that the Czecho-Slovak revolutionaries, in addition to their superb organization of the legions, had waged a long propaganda campaign to help secure support for the Allied cause in their homeland and abroad. As a result of these efforts, in the immediate aftermath of the First World War the Czechs and Slovaks enjoyed a soaring level of prestige among the victorious Allies that was unparalleled by other newly independent peoples.

The young Czechoslovak Republic managed to hold onto its favorable reputation during the interwar period, especially as it proved to be the most durable democracy among the successor states. Nevertheless, Western interest in Czechoslovakia declined steadily from its peak in late 1918. The cause of this can be traced to a number of factors from widespread disillusionment in the Versailles Treaty to isolationism in countries like the United States. The Czechs and Slovaks, along with their neighbors, were partly responsible for marring their image through their failure to live up to the wartime promises made by their revolutionary leaders, namely to cooperate towards peaceful and prosperous regional goals. Instead, a tense atmosphere fomented by nationalist pretensions and competing claims lingered in Central Europe throughout the interwar period and provided additional encouragement for powers like Great Britain and the United States to distance themselves from that area. At the same time, the fragmentation of interwar Central Europe made the region a susceptible target of Nazi aggression.

The trend of growing Western disinterest in Central Europe led to the bitter tragedy in which the Czechs and Slovaks were thrust into the center of the international stage. In September 1938, British, French and Italian statesmen sacrificed the integrity of the Czechoslovak Republic to the territorial ambitions of Nazi Germany, an act that would have been unthinkable two decades earlier. In the Second World War that followed shortly thereafter, another Czechoslovak liberation movement emerged abroad and in the Bohemian homeland. When the fighting ceased, the organization led by the veteran-exile Beneš managed to reestablish an independent Czechoslovakia; however, his accomplishment lacked the international acclaim and optimism inspired by his mentor in 1918. Indeed, in 1948 Beneš's new republic succumbed to a takeover by the Communist Party, confirming the country's position within the Soviet orbit. Subsequently, Western interest in Czechoslovakia ebbed during the Cold War, except during the brief thaw which the country experienced in 1968. When communism finally receded from Czechoslovakia a generation later, that event was cheered by the West but not with any particularly greater enthusiasm than the collapse of the Soviet system elsewhere in Europe.

The Czecho-Slovak struggle for independence during World War I was therefore unique not only for its accomplishments relative to other contemporary national separatist movements, but also for the fame it achieved in contrast to its later reincarnations during World War II and the Cold War. This was partly due to the fact that the impact of that liberation movement was felt far beyond the confines of the Czech and Slovak homelands. Amid the course of their revolutionary activity, the Czecho-Slovak exiles had acquired official statements of recognition and diplomatic statuses from various Allied nations that were withheld from the Poles, Yugoslavs and other national groups. These guarantees helped seal the doom of the Habsburg Empire, the disappearance of which would permanently alter the political map of Europe. Meanwhile, on the opposite end of the Eurasian landmass, the position of the Czecho-Slovak Legion in Russia became a *raison d'être* for the Allied military intervention in Siberia, an event that left a sour legacy on relations between the West and Soviet Russia.

Despite the importance of Czecho-Slovak activities during the First World War, relatively little has been published about the subject in the English language. Much of what has been written has been influenced by the period during which a particular work was published. The era between the two world wars saw probably the greatest number of books released on the subject, especially as the Czechoslovak leaders, various statesmen, military commanders and others published their wartime memoirs. Among the most important of these are Masaryk's memoir, *The Making of a State*, and Beneš's *My War Memoirs*. Besides memoirs and biographies focusing on the activities of the revolutionaries-turned-statesmen, other books presented the adventure of the Czecho-Slovak Legion in Russia, the best of these being Henry Baerlein's *The March of the Seventy Thousand*. Generally, works from this period are laden with admiration for the legionaries and especially for the exile leaders. As a result, they tend to avoid critical assessments of the activities of Czecho-Slovak exiles—except for Masaryk's onetime rival, Josef Dürich—and readily accept a number of émigré propagandists' claims, from supposed abuses perpetrated by the Austrian government to the alleged disloyalty of Czech and Slovak conscripts serving in the Austro-Hungarian Army.

With the onset of the Cold War after World War II, the earlier Czecho-Slovak liberation movement was reexamined from a new angle, especially the campaign of the Czecho-Slovak Legion in Russia. With U.S.–Soviet relations frequently on edge, interest increased in the record of interactions between these two governments, beginning with the American and Allied intervention in Russia's civil war. The most masterful account on this subject is George F. Kennan's two volume *Soviet-American Relations*. While the Czecho-Slovak liberation movement was only a peripheral topic to studies covering the Allied intervention in Siberia, these histories nevertheless provided a fresh viewpoint and evaluation of the fighting between the Czecho-Slovak legionaries and the Bolsheviks that played an integral role in the decision of Allied leaders to land troops in Siberia.

Cold War–era historians writing specifically about Czecho-Slovak affairs in the First World War took a more analytical approach toward their subject than their predecessors in the 1920s and 30s. Two factors contributed to this change. First of all, the deaths of key personalities and their most visible supporters removed the influence which they and their writings had wielded on the topic during the interwar period. Masaryk had died in 1937 and his close confidant, Karel Čapek, a highly-respected writer, outlived him only by nine months. Beneš passed away in 1948 followed by Robert Seton-Watson and Henry Wickham Steed during the following decade. The second factor behind the new approach was the domination of Czechoslovakia by foreign powers, first Germany and then the Soviet Union, since 1938. Given these developments, historians openly considered whether the disappearance of the Habsburg Monarchy in 1918 had indeed left the Czechs, Slovaks and other Central European peoples better off. After all, the totalitarian regimes imposed by Hitler and Stalin were far more murderous and oppressive than the exaggerated atrocities attributed to the Habsburgs in émigré propaganda.[1]

Among those accounts providing a balanced approach to the liberation movements among Austro-Hungarian nationalities are Zbyněk Zeman's *The Break-Up of the Habsburg Empire 1914–1918* and Victor Mamatey's *The United States and East Central Europe 1914– 1918*. Both books address the wartime activities of not only Czecho-Slovak separatists but also of those belonging to other ethnicities in the Habsburg Monarchy. Zeman's book, in particular, shed some much-needed light on the politicians and dissidents who led the struggle for independence from inside Austria-Hungary. The works of Victor Fic, including *The Revolutionary War for Independence and the Russian Question* and *The Bolsheviks and the Czechoslovak Legion*, also provide a mostly objective and detailed analysis of the political and military activities of the Czecho-Slovaks in Russia from 1914 to 1918.

Some Cold War-era historians also presented strong challenges to widely-accepted viewpoints propagated by the exiles and earlier historians. In *The Czechoslovak Legion in Russia 1914–1920*, John Bradley argued that even most Czechs were loyal to the Habsburg Monarchy at the outbreak of the war and that few Czech or Slovak soldiers serving in the Austro-Hungarian Army willingly entered Russian captivity.[2] Josef Kalvoda, in *The Genesis of Czechoslovakia*, took an even more audacious approach by offering a scathing critique of Masaryk's wartime activities while presenting a rather sympathetic portrait of Dürich.[3] At times, Kalvoda even appears to go as far as to fault Masaryk for passing up the earliest opportunity "to strangle the Bolshevik baby in its cradle" by ordering his troops to remain neutral instead of sending them against the newborn Soviet regime in late 1917 and early 1918.[4] Nonetheless, his book is remarkable since it is one of the few studies to examine all three spokes of the Czecho-Slovak liberation movement: the exiles, the legionaries and the domestic resistance.

Only a few English-language books directly covering the Czecho-Slovak liberation movement have been released since the collapse of the Soviet Union and the peaceful dissolution of Czechoslovakia into two separate states. With the Czech and Slovak peoples again basking in democracy and self-determination after nearly a half-century of oppression, the latest generation of historians can optimistically view the independence struggle led by Masaryk as the first leg on the Czechs and Slovaks' long road to freedom. Still, post–Cold

War works follow the pattern set by most before them by concentrating on either the exiles, the legionaries or the domestic dissidents. For example, *The Czechs During World War I* by H. Louis Rees details the activities of the Czech resistance in Austria-Hungary—a neglected topic in the English language. Andrea Orzoff's *The Battle for the Castle*, though focused primarily on political struggles in interwar Czechoslovakia, offers valuable insight into the propaganda machine of Masaryk, Beneš and their allies. Finally, *The Czech and Slovak Legion in Russia and Siberia, 1917–1922* by Joan McGuire Mohr is a fresh survey of the campaign of the Czecho-Slovak legionaries in Russia.

Drawing upon these diverse perspectives that have accumulated over the last century, *The Czecho-Slovak Struggle for Independence, 1914–1920* seeks to present a revealing and modern view of the personalities and events that contributed to the establishment of the First Czechoslovak Republic. Its aim is to enlighten readers on how the Czecho-Slovaks won their independence and why their revolutionary activity had such a profound impact on world events. To avoid the impression that either the exiles, the soldiers or the revolutionaries in Bohemia by themselves engineered the establishment of the Czechoslovak Republic, the book follows the wartime activities of all three groups. It is the author's hope that this ambitious and sometimes complicated approach will ultimately lead to a better understanding of the significance of the early twentieth century Czecho-Slovak liberation movement.

The author has chosen to use the hyphenated "Czecho-Slovak" instead of the amalgamated "Czechoslovak" throughout most of the text. One reason behind this decision is the acknowledgement that the Czechs and Slovaks, despite their similarities, are indeed two separate ethnicities. Moreover, "Czecho-Slovak" was commonly used during the years 1914–1918, in part due to agreements among émigré groups that the Slovaks would be granted some measure of autonomy in the projected state. After October 1918, the "Czechoslovak" form is used since the government of the new state was centralized in Prague, an arrangement which Masaryk showed no inclination to change.

A number of events in the book take place in Russia before that country adopted the Gregorian calendar in February 1918. Prior to then Russia used the old Julian calendar which was thirteen days behind the West. Thus the revolution that deposed the Tsar began on 8 March 1917 according to the Western calendar, but Russian timekeepers recorded the uprising as having started on 23 February 1917. Likewise, the Bolshevik seizure of power occurred on 7–8 November 1917 in the West and 25–26 October 1917 in Russia. All dates in the book are given according to the Western (Gregorian) calendar, but the two events mentioned here are frequently referred to as the February Revolution and October Revolution since that is how they are remembered in Russia.

Finally, a number of cities, towns and rivers in Central and Eastern Europe are known by multiple names, especially in regions where several languages are commonly spoken. For example, the provincial capital of Galicia is L'viv in Ukrainian, Lvov in Russia, Lwów in Polish and Lemberg in German. In these instances I have generally favored the name given by the predominant ethnicity in the region, in this case L'viv. The exceptions to this rule are those proper names which are already familiar to English readers; therefore I have used the German Prague instead of the Czech Praha when referring to the Bohemian capital. I apologize in advance for any confusion that may result from this design.

Terms, Abbreviations
and Acronyms

AEFS (American Expeditionary Force to Siberia): The U.S. forces sent to Siberia during the Allied intervention from summer of 1918–April 1920.

Agrarian Party: Rural-oriented Czech political party with large following.

ARPG (All-Russian Provisional Government): Anti-Bolshevik government established by the Ufa State Conference that lasted from September into November 1918.

AOK (Armee Oberkommando): Austro-Hungarian Army High Command.

Ataman: Cossack chieftain.

Ausgleich: German word for "compromise." In this text *Ausgleich* refers to the 1867 agreement that reorganized the Habsburg Empire into two semi-independent states, Austria and the Kingdom of Hungary, which shared a common ruler, army, foreign policy and finances.

Austro-Slavism: Slav movement professing loyalty to the Habsburg monarchy; often associated with the aim of reorganizing of the monarchy on a federal and democratic basis.

Ballhausplatz: Austro-Hungarian Ministry of Foreign Affairs.

Bohemian National Alliance: Organization of Czech-Americans founded in the United States in the early part of World War I.

Bolshevik Party: Radical faction of the Russian Social Democratic Labor Party led by Vladimir Lenin. In 1918, the party renamed itself the Communist Party.

Cheka: Soviet secret police.

Comando Supremo: Italian Army Supreme Command.

Congress Poland: The Polish Crownlands controlled by the Russian Empire per the terms of the Congress of Vienna (1815) until the Russian Army's retreat from those lands in 1915.

Consulta: Italian Ministry of Foreign Affairs.

Crewe House: Britain's Department of Propaganda in Enemy Countries; formed in 1918 and based in Crewe House in London.

Czech Union: Block of Czech deputies to the Reichsrat formed in November 1916.

Czecho-Slovak National Committee: A Prague-based group consisting of Czech political and non-political notables originally set up in November 1916 to complement the Czech Union. After it fell into inactivity during the summer of 1917, domestic Czech political leaders reformed the Czecho-Slovak National Committee in July 1918 and committed it to the goal of Czechoslovak independence in cooperation with the Czecho-Slovak National Council in Paris.

Czecho-Slovak National Council: Émigré organization headquartered in Paris which led the Czecho-Slovak liberation movement abroad, 1916–1918.

OHL (Oberste Heeresleitung): German Supreme Army Command.

Drang nach Osten: German for *Drive toward the East*, phrase used by Slav nationalists to describe alleged German aggression and colonization of Central and Eastern Europe.

Družina: *Česka Družina* (Czech Company), the Czecho-Slovak battalion formed shortly after the outbreak of World War I that eventually grew into Czecho-Slovak Army Corps in Russia.

Frontoviki: Russian term for world war veterans returned from the front. Many *frontoviki* joined or led the partisan detachments which engaged both sides in the Russian Civil War.

Hrad: Masaryk and Beneš's informal but powerful political organization in postwar Czecho-slovakia. Named after Prague (Hradčany) Castle; the president's residence.

Kappelovtsy: "Kappelites," anti–Bolshevik troops who served with devotion under General V. O. Kappel during the Siberian Whites' winter retreat of 1919–1920.

Kadet Party: Also known as the Constitutional Democratic Party; a center Russian political party.

Komuch: Russian acronym for "the Committee of Members of the Constituent Assembly," an anti–Bolshevik government based in Samara during the summer of 1918.

Kornilovtsy: "Kornilovites," troops who served with devotion under General Lavr Kornilov in the Russian Army and later in the White army in South Russia.

Kulak: Soviet demagogic term for a well-to-do peasant or rural petty bourgeoisie.

Maffie: Underground organization of Czech politicians and leaders formed in Prague during World War I (1915–18).

National Socialist party: Czech party that blended socialist causes with staunch nationalism. This party renamed it itself the Socialist Party in 1918.

Neo-Slavism: Early twentieth-century Pan-Slav movement led by Karel Kramář.

Ober Ost: Supreme Command of German Forces in the East (1914–1918).

Pan-Slavism: A supranational movement that sought the cultural and/or political unification of all Slavic-speaking peoples.

Quai d'Orsay: French Ministry for Foreign Affairs.

Reichsrat: "Imperial Council" or parliament representing all Austrian lands in the Habsburg Monarchy.

Revkom: Bolshevik Revolutionary Committee.

Rada: Ukrainian national parliament.

SCSR: *Svaz Československých Spolků na Rusi* (Association of Czechoslovak Societies in Russia). The league of Czech and Slovak groups responsible for leading the Czecho-Slovak liberation movement in Russia from 1914–1917.

Semenovtsy: "Semenovites," anti–Bolshevik soldiers who served under Ataman Grigorey Semenov.

Sibobduma: All-Siberian Regional Duma (parliament) organized in Tomsk 1917–1918.

Social Democratic Party: European-wide Marxist party. The Social Democrats in Western and Central Europe tended to be more moderate than their counterparts in Russia who were irreconcilably divided between the Menshevik and Bolshevik factions.

Socialist Revolutionary Party (SR): Loosely-organized socialist party popular with the Russian peasants and the largest political party in Russia prior to 1918.

Soviet: Council nominally formed to defend or promote class interests (e.g. workers, soldiers, peasants). When the proper form is used in the text, "Soviet" designates the Petrograd Soviet which operated parallel to the Provisional Government in 1917. Other soviets are paired with the region or municipality to which they claim authority (i.e. "Chelyabinsk Soviet" is the soviet operating out of city of Chelyabinsk).

Slavophilia: A variation of Pan-Slavism with intensely pro–Russian and often anti–Western views. In some cases Slavophile programs were equivalent to Russian domination or imperialistic expansion.

Slovak League: Organization of Slovak-Americans founded in the United States in the early part of World War I.

Sokol: Czech patriotic-gymnastic organization.

Sovnarkom: Russian acronym for the Council (Soviet) of People's Commissars, the leading governing body in Russia under the early Bolshevik regime.

Starets: A wandering monk or self-proclaimed holy man in the Orthodox faith.

State Duma: Parliament in tsarist Russia.

Stavka: Russian Army general headquarters.

Teplushka: Russian freight car outfitted to transport 20–30 troops. Most included a stove and rows of bunks; some also had latrines.

Trakt: The Great Siberian Post Road, an unpaved road between the cities of Tobolsk and Irkutsk which lies parallel to the Trans-Siberian Railway for much of the route.

Tsentrosibir: Central Siberian Soviet executive committee based in Irkutsk in 1918.

Wellington House: British War Propaganda Bureau.

Young Czech Party: Nickname for the National Liberal Party formed in 1874. For most of its existence the Young Czech party was nationalist-oriented with strong appeal to middle-class voters.

Introduction:
A Brawl at Chelyabinsk

As the summer of 1918 approached, nearly three years of war followed by a year of revolutionary turmoil had left the Russian Empire in a state of ruin. The blockade of the country's main ports and conversion of its industries to meet the needs of the army had crippled railway transportation and suppressed overall economic output. It was a vicious circle: thousands of locomotives sat idle on sidings and in train yards in need of repair, but mechanics had no spare parts since the factories, which relied on train-delivered coal and ore, were starved of the materials needed to produce them. The decline in rolling stock was felt throughout the country and by every class. Without the required stocks of coal, grain, textiles and other commodities reaching the cities, factories shut down, unemployment skyrocketed and hunger stalked many city dwellers. Russia's northern industrial centers, including Petrograd and Moscow, were especially hard hit by the scarcity of foodstuffs and were in the process of hemorrhaging their populations as residents left to search for something to eat in rural districts.[1] Those fleeing the cities often found the villages little better off. The peasants, who constituted the vast majority of Russia's population, were frustrated by the lack of the tools they needed to work their fields, the soaring inflation caused by the war and the price-controls which the tsarist regime had imposed on the grain they sold to market. Many had reverted to subsistence farming or distilled their surplus grain. On top of the steep economic decline was the added confusion and chaos caused by millions of uprooted persons scattered throughout Russia's vast lands. Besides foraging urban residents, these included war refugees from the western borderlands, landowners burned out of their manors by rebellious peasants, prisoners of war from the Central Powers, demobilized soldiers trying to return to their homes, and a multitude of foreigners, including troops, military missions and relief workers who were unsure what to make of Russia's new government.

The government in question styled itself as a Soviet Republic, claiming its authority in the name of the toiling masses; in actuality, the levers of power were dominated by a single political party: the Bolsheviks. Under their gifted but ruthless leader, Vladimir Ulianov, better known by his pseudonym Lenin, the Bolsheviks had seized power from the feeble Provisional Government in November 1917. In the following several months, they had embarked on an ambitious project of erasing the last traces of the *ancien régime* while building a new classless utopia that would merge with a worldwide social revolution, the outbreak of which they forecasted to be imminent. Unconcerned by whether they antagonized Russia's nominal allies or enemies, the Bolsheviks called upon workers serving in the armies of other countries to turn their weapons against their monarchs and bourgeoisie leaders, repudiated

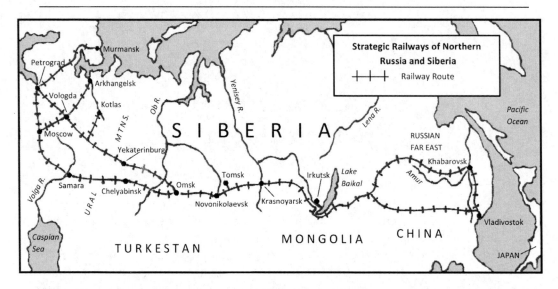

The strategic railways of northern Russia and Siberia in 1918.

Russia's substantial foreign debts and nationalized banks and industries, including foreign-owned enterprises. It was not this open ideological hostility, however, but rather the Soviet government's decision to conclude a separate peace with the Central Powers which earned it the animosity of Russia's former allies. Through the Treaty of Brest-Litovsk, signed on 3 March 1918, the Soviet regime obtained its desired peace but at an obscene cost: a vast arc of territory, starting at Finland, bending west into Poland and ending in the Caucasus Mountains, was effectively surrendered to the Central Powers.

Despite Russia's inglorious exit from the world war, Russian blood continued to be spilled, albeit in smaller quantities than on the former Eastern Front. From the Bolsheviks' first days in power, a series of civil wars began to flare up throughout the lands that had once constituted the empire of the tsars. The opponents differed from one region to another: Bolshevik Russians against anti–Bolshevik Russians, Russians against non–Russians, non–Russians against other non–Russians, and so on. Despite the widespread violence and the virtual anarchy which prevailed in some districts in early 1918, the Bolsheviks had nonetheless managed to cling to the seat of power and had seemingly prevailed against the most threatening of their enemies. That spring, Lenin had even confidently declared, "It can be said with certainty that, in the main, the civil war has ended."[2]

Undoubtedly many of Russia's war-weary and hungry masses hoped that Lenin was correct in his prognosis that the worst of the violence was past. With the winter snows receding, it was the season for optimism: warmer days, favorable growing weather for crops and dreams of replenishing the empty granaries with bountiful yields. Their anticipation, however, was soon to be crushed by a seemingly minor scuffle in a remote train depot.

The setting to this extraordinary incident was the station which straddled the Trans-Siberian Railway a few miles outside of Chelyabinsk, a town on the Siberian side of the low-lying Ural Mountains. On 14 May, a westbound train packed with wandering refugees pulled into the station and came to a halt alongside an idle troop train. The sight of soldiers milling about carriages and depots at that time was not an unusual one as Russian veterans made their way home from the front, and few travelers may have bothered to give the troop train a second glance. The soldiers standing around those railcars were outfitted in the olive-green tunics and visor caps typical of the tsarist army, but a keen eye would have detected something different about them. They might have noticed the absence of shaggy hair or beards among the soldiers, or that their uniforms were worn according to code. Such formal appearances were by then rare among Russian troops. Most telling of all—if the observer was close enough—were the red and white cockades pinned to their caps and uniforms. These, along with the rearing lions featured in the badges sewn to the soldiers' sleeves, were the insignia of Czecho-Slovak legionaries, former POWs from Austria-Hungary who, in an attempt to liberate their homelands, had volunteered to fight on behalf of the Allies. With Russia out of the war, the leadership of the Czecho-Slovak Legion had decided to evacuate that country through the Pacific port of Vladivostok. Thus the legionaries at Chelyabinsk were in the first leg of an epic journey in which their army of approximately 40,000 men was supposed to circumnavigate the globe so that it could serve on the Western Front in France. Needless to say, it was an ambitious plan, one that was, from the legionaries' point of view, in the process of being sabotaged by the constant delays in which the Bolsheviks, without apparent reason, forced their trains to sit idle for days or even weeks.

The warm weather that day enticed the travelers to exit their carriages and bask in the glow of the spring sunshine. Inevitably, they mingled with the legionaries, who soon discovered that the last three railcars of the newly-arrived train were carrying Magyar POWs. Neither the Czechs nor the Slovaks were known to be particularly fond of the Magyars. As a disproportionately powerful nationality in Austria-Hungary, the Magyars had long been resented by the Czechs and especially by the Slovaks, who suffered considerably under the discriminatory policies advocated by the Magyar magnates who effectively ruled Hungary. Yet, none of that traditional animosity was initially apparent among the Czecho-Slovaks or the Magyar prisoners that day. The legionaries, who had retained some of their arms under a delicate agreement with the Soviet government, were under strict orders from their officers not to provoke any incidents with either the Bolsheviks or the war prisoners who, under the terms of the Brest-Litovsk Treaty, were due to be repatriated to the Central Powers. Besides, the majority of the Czecho-Slovaks were familiar with the sometimes appalling conditions inside Russia's POW camps. It was perhaps this knowledge which made them sympathetic enough to lend the underfed Magyar prisoners spare food and cigarettes.

The encounter seemed destined to end on this rather amicable note right up until the refugee and POW train began to lurch out of the station to continue its westward trek. Suddenly, a piece of iron flung from one of the rear railcars struck a Czech soldier and severely wounded him.[3] Enraged, his comrades boarded the train before it had time to gain speed, forced the locomotive to a stop and ordered the prisoners out of the rear railcars. They then demanded to know the person responsible for throwing the projectile, and once the culprit was identified, the legionaries immediately lynched him. In the meantime, a scuffle had broken out between the legionaries and the other POWs, but order was restored by a few armed Bolshevik militiamen arriving on the scene. After the fighting between the Czecho-Slovak troops and Magyar prisoners was quelled, the latter, minus their executed comrade, were allowed to board the refugee train and leave Chelyabinsk.[4]

This ugly but seemingly minor skirmish would not have been of any historical significance if it were not for the reaction of the Chelyabinsk Soviet. Upon learning of the disorder in the railway station, the local soviet, which included a Bolshevized Magyar among its deputies, set up an investigative commission. The commission subsequently subpoenaed ten legionaries to give their testimonies as eyewitnesses, but when these men entered the soviet headquarters in Chelyabinsk on 17 May they were immediately placed under arrest. When the local commander of the legionaries, Lieutenant Colonel Sergey Voitsekhovsky, learned of his soldiers' imprisonment, he dispatched two Czech emissaries from the train station to ask for the release of the innocent men while promising to bring those actually responsible for the lynching to justice. The soviet reacted to this offer by taking one of the messengers hostage while permitting the other to return to his unit. The soviet, it seemed, had drawn its own conclusions on the culpability of the Czecho-Slovaks.

When the spared emissary returned to the Czecho-Slovak trains outside of town and recounted his experience with the soviet, the legionaries were outraged. Lacking confidence in the judgment of revolutionary tribunals and unable to free their incarcerated cadres through peaceful means, they resorted to force. That evening, the Czecho-Slovak troops, approximately 3,000 strong, marched into Chelyabinsk. Since they were lacking rifles due to earlier disarmament agreements, most of the soldiers initially wielded only clubs, sharp objects or any other weapons they could improvise from the tools available to them. Nevertheless, this bold display of strength was enough to subdue the town's Red militia who, like many Russians that were to serve in their country's civil war, preferred to lay down their arms without firing a shot rather than risk their lives in combat. The Czecho-Slovaks effectively took control of the streets, distributed among themselves some 800 rifles seized from an arms depot and were even greeted with an enthusiastic reception by some local bystanders. The soviet, however, was not deposed, and the legionaries explicitly announced that it was not their intention to do so. When their formations assembled before the soviet's headquarters, they merely demanded the release of the eleven Czecho-Slovaks. Having no realistic alternative, the chairman of the soviet consented and set free the imprisoned legionaries. This satisfied the Czecho-Slovaks, who withdrew from the town and returned to the depot bellowing patriotic hymns along the way.[5]

By the next day, the situation in Chelyabinsk appeared to have been returned to normal. The local soviet was in control of the town while in the vicinity of the station were the Czecho-Slovak troops, whose trains remained shunted from the main railway. Yet, relations between the town soviet and the legionaries were changed. The local commissars, who just a day earlier had treated the Czecho-Slovaks in a high-handed manner, were awed by the ease in which the legionaries had cowed their militia and now sought to expedite their evacuation. In a report of the incident cabled to Moscow during the night, the chairman of the Chelyabinsk soviet pleaded with his superiors to allow the legionaries to continue to Vladivostok. "It is absolutely necessary," he warned, "to transfer the Czechs to Siberia; the long delay in the movement of their trains, lasting already for several months, and the uncertainty whether they will be transported at all, could in the end provoke a powerful rebellion."[6] This change of heart impressed the legionaries, and of all the municipal and provincial soviets the Czecho-Slovaks were to encounter, the Chelyabinsk soviet became one of the most accommodating towards their goal of reaching Vladivostok.

While the legionaries' armed demonstration in Chelyabinsk caused the soviet there to adopt a cooperative attitude towards them, it had the opposite effect on the central Soviet leaders in Moscow, particularly the fiery Commissar of War, Leon Trotsky. He, more than anyone else, was personally responsible for the delays and complete stoppages of the eastward movement of the Czecho-Slovaks. He had always opposed the planned evacuation of the Legion from Vladivostok, primarily on his assessment that a sizeable armed outfit of foreigners should not be allowed to concentrate in eastern Siberia, far from the center of Soviet power, where they could ally with the anti–Bolshevik groups already operating there. In March, it was he who had urged that the Legion be completely disarmed and their movement halted, despite Lenin's earlier consent that the Czecho-Slovaks were free to leave for the east. Since then, the Commissar of War had at times moderated his views, but upon receiving news of the legionaries' temporary occupation of Chelyabinsk, Trotsky was outraged.[7] Not only did the Czecho-Slovak action there appear to verify his warnings of the danger that the Legion posed to the Siberian soviets, but he was also determined to punish what he regarded as an affront to Bolshevik sovereignty. Thus both the Czecho-Slovaks and Trotsky grew convinced that a bold demonstration of strength was the solution to the existing impasse. Unless one side displayed a willingness to back down, conflict between the two was inevitable.

The skirmish at Chelyabinsk marked neither the beginning nor finale of the Czecho-Slovak campaign for liberation of their homelands; rather, it helped usher in a new and crucial stage of that struggle. For the legionaries, their subsequent action in Russia would win them fame far beyond what they could have ever hoped to achieve on the Western Front; in a bizarre twist of events their most famous military campaign was to be not against their Austro-Hungarian oppressor but rather against their Soviet host. Their feats would be no small contribution to the independence which their homeland soon attained, but the legionaries were far from alone in working towards that goal.

The legionaries owed much of their superb organization to a group of Czech and Slovak political exiles led by Tomáš Masaryk and his two main accomplices, Edvard Beneš and Milan Štefánik. These men were responsible not only for growing a few regiments of Czech and Slovak volunteers into a seasoned army corps, but also for kindling the intense British and French interest in the Legion. In return, the Legion's valiant record against the Central Powers and later against the Bolsheviks provided Masaryk's émigré organization, the Czecho-Slovak National Council, considerable leverage amid its negotiations with Allied governments for recognition of Czecho-Slovak national aspirations.

By the summer of 1918, the Czecho-Slovak National Council, from its Paris headquarters, was not only coordinating the progress of the legionaries across Siberia, it was also guiding the upsurge of revolutionary ferment in the homelands. In the Viennese Reichsrat, Czech deputies were boldly announcing their desire for national self-determination and wishing defeat upon Austria-Hungary. Meanwhile, Prague became the site for popular street demonstrations against the war and monarchy. News of these rallies soon spread outside of Austria-Hungary and helped to convince Allied statesmen that the majority of Czechs and Slovaks, not just the exiles and legionaries, truly desired their national independence.

Together, the political exiles, the legionaries and the domestic resistance comprised the three branches of the Czecho-Slovak liberation movement during the First World War. It was a movement derived from very humble beginnings and requiring constant improvisation—especially in the summer of 1918 when events precipitated rapidly and the campaign achieved some of its greatest victories. Its success was far from guaranteed at the outbreak of the war or throughout most of the conflict's endurance. Contrary to some assumptions, the dismemberment of the Austro-Hungarian Empire was not originally an Allied objective. To the surprise and occasional frustration of the revolutionaries from Bohemia, it took a heavy dose of driven leadership, impeccable organization, clever propaganda, an unwanted military campaign and some fortunate accidents to finally sell the purported benefits of the

Monarchy's disappearance and their national liberation to Allied statesmen. Even the Czech and Slovak peoples for whom the émigrés claimed to speak needed plenty of convincing that their severance from the Habsburg dynasty was an achievable and a desirable outcome.

The Czech and Slovak peoples were not alone in their revolutionary activity. Numerous other peoples also sought to exploit the crisis of war by launching liberation movements of their own and bargaining with the various belligerents. From the earliest days of hostilities, Polish leaders began agitating for the revival of their state that had been partitioned out of existence at the end of the eighteenth century. Croat and Serb politicians voluntarily went into exile to garner foreign support for the establishment of a Yugoslav state. Finnish and Ukrainian nationalists eager to free their people from tsarist Russia found sympathetic ears in Germany, as did Irish nationalists seeking independence from Great Britain. Jews, Arabs and various Asian peoples also sought to establish independent states of their own, sometimes through cooperation with colonial powers and at other times by rebelling against them. None of these movements, however, attracted the impressive levels of confidence, enthusiasm and official pronouncements which the Czecho-Slovaks had obtained by the autumn of 1918. In nearly all aspects of their struggle, the Czecho-Slovaks had defied their critics, confounded skeptics and exceeded the expectations of their supporters.

After World War I, as various historians and participants looked back on the Czecho-Slovak struggle for independence, each tried to assign explanations for the movement's uncanny success. Many were inclined to attribute the revolution's achievements to the political warfare propagated by the exiles. "Most states have been fashioned by the sword or have grown out of colonization," wrote the historian H. A. L. Fisher, but "Czecho-Slovakia is the child of propaganda."[8] This assessment was, without any doubt, what Masaryk and Beneš wanted their countrymen and foreigners to believe. As longtime president and foreign minister, respectively, of the postwar Czechoslovak Republic, they staked their political careers in the legend that their wartime activities, more than anything else, contributed to the country's establishment. This view was encouraged by media released by their publishing house in the Czechoslovak Ministry of Foreign Affairs which was in many ways a continuation of the propaganda they had generated during the world war.[9] Although their arguments were probably the most widely accepted of those put forward, the controversy over which group— the political exiles, the domestic resistance or the legionaries—could claim to have had the most impact in liberating the country remained heated in interwar Czechoslovakia.

The debate was somewhat superfluous: each branch of the Czecho-Slovak liberation movement was important in its own way; without the exiles, the legionaries or the domestic resistance, it is highly unlikely that the Czech and Slovak peoples would have enjoyed the highly favorable international position that they held in the postwar scene. The Poles, for example, had their own set of esteemed exiles and troops enlisted behind the Allied cause, but the lack of harmony between those advocating for Polish independence abroad and those working towards the same goal in the homeland impeded their liberation movement. The Yugoslav émigrés had plenty of leaders abroad but lacked direct communication with their homeland and had no real army they could call their own.[10] Although both groups managed to set up independent states after the war, neither of the liberation movements came close to matching the achievements of the Czecho-Slovaks. The Czecho-Slovak liberation movement, it will be shown, owed its success not to the pen or the sword but rather to the pen *and* the sword.

Like any subject charged with emotional and political controversy, the Czecho-Slovak struggle for independence, from its inception to its outcome, has been partly enshrouded in myths. To begin, it is necessary to separate the facts from fiction regarding the true status of the Czechs and Slovaks in Austria-Hungary, for to make the blanket statement that they were two of many oppressed nationalities in the Monarchy is simply untrue. Although they pledged allegiance to the same monarch, the Czechs and Slovaks experienced very different levels of rights, representation and prosperity within the empire. To explain how this circumstance developed, and why certain personalities among them decided they must break away from the empire, one must examine the earliest historical experiences of these two fascinating peoples.

1

In the Shadow of White Mountain

The Czechs and Slovaks trace their origins to Slavic tribes who, during the great migrations of the sixth and seventh centuries, burst into Central Europe and settled in the heart of the continent. The lands of Bohemia and Moravia, ringed by mountains and once-impenetrable forests, became the homeland of the Czechs. To the east of Moravia, the ancestors of the Slovaks occupied the southern slopes of the Carpathian Mountains.[1] The geographic position of the Czech and Slovak lands in the center of Europe determined that throughout their history both peoples would be influenced by the divergent cultural, political and religious movements that developed to their east and to their west.

It was not long before such foreign intrusions were felt by the two peoples. Around the turn of the eighth and ninth centuries, the Frankish armies of Charlemagne invaded Bohemia and Moravia, introducing western Christianity as they marched eastward. Before the Roman Church consolidated its hold in the region, however, two missionaries from Constantinople, Constantine (Cyril) and Methodius arrived and preached the Greek rites of Christianity. Ultimately, Roman Catholicism prevailed among the Czechs and Slovaks but the Byzantine missionaries did manage to leave a stamp of eastern and Slavic traditions on the two peoples.[2]

During the region's Christianization and domination by the Franks, several Slavic princes expanded the territories under their administrative control and even challenged their Frankish overlords.[3] The Moravians led this trend, and one Moravian prince, Pribina, became a hero to later Slovak nationalists for building the first Christian church in their homeland.[4] By the end of the ninth century, the Moravians had constructed an impressive empire in Central Europe, but it was not to last. In the year 896, the Magyars, a nomadic steppe people from Central Asia, crossed the Carpathian Mountains and a decade later they destroyed a Moravian army on a battlefield in present day Slovakia. The Great Moravian Empire soon vanished and the Slovak lands would remain under Magyar control for the next millennium as an integral part of the Kingdom of Hungary.[5]

While the Slovaks began a long period of subservience to the Magyars, the Czechs emerged under the Přemyslid dynasty to continue the process of state-building where the Moravians had left off. The best known representative of this dynasty, Wenceslas (Václav), ruled as duke from 921 to 935 and later became the patron saint of the Bohemian lands. Wenceslas and most Přemyslids were careful to avoid the wrath of the powerful East Frank (German) princes and kings to their West by paying them tribute or declaring allegiance to the Holy Roman Emperor.[6] Indeed, although the dynasty was Slavic, it was on the whole

The Czech and Slovak homelands in 1914. Shaded areas indicate the predominantly German-speaking areas in the Bohemian lands.

quite friendly to German influences. In the twelfth and thirteenth centuries, Přemyslid rulers even encouraged German immigration to their Bohemian lands in order to stimulate economic development there.[7] Their policy was successful in that it attracted German farmers, merchants and artisans who introduced skills and methods hitherto unknown to the indigenous Slav population, but it also became a source of lasting tension since the settlers refused to assimilate into the "backward" Slav population of their new homeland.[8]

Although the Bohemian lands were included in the loose confederation that comprised the Holy Roman Empire, the Přemyslids made great progress towards achieving complete independence for their realms, often by playing off one claimant to the elective imperial title against another. This strategy reached its culmination during the reign of Přemysl Otakar I in the early thirteenth century, when he supported the successful imperial candidacy of Friedrich II of Hohenstaufen and received a royal title in return. As a sovereign kingdom, Bohemia from there on was required only to maintain a fragile association with the Holy Roman Empire. In the meantime, Bohemian kings focused their energies on expanding their territories; by the late thirteenth century, they controlled not only the traditional crownlands of Bohemia, Moravia and Silesia, but also Lusatia and Austria. The growing power of the Bohemian kingdom, however, aroused fear and envy among its neighbors. In 1276 and again in 1278, the Holy Roman king and founder of the Habsburg dynasty, Rudolf I, led a coalition against Bohemia's King Přemysl Otakar II. Neither of these engagements was successful for the Bohemians and the latter defeat, at Marchfeld, proved decisive when it claimed the life of their king. Stripped of its Austrian lands as the price of defeat, the Bohemian kingdom slipped into a period of decline and the Přemyslid dynasty itself died out early in the following century.[9]

The fortunes of the Bohemian kingdom recovered when the Crown of St. Wenceslas passed onto the Luxembourg dynasty. The kingdom experienced a golden age during the reign of that dynasty's second king, Charles IV (1346–1378). In 1355, Charles was crowned Holy Roman Emperor in addition to his title of King of Bohemia, and he subsequently made Prague the capital of the empire. Several famous landmarks of the city were constructed or at least begun during his reign: St. Vitus Cathedral, the elegant Charles Bridge over the Vltava River and Charles University, which was one of the first universities to be founded east of the Rhine. Moreover, his own three marriages and the matrimonial unions of his seven children expanded the territory and influence of Bohemia in Central Europe and beyond. After Charles' death, however, turmoil began to build in Bohemia as his son and successor, Wenceslas IV, quarreled with the Roman Catholic Church over the extent of his secular and religious powers in the kingdom. Simultaneously, Wenceslas IV also entered into a long struggle against his younger brother, Sigismund, for the title of Holy Roman Emperor.[10]

In the early years of the fifteenth century, the unrest in Bohemia was aggravated by the emergence of Jan Hus, a religious reformer influenced by the writings of the English theologian John Wycliffe. As dean of the theological faculty at Charles University and a priest at Bethlehem Chapel in Prague, Hus amassed a loyal following among Czechs as he railed against the flagrant corruption of the Catholic clergy. Even King Wenceslas IV lent Hus support as long as it was politically advantageous for him to do so. Although he was condemned as a heretic by the Church, Hus nonetheless accepted an invitation to defend his views before the Council of Constance, which had been convened to unify the Church under one of its three competing popes.[11] Despite a guarantee of safe-conduct from Emperor Sigismund, Hus was arrested immediately upon his arrival in Constance. After an imprisonment lasting several months and a hearing which amounted to little more than a show trial, Hus was convicted of heresy and burned at the stake on 6 July 1415.

Predictably, news of Hus's execution transformed him into a martyr among his followers in Bohemia. It also confirmed to them the veracity of the reformer's allegations of moral decay in the Church and served as a warning that Sigismund, who was in line for the Bohemian throne after Wenceslas's death in 1419, could not be trusted. Thus the Hussite Estates launched a rebellion that at times assumed the forms of a national, social and religious revolution. In response, a papal legation met in April 1420 and declared the first of five crusades that were launched against the Bohemian "heretics" over a span of only fifteen years.[12]

The motley peasant armies which the Hussites mustered during their rebellion hardly seemed adequate against the heavily-armored and better-trained invaders from neighboring German and Hungarian lands. But what the Hussites lacked in equipment and training was more than compensated by the brilliance of their one-eyed commander, Jan Žižka of Trocnov, and a fanatical devotion to their cause. Fighting under banners emblazoned with images of the chalice, the Hussite warriors soundly defeated one crusading army after another. Sharp disagreements, however, existed among the Hussite factions regarding religious doctrines. Although they were able to gloss over these disputes when fighting the foreign enemy, the two main sects, the moderate Utraquists and the radical, egalitarian Táborites, frequently battled each other during the lulls between invasions. Initially, this internecine struggle favored the Táborites thanks to gifted commanders such as Žižka and Prokop the Great, but their role in the rebellion was marginalized after 1434, when they were dealt a crushing defeat by a coalition army of Utraquists and Bohemian Catholics. The elimination of the radical element in the Hussite camp paved the way for negotiations with the Church as neither side was strong enough to settle the dispute by arms alone. In 1436, the two sides agreed to the *Compactata* of Basel in which Bohemia's rulers were bound to uphold religious freedoms for all confessions and classes; in return the Bohemian Estates were obligated to recognize the now aged Sigismund as their king.

Despite this settlement, fighting between Catholics and Hussites continued to flare up in Bohemia throughout the remainder of the fifteenth century. When peace delegations met to settle these conflicts, they invariably returned to the terms of the Basel *Compactata*. During the following century, when the Protestant Reformation sparked a series of religious wars that wrought misery upon a much wider swath of Europe, Bohemia was relatively quiet. Martin Luther, who announced his call for reforms in the Catholic Church in 1517, drew inspiration from Hus and his hero, Wycliffe.

In the meantime, a new dynasty, the Polish Jagiellons, was offered the Bohemian crown. In 1490, King Vladislav of Bohemia was elected by the Hungarian Estates to wear the Crown of St. Stephen, beginning a period lasting four centuries where the Czech and Magyar lands were to be ruled by the same monarch. The endurance of the Jagiellons, however, proved much shorter. In 1526, the heirless King Louis of Bohemia-Hungary died alongside his fleeing soldiers after being routed by the Ottoman Turks at the Battle of Mohács. The vacant thrones were quickly claimed by Ferdinand von Habsburg, a cousin to the fallen king's wife. Eager to find protection from the possible threat of an Ottoman invasion, the Bohemian Estates agreed to elect Ferdinand as their king on the stipulation that the Habsburg rulers would respect the kingdom's "ancient liberties," which meant preserving the authority of the Estates. Ferdinand grudgingly accepted these restrictions, was crowned King of Bohemia and thereby initiated a period of dynastical rule for the Czech lands that would persist into the twentieth century.[13]

The Kingdom of Bohemia flourished after its inclusion into the Habsburg realms, but religious differences once again threatened the peace of the crownlands as new Protestant confessions, Lutheranism and Calvinism, made inroads among a population already divided among Catholics, Jews, Utraquists and radical Hussites, now known as the Bohemian Brethren. Added to this volatile mix were the efforts of the Catholic Habsburg rulers to strengthen royal authority at the expense of the Estates, which caused Bohemian Protestants to fear that their religious liberties, guaranteed by the terms of the *Compactata*, might be violated by Habsburg policies favoring the Counter-Reformation. They were especially alarmed when the Jesuit-educated Archduke Ferdinand was poised to succeed their current king, Mathias, to the Crown of St. Wenceslas. Thus on 22 May 1618 a group of Protestant landowners staged a dramatic break with the dynasty by tossing two of their Catholic opposites out of a window from Prague Castle. Although the victims of this defenestration were saved by a heap of refuse that cushioned their landing, the act still plunged Bohemia into rebellion.

At first, the uprising appeared to be destined for success. During the next year the provinces of Moravia, Silesia and Lower and Upper Lusatia declared their solidarity with the Bohemians and together formed a confederation. In the summer of 1619 a rebel army swept through Austria and camped outside the gates of Vienna for a few weeks. The rebellious provinces also drafted a new constitution for themselves and nominated the Elector of the Palatine, Friedrich V, as their sovereign.[14] The appeal of the new king rested not on his abilities but rather on the foreign allies he might enlist behind the rebels' cause. The Protestant Estates of Bohemia, where Lutherans were the majority, shrewdly calculated that by electing a Calvinist monarch they would receive aid from the Calvinist-dominated Protestant Union of German princes and from the king's father-in-law, King James I of England. These expectations did not pan out. The English king had no desire to meddle in the affairs of Central Europe and the Protestant Union was inclined to regard Friedrich as a usurper to the Bohemian throne.[15] Consequently, the honeymoon between the monarch and his subjects was to be brief as the funds and troops which Friedrich secured for the Bohemian cause were woefully low. The solidarity of the rebels also broke down: the peasants and lower classes, unlike the nobles, felt that they had little to gain by defending Estates' rights; they also resented the presence of the Confederation's unpaid mercenaries who were despoiling the towns and countryside. Meanwhile, as the Calvinists desecrated Catholic shrines and icons in the latter part of 1619, Lutherans and Utraquists who initially supported the uprising were left wondering whether their holy sites might be next.[16]

Compared to the paltry foreign aid sent to the rebels, the rejected Bohemian monarch, Ferdinand II, received valuable aid from scion Habsburg courts in Madrid and Brussels. After he was elected Holy Roman Emperor in August 1619, he could also count on support from Bavaria and Saxony. In autumn of the following year Ferdinand and his allies finally launched an offensive. After bottling a confederate army inside the walls of Plzeň, Bavarian and imperial troops marched onto Prague. On a hill just a few miles west of that city, on 8 November 1620, the opposing sides clashed in the Battle of White Mountain. The rebels were so badly defeated in this engagement that their surviving troops did not even bother to defend the fortified capital against the invaders. Friedrich and his court had barely enough time to escape from Prague as imperial troops were pouring through its western gates. They fled into exile and eventually settled at The Hague in the Netherlands, from where they would continue to make futile attempts to drum up the foreign support they needed to regain their lost crown. Although the rebellion in Bohemia and adjacent provinces died out in the months following the Battle of White Mountain, the fighting which began there continued as the Thirty Years War and wrought similar devastation across Central Europe.[17]

The Battle of White Mountain, and especially its aftermath, later became a focal point for Czech nationalists who depicted the entire rebellion as a contest between the Czech people and German despotism. In their version, it was the Czech nation as a whole that was made to suffer the consequences of defeat as their property was appropriated and the people were forced to choose between accepting Catholicism or exile. The Habsburgs were even said to have replaced the native Czech nobility of Bohemia with Spanish, Italian and German servants of the dynasty. Although there was perhaps a kernel of truth behind some of these tales, the actual course of events appears quite different. First of all, ethnic ideologies counted for little if anything in the rebellion. Czechs and German-Bohemians fought alongside each other on both sides of the conflict and it is worth remembering that the confederation's elected king, Friedrich, was a German.[18] And while the victorious Ferdinand II was ruthless in meting out retribution upon the defeated rebels, their ethnicity was not taken into consideration. He saw himself first and foremost as a defender of the Church and was intolerant of Protestants regardless of their ethnicity. "Better a desert," he supposedly told his uncle's confessor, "than a country full of heretics."[19] The leaders of the rebellion, whether Czech or German, were executed and their heads were impaled above the gates of Prague for the next decade. Protestants, from Utraquists to Calvinists, were forced to either convert to Catholicism or emigrate outside the Bohemian lands. Hundreds of Protestant nobles and even some burghers were stripped of some or all their property; between one-half and two-thirds of Bohemian lands changed hands during this period. While some Bohemian estates were indeed turned over to foreign clients of Ferdinand, the native Catholic Czech and German nobles who remained loyal to the Habsburgs during the revolt were also handsomely rewarded.[20]

Even though Ferdinand's reprisals in the wake of White Mountain did not discriminate against either Czechs or German-Bohemians, it can be said that their aftermath left the Czech people much worse off than their German neighbors. Regardless of the fate of the German-Bohemians, German culture would still thrive in other parts of Europe outside the Emperor's reach. The Czech culture, largely confined to Bohemia and Moravia, did not enjoy this advantage. The forced and voluntarily emigration of many Protestant nobles, burghers and intellectuals deprived the Czechs of many of their political and cultural leaders.[21] The aristocracy was transformed by the influx of foreigners who were easily Germanized amid their desire to maintain social contacts with the Viennese court.[22] As German became the *lingua franca* of the upper classes, the Czech language virtually disappeared from the town and cities and could be heard only in servants' quarters, villages and crop fields.[23] Czech culture also lost its hitherto considerable Protestant influences. The success of the Counter-Reformation practically wiped out the Hussite movement in the Bohemian crownlands. A few radical Czech Hussites, along with other Protestants, did continue to practice their faith after immigrating to Poland and Upper Hungary, where the arrival of the refugees strengthened the Protestant element among the predominantly Catholic Slovaks.[24]

In the aftermath of the failed rebellion, it was only natural for Ferdinand to bring the Bohemian crownlands more firmly under his control. The Crown of St. Wenceslas, which for centuries had been nominally elective, was now rendered a hereditary possession of the Habsburg dynasty.[25] This and other measures dismantled the last of the Estates' "ancient state rights" that were supposed to be respected by terms under which Bohemia entered Habsburg domains in 1526.[26] The loss of Bohemian kingdom's special position in the Habsburg Monarchy meant that it could be subjected to the centralizing reforms of Empress Maria Theresa in the mid-eighteenth century. Under the new code, the administrations of Bohemia, Moravia and Silesia were responsible directly to Vienna, not Prague. The latter city was reduced to mere provincial capital and the Kingdom of Bohemia from then on really existed in name only.

Maria Theresa's son and successor, Joseph II, continued his mother's work of building a strong, modern and centralized government in Vienna. To simplify communication among the expanding bureaucracy, in 1784 he decreed German to be the official language of the empire. This step made him a hero to later German nationalists even though Joseph's intentions were centered on increasing the efficiency of the bureaucracy and had nothing to do with assimilating non–Germans.[27] Nonetheless, the reforms of Maria Theresa and Joseph II decreased the likelihood that the Czechs, while under the Habsburgs, would ever regain their former political power. Hence, the period from the Battle of White Mountain to the end of Joseph II's reign was mourned by later Czech nationalists as a "time of darkness."

The Czech national reawakening was sparked at the end of the eighteen century by the explosion of the revolution in France, which scattered embers of liberal and national ideology across the European continent. Although the Austrian statesmen, under the influence of Count Klemens Metternich, increasingly favored strict censorship to insulate the existing absolutist order from the dangerous ideas seeping out of revolutionary France, the early Czech nationalists were not seriously inconvenienced by the government's meddling. Metternich and his cohorts were most alert to political activism that might lead to revolutionary expressions, but the Czech movement at that time was a long ways from having such aims in mind. The Czech nationalists concerned themselves primarily with revitalizing their people's culture; in any case, their following was so paltry that few authorities bothered to take them very seriously.[28] Among the notable achievements of these early nationalists was the construction of the Bohemian National Museum in Prague, which opened in 1818, and the publication in 1836 of František Palacký's first volume of his sweeping account of Czech history. Palacký rose to become a leading Czech nationalist of the mid-nineteenth century, but like most early Czech nationalists, most of his support came not from the Czech masses but rather from the Bohemian nobility. These unlikely benefactors not only made funding of new projects possible, their influence also helped to convince Austrian authorities to turn a blind eye to some of the more controversial aspects of the Czech national movement.[29]

Why did Bohemian nobles, a substantial number of whom were anational or had foreign origins, bankroll the activities of the early Czech nationalists? Philanthropic feelings provide only a partial answer; a more important consideration for many nobles was Bohemia's lost state rights. While some Czech nationalists desired the reinstatement of these state rights to gain autonomy for the historical crownlands of St. Wenceslas, the Bohemian nobles saw these demands as a means of increasing their own political power, a sort of "feudal nostalgia."[30]

Not all Bohemian aristocrats, however, lent support to the Czech national revival. Many if not most were leery of the liberal and bourgeois connotations implicit in nineteenth-century national movements. Instead, they were more comfortable with a provincial, supranational patriotism known as Bohemism that viewed both the German and Slav population of Bohemia as fundamentally equal. This ideology found enthusiasts among intellectuals in both ethnic groups and formed the principles behind the initial demands made by German-Bohemians and Czech representatives on the St. Wenceslas Committee in the early days of the Revolutions of 1848.[31] However, after the extent of the uprisings elsewhere became known in Prague, the committee made more strident demands with nationalistic tones, thereby arousing suspicions and driving a permanent cleft between the two ethnic groups.[32]

As they went their separate ways, the earlier fraternal spirit between the German-Bohemian and Czech activists was quickly supplanted by irreconcilable passions inflamed by radicals among both peoples. The German-Bohemians sent a delegation to Frankfurt, where representatives from across the German Confederation were meeting, so that they might be included in a unified German national state. Although there were widely opposing views among the assembly as to where the geographical boundaries of the proposed German nation should lay, the most radical delegates desired the inclusion of not only the former lands of the Holy Roman Empire, but also those of the ethnically-diverse Habsburg territories as well. With the exception of a faction that sought an ethnically-pure, "lesser" German state (*Kleindeutschland*), many delegates automatically assumed that the Bohemian lands, once an important component of the Holy Roman Empire, would be incorporated into a Greater Germany.[33] The Czechs, having no desire to join a German national state, boycotted the proceedings in Frankfurt. Palacký, who was invited to attend the assembly, made clear his views that Austria, and not a unified Germany, presented the Czechs with the surest opportunity for freedom and security in Central Europe. "Certainly, if the Austrian state had not existed for ages," he wrote in his open letter, "we should be obliged in the interests of Europe and even of mankind to endeavor to create it as fast as possible."[34]

The Czech historian's Austrian patriotism, if one should call it that, stemmed from his conviction that small states were unviable and obsolete. Without Austria, he feared that the

Czech homeland would inevitably succumb to domination by its stronger neighbors, meaning a German state or Russia. In either case, the Czechs might be faced with the threat of assimilation and a more oppressive regime. Therefore, he found it imperative for Czechs and other small nationalities to reconcile themselves with an existence in a larger polyglot state that under ideal conditions would permit all nationalities equal rights and representation. It was his earnest hope that the crisis of 1848 would impose such liberal and federal reforms in Austria.[35]

In order to emphasize Czech support for Austria and ward off the possibility of Bohemia's inclusion into Germany, Palacký and his supporters convened a Slav Congress in Prague on 2 June 1848. This conference intended to counter the assembly at Frankfurt by galvanizing the Habsburg Slavs behind the dynasty in a movement that was to become known as Austro-Slavism. The Slovenes, like the Czechs, also faced a high risk of being included in a national German state and were eager to follow Palacký's lead, but many Slavs in attendance had other issues on their minds. Most of the Slovak and Croat delegates arrived in Prague as refugees from violent national repression in Hungary, and though they too were willing to support the Habsburgs, they perceived the Magyars, not the Germans, to be the main threat to their national development.[36] Other distractions included mutual distrust among the Slav delegations, especially between the Galician Poles and Ukrainians, and the arrival of Slavs from outside the Monarchy, including anarchists, whose aims were completely antagonistic towards Austro-Slavism. In the ten days over which it met, the 385 delegates of the Slav Congress drafted various and sometimes contradictory resolutions, none of which were passed before the conference was abruptly dissolved after student demonstrations in Prague degenerated into a violent uprising. For five days, poorly-armed Czech students and laborers fought Austrian troops from rooftops and makeshift street barricades. On 17 June, the Czech resistance collapsed after the military commander of Bohemia, Field Marshal Prince Alfred zu Windischgrätz, ordered his heavy artillery to begin shelling the center of Prague. Following his victory, Windischgrätz immediately set up an investigatory commission to uncover the origins of the insurrection. With the field marshal's prodding, the commission quickly blamed the revolt on the congress and alleged that both were part of a Slav conspiracy to dissolve the Monarchy. Not only was this falsification absurd, it was a slap in the face for Palacký and other Czech moderates who faithfully stood by the dynasty and were actually relieved by Windischgrätz's suppression of the radicals who led the uprising. It was an omen of what sort of "rewards" the old order was prepared to dole out if it survived the crucible of 1848.[37]

The Prague uprising ended the dynasty's retreat and began its triumphant march toward restoring order in lands with much more serious insurrections, namely Italy and Hungary. The latter entered the Habsburg dominions in 1526, the same year as Bohemia and under similar conditions that preserved the privileges of Hungarian Estates. Since Hungary never experienced a debacle on par with White Mountain, its state rights remained largely intact into 1848, allowing the aristocracy to continue to wield considerable power inside the kingdom.[38] Yet, despite the feudal character of its institutions, Hungary still contracted the nationalist germ during the first half of the nineteenth century and the result was a movement that intended to ensure Magyar supremacy in the historical crown lands of St. Stephen while preserving the power of the magnates.[39] The leading spokesman of this rapacious form of Magyar nationalism was Lajos Kossuth, who did not allow his own mixed ethnicity to temper his intense chauvinism.[40] Having declared that the historic Kingdom of Hungary belonged solely to the Magyars, Kossuth and his troupe were willing to grant the kingdom's minorities individual rights as Hungarian citizens but refused to extend any guarantee that their languages and customs would be respected. This policy, which aimed to assimilate the minorities, won the Magyars no friends among Hungary's considerable populations of Slovaks, Romanians, Germans, Ukrainians, Croats and Serbs.[41]

The Magyars' original goal in 1848 was to achieve the virtual independence of the kingdom while allowing the Habsburgs to retain the royal title. During the dynasty's dark days at the beginning of the revolution, the court initially consented to the Magyars' demands. However, after the court regained its confidence following the victories of the counterrevolution in Bohemia and Italy, the Habsburgs were determined to bring the Magyars to heel.[42] During this period of uncertainty, a small group of Slovak leaders had fled Upper Hungary to Vienna, where they founded a Slovak national council intent on supporting the dynasty against the Budapest government. Like the Croats in the southern regions of the empire, the Slovaks organized a force of armed volunteers, which many Czechs joined, to liberate their homeland from the Magyars.[43] The Hungarian rebels successfully resisted these and other expeditions launched against them from western areas of the Monarchy, and a year after the outbreak of the insurrection, they completely severed their ties with the Habsburgs by declaring the king deposed and electing Kossuth as their president.[44] Although considerable forces were preparing to move against them, not only from Austria in the west but also from Russia in the east, the Magyars refrained from making any overtures to Hungary's minorities in order to win their support. Instead, they attempted to terrorize the Slovaks and other ethnicities into submission, a policy which spilled blood on a genocidal scale in southern and eastern areas of Hungary.[45] This violence ended only when the Magyars were crushed by the combined military might of Austria and Russia. Through this victory, the Habsburgs and their supporters overwhelmed the last vestige of revolutionary opposition and preserved the pre–1848 integrity of their empire.

The widespread rebellions in 1848 did little to alter the established order in the Habsburg Empire. The crown had a fresh face after the eighteen-year-old Franz Josef ascended to the throne in December, but neither the new emperor nor his ministers were prepared to fulfill any of the promises made by the court in the desperate days of the revolutions. Among the earliest casualties of the reaction was the Kroměříž Constitution, which had been drafted in the Moravian town with the same name. Its sensible provisions were too much for the authorities to stomach and subsequently the moderate and loyal delegates who authored it—among them Palacký—were sent home. Had it been accepted by the government, the constitution's reorganization of administrative divisions along ethnic, instead of provincial, frontiers might have resolved, or at least eased, the turmoil among the nationalities that would cause the government so many headaches in the coming decades.[46]

The liberal aspirations and national grievances that had boiled to the surface during the unrest did not evaporate after the failure of the insurrections; instead they continued to simmer beneath the lid of Habsburg despotism. This was especially true of nationalism. In 1848, national consciousness among many peoples was primarily limited to intellectuals and the upper crust of society. Particularly among the Slavs of the empire, it was far from a mass movement despite the impressive boasts of some national leaders.[47] However, as the middle-class grew and literacy became more common during the latter half of the nineteenth century, nationalism connected to a wider audience, a trend which the Emperor and his entourage could not ignore. The situation was only aggravated by the emergence of the Italian and German nation-states at the expense of Austria. Moreover, the military defeats which Austria experienced during its neighbors' wars of unification were in part blamed by the army's need to maintain a large garrison in Hungary to prevent any outbreak of a rebellion there. Clearly, this state of affairs was unsustainable, and the Emperor soon decided that the Monarchy needed to cultivate support among at least some of its peoples if it was to maintain its Great Power status.

A constitution, approved in 1860, was the first of the Emperor's concessions to his subjects. Among other provisions, it bound the monarch to share some of his power with a Reichsrat that would function as a legislative and crudely representative organ of the empire. Although the inauguration of constitutional government ended the hated absolutism of the previous decade, it still failed to satisfy the hopes of any of the Monarchy's ethnic groups. Subsequently, in his search to put his empire on more sound footing, Franz Josef turned to the Magyars, who had never really accepted the consequences of their defeat in 1849. The result was an agreement between the Emperor and the Magyar ruling elite known as the Ausgleich, or Compromise, of 1867 which resurrected the Kingdom of Hungary and transformed the empire into two semi-independent states sharing only a common ruler, military, foreign policy and finances.[48]

Since the Ausgleich fell short of what was briefly promised to Hungary during the turbulent days of 1848, it was acceptable to the majority of Magyar nationalists only as a milestone on the path towards full independence.[49] The settlement was even more unpopular among other ethnic groups, particularly those Austrian Slavs who had stood behind the dynasty in 1848.[50] Among Czech nationalists, the Ausgleich ignited dreams that they might attain an analogous agreement for the historic Kingdom of Bohemia. To bring this about, they boycotted the Reichsrat and their scheme nearly worked. In 1871, the Austrian Prime Minister, Count Karl Hohenwart, toyed with a solution to appease the disgruntled Czech representatives by recognizing Bohemia's lost state rights. These so-called "Fundamental Articles" were dropped, however, when the plan was confronted with staunch resistance by the German-Bohemians, who rejected the proposals out of the fear of being demoted to the status of an ethnic minority in an administration embracing the Bohemian lands. Their opposition to the Fundamental Articles was even backed by Hungarian leaders who knew that the best means of protecting their exalted position in the Monarchy was to keep Austria in a state of ethnic ferment. That indeed was the result as the frustrated Czechs continued their boycott of the Reichsrat throughout the 1870s. Yet, despite the Czechs' disappointment, the biggest losers of the Ausgleich were the Slovaks and other minorities residing in the historic lands of the Kingdom of Hungary. By granting the Magyars complete control over the kingdom's domestic affairs, the dynasty had effectively abandoned them to Magyar pretensions, which had haunted Hungary's minorities since 1848–49.[51] This new direction would significantly handicap the budding national movements of the Slovaks and other Hungarian minorities.

Despite having recognized minority rights in the Nationalities Law of 1868, Hungary's oligarchy blatantly ignored its provisions as they sought to keep as much political power in Magyar hands as possible.[52] To succeed, the ruling class needed to prevent the non–Magyar nationalities, who collectively comprised over forty percent of Hungary's population, from being properly represented in the kingdom's Diet.[53] The Magyars therefore systematically prevented the cultural and political affairs of the Slovaks and other minorities from graduating beyond a sophomoric level of thought and activity. The only exception was the Croats, who were permitted to retain a limited form of autonomy that included their own provincial assembly in Zagreb. Outside of Croatia-Slavonia, Magyar was the only legal language within the Hungarian kingdom, meaning minority languages, like Slovak, were banned from public spaces—even in counties with a completely non–Magyar population. Cultural organizations and printing presses dedicated to preserving the heritage of ethnic minorities were also shut down by Hungarian authorities.[54] By the end of the nineteenth century, these policies had largely achieved the oligarchy's aims in Upper Hungary where Slovak cultural and political progress had been brought to a virtual standstill.

Traditionally, the few politically active Slovaks had identified with the Slovak National Party, a loose and unstable conglomeration of conservative clericals and democratic liberals. Included in the latter wing were Vavro Šrobár, a one-time student of Czech professor Tomáš Masaryk, and a small group of Slovak intelligentsia who edited the paper *Hlas* (*Voice*).[55] By the eve of World War I, however, three other political trends emerged among Slovaks to challenge the primacy of the National Party. The strongest was a populist movement led by the fiery Roman Catholic priest, Andrej Hlinka, who amassed a dedicated following among Slovak Catholics. Hlinka's political activism not only landed him in trouble with the royal government, it also led to friction with Hungary's Catholic Church hierarchy that more or less supported Budapest's Magyarization policies. Besides Hlinka's party, socialism and an agrarian movement also took root among Slovaks.[56]

The extent of support which any of these political parties could truthfully claim is difficult to gauge since the Slovaks, who comprised about ten percent of Hungary's population, were badly underrepresented in the Diet. After the 1906 elections, for example, they sent seven deputies to Budapest, but this was still less than two percent of the 413 seats in the lower house of the parliament.[57] Worse was yet to come. The new government in Budapest reacted to the flicker of Slovak political consciousness by jailing Šrobár, Hlinka and other leading figures. In the 1910 elections, it practiced even greater interference and subsequently the Slovaks managed to send only three of their own to the Diet.[58] One British observer of those elections in Upper Hungary was appalled by Magyar intimidation tactics of barricading electoral booths with pickets of gendarmes or obstructing the roads which Slovak peasants normally used to reach the towns on election day. Around this time, the Magyars were also keen to prevent the Slovaks from forming a united political front, a feat which they accomplished by paying the organs of Hlinka's clerical party to defame Šrobár and other Slovak liberals as atheists, a word that profoundly tarnished their image among the multitudes of devout Slovak Catholics.[59]

Such political oppression, combined with other assimilation policies directed at Hungary's minorities, compelled many Slovaks to immigrate to other lands, especially the United States, in the latter nineteenth century. This exodus of peoples did not concern the Magyar ruling class since it often meant the removal of the most resourceful, and possibly the most troublesome, element among the minorities. The Magyars therefore experienced little difficulty in keeping the Slovaks confined to the peasant and lower classes of Upper Hungary. Yet, despite the discrimination which they faced in their homeland, the Slovaks were generally considered very loyal to the Habsburg dynasty. This was due in part to their devout Catholicism, a traditional pillar of the dynasty, as well as a belief common to most peasants that it was the landlords and bureaucrats, not the divinely-anointed monarch, who were responsible for their misery. Overall, the national and political immaturity of the Slovaks was rivaled in the Habsburg Monarchy only by the Ukrainians in neighboring Ruthenia.[60]

In contrast to the cultural, political and economic stagnation of the Slovaks in the late nineteenth century, the Czech experience was almost precisely the opposite. The reason for this dissimilarity lay mostly in that fact that no ethnic group in Austria achieved a level of supremacy equivalent to that enjoyed by the Magyars in Hungary. Although the German-Austrians were dominant in the imperial government as well as the administration of most Austrian lands, they, unlike the Magyars, possessed a significant and increasingly liberal middle-class that had no desire to submit to an oligarchic regime.[61] While the German Liberals did not necessarily stand for the equal rights of all ethnic groups, their ostensible advocacy of modern principles was enough to make them suspect to Franz Josef, who was more comfortable dealing with the stubborn but well-bred Magyar landowners than with bourgeoisie representatives from Austria. Subsequently, the Emperor never accorded the German Liberals the extensive power which he had entrusted to the Magyar elite and soon he sought to thwart their political ambitions by playing off the Czechs and other minorities against them.

For the Czechs to be useful in this policy of *divide et imperia*, the Emperor and his ministers needed their representatives to enter the Reichsrat. Since 1867, the Czech National Party had boycotted the parliament in the hope that the Emperor would restore Bohemia's "historical state rights" that were lost in 1620. This strategy, however, was increasingly being challenged by a rising liberal wing of the party known as the Young Czechs. This group lacked their elders' devotion to Bohemia's lost state rights since these would provide the greatest benefit to the Bohemian aristocrats. Instead, they prioritized an active participation in politics and a broadening of franchise. In 1874, the Young Czechs finally broke with the "Old Czechs" and established their own party, the National Liberals.[62] The growing influence of the Young Czechs was aided by the rapid industrialization then occurring in Bohemia and Moravia. Along with this development came the migration of the population from rural locales to urban settings, transforming the cities, once islands of German language and culture, into centers that were predominantly Czech. Both education and incomes increased drastically among Czechs, and so did their national consciousness.[63] As Czech nationalism found genuine mass appeal, its original form that had been conservative in outlook and focused on state rights was replaced with a new movement that emphasized the upward mobility of the Czech lower classes. As they closed the economic gaps that had once left them disadvantaged in the private sector, the Czechs began seeking parity with German-Bohemians in the public service sector. In order to access these lucrative and influential careers, the Czechs realized they needed to give up the fruitless boycott of the Reichsrat and cooperate with the imperial government.[64]

By 1879, the Old Czechs were ready to admit the failure of their boycott and agreed with the new Austrian Prime Minister, Eduard Taaffe, to enter the Reichsrat, thereby ending the reign of the German Liberals. In exchange for their support of Taaffe's government, the Czechs received concessions ranging from an extension of franchise to new language ordinances which permitted the use of Czech in the "outer language" of the bureaucracy.[65]

These concessions compounded the woes of the German-Bohemians. The expanded electorate soon lost them the majority in the Bohemian Diet, which they could not hope to regain unless Austria returned to a stricter curial system. The language ordinance which raised the demand for bilingual public employees also left them at a disadvantage: many Czechs were familiar with their language and German, but far fewer Germans were inclined to learn Czech.[66] Fearing that they might be reduced to an impotent minority in Bohemia, the ethnic Germans boycotted its diet and demanded the administrative division of the province into

Czech and German areas.[67] Though such a division resembled the solution once put forth by Palacký, it was anathema to Czech nationalists who were committed to the "indivisibility" of the lands under the Crown of St. Wenceslas. Any fragmentation of the crownlands, they feared, would harm what they perceived as Bohemia's overall Czech character.

The changing political, social and economic landscape of Bohemia, by kindling pride in Czechs while prompting alarm among German-Bohemians, fueled extreme national passions in both peoples by the last decade of the nineteenth century. Each side had their set of academics and historians who bickered over whether legendary historical figures, such as Charles IV or Joseph II, preferred Czechs or Germans.[68] Public space was viewed as a chess board and was fiercely contested: one side's project to erect a school or monument was resolutely opposed by the other.[69] As the Old Czechs soon learned, compromises to ethnic rivals were detrimental to political careers. By 1890, the Old Czech deputies had moderated their position on Bohemia's state rights to the point where they were lining up behind Taaffe's proposal to carve Bohemia into Czech and German districts. This scheme was intended to woo the German-Bohemians back to the diet in Prague, but it was targeted by the Young Czechs as an unacceptable concession to the German nationalists. Their campaign against the compromise paid off in the next year's parliamentary elections when the Young Czechs sailed to victory to become the leading party among their nationality. Their renewed interest in Bohemia's state rights was now more than ever intended to further Czech autonomy within the Habsburg Monarchy. Upon these developments, the compromise was ultimately rejected by both the Czechs and the Germans, forcing Taaffe to resign his post.[70]

The growing reluctance of either side to give in was also reinforced by the attention which the national question in Bohemia garnered from other parts of the empire. Due to the prosperity and high-level of education attained by the Czechs relative to other Habsburg Slavs, they became role models to the national movements of nearly all Slav minorities in Austria-Hungary. The Czechs were, after all, but one of many Slavic ethnic groups in Austria who were in the throes of a mass national awakening. In the southern areas of the Monarchy, the Slovenes, Croats and Serbs were stirring while in Galicia Ukrainian nationalists were seeking to improve their lot as well. Political activists among these ethnicities eyed Bohemia carefully since any achievements by the Czechs, whether on the basis of "historical" or "natural" rights, might provide them with a roadmap on how to advance their own cause. Likewise, German-Austrian nationalists understood the precedent which Bohemia represented in the Monarchy: any setback of Czech national aims might discourage similar campaigns among other minorities, but if the Czechs were successful the Germans feared they might be demoted to a "subject race," not just in Bohemia, but within the empire at large.[71]

The profound interest with which the rest of the Monarchy followed "the Bohemian question" became evident in April 1897 after the Austrian Prime Minister, Count Casimir Badeni, sought to settle the ongoing dispute by placing the Czech language on an equal footing with German in Bohemia's administration. Upon the announcement of these language ordinances, outraged German-Austrians took to the streets in Bohemia and even in Vienna.[72] In the Reichsrat, German deputies conveyed their disapproval by paralyzing the parliament through obstruction and refused to let up until the ordinances were withdrawn. Badeni's hopes that the deputies' passions would cool after a long summer recess were not realized and he turned in his resignation that autumn. By then nationalists among both Czechs and Germans were haranguing their followers not to shop at stores owned by the other, and in December violent Czech demonstrations in Prague compelled the government to impose martial law there. In the meantime, the ministers in Vienna activated the loophole in Article 14 of the Austrian constitution which allowed them to bypass the parliament and govern by emergency decree.[73] To placate the German-Austrians, the Badeni language ordinances were quietly withdrawn in 1899 without ever having been put into effect. Nonetheless, the shockwaves from the explosive controversy continued to reverberate throughout Austria for years afterward. In the Reichsrat and the provincial diets, obstruction became a favorite tactic among recalcitrant deputies who copied the example set by the German-Austrian deputies in 1897. The government, in turn, grew quite comfortable with resorting to Article 14. These actions, however, undermined the authority of the Reichsrat and impeded the development of responsible representative government in Austria.[74]

Despite the outpouring of extreme national sentiments that were unleashed by the Badeni language ordinances, the imperial government did manage to show that ethnic Germans and Czechs could peacefully coexist in the same province. In 1905, the Moravian Diet approved a settlement which tempered the national competition in provincial elections by dividing itself into three separate houses where the aristocracy, Czechs and Germans were each represented.[75] Because of its success, the Moravian Compromise became a model for similar agreements applied in ethnically-divided areas such as Bukovina and the Tyrol, but it was wrong to believe that such an accord could be reached in neighboring Bohemia, where the contest was simply wrapped in too much emotion and prestige for a rational settlement to be considered by either side. Unlike their Bohemian counterparts, the Moravian Czechs and Germans had few extreme nationalists to contend with.[76] Negotiations for a similar compromise between the Czechs and Germans in Bohemia were encouraged by all of Austria's last peacetime premiers, but none of them had much faith that the talks would lead to any success.[77] Overall, the German-Bohemians clung to their demands for the administrative partitioning of the province along ethnic lines while the Czechs would accept nothing less than linguistic and civic equality within the historic frontiers of the Bohemian lands. In order to give their claims a sense of legitimacy, Czech delegations to the Reichsrat reminded other deputies of Bohemia's lost state rights through a token reference at every opening parliamentary session. With few exceptions, it was a tradition upheld by nearly all Czech parties into 1918.[78]

In the central parliament, no settlement or compromise seemed able to reverse the trend of national polarization. The obstructions and poor behavior which the Reichsrat deputies from liberal middle-class parties had regularly engaged in since 1897 frustrated Franz Josef and his ministers to the point that they felt they had nothing to lose by enfranchising the lower classes.[79] They may have even calculated that the Social Democratic Party, which was popular among the working class, would obscure the national quarrels. After all, socialist dogma was theoretically concerned with class interests and possessed an internationalist outlook: the Marxist ideal of universal socialism envisaged a Europe, indeed a world, unburdened by national borders.[80] Spurred on by the 1905 revolution in Russia and a crisis with Hungary over the language of command in the joint army, Franz Josef decreed universal franchise for all male Austrian subjects over the age of twenty-four, including those in the Bohemian lands. This gamble seemed successful at first: the 1907 parliamentary elections swept the socialist parties into power in the Reichsrat. Among Czechs, the Young Czech Party, which had held political dominance since 1891, was eclipsed by the less nationalistic Social Democrat and Agrarian parties.[81]

Despite the political realignment of the Reichsrat after the adoption of universal male suffrage, the experiment failed to meet the expectations of the Austrian ministers. In the coming years, the parliament was again wreaked with havoc and stalemates as the deputies from lower class parties demonstrated that they were nearly as susceptible to the fragmentary effects of nationalism as their middle-class peers.[82] The existence of national sentiments among working classes should not have been a surprise to anyone observing political movements among Czechs in Bohemia. In 1897, Czech socialists unhappy with the predominately German leadership in the Austrian Social Democratic Party formed an autonomous party of their own. Later, more radical Czech workers went further by founding the Czech National Socialist Party. The rhetoric of this party was especially resentful of German capitalists whose Bohemian firms were perceived as exploiting Czech labor; in this way the national and social questions of Bohemia went hand-in-hand. Before long, the Czech National Socialist Party amassed a dedicated following in districts where ethnic rivalry between the Czechs and Germans was the sharpest.[83]

While universal franchise failed to eradicate ethnic rivalry from Austrian politics, it did reduce the influence of some of the least compromising, most nationalistic parties. Among Czech delegations to the Reichsrat on the eve of the world war, that of the Social Democratic Party was second in size only to the Agrarian Party, which championed rural interests and possessed a broad appeal to both small and large farm operators.[84] Along with the smaller Czech clerical parties, these political parties were steadfastly loyal to the Monarchy and either opposed or had little interest in the notion of Bohemian autonomy.[85] It also bears mentioning that no major Czech political party was overtly disloyal to the dynasty prior to the war. Many, from the highly nationalistic Young Czechs to the tiny Realist Party led by Tomáš Masaryk, were perennial opponents of the government in power, but overall these parties accepted Palacký's premise that the Habsburg Monarchy offered the Czech people the best security against German or Russian oppression. Like the great historian, most Czech parties advocated reforms that would end dualism and reorganize the entire empire—Hungary included—into a federation of autonomous and equal nationalities.[86] Only one Czech political party, the State Right Party, openly advocated the complete independence of the Bohemian lands from the Habsburgs. This party, however, was limited to a radical fringe of Czech politics: it occupied only four of the 108 seats held by Czech deputies in the Reichsrat on the eve of the war. By comparison, the more mainstream Agrarians sent 36 deputies there while the Social Democrats held 26 seats.[87]

Although the Czechs were on the whole loyal to the Monarchy, it could be said that they were not enthusiastic patriots of the dynasty. They could not escape the feeling that Austrian authorities were biased towards ethnic Germans in any dispute. They also hated the dualist system, not only because they felt that the Kingdom of Bohemia deserved the same autonomous status as Hungary, but also because it abandoned their ethnic kin, the Slovaks, to the assimilation policies of the Magyar elite. Indeed, the plight of their Slovak neighbors served as an ever-present reminder for Czechs of the high stakes behind ethnic rivalries. Thus the Czechs searched for ways to initiate reforms that would mold the Monarchy into their own ideal. Some of these ideas, as we will see, were incompatible or impractical. Moreover, a few of these misguided notions and conflicting schemes would raise another set of obstacles when a handful of Czechs and Slovaks finally did begin seeking more workable solutions to their people's predicament.

2

On the Eve of the Storm

By the twentieth century, the polyglot Austro-Hungarian Empire appeared to be an anachronism on the map of Europe. While the diverse peoples of the Monarchy were linked together by the Habsburg dynasty, the relatively homogenous populations of the surrounding states were bound by a common language or national identity. To the south and east of the empire's borders were the kingdoms of Serbia and Romania, both of whom could potentially attract the loyalties of the ethnic Serb and Romanian populations inside the empire. The same could be said for Italy, on Austria's southwestern border, and the Italian populations living within the Monarchy. To the northwest was the most robust nation in continental Europe, Germany. Although Berlin was allied to Vienna, the prospect of a Greater Germany (*Grössdeutschland*) that might encompass all the former lands of the Holy Roman Empire continued to entrance Pan-German radicals in Austria. Finally, the refractory national movements in the Habsburg Empire itself seemed to foreshadow the end of the Dual Monarchy. With constant tension between the Czechs and German-Bohemians, the Galician Poles and the Ukrainians, and the Magyars and Romanians, it is not surprising that some contemporary observers thought that the Monarchy's expiration date was near.[1] Still, Austro-Hungarian leaders, as well as many representatives of the nationalities, were unwilling to accept the notion that the empire had outlived its usefulness. Most believed that the Habsburg Empire could serve a purpose, although they encountered difficulty in defining or agreeing on what that purpose was or should be. Nearly all were unanimous that some type of reform was needed to assure its survival in the twentieth century, but ideas as to what form these changes might take varied widely.

Hardly anyone expected that the necessary reforms would occur under the reign of Franz Josef. In 1908, the aging Emperor celebrated his sixtieth year on the throne, and while he was revered by most of his subjects, his resistance to change was widely known.[2] The same could not be said for his nephew and heir, the Archduke Franz Ferdinand, who clearly foresaw the need to reorganize the Monarchy on a sounder basis. What the Archduke viewed as his desired objective, however, was less obvious. He was prejudiced against several groups, including Jews and Italians, and was best known for his intense hatred of the Magyars. Influenced by an advisory circle which included conservative Czechs, Croats and Romanians, he became convinced of the need to thwart the disproportionate power which the Magyars had wielded in the Monarchy since 1867.[3] The rumors that he was prepared to end dualism were probably true, but the claims that he desired a trialist solution by raising an autonomous state of South Slavs or that he later favored federalist reforms do not fit his character. To the end of his life he remained attached to autocratic and centralist principles. Indeed, he hated the liberal middle-classes almost as much as he despised the Magyars.[4] Nevertheless, Franz Ferdinand's enmity towards the Magyars won him the affection of some Hungarian minorities. For example, to Milan Hodža, one of the rare Slovak deputies in the Hungarian Diet after 1906, the Archduke represented a beacon of hope for Slovaks seeking a reprieve from the Magyars' chauvinist policies. Hodža, along with the Romanian deputy Iuliu Maniu, forged important links with the heir-apparent and even submitted a plan to his court where the Archduke, upon his ascension, would avoid the entrapment of taking the oath to the Hungarian constitution and instead ram through reforms in Hungary's political system that would directly benefit the kingdom's non–Magyar ethnic groups.[5]

The Czechs too desired to reduce Magyar power in the Monarchy, but their leaders were less inclined to line up behind the heir apparent. Instead, many hoped that the Czech cause might obtain foreign backing, just as some ardent German nationalists in Bohemia yearned for their ethnic kin in the neighboring Reich to offer them a few words of encouragement. Since Palacký's time, some Czech leaders had looked to the French, who typically shared the Czechs' anti–German biases and were seen as purveyors of liberal, national and revolutionary thought.[6] After France's humiliating defeat by Prussian-led Germany in 1871, however, that country was in no position to exert pressure deep in Central Europe. Forced to look elsewhere, many Czech leaders turned to Pan-Slavism as a means of attracting support from outside the Monarchy. This movement was founded on the idea that all Slavs truly belonged to one nation and were separated by only minor differences in dialects, creed and geography. Although its origins lay with Lutheran Slovak writers in the early nineteenth century, it found more lasting support among Czech nationalists.[7]

Throughout its history, Pan-Slavism underwent several mutations. The Austro-Slavism which Palacký marketed at the Prague congress in 1848 was really a form of Pan-Slavism limited to the Slav ethnicities of the Habsburg Monarchy. Its appeal rested mainly in numbers: the various Slav ethnicities of the empire were by themselves too weak to seriously oppose the whims of the ethnic Germans and Magyars, but by coming together, they could speak more forcefully and from a stronger position. As we have seen, the congress was abruptly adjourned after the uprising in Prague; that, along with the general failure of the Revolutions of 1848, caused Pan-Slav enthusiasm to subside in the following years. The movement, however, experienced a revival after the 1867 Ausgleich prompted fears among Habsburg Slavs that the empire would be effectively divided between Germans and Magyars. That year, a second Pan-Slav congress was called into session in Moscow. Palacký again led the Czech delegation and he hoped that the presence of the congress in the heart of the tsarist empire, along with the active participation of a Russian delegation, would give the impression that Russia was concerned for the welfare of the Habsburg Slavs. This congress, however, was even less successful than the one held in Prague twenty years earlier. The Poles, with the Russians' brutal suppression of the 1863 rebellion in Congress Poland[8] fresh in their memory, were conspicuously absent from the assembly. The smaller Slav nationalities that did attend were soon horrified when the Russian delegation explained their concept of Pan-Slavism: that all Slavs should conform to the Russian language and church. The Russian Slavophiles extolled the virtues of their country's rural communes and declared Orthodoxy as the only true Christian faith since it, unlike Catholicism or Protestantism, was uncorrupted by classical and modern influences. Their Pan-Slavism was really a program of Russification. The 1867 congress, therefore, did nothing to bring the Slav ethnicities closer together. Nor did it give the impression that the Russian government had any interest in becoming a protector of Slavs outside its empire since the Russian delegation at the congress attended as private individuals and represented no one but themselves.[9]

The Russian Slavophiles were typically members of that country's tiny intelligentsia who were squeezed in a limbo between the ruling class and the mass of peasants, both of whom were inclined to look upon them with suspicion.[10] Although the Russian government and court at times showed concern for other Slavs, especially those belonging to the Orthodox faith, they were leery of the liberal principles which infiltrated most versions of Pan-Slavism.[11] The tsars could also not overlook the fact that a movement promoting the equality of all Slav ethnicities might be disruptive to the existing order of their empire, which included millions of Slavs—Poles, Belarusians and Ukrainians—who were stifled politically and threatened culturally by Russification policies.[12] Ultimately, the tsarist authorities were unwilling to lend the Slavophiles their unqualified backing; their interest was limited to how the movement might be exploited to advance Russian aims in Central Europe and the Balkans.[13] Meanwhile, among the lower classes, the Slavophiles found even less support. Prior to World War I, the vast majority of Russians belonged to the peasant class that had been unchained from the bondage of serfdom in only 1861. Most were illiterate and lived as they had for centuries in a world dictated by village communes, alcohol, superstition and seasonal work. At the end of the nineteenth century, as Russia entered a period of rapid industrialization, waves of peasants began flooding the larger cities to find work. There they found wretched working environments and intolerable living conditions in the slums.[14] Generally, the Russian lower classes neither understood nor cared for matters of foreign policy. For them, social questions were a far more pressing matter as the peasants and workers desired to be rid of landowners and factory owners, respectively, who were perceived as exploiting their labor.

Despite the failures of the 1848 and 1867 congresses, Pan-Slavism never quite dissipated among the Czech people and surprisingly the movement experienced a revival in the decade prior to the outbreak of the First World War. International events at the time factored into this resurgence. In 1893, Russia signed a military entente with republican France, forming a significant counterweight to the existing alliance between Germany and Austria-Hungary. Twelve years later, revolution erupted in the Russian Empire and forced Tsar Nicholas II to grant a constitution and a parliament, the State Duma. To some Pan-Slavs, the French alliance and more liberal regime raised the possibility that Russia might be destined to guide the Slav nations towards equality and freedom after all. Other occurrences, such as the Moroccan crisis of 1905 and the Anglo-Russian Entente of 1907 pointed to the need of a greater understanding with Russia if the Slavs of Austria-Hungary were to avoid taking up arms against their eastern cousins. War seemed more likely not only with the Russians, but with the Serbs as well. In 1903, a brutal regicide in the Serbia brought the Karadjordević dynasty to power and set the kingdom on an aggressive course to unite all Serbs, including those in Austria-Hungary, under its scepter.[15] Amid these worsening relations, Pan-Slavs in the Monarchy saw it as their duty to ward off war with the neighboring Slav states.

The spokesman for this new twentieth century form of Pan-Slavism was Karel Kramář, a lawyer whose name was recognized throughout the Bohemian lands as the seasoned leader of the Young Czech Party. His Russophilism defined more than just his career; it was also a lifestyle as he had married the daughter of a wealthy Moscow industrialist and vacationed regularly at her family's villa in the Crimea.[16] Yet, it was only after his political career peaked that Kramář turned to Pan-Slavism. Prior to 1907, he reveled in the supremacy which his party had enjoyed in Czech politics since 1891. He even aspired to become the Austro-

Hungarian Minister of Foreign Affairs and use that office to reorient the Monarchy's diplomacy away from Germany and towards Russia.[17] This ambition, along with his entire political fortunes, experienced a major setback when Austria held its first parliamentary elections under universal male suffrage. In those electoral returns, the Young Czech Party lost nearly two-thirds of its seats in the Reichsrat.[18] Disillusioned and perhaps most of all afraid that the sun was setting on his party, Kramář sought to reinvent himself in order to maintain his relevancy in the new era of Czech politics. The result was an updated version of Pan-Slavism rebranded as Neo-Slavism. Its aim was to establish an international committee composed of Slav politicians and bureaucrats who would guide their countries' foreign policies away from confrontation with one another.[19]

Kramář kicked off his movement by summoning—with the approval of Austrian authorities—Slav representatives to Prague for a new congress. The assembly met in July 1908, sixty-years and one month after the first Pan-Slav congress had convened there. It brought together an array of distinguished individuals, including deputies not only from the Austrian Reichsrat, but also from the Russian State Duma. Unlike the 1867 congress, both Polish and Russian delegations were in attendance, and their presence seemed to signify an impending rapprochement between two peoples who long regarded each other as natural enemies. If the Poles and Russians could set aside their ancient grievances, there seemed to be no reason why the Poles and Ukrainians, the Serbs and Croats, or the Serbs and Bulgarians could not do the same.[20]

Despite the appearance of Slav solidarity at the congress, there were some notable absentees. Ukrainian representatives had boycotted the congress due to the attendance of the Poles and Russians, whom they regarded as their oppressors, and subsequently their interests were ignored. The Slovaks too were also unrepresented, even though 1908 marked the beginning of regular contact between Czech and Slovak national leaders.[21] The absence of these ethnicities, however, did not trouble the assembled delegations. When it was all over, they had succeeded in accomplishing one of the congress's goals of electing an international Slav committee, with Kramář as an honorary chairman, and designated that a future Pan-Slav congress was to be held in the Bulgarian capital of Sofia two years later.[22]

The optimistic outlook of the Pan-Slavs following the Prague congress did not last long. Later that year, two developments, both originating with St. Petersburg, shattered their faith in the new direction of Russian politics. The first was the decision of the tsarist regime to intensify its Russification policies in Congress Poland as part of a wider reaction stemming from the 1905 Revolution. Alongside the crackdown against the nationalities, the government sent Cossack punitive expeditions into the countryside and manipulated electoral laws in order to maintain only a figment of democracy. This display of intractability repelled the autocracy's would-be supporters inside and outside of Russia. The moderate opposition inside the country, whether they were ethnic minorities eager for autonomy or liberals seeking more democratic freedoms, was now driven into the arms of the extremists.[23] Meanwhile, foreign Slavs deduced that regardless of the reassurances offered by the Russian Pan-Slav delegations, post-revolutionary Russia was not a messianic liberator.

The second event which revealed the tsarist government's complete disinterest in Pan-Slav ideals began earlier that year as a proposal from the Russian Foreign Minister, Aleksandr Izvolsky, to his Austro-Hungarian counterpart, Count Alois von Aehrenthal. Desperate to salvage some of Russia's lost prestige after the twin embarrassments of defeat in the Russo-Japanese War and the 1905 Revolution, Izvolsky hoped to score a diplomatic triumph that would revise a stipulation which closed the internationally-controlled Black Sea Straits to all foreign warships. Hoping to buy Vienna's support for such a revision, Izvolsky suggested that Russia was prepared to allow Austria-Hungary to formally annex the Turkish provinces of Bosnia and Herzegovina, which had been policed by Monarchy since 1878. Aehrenthal, as Izvolsky had calculated, was eager to seize the provinces since he believed their retention would deal a fatal blow to dreams of Pan-Serbs in Belgrade who claimed the provinces on historic and nationalist grounds.

On 6 October 1908, three weeks after the two foreign ministers met secretly to discuss the proposals, Franz Josef announced the annexation of Bosnia-Herzegovina into his empire. Izvolsky, who had just arrived in Paris after a vacation in Bavaria, was outraged since as of yet he had no guarantee from Britain or France that a revision concerning the straits would even take place. Ultimately, neither of Russia's entente partners welcomed the idea of a Straits revision, leaving Izvolsky to return to St. Petersburg empty-handed. In the meantime, the Russian Foreign Minister accused Aehrenthal of negotiating in bad faith, and the Austro-Hungarian statesman responded in kind. From the crisis emerged the threat of war as Serbia regarded the Monarchy's annexation of the neighboring provinces as a hostile act and mobilized its army; Vienna also began calling up its troops and Europe held its breath and waited to see what Russia would do. Although Russian officials and the court sympathized with the Serbs, the Tsar and his ministers knew that the country could not risk war so soon after the losses suffered in the Russo-Japanese War and 1905 Revolution. Nor were Britain and France eager to stand by Russia and risk a conflict over two impoverished Balkan provinces. Thus, in March 1909, St. Petersburg recognized Austria-Hungary's annexation of Bosnia-Herzegovina and counseled Belgrade to do the same.

The Bosnian crisis revealed once for all that Russia's motivation to support other Slavs was anything but altruistic. As long as the prospect of revising the Straits convention remained alive, Izvolsky showed no concern for the aspirations of the Slavs of Bosnia-Herzegovina. Only when they realized that Russia would not get its end of the bargain did the tsarist government discover its affection for Serbia.[24] Nonetheless, Pan-Slav ideals continued to have traction among Austrian Slavs. Their deputies in the Reichsrat, including those of the Czechs, voted in favor of the annexations as a means of strengthening the Slav element in the Habsburg Monarchy. Unlike their representatives, however, the Czech public took a negative view of the annexations, especially when the Pan-Slavic nightmare of war with Russia and Serbia seemed imminent. This was apparent in December 1908 when crowds of demonstrators marred the Prague celebrations of Franz Josef's diamond jubilee with jeers of "Long live Serbia!" The disturbances were so bad that nervous Austrian authorities imposed martial law on the Bohemian capital for twelve days.[25]

It would be wrong, however, to infer that the Czech response in the Bosnian crisis is completely attributable to Pan-Slav sentiment. Certain working districts of Prague had long been saturated with anti-military propaganda generated by the Czech National Socialist Party, which may explain some of the unrest when war loomed in December 1908. The Czechs also had an economic interest to desire peace: Russia and the Balkan countries were becoming important export markets for emerging Czech industries. Any conflict with either Russia or Serbia was certain to disrupt these trade outlets.[26]

While Pan-Slavism was compatible with the economic interests and peaceful desires of the Czechs and many other Slavs, it never became the primary guiding principle of those peoples. Nationalism, in particular, would always take precedence over Pan-Slavism. This was evident by the time that the 1910 Pan-Slav congress was held in Sofia: the Poles, frustrated by the continued assimilation policies of the tsarist government, had severed their ties with the Pan-Slav movement. Little of the optimism seen at the Prague congress two years earlier was echoed in Sofia.[27] The Bosnian crisis and other events since 1908 demonstrated that the movement had no practical means of attaining its goal of warding off bloodshed between Slavs ruled by different monarchs. This deficiency was of no surprise to one of the Czechs' most prominent thinkers, Tomáš Garrigue Masaryk, who never had much faith in Pan-Slav ideals.

Born into humble surroundings in Moravia in 1850, Masaryk was a complex individual in both his background and beliefs. He considered himself a Slovak by his father's lineage even though his mother was Germanized and he himself would spend most of his life among Czechs.[28] Having been raised on an imperial estate on which his father worked, the young Masaryk observed firsthand the gulf separating the opulent lifestyle of the Germanized nobility from the meager existence of the Slav peasantry. Many of these sights left an indelible impression upon him. As an exile during the First World War, for example, he bitterly recalled a pitiful scene of hungry Slovak villagers clawing and swinging at each other to seize the table scraps leftover from the feast of an aristocratic shooting party.[29] Aside from witnessing such great socio-ethnic inequalities, Masaryk's early childhood was unremarkable and his schooling nearly ended in his early teens, when he began apprenticeships under a locksmith and then a blacksmith. It was at this point that a priest who had taught the youth and recognized his prodigious thinking skills urged his parents to continue their son's education.[30] Following this advice, Masaryk was subsequently enrolled in a gymnasium[31] in Brno and later, in 1872, in the University of Vienna to study philosophy.[32] Since his parents had little money to spare for his studies, he had to support himself throughout these years by working as a private tutor for a student from a more affluent background. It was in cosmopolitan Vienna where Masaryk, raised in Slovak-German surroundings, began to become "Czechified" through his contact with the large population of Czech students and workers[33] residing there.[34] His time in the Austrian capital was interrupted in 1877 by a year-long sojourn in Leipzig, where he met and fell in love with the American-born Charlotte Garrigue.[35] In the following year he traveled to the United States, married her and in her honor assumed her maiden name as his middle name. The couple then returned to Vienna where Masaryk completed his doctoral thesis on the subject of suicide. In the summer

Tomáš Masaryk, undated. His familiarity with the English language and customs made him an ideal spokesman for the Czecho-Slovak cause in Britain and the United States.

of 1879, he was hired as an assistant professor at the university, where he remained for three years until accepting a professorship in philosophy in the newly-opened Czech section of Charles University in Prague.[36]

Once in the ancient Bohemian capital, Masaryk gained a reputation as a controversial figure that did not shy from advocating unpopular positions. His thesis on suicide, which he had published as his first book in 1881, drew fire from the Roman Catholic clergy due to its taboo subject.[37] Although raised Roman Catholic himself, Masaryk had become disenchanted with the Church in his early twenties and, after a brief flirtation with Uniatism,[38] he joined the Evangelical Reformed Church. Despite this conversion, his genuine adherence to any particular denomination remained ambiguous throughout his life despite his intense fascination with spirituality.[39] He never reconciled with the Catholic Church, however, and he maintained more or less openly anticlerical views throughout his careers as an academic and as a politician. By comparison, his attitudes towards Protestantism were nearly the opposite since, according to his world view, these denominations were more likely to foster individualism and democratic values among their followers. Recalling the fifteenth-century Hussite Reformation, he believed that the Czech people were Protestants in their hearts and only returned to Catholicism at the point of a sword. He dreamed that one day a new, modern reformation might take place among Czechs that would sever their spiritual allegiance to Rome and found a sort of national church.[40] Ultimately, his unwillingness to accept the predominance of Catholicism in the Bohemian lands was just one of several ways he estranged himself from many Czechs. His grudge against the Catholic Church was also reciprocated by its clergy, and they were far from the only group that was critical of the philosophy professor.[41]

The first major controversy which embroiled Masaryk after his move to Prague concerned the authentication of supposedly ancient manuscripts written in an old-style Czech. The first of these documents was "discovered" in 1817 and had been declared by a respected Czech philologist to be at least five centuries old. Seizing upon that assessment, Czech nationalists began citing the manuscripts as evidence of their people's great literary past. However, doubt concerning the manuscript's authenticity rose after the appearance of another supposedly ancient document just a year later. Both were found by same person, who also happened to be knowledgeable in Slav philology. From then on, debate raged in Bohemia over whether the manuscripts were genuine with most Czech nationalists defending their authenticity while German nationalists deemed them forgeries. In the mid–1880s, Czech academics, including Masaryk, began supporting extensive analysis of the documents to establish their veracity. His reasoning, as he later put it, was that, "Our pride, our culture, must not be based on a lie."[42] For unquestioning Czech patriots, the doubt raised by Masaryk and his colleagues was nothing short of blasphemy and subsequently the skeptics were reviled by the nationalist politicians and leaders. Eventually, it was verified that the manuscripts were nothing more than a clever fabrication.[43]

A second imbroglio at the turn of the twentieth century subjected Masaryk to an even greater public flogging. This controversy began in the spring of 1899 after a twenty-two-year-old Jewish drifter, Leopold Hilsner, was accused of committing a ritual murder after the body of a missing Czech seamstress was found near Polna in southeastern Bohemia. The case garnered wide publicity and ignited a firestorm of anti–Semitism in Czech public opinion, especially among the Catholic and nationalist presses, which factored into Hilsner's subsequent conviction and sentence of capital punishment. This verdict, however, was overturned after a thorough re-examination of the evidence and retrial was ordered. In the meantime, a new additional murder charge was brought against Hilsner after the remains of a second girl, missing since 1898, were unearthed near Polna.[44]

By the time Hilsner's new trial commenced, Masaryk was mired in the ensuing controversy. Writing in his party's paper, *Čas* (*Time*), after the first trial verdict, he refuted the allegations that the crime was a ritual murder and lamented the fact that the blood libel rumor still found wide acceptance among such a relatively sophisticated people as the Czechs.[45] He was immediately targeted for these remarks by the Czech Catholic clergy, National Socialists and other anti–Semites. His opponents even organized a campaign of intimidation against him by holding loud student demonstrations in his lecture halls and hurling rocks through the windows of his home.[46] The disruptions were so bad that Charles University suspended Masaryk's lectures for over a week. Although experts in law and forensic medicine quietly sided with Masaryk's assessment that Hilsner had not committed ritual murder, the professor continued to bear the brunt of the backlash and for a time he even considered immigrating to the United States with his wife and their four children. Ultimately, he stayed in Bohemia and would be rewarded for these hardships years later while he was actively lobbying for Czecho-Slovak independence abroad. Remembering his bold stand against anti–Semitism in the Hilsner case, Jewish organizations in the U.S. and Western Europe made no effort to hinder Masaryk's liberation movement and sometimes even lent it valuable support. Some of these same organizations, in contrast, were responsible for propaganda that partially disabled the Polish liberation movement in response to the anti–Semitism of some prominent Polish exiles.[47]

As a public figure, Masaryk was much more than an outspoken professor with a habit of taking up unpopular causes. He had begun his political career in the late 1880s by operating a periodical, *Čas*, with two associates, one of whom was Karel Kramář. In 1890, after declaring their affinity with the Young Czech Party, Masaryk and Kramář rode the wave of popular enthusiasm for the Young Czechs and were elected to seats in the Reichsrat and Bohemian Diet. During his tenure, however, Masaryk entered into sharp disagreements with the Young Czech leadership and as a result in 1893 he quit the party and resigned his mandates. Afterwards, he still continued to be active with *Čas* but he lost the cooperation of Kramář, who remained with the Young Czechs, eventually becoming that party's chairman and one of Masaryk's most enduring political rivals.[48]

Masaryk's withdrawal from the Young Czech Party was a direct result of his unorthodox political views. He had long been uncomfortable with the uncompromising nationalist platform promulgated by the more fanatical element of that party. His own sympathies were those of a democratic humanitarian and he was put off by the chauvinism evident among some nationalists.[49] "Morality and humanism must be the goals of every individual nation," he advised, "No nation has a right to its own special set of ethics."[50] His political outlook often appeared to blend contemporary liberal and socialist principles, but he liked neither label for himself. The liberals of his day, he complained, were "excessively rationalistic" while Marxists, in his opinion, grossly underestimated the importance of individual human will.[51] He was even less affectionate towards Czech Slavophiles. Having made several scholarly visits to Russia, the findings of which he later compiled into a three-volume book entitled *Russland und Europa*, he was well aware that the Slavophiles' adoration of the tsarist empire was based on mythical notions of the political, economic and social realities there.[52]

Masaryk's hiatus in active politics lasted less than a decade. At the turn of the twentieth century, the professor founded his own political party, the Czech People's Party, better known as the Realist Party, which employed *Čas* as its official organ. During the 1907 elections, Masaryk, as a candidate for his party in a district in eastern Moravia, managed to pull an upset in his contest and won a seat in the Reichsrat.[53]

Although the popularity of the Realist Party was far below that of more mainstream parties such as the Social Democrats, Agrarians or even Young Czechs, it still managed to wield an influence disproportionate to its tiny size thanks to its strong following among the intelligentsia community.[54] Besides these influential contacts which he cultivated in Bohemia, Masaryk also found favor with many prominent men outside the Czech homeland. A number of future Slovak, Croat and Slovene leaders studied under him at Charles University and some, like the Slovak nationalist Vavro Šrobár, would cooperate closely with his liberation movement during World War I.[55] Other admirers of the professor lived well beyond the Slav ethnographic frontier. Especially important was Charles Crane, an American entrepreneur who had earned a fortune in manufacturing plumbing and bathroom fixtures. As a philanthropist, Crane displayed an almost eccentric passion for Slavic causes and had even funded the School of Slavonic Studies at the University of Chicago. During the 1890s, Masaryk and Crane had met during one of the latter's wanderings in Eastern Europe and they struck a lasting friendship that would be especially opportune for the Czech professor during the coming war.[56] Another foreign contact, the London *Times* correspondent Henry Wickham Steed, whom Masaryk met during the high-profile Zagreb treason trial in 1909, would also provide countless benefits to the Czech liberation movement during the war.

Like Palacký, Masaryk had long believed that the multinational Habsburg Monarchy was the best solution for the Czechs and other small nationalities squeezed between the mighty German and Russian Empires. After 1907, however, a number of events challenged his loyal inclinations.[57]

Like nearly all Habsburg Slavs, Masaryk regarded the dualist structure of the Monarchy as a great abomination and desired the termination of unbridled Magyar rule in Hungary. Incidentally, the year which marked his return to the Reichsrat also saw the decennial debates over renewal of the Ausgleich, which always prompted sharp disagreements between politicians of the two halves of the Monarchy. Thanks to the many Slovak students who had studied under him, Masaryk was not oblivious to the plight of Hungary's minorities and he used the occasion to declare in the parliament that the Czechs would not abandon their Slovak compatriots to Magyar pretensions. Indeed, he essentially claimed that the Czechs and Slovaks represented one nation whose differences lay primarily in geography rather than culture or language. His support of Czecho-Slovak unity, however, resonated only with a small minority of Czech politicians. Many Czechs were sympathetic to the Slovaks, but few were willing to complicate their agenda and incur the ire of influential Magyar leaders on the Slovaks' behalf. Any plan that would wrench the Slovak homeland away from Budapest was considered an infringement upon the integrity of the historic Kingdom of Hungary, and such a scheme would undermine the demands of Czech nationalists for autonomy within Bohemia's historic frontiers.[58]

Against the opposition of Masaryk and others, the Ausgleich was renewed in 1907, dashing their hopes for reforming the governing system of the Monarchy. The precise form of government they would have liked to have seen in the empire remains unclear. The idea of replacing dualism with a "democratic federation of nationalities" was widely acclaimed by Czech politicians, but at the same time their own record of opposition to dividing the

Bohemian crownlands into ethnically-homogenous administrative districts made the federal solution unworkable in practice. The Pan-Slavs, it is true, supported democratic and federal reforms since in their mind the empire, with about twenty-four million Slavs against twenty-two million ethnic Germans and Magyars, appeared destined to become Slavic in outlook.[59] Of course, whether the Habsburg Slavs could have ever become a monolithic voting block is doubtful; nevertheless the notion brought hope and concern to both sides of the national question. What can be said with certainty is that the majority of Czechs did not contemplate complete independence, a possibility which even Masaryk spoke out against in 1909. "We cannot," he warned, "be independent outside of Austria next to a powerful Germany, having Germans on our territory."[60] He and most moderate Czechs recognized that their claims to exclusivity in the Bohemian lands could not be realized without offending the considerable German minority.[61] Moreover, Czech assertions of the historical state rights of the Kingdom of Bohemia could be countered with similar claims from the Germans regarding the frontiers of the former Holy Roman Empire, which encompassed the Bohemian lands.[62] Therefore, Masaryk, like Palacký, remained a mild supporter of Habsburg Monarchy, if for no other reason than the absence of any better options.

Maintaining that loyalty towards Vienna, however, was becoming increasingly difficult as the years slipped by. After the 1907 renewal of the hated Ausgleich came the 1908 Bosnian crisis, indicating that Austria-Hungary's foreign policy was on a collision course with Russia. Although Aehrenthal had predicted that the annexation of Bosnia-Herzegovina would deal a fatal blow to Serbian irredentism, the Austro-Hungarian Foreign Minister continued to obsess over suspicions of a Pan-Serb or "Yugoslav" conspiracy. In 1909, the Ballhausplatz claimed to have intercepted documents proving the existence of such a conspiracy, and these papers were the key evidence used to bring treason charges against fifty-three Serbian and Croat politicians from the Monarchy. Their trial was held in the Croatian provincial capital of Zagreb and its proceedings attracted interest from all over the Monarchy and Europe. Masaryk, as the head of a Reichsrat inquiry into the alleged South Slav conspiracy, testified at the trial that the documents were written by someone with a poor understanding of the Serbian language and almost certainly did not originate from Belgrade as alleged by the prosecution. The Reichsrat inquiry into anti–Habsburg movements among the South Slavs uncovered only a clumsy student gang—hardly the dangerous underground organization with highly-placed agents as claimed by Aehrenthal. With the documents shown to be forgeries concocted by the Austro-Hungarian Embassy in Belgrade, the Serbian and Croat politicians were acquitted. The Zagreb trial succeeded only in proving that the Austro-Hungarian Foreign Minister was willing to believe anything that supported his conviction that a "Yugoslav conspiracy" existed.[63]

Even after their worst fears were proven unfounded in Zagreb, Austro-Hungarian officials remained haunted by the Pan-Slav bogeyman. They were convinced that this menace had at last reared its head in October 1912, when the independent Balkan Slav states of Serbia, Montenegro and Bulgaria joined Greece in a military campaign against the Turks. Their alarm did not even dissipate in the following summer when Bulgaria fought her former allies over the spoils.[64] The Ballhausplatz was right to be concerned by these wars, not because of an international Pan-Slav conspiracy, but rather because they demonstrated that the status quo in the Balkans which it had attempted to preserve since 1908 was finished. Each of the Balkan nations expanded their domains at the losers' expense, and Vienna adopted the unpopular role of referee as it sought to limit the gains of certain victors. However, the

Austro-Hungarian government quickly learned that it was not enough to enforce its authority by simply blowing its whistle; it had to resort to the threat of military action to coerce the Montenegrins, Serbs and Greeks to withdraw from Albania and other disputed territories. The reorganization of the Balkans, having deprived the Turks of practically all their holdings in Europe, left Austria-Hungary as the only remaining imperial power there. Moreover, the Monarchy's most resolute enemy, Serbia, had more than doubled in size after the two Balkan Wars and increased its attractiveness to irredentist South Slavs who believed the virile little kingdom was destined to liberate all South Slavs from alien rule.[65] Given these foreboding developments, combined with their perpetual concerns of a Pan-Slav conspiracy, it is hardly surprising then that Austro-Hungarian authorities immediately suspected Belgrade's complicity in the assassination plot successfully carried out by a group of Bosnian Serb teenagers against the heir to the throne, Archduke Franz Ferdinand, and his wife during their visit to Sarajevo at the end of June 1914.

In the weeks following the Sarajevo assassinations, Europe's cables buzzed with proposals, ultimatums, mobilization orders and finally declarations of war, ushering in the greatest calamity that the continent had known up to that time. As their sons were called to serve the Emperor, the loyalties of Czech socialists, nationalists and Pan-Slavs were put to the test.

As the young men of Europe marched off to war in the summer of 1914, many diplomats, journalists and other foreign observers doubted whether Austria-Hungary could effectively launch much less sustain a major military campaign.[66] They predicted that the centrifugal national movements of the Austro-Hungarian ethnicities, when combined with the strains of mobilizing the economy and population for war, would tear the empire asunder. Their assessment was encouraged by perennial crises caused by the national question. In Bohemia, a caretaker committee was responsible for the province's administration after years of impasse between Czechs and Germans on the Bohemian Diet left the province's finances in ruin. The ongoing quarrel between those two nationalities eventually spilled over into the Reichsrat, where the Czech parties readily joined the Ukrainian deputies in a new round of obstructions. On 16 March 1914, Austrian Prime Minister Count Karl Stürgkh responded to this latest holdup by proroguing the Reichsrat and legislating by emergency decree. This bureaucratic dictatorship continued into the summer as the empire went to war, and with the onset of the great struggle the Emperor, his ministers and especially the military leaders saw even less reason to recall the Reichsrat.[67] Pan-Slavism, like nationalism, was also considered a force too great for any habitual dynastic loyalty to overcome. One Russian general, a supporter of the tsarist general staff's plan to send the bulk of its forces into Galicia at the outset of war, was convinced that the Habsburg Slavs would desert Austria-Hungary at the first sign of a Russian victory.[68]

The inherent difficulties of molding recruits from ten languages into a cohesive fighting force left even the Chief of the General Staff of the Austro-Hungarian Army, Franz Conrad von Hötzendorf, pessimistic in regards to the performance of his military machine.[69] Outwardly, the army appeared German but in the years prior to the outbreak of the world war controversies had arisen in the armed forces to remind the generals that the rows of men beneath the pike-gray uniforms hailed from diverse ethnic backgrounds.[70] Among Czech soldiers, acts of defiance during this period ranged from mild demonstrations, such as answering roll-call in their native tongue instead of German, to more serious ones, including mutinies in certain regiments mobilized during the crises of 1908 and 1912.[71] The memories of these incidents concerned the Armee Oberkommando (AOK) since the Czechs, with their high level of education, were an important source of cadets for the officer corps. Czech representation was strongest in the reserve officer corps, but this was to be no consolation for the AOK since the high casualty rates suffered by the regular officers, particularly at the outset, magnified the importance of the reservists.[72]

All of these expectations that Austria-Hungary's disaffected nationalities, particularly the Czechs, were liable to revolt at the outbreak of the war proved unfounded. In Prague, both Czech and German residents organized processions to show their support for the Monarchy.[73] Troops traveling through Bohemia on their way to the front were greeted at rail stations by crowds of cheering women extending offerings of bread and tea.[74] While it may wrong to suggest that the Czechs were wholly enthusiastic about the war, many at this stage were prepared or at least resigned to accept their wartime duties as Austrian soldiers and civilians. Patriotism—a dubious quality in a multinational state—was at least initially on the side of the Habsburgs.

The first acts of open defiance among Czech units appeared one month after war had been declared. When reservists from the 8th and 28th Prague Infantry Regiments were called up, soldiers from these units engaged in disorderly conduct as they marched to the train stations. Observers noted that these soldiers, many of whom appeared to be inebriated, waved banners emblazoned with Slav colors while others vandalized the railcars with demoralizing graffiti. The origins of this demonstration may lie in the fact that the two regiments were comprised mostly of recruits from working-class districts around Prague that were targeted by socialist anti-military propaganda in the years prior to the war. Military authorities, however, viewed the incident as part of a wider problem of Czech nationalism and general disloyalty to the throne. They quickly regarded the Czechs, and sometimes all Slavs, as either traitors or potential candidates of treason. For this reason, from September 1914 onwards, they engaged the civil servants in tug-of-war contest for complete control over Bohemia's administration.[75]

What certain military authorities failed to realize was that the Slavs of the Habsburg Monarchy were far from unanimous in the attitude towards their war. Unlike the Czechs, other Slavs, including the Croats, Poles and Slovenes, welcomed the war as an opportunity to settle scores with Serbia, Russia and later Italy. Slovak peasant-soldiers were also sturdy fighters until the last months of the war.[76] Throughout most of the conflict, it was not the rank-and-file that was responsible for the army's considerable defeats but rather its leadership. Archduke Franz Ferdinand, as the Inspector General of the army in the years leading up to the war, had emphasized aesthetic parade drills over more practical field exercises. Meanwhile, Conrad possessed a fanatical hatred of Serbia that seems to have clouded his judgment in the critical opening days of the war.[77] By first sending his reserves southward towards Serbia instead of eastward against the much larger Russian enemy, and then reversing his decision during their deployment, he ensured that those forces would not be available for the opening battles on either front.[78] This inept leadership, when combined with years of low defense expenditures that cut training programs and stalled equipment upgrades, was a recipe for military disaster.[79]

The catastrophe did not take long to materialize. In September 1914, after some short-lived tactical successes, the operations of the Austro-Hungarian Army met failure on both the Serbian and Eastern Fronts. The defeat in the latter theater was especially staggering: Russian forces overran most of Galicia after inflicting 350,000 casualties on the Habsburg army. These losses not only deprived the army of some of its best officers and men from the outset, they also cost it hundreds of valuable artillery pieces and ammunition stockpiles that would soon be in short supply. Hundreds of thousands of Galician refugees flooded the roads and rails westward to escape the Russian onslaught, rendering it impossible for AOK to hide the immense scale of the disaster from the public. Fearing that the Russians might resume their offensive as soon as their supplies caught up, a desperate Conrad made the first of what would become many ignominious pleas to the German Oberste Heerlesleitung (OHL) for military assistance.[80]

Naturally, the Austro-Hungarian commanders were unwilling to admit the role of their own shortcomings in the military debacle. Eager to find a scapegoat, they quickly concluded that the unreliability of the army's Slav troops, and the Czechs in particular, was undermining the fighting capacity of the entire army. This allegation, however, does not corroborate with the Russians' initial assessment of Czech formations on the Eastern Front. While Czech soldiers may have lacked the *élan* of their German-Austrian, Magyar or even Polish comrades, there is no evidence in the early stages of the war that manifestations of disloyalty were anything beyond isolated occurrences.[81] Yet, the generals would continue to nurture the myth that their Slav troops were prone to desert to their "racial allies" in order to preserve their own standings and deflect criticism. It also gave them leverage in their continued struggle with the civil service of Bohemia and Moravia to surrender the administration of Czech homeland to the whims of the military.[82]

The crushing defeat of the Austro-Hungarian Army in the opening phase of the war was bound to have a profound effect on Czech attitudes towards the conflict and the Monarchy. Not only were the early hopes of a quick decisive victory over the Entente dashed, but the inhabitants of the Bohemian lands were forced to consider the possibility that Austria-Hungary might lose the war and that they might have to reckon with an occupation by the Russians. Not all Czechs considered such an outcome to be undesirable. Ardent Pan-Slavs took secret delight in the Austrian retreat and looked forward to the "liberation" of Bohemia by the tsarist army. Their anticipations were buoyed by two manifestoes issued by the Commander-in-Chief of the Russian Army, Grand Duke Nikolay. The Grand Duke's first proclamation merely sought to secure Polish loyalty to the Russian cause by vaguely supporting a reunited and autonomous Poland; but the second of these, which was issued on 16 September 1914, made a similar guarantee to all Slav nationalities of Austria-Hungary. Pan-Slav propagandists inside the Bohemian lands helped disseminate the Grand Duke's message by reprinting Russian leaflets; in some instances they even edited his statements to enhance their appeal among Czechs.[83] Meanwhile, the war itself quickly became unpopular as older reservists were summoned to the colors in order to replace the steep losses incurred by the army on the Eastern Front. The absence of parliamentary government combined with the threatened imposition of military dictatorship, not to mention the evident hostility of the top commanders towards the Czech people, wrecked any chance that the dynastic patriotism seen in the population at the war's outbreak might be sustained.[84] Indeed, the realization that Bohemia might be subjected to the will of Austro-Hungarian generals, who themselves were beholden to the German Reich in order to keep the Russian armies at bay, kindled the fear that the lingering national question in the province would be settled once and for all in favor of the ethnic Germans. What was clear was that the bureaucratic-military administrators were no longer interested in formulating a compromise to settle the national question, and this could only work to the advantage of the ethnic German parties who sidled close to the government.[85] It is little wonder then that a few Czechs began to look outside the Monarchy for solutions to their people's predicament.

3

Contriving for a New Europe

Like many Europeans, Tomáš Masaryk had been enjoying a vacation with his family when war broke out in the summer of 1914.[1] As he made his way back from the Saxon resort where his family had been staying, the Czech professor was able to observe the perfunctory mobilization of Germany. He returned to Prague in time to witness the drunkenness and rowdiness of the 8th and 28th Prague Infantry Regiments, and the stark differences in the mobilization of the two empires left an indelible impression on him.[2] The Monarchy, unlike its meticulous ally, seemed unprepared to fight a war which it had done much to precipitate.

Over the following weeks, the loyalty that had kept Masaryk's political aspirations within the empire quickly unraveled. The weakness of the Monarchy that was evident after the military catastrophe in Galicia raised concern that the empire might become a dependent of Germany, an outcome that could have profound implications on the nationality question in Bohemia if not throughout Austria. As German troops were trucked southward to stiffen their flailing ally, Masaryk concluded that Austria-Hungary was no longer an obstruction to but rather an instrument of German hegemony. At the same time, he saw an opportunity that could improve the general livelihoods of Czechs, Slovaks and millions of others in Central Europe. He understood that the war—especially if it was to be prolonged—presented a substantial threat to the established order throughout Europe. After all, a much smaller conflict between Russia and Japan a decade earlier had unleashed a revolution that nearly toppled the most autocratic regime then in Europe. Therefore, it was reasonable to assume that a war involving not one or two but all five of Europe's Great Powers would have broad implications far beyond the battlefields. The social and ethnic questions that troubled Russia in 1905 could be found in all belligerents to some degree. Masaryk felt that if new governing systems closely aligned on liberal, democratic or even socialist principles emerged from the ruins of a general European war, then small independent states would no longer have to fear the imperialistic aims that defined the old order in Central Europe. In other words, Czechs, Slovaks and other small nationalities would no longer need the security of Austria-Hungary and could establish small, viable nation-states of their own.[3] These realizations sealed his opposition to the continued existence of the Habsburg Monarchy.

Most Czechs were much slower in arriving to the conclusion that the empire had outlived its usefulness. Masaryk quickly found this out when the Czech Social Democrat leaders rebuffed his pleas for them to use their contacts in the Second International to communicate with anti–Habsburg dissidents abroad.[4] Fortunately for the Czech professor, the outbreak of hostilities coincided with the visit of a group of Czech-Americans to Prague. Among these individuals was Emanuel Voska, who as a young exiled socialist went to the United States where he became a wealthy businessman. Over time Voska had abandoned his ardent socialism for the cause of Czech national freedom, and he was a deep admirer of Masaryk. Having known Voska prior to the war, the Czech professor entrusted his American guest to deliver the first of several letters he would send to acquaintances in enemy countries. As U.S. citizens, Voska and his group were able to move freely from one belligerent camp to the other via neutral Holland. On 2 September, an unkempt Voska, wearied by five days of travel from Prague, arrived in London and handed Masaryk's message to Henry Wickham Steed, then the foreign editor of *The Times*.[5]

During the decade prior to 1913, Steed had served as *The Times* correspondent in Vienna and had become acquainted with the Czech professor while covering the Zagreb treason trial.[6] In his letter, Masaryk gave Steed an exaggerated account of conditions inside the Habsburg Empire, claiming that Czech and South Slav leaders were being persecuted[7] and that there was widespread demoralization among Czech soldiers.[8] He also asked the Briton for a forecast regarding the duration of hostilities. At the time, it was widely accepted among academics and economists that a general war, for reasons pertaining to economics, finances and popular support, could not endure beyond a few weeks or a year at most. Lord Kitchener, the British Secretary of War, discounted these assessments and predicted that the conflict would last upwards of two or three years.[9] Steed reported Kitchener's view in his courier-delivered reply to Masaryk, bolstering the

Henry Wickham Steed, undated. As a journalist and propagandist, Steed was a strong advocate of dismembering Austria-Hungary.

professor's confidence that he might have the time needed to campaign for the liberation of the Czech people.[10] "For me this question was very weighty," he later recalled, "since the character of the work I meant to do abroad depended largely on the duration of the war."[11]

During these uncertain weeks of hostilities, when the early offensives brought mixed fortunes to both camps, Masaryk continued his relentless quest to gather as many perspectives as possible before embarking on a definite course of action. Eager to see for himself the wartime atmosphere beyond the Central Powers, Masaryk traveled to Holland under the pretext that he was escorting his visiting sister-in-law to Rotterdam, from where she was to embark on her return voyage to the U.S. He arrived in the Netherlands on 12 September and spent a fortnight pouring over uncensored foreign newspapers in order to gain a sense of the real direction of the campaigns. He also hoped to meet with Steed, but this proved impossible to arrange during his limited time in the country. He had better luck in a second trip to Holland during October, when he rendezvoused with one of Steed's trusted associates, Robert Seton-Watson, a thirty-five-year-old Scotsman and scholar on Austria-Hungary. A longtime champion of South Slav unity and a staunch opponent of Magyar assimilation policies, Seton-Watson had never devoted a considerable amount of his studies to the national question in Bohemia. He had met Masaryk during the professor's bold defense of the Serb and Croat politicians during the Zagreb treason trial, and the two men had since discussed launching a periodical that would enlighten English readers on the challenges facing small nationalities in Central Europe.[12] Now confronted with more urgent matters, Masaryk used his limited time in Rotterdam to acquaint Seton-Watson with his newly-formulated ideas for Czech independence. Amid their meeting inside his hotel room, the professor emphasized Bohemia's historical state rights as the most recognizable basis for Czech independence.[13] Seton-Watson quickly stated his disapproval since this argument would appear to justify the Magyars' domination over the Slovaks, whose plight he was especially sympathetic towards. Instead, he suggested that the case for Czecho-Slovak independence should be centered on the principle of nationality, but with the provision that such a state must be allotted borders that were economically and strategically viable.[14] This argument would imply the inclusion of Bohemia's historical frontiers—with its mountainous borderlands, valuable industries and, not to be overlooked, a German minority approximately three-million strong—into the proposed Czecho-Slovak state.

Masaryk's proposal to include the large ethnic German minority in an independent Slav state would essentially match that long advocated by radical Czech nationalists. The probable reason why he, with a record of rather moderate nationalism, suddenly backed such an extreme and controversial solution was that he needed to ensure his activities a measure of political backing in the homeland. Prior to the meeting with Seton-Watson, Masaryk had discussed possible outcomes of the Czechs' future without Austria-Hungary in secret meetings with politicians from the National Socialist, Moravian People's Progressive and State Right parties. One item which all these politicians agreed upon was that the integrity of the Bohemian lands must be preserved.[15] Hence, to avoid the risk of disavowal, Masaryk felt bound to uphold Czech claims to the entire provinces of Bohemia, Moravia and Lower Silesia. Since any division of the Bohemian crownlands was seen as rendering them militarily indefensible and economically unsustainable, he may have regarded the inclusion of the German minority as a necessary injustice. "The question arises," he later wrote, "whether it is fairer that a fragment of the German people should remain in a non–German state or that the whole Czechoslovak people should live in a German state."[16]

By the end of his meeting with Masaryk, Seton-Watson was sold on the desirability of liberating the Czech and Slovak homelands. Upon his return to the other side the Channel, the Scotsman outlined his conversations with Masaryk, whom he did not mention by name, into a memorandum which he submitted to Britain's Foreign Office. With the help of Steed, he saw that other copies of the document reached the foreign ministries in Paris and Petrograd. Besides claiming that the whole Czech nation is in "favour of the Allies," Seton-Watson noted that his informant admitted that Czechs would have preferred a monarchy over a republic as the form of government for their projected independent state. The document also assumed a Russian occupation of the Czech and Slovak homeland to be imminent and included suggestions on how the tsarist government should administer the conquered territories.[17] This and other schemes presented by the memorandum were destined to become obsolete in the coming months as the direction of the war veered drastically; nonetheless, it remained significant since it increased the standing of Seton-Watson with the Foreign Office, where he was seen as an unofficial advisor on Austria-Hungary.[18] Thus from this early stage a close ally of Masaryk's had secured the ear of the British government.

After his return to Prague, Masaryk continued to take the first steps in conspiring against the Monarchy. By then, the armies on the Western Front were entrenching themselves in the chalky soil of northern France while the conflict expanded to new theaters as the Ottoman Empire entered the fray as an ally to Germany and Austria-Hungary.[19] As the prospect that the war would be a protracted struggle grew more likely, the professor continued to meet with Czech politicians and leaders, including Josef Scheiner, the Slavophile chairman of the Sokol organization. He even met with Austrian officials, including Count Thun, Bohemia's governor, and a former Austrian prime minister, Ernst von Körber.[20] Of course, in his talks with Thun and Körber Masaryk concealed the revolutionary action he was then contemplating.[21]

Masaryk never seriously considered a "domestic" uprising in the Czech homeland. With Bohemia sandwiched between Germany and Austria, he and other conspirators expected such a revolt would be instantly squashed. Though they may have been unwilling to admit it, they may have also had lingering doubts whether any open challenge to Habsburg rule in Bohemia would receive widespread support from the Czech masses. Masaryk was also mindful that an insurrection might actually please the Slavophobes in the government and military who already expected nothing short of the worst from the Czechs and would welcome any excuse to impose a military rule in Bohemia. Therefore he had long ago concluded that the banner of Czech liberation would have to be raised abroad, where the revolutionaries would be outside the reach of Austrian police and censors. Moreover, a clandestine courier service between Prague and the neutral states had been organized by Voska early in the war, and through these secret messages Masaryk had learned of the embryonic liberation movements forming among Czech and Slovak émigrés in the U.S., France and Russia. By positioning himself outside of the Central Powers, he could hope to draw upon their resources while consolidating them into a unified body with a consistent program for a future Czecho-Slovak state.[22]

In mid–December 1914, Masaryk crossed the frontier of the Habsburg Empire for the last time. Accompanied by his daughter Olga, the pair traveled through neutral Italy on a fact-finding mission to Rome. He was eager to make contact with the fledging anti–Habsburg movement that had been formed there by a group of South Slav émigrés, among whom were a few of his former colleagues from the Austrian Reichsrat. After meeting with them and reviewing their plans, Masaryk was considerably impressed with their preparations and thought that the Czechs and Slovaks, in contrast, had much work to do.[23] Masaryk seems to have intended to return to Bohemia after his trip to Rome, but his indiscreet contact with the South Slav émigrés was apparently noticed by Austrian agents and reported back to Vienna. Through a message relayed from an informant in the Austrian government to Edvard Beneš in Prague and then to Steed in London, Masaryk was warned to remain abroad. Whether he liked it or not, his period of exile had begun.[24]

After nearly three weeks in Rome, Masaryk left Italy for Switzerland, settling in Geneva, which would serve as the base of his activity for the better part of the following year. With help from the community of Czech émigrés residing there, he embarked on his first task which was to maintain the secret communication network with accomplices in Prague. The émigrés employed their talents and skills into developing a cipher machine and crafting briefcases, chests and garments with hidden compartments.[25] Unlike most other exile leaders that would emerge during the war, Masaryk emphasized from the very beginning the need to maintain contact with the homeland. Prior to his trip to Italy, Masaryk had begun laying the groundwork for an underground organization that would complement the independence movement abroad by furnishing the exiles with intelligence and sanctioning their political activity. Since this secret society was incomplete when he left Austria-Hungary in December 1914, Masaryk relied on trusted members of his Realist Party to put the final touches on this nucleus of a domestic resistance. One of the men leading this effort was a rather obscure sociology professor less than half his age, Edvard Beneš.[26]

At the time of the war's outbreak, Beneš was only thirty years old and would later feign a limp to avoid conscription into the Habsburg Army. Just several years earlier, he had been a student in Masaryk's lecture halls, though the two men seemed to have limited interaction prior to the war. Although he had strong socialist sympathies, Beneš identified with Masaryk's Realists and took an active role in the party by volunteering his services to *Čas* after the war began. In the following weeks, the two men gradually learned of their shared desire to liberate the Czech people from Habsburg rule, beginning one of the most dynamic partnerships seen in the war.[27]

Of the three figures who would dominate the campaign for Czecho-Slovak independence abroad, Beneš's outward personality and credentials seemed least suited toward such a prominent role. He was a rigid introvert devoid of any charm; throughout his lifetime he had few friends beyond his wife, Hana. Even his collaboration with Masaryk, which would prove lifelong, never managed to shed the formal appearance of a relationship between an instructor and a pupil. With a delicate pair of spectacles and a thin mat of dark hair neatly

parted from the left, his appearance was neither imposing nor remarkable; he resembled every dapper gentlemen of the day. His writing was equally uninspiring. Yet, behind these drab features was a man of boundless energy, dedication and efficiency that made him willing to tackle any workload. It was these qualities which would make Beneš an invaluable asset to Masaryk's campaign, particularly in the early stages of the movement when resources were limited.

Ironically, Beneš had written his doctoral dissertation on—of all things—the need to preserve the Habsburg Monarchy.[28] By the autumn of 1914, however, he had reversed those views and now began coordinating an underground resistance against the empire whose existence he once defended. The organization, called Maffie, met for the first time in March 1915 and included among its earliest members respected figures such as Kramář, Scheiner, and another prominent Young Czech politician, Alois Rašín.[29] The lesser known Přemysl Šamal, a lawyer who was designated to lead the Realist Party in Masaryk's absence, frequently hosted Maffie's

Edvard Beneš, general secretary of the Czecho-Slovak National Council, undated.

meetings at his Prague residence.[30] Besides the parties whose politicians were directly involved in the underground, Maffie also had contacts with the Czech Social Democratic, Agrarian and State Right parties. On the other hand, the National Socialists were excluded from having any role in the group at the insistence of the Young Czechs while Masaryk made the same stipulation for the clerical parties.[31]

By the time of the first Maffie meeting in the spring of 1915, Kramář had already taken his own steps to free the Czechs from Habsburg rule. Although he did not venture outside of Austria-Hungary, through the employment of secret couriers he was able to transmit proposals for the inclusion of the Bohemian crownlands into a Russian-dominated Slav confederation. Vsevolod Svatkovsky, a Russian correspondent stationed in Berne who had been acquainted with Kramář prior to the war, had made certain that the Young Czech leader's memorandum reached Petrograd.[32] Masaryk had learned of Kramář's proposal when he personally met with Svatkovsky in early 1915. This encounter between the professor and the Slavophile journalist could have been potentially rocky: Masaryk's contempt of the tsarist system was well known from his recent work, *Russland und Europa*, and as a result he was classified as a *persona non grata* in Russia. Both men, however, put their ideological differences aside; the well-connected Russian correspondent even entrusted Masaryk with access to his own secret courier system into the Habsburg Empire.[33] This meeting, at which a visiting Beneš was also present, had one other important outcome in that it convinced Kramář to merge his activity with that of Masaryk and Beneš though his participation in Maffie.

Although both Masaryk and Kramář covertly opposed Austrian rule over Bohemia at this stage, collaboration between the two men was anything but certain. Throughout their careers, they had looked to opposite directions for their inspiration: Masaryk was an admirer of the democracies of the West while Kramář sought a protector in the colossal Russian Empire to the East. Their differences continued after the outbreak of World War I as they disagreed on the fundamental nature of the conflict. Kramář accepted the Pan-Slav version that the struggle would decide whether the Slavs or Teutons would be the masters of Europe.[34] Masaryk, however, eventually rejected this thesis of a race war and instead regarded it as a contest of two political ideals: the liberal and democratic nations of the Western Allies versus the medieval autocracies of the Central Powers.[35]

Despite their differences, Masaryk was eager to ensure that Kramář, whose party was far larger than the Realists, was on his side in the struggle for an independent Czecho-Slovak state.[36] The Young Czech leader seems to have accepted his invitation into Maffie only after learning that Masaryk had been in touch with Svatkovsky.[37] According to Beneš, at the first Maffie meeting Kramář was primarily interested in the conversation between the exiled professor and Russian journalist. Their discussions apparently buoyed his hope that Masaryk, despite his decision to remain in Western Europe, was not discounting the Slavic big brother in his scheme for Bohemian independence. During the remainder of the Maffie gathering, Kramář reiterated his belief that the Czechs' liberation would be achieved through Russian arms and he rejected Masaryk's suggestion, relayed by Beneš, that the Young Czech leader should join him in exile. Kramář dug in his heels and refused to be absent from Bohemia when Russian troops arrived. While these ramblings certainly annoyed the two men present at the meeting closest to Masaryk, Beneš and Šamal, both were relatively unknown and sorely lacking credentials to voice any opposition to such a respected politician. For the time being, they suppressed their objections and quietly tolerated Kramář's Russophile fantasies.[38] Such was the uneasy and delicate foundation upon which the existence of the early Maffie rested.

Kramář's importance to Masaryk and the Prague underground might have been diminished had a leader of a larger Czech political party, such as the Social Democrats or Agrarians, joined Maffie, but this failed to materialize despite Beneš's efforts. In November 1914 Beneš had personally sought an endorsement for Masaryk's planned revolutionary activity from the chairman of the Czech Social Democratic Party, Bohumír Šmeral. The latter's response to this overture was harsh: he denounced Masaryk as "irresponsible" and predicted that the professor's actions would lead to a "second White Mountain" for the Czechs.[39] As for the Czech Agrarians, they were unwilling to completely abandon their loyalty to the dynasty as long as the direction of the war remained in doubt.[40] These rebuffs were certainly disappointing for Masaryk and Beneš, but they did not deter the former from conveying the impression abroad that the Czech Social Democrats were among the multitude of parties that had approved of his revolutionary activity.[41] Fortunately for him, most of the Entente officials he dealt with had little if any reliable knowledge of Czech attitudes either prior to or during the war.

The difficulty which Maffie had in attempting to persuade Kramář, or any other Czech politician for that matter, to join Masaryk abroad in the spring of 1915 stemmed in part from forecasts that Austria-Hungary's total defeat was imminent. These assessments were not without foundation. On 22 March, the garrison inside the besieged Galician fortress of Przemyśl, after butchering the last of their horses for food and blasting their remaining stock of munitions, hoisted white flags above their ramparts. The fall of this modern fortress was major blow to the Austro-Hungarian Army, not only because over 117,000 troops and officers were lost to Russian captivity, but also because its heroic resistance had been cited as an example for the soldiers to follow.[42] Moreover, the considerable number of tsarist troops that had invested the fortress could now be deployed elsewhere; many took part in the subsequent Russian offensive that carried the attackers to the summits of the Carpathian Mountains, the last major obstacle standing between them and the Hungarian plains. Pummeled by the intense cold and a relentless fighting, tens of thousands of Habsburg troops simply gave up and surrendered, and AOK was at a loss on how to contain the enemy. It was only a matter time until supplies and reinforcements caught up to the Russian frontline and would enable the tsarist armies to descend into the Danube valley.[43]

Even though the Habsburg Empire's defeat appeared imminent, the Maffie conspirators finally did stumble across a politician who was prepared to go abroad. This man was Josef Dürich, a sixty-nine-year-old Agrarian deputy whose appeal rested mainly with his affiliation to one of the largest Czech political parties.[44] Although the Agrarians' leader, Antonín Švehla, was at this stage highly skeptical about the odds for Masaryk's success, he nevertheless was shrewd enough to realize that his party should have a foot in the revolutionaries' camp just in case they prevailed.[45] Dürich himself was not enthusiastic about the mission and agreed to it only because he was planning to go abroad anyway to visit his daughters in neutral Spain. Conscious of Austria-Hungary's reverses on the Eastern Front, he may have believed that peace talks might soon be underway and therefore he would not need to be absent from his homeland for very long.[46] Since he was also known to have Slavophile sympathies, Dürich received the approval of Kramář and other Russophiles who felt that Masaryk was wasting his time in Western Europe.[47] After being secretly instructed by Kramář to concentrate on coordinating his revolutionary activity with Russia, even at the price of disregarding Masaryk's intentions, Dürich left Austria-Hungary and on 9 May arrived in Zurich.[48]

While Czech politicians were busy combing their ranks for someone to strengthen

Czech representation abroad, Masaryk was trying to develop a formal, centralized program for Czecho-Slovak independence. His first objective was to win the backing of the disparate Czech and Slovak societies that had sprouted in Switzerland, France, the U.S. and Russia since the beginning of the war. He was not the first person to attempt this feat. In late January, a Czech-Russian from Moscow, Svatopluk Koníček, had gone to Paris to unite Czech organizations in Russia and Western Europe into a supreme Czech national council. An ardent Slavophile, Koníček's repeated adorations of the Tsar did not resonate well with more liberal Czech émigrés living in Great Britain, France and Switzerland. Denied their confidence and support, Koníček's national council withered away that summer and he eventually returned to Russia.[49] His failure demonstrated the difficulty facing any organization that aspired to encompass the diverse views of Czecho-Slovak émigrés from around the world.

The liberal Czech groups in the West that had shunned Koníček were more predisposed to support Masaryk, and in March 1915 he began collecting statements of support from these organizations. Still, even he, an author and politician with considerable democratic and liberal credentials, was not without his critics in Western Europe and the U.S. Especially in America, he encountered opposition from Catholic Czechs who thought that the professor's record of anticlericalism should disqualify him as a representative of a people who were predominantly Catholic. Over the course of the war, however, these and other foes of Masaryk were neutralized by propaganda generated by his backers. In some instances, the pro–Masaryk cabal resorted to branding the professor's critics as "Austrophiles" and even went as far as to forge evidence that such men were paid agents of Austro-Hungarian consulates.[50]

While he was working to unite the efforts of Czech émigrés, Masaryk also sought to win the confidence of Slovak immigrants as well; he did, after all, style himself as a leader of "Czecho-Slovaks." Although Russia and especially the U.S. had large colonies of Slovaks, they, even more than their Czech counterparts, were uncertain as to what future aims best reflected the will of the people in their homeland. This was in no small part to due to the oppressive Magyar policies that had muted Slovak nationalism and kept the Slovak peasantry in a limbo of political confusion.[51] Subsequently, Slovaks living abroad invented their own ideas as to what their kin in Upper Hungary would want. Some believed the Slovaks were ready for their own independent state separate from the Czechs; others took a more Pan-Slavic view by claiming that their homeland should be annexed into the Russian Empire. Many were not averse to the union of the Slovaks with the Czechs in a joint nation-state, but most were adamant that such an arrangement would have to be federative with both peoples enjoying equal rights and powers. Throughout the war, Masaryk and his supporters were willing to meet this condition to assure Slovak cooperation.[52] Slovak émigrés in Russia, like the Czech émigrés living there, proved among the least susceptible to Masaryk's overtures. Although some Czech-Russians recognized Masaryk's leadership over the wider liberation movement in early 1915, the professor's control over the organizations in Russia would remain fictitious for some time. As we will see in the following chapter, those groups faced a unique set of obstacles stemming from political infighting among themselves combined with the intrigues of tsarist officials.

With the Czecho-Slovak organizations in the West coalescing around his person, Masaryk's next task was to publicize the cause of liberating the Czech and Slovak homelands. With the help of Ernest Denis, a French scholar on Slavic issues, he organized a gala in Geneva commemorating the fifth centenary of the execution of Jan Hus on 6 July 1915.[53] The following month, Masaryk and his supporters began publishing the newspaper

Českaslovenská Samostatnost (*Czechoslovak Independence*) to serve as the official voice of the movement. Of course, all of these enterprises came with a price tag, and a lack of funds continued to trouble the exiles. Their financial problems had been temporarily alleviated earlier in the year by personal donations from Beneš, Scheiner and Šámal, but the amounts which these men could spare was far below what Masaryk projected as necessary to wage an effectual propaganda campaign. To raise the desperately needed money, Maffie decided to send Vojta Beneš, brother to Edvard, to the U.S. in order to coordinate fundraising efforts among the Czech and Slovak immigrants living there. That summer, Beneš slipped out of Austria-Hungary and crossed the Atlantic to begin his work. With his help, Czech- and Slovak-American groups donated $37,841 to Masaryk's organization in 1915, but this sum was just three-quarters of the amount desired by the professor. However, the Czecho-Slovak Americans made up for any shortcomings that year by surpassing Masaryk's financial goals for 1916. By the end of the war, millions of dollars worth of donations from Czech and Slovak communities in the U.S. would flow into the coffers of Masaryk's organization, making them one of the primary sources of income for the exiles' activities.[54]

Not long after Vojta Beneš began his fundraising campaign in the U.S., reports of his activity reached Vienna and soon his brother Edvard was placed under police surveillance. It is possible that the Austrian police had other reasons to suspect that the young instructor might be enmeshed in treasonous activity. According to one of his biographers, Beneš was rather sloppy in his Maffie work and this was exemplified by his habit of not rigorously vetting the couriers he hired to carry his sensitive messages abroad.[55] Apparently, he was obscure enough to avoid the attention of key Austrian authorities, but the same could not be said for other Maffie members. On 21 May 1915 Kramář and Scheiner were apprehended on the orders of the army's Commander-in-Chief, Archduke Friedrich. Earlier that month, Kramář had provoked the archduke's ire by dissuading his fellow Czech party leaders from dispatching congratulatory telegrams to AOK for the army's recent successes on the Eastern Front. Although Scheiner was released after a few weeks, Maffie lost another member in July when Rašín was detained by police on charges of treason.[56]

Despite these arrests, the existence of Maffie itself continued to elude Austrian authorities. Nonetheless, by late summer, Beneš was growing uncomfortable as detectives continued to follow his tracks. After acquiring a false passport and appointing Šámal to replace him as the leader of Maffie, Beneš left for Germany and from there crossed into Switzerland on 3 September. To his surprise, his reception by Masaryk was cool. The elder revolutionary initially thought that the arrangements which his accomplice had made with Maffie before his departure were insufficient, and he even contemplated sending Beneš back to Prague. Fortunately for Beneš and possibly the entire Czecho-Slovak liberation movement, Masaryk soon decided against that idea. During the following month, Austrian police intercepted a female courier in Prague as she was trying to deliver a message to Maffie. With evidence that some sort of treason was afoot, the police quickly apprehended Masaryk's adult daughter, Alice; Beneš's wife; her brother; and others who were linked to the exiles.[57] Although the roles of Šámal and a few others in the underground remained undetected by Austrian authorities, the spate of arrests did succeed in disrupting the regular chain of communications between Prague and Geneva; they also had the added effect of reducing Maffie to a shell of its former self for the time being.[58] In the meantime, Beneš's talents were put to better use among the busier exiles.

Soon after Beneš joined Masaryk in Switzerland, the latter decided it was time to relocate the center of the Czecho-Slovak liberation movement to an Entente country. The reasons for this were twofold: Switzerland was easily accessible to Austrian agents and its authorities looked unfavorably upon the exiles' increasingly anti–Austrian stance.[59] He ultimately settled on the arrangement that he would establish his office in London while Beneš, who had studied in France before the war, should reside in Paris.[60] That city, with a thriving Czech organization, was to be headquarters of their liberation movement for the remainder of the conflict. Upon arriving there, the frugal Beneš rented out an attic as his living quarters and sought help from his former professors, including Denis and Louis Eisenmann, who helped him contact French government and military officials.[61] It did not take the young revolutionary long to figure out that he could penetrate those elite circles and gain their confidence by feeding them bits of intelligence which he gleaned from incoming Maffie reports.[62]

While his protégé settled in Paris, Masaryk continued onto London. With his fluency in English and familiarity with Anglo-Saxon customs, he was a perfect spokesperson for a foreign people in the British capital. A true Anglophile, from the earliest days of hostilities he regarded Britain's role in the conflagration with the utmost importance: he was pessimistic about Russia's ability to withstand the strains of a prolonged war and doubted whether France could fend off the Kaiser's army, but he was certain that Britain could hold out thanks to the Channel and the strongest navy in Europe.[63]

The British Isles, however, were not impervious to the terrifying bombing raids of German zeppelins. Masaryk realized this when he first crossed the Channel in April 1915 and arrived in a dark London train station surrounded by unlit streets—the city was blacked-out to avoid being targeted from the air. During that trip, he was, with Seton-Watson's help, granted an opportunity to personally submit a memorandum to the Foreign Office explaining his program for an independent Czecho-Slovak state.[64] Entitled *Independent Bohemia*, the document reiterated many of the points made in Seton-Watson's earlier memorandum but with greater detail. Condemning Austria-Hungary as "an artificial state" which "exists only as the vassal of Berlin," it urged the Entente to assist in the creation of independent Czecho-Slovak and South Slav states that would act as a barrier against the dual threats of Pan-Germanism and *Drang nach Osten*.[65, 66] Although the members of Foreign Office who read the memorandum did not dismiss its aims outright, they remained very skeptical of the practicality of Czecho-Slovak independence.[67]

During that initial trip to London, Masaryk had politely refused Seton-Watson's suggestions that he should work for the cause of Czecho-Slovak independence from Britain. At the time, he was particularly concerned with keeping in touch with the Prague underground, which was easier from Switzerland. Besides, Britain had only a tiny community of Czech émigrés compared to those in France and Switzerland, but despite its small size it was not unimportant. After the outbreak of war, the London Czech Committee, like other ethnic organizations in Britain representing the Poles and South Slavs, proclaimed its loyalty to the Entente cause and sought to spare its compatriots from internment as enemy aliens. With Steed's help, the committee was successful in these early endeavors, and soon the group undertook more tasks that evolved into a partnership between various branches of the British government and Czech émigrés.[68]

The cooperation between British officials and the émigrés was a relationship of convenience in a fight against common enemies. The various branches of the British government which accepted the help offered by organizations like the London Czech Committee and later the Czecho-Slovak National Council did so unilaterally and without the authorization of the cabinet. The government itself had no definite policy towards the national question in Central Europe. While the Liberal politicians who dominated the cabinet during the first two years of the war were somewhat sympathetic towards national movements, they did not lead their country into the conflict to win independence for the Czechs and Slovaks, who were unknown to many Britons, or for any other stateless people. They were largely uninterested in Central Europe as long as any territorial reorganization there did not tip the continent's balance of power irrevocably in favor of either Germany or Russia.[69] Without any commitment from London regarding the future of Central Europe, the Czech émigrés who collaborated with British officials throughout most of the war did so without any guarantee that their work would be rewarded with the liberation of their homeland.

By the time Masaryk settled in London in the autumn of 1915, Slav émigrés—not just Czechs but also Poles and South Slavs—were deeply involved in the propaganda and espionage activity of various government departments. Of all the nationalities who offered their services to His Majesty's government, the Czechs were the most trusted from the very beginning.[70] The reason for this preferential treatment is unclear; perhaps it was because the Czech movement, unlike that of the Poles or South Slavs, had no anti–Russian or anti–Italian sentiments that could complicate Britain's relations with her allies. The devout backing of respected men like Steed and Seton-Watson may have also played a role, while another factor may have been the esteemed services of Emanuel Voska in the U.S. After delivering Masaryk's first wartime correspondence with Steed, Voska had returned to the U.S. and, under the guidance of a British naval attaché to Washington, set up a spy network which monitored the activities of German and Austrian officials in the U.S., infiltrated German- and Irish-American organizations and distributed propaganda printed in Great Britain. His cover organization, the Bohemian National Alliance, was given considerable leeway by the British in contrast to other Slav groups.[71] Voska's elaborate spy ring, however, was an exception among the émigré collaborators; more commonly, their activity was limited to the production and distribution of propaganda intended to blacken the reputation of the enemy, attract sympathy to their national cause and encourage their compatriots abroad to support the Entente.[72]

Propaganda was Masaryk's first order of business in England. Finding sufficient personal funds were no longer a pressing matter for the revolutionary since through Steed he gained access to an open bank account financed by Charles Crane.[73] He also had an excellent cover for his presence in Britain after he accepted a lectureship at the newly-established School of Slavonic Studies at King's College.[74] On 19 October, he delivered his inaugural lecture entitled *The Problem of Small Nations in the European Crisis* in which he tried to dispel the fear of "Balkanization" of Central Europe. He was scheduled to have the honor of Britain's Prime Minister, Herbert Asquith, in the audience, but an illness prevented Asquith from attending and instead Lord Robert Cecil, the Permanent Under-Secretary of State for Foreign Affairs, stood in for him. Masaryk, of course, was delighted at the opportunity to present his case to such influential persons.[75]

The series of lectures which Masaryk gave at King's College were just one aspect of the propaganda campaign he helped launch to bring the question of Czech and Slovak self-determination to the attention of the West. It was to be his fortune that the British government, especially the Foreign Office, turned increasingly to the weapon of propaganda the longer the war dragged on.[76] Britain entered the conflict without any governmental department designated for public opinion manipulation; therefore, the propaganda apparatus which it constructed during the war was an *ad hoc* creation intended to maintain support for the war at home and sell the Entente cause abroad. Its propagandists worked in that capacity as free-lancers; most were novelists, playwrights, poets, journalists and scholars who otherwise made their living outside the bureaucracy. Many served under the War Propaganda Bureau at Wellington House, which coordinated the activities of writers, publishers and advisors to generate pamphlets, books and other media. The existence of this bureau was a closely guarded secret during the war; the government correctly calculated that propaganda was most effective if it could not be traced to official sources. Thanks to his friendship with Steed and Seton-Watson, who themselves found employment in various government propaganda departments, Masaryk was able to draw upon the resources of Wellington House for his own propaganda campaign on behalf of Czecho-Slovak independence.[77]

Through the War Propaganda Bureau, Masaryk published two pamphlets, *The Slavs among Nations* and *Austrian Terrorism in Bohemia*, during his stay in Great Britain.[78] Much of the propaganda which he and other émigrés authored was aimed at Slav immigrant communities in the U.S. British officials encouraged this as a means to counter the activities of German- and Irish-American groups who they feared might sway Washington to adopt a policy of strict neutrality or, less likely, a preference for the Central Powers. Britain therefore viewed America's Slav immigrants as a potentially anti–German, pro–Entente voting bloc that would help encourage Washington, which was ostensibly neutral at this stage, to maintain its exports of raw materials, munitions and loans that were vital for keeping the Entente in the war. The émigré propagandists had the advantage of understanding their compatriots better than any Briton and therefore they could more effectively attract the attention and sympathy of their intended audiences. Moreover, they were not strictly bound to accurately depict British or Entente policy in their works. They could, for example, truthfully point out that Asquith spoke of safeguarding the rights of small nations when he led Britain into the war in 1914. However, they omitted mentioning that Asquith's words were intended to apply to existing small states, such as Belgium or Serbia, and not long extinct ones such as Bohemia or Croatia. Finally, the émigrés also had a major role in the distribution of the propaganda. Organizations like the Bohemian National Alliance were one of the main distributors of Wellington House propaganda in the U.S., and this system made it difficult for anyone to trace its origins to the British government.[79]

Masaryk and his associates also developed their own propaganda campaign outside of the War Propaganda Bureau. Following the patterns of the British model, they aimed their pieces at a certain audience, often politicians, journalists and academics, rather than at the general masses.[80] They believed that if this influential tier could be converted to their cause, the rest would sheepishly follow. One of the flagships of this non-government sponsored propaganda was the weekly periodical which Seton-Watson launched in October 1916, *The New Europe*. Its circulation eventually spanned to Italy, France and the United States yet it never exceeded a printing beyond 4,000 copies per issue. It did, however, cultivate an elite readership, and while its effectiveness in converting any official to an anti–Habsburg mindset is dubious, it certainly did kindle an awareness of the ethnic problems in Central Europe.[81] Alongside the émigrés' own mouthpiece, *Československá Samostatnos*, and *The New Europe*, a third periodical, *La Nation Tchèque*, was published in France by Denis, the Slavophile Sorbonne professor. Together, these organs comprised the main pro–Czecho-Slovak publications in Western Europe.[82]

While Masaryk placed high expectations in his propaganda, he knew that it was no substitute for concrete action. Since early 1915, he had been seeking approval from various Czecho-Slovak groups for publishing a manifesto outlining the aims and justifications for the planned independent state. It was no easy task: in a single document he would have to cater to the ideals of the democratic, liberal organizations in the West who entrusted him with their support while not alienating the considerable Pan-Slav element present among the Russian groups, Maffie and in the person of Dürich. Masaryk was eager to publish the manifesto—which amounted to a declaration of war on the Habsburg Empire—as soon as possible, but Maffie's approval of the document reached him only when Beneš crossed into Switzerland in September.[83] By late autumn he could wait no longer; he felt that some sort of demonstration was needed to sustain the morale of the Czech liberation movement in the homeland and abroad.

Masaryk's urgency was prompted by the Entente's military outlook which had gone from favorable to bleak over the course of 1915. The tide had begun to turn in May when a German-led breakthrough on the Eastern Front unleashed a calamity in the tsarist war effort that foiled the Russian Army's plan to steamroll down the Carpathians and across the Hungarian plain. The Russians retreated throughout most of the summer; by autumn they had suffered nearly a million casualties and had lost most of their Polish and Lithuanian territories.[84] The sudden reverse of Russia's military fortunes, especially at a moment when victory seemed so near, was particularly disheartening for Russophile Czechs like Kramář who, as Seton-Watson put it, had been "waiting with folded hands in Prague for the coming of the Cossack liberator."[85] The retreat also caused plenty of anxiety among Masaryk's friends in the West who feared that the tsarist empire might be compelled to quit the war.[86] On top of the bad news from the Eastern Front, the Gallipoli operation was proving to be a failure while Serbia was overrun by the Central Powers that autumn. These two developments ended the Entente's hopes of breaking the general stalemate by consolidating the neutral Balkan states into a league that would declare war on the Central Powers. This setback was especially injurious for the Yugoslavs whose movement had benefited considerably from the attention focused on their region.[87]

Hence, Masaryk aspired to offer the dejected Czecho-Slovak nationalists and their supporters a new hope from his base in the West.[88] On 14 November, his organization, designating itself as the Czech Committee Abroad, released a manifesto formerly declaring war on the Austro-Hungarian Empire. It was endorsed through the signatures of Masaryk, Dürich and numerous other Czech and Slovak émigrés based in France, Great Britain, Russia and even the U.S. As a consequence for the need of a broad appeal, the document bore strong hints of Pan-Slavism but otherwise it repeated the arguments which Masaryk had already presented among his travels in Western Europe. Among its more memorable statements was a declaration that the entire Czecho-Slovak people was resolved to take up arms for its liberation.[89] This was a dubious exaggeration to say the least; the majority of Czechs and Slovaks had as of yet given no indication that they yearned for a future outside of the Monarchy, and it would be sometime before the bulk of their representatives would even consider making such a statement.

Naturally, the Czecho-Slovak émigrés and their foreign supporters, such as Seton-Watson, Steed and Denis, were enthralled by the November proclamation. While the publication of the manifesto was indeed a milestone, it was anything but a game-changing one. None of the Entente governments bothered to utter a word of sympathy for Czecho-Slovak aspirations after the declaration was released. As far as the priorities of British and French officials were concerned, the nationality question in Austria-Hungary ranked far behind their more immediate predicament of how and on what terms they could defeat Germany. We have already seen how the British government, despite its employment of émigrés from Central Europe, was unwilling to make any future commitments there. Outside of official policy, the private opinions and advice proffered by politicians, bureaucrats and other parties varied. Many of those who supported the preservation of the Monarchy did so from the familiar geopolitical assessment that that any void vacated by the empire would be inevitably filled by either Germany or Russia, and neither scenario was regarded favorably by the Western Entente.[90] Others, particularly British Conservatives annoyed by Irish demands for home rule, lacked any sympathy for national movements.[91] Although in 1915 and 1916 the Entente had agreed to rectifications on the southern and eastern frontiers of the Monarchy to buy Italy and Romania's intervention, these extensive territorial losses were not viewed—perhaps unrealistically—as mortal to the existence of Austria-Hungary.[92] The Czech homeland, however, was different. Bohemia was the Monarchy's industrial heartland and a major source of grain and coal; without it the empire was doomed. The Bohemian question, therefore, was unique in that it was a matter of life or death for the Monarchy; those who wished to see Austria-Hungary survive inherently opposed Czecho-Slovak independence.

The émigrés did of course have many supporters and sympathizers in and outside the bureaucracy. Steed and Seton-Watson were two of their most important backers. During the war, they vacillated between private and public sectors and provided many openings for Masaryk and other exiles into official, academic and elite circles in Britain and abroad. Some in Foreign Office, such as Lord Robert Cecil, were irritated by what they regarded as the intrusiveness of Steed, Seton-Watson and their exile friends, but even the Under-Secretary conceded that the national principles for which they agitated "would be a folly to disregard."[93] In the summer of 1916, a commission set up by Foreign Office to identify possible war aims in Central Europe arrived to a similar conclusion by recommending the dissolution of Austria-Hungary into nation-states.[94] The nationalities also garnered sympathy from unlikely individuals, such as Arthur James Balfour, a Conservative cabinet member who on 5 December 1916 became Britain's Secretary of State for Foreign Affairs. In a memorandum completed that October, he too recognized that some application of national self-determination was needed to stabilize Central Europe, but at the same time he acknowledged the practical limitations of that ideal.[95] Although this was a mild endorsement of the solution touted by Masaryk and his fellow émigrés, time was on their side. The sympathies which the nationalities enjoyed inside the British bureaucracy became more pronounced the longer the cooperation between the émigrés and the government continued. Admiration for certain nationalities reached a new level altogether after some of their feats became known to the general public; the Czecho-Slovaks would especially benefit from such a circumstance in the summer of 1918.[96]

French opinion towards Austria-Hungary followed an uncertain pattern similar to that in Britain.[97] Since both countries were colonial powers, they had to exercise caution when championing nationalist principles. Moreover, neither the statesmen nor the general public of either country was willing to prolong the war simply to secure the freedom of Czecho-Slovaks or any other nationality in Austria-Hungary. Their attitudes towards the Habsburg Monarchy were moderate compared to their hatred of Germany, which was regarded as the main villain in the enemy alliance. The Entente's obsession with Germany explains why the propaganda of the anti–Habsburg exiles constantly tried to link the central empires as close as possible, such as by declaring Austria-Hungary to be a "vassal" or "outpost" of Berlin.[98] Throughout most of the war, this argument was an unabashed stretch of the truth. The two empires, far from acting in unison, were frequently at odds over the persecution of the war and foreign policy, their divergent plans for the future of occupied Poland being a primary example. As the conflict wore on, however, there can be no doubt that the Monarchy became increasingly dependent on its northern ally to sustain its war effort, a trend that weakened Vienna's ability to press its aims in the alliance.[99]

While Germanophobe themes were popular in the émigré propaganda, the Czecho-Slovak exiles and their supporters were careful not to overlook the Magyars. Owing to the difficulty of their language and the seasonal travels of their cultivated nobility, the Magyars were not very well understood by most peoples in Western Europe and America. Kossuth, for instance, was far more likely to be remembered as a freedom fighter against Austrian tyranny in 1848 and not as a demagogue who sought to forcibly assimilate Hungary's ethnic minorities. Although a few scholars such as Seton-Watson attempted to unveil the true plight of Hungary's minorities, his condemnations of "Magyar racial tyranny" were easily forgotten amid feelings of contempt and outrage towards the Germans.[100] Nonetheless, émigré propaganda went to some lengths to dispel the myths which encapsulated the Magyars in the West. In his 1917 publication, *Bohemia's Case of Independence*, Beneš reserved some of his sharpest criticism for the Magyar ruling class. "The Balkan policy of the Monarchy was above all things a Magyar policy," he alleged, "It is on them principally that the responsibility falls, of letting loose the present war."[101] His argument exemplifies the misconceptions and half-truths that were woven into émigré propaganda: while the Magyar elite had many faults, warmongering was not one of them. Among Austro-Hungarian leaders during the July 1914 crisis, István Tisza, Hungary's Prime Minister, was among the least willing to favor war due to his anxiety that any addition or cessation of territory resulting from hostilities might upset the delicate balance of the dualist system in the empire.[102]

Regardless of how well the émigrés crafted their propaganda, their allegations of atrocities and terrorism by the Austrian government might still have rung hollow without some concrete examples. Fortunately for them, the actions of Austrian authorities gave them considerable fuel with which they could ignite controversy. The suspension of parliamentary immunity early in the war, followed by the arrests of politicians like Kramář, Rašín and the leader of the Czech National Socialists, Václav Klofáč, strengthened Czech exiles' portrayal of Austria as a genuine authoritarian state. Although there were many political prisoners who were indeed guilty of treasonous activity, the fact that many were not given normal due process lowered Austria-Hungary's image abroad. Because Kramář was relatively well-known abroad as far as Czech politicians go, his six-month trial behind closed doors was followed with interest in the Allied camp. On 3 June 1916 the court passed the sentence of death by hanging upon him, Rašín and two other defendants. In the meantime, Klofáč, whose arrest dated back to September 1914, continued to be held in prison without any formal proceedings brought against him. Another high-profile arrest was that of Masaryk's daughter, Alice. Her plight received much publicity in the U.S. in no small part due to the efforts of Charles Crane, various Czecho-Slovak immigrant societies and women's advocate groups. This unwanted attention may have factored in Vienna's decision to finally release the professor's daughter in the summer of 1916.[103] While her few months of imprisonment caused Masaryk great concern, he did note that the incident, along with the arrest of other well-known figures, had done a great service for the liberation movement. "Martyrdom, and especially blood," he later wrote in his memoir, "win sympathies."[104]

According to Beneš, the Czech Committee Abroad was conceived in an expedient manner for the purpose of providing signatures for Masaryk's manifesto. It was not until February 1916 when the organization was reconstituted into a more permanent form as the Czecho-Slovak National Council.[105] Paris was designated as the headquarters of the National Council while Masaryk's office in London was to serve as the organization's branch in Britain. He hoped that similar branches would soon follow in Rome, Petrograd and even in neutral countries with active Czecho-Slovak groups, such as the United States. Masaryk and Dürich were named co-presidents and were theoretically on equal footing despite the professor's claim that Dürich was actually a vice-president. It is likely, however, that from its inception Masaryk had more leverage in the National Council than the elder Agrarian deputy. One reason for this was that the Czecho-Slovak groups in the West which lent it their support were warmer to Masaryk's democratic ideals than to Dürich's Pan-Slavism. Moreover, Masaryk's protégé, Beneš, was named the National Council's general secretariat and would be a fixture in the Paris office throughout the war.[106]

To give the Czecho-Slovak National Council the appearance of a genuine Czech *and* Slovak movement, it was imperative to bring a representative of the latter ethnicity, or at least someone who could be passed off as such, into the upper tier of the group. Even though Masaryk always considered himself a Slovak and frequently emphasized his ethnic origin, his life and career in Prague had left him "Czechified" in the eyes of observers both at home and abroad. The National Council needed a Slovak who was lacking Masaryk's Bohemian taint, and the group found that representative in the person of Milan Ratislav Štefánik.[107]

By the time Beneš had settled in the French capital in September 1915, Štefánik was already a name recognized among the city's elite despite the fact that he was a Slovak from rather obscure origins. Born in 1880, Štefánik, like Beneš, was a former pupil of Masaryk's at the University of Prague, which he attended until 1904. Afterwards, the sprightly Slovak began a brilliant career in astronomy and meteorology by working at an observatory in Paris and embarking on scientific expeditions to exotic locales in South America, Asia and Africa. Partly because of his research, which had earned him the respect of French scientists, but also because of his charming and lavish personality, he became a fixture in the upper strata of Parisian society and was especially popular with women. In 1912 he became a French citizen and, in early 1915, he volunteered in the army air force of his adopted country. He quickly proved to be a remarkable aviator, and his fame in France widened even further when he achieved the status of an ace in the skies above the Western Front. Later that year, however, he was badly wounded in a plane crash on the Balkan front.[108, 109] In December, after being brought back to Paris to recuperate, he met with Beneš through a mutual friend and soon began an active role in the Czecho-Slovak revolutionary movement.[110]

Although he was to serve as the representative of the Slovaks in the National Council, Štefánik was a dubious spokesman of the long-submerged Slavs of northern Hungary. He actually claimed his ancestry from Czech Lutheran nobles who fled to Upper Hungary after the Battle of White Mountain, which might explain his penchant for aristocratic flair.[111] His Protestant faith, when added with his excellent education, broad travel experience and French citizenship, made him anything but a typical representative for the Catholic and village-centric Slovak majority. Nationalists among Slovak Protestants and their Catholic compatriots had always sharply disagreed over the prospective goals of the Slovak national revival, and the Czechophile leanings of the Slovak Protestant minority mirrored those of Štefánik.[112] Fortunately for the National Council, these differences were unknown to Entente statesmen and no elected Slovak leader ventured abroad during the war. The Slovaks were even more obscure than the Czechs to most persons in the West, the most famous example of this being British Prime Minister David Lloyd George's admission in late 1916 that he had never heard of the Slovaks.[113] Naturally, Masaryk and his supporters were only too eager to provide the befuddled Entente statesmen with their version of who the Slovaks were and what they desired.

Štefánik's importance to the National Council went beyond acting as a Slovak figurehead for the organization; his esteemed reputation and connections among French elites enabled the Czecho-Slovak revolutionaries to access new and influential circles. It was through the Slovak aviator that Masaryk obtained his first audience with a head of state since entering exile. In his meeting with the French Prime Minister, Aristide Briand, on 3 February 1916, he

Milan Štefánik in the uniform of a French general, undated.

declared that the dissolution of the Habsburg Monarchy "into her historical and natural elements" would enfeeble Germany and enhance French security. After the meeting with Briand, the Czech professor was soon granted audiences by France's President and Minister of Foreign Affairs. While Masaryk and Štefánik both regarded these encounters as successes, in every case the statesmen were unwilling to commit to including Czecho-Slovak independence as a condition in the postwar settlement.[114]

Masaryk was too wise to believe that clever propaganda and tea breaks with heads of states would be enough convince the Entente that the Czecho-Slovak homelands must be free. He knew that the Czecho-Slovaks would have to make a major demonstration to show not only their sincerity to the Entente's cause, but also their fitness for self-rule. While an anti–Habsburg uprising among the Czech or Slovak people might have been an acceptable demonstration, it was too fraught with risks from Masaryk's viewpoint: if it succeeded, the new leaders might be Slavophiles unfriendly to his democratic, Western-oriented program; if it failed, the Austrians might completely crush the domestic resistance and leave the Czecho-Slovak liberation movement in an even weaker state. Instead, what he had in mind was to create an independent Czecho-Slovak army from émigrés and war prisoners that would march alongside the Entente to victory. As he put it in a message to Maffie in February 1915:

If we establish an army we shall acquire a new juridical status as regards Austria and the Allies. A further step might possibly consist of a formal declaration of war upon Austria-Hungary. This will create a political situation enabling us to attain at least our minimum demands when peace is negotiated. In any case, neither the Allies nor Vienna will be able to pass us by in silence if we have soldiers. The Allies and our people at home will have a compensatory means of attaining concessions to our national cause, even if it were to turn out badly. But without a decisive and military struggle we shall obtain nothing from anybody.[115]

Shortly after sending that message, he learned that a battalion of Czech immigrants—the Družina—had been established by the Russians early in war. He soon sent another message to Maffie emphasizing that the formation of Czech and Slovak military units was the most important task in their unfolding revolutionary activity. For this reason, he urged a figure in Maffie to escape to Russia and aid in the organization of the Družina, which he erroneously believed was being expanded to a strength of twenty-thousand troops.[116] While he was encouraged by the few hundred Czecho-Slovak émigrés in the West who had joined the French Foreign Legion, he knew that only Russia, with its tens of thousands of prewar Czecho-Slovak immigrants and recently-arrived war prisoners could provide the impressive quantity of troops which he envisaged.[117] However, the initial optimism he had towards the goal of building a sizeable Czecho-Slovak army in Russia would soon to be shattered. Conditions inside the tsarist empire, known for its unwieldy backwardness and rigid autocracy, presented a whole unique set of challenges that few Czecho-Slovak émigrés could have foreseen.

4

The Slavophile Challenge

Since the late nineteenth century, the Russian Empire had been a popular destination for some Czech and Slovak immigrants. While Pan-Slav sentiment might have drawn a few of these Czecho-Slovaks eastward, a more likely motivation was new career opportunities. Russia was a growing market for Czech goods; moreover, Czech professional and skilled workers who moved to Russia found the job competition in their fields much more favorable in a country with a significantly lower literacy rate than Bohemia.[1] Together, the Czech and Slovak immigrants made their homes in Russia's major cities, including Warsaw, Moscow, St. Petersburg and Kiev, or took up farming in the Volhynia region of the western Ukraine. Some assimilated into their Russian surroundings, but a few organized national societies and even established Sokol gyms to keep their heritage alive in their adopted motherland. These efforts were made possible by the unusual leniency of the tsarist government, which otherwise was known for enacting assimilation policies on its own native minorities.

By the time war broke out in 1914, there were about 100,000 Czech and Slovak immigrants in Russia.[2] Since many were not yet naturalized citizens, they were categorized as enemy aliens and were subject to detainment and property confiscations. Although alien Slavs were generally treated more lightly than those who were German, some Czechs and Slovaks were still among the 200,000 German and Austro-Hungarian citizens in Russia who were interned, placed under house arrest or deported from zones of military operation.[3] In response to the tsarist government's crackdown against enemy aliens, many Czech and Slovak patriotic societies sought to shield their members from persecution by publicly expressing their loyalty to Russia and the Entente cause. After toying with ideas ranging from mass religious conversions to public rallies in support of the government, many of these groups eventually concluded that the formation of an army unit comprised of Czech and Slovak volunteers was the best means to show their devotion to Russia.

The Czech Auxiliary Association, a national society located in the Russian capital of St. Petersburg, was the first such group to assure top tsarist officials of their members' allegiance to Russia. In early August, their representatives met with the Minister of the Interior, V. A. Maklakov, who agreed to grant special protection for Czech immigrants in Russia. In another meeting, they convinced the Minister of War to approve the formation of a Czech national unit.[4] They also secured an audience with the Foreign Minister, Sergey Sazonov, who requested a written memorandum on their proposals for a Czecho-Slovak state. It was duly submitted and became the first program of the Czecho-Slovak liberation movement presented to an Entente government.[5]

Although there was some collaboration between a group of Moscow Czechs and those in St. Petersburg, for the most part the early activities of the Czech and Slovak societies were pursued singularly and clumsily. In late August, for example, a delegation of Moscow Czechs submitted to Tsar Nicholas II what were largely the same pledges and proposals presented earlier by the St. Petersburg Czechs. Like any responsible statesman, the Russian autocrat showed interest in the delegation's presentation but avoided any binding commitment to the liberation of Bohemia.[6]

After this meeting, the Czech- and Slovak-Russians recognized a need to consolidate the military and political activities of their scattered organizations. Between 10–18 September, representatives from the largest and most influential Czecho-Slovak groups in Russia met in Petrograd with the goal of establishing a common policy. With the approval of Maklakov they established an umbrella organization of Czech and Slovak groups in Russia. Initially known as the Czecho-Slovak Council in Russia (*Rada Čechů a Slováků v Rusku*), in December 1914 it assumed the permanent name of the Association of Czechoslovak Societies in Russia (*Svaz Československých Spolků an Rusi*, SCSR) The conference experienced further successes when a three-man delegation from it was received by the Tsar and, on a separate occasion, by Sazonov.[7]

The government's attitude towards the Czech and Slovak immigrants pressing for the liberation of their national homeland was conflicted. The most right-wing of the Tsar's advisers, particularly Maklakov and a former prime minister, the eminent Sergey Witte, were concerned with preserving the status quo within the Russian Empire. They believed that if the tsarist government espoused self-determination for Czecho-Slovaks and other peoples outside the empire, whether on the basis of national or historic state rights, it would encourage separatist movements among Russia's many subject nationalities, such as the Poles, Lithuanians and Ukrainians, who could advance similar claims of their own.[8] Moreover, the tsarist government had reason to fear that its own minorities might collaborate with its enemies in the same manner as the Czecho-Slovak émigrés who were extending offers of cooperation to the Entente powers. In the years leading up to war, Austrian authorities in Galicia permitted Józef Piłsudski, a Russian Pole, to train paramilitary formations there. Piłsudski was a militant nationalist who believed that Russia's defeat was a prerequisite for Polish independence, and he looked forward to the day when his sharpshooters would cross the border into Congress Poland and trigger a national insurrection against tsarist rule. To his disappointment, his incursion into Congress Poland in early August 1914 did not spark any rebellion, but nonetheless he continued to build his movement. Over the next eighteen months his legion, which had begun the war with only several thousand men, would swell into a force of three infantry brigades.[9] Nor were the Poles alone in turning to the Central Powers to achieve some form of self-rule. Émigrés from Ukraine sought help from Berlin to organize national committees and generate anti–Russian propaganda while Finnish nationalists formed the Jäger battalion that would fight alongside the Germans on the Eastern Front.[10] The reactionary tsarist ministers, it seemed, were correct to view the weapon of national foment as a double-edged sword.

Still, not everyone in the tsarist government was inflexibly opposed to accommodating national movements. Sazonov, who was eager to cement the alliance with Britain and France, understood that proclamations promising greater freedoms toward oppressed peoples, especially the Poles, resonated well with the more liberal governments and public opinions of Western Europe. In his list of Russia's war aims known as the Twelve Points, he went as far as to openly state that "territorial modifications ought to be determined by the principle of nationalities." As for the Czecho-Slovaks, his Twelve Points recommended an autonomous status for them in a tripartite Habsburg Monarchy consisting of Austria, Hungary and Bohemia.[11] While this condition was far short of the goal of independence advocated by the Czech- and Slovak-Russian groups, it does indicate that their activities in the first weeks of the war had grabbed the attention of the Russian Foreign Minister.

At the Petrograd conference in September 1914, the Czech- and Slovak-Russian groups identified a number of immediate tasks to be addressed by their association. These ranged from drafting a constitution for their movement to enlarging their membership by including other Czech and Slovak organizations in Russia. One of the most important undertakings they agreed upon was to guard and advance the interests of a battalion of Czecho-Slovak volunteers that was training to fight alongside the Russians. As we have already seen, many of the various Czecho-Slovak societies in Russia had seized upon the idea of forming an autonomous Czecho-Slovak military unit as a powerful expression of devotion to the tsarist government. A group of Czechs in St. Petersburg, evoking their ancestors' legendary feats on the battlefield, had called upon their members to enlist into a Czech Hussite Volunteer Corps a few days after the war began. Their compatriots in Moscow also made an effort to organize a similar armed force. Surprisingly, it was not these groups but rather the Russian Stavka (Supreme Command) which decided to set up the unit that was to become the nucleus of all subsequent Czecho-Slovak national military formations in Russia. On 5 August 1914, Stavka ordered the formation of a Czech military unit and ten days later this force became a reality when a battalion was assembled at the Mikhailov Monastery in Kiev.

The battalion, dubbed the Česká Družina (Czech Companions), was intended by Stavka to serve as an administrative military unit once the Russian Army occupied the Czech and Slovak homelands.[12] The young volunteers who formed the unit's earliest recruits under-

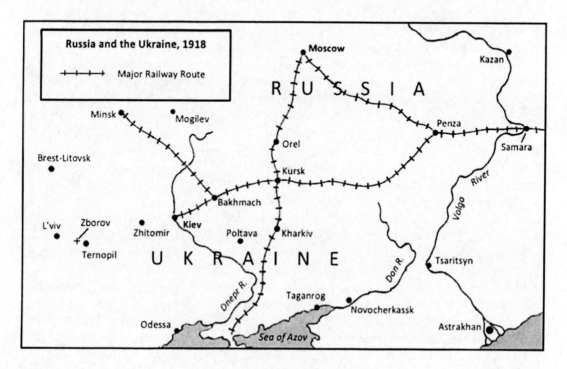

Southern Russia and Ukraine in 1918.

went many strains long before they saw action at the front. Not only were they given poor accommodations in the Mikhailov Monastery, but the Družina's Russian officers were quite insensitive to their men's Czecho-Slovak patriotism. Relations between the ranks were not helped by the fact that the Russian officers were accustomed to instructing barely literate peasant conscripts while many of the Czech volunteers had university educations.[13] Against these initial difficulties, however, the Družina approached a strength of 1,000 troops by the end of September 1914. Of these, about 800 were Czecho-Slovak volunteers and the remaining 200 consisted of Russian irregulars and officers.[14] At this stage all of the members of the unit were required to possess Russian citizenship. Among the names of the Družina's earliest soldiers were several that would gain fame over the course of the war: Stanislav Čeček in 1st Company, Vladislav Klecanda in 2nd Company and Jan Syrový in 4th Company. In mid–September Klecanda and three other volunteers were promoted to become the battalion's first Czech officers, and although more promotions soon followed, the officer caste, and the higher ranks in particular, remained dominated by Russians.[15]

On 28 September, the feast day of St. Wenceslas, the Družina was presented with a flag and took the Russian oath of allegiance in Kiev's St. Sophia Square. Christened the battalion of St. Wenceslas after the Czech patron saint, the Družina left Kiev on 9 October for Russia's Southwestern Front, where they were attached to the Third Army under General Radko-Dmitriev.[16] By then, the Russian advance in Galicia had stalled and there was no immediate prospect of the battalion fulfilling the occupational role originally intended for it. As a result, the Third Army decided to employ the Czecho-Slovak unit in a reconnoitering role at the front. Before long, the Družina was dispersed into an array of patrols along Third Army's sector gathering intelligence on enemy units and even infiltrating behind enemy lines.[17] In one of its most ambitious missions, four Družina soldiers were sent across the front to contact Kramář in Prague and urge him to organize a revolt once the Russian Army approached Bohemia's frontier. Only one of the soldiers, Vladimír Vaněk, reached the Bohemian capital in November 1914. The Young Czech leader, though surprised and impressed by the soldier's mission, promised only to continue his people's "passive resistance." Disillusioned by Kramář's apparent lack of nerve, Vaněk recrossed the frontline back into Russia from where he eventually went onto Western Europe and assisted the Czecho-Slovak National Council.[18]

Vaněk's daring exploit was an exception among Družina missions; most of the time the patrols did not penetrate beyond no-man's land and merely limited their contacts with Slav, especially Czech, infantrymen serving in the Austro-Hungarian Army. By communicating with such troops and targeting them with propaganda, the Družina soldiers hoped to induce them to desert to Russian lines. Their effectiveness at this form of subversion is debatable. For example, one of the most famous feats credited to their activities was the capture of nearly two entire battalions from the 28th Prague Infantry Regiment during the battle of Štebnická Huta in early April 1915. The incident caused a sensation on both sides of the front. In Austria-Hungary, the military cited the loss of the battalions as an example of the unreliability of its Czech soldiers. Later that month, Franz Josef disbanded the entire regiment altogether.[19] Meanwhile, émigré folklore quickly romanticized the incident by depicting the regiment as having crossed over the Russian lines with its banners unfurled and its band blaring Pan-Slavic hymns.[20] After the war, however, historians who examined the incident have uncovered plenty of reason to doubt whether national or Pan-Slav motivations played the decisive role in the battalions' demise. Observers of the battle claimed that the regiment had offered resistance to the Russian attack, although it may have been only of a token

Czecho-Slovak soldiers in trenches on the Eastern Front, undated.

nature. Others have pointed out that morale in the 28th Regiment had never been high; its troops were among those who caused disturbances in Prague the previous September and it had been badly mauled by intense fighting along the Carpathian front in the weeks prior to the battalions' capture. Large catches of Austro-Hungarian troops by the Russians at this time were not unusual on the Eastern Front; the only real difference was the amount of publicity focused on the fate of the 28th Regiment.[21]

Regardless of whether the battalions laid down their arms due to exhaustion or the successful agitation of Czech soldiers on the Russian side of the front, the incident won the Družina much prestige among Russian commanders. They valued the unit's troops as specialists in intelligence gathering and prisoner interrogation. In the meantime, as Czech- and Slovak-Russian groups combined their activities under the SCSR, a number of modifications were made to the Družina with Russian consent. In November 1914, the forerunner to the SCSR was permitted to assign four commissars, three Czechs and one Slovak, to each company in the battalion. In order to preserve the authority of the officers, the responsibilities of these commissars was strictly confined to economic and social issues of the unit. They could, and did, however, influence the appointment of officers to the unit.[22]

Buoyed by the Družina's successes at the front, the SCSR and some Russian officers began seeking ways to expand the unit. Since the battalion's members were required to possess Russian citizenship, the pool from which the SCSR could recruit from appeared quite limited. In the three years from autumn 1914, the Družina and its successive formations never

A *Družina* patrol attempts to build a campfire amid a snow-covered birch forest, undated.

attracted more than 2,000 Czech- and Slovak-Russian volunteers.[23] Since that number was hardly sufficient to replace the battalion's losses, the unit's patrons needed to seek manpower from another quarter. The most obvious solution was to recruit volunteers from Austro-Hungarian prisoners of war, who began entering Russia by the tens of thousands beginning in September 1914. By the end of that year, about 250,000 Austro-Hungarian POWs would be detained in Russia, and their numbers continued to swell during the next two years. Among these captives were soldiers of Czech and Slovak nationality who were regarded by both the SCSR and the Russians as a disaffected element that might be exploited against the Habsburg Monarchy.[24]

The prisoner of war statistics from the Eastern Front in World War I are quite revealing about the deplorable condition of the Austro-Hungarian Army. By 1917, after two and a half years of fighting, approximately two million soldiers from the Habsburg Army were being held in Russian POW camps. In contrast, only 167,000 soldiers and officers from the German Army went into Russian captivity. The reasons why Austria-Hungary lost so many men as prisoners may be attributed to the army's inadequate training, obsolete equipment and poor commanders, all of which took their toll on the soldiers' morale. The Russians quickly detected the Austro-Hungarians to be the weaker of the two enemies it faced on the Eastern Front; subsequently, the sectors manned by Habsburg troops were more attractive targets for Russian attacks than those defended by Germans. On the relatively fluid Eastern Front, offensives often led to large encirclements of defenders. Among the belligerents, Austria-Hungary's total losses as POWs were exceeded only by that of Russia.[25]

The molding of soldiers from so many ethnicities, many of whom were unfriendly to each other, into a single army was bound to put the Austro-Hungarian Army at a disadvantage versus the relatively homogenous armies of nation-states such as Germany, Great Britain or France. The multiethnic formations simply lacked the cohesion and overwhelming sense of patriotic duty possessed by national units. Yet, the proclivity of the Habsburg Slavs to avoid fighting or desert to the enemy was probably exaggerated by both the AOK and émigrés, the latter claiming that their compatriots "openly vowed to each other not to fire on the Russians and Serbs and to surrender at the first opportunity."[26] If these claims were true, one might have expected to find a disproportionately high number of Habsburg Slavs in Russian POW camps. Studies on this subject, however, have shown that no ethnic group was overly represented among the POWs relative to its proportion of the population in the Monarchy. For example, between 1914 and 1917 an estimated 250,000 Czech and Slovaks were taken captive by the Russians. Out of the roughly two million Austro-Hungarian prisoners held in Russia, this meant that only about thirteen percent consisted of Czechs and Slovaks. This is close to the combined percentage of Czechs and Slovaks in the Monarchy, which according to the 1910 census data stood at about sixteen percent.[27] In other words, no single ethnic group was responsible for the obscenely high number of POWs taken from the Habsburg Army; the problem encompassed the entire army and every nationality.

The assessment of Czecho-Slovak émigré organizations and some Russian officers that Czecho-Slovak POWs were conscious deserters of Austria-Hungary led them to believe that this element could be exploited for their own purposes. On 22 October 1914 Stavka designated that preferential treatment should be accorded to all prisoners of Slav ethnicity. The extent to which Slav POWs actually benefited from this regulation is arguable. For example, a Hungarian officer taken captive during the opening battles in Galicia later wrote that the Czechs, whom he called "the pet prisoners of the Russians," were given the best food, medical treatment and the warmest railcars during their transit to distant POW camps.[28] Experiences varied, however, and the decree appears to have mainly affected the destinations of the various groups of prisoners. Slav POWs were mostly penned in camps in European Russia while German and Magyar POWs were more likely to be sent to Siberia even though camp conditions were not necessarily worse east of the Urals.[29]

A more significant step toward utilizing enemy POWs was taken by the Russian Third Army in December 1914. Acting upon the suggestions of the SCSR commissars, General Radko-Dmitriev issued an order allowing newly-captured Czech and Slovak war prisoners to volunteer for service in the Družina.[30] At first this allowance applied only to the front of the Third Army, but later that month it was expanded to other sectors by the Russian Army's Commander-in-Chief, Grand Duke Nikolay. Opposition from other ministries in the government soon compelled Stavka to repeal the order, but in the meantime 350 POWs were able to enter the Družina.[31] Although it affected only a small number of POWs for the time being, the SCSR nurtured hopes that the order might soon be reinstated, thereby allowing the POWs to become a wellspring of manpower to reinforce and expand the Družina.

The department of government that bore the most responsibility for obstructing the recruitment of POWs into the Družina was the Ministry of Foreign Affairs. Sazonov, while unwilling to make any commitment to Czecho-Slovak independence, had initially looked upon the émigrés' goals more kindly than other figures in the Russian government. At the end of 1914, the Foreign Minister had even quietly decided that the Czecho-Slovaks, along with the rest of the Monarchy's Slavs should be freed from Habsburg rule.[32] The increasingly favorable attitude in the Russian government towards Czecho-Slovak national aspirations dissipated in the aftermath of two incidents the spring of 1915. The first was of the émigrés' own making. In March 1915, the SCSR held its first congress of Russian Czecho-Slovak groups in Moscow and elected an executive committee that, among other items, was responsible for cultivating support among Russian ministers and Duma deputies.[33] In the following month, the SCSR executive committee sent an imprudent memorandum to the Russian Ministry of Foreign Affairs demanding a public statement supporting Czecho-Slovak independence and for the uninhibited recruitment of POWs into a full-strength Czecho-Slovak army. When confronted with this memorandum, Sazonov regarded it as an encroachment upon the prerogatives of his department and lost all patience with the SCSR. He soon threw his weight against the Czecho-Slovak cause by blocking any expansion of the Družina with war prisoners on the grounds that it would violate the terms of POW treatment under the 1907 Hague Convention.[34]

On the heels of the SCSR's mishap came the German breakthrough on the front between Gorlice and Tarnów on 1 May.[35] The attackers had selected their target well: the Russian Third Army defending that sector was starved of manpower since its reinforcements were diverted to the south to support the planned drive into Hungary. The Russians' problems were compounded by having too few adequately-trained reserves, low stocks of shells and incompetent commanders, and soon this localized defeat snowballed into the Great Retreat that affected nearly every sector of the Eastern Front and lasted throughout the summer. Amid the ensuing crises, the Russians were forced to evacuate most of Congress Poland and Galicia.[36] Suddenly, the tsarist armies found themselves far away from Bohemia and the prospect of occupying the Czecho-Slovak homelands no longer appeared on the horizon. The Russian Stavka, which had looked favorably upon Czecho-Slovak national aspirations in the hope they might lead to rebellion behind the enemy front, now lost interest as its troops were pushed further back from Bohemia.

With the reversal of attitudes in the Russian Foreign Ministry and the Stavka's waning interest in "the Czecho-Slovak question," the émigrés had lost most of their leverage in their efforts to open the POW camps to SCSR recruiters. Therefore the Družina grew much more slowly than the émigrés had hoped. During the summer of the Great Retreat, the formation added a fifth company of Czech- and Slovak-Russians mostly from the Volhynia region. The commander of the new unit was Lieutenant Stanislav Čeček, who prior to the war had worked in Russia as a representative of a Bohemian automobile firm. Since volunteer-

Stanislav Čeček, undated. Čeček was an early hero among Czecho-Slovak troops in Russia and later became one of their most famous commanders.

ing in the Družina, Čeček had performed a number of distinguishing feats on the frontlines. His most impressive operation was on Christmas Eve in 1914, when he bluffed 127 Austro-Hungarian troops manning an outpost into giving themselves up to his patrol—which numbered only eight men including himself.[37]

Čeček was far from the only Družina soldier to serve the Russians admirably. The retreat in the summer of 1915 was a trying time for the tsarist army; the morale of its peasant soldiers was demolished by their seeming inferiority against a better-equipped enemy. In the rear, tsarist gendarmes burnt fields, farms and villages in an effort to leave nothing to the enemy, meanwhile starvation and epidemics took a heavy toll on the Polish and Ukrainian refugees flooding the roads eastward. This scale of destruction and death was unjustifiable in the eyes of a people who understood neither the war's underlying causes nor what their government hoped to achieve in its aftermath. Subsequently, hundreds of thousands of Russian troops surrendered to the enemy over the course of the summer.[38] As the peasant soldiers retreating alongside them lost heart, however, the Czecho-Slovak volunteers remained steadfast. For them, surrendering or allowing themselves to be captured was unthinkable. Despite their Russian citizenship, Družina troops captured by the enemy were regarded as traitors to the Habsburg Emperor and hung.[39]

The Družina's renowned fighting qualities alone sustained enough Russian interest in the unit to continue its slow expansion. In autumn of 1915, the battalion added three more companies of Czech- and Slovak-Russians, and in the following January, it was renamed the 1st Czecho-Slovak Infantry Regiment.[40] While this development was welcomed by the soldiers and SCSR alike, it was disappointing for those who expected a much larger Czecho-Slovak force to be in place by that time.

The causes behind the underwhelming planned expansion of the Družina were not entirely

Czecho-Slovak troops wearing Russian gas masks, undated.

clear to the Czecho-Slovak émigrés at the time. Many factors which played a part were beyond the SCSR's control: the cautious and noncommittal approach of tsarist authorities to the Czecho-Slovak question, the inefficiency of the tsarist bureaucracy in processing the immigrants' applications for citizenship, and the abysmal supply situation in 1915 that left Russian quartermasters unable to properly arm their regular soldiers much less Czecho-Slovak volunteers.[41] The SCSR leaders' disastrous memorandum also set back their cause, and whether it deserved it or not, the organization's executive committee received most of the blame for the Družina's agonizingly slow growth.

The March 1915 congress of the SCSR had identified the expansion of the Družina, particularly through the recruitment of Czech and Slovak POWs, as one of its immediate goals. Afterwards the organization had dispatched emissaries to Russian camps to contact and begin registering Czecho-Slovak POWs. The recruiting campaign found considerable enthusiasm among the war prisoners; besides patriotic motivations, many POWs may have viewed entry into a Czecho-Slovak army as an escape from the often inhumane conditions of the camps. The Russians had not expected to capture so many enemy troops, particularly at the outset, and as a result POW camps were sometimes nothing more than makeshift holding pens which quickly became crowded and unsanitary. The SCSR, however, could not overcome the tsarist government's opposition to mobilizing POWs. Meanwhile, the recruiting efforts had given the POWs a false hope of imminent release, and when the camps' gates remained closed to them over the following weeks and months, their spirits soon sank into despair and resentment.[42]

With nothing becoming of the SCSR's efforts to enact a widespread mobilization of POWs, many Czecho-Slovaks turned to localized solutions. For example, as Czech and Slovak POWs saw their chances of entering the Družina diminish, approximately 1,000 of them joined the Serbian Volunteer Corps in Odessa, which had much more lenient admission policies.[43] In the meantime, the SCSR's military commission, based in Kiev, sought to help the POWs through agreements with local military officials. Through their efforts, a number of Slav POWs were able to gain employment in defense industries while those in the camps saw their living conditions improve. By spring of 1916, representatives of the Czecho-Slovak POWs and émigrés, impressed with these achievements, were clamoring for a turnover of the SCSR's leadership. They desired the replacement of the original executive committee with the seemingly more effective military commission in Kiev. They got their wish at a second congress of the SCSR held in Kiev at the end of April.[44]

The new executive committee of the SCSR was headed by Václav Vondrák, one of the original four commissars to the Družina. Vondrák and his party, however, were no more successful than the previous SCSR leaders in convincing the central Russian authorities to permit the widespread mobilization of Czecho-Slovak POWs. Although the Czecho-Slovak army unit continued to grow by adding another regiment during the course of the year, these successes were only made possible by their agreements with the district military authorities in Kiev. Moreover, while Vondrák possessed a gift for military organization, he was less decisive as a political leader. Unfortunately, his leadership of the SCSR coincided with a time when the organization was to undergo a period of considerable political turmoil. This was prompted in part by the Kiev congress's recognition of the Czecho-Slovak National Council in Paris as the supreme authority in the Czecho-Slovak liberation movement.[45] Although Masaryk's control over the SCSR was to be more nominal than real, this declaration alarmed Slavophile-extremists among Czech- and Slovak-Russians as well as some elements of the tsarist government. The Czech professor was simply too liberal, too Western-oriented for their tastes, and soon they combined their efforts to seize the political direction of the liberation movement. In the ensuing crisis, Vondrák's policies resembled a weathervane shifting amid currents of varying intensity.

The scheme of the Czech and Slovak Slavophiles in Russia probably would have never made it far off the drawing board without help from the tsarist government. Having lost interest in the Czecho-Slovak question after the reverses suffered by the army in 1915, the Russian Ministry of Foreign Affairs reexamined the issue the following year. The ministry's reason for doing so seems to rest with the attention that Masaryk was attracting in Western Europe: his organization by then had openly declared war on Austria-Hungary, he had met with Briand and other French statesmen, and émigré-inspired propaganda was appearing in Western media. This activity alarmed Russian observers who feared that unless their country patronized those Czecho-Slovak groups favorable to Russia, London and Paris might outmaneuver Petrograd for influence in an independent Czecho-Slovak state in a reorganized postwar Central Europe.[46] After these concerns were reported to the Russian Foreign Ministry, Sazonov turned to one of his experts on Austria-Hungary, a man by the name of Priklonsky, to research and formulate a definitive policy towards "the Czecho-Slovak question."

Sazonov did not remain in office long enough to see Priklonsky's final product. At the end of July, he was suddenly replaced by Boris Stürmer, whose appointment came to symbolize everything that was wrong with the tsarist government. Stürmer's main qualification for the post was that unlike Sazonov and other esteemed individuals, he was willing to tolerate the malignant presence of the Tsarina's spiritual guru, Grigory Rasputin, at the court. Rasputin's critics opposed him on the grounds that the fraudulent Siberian holy man was undermining the venerable image of the monarchy through his nightly drunken escapades and orgies. The Tsarina, however, remained devoted to the *starets* due to his mysterious ability to relieve the hemophilic symptoms of her son. Through her, Rasputin bombarded the Tsar with unsolicited, reactionary advice; it was in this way that he had—not for the last time—engineered the shake-up in a top government post. Stürmer was a particularly bad choice to serve as foreign minister; his Germanic name alone was enough to convince Russia's distrusting soldiers that treason existed in the highest circles of the government. He was also incompetent and overworked—he served as Russia's Prime Minister while Foreign Minister—and subsequently he could be more easily swayed than Sazonov by the bureaucrats, like Priklonsky, working under him.[47]

Priklonsky's first of three memoranda on the subject of Czecho-Slovak independence was submitted to his superiors in the Foreign Ministry on 19 September 1916. It examined the national aspirations of the Czechs and Slovaks separately and offered a distinctly different solution for each ethnicity. He opposed the SCSR and thought that both groups should each have their own separate organization. He showed a particular fondness for the Slovaks, and the ultimate goal he set for them mirrored that advocated by Slovak-Russian Slavophile-extremists who thought their national homeland should be included into an enlarged Russian Empire. As a simple peasant folk, they felt that the Slovaks could be easily assimilated into the Russian culture.[48] Priklonsky, however, harbored no such illusions about the Czechs. From his point of view, they were too urbane and corrupted by German influences, meaning he thought them susceptible to "heretical" and liberal tendencies. Rather than assimilation into Russia, Priklonsky believed that the Czechs should have their own independent state, but one that was oriented towards Russia and not Great Britain or France.

The possible future relations between an independent Bohemia, Russia and Great Britain were a prominent theme in all three of Priklonsky's memoranda. He feared that Masaryk, whom he regarded as a British agent, was placing the entire Czecho-Slovak liberation movement, including the SCSR, at London's disposal. Moreover, he claimed that the Czech professor was unfit to lead the movement since his own political party was minute and his activities did not appear to be authorized by any significant group in the Czech homeland. If an independent Czech state were created according to Masaryk's program, it might establish dynastical ties with Britain and Central Europe might become a new area of friction between the two empires who were already rivals in Asia. Instead of Masaryk, he thought Josef Dürich a much more suitable candidate for the Czech independence movement since not only did he belong to one of the largest Czech political parties, but his Slavophile leanings might also protect Russian interests in an independent Czech state.

The Russian Ministry of Foreign Affairs began to heed the advice in Priklonsky's memoranda beginning in October 1916.[49] By then Dürich was in Russia and Slavophile elements among the Russians and Czecho-Slovaks were already swarming around the exile from the Bohemian homeland.

If Masaryk is to be believed, Dürich had failed to endear himself to most of the émigrés during the year he spent in Switzerland and France.[50] Heeding his instructions from Kramář, the Agrarian deputy gravitated towards a cell of Slavophile Czechs residing in Paris and became a frequent visitor at the Russian Embassy.[51] Despite his solid recommendations from known Pan-Slavs, Dürich, probably as a result of his association with Masaryk, was first denied a visa to enter Russia. It was only in the summer of 1916, after Russian bureaucrats recognized Dürich's true political sympathies, that he was finally issued the documentation he needed to travel into the tsarist empire.

The ostensible purpose for his mission to Russia was to negotiate the transfer of Czecho-Slovak volunteers from Russian POW camps to France as a new source of manpower. The idea had its origins in an agreement between Paris and Petrograd where Russia was to furnish soldiers from its seemingly inexhaustible reserves of "human materiel" to fight on the Western Front. Only a tenth of the expected 400,000 Russian troops, however, actually arrived in France. When the German Army launched its major offensive around Verdun in late February 1916, the ensuing butchery strained France's manpower resources to the limit. Štefánik, upon learning of this predicament, proposed a plan to substitute Czecho-Slovak POWs for the tardy shipments of Russian soldiers. The idea was quickly accepted by the French government, though its outcome ultimately depended on the consent of Petrograd. To facilitate the necessary talks with tsarist officials, Dürich, with funding from the French government and military, was sent to Russia.[52] In addition to the negotiations with the Russian government, he was also instructed by Masaryk to establish a Russian branch of the National Council that would improve cooperation between the Czecho-Slovak Russians and the émigrés in the West.[53]

The decision to send Dürich to Russia was not popular with Štefánik, who envisaged himself leading such a mission, or Beneš, who thought the Agrarian politician was unsuitable for the task.[54] Masaryk, however, ignored their objections. He seems to have doubted whether anything of value could be accomplished in the reactionary climate of tsarist Russia and considered Dürich's services expendable. The two younger revolutionaries then took it upon themselves to obtain the permission of French and Russian officials for Štefánik to go to Russia.[55] Once this was done, they then presented Masaryk with a *fait accompli*. The elder professor feared that if he offered any further resistance, he might provoke a heated confrontation with Štefánik that might compel the short-fused Slovak to withdraw from the National Council.[56]

Upon his arrival in Petrograd in early July, Dürich seems to have immediately forgotten the missions which the French government and Masaryk entrusted him with. He certainly found a number of distractions in the Russian capital as he met with officials in the Russian Foreign Ministry and Czecho-Slovak Slavophiles opposed the political program of the SCSR. To Stürmer, the new Russian Foreign Minister, Dürich submitted a detailed memorandum that mirrored Kramář's proposals for a Russian-led Slavic Confederation that would encompass Bohemia and most of Central Europe.[57] Although this plan did not match Priklonsky's designs for a more surreptitiously Russian-controlled Central Europe, the Russian Slavophiles no longer had any doubt that Dürich was the candidate they needed to reign in the Czecho-Slovak nationalists on their soil. The compliant Dürich soon adjusted his program to match the objectives Priklonsky had in mind.

Later that summer, Dürich went to the army headquarters at Mogilev and broached Priklonsky's plan of forming an entirely new and separate Czech and Slovak organizations in Russia to the Russian Army's Chief of Staff, General Mikhail Alekseev. A practical military man, Alekseev was put off by the proposal to completely rebuild the Czecho-Slovak organizations in Russia. Like the French, he too was in need of soldiers. Although the Russians were gaining considerable ground and inflicting severe casualties on the enemy that summer amid General Brusilov's offensive, these successes were coming at a hefty cost for the attackers.[58] On top of these immediate manpower needs, he knew that the French were still badgering the tsarist government for the promised 400,000 soldiers.[59] Alekseev, therefore, appears to have supported the widespread mobilization of POWs as quickly as possible. He knew that to erect a new Czecho-Slovak national committee would take precious time and might even undo the valuable work that the SCSR had already done in contacting and registering POWs. Unfazed by the Foreign Ministry's unfavorable attitude towards the SCSR, the general urged Dürich work with, rather than against, the existing émigré organization.[60]

Shortly after his visit to Stavka, Dürich learned that he was not the only member of the National Council to enter Russia. On his heels followed Štefánik, who was relying more on his credentials as a French officer than as a National Council member to negotiate for the release of 150,000 Czecho-Slovak volunteers from POW camps for service in France.[61] His goal was exceedingly optimistic: Russia never held more than 250,000 Czech and Slovak POWs and, as later events would show, it was doubtful whether 150,000 volunteers could be found among them to serve on the Western Front. Moreover, politically-minded tsarist officials instantly realized that if this body of troops were allowed to form, it would enhance the bargaining position of Masaryk's National Council in the peace settlement and endanger the goals set for Dürich. Finally, Stavka was unlikely to permit the transport of so many volunteers outside the country when Russia itself was in need of men to fill the trenches.

Soon after his arrival in Russia, Štefánik learned that Dürich was deviating considerably from the official purpose of his mission. In response, the Slovak aviator delayed his own planned negotiations in Petrograd and hastened to Kiev, the base of the SCSR. On 28 August 1916, both he and Dürich were given an official reception by SCSR leaders. The initial politeness of the event soon gave away to simmering tensions among the attendees, not just between the supporters of Štefánik and Dürich, but also between the representatives of the émigrés and POWs in the SCSR. The latter group was by now thoroughly disillusioned with the high hopes they placed in Vondrák and his committee earlier that year. The Czecho-Slovak regiments were growing only very slowly, and the majority of the volunteers among the Czecho-Slovak POWs continued to languish in camps. Despite their successes with the officials of the Kiev Military District, Vondrák and his group were proving to be just as ineffectual as their predecessors in getting the central tsarist authorities to budge on POW mobilization.

At this point neither Dürich nor Štefánik desired a split in the Czecho-Slovak liberation movement in Russia. The Czech politician may have not felt his support strong enough in the SCSR to openly challenge the Slovak revolutionary; on the other hand the latter wanted to avoid the negative publicity that would be the inevitable result of internecine fighting within the movement. Therefore, on the following day, a protocol was agreed upon by the two men and other émigrés. It defined several principles of the Czecho-Slovak movement in Russia, and among these was the amalgamation of the Czech and Slovak national movement that had been opposed by Priklonsky. The document also recognized the need of Czecho-Slovak émigrés throughout the world to coordinate their political, diplomatic, military and POW activities under one organization, and the Czecho-Slovak National Council was named as the group best suited to fulfill this need.[62] Confident that Dürich had been restrained, Štefánik proceeded to embark on his original mission of negotiating the POWs' release and transfer to France.

On 7 September, the Slovak aviator paid a visit to Stavka. Having been previously briefed about the Foreign Ministry's distrust of the revolutionary, Alekseev was pleasantly surprised to discover that Štefánik was quite reasonable in his proposals. The general learned that while his guest was eager to deliver Czecho-Slovak volunteers to France, Štefánik readily stated that any mobilization of the POWs must also take Russian interests into consideration. Štefánik's reputation at Stavka was further raised by the chief of the French Military Mission, General Maurice Pierre Janin. While observing Dürich's scatterbrained activity in Russia, Janin had grown pessimistic whether France would see any achievements from his mission. His hopes, however, were raised by the arrival of Štefánik, whom he recognized as a likeable and competent personality who would be more likely to see through the difficult negotiations for raising a Czecho-Slovak army. Both he and Alekseev concluded that Štefánik should lead a planned commission for mobilizing the Czecho-Slovak POWs. As for Dürich, they thought he should be granted an honorary title that would have marginalized him to the role of a figurehead on the commission.[63]

Dürich's handlers in the Foreign Ministry, however, did not want their man regulated to a powerless, ceremonial role. While they had every intention of making him their puppet, he at least needed to be forceful enough to assert his authority over the émigré organizations. The Kiev protocol which he had signed blocked this, so the tsarist officials prodded him into declaring the agreement invalid on the grounds that he had signed it under duress. Dürich was free to work against Masaryk once again.[64]

In early October 1916, when Priklonsky's memoranda were being circulated in the Foreign Ministry and his influence reached its height, Dürich convened a conference of Russia's leading Czecho-Slovak groups in Petrograd. It was there that he repudiated several principles enshrined in the Kiev protocol; he also renounced his chair on the Paris-based National Council. The tsarist government, he declared, distrusted Masaryk. Russian officials were eager to approve the POW mobilizations desired by the SCSR, but only if the latter recognized a suitable authority. The implied authority was, of course, Dürich himself. Many of the Czech- and Slovak-Russians at the conference were not opposed to such a solution; their primary goal was simply to overcome the inertia in their activity. The representatives of one key group, however, were unwilling to yield to Dürich's proposals. These men belonged to the POWs, whose numbers were subjected to effective press and propaganda campaigns that were both liberal and pro–Masaryk in orientation. After the conference, they reported Dürich's mild ultimatum to the SCSR executive committee in Kiev, but Vondrák and his cabal were themselves undecided about whom they should support. They held a series of debates in a vain attempt to reach a compromise, but what ultimately ensued was a schism in the SCSR into two camps divided by their support or opposition to Dürich.[65]

The Russian Foreign Ministry was playing a zero-sum game in regards to the SCSR; it did not want compromise but rather submission. Only in this way could the organization be purged of its distasteful influences and rendered into pliable instrument. As the debate raging within the SCSR grew more protracted following Dürich's October conference, Priklonsky became more pessimistic over whether his candidate could ever completely control the SCSR. He decided that the establishment of an entirely new organization, which he had long advocated, was the only realistic solution. In late January 1917, the Russian Council of Ministers authorized his plan to found a new Czecho-Slovak national organization with Dürich as chairman. The constitution of the organization was to be drafted by the Russian Ministry of Foreign Affairs, and the government would furnish the committee with a spending allowance of 7,500 rubles per month. On 30 January, Dürich announced the impending formation of his new national council.[66]

Between October 1916 and January 1917, Štefánik had been in Romania negotiating with that government for the release and transfer of its Czecho-Slovak POWs.[67] When he returned to Russia, he was dismayed to learn that the POW commission agreed to by Stavka had been delayed indefinitely pending the confusion within the SCSR. In an effort to bypass attacking Dürich directly, he sent a letter to the Russian Minister of War pleading for the recognition of the earlier agreement. Dürich's new committee, he warned, would only delay the reinforcement of the fronts with Czecho-Slovak volunteers. This last-ditch effort, however, failed to have its intended effect. The Minister of War proved unwilling to intervene on his behalf against the Ministry of Foreign Affairs.

The breach with Dürich that Štefánik had tried to avoid was now inevitable. While the Agrarian deputy had powerful backers in the Russian Foreign Ministry, the Slovak aviator was not without his own network of eminent supporters. One was General Janin, who was so impressed with Štefánik's unceasing efforts to mobilize POWs for the Entente cause that he recommended his decoration with the Order of St. Vladimir to Stavka.[68] Another group Štefánik could rely upon was a well-connected ring of liberal Czech- and Slovak-Russians in Petrograd. These émigrés had contacts with progressive-minded parliamentarians in the State Duma, and through them they obtained the minutes of the Council of Ministers' meeting regarding the Czecho-Slovak liberation movement. Armed with these documents, Štefánik went on the offensive. He showed them first to General Janin, who was outraged to learn that the goal of recruiting Czecho-Slovak POWs for service in France was being delayed by the tsarist government's tampering. The revelation in the papers that Petrograd was playing shady political games at a time of national crises for the Entente was embarrassing for the tsarist government.[69] Štefánik also brought the incriminating papers to a SCSR conference in Kiev on 7 February. The evidence that Dürich's activities were being directly funded by the tsarist government completely evaporated his support among the gathered representatives.

Vondrák, now certain of the prevailing political winds, turned decisively against Dürich and asked Russia's new Foreign Minister, Nikolay Pokrovsky, to terminate Dürich's committee. Although the humbled official was not prepared to liquidate Dürich's group, he slowly backed his department away from further meddling in Czecho-Slovak affairs and left the émigrés to sort out their own disputes at an SCSR congress scheduled for later that year. For the time being, two rival organizations claiming to represent the national aspirations of the Czecho-Slovak peoples lingered in Russia.

After the February SCSR conference, Dürich's national council was deprived of most of its support among Czecho-Slovak émigrés and subsequently depended completely on the patronage of the tsarist government. That regime, however, was undergoing its own struggle for survival. With each passing day of hostilities, Russia's army, economy, infrastructure and society was buckling more and more under the strains of a modern war. The railroads were unable to maintain the hauling capacity to feed the cities and the armies, so the cities went hungry. The peasants saw the purchasing power of their rubles plummet, so they refused to sell their grain at the government's fixed prices. The men who had once comprised the flower of the regular army and officer corps were now lying beneath the snow in Galicia and Poland; in their place stood workers and peasants who were no longer inspired to die in the trenches for their Tsar. Strikes and demonstrations had become a somewhat regular occurrence in the major cities, including the capital; not even the frigid Russian winter was enough to discourage the angry masses from taking to the streets.[70]

Resolving Russia's domestic woes would have been a challenge for even the ablest of the country's administrators, but such a person was unlikely to be appointed by the Tsar as long as the Tsarina and, by proxy, Rasputin swayed his decisions. On 30 December 1916, a group of devoted monarchists tried to save the Romanov monarchy from itself by murdering the *starets*. Their sloppy assassination did not have its intended effect since the imperial couple became even more withdrawn and Rasputin's lackeys continued to occupy important ministerial posts. One of them, the Minister of the Interior, even improved his position with the Tsarina by claiming that he regularly held séances with the spirit of the slain *starets*.[71]

Under these circumstances, nearly everyone in Russia sensed that the days of the autocracy were numbered. The only exceptions, aside from the alienated imperial couple, were Dürich and his small circle of Slavophile supporters. Even though his activities were confined within the boundaries of the tsarist empire, his defection from the National Council had not gone unnoticed in the West. For Masaryk and Beneš, the timing of this unwanted publicity could not have been worse since the two men were then pushing hard in Paris to obtain a degree of recognition for Czecho-Slovak national aspirations.

Like Štefánik, Masaryk was reluctant to make a formal break with Dürich. He knew that the Entente would only gain confidence in the Czecho-Slovaks' readiness for self-rule if the liberation movement presented a united front. Indeed, this was one area where the Czecho-Slovaks possessed some advantages over the parallel liberation movements launched by the Poles and the Yugoslavs. The former were irreconcilably split between the left, which idolized Piłsudski and was anti–Russian, and the pro–Entente right arrayed around Roman Dmowski. Among the South Slavs, the main dispute was centered on the partition of power in their planned independent state. The Yugoslav Committee in London sought a federal state where Croats, Serbs and Slovenes would be theoretically equal; the Serbian government of Nikola Pašić, however, desired Serbian dominance in a postwar South Slav state.[72] In contrast, the open rivalry that emerged between Masaryk's National Council and Dürich's committee was a mild disruption. Nonetheless, the internecine strife among the seemingly level-headed Czecho-Slovaks reinforced doubts among some Western observers over whether the Slavs of Central Europe were fit to govern themselves.

Štefánik had cabled Masaryk and Beneš in Paris to formally expel Dürich from the National Council only after he obtained the incriminating papers which exposed the elderly Czech politician as a tsarist tool.[73] While Masaryk was already aware of Dürich's erratic behavior in Russia, he avoided openly condemning his colleague's activities there. His slow repudiation of Dürich have led some historians to paint Masaryk as an opportunist; in other words that he was leaving the door open to Dürich's Slavophile program if he were left with no other choice.[74] The more plausible explanation is that it was pragmatism, not opportunism, behind Masaryk's reluctance to more forcefully assert the democratic, Western-oriented program for Czecho-Slovak independence. Not only did he desire to uphold the guise of Czecho-Slovak unity, he also wanted to avoid offending the sensibilities of the tsarist government by appearing too anti–Russian or anti–Slav. He knew that the Western governments he was counting on for support would never back Czecho-Slovak aspirations if it meant alienating one of their most important allies in the war. Indeed, anti–Russian sentiment among some Polish émigrés was one reason why London and Paris approached the Polish question with considerable restraint up to 1917.

When the breach between Dürich and himself could no longer be glossed over, Masaryk turned to propaganda to neutralize his rival in Russia and brush the matter aside in the West. According to him, Dürich had "succumbed to the pressure of reactionaries and of foolish officials."[75] In the war of words that raged between the two men, Dürich was completely outgunned. The Czecho-Slovak émigré press abroad overwhelmingly favored the Czech professor, as did some key organs in Russia. Dürich himself had no desire to verbally abuse his fellow exile. Like the old-fashioned politician he was, he appeared to have viewed the dispute between him and Masaryk as a gentlemen's disagreement where each was doing what he thought best for Czecho-Slovak interests.[76]

While the National Council's presence in Russia rested on less-sure footing than Masaryk had hoped at this point, he and Beneš were expending most of their energy on advancing their cause in Western Europe. In December 1916, a unique opportunity presented itself for the National Council to obtain the Entente's public recognition, or at least its acknowledgement, of Czecho-Slovak national aspirations. That month, U.S. President Woodrow Wilson, having recently won reelection on his record of keeping America out of the war, attempted to initiate negotiations towards ending the conflict by asking all belligerents to identify their conditions for peace.[77] Wilson's motivation for sending the note was likely due to his fear that if the war did not end soon, Germany would recommence her unrestricted submarine campaign in the Atlantic and thereby draw the U.S. into the war. The Central Powers were the first to reply to the inquiry although their ambiguous terms and reiteration of their faith in final victory probably did not impress the President.[78] The Entente, on the other hand, realized that they needed to be more prudent in their answer to Wilson. Although irritated by the President's meddling, they were painfully aware that the U.S. was for them a vital source of munitions and credit. They needed to furnish an answer that would appeal to the President's conscious in order to ensure their uninterrupted access to armaments, foodstuffs and financial loans from the other side of the Atlantic.[79] Hence, the Entente's reply was to be more akin to a propaganda exercise than a genuine declaration of war aims.

When Masaryk and Beneš learned of Wilson's peace note, they saw it as a golden opportunity to advance their cause. At the end of December, Beneš sent a memorandum to the French Ministry of Foreign Affairs claiming that if the Entente listed Czecho-Slovak independence among its war aims, the Czech opposition in Austria would be strengthened, leaving the empire "completely disorganized."[80] The French and their allies were unconvinced by Beneš's argument. Originally, they intended to call for the liberation of the Italians, Romanians and Slavs in the Monarchy as a condition for peace. This appeal to national self-determination may have been deemed necessary by Britain's own secret propaganda campaign, which by then had aroused considerable sympathy in the U.S. for the subject nationalities of Austria-Hungary. The Entente's statement on the nationalities was meant to be deliberately vague; most did not want the principle of national self-determination to be applied evenly across the board. Therefore, by using the word "Slavs" it avoided singling out any particular nationality; at the same time, "liberation" might have been construed as mere autonomy. Ultimately, it did not commit the Entente to the dissolution of Austria-Hungary.[81]

Beneš was unsatisfied by this version of the draft and remained committed to his original goal of seeking a specific endorsement of Czecho-Slovak national aspirations. After expounding his arguments personally in three interviews with various officials in the French Foreign Ministry, his persistence paid off.[82] In the final version of this statement, the Entente demanded "the liberation of Italians, Slavs, Romanians and Czechoslovaks from foreign rule."

The Entente's reply to Wilson was released on 12 January 1917 and its mention of the Czecho-Slovaks caused much celebration and optimism among the émigré organizations abroad.[83] The statement also did not go unnoticed in Bohemia, where the Czech clerical parties readily repudiated the condition. This was soon followed by a much more damaging disavowal of the émigrés' activities released on 23 January by the Czech Union (*Český Svaz*), a coalition consisting of Reichsrat deputies from all Czech political parties with the exception of the State Right and Realist parties.[84] They declared not only that the émigré program of Czech liberation was based on "entirely false suppositions," but also that "the Czech nation envisages the conditions of its development only beneath the scepter of the Habsburgs."[85] Altogether, its contents were a bitter reward for Beneš and others who had labored so hard to obtain the Czecho-Slovaks' mention in the Entente note.

The disavowal from elected leaders in the Czech homeland put the National Council on the defensive. To the Entente press, Beneš explained the repudiation as having been squeezed out of the Czech politicians by the Austrian government. Masaryk struck a similar note by asserting that the Czechs made the statement of loyalty to Vienna in the hope that the authorities might yet spare their imprisoned leaders, such as Kramář, from the gallows. These claims were mostly untrue. The Czech Union had opted for the repudiation largely by its own accord. The new Austro-Hungarian Foreign Minister, Count Ottokar Czernin, did persuade the deputies into signing a more strongly-worded disavowal than they originally drafted and it was this sharper version that was subsequently made public. The exiles were unable to admit that the majority of Czech politicians in the Bohemian lands still maintained the mentality of Austrian citizens, not of revolutionaries. For now at least, the domestic leaders attached little importance to the sympathies which the exiles had conjured abroad for the Czecho-Slovak peoples. They were more concerned with cultivating the goodwill of Vienna in the hope that the new emperor might reinstate parliamentary government in Austria.[86]

The Dürich affair and the disavowals from Bohemia had the potential to seriously undermine the credibility of the Czecho-Slovak National Council at a time when the organization had finally found its way into the spotlight. Both incidents were indicative that the Czecho-Slovaks at home and abroad were not as united in a common goal as the émigrés would have liked the Entente governments to believe. Fortunately for Masaryk and his accomplices, these setbacks would soon be overshadowed by the Russian Revolution and the entry of the United States into the world war. These two events would not only shakeup the military outlook of the conflict, but also its economic, social and political balances. They also transformed how the Czechs and Slovaks at home and abroad viewed their national aspirations in context of the global struggle. Generally, these changes were to work in Masaryk's favor although he and his National Council would still encounter many challenges along their path.

5

Deliverance at Zborov

The food riots in Petrograd that began on 8 March 1917[1] were initially neither extraordinary nor alarming to the tsarist authorities. Only in the course of the following days as the capital's garrison began shifting their allegiance from the government to the demonstrators did the authorities appreciate the seriousness of the disturbances. On 12 March in the Tauride Palace, a group of deputies to the State Duma organized themselves into a committee to restore order in Petrograd. Simultaneously in the opposite wing of that palace, a Soviet of workers' representatives was established on the same model used in the abortive 1905 Revolution. Three days later, after the revolt had spread to Russia's other Baltic ports and to Moscow, the Tsar acknowledged the futility of his attempts to regain control of his realm and abdicated in favor of his son and then his younger brother, the Grand Duke Mikhail. When this last would-be successor declined the crown on the following day, three centuries of Romanov sovereignty arrived to an end. The autocracy was replaced by a dual system of government. The committee established by the Duma members claimed its authority as the Provisional Government, but it was obliged to share power with the Soviet that commanded the loyalty of the workers and soldiers. Originally, these two organs agreed to collaborate towards establishing a permanent Russian government in the form of a democratically-elected Constituent Assembly.[2] The Russian masses, for whom serfdom was still a living memory, were now promised a latitude of freedom that rivaled the most progressive of Western democracies.

From London, Masaryk celebrated the news of the revolution in Russia. The downfall of the Romanovs not only removed the regime that had been unwelcoming to his person and program, it also appeared to vindicate his initial assessment that the war was a conflict between democratic and autocratic ideologies, not between the Slav and Teutonic races. Moreover, his academic acquaintance, Pavel Miliukov, a historian and the chairman of the liberal Kadet Party, was named foreign minister in the Provisional Government. On 18 March he sent a congratulatory telegram to Miliukov stating his confidence that the new, free Russia will liberate the Slavs from "German-Magyar-Turkish domination."[3] Miliukov reciprocated these tidings five days later at a press conference when he announced his support for an independent Czecho-Slovak state.[4]

The new Russian Foreign Minister was also crucial in emasculating Dürich's operation. Shortly after Miliukov took office, Štefánik had successfully requested the severance of the subsidies to Agrarian politician's rival committee. Even if the new foreign minister had not been personally affiliated with Masaryk, it is unlikely that Dürich would have lasted very long on the Provisional Government's payroll; his brand of conservative Slavophile politics was more likely to arouse suspicions, not sympathies, in revolutionary Russia. He was slow to grasp the significance of the changes taking place in the country; subsequently, he was thunderstruck when his funds dried up and Priklonsky, the mastermind behind his organization, suggested that he cease his activities.[5] His Slavophile committee gradually faded away during the spring of 1917. For Masaryk, it was another reason to celebrate the disappearance of tsarism. In a letter to a supporter, he made the laconic observation, "The revolution buried absolutism, its Slavic policy, and hence also our colleague Dürich."[6]

No longer prohibited from entering the country, Masaryk now felt that the time had come for him to go to Russia and steer the Czecho-Slovak liberation movement there on a proper course. The British Foreign Office, which was eager to send anyone to Russia who might help keep that country in the war, quickly issued the Czech professor a passport under the alias Thomas George Marsden.[7] He originally intended to board a ship from Britain on 17 April but instead he delayed his departure to meet with Štefánik, who had just returned from Russia. He would not regret this move since not only did he get an up-to-date briefing on the Russian situation from his Slovak accomplice, but the vessel upon which he was planning to travel was sunk by a German U-boat. The realization that he may have escaped an early demise in the frigid waters of the North Sea seems to have caused him anxiety to the point of physical illness.[8] He recovered, however, and finally left for Norway early in the following month. His nerves were put at ease by the fact that the ship upon which he sailed was escorted by two destroyers.[9] After a train ride across the peaceful, snow-draped landscapes of Scandinavia, he was jolted when he arrived into a tumultuous Petrograd on 16 May. His optimism in the new democratic Russia was quickly transformed into a sense of foreboding.[10]

Much had changed since the early days of the Revolution when the Petrograd Soviet and the Provisional Government had resolved to work together to build a new democratic Russia. The two bodies vehemently disagreed on what terms they were to continue prosecuting the war. Since taking office as foreign minister, Miliukov wanted to adhere to the previous treaties between the Entente powers and the tsarist government; this meant Russia would continue the fight until final victory and obtain territorial rewards, such as eastern Galicia and the Black Sea Straits. To the Soviet leaders, however, this policy reeked of old-fashioned imperialism. They and the socialist parties desired a peace without annexations or indemnities. Subsequently, at the end of March, the Soviet turned up the heat on the government by releasing a general declaration calling upon the proletariat in all countries to end the war by refusing to serve "as an instrument of violence and conquest." The Provisional Government, despite the disapproval of Miliukov and other ministers, caved to the pressure from the Soviet. On 9 April, it released a diplomatic note to the Allies which attempted to harmonize its war aims with those of the Soviet by renouncing Russia's claims to any foreign territory. The Foreign Minister, however, refused to associate his office with that statement and continued to publicly insist that Russia would observe her treaty obligations. His unwillingness to conform to the new order triggered an outbreak of turbulent street demonstrations in the Russian capital. On 14 May, two days before Masaryk reached Petrograd, Miliukov resigned as foreign minister. Four days later, the Provisional Government was reconstituted with a coalition cabinet that included a larger number of socialists.[11] Miliukov's fall and the general unrest in the capital were the first of many unpleasant surprises which Masaryk encountered during his first days in Russia.[12]

Russia by then was already teeming with foreign socialists, propagandists and amnestied exiles fervently pushing their agendas. Many had been sent there by Russia's allies who had listened to the pacifist rhetoric of the Soviet with trepidation. If Russia quit the war, the Central Powers would be able to concentrate their full might in Western Europe. Subsequently, in order to galvanize their ally's war effort, Britain sent, in addition to Masaryk, Labour Party leader Arthur Henderson. Belgium and France followed suit by sending their respective leading socialists, Emile Vandervelde and Albert Thomas.[13] The United States, Petrograd's newest ally in the war, sent two advisory commissions to Russia. One consisted of a group of railway experts who sought to rehabilitate the country's deteriorating transportation network, the second was headed by Elihu Root, a former U.S. Secretary of State, and recommended ways to stiffen Russian resolve to fight on to final victory.[14] Emanuel Voska, with British connivance, also went to Russia from the U.S. to carry out a pro-war propaganda campaign.[15]

Arrayed against this impressive collection of foreign spokesmen and propagandists were amnestied revolutionaries who viewed the overthrow of tsarism in Russia as the first salvo of a worldwide social revolution against capitalism. Most prominent among these extremists was Vladimir Ilych Ulianov, better known to history by his alias of Lenin. His faction of the Russian Social Democratic Party, known as the Bolsheviks, was the most consistent in their opposition to the "capitalist war." Lenin wanted the working classes in all countries to turn their arms on the monarchs, aristocrats and bourgeoisie, and he viewed the February Revolution as the opening act in the desired civil war among classes. German agents quickly recognized that Lenin and his circle of émigrés residing in Switzerland might be a useful weapon to undermine the resistance of their eastern adversary. Subsequently, they agreed to whisk the Russian revolutionaries across the Reich and to Stockholm, from where the Bolshevik leader reached Petrograd on 16 April after seventeen years of foreign exile.[16] From the moment he arrived in Russia, Lenin began agitating for the termination of the present conflict in favor of a war against capitalism. His ideas proved unpopular at the moment; he even had trouble convincing his own followers of their correctness.[17] This lack of support, however, did nothing to deter the willful revolutionary from further activity.

Masaryk too began his agitation almost from the moment he left Petrograd's Finland Station. Relying on his reputation as a respected scholar and current revolutionary leader, he warned against the pacifist movement overtaking Russia in press interviews and public debates.[18] While he remained in Petrograd to help organize pro-war propaganda to keep Russia in the war, he kept an eye cocked on the cause dearest to him, the Czecho-Slovak liberation movement. He found the political direction of the movement in Russia to be headed in the right direction. When he arrived in the Russian capital, a third SCSR congress had just wrapped up in Kiev from which Dürich and his few remaining supporters were barred. During its proceedings, the gathered delegates had cast aside the executive committee led by Vondrák in favor of a newly-established Russian branch of the Czecho-Slovak National Council. From now on, the dominant element in the Czecho-Slovak revolutionary activity in Russia was not the immigrants, many who were Russian citizens, but the POWs and exiles who were still technically soldiers and citizens of Austria-Hungary. With the political turmoil in the movement finally settled in Masaryk's favor, the Czecho-Slovaks needed to turn their attention to their small army, whose outlook was very uncertain.[19]

Although the intrigues of the Russian Foreign Ministry blocked the SCSR from enlisting volunteers from POW camps, the battalion of volunteers known as the Družina early in the war had, by late 1916, expanded to the size of a brigade. This was made possible through agreements with local military officials on Russia's Southwestern Front who permitted the

Czecho-Slovaks to recruit among freshly-seized prisoners on their sector. During this time, the Czecho-Slovak Brigade (*Českaslovenská brigáda*), probably owing to the questions surrounding Czecho-Slovak activity in Russia, had been idled in Ukraine into early 1917.[20] The confusion and disintegration of the central authority in the aftermath of the February Revolution eased the pressure on the Brigade. Its troops undertook a new oath of allegiance, now to Masaryk, the National Council and the concept of Czecho-Slovak statehood, and a new effort was made to organize the POWs in the camps.[21]

The enlargement of the Brigade through Czech and Slovak volunteers in the POW camps remained a foremost yet elusive aim of the new Russian branch of the Czecho-Slovak National Council. The Provisional Government's first Minister of War, Aleksandr Guchkov, preferred to keep the Czecho-Slovak volunteers in the prison camp system where they could serve as laborers in Russia's war industries.[22] Since late 1915, war prisoners were replacing conscripted Russian workers in everything from agriculture to industrial labor. Certain nationalities among the POWs, including the Czechs, were popular with Russian employers for their abundance of skilled laborers.[23] The tasks required of the POWs varied considerably. While many probably found employments in the factories and on peasant farms preferable to the danger of the trenches or the monotony of the camps, others, particularly those pressed into mining or construction duty in the frozen north or in the baking deserts of Central Asia, resented their assignments.[24]

Guchkov lost his office along with Miliukov in the first cabinet crisis of the Provisional Government, but his replacement, Aleksandr Kerensky, was no friendlier to the goal of enlarging the Czecho-Slovak military formation. Kerensky, a thirty-five-year-old lawyer who exuded personal charisma along with a talent for stirring oratory, was perhaps the Provisional Government's only popular figure. As a member of the Soviet's executive committee, his presence in the government allayed the fears of Russia's workers and soldiers who suspected that the liberal politicians, such as Miliukov, might betray the revolution to the bourgeoisie. For a brief moment, it seemed that his inspiring words alone might be enough to bolster Russia's sagging enthusiasm for the military effort at home and at the front.[25]

Some historians have blamed Kerensky's opposition to the enlargement of the Czecho-Slovak Brigade on the pacifist policies which he and other socialists tried to implement after assuming their new offices in the Provisional Government in May 1917.[26] That explanation, however, is inconsistent with Kerensky's own considerable efforts as Minister of War to gear the army and country for the summer offensive which Russia had promised her allies. The more likely reason why Kerensky was opposed to augmenting the Czecho-Slovak Brigade was that he and others saw nationalism as a growing threat to the army's unity. Since the disappearance of tsarism, Russia's minorities were steadily becoming more assertive in their demands for autonomy, not only in their regional administrations but also in the armed forces. The Ukrainians, who were one of the largest minority groups in Russia and had sent many men into the army, were particularly disruptive by the summer of 1917.[27] Therefore, to stamp out Ukrainian aspirations of forming their own autonomous, nationally-homogenous units in the army, Kerensky soon banned all recruiting activities—including those of the Czecho-Slovaks—for national armies.

The War Minister's injunction had the potential to lead to the complete disbandment of the Czecho-Slovak Brigade. Many Russian socialists looked disapprovingly on the Brigade, and Kerensky catered to their sentiment by labeling the national movements a "manifestation of an unhealthy coloring of the national question bordering on chauvinism."[28] In Russia's interior, Czecho-Slovak emissaries attempting to register POW volunteers soon found their efforts obstructed by local soviet chairmen who complained that a larger Czecho-Slovak force would only prolong the conflict.[29] Fortunately for the Brigade itself, the military authorities on the Southwestern Front made no effort to disarm it or prevent it from fighting. On the contrary, the commanders and commissars who were preparing for the upcoming offensive were pleased to accept an offer from the Brigade to fight in the attack's first wave.[30]

While the Czecho-Slovak Brigade maintained relatively good spirits and discipline, the same could not be said for most of the Russian Army by summer of 1917. Kerensky and many others hoped that the new freedoms which the Russian masses had won in the revolution would galvanize the troops to fight until final victory, but instead it had the opposite effect. The earliest decree of the Soviet, the infamous "Order Number One," bestowed on soldiers and sailors the right to elect their own committees which would then decide whether to follow their officers' orders.[31] Originally, Order Number One was intended to apply only to the Petrograd garrison, but it quickly became known on every corner of the front and undercut the authority of the officers and Stavka. The commanders did not dare to openly resist the implementation of the decree due to their fear of provoking the troops to more violent rebellion.[32] Desertion, already a perennial problem for the tsarist army, increased fivefold in the months after the February Revolution.[33] Meanwhile, those who remained at the front caused their commanders plenty of headaches. In the spring of 1917, the German command launched an organized campaign of fraternization and propaganda in order to subvert the Russian troops. All across the Eastern Front, German intelligence officers distributed leaflets and even a Russian-language newspaper to convince the peasant soldiers that they needed to return home in order to obtain the fruits of the revolution. In no man's land and even behind their lines, the Russian infantrymen gathered to listen to emissaries from the Central Powers who promised peace and offerings of rum and vodka. Their helpless officers could only look on with grim faces—their attempts to break up these meetings by firing pistols or artillery into the crowds merely incited a mutinous backlash.[34]

Despite the steady unraveling of discipline in the Russian Army, Kerensky was determined to launch the scheduled offensive. To sell its merits to the soldiers, he embarked on a whirlwind speaking tour of the front where he gave dramatic performances to inspire the demoralized troops to defend their motherland and the revolution.[35] General Brusilov, the mastermind of the stunning offensive during the previous summer and who had a reputation for accommodating the army committees, was promoted to Commander-in-Chief at Stavka. Great effort was also made to achieve artillery superiority across the front; for the first time in the war, the Russian soldiers would be supported by batteries of heavy howitzers.[36]

The attack that would be remembered as the Kerensky Offensive began on 1 July 1917 along a forty-mile sector of the Southwestern Front, where the main effort was to be made. On that morning, after a massive two-day bombardment of enemy lines, infantrymen from the Russian Seventh and Eleventh Armies stormed out of their trenches and charged across no-man's land with an *élan* not seen for months.[37] It was an encouraging start made all the more surprising by the fact that many areas of the Russian rear continued to be a seething quagmire of insubordination and outright mutiny up to the eve of the attack.[38]

The operation planned for the Czecho-Slovak Brigade, which was to be its first major action as a united formation, was of secondary importance and began one day after the initial infantry assaults. In preparation for the attack, the Czecho-Slovaks were deployed with the Eleventh Army on a four-mile stretch of the front west of the town of Zborov, from which

Russian artillery in action on the Eastern Front, undated. The Czecho-Slovaks were barred from forming artillery units until after Kerensky's offensive.

the ensuing battle took its name. Each wing of the sector was covered by a Finnish division; in between them the Czecho-Slovak infantry regiments were deployed north to south in the following order: 1st Regiment, 3rd Regiment and 2nd Regiment. With a total strength of about 7,000 men, the Brigade was outnumbered by the formations of the Austro-Hungarian Second Army dug into the opposing high ground: the 86th Infantry Regiment comprised of Croat-Hungarians and two predominantly–Czech infantry regiments, the 35th Plzeň and the 75th Jindřichuv Hradec. With their reserves, these Austro-Hungarian formations totaled 12,000 men. The soldiers of the Czecho-Slovak Brigade were supposed to advance only after the Fourth Finnish Division to their north broke through the enemy lines. The Czecho-Slovaks, however, proved too impatient to wait for a successful outcome on their right wing and subsequently they advanced prematurely against the enemy positions. Thanks in part to the token resistance given by the Czechs serving in two of the opposing regiments; the Czecho-Slovak Brigade overran the Austrian defenses within hours and successfully fought off enemy attempts to regain the heights. Although accounts of their battlefield success vary, low figures place the number of enemy soldiers captured by the brigade at 1,200 and several dozen officers while higher estimates tally the number of prisoners taken by the Czecho-Slovaks at over 4,000. In addition to the prisoners, numerous enemy machine guns and field pieces were also captured at a cost to the attackers of slightly less than 200 dead, 700 wounded and several missing. Although the breakthrough at Zborov was an impressive achievement for the Czecho-Slovak Brigade, it was a minor action in the overall offensive that might have been overlooked had it not been for the dismal reports relayed to the Russian generals and Minister of War from other sectors of the front.[39]

The potent Russian advance seen at zero-hour of the attack quickly ran out of steam within a couple of days.[40] As the dedicated frontline troops fell amid the fighting, the plentiful reinforcements behind them debated whether or not to accept their orders to move up into the firing line. Many refused and those that did go forward were easily stalled by the slightest enemy resistance.[41, 42] Even with the attack bogged down, Stavka hoped to renew the offensive on that part of the front. The enemy, however, was not about to give the Russian commanders that chance. Having obtained advance knowledge of the offensive, the Central Powers carefully prepared for the assault by organizing a defense in-depth and posting second-class formations to the forward trenches wherever possible. While holding their most fit troops in reserve, the Central Powers patiently waited for the Russian drive to sputter out. Then on 19 July nine German divisions commanded by General Winckler struck against the left wing of the Russian Eleventh Army.[43] The salient formed by the Czecho-Slovak Brigade west of Zborov lay directly in the path of the attacking forces and was immediately erased. Alongside the bewildered Russians, the Czecho-Slovak soldiers were forced to beat a hasty retreat eastward. As one of the few remaining disciplined units, the Brigade was called upon to serve as a rearguard and took heavy casualties in a stand outside the important junction of Ternopil. Even though that town, on Brusilov's orders, was to be held at all costs, the Russian guards division designated to defend Ternopil never took up its positions. Many Russian formations had become completely disorganized in the headlong flight, and as they converged on the town, the soldiers went on a looting spree. After setting fires to what they were unable to carry, the mob of troops then piled onto eastbound trains. Not surprisingly, the resistance offered by the Czecho-Slovaks and the few Russians willing to stand with them was doomed, and Winckler's force captured Ternopil on 24 July. From there, the Germans swooped southward between the Strypa and Sereth rivers into the rear of the Russian Seventh Army. By then that army was under attack by the Third Austro-Hungarian Army to its west and subsequently it withdrew to avoid envelopment. Further to the south, the Russian Eighth Army was also obligated to give up its considerable gains and fall back to avoid exposing its right flank. By the time the line stabilized in early August, the Russians had lost nearly all the ground they had gained since the previous summer.[44]

By First World War standards, the losses inflicted upon either side in the Kerensky Offensive were not terribly high: the Russians suffered 40,000 killed compared to 12,500 for the Central Powers.[45] Yet, in the aftermath of the half-hearted attack and devastating retreat, few doubted that the Russian Army had fired its last bolt. Demoralization and indiscipline were rampant among the retreating Russian units, not just around Ternopil, but all across along the beleaguered front as the troops resorted to pillage, rape and in some cases pogroms against Jewish civilians. Although Russian resistance against the attackers stiffened as they were pushed out of Galicia, neither the reshuffling in personnel at Stavka nor reinstitution of the death penalty at the front repaired the broken relations between the officers and the rank-and-file. The former blamed the proliferation of Bolshevik propaganda in the trenches, which supposedly went in hand with German subterfuge, for undermining the will of the troops to hold firm before Ternopil; meanwhile the soldiers suspected that their officers allowed the Germans to take the town so they could justify squelching their recently-won freedoms. Similar assessments were made by each side after the Germans captured the Baltic port of Riga in September, bringing the enemy dangerously close to the Russian capital.[46] It only remained to be seen whether the country would linger in the war or sue for peace.

At Zborov, the Czecho-Slovak Brigade proved not only that it was one of the few units in Russia still willing to fully engage the enemy, but also that was a respectable and effective fighting force. Its performance caught the attention of both their allies and their enemies. Among the foreign observers of the offensive were some Americans with the Root Commission.[47] In their assessment, the Czecho-Slovaks were given every bit of praise while the Russians were derided for having "failed to come up to their support."[48] In Austria-Hungary, reports of the battle unveiled to Habsburg subjects for the first time that some of their fellow citizens had actively taken up arms against their state.[49] The most important recognition of the Czecho-Slovaks' feats came from Kerensky, who personally visited their Brigade and lavished its officers and men with banners and medals. In a decision that would prove monumental for the Czecho-Slovak liberation movement, the Minister of War completely reversed his earlier opposition to the national armies and now encouraged their development.[50] Taking advantage of this change of heart, the Czecho-Slovak National Council in Russia immediately sent out some 300 recruiters to enlist Czechs and Slovaks in the POW camps. That summer, the brigade's strength, which had been under ten thousand men, more than tripled by September through the addition of 21,760 volunteers.[51] A fourth regiment was added to the brigade, which was renamed the First Division of the Czecho-Slovak Army Corps, or the Czecho-Slovak Legion (*Československá legie*) as the men preferred to call their force. The foundations of an additional four regiments were laid that summer, and these would eventually form the Second Division of the army corps.[52] Each of the regiments continued to be named after heroes or symbols from Czech or Slovak history, but at Masaryk's insistence these names could not be associated with Catholicism. In his view, names evoking the Hussites' glory were much more suitable. Consequently, the 1st Saint Wenceslas Regiment was renamed after Jan Hus, the 2nd Regiment after Jiří of Poděbrad. It was yet another example of the professor's rabid anti-clericalism.[53]

Despite the massive growth which the Czecho-Slovak corps experienced in those months, the results of the recruiting drive were still somewhat disappointing. By 1917, Russia held an estimated quarter million POWs of Czech or Slovak ethnicity; of this number, 83,000 had been contacted by a recruiter that summer and 21,760 enlisted. This rate of one enlistment for every four prisoners contacted, as bad as it was, only got worse in later recruiting drives. The call for volunteers was met with particular indifference by Slovaks, who comprised less than ten percent of the total number of men who enlisted that summer.[54]

Why did so many Czech and Slovak prisoners opt to remain in the camps instead of joining the army? The answers to this question are varied, but to start, many Czech and Slovak soldiers were not the traitorous, revolutionary-prone soldiers that the AOK—and émigré propaganda—made them out to be. Many were apolitical and probably more than a few thought that the notion of an independent Czecho-Slovak state squeezed between Germany and Austria was pure lunacy. Due to their proximity to events occurring on the Eastern Front and in revolutionary Russia, many were pessimistic about the Allies' chances for victory. They probably thought it would be superfluous of them to join a new army when peace seemed imminent, especially if that army appeared to be on the losing side. Many in work programs, particularly those assigned to factories and peasant farms, did not find life as a war prisoner unbearable. It was certainly more tolerable than a troglodyte existence in muddy trenches surrounded by rats, lice and putrefying corpses. It is probably no exaggeration to say that those men who risked going back into such a hellish environment by signing with the Czecho-Slovak Army Corps had to be, more often than not, fanatical to the national cause.

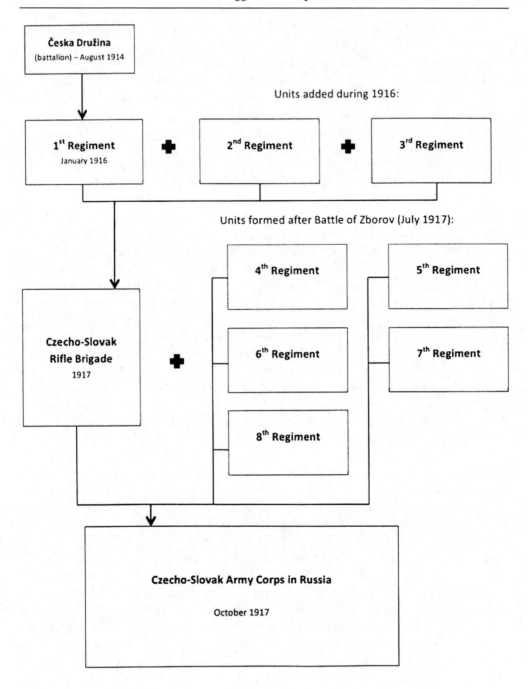

Diagram showing the development of the Czecho-Slovak Army in Russia, 1914–1917.

The quaint lifestyle which many POW laborers in Russia had grown accustomed to was soon to end. Those in the factories began to find it difficult to remain neutral in the labor disputes between native Russian workers and employers.[55] In the countryside too, the POWs were exposed to increasing violence as the peasants took advantage of the near-absence of authority to drive out anyone who did not belong to their close-knit communities. Deliveries of food and other supplies arrived with less regularity in the camps, while guards deserted their posts, leaving the prisoners to fend for themselves in a hostile environment.[56] Yet, additional recruiting drives in the following autumn and winter had diminishing returns. By spring of 1918, only about 40,000 Czecho-Slovak POWs had joined the Legion, amounting to only sixteen percent of the total number of Czech and Slovak prisoners in Russia.[57]

Masaryk worked tirelessly throughout the summer of 1917 to expand his brigade into a full-fledged army corps. As one who was careful never to let an opportunity go to waste, he readily capitalized on the good press which the Brigade had won at Zborov. The military commanders he dealt with at Stavka, first Brusilov, then his successor General Lavr Kornilov, followed by Alekseev and then General Nikolay Dukhonin, were all generally accommodating of Masaryk's efforts to enlarge the army and increase the National Council's jurisdiction over it. With the reliability of the Russian Army increasingly questionable, these commanders were not in a favorable position to reject help from any quarter. In another agreement with Stavka, the Czecho-Slovak leader eventually appointed two Russian officers to lead his army corps: General Vladimir Shokhorov as its Commander-in-Chief and General Mikhail Diterikhs as the Chief of Staff.[58]

In between his negotiations with Stavka, Masaryk attended directly to the needs of the army. In order to cement his authority over the troops while at the same time boosting their morale, he embarked on an ambitious speaking tour in August 1917. Visiting one regiment after another in the Ukrainian towns where they were billeted, Masaryk reiterated that the army's objective was to help the Allies liberate the Czech and Slovak homelands from foreign tyranny. Great sacrifices, he warned, might be asked of them to achieve this end. He also attempted to smooth over controversies brewing in the army, including politicization and relations between the officers and men, that were exacerbated by the Czecho-Slovaks' exposure to neighboring Russian units, their soldier committees and revolutionary agitators. He especially emphasized that the Czecho-Slovaks must remain neutral in Russia's increasingly volatile domestic affairs, a theme he had consistently advocated since his arrival in Petrograd.[59] As the central authority of the country continued to fade into autumn, the potential for civil war increased as challengers to the rule of the Provisional Government cropped up on both ends of the political spectrum and in Russia's borderlands.

Although Masaryk exuded confidence when speaking in front of his troops, he continued to be troubled by the question of how war on the Central Powers could be sustained amid the increasingly chaotic situation in Russia. The country's government was breaking down, its infrastructure was in a state of disrepair and its army would not fight. The Russian soldiers were demanding peace before the first freeze and in order to enforce this desire they refused orders to prepare winter quarters.[60] He knew that if Russia made peace with Berlin and Vienna, it could not permit an outfit hostile to the Central Powers to operate on its territory; it might even be compelled to turn over such forces to the enemy. As he grew more pessimistic over the war's outlook on the Eastern Front, he became increasingly entranced by the old dream of shipping the Czecho-Slovaks to France. Although little had come of the Štefánik's mission to negotiate the transfer of POW volunteers to France, Masaryk undertook his own effort to accomplish that goal. Shortly after arriving in Petrograd in May 1917, he broached the idea to Albert Thomas, the French socialist Minister of Labor who was then amid his own propaganda mission to Russia.[61] He found Thomas open to the proposal; France was still in need of soldiers and at the time nearly half of its army was on the verge of mutiny following the abortive offensive of April 1917.[62] On 27 May, the two men signed

Masaryk addresses his troops in Ukraine, late summer 1917. His speaking tour helped lift their morale as the Russian forces around them disintegrated.

an agreement for 30,000 Czecho-Slovak volunteers to be shipped to France for service in the trenches with a provision for thousands more to go there to work in the war industries.[63] Although its goal was much more modest than Štefánik's earlier expectations, it was still asking too much when the Russian commanders themselves did not have enough reliable troops at hand. Nonetheless, in July Masaryk requested that Stavka honor the agreement between him and Thomas by releasing Czecho-Slovak troops for transport to France.[64] Although a handful of Czecho-Slovak troops from Russian camps were eventually permitted to depart for France, the bulk of the Czecho-Slovak corps remained on the Eastern Front and indecision over its future continued beyond the existence of the old Russian Army Stavka.

The first group of Czecho-Slovak soldiers to leave for France was a contingent of less than 400 volunteers who had been POWs in Romania and sailed from Archangelsk in June 1917. Their transfer had been arranged several months earlier by Štefánik in meetings with Romanian and Russian officials. Later that autumn, about 1,500 Czecho-Slovak volunteers were allowed to depart from Russia for France under the terms of the Masaryk-Thomas agreement. Another detachment of 500 troops headed north from Ukraine in late

November but they did not reach Archangelsk before the port was locked in ice. Throughout the winter of 1917–18, they remained stranded in North Russia and eventually moved towards Murmansk, where they joined the few local Bolsheviks and British marines there in a standoff against pro–German Finnish forces operating in nearby Finland. It was not until late March, four months after leaving Ukraine, when they were finally permitted to board a British steamer.[65] Clearly, transporting the legionaries across vast distances surrounded by near-anarchy and then finding adequate tonnage for them among the Allies' already strained shipping resources were more daunting tasks than either Masaryk or the French had anticipated.

While the months following the Battle of Zborov brought great progress to the development of the Czecho-Slovak Legion, they were also menacing. It became evermore apparent that the Provisional Government enjoyed the confidence of neither the right nor left in Russian politics. Each side had its own answers on how to save Russia; the conservatives appealed to a sense of patriotic duty while the socialists emphasized the need for land reform and the convocation of a constituent assembly. The middle ground which the Provisional Government tried to stake for itself became an increasingly untenable position.

The Bolsheviks emerged as the greatest beneficiaries of the polarization of Russian politics. Although Lenin was as foreign to most Russians as were Masaryk, Voska and Thomas, he nevertheless became the only propagandist out of a crowded field of public opinion manipulators and agitators to attract any sizeable following. While the pro-war propagandists sent from Western Europe and America attempted to persuade their wavering ally to remain in the war by evoking a sense of national pride or accentuating the wickedness of the enemy, Lenin's simpler promise of bread, land and peace more accurately captured the mood of the Russian masses who were fed up with the seemingly endless sacrifices being demanded from them. That does not mean that the Bolshevik Party commanded any sort of political majority among Russians; that distinction belonged to the loosely-organized Social Revolutionary (SR) Party that was popular with the rural peasantry. Lenin's base was the urban proletariat, a class that was much smaller than the peasantry but strong in Russia's industrial centers, including the capital. The Bolsheviks proved themselves to be highly motivated revolutionaries and made great inroads among the sailors and soldiers of the armed forces. After September 1917, they also effectively had their own paramilitary forces in the capital—the Red Guards—which had been armed by Kerensky to avert the threat of counterrevolution from the right. In doing so, he had rendered the Provisional Government vulnerable to the extreme left.[66]

While more moderate socialists, such as Mensheviks or SRs, made no attempt to concentrate authority in the Soviet out of the belief that Russia had to undergo a period of "bourgeoisie" rule before the country would be ready for socialism, the Bolsheviks had no qualms against seizing power.[67] On the night of 7 November 1917, the latter finally made their bid to launch Russia into a new era of socialist utopia. By this time the Provisional Government could muster few reliable troops to its defense and as a result Petrograd's railways stations, post offices, police stations and telegraph offices all succumbed rather easily to armed Red Guard patrols. The only resistance they met was at the Winter Palace, where a hodge-podge garrison of inexperienced cadets, Cossacks and members of a women's shock battalion half-heartedly defended the government ministers gathered there while Kerensky attempted to summon troops outside the capital. When Kerensky finally returned to the outskirts of the capital a few days later behind a squadron of Cossacks, the Winter Palace had fallen and Petrograd was completely in Bolshevik hands. His attempt to regain Petrograd quickly failed while Red Guards in other major cities deposed local authorities to spread Bolshevik rule across the breadth of Russia.[68]

Masaryk bemoaned the October Revolution,[69] which was not a revolution but rather a *coup d'etat* staged by the Bolsheviks. Writing to Georgey Plekhanov, a founder of Russian Social Democracy and a Menshevik, the Czech leader complained, "As soon as Russia was rid of absolutism, a republic declared, a parliament organized, and constitutional freedoms introduced, there was no moral basis for the [October] revolution, even if one admits the weakness and incompetence of the Provisional Government."[70] His own travels in Russia were complicated by the Bolshevik action in Moscow, where fighting between the Bolsheviks and government loyalists was far bloodier and more protracted than the skirmish in the capital. At one point, he, his bodyguard and other guests at the hotel where they were staying had to shut themselves in for six days as they tried to avoid getting caught in the crossfire.[71] Aside from these personal inconveniences, however, Masaryk was troubled by the implications which the regime change in Russia held for his army there. Lenin made no attempt to hide his desire to seek peace—he announced that intention during his second day of power in Petrograd.[72] As troubling as Lenin's Decree on Peace was for Masaryk, a more immediate concern for him was the Legion's need to observe strict neutrality amid the street fighting and insurrections which broke out all over Russia. Despite reminding the Legion's commanders of this order in telegram, the Russian commander of the 2nd Czecho-Slovak Regiment, Colonel Mamontov, permitted his troops to be used to guard public works in Kiev at the instigation of the Ukrainian Rada. This arrangement allowed the Ukrainian nationalists to throw their full weight against the city's Bolsheviks, composed mostly of Russian workers, and the residual Russian Army units vying for power in the city. When Masaryk learned of this violation of his directives, he immediately ordered the 2nd Regiment to stand down and dismissed Mamontov.[73] This incident was the first entanglement of Legion in the civil war that was engulfing Russia, and it foreshadowed the difficulty of keeping the army outside the fray.

Although the Bolshevik insurrection failed in Kiev, Lenin's followers prevailed in the following weeks throughout most of Russia. From Petrograd to the Pacific, and from Astrakhan to Archangelsk, Bolsheviks Party members reconstituted soviets and soldiers' committees to attain an unassailable majority. On 26 November, a Soviet delegation, acting in accord with Lenin's Decree on Peace, crossed the Eastern Front and began parlaying with the Central Powers at Brest-Litovsk.[74] With this development, Masaryk felt that the Czecho-Slovaks' obligations to Russia had come to an end. The National Council claimed undisputed authority over the Czecho-Slovak Legion and new badges specific to the Czecho-Slovaks were sewn over the Russian insignia on the left sleeve of their uniforms.[75] Yet, no matter how badly the Czecho-Slovak leaders desired to keep their soldiers outside of the Russian morass, the Legion could not be simply ignored. Their army, which at the beginning of the year had been a brigade of less than 10,000 men, was by the winter of 1917–18 an army corps consisting to two divisions, each with artillery and engineer battalions, a reserve regiment and a storm battalion for a total strength of 40,000 troops.[76] It was inevitable that the Bolsheviks and their enemies would attempt to woo this highly-reputed force to their respective sides.

The year 1917, as we have seen, was a drastic turning point for Czecho-Slovak revolutionary activity in Russia. The émigrés and troops operating in that country, however, were not the only ones affected by the tremendous events occurring around them. For their compatriots in Austria-Hungary, the year had heralded a new phase of rule under the Habsburgs, one that promised so much but could only deliver little. During the course of the year, the attitudes of the Czechs inside Austria-Hungary underwent profound changes that were as critical to the liberation movement as was the émigrés' progress in Russia.

6

Prague on the Brink

For the populations of Germany and Austria-Hungary, the war was a vast siege with no end in sight. Surrounded by enemies on all sides, the central empires were denied access to the overland and seaborne trade routes which their economies had grown dependent on. Items once taken for granted, such as cotton, tobacco and rubber, became scarce or unavailable only months after hostilities began. Despite the implementation of strict rationing systems and the development of *ersatz* products, the crisis only deepened and black-market trading became more problematic. Soon even food supplies were affected, especially in Austria-Hungary. Galicia was a major domestic source of cereal grain for the Habsburg Monarchy, but its output was reduced by the fighting which took place there from 1914 to 1917. The loss of its commodities could not be made good anywhere else in the empire since agricultural output declined as rural labor was conscripted, draft horses were requisitioned and nitrates were diverted from the production of fertilizers to munitions.[1]

Morale in these lean times was partly sustained by the considerable gains which the Habsburg and Hohenzollern armies had made on the battlefields: Belgium and Serbia were overrun while northern France and Russia's western borderlands were occupied. By early 1917, they held most of Romania as well after that country entered the conflict on 27 August 1916. Some experts in the Entente camp had predicted that the intervention of Romania and her army of 800,000 soldiers would finally tip the scale in their side's favor, but in fact it did nearly the opposite.[2] The Central Power's conquest of southwestern Romania not only won them access to a new trove of food and fuel resources,[3] but their success also forced Russia to buttress the Romanian front with forty divisions that she should hardly afford to spare.[4] Still, the victory in Romania was not enough to break the enemy noose that was slowly strangling the economies of Germany and Austria-Hungary. Larger operations undertaken in 1916 with this goal in mind, such as at Verdun or in northern Italy, were abject failures. The final victory which everyone desired appeared no closer at the beginning of 1917. By then, all the peoples the Habsburg Monarchy, regardless of creed or ethnicity, had made immense sacrifices: of almost the five million men mobilized, approximately 800,000 had been killed, one million had been infirmed by serious wounds or illness and over two million were held in enemy captivity.[5, 6]

In spite of these many hardships, the Czechs, who at times seemed prepared to revolt on the slightest pretext prior to 1914, caused the Austrian government no major difficulties in the first years of the war. "The Bohemian national spirit which was so rampant before the war," observed the U.S. Consul to Prague in January 1916, "has completely evaporated."[7] The reasons for the Czechs' apparent loyalty to Vienna at this stage might be attributed more to complacency than enthusiasm for the war or dynasty. The national extremists among the

Czechs were cowed by the arrests of high-profile political leaders such as Kramář, Rašín and the National Socialist Party chairman, Václav Klofáč. Their party committees that were known for taking bold stances prior to war now made declarations that were tame by comparison.[8] It helped also that the privations caused by the war were mostly inconveniences up to this point; although luxuries were few, the people's basic needs were, for the most part, being met.[9] Finally, there was the uncertain outlook of the war itself. Like the Central Powers, the Entente demonstrated that they too were unable to break the stalemate on the Somme and in Galicia in 1916, and as a result neither side appeared stronger than the other. With the Reichsrat as well as the diets of Bohemia, Moravia and Silesia all closed, the Czech politicians had no pertinent reason to publicize their views on the war, the future of the Monarchy or even the revolutionary movement abroad.[10] It was much safer for them to await further developments and endure present conditions.

This precarious status quo in the Habsburg Empire was upset in late 1916. First came unseasonably cold and wet autumn weather which wreaked havoc on the harvest of potatoes, a crop that had become a major staple in the wartime diets of Germany and Austria-Hungary.[11] In addition to the hunger which inevitably followed, the Habsburg Monarchy experienced its first major coal shortages which left the empire's cities dark at night, its factories idle and its citizens shivering in unheated dwellings. This deterioration of living standards was too intolerable for many Czechs by late winter, and their disgust culminated into strikes and anti-war demonstrations that erupted in the working-class districts of Prague in mid–April 1917.[12]

As though these privations were not enough strain on the loyalty of the Monarchy's subjects, late 1916 also saw changes at the highest levels of the Imperial government. In late October, the Austrian Prime Minister, Count Stürgkh, was gunned down by an assassin. His replacement, Ernst von Körber, was not a bureaucrat of the same mold and quickly made known his desire to recall the Reichsrat.[13] A loss of much greater magnitude occurred a month later when the eighty-six-year-old Franz Josef passed away on 21 November. The aged Emperor died just a few weeks shy of the sixty-eighth anniversary of his coronation and very few of his subjects had known any other head of state. His grandfatherly figure, which had provided a stable link between generations and among the empire's diverse peoples, was now reduced to a fond memory.[14]

Months before his death, Franz Josef acknowledged the predicament of his realm and had resolved to not let it "drift into irretrievable rack and ruin."[15] Now that weighty mission fell on the narrow shoulders of his great-nephew and heir, Karl. The new emperor was a sober, trim and devout Catholic; although he was only twenty-nine years of age, he had no illusions about the difficult circumstances under which he assumed his new title. Despite his family's exalted status, he refused to allow them to be padded from the privations of the war: once common but now scarce entrées were struck from the royal menu and only a few rooms in the family's residential palace were to be heated during the winter.[16] He knew the empire was exhausted by the war and he needed to secure a timely peace in order to resolve its economic and ethnic troubles. Yet, while the young emperor possessed ample energy to pursue these ambitious goals, he was uncertain as to how they might be attained. Subsequently, at times he appeared to be weak-willed and vacillating.[17]

Karl aspired to rule as a modern monarch who heeded constitutions and was mindful of public opinion. In order to gain the confidence of the various nationalities and make them open to compromise, he eased the military's encroachment on provincial administrations far behind the front, including Bohemia, and at the beginning of January 1917 he commuted the death sentences imposed on Kramář, Rašín and other political prisoners.[18] Despite his somewhat liberal intentions, however, Karl surrounded himself with conservative stalwarts who had belonged to the late Franz Ferdinand's circle of advisors. Two of his leading ministers, Counts Heinrich Clam-Martinic and Ottokar Czernin, were products of the ancient Bohemian aristocracy but tended to be German in their outlook[19]; as a result their appointments aroused grave concern among Czechs.[20] Their suspicions were justified as both men favored an internal reorganization of Austria similar to a scheme backed by most of the German-Austrian political parties. This program, dubbed the "German solution," urged Austria to adopt German as the official state language, divide Bohemia into Czech and German districts, and separate Galicia from Austria to ensure the ethnic German parties a supermajority over Slavs in the Reichsrat.[21] Clam-Martinic, the Prime Minister, was astute enough to know that the non–German representatives in the Reichsrat, if that body were recalled, would never permit the ratification of such program and instead he advised the Emperor to implement it by imperial decree. The outbreak of the revolution in Russia, however, unnerved Foreign Minister Czernin, who demanded the Emperor to summon the Reichsrat before an imperial decree could be issued. Karl needed little convincing to return to parliamentary government as he naturally did not want his birthright to share the fate of the Romanovs'.[22]

The Reichsrat, despite its long record of dysfunction, had embodied a certain unity among Austria's heterogeneous peoples and imparted a moderating influence on the deputies who served in it.[23] Both of these qualities, which were desirable for the polyglot state, were lost when the Ukrainian-led obstruction in March 1914 caused it to be shuttered and not reconvened in the following years. By the time they were recalled in the spring of 1917, the deputies had spent the intervening years in the provinces or in a few instances at the front, where they were exposed to powerful nationalist and pacifist trends as the living standards of their constituents dropped. In the Bohemian crownlands, Czech workers whose families were underfed and living in cold homes grumbled when they saw trainloads of grain and coal being shipped from their province to other areas of the Monarchy.[24] The empire's increasing dependence on Germany was also a growing anxiety for many Czechs who feared that the dominant ally might coerce Vienna into adopting the "German solution." Thus the radical nationalists, though they may have been less vocal in 1916 than they had been in 1913, found increasing acceptance for their message among Czechs alarmed by the prospective deterioration of their economic and political lot. This trend would continue as the war ground on.

The accession of the new Emperor and the prospect of returning to parliamentary government temporarily resuscitated the hopes of those Czechs who still placed the future of their people with the Habsburgs. It was they who were behind the Czech Union's public disavowal of the inclusion of their people's liberation in the Entente note to Wilson, an action that was undertaken in part to encourage the government to summon the Reichsrat. Despite the powerful statements of loyalty made in the disavowal, those groups that had positioned themselves close to the dynasty, such as the ethnic German parties and military authorities, continued to doubt the Czechs' sincerity and feared that their representatives would use their parliamentary immunity to make proclamations against the state.

The Austrian-German politicians and the military elite were not the only ones who opposed the thaw of the bureaucratic dictatorship in Austria. The prospect of the Reichsrat returning into session also troubled the exiles, who feared that their compatriots might show themselves to be too loyal and cooperative towards the Austrian government.[25] It was much easier for the émigré propagandists to whip up enmity against Vienna when the Imperial government was practicing authoritarian rule and imprisoning their politicians. However, the new Emperor's relaxation of military rule, his amnesties of political prisoners and his openly-stated desire for peace made it difficult for them to depict Austria-Hungary as a "prison of peoples" ruled by warmongering leaders. The disavowal was also fresh in the émigrés' memories, and for this reason in April 1917 Beneš sent a tersely-worded message to Maffie to remind the politicians that not only the exiles but also the Entente countries would be scrutinizing their actions in the Reichsrat. He wrote to them:

> If the Austrians were able to say that they are entitled to speak in your name, if you were able to make a declaration of loyalty, if you failed to show clearly that you are opposed to Austria, you will deprive us of our last weapon, and justify the Entente in concluding with the dynasty a separate peace, in the framing of which we should not be able to express any opinion. The present situation makes it imperative for us to show whether it is the dynasty and the diplomats, or whether it is the nations themselves who are entitled to negotiate on behalf of the Austrian nation. Unless you make it clear at the present moment that the dynasty and its diplomats are not entitled to do so, we are lost.[26]

Despite this message, Beneš seemed to harbor doubts whether his instructions to the politicians in Bohemia would be followed. As the opening session of the Reichsrat approached, he looked for any way to discredit it; at one point he declared that it would have an insufficient quorum since about fifty elected deputies in the lower chamber, including some anti–Habsburg exiles like Masaryk, could not be in attendance.[27]

Beneš did not then know that Maffie conspirators had heeded his advice and were busily mobilizing celebrities among the Czech nation to provide the radical nationalist program a significant endorsement. Their clandestine efforts were responsible for a manifesto signed by 222 Czech authors, playwrights and writers that was published on 17 May.[28] Written in language ambiguous enough to pass the inspection of the Austrian censors, the declaration implored the Czech Reichsrat deputies, especially those in the Czech Union, to defend and insist on "Czech rights." It also referred to the "Czechoslovak nation" even though no Slovaks were represented among the signatories.[29]

This "Manifesto of Czech Authors" was deliberately released at a time when it would encourage the Czech politicians to pause for careful thought. They had been busily preparing for the opening of the Reichsrat at the end of the month by meeting with their parties and others to formulate a program to be announced at the inaugural session. For the coalition of political parties in the Czech Union, this meant deciding on a joint program acceptable to the member parties. While they generally agreed that the opening statement of the Czech Union should include the traditional recitation of Bohemia's state rights, fewer consensuses existed over the question of whether or not to mention the Slovaks in their proclamation. Most of the Union's delegates initially opposed the idea to include the Slovaks on the grounds that its attack on Hungary's historic boundaries would complicate the Czech argument over Bohemia's historic state rights. Antonín Švehla, the wily leader of the powerful Czech Agrarian Party, initially agreed with this view. He changed his mind though after meeting with Vavro Šrobár, the Slovak physician-turned-politician, who prevailed upon the Czech leaders not to abandon their eastern kinsmen. Through Švehla's conversion and influence, the "Czecho-Slovak" program was adopted and read at the opening session of the Reichsrat on 30 May. The Czech Union's declaration condemned the dualist system of the empire as "detrimental to the interests of the whole" and demanded the "transformation of the

Habsburg monarchy into a federal state consisting of free and equal nation states" as well as the unification of the Czech nation with the "Slovak branch." Although it did not openly state full independence as a desirable goal of the Czecho-Slovaks, its wording was a drastic shift from the submissive disavowal issued in the name of the same group barely six months earlier.

The bold declaration of the Czech Union confirmed the anxieties shared by the Austrian-German parties and Clam-Martinic regarding the return to parliamentary government.[30] Even worse for them, the Czech parties were not alone in making seemingly radical opening statements. The Yugoslav Club, like the Czech Union, made a verbal assault on the dualist system by declaring its objective to be the union of all Serbs, Croats and Slovenes in the Monarchy. They and the Czech Union also strengthened their hand by forming a close parliamentary alliance. Even the Polish deputies, who had a record of traditionally siding with the government, made waves by explicitly refusing to accept an Austrian proposal of greater autonomy for Galicia. Instead, they desired to become part of a united and independent Poland.[31] Against these challenges from all directions, Clam-Martinic was at a loss on how to drum up support for his government. On 12 June, he addressed the Reichsrat and pathetically declared, "The government's program is Austria. Let us all be Austrians."[32] To the various Slav deputations, the prime minister's refusal to even entertain their proposals indicated that he was offering their people nothing in return for the perseverance and sacrifices the government was asking of them during the war.

Clam-Martinic's speech revealed the extent of lethargy present in his government. He showed no imagination or willingness to work out the compromises to keep at least the moderates among the nationalities in the Habsburg fold.[33] Some fault also must rest with the young Emperor. Even though he once expressed his desire to grant equal rights to all ethnicities inside his realm by stating that "a father has no favorites among his children," he was relying on ministers who were unable to think outside the "German solution."[34] Moreover, any hopes the Slavs might have had that Karl would assume a tough stance towards the Magyar oligarchy in Hungary were soon dashed when he allowed himself to be coaxed into undergoing a coronation ceremony at Budapest where he swore to preserve the integrity of the Hungarian constitution and her existing boundaries.[35] This oath to effectively uphold the dualist system ended any likelihood that the Emperor would actively seek to reorganize the Monarchy as desired by most of his Slav subjects. In the meantime, the Slavs in Austria had to reckon with the painful realization that Vienna was becoming a virtual prisoner to its Hungarian partner. Amid the crises caused by food shortages, the capital and other non-agricultural regions of Austria had grown reliant on grain imports from Hungary to feed their populations. The Magyar elite soon learned to exploit this dependency in their disagreements with Vienna by cajoling the Austrians into submission with the threat of a grain embargo.[36] This practice was deeply resented by the nationalities in Austria and worsened interethnic relations in the empire as a whole.

Even as Karl strived to put the Monarchy on a sounder footing in the domestic sphere, his overriding concern from the moment he ascended the throne was to end his empire's involvement in the war. While the heir-apparent, he had commanded army formations various fronts and saw firsthand the war's immense toll on men.[37] He also deplored Austria-Hungary's increasing dependence on Germany as war continued, and he harbored fears that his realm might be reduced to a puppet of the Reich.[38] For these reasons, his first proclamation to his hungry and deprived subjects included a passage where he assured them of his commitment "to put an end to the horrors and sacrifices of the war at the earliest possible moment, and to restore the sadly missed blessings of peace."[39]

The Emperor's openly stated desire for peace was music to the ears of Entente statesmen, and soon began the first of what would be many secret exchanges between the Entente and Austria-Hungary. This first round was initiated by Karl himself when he reached out to his wife's brothers, Sixte and Xavier of Bourbon-Parma, who were then serving in the Belgian Army.[40] After securing permission from French and Belgian authorities, the two princes secretly entered Austria via Switzerland and met the imperial couple at Laxenburg castle on 23 March 1917. Karl, accompanied by Foreign Minister Czernin, informed the princes of his conditions for a general peace, which included restoring the sovereignty of Belgium, Serbia and Germany's cessation of the provinces of Alsace-Lorraine to France.[41] The Emperor made clear his refusal to entertain a separate peace that would leave his Germany ally the lurch, nor did he offer to satisfy Italian war aims with territory along the Adriatic littoral.[42] Before their departure, Sixte and Xavier received an official note of the proposals from Czernin while Karl slipped them a hand-written letter that was to have significant repercussions a year later.

Upon their return to Paris, the Bourbon-Parma princes dutifully presented their papers to French and British officials. The British Prime Minister, David Lloyd George, was so impressed with the documents that he reportedly exclaimed, "This is peace!"[43] By then the Entente was finding more reasons than ever to seriously consider peace proposals. The revolution in Russia was well underway and was raising doubts about the prospects of that country's continued contribution to the Entente war effort; meanwhile France was about to launch a disastrous attack along the Chemin des Dames that would lead to considerable insubordination in its army. At the beginning of April, the Entente nations had gained a new military partner in the United States in the struggle against Germany. President Wilson, however, refused to declare war on Austria-Hungary and was a proponent of the diplomatic strategy to detach the Monarchy from the central alliance.[44] Throughout the remainder of 1917 and into the following year, long after the Bourbon-Parma princes ceased acting as middlemen between the Entente and Vienna, agents representing the two sides continued to rendezvous in Switzerland in the hope of finding some common ground from which they could begin peace negotiations.

The missions of the Entente peace feelers were hidden from the Czecho-Slovak National Council and other émigré organizations in Western Europe. For Beneš, the first clue that something was afoot was the sudden appearance of "suspiciously Austrophile articles" in a French newspaper known for its reliable contacts in the Quai d'Orsay.[45] Not even Robert Seton-Watson, who was newly employed in Britain's Intelligence Bureau, was let in on the secret.[46] No one could have had any doubt how such news would had been received by émigré organizations and their backers; as Beneš later wrote, "Any compromise with Vienna in the summer of 1917 would have been an unmitigated disaster to us."[47] An independent Czecho-Slovak state would have been out of the question in a negotiated peace with Austria-Hungary, and it is difficult to say whether the Entente would have even pushed for Czecho-Slovak autonomy in such a settlement. Early that year, the Foreign Office did circulate a memorandum recommending that any peace terms with Austria-Hungary should include autonomous statuses for the Czecho-Slovaks and Yugoslavs, but it seems unlikely that senior British officials, amid their growing pessimistic military outlook, would firmly adhere to such advice if Vienna indicated a strong desire to conclude a separate peace.[48] In the meantime, the

British continued to play a double-game by collaborating with anti–Habsburg exiles in propaganda and intelligence while continuing to initiate peace talks with Vienna. France did much the same and even took its cooperation with the exiles to a new level. On 4 June 1917, the French president announced his country's plans to establish a Polish army to fight with the Allies on the Western Front. Around that time, Beneš began negotiations with Paris to implement a similar project for the Czecho-Slovaks.[49]

Fortunately for the Czecho-Slovaks and other exiles, the Entente and Vienna were further apart in their negotiations than either side was willing to admit. Karl's proposal to restore Belgium and Serbia and return Alsace-Lorraine to France was not in synch with his ally's attitude towards these questions.[50] Without any means to compel Germany to yield on these issues, the only route left for him to extract his realm from war was to seek a separate peace. Karl, however, consistently refused to even consider such a scheme; he may have been too much of a gentlemen to forsake his country's closest partner in the thick of the fighting, or it's quite possible he lacked the strong personal initiative that would have been needed to oppose the will of his overbearing ally and the pro–German cabal in Vienna. Because of the Monarchy's military reliance on Germany by this time, some Austro-Hungarian officials even doubted whether Vienna could have pulled out of the war without succumbing to a hostile takeover by Germany.[51, 52]

In the Entente camp, the peace initiatives encountered staunch opposition from Italy. That country had entered the war in May 1915 after diplomats on both sides engaged each other in a fierce bidding competition for Rome's intervention or neutrality. The contest favored the Entente from the start since Italy's Foreign Minister, Giorgio Sidney Sonnino, and like-minded Italian nationalists desired Habsburg territories along the Alpine frontier and the eastern coast of the Adriatic Sea. Control of these areas would not only redeem Italian enclaves in those areas, it would also ensure Italy complete supremacy in the Adriatic.[53] This price was too high for Vienna but the Entente, while privately scorning Italy's naked imperialism, bowed to Sonnino's demands out of "war necessity."[54] The result was the secret Treaty of London, signed on 26 April 1915, that guaranteed the peninsular nation the southern Tyrol, the provinces of Istria and Dalmatia along with the port of Trieste.

As the most powerful European entity not yet involved in the war, the Entente nations had great expectations for their new partner, but their optimism quickly turned to disappointment.[55] The mountainous frontier between Italy and Austria was not an ideal theater for conducting military operations, and the Italians were disadvantaged by the Austrians' general control of the higher ground. The Italian Army further suffered from shoddy training of its soldiers, a weak artillery corps, unimaginative commanders and a system of discipline that was the most draconian of all major combatants in the war.[56] By the time Sonnino was informed of Austria's first peace initiatives in April 1917, the Italian Army had bludgeoned itself against Austrian lines on the Isonzo front in nine unsuccessful offensives since entering the war two years earlier.[57] Although the army's casualties were soaring upwards of a million and its soldiers had little to show for their sacrifices, Sonnino still refused to consider any peace terms that offered his nation anything less than the extensive prizes promised by the Treaty of London.[58] For British and French statesmen who just a month earlier saw the prospect of peace just over the horizon, Sonnino's unbending attitude was to be the first of many disappointments in their quest for peace with Vienna.

Prince Sixte went back to Laxenburg in May with Rome's conditions for ending the war and soon returned to France without having brought the two sides any closer together.[59]

The Austrian government refused to make any concessions to Italy and would only consider a general, not separate, peace. The Allies correctly gauged that Berlin was as of yet unwilling to consider what they felt were acceptable terms for a general peace, as a result they continued to woo Vienna in the hope eliminating the Monarchy as an enemy by way of a separate peace. It was a pattern that was to be repeated on several occasions into spring of 1918.

Italy's strict adherence to the terms of the Treaty of London was an important asset to the Czecho-Slovak liberation movement since it reduced the chances that the Allies and Vienna would enter into peace negotiations. Quite simply, Italy's claims to the Tyrol and the Adriatic littoral were unlikely to be realized unless a shattering defeat were inflicted on the Habsburg Empire, and such an event could only bode well for Masaryk and other émigrés who were bent on destroying the Monarchy.

Although the Italian statesmen and the anti–Habsburg exiles were unique among the Allies since they both looked at Austria-Hungary, and not Germany, as their main enemy, their relations were far from cozy. Italy's entry into the war had greatly complicated the post-war possibilities in the event of the Habsburg Empire's defeat, especially where the South Slavs were concerned. The Yugoslav Committee's vision of a future South Slav state straddling the eastern Adriatic coast directly clashed with Italy's territorial ambitions. Although no similar quarrel stood between the Czecho-Slovak National Council and the Italian government, Sonnino was nonetheless cool to the idea of Czecho-Slovak independence since it would naturally be interpreted as a precedent for the South Slavs.[60] He wanted to amputate a few peripheral territories from the Monarchy while leaving the body intact, but there were a few leading men in Rome who were willing to challenge this policy. Leonida Bissolati, a minister without a portfolio since late 1916, supported the complete dismemberment of the empire into nation-states.[61] His views were complemented by another minister without a portfolio, Ubaldo Comandini, who invited Beneš for an official visit to Rome in January 1917.

Beneš's first meeting with the obstinate Sonnino during this trip did not go as well as he had hoped. "All my explanations and endeavors to bring forward the Czechoslovak question," he wrote of that visit, "merely brought a reiterated statement of the Italian case against the Yugoslavs."[62] The only consolation he had from the trip was that he had been permitted to establish a Czecho-Slovak press bureau in Rome and was allowed access to Czech and Slovak POWs held in Italy.[63] What he did not know was that Sonnino was subjected to increasing pressure from the liberal press, which feared that Italy might fall into diplomatic isolation unless it moderated its official opposition to the national movements, and army intelligence officers who appreciated the reports originating from the underground cell in Prague that were passed onto them. At their urging, Beneš was extended another invitation to come to Rome in September 1917.[64]

Beneš's objective in his next visit was to convince the Foreign Minister to agree to the repatriation of Czecho-Slovak POWs from Italian camps so they could be transported to France to fight in the Czecho-Slovak army being planned there. After submitting this request to the Consulta, Beneš remained in Italy for a month as he waited for Sonnino's reply with great anticipation. During this interval, he visited Czech and Slovak war prisoners in the country who had begun organizing themselves into volunteer corps earlier that year. He found the POWs frustrated and cynical at their idleness in the camps while the terms of their service were being hashed out between the Italian government and the National Council. As in Russia a year earlier, the process of forming armed units from the camps would be a much more complicated process than anticipated by either the prisoners or the émigrés.[65]

To Beneš's bitter disappointment, Sonnino rejected his request to release Czecho-Slovak volunteers for service on the Western Front. The Foreign Minister argued that if he allowed POWs to be transferred from Italy to France, then Austria-Hungary might retaliate by shipping Italian POWs to the desert wastes of the Ottoman Empire.[66] It is unlikely that this was the true reason behind Sonnino's decision as the Italian government tended to regard prisoners from its armies as deserters and made no effort to alleviate their suffering through shipments of food or clothing for their use.[67] The more probable explanation was that the Foreign Minister feared that anything which might strengthen the Czecho-Slovak liberation movement would give a corresponding boost to the South Slavs' efforts as well. Still, Beneš did not leave Italy empty-handed. His efforts did persuade Italian officials to at least organize the Czecho-Slovak POWs into labor units that would eventually be employed in improving roads or building defensive works behind the front.[68] Although such work was important to the war effort, it was a thankless task that would not, as Beneš very well knew, win the Czecho-Slovaks appreciation from the Allies. He and other émigré leaders accepted the decision not as an end to their quest but as a step in a favorable direction.

Beneš's negotiations with the Consulta that autumn foundered on the Foreign Minister's confidence that his country's military campaign was progressing towards a successful finality. During the spring and summer of 1917, Italy had launched two more offensives—the Tenth and Eleventh Battles of the Isonzo—to break through the Austro-Hungarian front. Both attacks failed to achieve their objectives and were costly to the Italians, but the latter did succeed in forcing the Habsburg troops to withdraw to their last mountainous defensive line before Trieste.[69] In order to prevent a possible Italian breakthrough, the OHL responded to the crisis by diverting considerable forces of troops, artillery and munitions to the threatened sector. On 24 October this gathering storm broke on the unsuspecting Italians in the

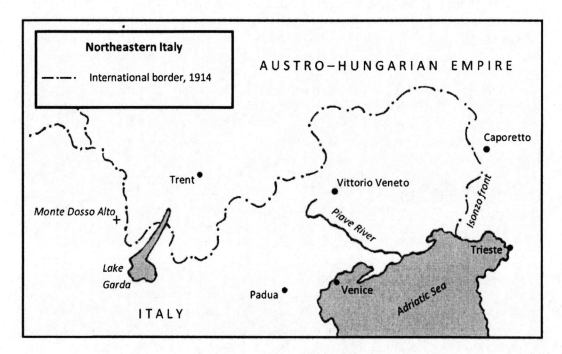

Northeastern Italy with 1914 borders.

form of a thunderous bombardment and a lightning advance of infantry. The offensive, remembered as the Battle of Caporetto, was one of the few operations in the Great War to exceed the attackers' expectations: the Germans and Austro-Hungarians had planned to push the defenders back only thirty miles, but instead they advanced over twice that distance to the Piave River. In the meantime, the supremacy of the attackers' artillery and their infantry's employment of infiltration tactics completely stunned the Italian troops, who gave themselves up in droves. Of the 300,000 casualties incurred by the Italians during the offensive, over 265,000 were captured by the enemy. A similar number of troops deserted to the rear; some of them even warbled the revolutionary *Internationale* along the way. In addition to troop losses, the Italians also gave up irreplaceable quantities of artillery, shells and other war materiel, leaving Britain and France with no other choice than to buttress their ally's sagging lines with soldiers and batteries sorely needed on the Western Front.[70]

Austria-Hungary's great victory at Caporetto, which was made possible with substantial German help, did nothing to improve the empire's domestic woes. Since the recall of the Reichsrat, opposition to the government continued to mount as the Slavs' demand for internal reorganization of the empire were not even given consideration. Emperor Karl attempted to placate them by proposing a "ministry of nationalities," but he quickly retracted the offer when the plan ignited an outcry among German-Austrians and even the Magyars, who repeated their familiar threat to halt grain exports to Austria.[71] Clam-Martinic, who had been unable to secure a majority in the Reichsrat, resigned in late June and a new government, but one no more sympathetic to the Slavs, was formed under a reluctant stand-in, Ernst von Seidler.[72] In the meantime, the Reichsrat did prepare to tackle the question of constitutional reform, and the Czech Union was invited to appoint delegates to a subcommittee that would examine the issue. When the Maffie conspirators learned of this plan, they quickly dispatched agitators among the parties to dissuade the politicians against sending delegates to the subcommittee. Their efforts proved decisive on 25 July when a conference of prominent Czech politicians and figures opted to abstain from the subcommittee.[73]

Even more inflammatory than the ethnic politics were the rampant food shortages that lingered in many areas of Austria throughout 1917. By August, the government was unable to supply the meager weekly meat and milk allowances, and in some urban districts of Bohemia daily flour rations were cut to 165 grams per person. In Plzeň, the announcement of the latest ration reduction sparked riots and looting, especially against property owned by ethnic Germans and Jews, and the majority of the workforce at the Monarchy's largest armament plant, Škoda Works, went on strike for several days.[74]

This radicalism which had burst forth in the factories and streets of Bohemia was echoed in the political parties. The Czech Social Democrats, whose official party program had long recoiled from the nationalist agenda despite their break from their Austrian comrades, experienced considerable internal dissension that summer. It will be recalled that early in the war the party's chairman, Bohumír Šmeral, had rebuffed Beneš's plea that he conspire with or at least endorse Masaryk's planned revolutionary activity abroad.[75] In the years since, Šmeral continued to stonewall nationalist agitation and guided his party to remain faithful to Marxist internationalism and by default, Austria-Hungary. His loyalist brand of leadership, however, was challenged soon after a party delegation attended an international socialist conference in Stockholm. Masaryk, recognizing the conference as a golden opportunity to impress his feats on Czech politicians not directly involved in Maffie, had arranged for two of his trusted associates from the Russian branch of the Czecho-Slovak National Council,

Bohdan Pavlů and Prokop Maxa, to meet the socialist delegation from Prague.[76] A similar rendezvous took place around the same time in Switzerland between Beneš and another leading Czech Social Democrat, Vlastimil Tusar. In both of these meetings, the Czech exiles impressed their audiences with their accomplishments to date and convinced them that the future of the Czechs lay outside the Monarchy. After their return to Prague, the awed socialists helped reconstitute the Czech Social Democrat Party executive committee in favor of Masaryk's program for Czecho-Slovak independence. Šmeral, whose loyalist policies appeared increasingly out of touch with the rising agitation of the Czech working class, resigned as party chairman and was ruthlessly vilified by right-wing national propagandists.

The Czech clerical parties, which had been the first to reject the mention of Czecho-Slovak liberation in the Entente note to Wilson, were slow to perceive the winds of change in Czech politics as public opinion moved closer to the national extremists. By the time they adopted a program in favor of independence in the spring of 1918, they had lost much of their former influence.[77] Other Czech parties made the transition effortlessly. As 1917 drew to a close, the Agrarians, who pursued an opportunist policy of lending support to both the national radicals and the Habsburg loyalists, quietly ended this strategy and collaborated with the revolutionaries for the remainder of the war. The Young Czechs and National Socialists, both of which displayed bouts of hyper-nationalism prior to war but nevertheless joined the Czech Union in 1916, also lined up behind the revolutionaries. Ironically, their extremism was unwittingly abetted by one of the Emperor's own conciliatory gestures. In early July 1917, Karl, in order to procure support for Seidler's government among the nationalities, decreed the release of most political prisoners, including Kramář, Rašín and Klofáč.[78] This token of goodwill was destined to backfire, not least because the men were embittered by their experiences of prison and military tribunals. Moreover, their plight made them martyrs to the Czech people and, especially in Kramář's case, significantly boosted their political popularity. The freed men had no trouble returning to the helms of their parties and effortlessly brushed aside the relatively moderate members who had sat on the executive committees during their imprisonment.[79]

In December, when the news that Soviet Russia was suing for peace appeared in the Austrian press, the Czech Union and their Yugoslav allies in the Reichsrat soon put the government to the test. Since the German and Austro-Hungarian delegations at Brest-Litovsk ostensibly agreed with the Bolshevik proposal to make self-determination a guiding principle of the peace talks, the Prague politicians took the government at its word and pressed the ministers to allow representatives from each of the empire's nationalities to participate at the peace conference. On 19 December, Prime Minister Seidler denied this request out of hand, while a few days later Czernin was even more explicit by declaring that nationalities without political independence could not send delegations to an international forum. For the majority of the Czech politicians, this arrogant reply was the last straw. On 6 January 1918 the Czech Union issued a manifesto known as the Epiphany Declaration in which any mention of future ties between the Czech nation and the Monarchy was notably absent.[80] It closed with an ominous warning to the Austrian government:

> We, the representatives of the Czech nation, proclaim that a peace which would not bring justice and freedom to our nation would not be for us a peace, but only the beginning of a new, powerful, and consequential struggle for state independence in which our nation would exert to the limit its entire material and moral strength and would not desist from this ruthless struggle until its successful resolution.[81]

The publication of this declaration provoked an outcry among Habsburg patriots. Seidler dismissed it as "a fruit of war psychosis" while an Austrian-German deputy in the Reichsrat drew attention to the contradictions in Czech aims that upheld the integrity of Bohemia's historic lands but not those of Hungary.[82] On the other hand, the Epiphany Declaration was considered a belated holiday present by the National Council in Paris. The Czech émigrés there and elsewhere eagerly cited it as compelling evidence that their revolutionary aims met the approval of the majority of Bohemia's general population.[83]

The Epiphany Declaration clearly indicated that Karl's relaxation of military rule and the return to parliamentary government was failing ensure the allegiance of the moderates among the disaffected nationalities. Although his decisions were made with high-minded intentions, he had reconvened the Reichsrat at a time when his own ability to direct the foreign and domestic affairs of the state was severely curtailed by the Monarchy's dependence on Germany and the Magyar threat to withhold food supplies. Those who did await for him to introduce internal reforms or initiate peace negotiations were disappointed throughout the year as they watched him take an oath to uphold dualism and then launch a crushing offensive against Italy. Added to this was the downward spiral of economic conditions in the empire, which was a radicalizing force by itself. Thus the Reichsrat, rather than serving as a platform for solutions as Karl intended, became a stage for dissent as Slav deputies took advantage of their parliamentary immunity in order to complain about the privations of the war and denounce the polices of the government. In the meantime, those elements that were traditionally the most loyal to the dynasty, such as the Austrian-Germans, upper classes and the military, lost faith in their monarch when he appeared oblivious to the fact that his efforts to appease the minorities merely emboldened them. "The emperor's warmheartedness and humanity," wrote a staff colonel in AOK, "became a liability instead of an asset."[84]

By the start of 1918, the empire's internal problems began to appear more ominous than its remaining external foes. From a military viewpoint, Austria-Hungary's outlook was encouraging. The great victory at Caporetto had, if only temporarily, eliminated Italy as a threat. With Serbia and most of Romania occupied, the Central Powers were essentially the masters of the Balkans, while Russia, under its new Bolshevik rulers, was negotiating its exit from the war. Since late 1916, casualties in the Habsburg army were declining, and the likelihood of peace in the East held not only the prospect of repatriating the two million Austro-Hungarian soldiers interred in Russian prison camps, but also the tantalizing possibility of alleviating the food crisis in the Monarchy through grain imports from Ukraine.[85]

Vienna's hope was the Allies' despair. While publicly maintaining their image as men confident in the ultimate success of their countries' war effort, some key Allied politicians and military commanders lost faith in achieving total victory. This pessimism provided considerable motive for the ongoing Allied quest to negotiate a separate peace with Austria-Hungary into early 1918.[86] With the Central Powers victorious on virtually all fronts except in France, the Allies had little doubt where the next enemy blow would fall. The one bright spot for the exhausted European Allies existed in the form of their new partner, the United States, and its vast reservoir of untapped manpower, but the Americans were far from ready to wrangle with the Germans when Congress voted in favor of war during the first days of April 1917. At that time, the strength of the U.S. Army stood at less than 130,000 men; in contrast Romania fielded an army over six times that size when its government made the disastrous decision to abandon neutrality in the summer of 1916. Worse, the Americans were short or completely devoid of hardware such as machine guns, tanks, modern artillery and aircraft that were needed to dominate the battlefield. They needed time to train their conscripts, ship them across the Atlantic and outfit them for service in the trenches.[87] Their accomplishments in this area were impressive: by March 1918 they had already landed 318,000 troops in France. However, that previous winter the Germans transferred fifty of their best divisions from the Russian front to France. Whereas the newly-arrived doughboys were untested in combat, the Germans were battle-hardened and ready to provide OHL's mastermind, General Erich Ludendorff, with the punch he needed to finally smash through Allied lines on the Western Front.[88] Hence, the military fortunes of the Allies were to get much worse before they got better. In the meantime, the Czecho-Slovak exiles, by closely monitoring the pulse of Allied officialdom, were able to detect the impending crisis and readily offered their services—but not without the expectation that they would receive some form of compensation in return.

7

The Rise of the Czecho-Slovak Legions in the West

Since the start of the war, Masaryk had differentiated his revolutionary movement from Pan-Slav competitors by concentrating his activity on the West rather than in Russia. Ironically, by 1918, his organization appeared to have accomplished more in Russia than in the West. This picture was somewhat misleading as Masaryk and his fellow émigrés' extensive work in the British propaganda machine was mostly hidden from view. Moreover, Masaryk and the National Council had won over their compatriots in Russia precisely because of the inroads they made among elite British and French circles earlier in the war. Yet as the conflict entered its final and most critical year, there was no disputing the fact that a Czecho-Slovak army, the formation of which Masaryk had set as one of his main goals almost from the outset, was only in service on the Eastern Front. In Western Europe, Czecho-Slovaks were not fighting in autonomous formations nor were the aims of the National Council officially recognized by any government.

With Masaryk in Russia for most of 1917 and into the spring of 1918, the task of improving the fortunes of the Czecho-Slovak liberation movement in Western Europe fell on Beneš and Štefánik, both of whom were eager to establish an autonomous Czecho-Slovak army. Because of Sonnino's reluctance to lend any hint of support to national movements among the Slavs of Austria-Hungary, they concentrated their efforts of forming an armed unit in France.

Shortly after the outbreak of the war, about 300 volunteers from the Czech émigré colony in France enlisted with the French Foreign Legion.[1] This group was eventually deployed into a separate Czech company called *Nazdar*. Tragically, this unit was virtually wiped out in May 1915 during the Second Battle of Artois and the few survivors had to be integrated into other units of the Foreign Legion.[2]

When the Czecho-Slovak National Council began drafting blueprints for constructing an autonomous army in France, it had to look outside that country for recruits. The Czech colony there was simply too small and the French military acquired no Czecho-Slovak POWs since Austro-Hungarian troops had no presence on the Western Front.[3, 4] One solution to this quandary was to import Czech and Slovak volunteers from Russian POW camps. As we have seen, this scheme ran into a new set of problems due to the machinations of the tsarist government and ultimately the outbreak of the revolution. Another limiting factor was the lack of available Allied transports to carry troops from Russia to France. Although 2,400 Czecho-Slovak troops were shipped from North Russia by the spring of 1918, the condition of the country's railways and the scarce availability of Allied shipping left sufficient reason to doubt whether a significant force of troops would arrive from Russia anytime soon.

Another potential source of Czecho-Slovak prisoners existed with Serbia. During the first year of the war, thousands of Czech and Slovak soldiers had been captured by the Serbian Army. When the Serbian front collapsed in late 1915, the entire nation was put to flight by the advancing Austro-Hungarian, German and Bulgarian armies. The Serbs, rather than let their 20,000 POWs be liberated by the enemy, forced the prisoners to march to the coast alongside their fleeing columns.[5] The three-week retreat in wintry conditions through mountainous wilderness was harrowing for everyone involved—Serb casualties soared as high as 60,000—and it was especially grueling for the prisoners since their captors had little food or supplies to spare on them.[6] By the time the Austro-Hungarian POWs were evacuated by Italian ships from the Albanian coast, their numbers had been reduced to about 11,000. Exhaustion and malnutrition, with the added horrors of typhus and dysentery, had taken their toll on the POWs, and they continued to perish at alarming rates even after they were unloaded on the island of Asinara. Beneš soon became aware of the plight of these unlucky POWs, and he successfully lobbied the Serbian government-in-exile for the transfer of the Czecho-Slovaks among them to France.[7] By then, only a few thousand Czecho-Slovak POWs were left and further time was needed not only for them to physically recover from their ordeal, but also for the National Council to obtain jurisdiction over the prisoners since they were still the nominal responsibility of Serbia.[8]

In Beneš's negotiations with the French Ministry of War during the latter half of 1917, he had mentioned Italy as a possible source of Czecho-Slovak volunteers for the planned army in France. However, Rome's continued frosty attitude toward the national movements of Habsburg Slavs, a position staked by Sonnino, upset this scheme.[9] Meanwhile, Štefánik, who had made his own attempt to reason with the Italians earlier that year, left for the United States to recruit Czecho-Slovak soldiers from the immigrant communities there. He had high expectations for his mission: war exhaustion was unknown in America since the U.S. had only recently entered the conflict, the Czech- and Slovak-Americans had thus far proved generous in their monetary support of the liberation movement and his activities were underwritten by the French government. In the end, though, his recruitment drive enlisted only 2,300 volunteers, far below the projections of the National Council.[10] There are several explanations for this disappointing result, not least being the U.S. government's stipulation that prohibited Štefánik from enlisting those who were eligible for the draft. Consequently, his recruiting pool was restricted to men above the age of thirty or who did not yet possess U.S. citizenship. Moreover, the U.S. Army held considerable appeal even for those eligible to join the planned Czecho-Slovak army in France since American troops were guaranteed higher pay and better rations. Additionally, many young Czech- and Slovak-Americans placed more importance in their American identity than their old Czech or Slovak heritage. The rapid assimilation of immigrants into American society seems have been overlooked by Štefánik and most Europeans—including the German leaders who miscalculated that most German-Americans would never take up arms against the land of their fathers.[11]

While Štefánik was trying to muster troops for a Czecho-Slovak army in France, Beneš was engaging the French Ministries of War and Foreign Affairs to construct the framework for such an army. The terms which the Czech revolutionary proposed mirrored the conditions which Masaryk had agreed to with the Russian Provisional Government: the National Council was to be given political control while officer appointments were to meet the approval of both the National Council and the host government. Beneš had intended to have an arrangement for an army ready by the time Czecho-Slovak troops began arriving from Russia, but this was not to be.[12] When the first Czecho-Slovak detachment from Archangelsk reached French shores in June 1917, the French authorities welcomed them by sealing them in trains and sending them to a prison camp alongside mutinous soldiers from the Russian expeditionary force.[13] The French authorities were suspicious of anyone arriving from the revolutionary cauldron of Russia, and it seems that they quarantined the Czecho-Slovak troops to protect the morale of their own shaky army. Unfortunately for these soldiers, the formal negotiations between Beneš and the French government had just begun and would continue throughout that year into the following winter.[14] A major sticking point in the parlays between the two parties was Beneš's insistence that the army's finances be guaranteed through a loan to be repaid by a future Czecho-Slovak state. The French, who were too wily to be roped into a condition that was tantamount to recognition of the Czecho-Slovak independence movement, would not agree to this condition.[15] Another reason for the slow progress of the negotiations, though not apparent to Beneš at the time, rested with French and Allied hopes to lure Austria-Hungary into a separate peace. As long as this possibility existed, the French were reluctant to offend Vienna by forming a Czecho-Slovak army.

The event which caused the Allies to modify their attitude that winter towards the exiles was the rout of the Italian Army at Caporetto. The disaster precipitated two major changes in the Allied camp. The first was the establishment of the Supreme War Council, which was intended to better coordinate strategic decisions among the British, French, Italian and American commands.[16] The second was that the attack hardened Allied attitudes toward Austria-Hungary. It was the first time that any of them had been subjected to a large-scale, combined Austro-Hungarian and German attack. The experience seemed to confirm the claims of anti–Habsburg exiles that the Monarchy was an enabler of, rather than a bulwark against, German hegemony in Central and Eastern Europe.

As the spring of 1918 approached, the Allies were becoming increasingly worried about the expected German offensive on the Western Front and the supporting role Austria-Hungary might assume during the attack. To address this concern, the British began looking for a way to weaken the Habsburg army without expending precious troops or ordinance in a military operation. The weapon they resorted to was propaganda, which was by now an ever-expanding enterprise of His Majesty's government. In February, Lloyd George set up the Department of Propaganda in Enemy Countries. The new section was to be based at the London mansion of Crewe House and its operations were placed under the responsibility of the newspaper tycoon Lord Northcliffe.[17] As the owner of *The Times* and several other British newspapers, Northcliffe, whose birth name was Alfred Harmsworth, was a wealthy, controversial but also influential entrepreneur who had helped make the press accessible to lower, newly-literate classes. His understanding of the popular press, as well as his own successful publicity efforts in the U.S. during 1917, made him an ideal candidate to lead Britain's latest exercise in propaganda aimed abroad.

Northcliffe's primary weakness was his health, which was ailing in early 1918. As a result the onus for generating the propaganda fell on his subordinates, including Henry Wickham Steed, who was also his employee at *The Times*, and Robert Seton-Watson.[18] The influence of these men in Crewe House was evident from the start. When Northcliffe accepted his new position, he immediately looked to Steed for advice on how to launch a propaganda offensive against the Central Powers.[19] Within twenty-four hours, Steed had replied to his boss with a memorandum stating that the easiest target for such a campaign was Austria-Hungary. He argued that the Allies had to choose between two exclusive policies towards the Monarchy: either pursue a separate peace with the Habsburgs or break their power "by supporting and encouraging all anti–German and pro–Allied peoples and tendencies." Since earlier attempts to seek a separate peace with Austria-Hungary were unsuccessful, Steed thought it logical to go the second route which, according to him, was "in harmony with the declared aims of the Allies."[20] He wrote that only the Austrian-Germans and Magyars were pro–German and that they were outnumbered by the empire's Slavs, Italians and Romanians who were actively or passively anti–German. "The pro–German minority rules the anti–German majority," he explained. "Apart from the questions of democratic principle, the policy of the Allies should be evidently to help and encourage the anti–Germans."[21]

After receiving these recommendations, Northcliffe forwarded the memorandum to Britain's Secretary of State of Foreign Affairs, Arthur James Balfour, who requested further details of the scheme. Steed replied to the Foreign Secretary by stating that the Allied governments should demand democratic freedoms for the ethnicities of the Habsburg Empire while avoiding phrases that implied the preservation of Austria-Hungary. He added that the Allies should utilize the experienced propagandists in the émigré organizations, specifically mentioning the Czecho-Slovak National Council and the Yugoslav Committee, and encourage Italy to relax her strict interpretation of the Treaty of London.

On 26 February Balfour stated his agreement with the course of action outlined by Steed but at the same time he made known his reluctance to drastically alter his government's policy towards the future of Austria-Hungary. "As you point out with unanswerable force," he wrote to Northcliffe, "everything which encourages the anti–German elements in the Habsburg dominions really helps to compel the Emperor and the Court to a separate peace."[22] In other words, Balfour's wishfully believed that the Allies did not have to choose between either of the policies mentioned by Steed; they could foment unrest among the disaffected ethnicities of the Monarchy *and* pursue a separate peace. The following day, the press lord drafted a note that was intended to force the Foreign Secretary to make a more definite decision. He informed Balfour that since the Italians were forecasting a major offensive on their front in the next two months, he was eager to launch a propaganda campaign in the hope that it might undermine the expected attack. The British War Cabinet agreed with Northcliffe and gave him and Steed permission to launch a propaganda campaign among the nationalities of Austria-Hungary but with the caveat that they were to avoid promising them independence. Although Steed was disappointed by this restriction, he nevertheless readily accepted the task before him.

The British decision to intensify propaganda activities against the Central Powers was echoed by representatives of the major powers at an inter–Allied conference on propaganda held in London in late February. Henri Moysett, the private secretary to the French Minister of the Marine, urged the Allies to unleash "a war of ideas" on Germany. To support his view, he pointed to the success of enemy propaganda on the Eastern Front, where the Central Powers had utilized "the shattering effect of Bolshevist doctrine upon Russian minds." A similar campaign, Moysett declared, should be aimed at Austria-Hungary by stirring the national aspirations of the empire's ethnic minorities.[23] His basic argument was that just as Germany had exploited Lenin to sabotage the Russian war effort, the Allies should do likewise to their enemies with the bountiful exiles from Austria-Hungary, among whom Masaryk was the most formidable.

On 19 March Steed, acting on an Italian proposal at the London conference, began his journey to Italy to begin coordinating the propaganda offensive against the Austro-Hungarian Army.[24] He expected his colleague in Crewe House, Seton-Watson, to accompany him, but Balfour held back the Scotsman at the request of Italy's Ambassador to Great Britain, who thought him to be too pro–Yugoslav.[25] Such inter–Allied intrigues seemed rather preposterous when two days later the German guns opened up in the pre-dawn hours along a fifty-mile section of the Western Front. When the shelling ceased five-hours later, masked German storm troopers surged through the clouds of smoke and noxious gasses into the nearly obliterated British trenches, where the survivors were often too few or too dazed to give serious resistance. In two days the decimated British Fifth Army fell back almost forty miles before the German onslaught, returning a pace of movement to the Western Front not seen since 1914. Moreover, the offensive had brought Paris within the seventy-five mile-range of a monstrous German artillery gun while confronting the Allies with one of the bleakest hours of their war effort.[26]

News of the German attack in France had cast a dark shadow over the Italian Army Comando Supremo in Padua by the time Steed arrived there. The enemy advance, combined with the painful memories of the Caporetto debacle only a few months earlier and the predictions of intelligence officers that the Habsburg armies might strike at any moment, all exerted untold strain on Italian morale. Amid this environment of acute anxiety, Steed briefed a meeting of Italian intelligence officers on the details of his mission and requested their views on the best means of completing it. To his surprise, the Italian officers were not only enthusiastic about his propaganda scheme against Austria-Hungary, they even suggested that the émigré organizations should proclaim independence on behalf of their peoples and that these declarations should be openly backed by the Allied governments. When Steed informed them that this course of action was explicitly prohibited by the British War Cabinet, they fell into a disappointment marked by silence. After a pause, however, the Briton asked for two days to gain his government's authorization to promise independence to the Habsburg ethnicities. "In view of the German offensive," he confided to them, "it may be possible to have this restriction removed. Meanwhile, let us go ahead and prepare leaflets on the assumption that it will be removed."[27]

While the Italian intelligence officers supervised the drafting of leaflets in the languages of Austro-Hungarian ethnicities, Steed lobbed an urgent telegram to Northcliffe requesting him to secure the British War Cabinet's assent to propaganda promising independence to the peoples of the Habsburg Empire. Thirty-six hours later, he received the authorization he needed through Northcliffe. From Paris, French Prime Minister Georges Clemenceau also approved the planned propaganda. Steed also made an attempt to gain Sonnino's support for the scheme, but the Italian Foreign Minister, while willing to tolerate the distribution of propaganda promising self-determination to the empire's ethnicities, refused to associate his office with such a policy. Although Steed was disappointed by Sonnino's duplicity, he initiated the operation as scheduled. By 7 April Allied airplanes were showering Austro-Hungarian regiments with leaflets promising independence to Czecho-Slovaks, South Slavs, Poles and Romanians.

When the front along the Piave River remained quiet that April, Steed and his accomplices claimed the enemy's passivity was due to the disruption which their propaganda barrage unleashed in the Habsburg army. In actuality, the Italian intelligence forecasting an imminent Austro-Hungarian offensive that month was faulty.[28] The extent to which the

Austro-Hungarian Army was affected by this propaganda is difficult to gauge. Although Steed's efforts produced considerable materiel—an estimated 15,000,000 leaflets in a half-dozen languages by the second week in April—the real difficulty lay in their proper distribution. Italian intelligence regarding the position of Czech, Croat, Slovene and Romanian divisions in the army was not always accurate; therefore it may be surmised that many leaflets landed on formations that would be unable to read their content. Moreover, leaflets dropped from airplanes frequently missed their target altogether.

Despite its dubious effectiveness, the propaganda offensive orchestrated by Steed was a very significant milestone for the anti–Habsburg émigré organizations. With the establishment of a Central Inter-Allied Propaganda Commission at Padua that included Czech, South Slav, Romanian and Polish delegates in addition to representatives from the Entente powers, the émigrés were brought into closer and more open cooperation with the Allies.[29] Not to be overlooked was the content of the propaganda itself. Although the propagandists probably at least suspected that the leaflets promising independence to the Slavs of Austria-Hungary did not accurately reflect Allied policy at the time, many became increasingly sympathetic towards the national movements. Even Northcliffe felt that the die was cast and later pressured the British government to clarify its policy towards the national aspirations among the peoples of Austria-Hungary. The press lord, it seems, was growing uncomfortable with having his name associated with printed items that might prove to be outright falsehoods.[30, 31]

Steed, along with Seton-Watson, who was finally permitted to travel to Italy at the end of March, performed another crowning achievement for the ethnic groups by convening a "Congress of Oppressed Nationalities of Austria-Hungary" in Rome during 8–11 April. The conference brought together Beneš and Štefánik for the Czecho-Slovaks, Ante Trumbić for the Yugo-Slav Committee, Polish émigrés, Romanian exiles from Transylvania and a delegation from the Serbian Skupština. The representatives of the various exile organizations arrived in the Italian capital with high expectations, primarily that their objectives toward national liberation would be recognized by the Allies in accordance with Steed's plan. Thus they were doubly piqued when these announcements were not only withheld, but also when Balfour publicly disavowed Steed and Seton-Watson's work to silence domestic critics.[32] The congress' only official response from an Allied government, a statement issued by the U.S. Secretary of State in late May that Washington had watched the proceedings in Rome with great interest, was still disappointing compared to the émigrés' initial hopes.[33] Still, the congress had its own propaganda value: it demonstrated the solidarity of the various nationalities, easing concerns of Balkanization in a fragmented Central Europe. It also ratified an earlier agreement intended to smooth over relations between Italy and the South Slavs, thereby lowering a barrier which had confronted the Czecho-Slovaks and others in their quest for official Allied support of their aims.[34]

The Congress of the Oppressed Nationalities revealed that the Allies, without question, were unwilling to officially endorse the statements printed in their own propaganda. This was a letdown for Steed; he later assessed in his memoirs that the Allies were willing to extend any guarantees amid their panic on the Western Front and the perceived threat in Italy regardless of whether they might default on them later once the crisis passed.[35] For Beneš and Štefánik, the absence of any Allied recognition following the Rome congress reinvigorated them with a sense of self-reliance that had been strong in their movement from the very beginning. That spring, they were closing in on a goal that was a propaganda coup larger than any political resolution: autonomous Czecho-Slovak armies would soon be serving in France and Italy.

As long as a separate peace seemed possible between the Allies and Austria-Hungary, the French were in no hurry to set up a Czecho-Slovak army on their soil. During the winter of 1917–18, however, they concluded that Vienna no longer felt an urgent need to make peace in light of her recent victory in Italy and the negotiations taking place at Brest-Litovsk. Realizing that the war was more likely to be settled by military rather than diplomatic means, the French finally accepted the necessity of utilizing every military resource at their disposal.

This shift in mentality led to the presidential decree of 16 December 1917 which announced the establishment of a Czecho-Slovak army in France, although the final terms for the unit were not worked out between Beneš and Prime Minister Clemenceau until the following February.[36] To reach this settlement, Beneš had to drop his earlier stipulation that the army be funded by a loan to be repaid by a future Czecho-Slovak state. Upon its initiation, the Czecho-Slovak Legion in France consisted of approximately 8,000 men welded together from the volunteers that arrived earlier from Russia, the U.S. and the Balkans.[37] The lack of available manpower continued to be a limiting factor for this corps, and its strength would never exceed 10,000. Though it fought bravely in several actions on the Western Front, it was simply too small to have a decisive role there.[38]

News of the establishment of a Czecho-Slovak army in France had a profound impact in Rome, where the Italian government found it difficult to maintain its antipathetic attitude towards such a project. Not only did the government feel pressured by the actions of its ally to mobilize its Czecho-Slovak POWs, but the Italian Army was also eager to raise a Slavic legion. The military was, in fact, already experimenting with volunteer soldiers recruited from Slav prisoners. They had begun employing POWs in April 1917 when František Hlaváček, a Czech deserter captured the previous summer, was released after the intelligence he provided regarding Austrian artillery placements along a sector of the Isonzo front was verified to be true. During the following months, Hlaváček helped the Italian Second Army with prisoner interrogation and operation planning, for which he was soon decorated. He also used his growing clout with the Italian military elite to push for the establishment of a Czecho-Slovak legion in Italy and aided Beneš and Štefánik in their negotiations with the Italian government.[39]

Even while the Consulta, led by Sonnino, blocked the National Council's efforts to draw upon Czecho-Slovak POWs in Italy for their planned army, the Italian Army set up a tiny unit of Slav deserters behind the government's back in the autumn of 1917. These soldiers, who initially numbered less than twenty men, were intended to function as specialists in reconnaissance and enemy subversion in a manner similar to the early Družina in Russia. With Hlaváček's help, the Slav detachment, consisting mostly of Czech along with a few South Slavs, added several dozen POWs to its ranks in the coming months.[40] Gradually, the military was warming to idea of a large mobilization of Slav POWs.

In the meantime, in February 1918, the Comando Supremo finally deployed the Czecho-Slovak labor battalions it had begun organizing the previous autumn. While this role was much less than what either Hlaváček or Beneš intended for the Czecho-Slovak POWs, both assented to it in the hope that it would eventually lead to a combat role for the volunteers.[41] Štefánik, however, was irresolutely opposed to the employment of the POWs in mere labor detachments. He went to Italy later that month determined to make nothing less than soldiers out of the Czecho-Slovak volunteers. After tedious negotiations, his persistence paid off

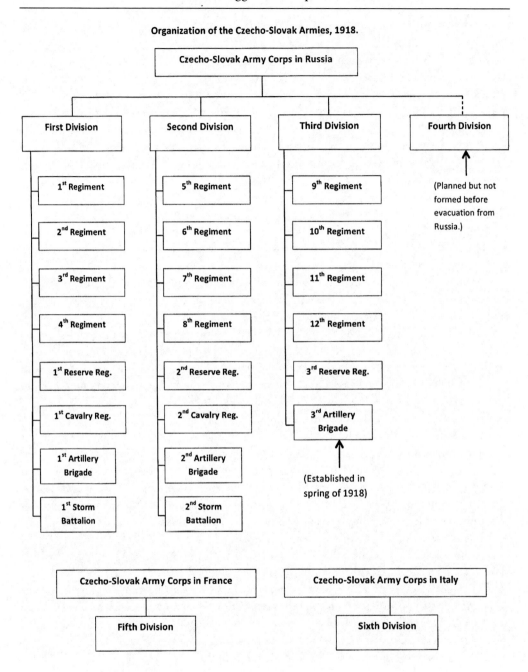

Organization of the Czecho-Slovak Armies, 1918.

Organizational chart of the Czecho-Slovak legions, 1918–1919.

with what Beneš praised as "his greatest success during his war-time activity."[42] On 21 April, the Slovak aviator signed an agreement for an autonomous Czecho-Slovak national army with the new Italian Prime Minister, Vittorio Orlando.[43] Under its terms, the Italians, unlike the French, agreed to finance the army through a loan to be repaid by a future Czecho-Slovak state.[44] These advantageous terms were made possible by Sonnino's continued aloofness to the project; he avoided endorsing either this or any of the other follow-up agreements concerning the Czecho-Slovak army.[45] His disdainful attitude towards the creation of a Czecho-Slovak Legion in Italy was an exception in that country as most of the cabinet and the Italian presses were enthusiastic over mobilizing the POWs.[46]

Once the agreement negotiated by Štefánik went into effect, the Czecho-Slovak labor battalions were quickly converted into frontline detachments. By the middle of May, the unit that would be known as the Czecho-Slovak Legion's Sixth Division[47] numbered over 11,000 and was growing.[48] At this stage, the legionaries continued to serve as scattered patrols along the front gathering intelligence or tempting their compatriots in the Austro-Hungarian Army to desert either by blaring Slavic hymns on gramophones placed in no-man's land or simply promising them abundant food. This work was fraught with danger. During the advance of the Habsburg troops in June, thirty-five Czechs wearing Italian uniforms and the tell-tale red, white and blue cockades were captured by the attackers. Most of them were soon hanged as traitors and their corpses were left dangling for several days to serve as a gruesome warning to legionaries and potential deserters alike.[49]

Even with the generous terms attained by the Czecho-Slovaks in their agreement with the Italian government, the build-up of their army was not without certain difficulties. The Legion's original Commander-in-Chief, Italian General Andrea Graziani, had one of the worst reputations among Italian generals in the war for summarily executing his men.[50] This was no mild achievement as no other army of the day, except for the Red Army, employed such draconian measures in order to terrify its troops into following orders.[51] As a result, discipline was strongly enforced in the Czecho-Slovak Legion in Italy and the slightest manifestation of insubordination or pro–Austrian sentiment could earn the soldiers a one-way ticket back to a prison camp—if they were lucky. On at least one occasion, eight Czech soldiers deemed unreliable were put before a firing squad by Graziani.[52] The general had other flaws besides his fearsome brutality as he also showed considerable insensitivity to the Legion's national character and demanded its appearance to conform with the rest of the Italian Army.[53] The controversy among Czecho-Slovak leaders concerning Graziani's behavior lasted throughout the summer and into the autumn of 1918 when, just days before Italy launched its final offensive, he was replaced by another Italian, General Luigi Piccione, as the commander of the Czecho-Slovak Legion in Italy.[54]

The reaction of Austro-Hungarian commanders to news that Czecho-Slovak war prisoners would be deployed against them also posed additional challenges for the legionaries. Habsburg troops were under orders to fire immediately whenever they spotted Czecho-Slovak patrols, and later AOK offered a reward of 300 *kronen* for each captured legionary.[55] As revolutionaries, the legionaries were not considered to be under the protection of international law; hence most of the captured Czecho-Slovaks were executed by the Austro-Hungarians. These killings, which were sometimes deliberately carried out within view of Italian lines, enraged Štefánik.[56] At one point the feisty Slovak had leaflets scattered over the enemy lines warning that ten German-Austrian or Magyar POWs would be slaughtered for every legionary executed. AOK quickly neutralized the threat by issuing leaflets of its own promising to kill ten Italian POWs for every Austro-Hungarian soldier sent to the gallows.[57]

The legionaries' first engagement in large, cohesive units occurred in mid–June when two Czecho-Slovak battalions from the 33rd and 34th Regiments engaged Habsburg troops as the latter commenced their long-awaited offensive across the Piave. One company from the 33rd Regiment was encircled by the enemy and annihilated; most were killed in the subsequent fighting while the fifteen men eventually taken captive were executed. The assessments of the legionaries' performance in this encounter are mixed, but they unquestionably proved their worth as soldiers later that month by leading an attack to recapture the summit of Mount di Val Bella, during which some 800 Habsburg troops of South Slav origin gave themselves up during the battle.[58]

The most significant engagement fought by Czecho-Slovak troops in Italy occurred in September 1918. During the previous month, the Czecho-Slovak Sixth Division was redeployed on a twelve-mile sector of the front from Lake Garda to the Adige River. The legionaries' position included Monte Dosso Alto, the commanding heights of which dominated the local terrain. On 29 August a sudden Austro-Hungarian attack was repulsed by the Czecho-Slovak 34th Regiment. Ten days later, the enemy made an unsuccessful attempt to dislodge the 33rd Regiment from its position. Sporadic fighting continued along the line over the following days until 21 September, when Austro-Hungarian artillery began raining gas and high-explosive shells on the Czecho-Slovak defenders. Once the bombardment lifted, Habsburg troops attacked the legionaries in force in an attempt to storm Monte Dosso Alto. The legionaries fought stubbornly for two hours and resorted to staving off the attackers with hand grenades after they ran out of ammunition. The Austro-Hungarians eventually overwhelmed the Czecho-Slovaks and seized the summit, but their triumph was short-lived. Early the next morning, the legionaries counterattacked and retook Monte Dosso Alto before daybreak. Although the Czecho-Slovak losses were severe, they ultimately retained their position and, more importantly for their cause, obtained the respect and admiration of their Italian sponsors.[59]

Some Czecho-Slovak units that had been formed as scouting and infiltrating parties, such as the loosely-organized 39th Regiment, continued their commando-like raids into the final days of the war. Many of these missions ended with the discovery and execution of the would-be saboteurs, but others were quite successful in wreaking havoc by blasting enemy ammunition dumps and even an aircraft hangar.[60] Thus the Czecho-Slovak soldiers in Italy fought in diverse roles during the last months of fighting, and their strength in that country approached 20,000 troops.[61] They would, as Masaryk had hoped early in the war, be on hand to march alongside the Italian, French and British units in a final, war-winning offensive.[62]

Timing, it seems, was a crucial factor behind the considerable accomplishments of the Czecho-Slovak liberation movement in Italy. Their greatest achievement, the Czecho-Slovak Legion there, was successfully negotiated by Štefánik from February to April 1918, in a window when the Italians felt particularly vulnerable. For about seven months after the catastrophe at Caporetto, Rome was willing to grasp at any available weapon to fend off the enemy, even to the point of weakening the rationale behind its war aims by embracing the national principle for Austria-Hungary's ethnic groups. After the Austro-Hungarian offensive along the Piave was checked in June, however, the Italians quickly regained their former intransigence. Subsequently, they tightened their reins over the Padua commission to the point of driving the Polish and Yugoslav delegates out while Sonnino successfully blocked another congress of oppressed nationalities from convening in Paris.[63]

The South Slavs were hit the hardest by this Italian change in attitude. The Yugoslav Committee had hoped to emulate the Czecho-Slovaks by establishing a legion of their own recruited from South Slav war prisoners in Italy, but such a proposal went too far for the Italians. Because of pressure from their allies, they did permit several hundred South Slav POWs, primarily Orthodox Serbs, to join Slavic formations already in existence, but there would ultimately be no formal Yugoslav force established in Italy.[64]

Not even the Poles, with whom the Italians had no direct quarrels, came close to matching Czecho-Slovak successes in Italy before the armistice. This was somewhat unusual since nearly all of the major powers wanted to avoid the appearance of standing in the way of Polish national aspirations. It all began with the Central Power's proclamation of an independent Polish kingdom on 5 November 1916 that initiated a tug-of-war between the two sides for Polish loyalties. General Ludendorff had hoped that the declaration would attract the volunteers from occupied Poland into the Polnische Wehrmacht that would serve alongside the Central Powers.[65] On the other hand, the Entente became more openly supportive of the Polish liberation movement not only to offset Ludendorff's scheme, but also to impress President Wilson. The U.S. President had developed a deep sympathy for the Poles, possibly due to the concerts staged by the touring Polish pianist Ignace Paderewski.[66] The Polish national movement scored a major success in June 1917 when France announced the establishment of a Polish legion on its soil, and this was followed by the creation of a Polish National Committee in August. Under the leadership of Roman Dmowski, this group was immediately favored by the Allies over the left-leaning Polish organizations and exiles associated with Józef Piłsudski, the Regency Council in Warsaw and other so-called German collaborators. A few months later, the Polish National Committee was granted official recognition by the governments of France, Britain and the United States.[67]

The Poles' recruiting efforts in France and the U.S. were more successful than those conducted by the Czecho-Slovaks in those countries, mainly due to the fact they had far larger pool to draw from. Still, the Poles could have benefited from mobilizing Polish POWs interned in Italy, but by the time they reached the organizational level needed to recruit POWs in that country and request their release from the government, Rome had lost much of its earlier enthusiasm for fostering Slavic national armies. Consequently, the 38,000 Polish POWs in Italy who volunteered for the Polish Legion in France were not allowed to physically join the unit until after the armistice.[68]

The progress of the South Slav and Polish national movements in Italy demonstrate that the accomplishments of the Czecho-Slovaks in the peninsular nation were not inevitable. Still, the work of the Czecho-Slovak National Council was far from complete. As Beneš noted of the army settlements, "none of these agreements contained any express political commitments as regards our future independence."[69] The legions could and would elevate the National Council's position *vis-à-vis* the Western Allies, but by themselves the armies could not guarantee that the political aim of an independent Czecho-Slovak state would be realized. Aside from the question of official recognition, the National Council had one other major issue to resolve in early 1918, that being what would become of the Czecho-Slovak Legion on the former Eastern Front, which was then mired deep inside Russia and surrounded by a turbulent sea of anarchy. The possibilities dreamt for the legionaries in Russia, who composed the largest Czecho-Slovak army formed during the war, were diverse. Some, like Masaryk, desired the legionaries to be transported to France and save it from succumbing to Russia's woes. Others, including many British and French strategists, wanted to use the Czecho-Slovak corps as a cornerstone for rebuilding a new anti–German front in the East. Ultimately, the legionaries would take on a role much different than anyone had envisaged, and in the course of doing so, they would help the National Council in the realization of its most cherished political goal.

8

Between Cossacks
and Commissars

The winter of 1917–18 was an especially trying time for the Czecho-Slovak legionaries encamped in Ukraine. Not only did they have to contend with bone-chilling weather, but they also faced the uncertainty of their future. Aware that the Bolsheviks were attempting to negotiate Russia's exit from the war at Brest-Litovsk, the Czecho-Slovak troops could only guess what peace on the Eastern Front would mean for their outfit. As they pondered this question during the long winter nights, an emissary from the Austro-Hungarian Emperor arrived with an offer of full amnesty for the troops if they laid down their arms. Without any hesitation, the Czecho-Slovak officers rejected this overture, but the emissary was not the only unwelcome visitor in their camps.[1] Bolshevik agitators, Ukrainian nationalists and couriers from the anti–Bolshevik army forming in the Don Territory all tried to attract the sympathies of either the Czecho-Slovak troops or their officers. Since many of the Legion's officers were Russian, they were divided between their devotion to the motherland and sub-ordination to Masaryk's order of noninterference in Russia's internal affairs. In some cases the officers themselves quarreled with each other and neglected their duties, forcing rounds of dismissals and new appointments. Overall, morale in the Czecho-Slovak Legion sank to dangerous lows that winter as snowstorms, rumors of impending peace and an unknown future all took a toll on the troops' condition.[2]

The question of where these troops might fight next, or perhaps if they would even fight at all, depended mainly on the Western Allies. The Allies, however, were unable to agree on any common policy in regards to the situation on the Eastern Front. At an inter–Allied conference in Paris that met in late November 1917, Britain and France both asserted that Germany and Austria-Hungary must be barred from penetrating the grain-rich lands of Ukraine. If they did so, it was feared that the Central Powers would neutralize the blockade, which was one of the Allies' most effective weapons to date. British and French hopes that resistance could be maintained on the southern end of the Eastern Front were encouraged by reports from their military missions that the forces there, consisting of the Romanian Army, Ukrainian forces and the Czecho-Slovak and Polish legions were in far better shape than the skeletal Russian formations to their north.[3] Still, these units could not be expected to fend off the Central Powers without assistance and supplies from a major power outside Russia. Since Britain and France were already dispatching forces at that moment to prop up the Italian Front, they had no men or materiel to spare for an expedition to Russia. Hence, London and Paris inquired whether the United States and Japan might be willing to undertake such a commitment in Russia. The task which they proposed—

transporting men and supplies across 6,000 miles of railway from Vladivostok to Ukraine—would have been a logistical nightmare. Both Washington and Tokyo quickly rejected the scheme.[4]

After their allies turned down their proposal for a large-scale intervention in Russia, British and French officials at the Paris conference stayed behind to forge their own strategy on how to block a German advance in the East. Each country decided to support forces deemed unfriendly to the Germans, including those that were explicitly anti–Bolshevik. The two allies then partitioned out two "spheres of influence": the British were to concentrate their efforts in the Caucuses and Central Asia while the French were responsible for the unoccupied areas of Romania and Ukraine.[5]

Long before this policy went into effect, the French Military Mission to Romania had already begun looking for ways to sustain an anti–German front in the East. In early autumn of 1917, as much of the Eastern Front began to lapse into inactivity, the French officials in Iaşi cabled Paris with the idea that the Czecho-Slovak Legion might be put to better use in Romania than in Ukraine. The French government quickly seized upon this idea and asked for permission from Beneš and Štefánik to begin the redeployment of the Legion. The two National Council figures both favored the proposal but left the final decision to Masaryk since he was closer to the fronts in question and could obtain more accurate information on conditions there.[6] The Czech professor, never one to make an important decision without a thorough investigation, soon embarked on a fact-finding mission to Iaşi, the seat of the Romanian government since its evacuation of Bucharest almost a year earlier.

After the Romanian Army's lamentable performance in 1916, it may seem surprising that just a year later Masaryk and several Allied generals contemplated its potential to act as a backbone to anti–German opposition in the region. Their confidence was not completely unwarranted after the French Military Mission to Romania overhauled the remnant of the Romanian force through reorganization and new equipment. These reforms were so successful that the combined Romanian-Russian units on that front mounted one of the most successful secondary attacks during the 1917 summer offensives.[7] Yet, by the time Masaryk personally toured the Romanian front in late October, he found the lines ominously quiet.

Masaryk reviews the Czecho-Slovak 1st Regiment, undated. To his left in the foreground is General Janin, then chief of the French Military Mission to Russia.

The three Russian armies in Romania, like the others to their north, were thoroughly demoralized by enemy and revolutionary propaganda. Tensions were high between the allied troops since generally reliable Romanian soldiers were prevailed upon to suppress mutinies in neighboring Russian formations.[8] Despite the evident problems at the front, Masaryk continued to consider the Legion's redeployment to Romania after meeting with various Romanian leaders, Allied diplomats and the chief of the French Military Mission, General Henri Berthelot.[9] He continued to explore the question after returning to Kiev, where he found the Legion's Commander-in-Chief, General Shokhorov, supportive of the project. Masaryk, however, could not ignore his lingering doubts about Romania's ability to provision an additional 40,000 troops, not to mention her willingness to continue the war if Russia made peace. His vacillation led to friction with Paris even though some senior French officers there considered the plan risky as well.[10] Eventually, Masaryk was vindicated in his refusal to authorize the project when Romania entered into armistice talks with the Central Powers in early December, only days after Russia.[11]

Not long after the Romanian scheme was put to rest, the Czecho-Slovak Legion began receiving invitations to make common cause with another force, the Volunteer Army. This so-called army, which numbered less than 4,000 bayonets throughout most of the winter, had been organized in the Don Territory by General Alekseev and several other commanders from the tsarist army. Although it counted the Central Powers among its enemies, the Volunteer Army's primary goal was to wrest Russia from Bolshevik control. Its leaders had hoped that the Czecho-Slovak and Polish legions in Ukraine would at least act as a "covering force" while the Volunteers and their Cossack allies mustered their strength for a march into the Russian heartland.[12]

When Masaryk first received a letter from Alekseev in December 1917 proposing cooperation between their forces, he did not reject the idea outright despite his own long-stated policy that the Czecho-Slovaks must remain neutral in Russia's domestic affairs. His second thoughts may have been encouraged by the French military attachés in Kiev, who were establishing their own contacts with Alekseev and General Kaledin, the Don Cossack ataman who was playing host to the Volunteers. In his reply to Alekseev, Masaryk avoided making any commitments to the Volunteer Army but did request more details on its politics.[13] This message was to be delivered to Novocherkassk by Captain Klecanda, who had been the Czecho-Slovak National Council's authorized representative to Stavka and knew many of the White generals personally, but he was unable to reach Alekseev's headquarters.[14]

There was a small group of Czecho-Slovaks who, unlike Masaryk, had no qualms against serving with the anti–Bolshevik Russians from the start. These included a handful of Czecho-Slovak POWs from the Romanian front that had fought under the charismatic General Lavr Kornilov in the summer of 1917. They remained devoted to the general over the following stormy months, which saw Kornilov rise to become the head of Stavka, then become Kerensky's prisoner and finally a fugitive of the Bolsheviks. The *kornilovsty* Czecho-Slovaks eventually followed their hero to the Don Territory, where they were joined by conservative, Slavophile Czecho-Slovaks, including some ex-members of Dürich's national council. One such former Dürich supporter, Captain František Král, sought to enlarge the Czecho-Slovak contingent under the Volunteer Army by attempting to enlist Czecho-Slovak POWs in the region.[15] Although he recruited in the name of the famed Czecho-Slovak Legion, Král had no intention of obeying Masaryk's directive of non-interference in purely Russian affairs. In the meantime, Václav Vondrák, the former chairman of the SCSR, and Pavel Miliukov, the onetime foreign minister in Russia's Provisional Government and Masaryk's friend, all turned up in South Russia.[16] These developments could only increase Soviet suspicions that Masaryk and his army might have counterrevolutionary sympathies, and subsequently the Czech professor was compelled to publicly denounce both Král's recruiting activities and any suggestion that the Legion should intervene in the unfolding civil war. He also broke off correspondence with the Whites in South Russia, including Miliukov.[17] Unperturbed by Masaryk's disavowal of him, Král continued his work and once again declared his allegiance to Dürich, who had opposed Masaryk's policy of neutrality in Russia's internal conflicts since November 1917.[18] This latest challenge posed by the Czecho-Slovak Slavophiles was not a serious threat to Masaryk's leadership of the National Council or the Legion in Russia. From early 1918 onwards, the White-controlled regions of South Russia were cut off from the main body of the Legion by hostile Red forces. The Slavophiles' fate was therefore tied directly to the fortunes of the anti–Bolshevik Russians, for whom the early months of the civil war brought mostly defeat and extreme trials.

Another organization that explored the possibility of a military alliance with the Czecho-Slovak Legion was the Rada, the central Ukrainian parliament in Kiev. Since its inception shortly after the February Revolution, the Rada had taken advantage of the decline of central authority in Russia to push for greater autonomy. After the overthrow of the Provisional Government, the Rada proclaimed a Ukrainian National Republic for its homeland without fully separating Ukraine from Russia. From this point on, the Rada considered itself on equal terms with the Soviet government and not bound to the armistice terms agreed by the Bolsheviks at Brest-Litovsk. For this reason, both the French military attachés in Kiev and Masaryk forged close ties with the Ukrainian leaders that winter in the hope that Ukraine would continue to oppose the Central Powers in the East. In some ways the Czecho-Slovak and Ukrainian national movements seemed compatible: both were Slav ethnicities with populations who were subjects of the Habsburgs.[19, 20] The similarities, however, mostly ended there. Whereas Czecho-Slovak nationalism was anti–German and anti–Magyar, that of the Ukrainians was mainly anti–Russian and anti–Polish. There was also a strong element among Ukrainian nationalists that was decidedly pro–German since Berlin frequently patronized their separatist activities to stir up discontent on the Russian home front.[21] Despite this knowledge, the commander of the French Military Mission in Kiev, General Tabois, seemed confident that the Ukrainian Rada could be enlisted as a much-needed ally on the Eastern Front.[22]

Since the Czecho-Slovak Legion was encamped on lands claimed by the Rada, Masaryk and the Russian branch of the National Council found it necessary to negotiate with the Ukrainian leaders in order to define the conditions of the legionaries' presence in Ukraine. These talks, which began on 5 January 1918, were a success from the Czecho-Slovak point of view. In exchange for a guarantee of the Legion's military support if Ukraine entered into hostilities with the Central Powers, the Rada agreed to allow provisions to reach the legionaries and permit the Czecho-Slovak corps a free exit if the Ukrainians concluded peace with the Central Powers.[23] During the negotiations with the Rada, Masaryk received another piece of good news: the French government had recognized the Czecho-Slovak Legions as an Allied army.[24]

The French Military Mission in Kiev was so confident that the Rada would declare its allegiance to the Allies that it began ordering the Czecho-Slovak and Polish armies in the region to prepare for joint military operations with the Rada's three infantry regiments.

Their plan called for the Czecho-Slovak First Division to take up positions west of Kiev with the First Polish Corps to its north and the Second Polish Corps and Ukrainians to the south. These forces, along with the Romanians who the French commanders hoped might yet be induced to stay in the war, would then form a contiguous front that would block the enemy's route into the granaries of Ukraine and South Russia.[25] The French, however, were more optimistic than they should have been regarding the Rada's desire to join their side.

The negotiations between the Rada and the French military attachés were complicated by the latter's consideration for Russian attitudes towards Ukrainian independence. They continued to hope that Russia might yet resume hostilities against the Central Powers if the peace talks at Brest-Litovsk floundered or if another party seized power in Petrograd. They knew that Great Russian patriots, which included the leaders of many anti–Bolshevik forces, remained committed to a "one and indivisible" Russia and opposed complete independence for Ukraine. They also realized that the Bolsheviks, who portrayed themselves as willing to recognize the right of Ukrainians and other national minorities to succeed from the former Russian Empire, did not necessarily look favorably on such tendencies. The Bolsheviks were convinced that all proletarians desired the Marxist ideal of international worker solidarity. To them, separatist movements were sponsored by class enemies and thus counterrevolutionary. The Soviet government, and in particular its Commissariat for Nationalities Affairs led by a Georgian Bolshevik named Iosif Dzhugashvili, better known by the pseudonym Stalin, subsidized propaganda and Marxist organizations among the minorities that sought to maintain unity with Soviet Russia. Therefore, the French refused to offer any formal recognition of Ukrainian independence to avoid offending Russian sensibilities, whether Red or White. This policy was successful since it left a door open between themselves and the various claimants to Russian power, however, it also undermined their chances of attracting the Rada to their camp.[26]

Disappointed by the cautious policy of the French, the Rada turned to the Germans, who readily recognized its authority as a sovereign government and then began separate negotiations with the Ukrainian delegation at Brest-Litovsk to turn up the pressure on the dithering Bolsheviks.[27] The French military attachés were aghast at this development, which signaled the collapse of their planned anti–German front in Ukraine.[28] The Soviet government was also furious with the Rada's action and, unlike the French, it was prepared to use force. In late January it dispatched Red Guard detachments under Lieutenant Colonel Mikhail Muraviev to depose the nationalist Rada and install a puppet government of Ukrainian Bolsheviks in Kiev. This attack put the strength of the Rada to the test, and it failed miserably. The Ukrainian nationalists did not attract any enthusiastic support among peasantry, who were the majority of the region's population, and their battalions were thoroughly inoculated with Bolshevist and pacifist ideology. Against Muraviev's troops, who were not very well equipped and possessed poor discipline, they put up little resistance. Indeed, the biggest hindrance to the Red Guards' advance was the decrepit condition of the railways.[29]

The Bolshevik offensive in Ukraine brought the legionaries into contact with the military forces of the Soviet regime for the first time. On 1 February 1918 the commanders of the Red troops and the Czecho-Slovak Legion met and worked out an agreement where the Bolsheviks accepted the armed neutrality of the Czecho-Slovaks.[30] The Polish Army in Russia, on the other hand, made no effort cultivate the goodwill of the Bolsheviks. This formation consisted of three corps recruited mainly from Poles who had been serving in the tsarist army. The largest of these was the First Polish Army Corps, consisting of about 20,000 men, under the command of General Józef Dowbor-Muśnicki. Like Masaryk, Dowbor-Muśnicki had declared his corps' neutrality after the Bolsheviks seized power in November 1917, but the Poles found it difficult watch passively as Ukrainian and Belarusian peasants plundered the manors of Polish landlords in their sector. Subsequently, the corps began defending Polish persons and property, a decision which resulted in open hostilities between the First Polish Corps and the Bolsheviks. Although the Poles successfully staved off the Red Guards, they found themselves pinched between two enemies: the Soviets to the east and the Central Powers to the west.[31]

Even after the Legion had settled the terms of its armed neutrality with Muraviev, the French military attachés in Kiev urged the National Council to assist the Rada's forces with the defense of the Ukrainian capital.[32] Masaryk refused the suggestion and remained faithful to the truce; nonetheless, the Bolsheviks' operations did test the limits of Masaryk's temperament. Once they reached the outskirts of the Kiev, the Red Guards bombarded the city with field artillery and engaged the Ukrainian nationalist troops in street fighting that lasted for several days.[33] Amid the confusion, a few Czecho-Slovak soldiers were apparently mistaken for enemy defenders by the Red Guards who killed them, stripped their bodies of clothing and mutilated their naked corpses. When Masaryk learned of this atrocity, he issued a terse protest to the Bolshevik commissars and was promised by them that the offenders would be brought to justice. Despite this tragedy, the neutrality between the legionaries and the Bolsheviks remained in effect and a large scale confrontation between them was avoided.[34]

On February 8, the Rada abandoned Kiev to Muraviev's forces, and two days later Masaryk led an Allied delegation of French, British, Czecho-Slovak and Serbian representatives through streets covered with shards of glass and mortar to meet with the Red commander. With Masaryk acting as an interpreter, the conference proceeded smoothly and cordially. It was here that Masaryk revealed to the Bolsheviks his decision for the Legion to leave Ukraine and Russia to fight in France. Muraviev made no objection to the proposal and agreed to seek authorization from the Soviet government for the project.[35] A few days later, on 16 February, the Red commander informed Masaryk that the Soviet leaders, in a telegram from Petrograd, had approved the Czecho-Slovak Legion's departure from Ukraine.[36] Ecstatic at this news, Masaryk immediately called upon the National Council to begin working out the finances and logistics for shipping approximately 45,000 soldiers across Russia and Siberia to Vladivostok.[37] The timing of Soviet government's consent to the project was significant; had they waited a few days they may have wanted the Czecho-Slovaks to remain in Ukraine and help the Red Guards halt the advance of the Central Powers.

The peace talks at Brest-Litovsk, a charred Polish fortress-town serving as the headquarters of the German Army on the Eastern Front (Ober Ost), began in the last days of November 1917 and continued intermittently over the following two months.[38] The difficulties amid the negotiations stemmed from the vastly different goal of the two sides. The delegations of the Central Powers, which were dominated by the German military elite, thought of their objectives in traditional terms. They wanted to permanently disable Russia as a threat to their security while simultaneously exploiting the resources in the occupied territories to sustain the German war effort in the West. The Bolsheviks, on the other hand, aimed to turn the Russian socialist revolution into a worldwide conflagration. They were confident that they could successfully exploit their debut on the international stage to persuade the proletariat classes in other countries, including the Central Powers, to over-throw their monarchs and bourgeoisie politicians.[39] Outside of the conference, the Bolsheviks were already working towards this goal by printing inflammatory pamphlets in German, Magyar and other languages and then distributing them to enemy soldiers at the front and in Russia's POW camps.[40] Ultimately, their strategy was not to seek the lightest terms possible from a subdued position, but rather to protract the negotiations long enough for the anticipated revolution to erupt in the enemy countries and thus render the conference irrelevant.

Throughout the deliberations, both sides adopted lofty principles in their oratory while implementing less idealistic policies in practice. The Bolsheviks, who declared themselves in favor of the principle of national self-determination, supported anti-nationalist forces in Ukraine and Finland.[41] Likewise, the delegations of the Central Powers accepted the Soviet call for self-determination but only as they saw fit. In other words, the formal declarations of the various land councils set up by Ober Ost in the occupied territories would serve as the justification for amputating these lands from Russia and binding them to Germany even though these councils were by no means representative of the native populations. Significantly, this undemocratic interpretation of self-determination spared the central empires, particularly Austria-Hungary, from having to make any concessions to their minorities.[42] The Bolsheviks were bewildered when they first learned of the full extent of German demands for territorial cessations and indemnities but they were unwilling to break off the peace talks since they desperately needed peace to remain in power.[43] Lenin resorted to a delaying tactic by sending the garrulous Trotsky to lead the Soviet delegation and prevent the conference from making any actual progress.[44] His antics succeeded in stalling the negotiations for four weeks, an excruciating period for the Austro-Hungarian Minister of Foreign Affairs, Count Ottokar Czernin, who was under considerable pressure from his emperor and events at home to conclude peace as quickly as possible.[45]

Czernin's sense of urgency to make peace with the Bolsheviks was aggravated by an outbreak of serious strikes across Austria-Hungary following the announcement of another reduction in the flour ration on 14 January.[46] Though the strikes were relatively mild in Bohemia, elsewhere in the empire worker soviets were formed and the threat of a Bolshevik-style uprising loomed.[47] These ominous developments put Czernin on the receiving end of a steady stream of messages from Austrian authorities complaining of dire food shortages and warning him that disaster was imminent unless peace was made.[48] From Brest-Litovsk, the foreign minister pleaded for the Emperor to take command of the situation since if the Bolsheviks perceived that the empire was on the brink of revolution, "they will not make peace at all."[49] To that, Karl only replied weakly that "the whole fate of the Monarchy and of the dynasty depends on peace being concluded at Brest-Litovsk as soon as possible."[50] By emphasizing the gravity of the situation, Karl hoped his foreign minister would muster the courage to convince their domineering German ally to make more reasonable demands that would be immediately accepted by the Bolsheviks. Czernin, however, had no leverage from which he could moderate German demands. He could not seriously threaten to conclude his own peace with the Bolsheviks since Austria needed to import German grain to help alleviate the crisis caused by food shortages. General Max Hoffmann, the chief of staff of Ober Ost, pitied the Austro-Hungarian Foreign Minister "whose nerves become worse every day."[51] The German command, by shrugging off Czernin's pleas for moderation, demonstrated to the world once and for all that the central empires were not equal partners in their alliance.[52] This revelation played into the propaganda generated by Czech and other émigrés which claimed that the empire had become a puppet of the Reich.

The news of the disorders in Austria-Hungary sparked much excitement among Soviet leaders; however, as the strike movement subsided in late January, the Bolsheviks had to face the reality that Central Europe might not be ripe for revolution after all. Moreover, the Central Powers were growing weary of Trotsky's theatrical delaying tactics, and pressed by the German commanders, they resolved to force a decision from the Bolsheviks when the conference resumed at the beginning of February.[53] By then, their aim to establish hegemony over the western borderlands of Russia was greatly aided by the delegation of the Ukrainian Rada, which signed the "bread peace" (*Brotfrieden*) with the Central Powers on 9 February. Under the terms of this treaty, Austria-Hungary and Germany agreed to protect the Ukrainian state in exchange for the delivery of one-million tons of grain.[54] In the meantime, the Bolsheviks were bickering amongst themselves over whether to accept the harsh peace or continue hostilities in the form of a "revolutionary war." The two sides eventually agreed to the compromise proposed by Trotsky of "no war, no peace," which he announced to the conference on 10 February. "In refusing to sign an annexationist peace," he declared, "Russia announces that the state of war with Germany, Austria-Hungary, Bulgaria and Turkey is at an end."[55] Having rendered the Central Power delegations speechless, he and the Bolshevik delegation walked out and returned to Russia that evening convinced that the Germans, despite their threats, would not launch a new offensive into Soviet territory.[56]

For a few days, it seemed that he was right. Then on 18 February the Austro-Hungarian and German formations in the east initiated Operation Faustschlag (Thunderbolt) across the entire front. Their forces advanced quickly and were pleasantly surprised by how easily they could dash along the roads and railways with minimal investments of troops. "The Russian Army is more rotten than I had supposed," wrote General Hoffmann two days after the offensive began. "There is no fight left in them."[57]

With the onset of the enemy offensive, the Bolshevik military commissars in Kiev immediately appealed to the Czecho-Slovak National Council for military assistance against the common enemy. Although the Czecho-Slovak leaders were by this time intent on leaving Ukraine, a delegation consisting of the Legion's Chief of Staff, General Mikhail Diterikhs, and National Council secretaries Prokop Maxa and Jiří Klecanda met with the Bolshevik command in Kiev and discussed the proposed alliance. The Bolsheviks, despite their best efforts, failed to convince the Czecho-Slovaks that their ragtag militias would be a reliable ally in the field against experienced and well-equipped enemy troops. On 21 February the National Council officially sanctioned the eastward retreat of the legionaries that was by then already underway.[58]

The First Czecho-Slovak Division, as the most westerly unit of the Legion, was the most exposed to the German attack. Its troops were based in the vicinity of Zhitomir, to the west of Kiev, and thus lay directly in the path of an enemy force headed for the Ukrainian capital. The 4th Regiment, which was the closest to the frontline, had begun marching east on 20 February and acted as the rearguard of the division.

The objective of the First Division was to cross the Dnieper River at Kiev, link up with the Second Czecho-Slovak Division already east of the city, acquire rolling stock and then begin the long journey by train to Vladivostok. While the most dangerous menace to the legionaries during this time was the armies of the Central Powers approaching from the west, they also faced a smaller threat from scattered Ukrainian detachments that harassed their line of retreat. On 1 March, as the last formations from First Division were passing through Kiev with the Germans on their heels, a company from the 3rd Regiment was forcibly disarmed by a Ukrainian militia. The Czecho-Slovaks, eager to simply leave the area without engaging in unnecessary hostilities with the Ukrainians, requested that they observe the earlier settlement of neutrality between the National Council and the Rada that was supposed to guarantee the legionaries an unmolested withdrawal if the latter allied with the Central Powers. Nothing became of these talks since the Ukrainian insurgents, emboldened by the approach of their German ally, refused to acknowledge the agreement and demanded the Legion's complete disarmament.

While the legionaries attempted to neutralize the Ukrainian threat by last-minute diplomacy, fighting broke out between the troops from the Czecho-Slovak 2nd Regiment and the German vanguard in Nikolska Slobodka, a suburb of Kiev. The fighting centered on a suspension bridge used by the First Division to cross the Dnieper. By the time the Germans reached the suburb, most of the legionaries were safely on the east bank but the 2nd Regiment retained possession of the crucial bridge to slow the enemy advance. After a sudden attack, the Germans managed to seize control of the western end of the bridge but were unable to dislodge the defenders from the other side. A company of Germans tried to break the ensuing stalemate in the battle by crossing the river south the bridge and attacking the Czecho-Slovaks in their rear, but even this ambush was unsuccessful. The legionaries held their position until nightfall, when they quietly evacuated the city and joined the main body of the First Division east of Kiev.

· The Second Czecho-Slovak Division, which had been encamped in the area around Poltava, was not immediately threatened by the Central Power's offensive. While their cadres in the First Division withdrew east and fought off German spearheads, the troops from the Second Division needed to secure ample provisions and rolling stock so the entire corps could begin its retreat across Russia.[59] They were also supposed to keep open a rail route for the both divisions to use in their withdrawal from Ukraine, and this became an issue when an enemy thrust from the direction of Minsk threatened to sever a key railway. On 5 March the 6th Regiment moved into position to defend the critical railway junction of Bakhmach. The two divisions of the Legion, after boarding trains south of Bakhmach, needed to pass through the junction to escape on the railway line that headed northeast towards Kursk. German units, however, were approaching the junction from two directions, the southwest and northwest. The operation was further complicated by desultory fighting between Ukrainian nationalists and Bolshevik Red Guards in the vicinity. When a patrol from the 6th Regiment reached Bakhmach station, they found the Bolsheviks there chasing away a small train of Ukrainian insurgents. The legionaries immediately made contact with the Red garrison at the station, alerted them of the German advance and persuaded them to agree to the Czecho-Slovak occupation of the junction.[60] The result was that the Battle of Bakhmach would become one of the few instances of military cooperation between the Czecho-Slovak Legion and the Bolsheviks.

Three days after the 6th Regiment arrived in Bakhmach, the first shots were exchanged near Mena station, about 35 miles northwest of the junction. Although the legionaries were dug in and the Germans were inferior in number, the latter's artillery succeeded in pushing the defenders back about seven miles.[61] On the same day, another attack by the German vanguard along the southwestern line was also repulsed by the legionaries. These skirmishes continued until 10 March, when the attackers were replenished with reinforcements. On that day, the Germans attacked in force along both lines. When recalling that date many years later, Gustav Bečvar, who fought with the 6th Regiment on the southwestern line, remembered how their positions were first approached by a suspicious train emerging from the early morning mist. Consisting of a locomotive and two carriages, the train had "lost a semblance of its normal appearance" as Russians and Ukrainians, many of them deserters and refugees, formed a cocoon of human bodies as they clung to the outsides of the railcars. When the Czecho-Slovaks fired a warning shot from a field gun, the layer of flesh peeled away as the passengers jumped from the coaches and took flight, revealing the flared coal-scuttle helmets of German troops inside the railcars. The legionaries took advantage of the enemy's disarray and charged the train, firing into the railcars and forcing the locomotive into reverse.[62]

Although they easily thwarted this German ruse, Bečvar and his fellow legionaries had little time to celebrate. Their scouts reported that the enemy was receiving significant reinforcements, rendering their position untenable. They decided to retire, but not without tearing up the tracks and leaving a small detachment behind to harass German attempts to repair the line. This tactic was repeated several times until the enemy stood only four miles from Bakhmach. Unable to retreat further without jeopardizing their hold on the town, the legionnaires were reinforced at that crucial moment with two additional companies and staged a successful counterattack. The Germans initially fell back and then made their own counterattack; this seesaw engagement across muddy fields next to the railway continued throughout the afternoon until passing troops from the First Division halted their train and assisted their beleaguered comrades from the 6th Regiment. By evening, the line southwest of Bakhmach was secure and Czecho-Slovak trains were passing safely through the junction.[63]

To the northwest of Bakhmach, the Czecho-Slovaks had an easier time of fending off their attackers. The line there was manned by detachments from the 6th and 7th Regiments under the command of the indomitable Captain Eduard Kadlec. A born soldier, Kadlec enlisted with the Belgian Army to fight in the Congo before the war, then served in the Austro-Hungarian Army until taken prisoner by the Russians and finally joined the Czecho-Slovak army in Russia from a POW camp in Turkistan. As one of the Legion's most experienced officers, he possessed a reputation as a harsh disciplinarian but was also recognized as an able field commander, which he proved at Bakhmach.[64] On the morning of 10 March, with the support of only a single field gun, he launched a spoiling attack against the concentrating enemy forces with only five companies. Later that day, his attack was assisted by Red Guards, whose main contribution was in the form of two additional artillery pieces. By evening, Kadlec's troops withdrew to their original positions, some twenty miles outside of Bakhmach. In the meantime, staff officers from First Division had dispatched a pair of emissaries to negotiate a three-day armistice with the German command to allow the Czecho-Slovaks pass through Bakhmach peacefully and unmolested. These negotiations, however, were only partly successful. The Germans, perhaps discouraged by Kadlec's fierce drive on the northwestern line earlier that day, agreed to a ceasefire along that sector but in the meantime they refused to halt their attacks on the line from Kiev.[65]

For the next three days, fighting raged between the Germans and Czecho-Slovaks southwest of Bakhmach. There were moments when the Germans fought their way dangerously close to the railway but the 6th Regiment, at various times assisted by other Czecho-Slovak units and Red Guards, managed to hold the attackers at bay. The legionaries faced their final difficulty at Bakhmach as the rearguard prepared to evacuate the station and the town. The

Red Guards, having finally realized that the Czecho-Slovaks did not intend to defend the junction indefinitely against the Germans, were indignant to learn that the legionaries were abandoning them. The Czecho-Slovaks might have been more sympathetic to their makeshift ally if the Red Guards had earned their respect on the battlefield, but the Bolsheviks militias had a tendency to run rather than hold their ground under enemy fire.[66] The legionaries had borne the brunt of the fighting and were eager leave since the armistice on the northwestern sector was due to expire; it was only a matter of time until the Germans amassed enough reinforcements to overwhelm the area. Still, the Red Guards could not comprehend why the legionaries insisted on traveling thousands of miles by rail and ship to fight the Germans in France when German divisions were pouring into Ukraine. The argument of the Czecho-Slovaks that the war, and thus the independence of their homeland, was being decided on the Western Front was of no consolation to the Bolsheviks.

The Red Guards' continued protests were of no use. The legionaries had lost nearly 600 men in the five days of fighting around Bakhmach, and this steep casualty list reiterated the assessment already made by Czecho-Slovak leaders that their small army could only resist the Central Powers in an auxiliary role.[67] They could fulfill such a role in France, but in the East there was no military force that could even remotely match the Germans in strength and resources. Even though they had transferred dozens of divisions to fronts in the West, the Germans and their Austro-Hungarian ally would maintain a formidable presence of a million troops in the East long after the signing of the Brest-Litovsk Treaty.[68] Therefore, on the evening of 13 March, under the cover of darkness, the last Czecho-Slovak trains departed from Bakhmach. The next day, the Germans moved in and finally took possession of the junction.[69]

While the legionaries were fighting to save their army from annihilation at Bakhmach, the leaders of the Czecho-Slovak National Council in Russia were making final arrangements with French and Bolshevik representatives for the Legion's journey to Vladivostok and eventually France. Masaryk had begun this process at the end of February when he traveled to Moscow to meet with French officials there.[70] Convinced that the Czecho-Slovaks' political and military activity in Russia was drawing to a close, and with Beneš and Štefánik making steady progress for the formation of legions in France and Italy, he decided that it was imperative for him to further the Czecho-Slovak cause in America. He had perceived that the United States and its president would have a momentous influence on the postwar world which he could not risk ignoring if he was to achieve his goal of an independent Czecho-Slovak state. On 7 March he boarded a train headed east out of Moscow and traveled to Vladivostok via the Trans-Siberian Railway, the very same span of railroad that he expected his troops would pass over in a few short weeks.

Prior to his departure, Masaryk appointed two young secretaries from the Russian branch of the National Council to supervise the Legion's trek across Siberia. Jiří Klecanda, a Czech-Russian who before the war was employed as a historian in a St. Petersburg academy, was charged to oversee political matters and met with Soviet leaders in Moscow. Meanwhile, Prokop Maxa was to be responsible for military affairs and headed negotiations with local soviet leaders in southern Russia as the Czecho-Slovak trains steamed towards the Russian-Ukrainian border.[71] These meetings were held just days after the Bolshevik leaders had emerged from their most trying crisis since their seizure of power.

The Central Powers' offensive demonstrated that Trotsky's solution of "no war, no peace" really meant war. The attack exposed the military impotency of Soviet Russia, and the Bolsheviks soon admitted their utter defeat by wiring their readiness to accept the earlier peace terms. On 23 February, however, the Germans replied with new and harsher demands. Once again, the Bolshevik Party's central committee was plunged into a series of agonizing debates over the question to conclude peace; the disputes were so heated at times that the divided leaders threatened to resign from the party. In the meantime, the invaders were approaching a distance of only 150 miles from Petrograd and German planes emphasized their side's seeming invincibility by dropping bombs over the Russian capital.[72] Amid these reminders of the seriousness of their predicament, Lenin was finally able to persuade his party leaders to accept the German conditions for peace. On 3 March a Soviet delegation arrived in Brest-Litovsk and affixed their signatures to the treaty laid in front of them; in doing so they surrendered a vast expanse of Russia's prewar borderlands to German hegemony.[73]

Even after submitting to the German peace terms, the Bolsheviks continued to fear the martial strength of their western neighbor whose outposts were uncomfortably close to Petrograd. Under these circumstances, Lenin decided it was prudent to transfer the seat of his government further into the Russian interior to a safe distance from the front. The city he chose for his new capital was Moscow, where he set up his office in the Kremlin.[74]

On 15 March, just four days after Lenin transformed the fortress of Russia's early tsars into the new hub of the Soviet government, Klecanda met with a deputation of Bolshevik leaders to iron out the final arrangements of the Czecho-Slovaks' evacuation. The timing of the meeting was not particularly favorable for the Bolsheviks; the government's move to Moscow was not a smooth transition and the departments faced difficulties not only in finding each other but also in locating the staff and archives that arrived on different trains.[75] In this jungle of confusion, it is doubtful that the Soviet leaders examined the legionaries' exit with the thoroughness that the matter might have otherwise warranted. In his meeting, Klecanda conferred with three Soviet representatives, among them Stalin, all of whom appeared supportive of his evacuation plan. On the following day, Lenin was consulted about the Legion's evacuation by telephone and he too agreed that the Czecho-Slovaks should leave as soon as possible.

The Soviet leader had good reason to want the Czecho-Slovaks out of Russia: by the terms of the Brest-Litovsk Treaty, all units from the tsarist army were to be demobilized and prisoner exchanges were to begin as soon as possible. Both clauses affected the Czecho-Slovak Legion, the first since it traced its origins to the Družina, the second because by 1918 the vast majority of the legionaries were technically Austro-Hungarian POWs.[76] Lenin knew he had no realistic means of compelling the Legion to disarm against its will—the only pro–Soviet forces remotely capable of taking on the Czecho-Slovaks, such as the 18,000-strong Latvian Rifle Division,[77] were badly needed to provide security in the capital and elsewhere.[78] He was also aware that the Czecho-Slovak Legion had been recognized as an Allied army by France, and he had no desire to antagonize the Allies at this time. Ever fearful that Germany might renew its attack on helpless Soviet Russia, he wanted to keep open the possibility of Allied aid and cooperation in a war against the Central Powers.[79] Lenin therefore felt he had little choice other than to acquiesce in the passage of an armed Czecho-Slovak Legion through Soviet territory so that they could reengage the Germans on the Western Front— even though the presence of a force hostile to Germany within Soviet Russia was strictly forbidden by the Brest-Litovsk Treaty. It is no wonder the Bolshevik leader thought that the sooner the Legion was out of Russia, the better.

Klecanda's negotiations with the Soviet government in Moscow were paralleled by those of Maxa at the headquarters of the Bolshevik military commander, Vladimir Antonov-Ovseyenko, in Kursk. As the trains bearing armed Czecho-Slovaks troops and their cache of weaponry approached the Ukrainian-Russian border, the local soviet commissars grew nervous. To assuage their fears, Maxa ordered the legionaries to turn over most of their heavy weapons, which included artillery and armored cars, to the Bolsheviks at Kursk. This "token of friendship," as Antonov-Ovseyenko phrased it, compelled him to order the soviets along the route to allow the Czecho-Slovaks to proceed to Penza, a railway junction about 400 miles southeast of Moscow.[80] Although Maxa's bargain was successful in accomplishing the legionaries' immediate goal of evacuation from Ukraine, his gesture of partial disarmament set a dangerous precedent that would complicate the rest of their journey through Russia.

The concept of hauling approximately seventy trains filled with Czecho-Slovak troops across the great expanse of Siberia to embark on transports that would then take them halfway across the globe to France was certainly an ambitious, but not necessarily impossible, project. Other military units had recently departed from Russia by the same route. Shortly after the October Revolution, a Belgian armored car division that was serving on the Eastern Front extricated itself from the Russian quagmire by taking the Trans-Siberian Railway to Vladivostok, where it boarded ships to Europe.[81] In early 1918, a brigade composed mostly of Serbian soldiers, with a handful of Croats and Slovenes, made the same overland journey to Harbin, from where it then traveled southward on the South Manchurian Railway to the Japanese-controlled port of Darien. From there the brigade was shipped to Salonika where they arrived in May 1918—well in time for the decisive battles that would later be fought on that front.[82]

The successful exits of the Belgian and South Slav troops through Siberia seemed to bode well for the Czecho-Slovak operation. There was, however, one stark difference between those previous evacuations and that of the Czecho-Slovaks: while hardly anyone batted an eye at the withdrawal of the Belgian and South Slav units, the Czecho-Slovaks attracted much more attention not only because they were a larger formation, but also due to their reputed fighting quality. Their military prowess was elevated even more after news spread of the Battle of Bakhmach. Although the Czecho-Slovaks incurred heavy casualties in that operation, the legionaries claimed to have killed at least three Germans for every one of their own dead. It is possible that German losses were inflated by the Czecho-Slovaks, but it was undeniable that the legionaries had fought admirably.[83] Their performance shone even more brilliantly against the ignominious fate of the Polish Army in Russia. When the Central Powers initiated their offensive, the First Polish Corps found itself wedged between two hostile forces. Its commander, General Dowbor-Muśnicki, decided he would rather submit to the Germans rather than the heathen Bolsheviks. His staff even went a step further by accepting German requests to defend railways and ammunition dumps from local partisans. This virtual defection of the Polish troops, when it became known in the West, was a major embarrassment for the Polish National Committee. Eventually, the First Polish Corps, along with the other two smaller corps formed from Poles serving the old Russian Army, were disarmed by the Central Powers.[84]

Many statesmen and military minds in Western Europe still believed that the only way the Allies could defeat Germany was by maintaining a threat on her eastern frontier. In light of the shaky peace obtained by the Bolsheviks, the armistice in Romania, the crushing of the anti–Bolshevik and Cossack armies in Southern Russia, the collaboration of the Ukrainians with the enemy and the neutralization of the Polish corps, the Czecho-Slovaks were the only force remaining in Russia that was willing to fight the Central Powers. Besides the Allies, the Czecho-Slovak presence in Russia inspired schemes among the warring Russian factions as well. The Soviet government and underground White organizations did not forget the fact that the Legion—as the largest cohesive military formation in Russia east of the German frontlines—could give either side that enlisted it as an ally an immediate advantage in the civil war.[85] As a result, Masaryk's rather small army became an object of intense Allied intrigue and Bolshevik subversion, and both of these factors are behind why the vast majority of the Czecho-Slovak legionaries in Russia would fail to reach the Western Front.

9

The Russian Muddle

As the Czecho-Slovaks set out amid their epic journey in March 1918, the conditions inside Soviet Russia had the potential to not only hamper their operation, but make it hazardous as well. When the autocracy went extinct in Russia, so did the strong if obsolete machinery of centralization. By the time of the revolution's first anniversary, much of the western borderland had been lost to Russia's new masters either through enemy occupation or the independence movements of their peoples. In the lands the Bolsheviks did claim to be under their control, their authority was fragile at best. Most of the larger cities from Petrograd to the Pacific Ocean were controlled by Bolshevik-dominated soviets, but in many areas the countryside was in a state of anarchy or outright revolt. The peasants' foremost goal in the revolution was to seize the private lands of their neighbors, regardless of whether the owners were nobles or simply well-to-do peasants disparagingly known as *kulaks*. After seizing power, the Bolsheviks maneuvered to distract the peasants, among whom they had only a weak following, by encouraging them to expropriate the lands they coveted. The ruse worked: the peasants were so preoccupied with staking their claims on their neighbors' fields that they hardly seemed bothered by the Red Guards' dispersal of their elected representatives to the Constituent Assembly when that body met for the first and last time in Petrograd on 19 January 1918.[1]

The Russian Civil War—in reality a conglomeration of smaller conflicts fought in disparate theaters—that had begun with the October Revolution continued in one form or another throughout nearly every corner of the country. At the most basic level was the class warfare incited by the Bolsheviks that pitted worker against bourgeoisie in the city and peasant against landowner in the countryside. In ethnically-heterogeneous regions, the fighting was sometimes three-sided or more with Russian peasant immigrants, Cossack farmers and natives all slashing at each other's throats.[2] Then there was the armed political and social struggle between the Red troops and the White armies. By spring 1918, however, the latter were confined mostly to a few distant frontiers and appeared on the verge of total annihilation. In some areas, the violence lacked any ideological foundation and was motivated by simple banditry. This was the case in the Russian Far East, where gangs of Manchurian outlaws, or *hunghutze*, frequently held-up train passengers on the Trans-Siberian Railway.[3]

Besides the general instability in the country, the legionaries faced another obstacle in the decrepit condition of Russian railways. Even before the war, the Russian railroads—especially the Trans-Siberian Railway—suffered from inputs of shoddy materials, including rails of poor durability, untreated ties and a lack of ballast that made them far less efficient than their American or European counterparts.[4] Passenger trains on the Trans-Siberian line, for example, averaged a speed of only 25 miles per hour and freight trains were even slower.[5]

The heavy demand placed on the railways during the war only exacerbated the existing problems. Insufficient maintenance and scarcity of replacement parts by 1918 caused many locomotives and railcars, though only in need of a light repair, to sit idle. During the katabasis of the Czecho-Slovak Legion, the corps' resourceful mechanics quickly learned to cannibalize disabled rolling stock for replacement wheels, gears and other parts to keep their trains moving.[6]

The deplorable conditions of Russia's railways was not overlooked by her allies, and after the U.S. entered the war, President Wilson dispatched a team of experts under John F. Stevens, a highly-esteemed American railway engineer, to look for ways to improve the efficiency of the Trans-Siberian Railway. The specific goal of his advisory commission was to increase the railway's capacity by as much as three times. After observing the railway's symptoms firsthand during the summer of 1917, Stevens recommended the deployment of 300 American engineers to act as troubleshooters. The fall of the Provisional Government in November disrupted these plans, and the taskforce of engineers, dubbed the Russian Railway Service Corps, had to wait in Japan to find out whether the new Soviet government would accept their services.[7]

The relations between the new Soviet government and the Allies were complicated at this time. In their first few months in power, the Bolsheviks had left little doubt that they considered the Western powers an ideological enemy on par with the central empires. Among the more provocative actions taken by the Soviet regime were their appeals to stir up social revolution in other nations, the publication of the secret treaties to expose the imperialist aims of the Entente and their refusal to honor Russia's substantial debts to domestic and foreign lenders. In Allied eyes, however, the most despicable act committed by Russia's new masters was their decision to take the country out of the war.[8] For them, the threat which the Bolsheviks posed to the existing order and traditional decency was momentarily inconsequential; their attitude towards the Soviet government hinged on whether it would continue the war, in which case they were ready to support it, or if it would conclude peace with the Central Powers and thus earn their enmity.[9] Even after the Soviet delegation signed the Brest-Litovsk Treaty, the Allies continued to hold out hope—one that was encouraged by the Bolsheviks themselves—that the Soviet government would soon find itself at war again with Germany.[10]

Communication between the Western governments and the Soviet Republic was fickle from the start. Although the Allies withheld official recognition to the Bolshevik usurpers, most of their ambassadors to the defunct Provisional Government stayed in Russia after November 1917. This was partly due to diplomats' assessment that the Bolsheviks were merely a passing aberration that would soon be replaced by a stronger, more centric party.[11] The Allies' chanceries also feared that a complete severance of communications with the Bolsheviks would simply drive them into the arms of Germany. The void between the ambassadors and Soviet leaders expanded when the latter relocated their government to Moscow. Rather than follow the regime to the ancient capital, where lawless gangs still roamed and widespread damage remained from the street fighting in November, the ambassadors instead set up their offices in the quieter northern town of Vologda.[12] In the meantime, the job of communicating directly with the Soviet leaders was left to three unofficial agents in Moscow: Bruce Lockhart, a Scotsman who served as the British Vice-Consul there; Raymond Robins, the chief of the American Red Cross Mission to Russia; and Jacques Sadoul, a captain with strong socialist sympathies on the French Military Mission. For the most part, these men were impressionable amateurs whose views were rather easily manipulated by top Soviet leaders.[13]

The Bolsheviks' wily revolutionary instincts made them reluctant to accept any support from the "bourgeoisie governments" of the Allies. Nonetheless, after the Central Powers began their attack in late February 1918, both the party and Sovnarkom voted to accept Allied aid on the grounds that German militarism was a more immediate threat to their regime than Western capitalism.[14] Trotsky, using Sadoul and Robins as intermediaries, appealed to the French and British governments to help Soviet Russia halt the German onslaught. The French proved that they were eager to help; within days officers from the French Military Mission in Russia were instructing Bolshevik military leaders on how to build a military force that could stand up to the German Army.[15]

The cooperation between the Allies and the Bolsheviks, though limited, continued even after the latter signed the Treaty of Brest-Litovsk. On 6 March, three days after the treaty was signed, a detachment of 170 British marines landed in Murmansk upon the Bolsheviks' invitation. Trotsky, who was under the impression that the Germans were going to continue hostilities against Soviet Russia, sought this assistance to protect the ice-free port and its stores of war materiel from possible Finno-German incursions.[16] The British were soon aided by the 500 Czecho-Slovak troops who had left Zhitomir the previous November, had been marooned in North Russia throughout the winter and were now attempting to exit the country through Murmansk. On 10 March the legionaries' trains encountered the British at Kola, south of the port, where they agreed to take up positions alongside the marines and the local Red militia while waiting for a transport to take them to France.[17]

From a military perspective, the Bolsheviks needed all the help they could get if they were to find themselves at war again with the Central Powers. They already had their hands full with their much less formidable enemies in the civil wars: anarchists, nationalists in the borderlands, the Cossack hosts along Russia's southern frontier and a few scattered bands of White soldiers. Despite their predicament, the Bolsheviks at this time were not easily swayed from their pure revolutionary ideals regardless of how impractical these may have appeared. For example, while the French officers and ex-tsarist generals mentoring them urged them to remodel a new force on the skeletal fragments of the old Russian Army, the Bolsheviks went ahead with their plans to create an entirely new "revolutionary" army of volunteer workers and peasants. This project to establish a Red Army was announced in early 1918 but quickly turned into an abject failure as it attracted neither the quantity nor quality of recruits needed. Even so, the first Soviet Commissar of War, Nikolay Krylenko, preferred to resign rather than betray revolutionary dogma by building an army of conscripts. His replacement was the more pragmatic Trotsky, who had just quit the Commissariat of Foreign Affairs.[18]

Trotsky's task of organizing and building the Red Army was one of the most formidable challenges the thirty-eight-year-old revolutionary icon had yet faced. The son of a relatively prosperous Jewish farmer from southern Ukraine, Trotsky had earned his revolutionary credentials in the upheaval of 1905, when he was one of the leading personalities on the short-lived Petrograd Soviet.[19] After the failure of that revolution, Trotsky had been sentenced to exile on the Siberian tundra, from where he escaped and lived abroad for the following decade. During his period of foreign exile he traveled to almost every corner of Europe and even made a brief sojourn to the United States, from where he departed for Russia following the collapse of the tsarist regime. The cosmopolitan outlook he acquired during his exile made him among the most qualified Bolsheviks to lead the Commissariat of Foreign Affairs, but he had no military training or relevant experience to recommend him for the post of

Commissar of War.[20] What he did possess was a brilliant mind, a gift for persuasion and a fanatical devotion to the international proletarian revolution.

When Trotsky began his stint as Commissar of War, the most cohesive force that the Bolsheviks had at their disposal was the Latvian Rifle Division of about 18,000 bayonets.[21] Besides the renowned Latvian troops, the Bolsheviks could also call upon the worker militias known as Red Guards, but these numbered perhaps 30,000 men total and were of questionable military value since many lacked military training and discipline.[22] Therefore, Trotsky had to build the Red Army mostly from scratch, and to accomplish this goal as quickly as possible, he was willing to consider unconventional means. His exploration of Allied offers of military aid was one example of this strategy. Another was his decision to employ ex-tsarist officers to enforce discipline and command Red troops in the field. This scheme was particularly distasteful to Bolshevik stalwarts since the party's propaganda among the rank and file had long denounced the officer corps as an enemy of the people. Against their outrage, Trotsky prevailed, and to ensure the loyalty of the officers, he made them politically subordinate to pistol-wielding commissars.[23] Another method through which Trotsky sought to grow the Red Army was more in tune with Marxist principles. Since he and his comrades expected the revolutionary gale in Russia to blow through Europe and knock down those governments at any moment, he saw no reason why the Red Army's ranks should be limited to Russians or the peoples of the former tsarist empire. Subsequently, the Bolsheviks launched campaigns to enlist German and Austro-Hungarian POWs in Russia into the Red Army. Since these prisoner-recruits already had basic military training and some measure of combat experience, the battalions which they formed, known as Internationalists, could theoretically be fielded faster and more effectively than units composed of untrained Russians.[24]

The formation of Internationalist battalions was encouraged by various Marxist émigrés and POWs cooperating with the Bolsheviks. Many of these foreigners also established autonomous Communist parties for their ethnicity on Russian soil, including one for the Czecho-Slovaks.[25] A radical left had first revealed itself among the Czecho-Slovaks in Kiev amid the revolutionary upheaval in early 1917. Before the summer, their numbers had grown to about 1,000 and their extremism was kindled by their contact with Russian Bolsheviks.[26] At first they had worked within the framework of Masaryk's Russian branch of the Czecho-Slovak National Council, but after Lenin's followers seized power in November, the Czecho-Slovak Bolsheviks were emboldened enough to pursue their own goals. They soon published their own newspaper, repudiated their earlier acceptance of Masaryk's leadership and called upon Czecho-Slovak workers and soldiers in Russia to openly support the Soviet regime.[27] Their activities complicated the work of Masaryk and his colleagues. While the professor and his supporters tried to undermine the appeal of the Czecho-Slovak Bolsheviks by discrediting them as being under the influence of German agents, they were careful to not denounce the upstarts too strongly in order to avoid aggravating the Soviet government.[28]

The National Council's desire to appease the Bolsheviks led them to permit a delegation of legionaries to attend a socialist conference in Kiev organized by the Czecho-Slovak Bolsheviks in late November 1917. The objective of the conference was to unite all Czech and Slovak socialists in Russia under a Bolshevik program. This meant emphasizing a violent social revolution over the national cause, and when the soldier delegates learned this, they immediately walked out of the assembly. Rather than bringing the Czecho-Slovak socialists in Russia closer together, the conference had instead driven them apart.[29]

The legionary delegation demonstrated that even though they may be proletarians and socialists, they were above all Czecho-Slovak patriots. Their repudiation of the conference left the Czecho-Slovak Bolsheviks without the soldiers they needed to provide military aid to Lenin's dictatorship. Moreover, the Ukrainian Rada had prohibited the Czecho-Slovak Bolsheviks from establishing an armed force of their own, but this restriction was lifted after the successful Soviet invasion of Ukraine in late January 1918.[30] After the regime-change in Kiev, the Czecho-Slovak Bolsheviks called on all proletarians of their ethnic groups to join a Czecho-Slovak Red Army to fight on behalf of the workers' revolution. Thus by mid–February there were technically three separate Czecho-Slovak "armies" in former Russian territory: the Czecho-Slovak Red Army, Král's Czecho-Slovaks serving alongside the Volunteer Army, and Masaryk's Legion, by far the largest of these formations.

The new Czecho-Slovak Red Army was inaugurated with a strength of less than 500 men. At least some of these troops, as with Král's regiment in the Don, were misled POWs who believed that they were serving Masaryk's cause.[31] While the Czecho-Slovak Bolsheviks had some luck in recruiting from nearby camps, the so-called "proletarian element" in the Czecho-Slovak Legion remained an attractive target for them.[32] Once again Masaryk, in order to appease the Czecho-Slovak Bolsheviks and more importantly their Russian masters, permitted Bolshevik agitators to ply their trade amongst his troops. This decision was unpopular with the Legion's Russian officers and its French attachés, but as the professor later wrote, the troop's firsthand exposure to Bolshevism opened their eyes "more thoroughly than I could have done by any prohibition of Bolshevist propaganda."[33] By the end of February, only 220 legionaries had defected to the Czecho-Slovak Red Army. Many probably later regretted this decision after they were sacrificed alongside Red Guards and Bolshevized sailors in a hopeless bid to stem the German-led invasion of Ukraine.[34]

After its recruiting campaign among the legionaries was cut short by the Central Powers' offensive, the staff of the Czecho-Slovak Red Army transferred its headquarters to Penza. It was no accident that they relocated to the same railway town which the trains of the Czecho-Slovak Legion were to pass through on their route to Siberia.[35]

Despite the failures of their earlier attempts at subversion, the Czecho-Slovak Communists, as the radical socialists rebranded themselves, refused to give up their courtship of the socialists and proletarians in the Czecho-Slovak Legion in Russia. They assessed—perhaps optimistically—that this element comprised almost seventy percent of the two divisions. From this, they predicted that they could convince 15,000 legionaries, or almost forty percent of the army corps, to desert to the Czecho-Slovak Red Army—but only if the "reactionary influence" of the Legion's officers was neutralized. This forecast soon reached the ears of Trotsky, who was probably delighted by the prospect of injecting his embryonic Red Army with the military experience and prowess of thousands of Czecho-Slovak soldiers.[36]

The Commissar of War was absent from Moscow when Klecanda met with Bolshevik leaders and arranged for the First Czecho-Slovak Army Corps to cross Siberia in order to reach Vladivostok. Trotsky finally arrived in the new Soviet capital on 17 March, one day after Klecanda wrapped up these negotiations. Upon learning of these talks, he was not pleased. On 20 March he issued the first of what would become many telegrams to soviets along the Legion's route to halt the Czecho-Slovak trains. After stopping the trains, the local Red militias were to disarm the legionaries—a bold instruction given that the Czecho-Slovaks, about 40,000 strong and fairly concentrated south and west of Penza, could have easily overwhelmed any force of Red Guards that the local soviets might have been able to scratch together. The soviets realized this too, and although the local commissars did command the railway workers to stop the legionaries' trains, they refused to risk a confrontation with the Czecho-Slovaks by attempting to disarm them.[37]

The legionaries were stopped just as their lead trains were approaching the city of Penza. Their sudden stoppage caused much confusion and the local commissars were unable to offer any explanation. The reason began to dawn on the Czecho-Slovak leaders on 22 March, after Bohumil Čermak, a secretary of the National Council in Moscow, was handed a request from Trotsky for the Czecho-Slovak corps to stay in Russia and support the Red Army. Although the French Military Mission and even the Allied generalissimo, Marshal Ferdinand Foch, looked favorably on the idea of keeping the Legion in Russia, the final decision was left to the National Council. Since Masaryk was en route to the Pacific and could not be consulted, the Czecho-Slovak leaders in both Paris and Moscow took it upon themselves to stick with the professor's plan of transferring the legionaries from Russia to the Western Front.[38]

In the meantime, Stalin, the Commissar of Nationalities who negotiated the original terms of the evacuation with Klecanda, changed his mind and sent a new order for the legionaries to turn over all their weapons at Penza. When confronted with this demand by the Penza commissars, the Czecho-Slovaks protested that it violated the earlier settlements concluded by Klecanda and Maxa. They also reminded the Bolsheviks that they already turned over their heavy weaponry to Antonov-Ovseyenko at Kursk. The legionaries had plenty of reasons to desire the retention of their remaining arms. It was apparent to them as well as everyone else that lawlessness prevailed in many locales; there was no way of telling whether they might find themselves targeted by rebellious peasants or Cossack marauders who were stirring up trouble in numerous areas along their projected route. Moreover, the Trans-Siberian Railway was lined with prison camps filled with German and Magyar POWs, many of whom were loosely watched at best and were potentially hostile to the Czecho-Slovaks.[39]

Since the Czecho-Slovaks would not disarm and the Bolsheviks would not let them proceed, the two sides entered into the first of what would be many serious impasses.[40] This standoff favored the Soviet leaders since the presence of the insolent Trotsky and the beckoning of Czecho-Slovak Communists to treat the corps harshly to compel its soldiers to desert all encouraged the Bolsheviks' increasingly uncompromising attitude.[41] On the other hand, the Czecho-Slovak leadership was becoming weaker as Masaryk, by then passing through Eastern Siberia, was putting more distance between himself and the legionaries with each passing day. The two young men he entrusted to lead in his absence, Klecanda and Maxa, were separated by a few hundred miles and sketchy communications. It was the latter who, while operating from Penza and other towns along the planned route for the katabasis, was to have a more direct influence on the Legion's progress.

Oblivious to the sinister calculations of the Czecho-Slovak Communists, Maxa led his associates in the National Council in a new round of negotiations with the Penza Soviet. A schoolteacher in his civilian life, Maxa was a former POW who was described by an American observer as "a very democratic fellow, fine mixer, and likes nothing better than to be the center of a room full of good companions and storytellers, amidst clouds of smoke."[42] He was unwaveringly loyal to Masaryk and his policy of neutrality in Russia, but in the coming weeks he was to demonstrate a lack of sound judgment regarding people and situations, a fault that would eventually be his undoing.[43] At this point, however, Maxa was far from alone in his belief that the Bolsheviks could be bargained with in good faith. Two French attachés traveling with the Legion, General Arsen Vergé and Major Marie Constantine Paris, encouraged the negotiations. Running parallel to these talks were Klecanda's own efforts to convince Soviet leaders in Moscow to allow Czecho-Slovak trains to start moving again. Unlike Maxa and the French attachés, he was beginning to doubt the trustworthiness of the Bolsheviks in light of their failure to honor the agreement he had made with them just a week earlier. In a letter to his colleagues in Penza, he advised them not to excessively weaken the Czecho-Slovak position by conceding to a drastic arms reduction.[44]

Maxa brushed aside Klecanda's warning in his conviction that accords, and not rifles, would most effectively facilitate the movement of the Czecho-Slovak trains towards Vladivostok. Believing that concessions were necessary to forge a compromise with the Penza Soviet, on 25 March he struck an agreement with the Penza commissars whereby the legionaries would surrender a whopping four-fifths of their arms, leaving them with only 168 rifles, one trench mortar and one machine gun per train. In addition, the munitions in their possession were to be reduced to 300 cartridges per rifle and 1200 shells per mortar. This was the minimum level of arms deemed necessary by the Legion's commanders to defend themselves against any hostile elements they might encounter. In return for the weapons, the Czecho-Slovaks were to receive certificates guaranteeing their free passage to Vladivostok.[45]

Under this settlement, the first Czecho-Slovak train began the trek towards Siberia and Vladivostok two days later. Inside its coaches were several notable functionaries, including a few National Council representatives as well as a commissar of the Soviet government who was to use his authority to overrule the objections the local soviets might raise against the passage of the legionaries through their districts.[46] The soviets along the route also received a telegram from Stalin informing them that the Czecho-Slovaks "shall proceed not as fighting units but as a group of free citizens, taking with them a certain quantity of arms for self-defense against the attacks of counter-revolutionists."[47]

The terms of the Penza Agreement provoked a mixed reaction from the Legion's political leaders, commanders and troops. The latter was particularly disdainful of surrendering the majority of their arms. "The equipment we turned over to the Bolsheviks," later remarked a Czech captain, "was logically our possession for we took it away from the Germans, to whom it was abandoned by the fleeing Russians."[48] Conversely, the representatives of the National Council, with the exception of Klecanda and Bohdan Pavlů, were enthusiastic over the settlement.[49] Both of the Legion's most senior commanders, Generals Shokhorov and Diterikhs, agreed that accommodation of the Bolsheviks through partial disarmament was necessary, and General Vergé seconded their opinion.[50] Likewise, Masaryk, who was in Tokyo when he heard the news that his Legion was to turn over most of its arms, welcomed the decision as well.[51] The troops and their officers, however, were unimpressed with their leaders' arguments for disarmament. Subsequently, many went to great lengths to conceal additional rifles and cartridges beyond what was allowed in the Penza Agreement. These hidden caches were stashed between the walls of boxcars, in the ceiling, under carriages or in any other secret compartment the men could devise.[52]

Besides the surrender of arms, the Penza Agreement bound the Czecho-Slovaks to meet one other condition. This was the dismissal of their "counterrevolutionary" Russian officers, a stipulation added to settlement by Stalin, perhaps at the behest of the Czecho-Slovak Communists. Since this demand had been anticipated by the National Council to some degree, the Czecho-Slovak leaders had been prepared to make some changes. As a result,

Legionaries watch with mixed emotion as their rifles are turned over to the Penza Soviet in spring 1918.

they immediately released a majority of the Russian officers in the Legion and retained only a handful whose expertise was regarded as invaluable, including General Shokhorov, the Commander-in-Chief; General Diterikhs, the Chief of Staff; Captain Stepanov, the commander of the 1st Regiment; and Lieutenant Colonel Sergey Voitsekhovsky, the commander of the 3rd Regiment. All other regiments were placed under the command of Czecho-Slovak officers, several of whom would gain unprecedented fame in the coming months.[53]

Even when the first Czecho-Slovak trains began steaming out of Penza on the afternoon of 27 March, omens arose that soon overshadowed the optimism of National Council members who believed that their complications with the Bolsheviks were resolved. That same day, Trotsky met with Klecanda and voiced his dissatisfaction with the Penza Agreement. The Commissar of War still wanted the legionaries *completely* disarmed; moreover, he wanted the Czecho-Slovak Communists to have access to the legionaries. Klecanda rejected the idea of complete disarmament but reluctantly acquiesced on the second issue. He was confident that the legionaries, insulated by the National Council's own propaganda and possessing an excellent *esprit de corps*, would resist communist indoctrination. He did, however, warn Trotsky that any aggressive action against the legionaries would be resisted.[54]

After this final, strained meeting with Trotsky, Klecanda left Moscow to join the staff of the National Council in Omsk. He carried with him an apprehensive attitude toward the Bolsheviks whom he felt could not be trusted. His cautious voice, which might have served the Czecho-Slovak leadership in Russia well in the weeks to come, was lost after the young secretary fell ill and died shortly after his arrival in Siberia.[55] With Klecanda's untimely passing, Maxa was left without an equal in the National Council in Russia.

Shortly after the legionaries' trains began heading towards the Urals, the quasi-sovereignty of the provincial soviets raised a new obstacle in the evacuation. The central committee of

Siberian soviets, or Tsentrosibir, in Irkutsk cabled all soviets between Omsk and Lake Baikal to halt the legionaries' trains and completely disarm the troops. This ignited a chain reaction as the Omsk Soviet wired similar orders at soviets to its west and those soviets in turn flooded the War Commissariat with demands that the legionaries be completely disarmed. On 2 April, Trotsky yielded to their pressure and sent orders for the legionaries to surrender the remainder of their arms. When confronted with this telegram, the Czecho-Slovaks whose trains were chugging through the Volga basin ignored the order on the grounds that it breached the terms of the Penza Agreement. When the lead train reached Samara, however, the Czecho-Slovak and Soviet representatives were forced to argue with that city's soviet to no effect. Ultimately, the Czecho-Slovak representatives decided to haggle with the soviet and agreed to turn over additional arms—leaving themselves with a mere thirty rifles per train.[56] It was a portent of the difficulties to come along the thousands of miles that remained between them and Vladivostok.

The reports from the lead train detailing the additional weapon demands of the local soviets as well as the presence of Czecho-Slovak Communist agitators at stations along their route were sent back to the National Council members in Penza, who in turn formally protested these actions to the Penza Soviet. Maxa, taking an uncharacteristically firm position, declared that the corps would surrender no more arms until it received new guarantees of the troops' unmolested passage to Vladivostok.[57] This announcement placed Penza's commissars in a bind since they were also being prodded by the Czecho-Slovak Communists to engender an uncompromising attitude towards the legionaries no matter the cost.[58] This time it was the Reds who backed down. Five days after Trotsky's latest telegram to disarm the legionaries, the chairman of the Penza Soviet, Vasily V. Kurazhov, personally informed Maxa that the War Commissar would to allow the Czecho-Slovak trains to proceed on the basis of the Penza Agreement after all. After blaming the latest stoppage on a misunderstanding, Kurazhov requested permission for the Czecho-Slovak Communists to agitate among the legionaries. Like Masaryk and Klecanda earlier, Maxa was troubled by the proposal but acceded to it amid his desire to appease the Bolsheviks.[59]

Although the movement of the Czecho-Slovak trains was renewed west of the Ural Mountains, the West Siberian Soviet in Omsk on the other side of the range continued to prohibit the entry of armed legionaries into its district. Its opposition, made known in telegrams to Moscow and soviets to its west, again paralyzed the progress of the Czecho-Slovak trains. On 12 April, a National Council delegation led by Maxa, with the assistance of the Samara Soviet, coaxed the Omsk and Irkutsk soviets to accept the legionaries' trains up to the rate of four per day. By evening, the Czecho-Slovak trains were creaking eastward again, although not without complications. In the following days, Maxa and his colleagues received a steady stream of cables from train commanders along the route informing them that various soviets were still demanding further arms from the legionaries, often down to a mere two dozen per train. Even the lead train, replete with representatives of the National Council and a commissar from Moscow, reported back that it had only fifteen rifles by the time it rounded the southern shore of Lake Baikal. These revelations frustrated Maxa. He wanted a comprehensive settlement that would eliminate the need for the legionaries to waste valuable time bartering their arms for passage across the districts of the provincial and municipal soviets. He decided, quite inexplicably, that such an accord could be reached by being even more accommodating to the Bolsheviks. On 18 April he concluded a new settlement with the Omsk Soviet stipulating the Czecho-Slovak trains were to avoid surrendering their arms after Penza until they reached Omsk, where they would turn over their machine guns. Further disarmament was to follow once the trains reached Irkutsk, where each train was bound to give up all but twenty rifles.[60]

Maxa's decision to appease select soviets along the route quickly backfired. He failed to appreciate the mentality of self-preservation inherent in each of the soviets the Legion encountered along its wayward journey. Decentralization prevailed in those early days of the Soviet Republic, and the provincial and municipal soviets knew that they could not count on arms or troops from Moscow to suppress the revolts that flared up in their hinterlands. Therefore the lesser soviets were eager to obtain rifles to build their own militias, and the promise that arms would be surrendered to other faraway soviets was no consolation to them. When the soviets in Samara, Syzran and even Penza learned of Maxa's willingness to drastically cut the number of rifles possessed by each train at designated points to their east, they immediately demanded that they receive the weapons that would otherwise be surrendered at Omsk or Irkutsk. Amid this dispute, the Czecho-Slovak trains, with few local exceptions, remained frozen in place.[61]

More interferences with the Legion's trains followed, and by the end of April its progress on the journey to Vladivostok was highly disappointing. The National Council, which had worked out what it thought to be a reasonable time table for the evacuation in order to avoid overburdening the Russian railways with Czecho-Slovak trains, had hoped that the legionaries' trains would be released from Penza at the rate of four per day with the last one leaving the city around mid to late April. Due to the unexpected interruptions, however, most trains did not depart from Penza until the latter half of April, and by the end of that month, seventeen of the original seventy-odd Czecho-Slovak trains were still sitting idle in yards west of the city.[62] While Maxa and much of the National Council continued their policy of appeasement to facilitate the evacuation, the Czecho-Slovak soldiers would have preferred their leaders to take the opposite approach. They knew, as everyone else did, that the Bolsheviks were militarily weak in the spring of 1918, and because of this they believed that if they remained well-armed, they could resort to forcibly punching their way through to Vladivostok.[63] There were some instances of Czecho-Slovak officers advocating a march on Penza in order to coerce that city's soviet into releasing their trains, but overall, except for their concealment of a few spare rifles, the troops obediently surrendered a majority of their arms in exchange for papers that were supposed to guarantee their free passage to the east. When these documents proved mostly meaningless, however, the legionaries became furious not only with the Bolsheviks, but also with the National Council.[64]

The legionaries' feelings of resentment for the Czecho-Slovak political leaders in Russia found an outlet at a preliminary session for the Congress of the Czecho-Slovak Army Corps. The congress, which had been planned in various forms since the autumn of 1917, was a by-product of the push for greater democratization in the corps. The debate centered on whether the powers of the army committees should be expanded or diminished; the controversy had raged in the old Russian Army and its presence in the Czecho-Slovak Legion demonstrated how revolutionary toxins secreted by one nearby body infected another. The issue was kept alive over the following months in the Czecho-Slovak corps through the troops' exposure to revolutionary propaganda; it was in fact a favorite topic among Czecho-Slovak Communist agitators.[65]

In the spring of 1918, the Czecho-Slovak Communists charged that the congress was deliberately delayed by the National Council to muzzle the voices of the legionaries, who they claimed did not want to fight in France.[66] This message was similar to one proclaimed by the Russian Bolsheviks throughout most of the previous autumn: they had claimed that the Provisional Government's procrastination in holding the election to the Constituent Assembly was merely a ploy to suppress the popular revolutionary zeal of the masses.[67] While the Bolsheviks demonstrated that they were neither friends of democracy nor sympathetic to popular will, the propaganda had fostered distrust towards the Provisional Government and may be counted as one of the reasons why so few rallied to its defense when Lenin and his party moved against it. This reminder troubled the Czecho-Slovak leaders, who did not want to become the Kerensky's of their own revolution. Hence, in order to outmaneuver the Czecho-Slovak Communists, the National Council decided to convoke the long-awaited army congress.

The news that an army congress was imminent did not dampen the spirits of the Czecho-Slovak Communists. They had observed with delight the legionaries' growing frustration at the slow progress of the evacuation and they believed that these feelings would boil over at the congress into a denouncement of Maxa and the National Council and compel great numbers of troops to join the communist cause. In reality, the Czecho-Slovak Communists had repeated their error of overestimating the effectiveness of their propaganda while underestimating the legionaries' loyalty to their corps. While they were right that the legionaries' patience with their political leaders was wearing thin, their growing anger also made them less amiable to the Bolsheviks.[68] Because of their overt support for Moscow, the Czecho-Slovak Communists were bound to remain unpopular as well and would have little chance of winning the confidence of the legionaries.

It was amid these circumstances that the preliminary conference for the congress was held in a Penza school building from 27 April through 1 May 1918.[69] In the days leading up to the opening session, delegates who had been elected earlier that month arrived from near and afar, the latter often by passenger trains. Rudolf Medek, a commissar in the Legion later famous for chronicling its fortunes in novels and movies, opened the conference by reiterating that the corps' main goal was to reach Vladivostok and then sail for France. His statement was immediately challenged by a group of delegates who were sympathetic to the Czecho-Slovak Communists. These extremists demanded that the congress should consider a resolution for the corps to remain in Russia and assist or perhaps be incorporated into Soviet military forces. This motion failed to secure a necessary majority, however, and in response the flustered extremists walked out of the assembly.[70]

The departure of the far-left radicals on the first day did little to render the remaining four days of the conference any less tense. The remainder of the assembly was split between delegates who continued to place confidence in the leadership of the National Council and those who wanted to end Maxa's policy of Bolshevik appeasement. One of the leading spokesmen of this latter group was Lieutenant Stanislav Čeček, a delegate and the commanding officer of the 4th Regiment which had spent the past month waiting for its turn to begin the transcontinental journey from Penza. At one point in the conference, Čeček proposed that the soldiers should repudiate the authority of the Russian branch of the Czecho-Slovak National Council and replace it with a commission of military leaders who would confront the soviets with an ultimatum to open the way to Vladivostok. To the relief of the observers from the National Council, his bold motion failed to pass as most of the delegates deemed it too extreme—for now.[71]

By the beginning of May, tensions were not only running high in the Penza school building hosting the preliminary army congress, but also throughout the city. Russian disaffection with the Soviet regime was growing apparent that spring as mutinies among Red garrisons and Social Revolutionary agitation became more commonplace in the region.[72] Although the soviet remained in charge of Penza, its commissars had reasons for concern. The city's parade celebrating May Day, one of the most revered holidays on the socialist calendar, attracted only a paltry turnout of residents. The same day, the National Council held a rally of its own at the city's train station, and more than a few curious Russians could be seen among the crowds of Czecho-Slovak troops and onlookers. Not to be outdone, on 2 May the Czecho-Slovak Communists decided to stage their own public demonstration at the same venue.[73] Despite the failure of their latest recruiting campaign, which yielded only 150 defectors from the Czecho-Slovak Legion, and their embarrassment at the preliminary army conference a few days earlier, the Czecho-Slovak Communists were still convinced that somewhere within the corps there was a silent element sympathetic to the proletarian cause.[74] Their exhibition was successful in attracting a large number of troops, but when the demagogic speakers at the rally began deriding the National Council, the legionaries drowned out the orators' messages with protests and then a chorus of national hymns. In essence, the demonstration, rather than revealing the soldiers' hidden sympathy for Marxism, instead confirmed their adherence to the struggle for Czecho-Slovak national independence. It was a rejection that not even the persistent Czecho-Slovak Communists could ignore, and it confirmed the suspicions of their Soviet handlers that the agitators would be unable to deliver the promised 15,000 "proletarian" legionaries—or even a fraction of that number—into the ranks of the Red Army.[75]

While distrust and intrigue between the Czecho-Slovaks and the Bolsheviks impeded the Legion's evacuation from Russia, there were other factors from outside the country that also affected the operation. These elements, while emanating from different quarters, were all related to the question of Allied intervention in Russia and particularly Siberia. Despite the utter collapse of the Eastern Front, the Entente still longed to somehow pin down enemy forces in Eastern Europe to prevent Germany from using them to reinforce the Western Front. We have seen how the Entente leaders, amid their desperation, were prepared to cooperate with the Soviet government if it renewed hostilities with the Central Powers. It was the earnest hope of many of these statesmen that the Bolsheviks would invite an Allied expeditionary force into their realm to fight the Central Powers alongside them. However, the Allied nation best positioned from a geographical and military standpoint to send a sizeable expedition into Russia was that country's old enemy from the war of 1904–05, Japan. Since entering the war on the side of the Allies in August 1914, Japan exploited the preoccupation of all European powers with the war to strengthen her hegemony in the Far East. The Japanese pursued this objective by first seizing German possessions in the Pacific and in China, and then by increasing her economic penetration of Manchuria at the expense of her nominal ally, Russia.[76] Not surprisingly, repeated French proposals for the deployment of Japanese troops on the Eastern Front garnered no support among Russians, including the Bolsheviks.[77] After several meetings with Soviet leaders, British agent Bruce Lockhart warned his government that "Japanese intervention in Siberia would destroy all possibility of an understanding with the Bolsheviks."[78]

As the crisis on the Western Front continued and the likelihood of the Bolsheviks renewing hostilities with Germany gradually faded after the Fourth Congress of Soviets ratified the Brest-Litovsk Treaty in mid–March 1918, the Entente governments grew less interested in remaining in the good graces of the Soviet government. There were long-held suspicions among the Allies that Lenin and Trotsky were German agents who concluded the peace treaty in order to make Russia subservient to Germany.[79] Moreover, Allied officialdom in and outside of Russia were becoming disheveled by reports that the Bolsheviks were arming Austro-Hungarian and German prisoners of war. Most did not understand or were antipathetic to the Internationalist ideology that led to the formation of the POW battalions; they simply regarded the POWs as *the* enemy whose arming was not to be tolerated. The cries for intervention from Paris and London inevitably increased.

The fear which armed prisoner detachments evoked among the Allies was partially due their knowledge that Russia held vast numbers of war prisoners—over two million of them by autumn of 1917.[80] The campaign to Bolshevize these men began when Bolshevik agitators started canvassing the POW camps shortly after the October Revolution. A month later, the Soviet government decreed that all POWs in the Soviet republic were to enjoy the same rights as Russians while establishing a committee in the Russian capital to oversee the recruitment of POWs to the communist cause.[81] The original assignment of the Bolshevized POWs was to export social revolution to Central Europe upon their repatriation. However, after Trotsky realized the vulnerability of the Soviet regime following the German attack in February 1918, the mission of the Internationalists was altered. Instead of returning to Central Europe to foment worker uprisings in their home countries, the Internationalists were to remain in Russia and defend the revolution already in existence.[82]

Incidentally, the efforts to recruit POWs into communist forces reached their pinnacle during the same period when the Czecho-Slovak Legion was attempting to withdraw from central Russia to Vladivostok, or from about mid–March to late May. Reflecting the general disorder and poor communications throughout revolutionary Russia, contemporary Allied observers inside the country and beyond it found it difficult to determine how great a threat the International battalions represented to Allied interests; some even disputed their existence. Historians too have had trouble separating fact from rumor in regards to POW activity in Soviet Russia, but the most thorough studies on the subject do agree on a few points. First of all, the number of POWs who joined the International battalions as a result of ideological motivation was probably low. The socialists among the Austrian and German POWs, like their Czech comrades, were generally of the moderate variety who typically felt a stronger attachment to their national allegiance than Marxist principles. The most effective recruiting tool for Bolsheviks was probably sheer bribery. After they took control of the camps, the Bolsheviks allegedly allotted higher food rations to those who enlisted in the International battalions. Another point of general agreement is that the recruiting campaign among the POWs was more successful in Siberia than in European Russia, and the nationality which responded the most positively to the communists' overtures were the Magyars.[83, 84] Finally, despite Allied perceptions at the time, the Internationalist battalions in no way served the interests of the Central Powers, and neither Berlin nor Vienna looked favorably upon the existence of these formations.[85, 86]

Historians differ on the actual number of POWs who served in the early Red Army. Low estimates place their number at no more than 15,000 men, an unimpressive force when scattered across the great expanses of Russian territory.[87] Less conservative estimates have placed the number as high as 200,000 POWs, while one in-depth study on the subject has given the extremely broad range that between 50,000 and 190,000 men joined Internationalist units, though some served only for a few days or weeks.[88] Even if these higher estimates are accepted, only a small minority of POWs took up arms for the communists and even fewer saw actual combat in the Russian Civil War. The Bolshevik recruiters, like the Czecho-Slovaks before them, found that most POWs were apolitical and tired of fighting. Many preferred to passively await their repatriation to the central empires, which appeared imminent after the signing of the Brest-Litovsk Treaty.

The Allies did make some attempts to learn how many POWs were being armed by the Soviet regime, or at least to verify whether they were being armed at all. Masaryk, after arriving in Japan in early April 1918, told attentive Allied representatives there that he did not see any armed POWs during his trip across Siberia.[89] Allied representatives who traveled the Trans-Siberian Railway to investigate the matter did report encountering small detachments of rifle-wielding POWs but they disagreed whether or not these should be viewed as a threat to the Allies. While one group of these fact-seekers looked at the Internationalists as mostly harmless, another reported that these detachments were "a positive menace through [the] inability of the Trotsky government to control them."[90]

By the end of April, the pessimistic view of the Internationalist battalions was gaining wider acceptance among the Allies. One reason for this was the irrational fear that anyone who was claiming that the Soviet regime was not a creature of Germany was likely infected with Bolshevism.[91] Moreover, it was difficult in any circumstance to ignore the disturbing tales of POW activity that continued to stream into Allied capitals from consuls and other representatives in Russia and Siberia. One erroneous report claiming that 80,000 German prisoners were set to converge on Irkutsk even caused U.S. Secretary of State Robert Lansing to waver in his opposition to military intervention in Siberia. Although Lansing's department was inundated with appeals for action from its European allies, as well from some of its own representatives in the Far East, for the moment Washington was unwilling to take any steps beyond its earlier decision to send the USS *Brooklyn* to Vladivostok harbor. Since arriving there on 1 March, the *Brooklyn* accompanied two Japanese warships and Britain's HMS *Suffolk*, all of which had been anchored in those waters since early January. The announced purpose for this Allied naval presence at Russia's main Pacific port was to guard the 600,000 tons of imported war materiel that had accumulated in the city's warehouses and wharves during the war. The Allies feared that these supplies, which included munitions, barbed wire, cotton bales and automobiles, would end up in German hands if the Bolsheviks or anyone else moved them into the interior. There can be little doubt, however, that the American, British and Japanese crews were as interested in monitoring each other as they were the war materiel.[92]

The U.S. attitude towards the Allied proposals for intervention was important for two reasons. First, the United States was the only Allied power besides Japan that could spare significant manpower and resources for a massive intervention in Russia. The governments which were the biggest proponents for intervention, Britain and France, needed every last man to contain the German attacks on the Western Front. The second reason why the U.S. position on the question of intervention was so important was that Japan, the only other country capable of sending a large force into Russia, would not do so without U.S. sanction. As economic contenders in the Pacific and Far East, tensions were frequently high between the Japanese and American governments. Both looked to the Far East as a rising market for their goods, and while each sought to obtain an economic edge over the other, neither wanted to provoke an open clash. Since a Japanese expedition to Siberia might be viewed as a threat to the existing balance of power in the region, Tokyo was reluctant to act on the fervent appeals from Britain and France without a nod from Washington.[93]

Despite its unwillingness to act without U.S. consent, the Japanese government was astute enough to leave itself with some wiggle room. Its Siberian policy included a provision that reserved it the right to enter Russian territory if Japanese lives or properties were thought to be at risk. On 5 April, it acted on this loophole after three Japanese nationals were murdered in Vladivostok a day earlier. In this operation, 500 Japanese troops were sent ashore. The British, not to be left out, landed fifty marines in the city on the pretext that they were needed to guard their consulate. Although these Allied detachments confined themselves to the city and its environs, the Soviet government regarded the actions of both nations as hostile and a forerunner of large-scale invasion.[94] Considering that agents from both countries were in contact with and financing the operations of anti–Bolshevik Cossacks in Eastern Siberia, Moscow's apprehension was not unjustified.[95] The landing also stoked Bolshevik concerns that the Russian Far East was becoming a hive of counterrevolution, and this provided them with yet another reason to bar the Czecho-Slovak Legion from going east.[96, 97] It was not unheard of for such travelers to make common cause with anti–Bolshevik forces in the region: some 150 Serb deserters from the South Slav brigade that had crossed Siberia earlier that year had joined the counterrevolutionary army of Grigory Semenov.[98] Gradually, the Bolsheviks' alarm at these initial landings receded, particularly after Allied forces made no preparations to move further inland. The Czecho-Slovaks, whose trains were stopped at the time for other reasons, were soon allowed to resume their journey.

The Bolshevik leaders remained uncomfortable with the Legion's withdrawal into Eastern Siberia, where their grip seemed to be growing more delicate with each passing day. They soon indicated to the French Military Mission their willingness to explore other options for the Czecho-Slovaks' evacuation.[99] Coincidentally, other parties were also seeking other alternatives for the Czecho-Slovak Legion in Russia. On 1 April the British, using the French government as an intermediary, broached a revised evacuation plan to Beneš in Paris to reroute part of the corps to North Russia to help guard the ports and stores of war materiel there.[100] The reasons for the British desire to alter the original plan are unclear, but London's interest in the legionaries had been growing since learning of their adept performance at Bakhmach. Convinced that Allied intervention in Russia was inevitable, many British leaders now thought that the skilled Czecho-Slovak troops might be more useful in that country than in France.[101] They calculated that the presence of Czecho-Slovak troops in an Allied intervention might make such an operation more acceptable to the Bolsheviks since the legionaries would give the expeditionary forces a multinational or even Slavic disguise. Another possible reason for the plan's revision was that British military leaders were pessimistic in regards to whether enough tonnage could be gathered in short time to transport the entire Czecho-Slovak corps from Vladivostok. Their bleak assessment stemmed in part from earlier French failures to locate the needed vessels. Japan, when asked to furnish some of the transports, claimed it had no ships available for the operation. This may very well have been true since any ships that could be spared had already been sent to the Atlantic to deliver supplies and troops to Europe. Ships from numerous countries, including Japan, were also chartered abroad to replace vessels sunk by German U-boats. In other words, the shipping lanes in the Pacific were left with minimal traffic. In light of this situation, the British were certain that the evacuation of the legionaries would be delayed at the very least. Subsequently, they decided preparations should be made to use the Czecho-Slovaks where they stood.[102]

When Beneš was confronted with the British proposal to deploy the legionaries in parts of Russia while waiting for their evacuation, he reacted cautiously and coordinated his response with the advice of General Maurice Janin, who had been appointed as the Supreme Commander of the Czecho-Slovak Armies. Janin, citing reports from French attachés, replied that the transfer of the corps to France was the foremost desire of the legionaries. He added that the evacuation of the Czecho-Slovak troops through Murmansk and Archangelsk should be considered if it would expedite their arrival in France. Beneš accepted his recommendations but did mention that the National Council would consent to the *temporary* deployment of its troops in Russia and Siberia until the required ships were found. This emphasis on the removal of the Czecho-Slovak Legion to France, allowing for at best their limited participation in Allied operations in Russia, essentially defined the National Council's formal policy until well into the summer of 1918.[103]

On paper at least, the rerouting of an entire division, or about half of the Czecho-Slovak Legion, to the northern ports seemed to offer the advantages of a drastically shorter overland and sea route for the legionaries while easing the demands on the limited tonnage in the Pacific Ocean. The disadvantages of the route, however, were less obvious. As the 2,400 Czecho-Slovak troops who used that route to depart from Russia in the autumn and winter of 1917–18 learned, North Russia had few provisions to spare on troops passing through the region. Starvation was a real threat in Archangelsk that winter as the port received little of the grain shipments from the interior which its residents normally depended upon. This forced the desperate city leaders to contemplate exchanging some of the war materiel that had accumulated on their quays for shipments of foodstuffs from Britain and the U.S.[104] Conditions at Murmansk were no better, especially after March 1918 when the port was flooded with trainloads of refugees from Petrograd seeking to escape the violent mayhem that was engulfing Russia.[105] Siberia, in contrast, had adequate stores of food and grain, and the Czecho-Slovaks had already obtained access to these supplies through previous arrangements made with the Siberian cooperatives.[106]

Despite the challenges of rerouting some of the legionaries to North Russia, nearly all parties involved in the Czecho-Slovak evacuation had informally accepted the proposal by late April. Their reasons for agreeing to the plan varied. The scheme appealed to the National Council and French leaders primarily because of its promise to deliver the troops to France sooner. The Bolsheviks liked the idea since it would cut down on the number of foreign troops in the sensitive zone of Eastern Siberia. The British, who were main advocates of the plan, liked its option of using the legionaries in Russia to keep strategic points and war materiel out of enemy—meaning German—possession. The War Office in London was especially concerned that the Finnish Whites, who with German aid were winning the civil war in their homeland against the Finnish Bolsheviks, might raid Murmansk in order to seize its stockpile of war materiel. Although their minds likely inflated the threat to the port, British leaders were soothed by the prospect of their few marines in the region being reinforced by a sizeable force of Czecho-Slovaks.[107]

Encouraged by this support of their revised evacuation plan, the British presented the scheme to the permanent military representatives of the Allied Supreme War Council in Versailles. Although the Allied military leaders gave the project their stamp of approval, it had much more difficulty clearing the agenda of the Allied statesmen when they met on 2 May at the Fifth Session of the Supreme War Council in Abbeville, France. Its proposals immediately aroused reservations in Georges Clemenceau, who was unyielding in his desire to bring every last man of the Czecho-Slovak Legion to fight in France. "This is not the hour," the French Prime Minister roared to the conference, "when English effectives are diminishing, when France has imposed upon herself the last sacrifices to maintain the numer-ical superiority of our armies, for you to think of depriving us of soldiers who are courageous, well-trained, and profoundly devoted to our cause."[108] While he was not opposed to redi-recting some of the legionaries to North Russia if it would facilitate the evacuation, he rightly suspected that the British were in no hurry to pull Czecho-Slovaks out of Russia. The British responded to his concerns with promises to make every effort to obtain the necessary trans-ports, but in the same breath they expressed their doubt over whether this was possible under the circumstances. The British Secretary of State for War, Lord Milner, even suggested that part of the Czecho-Slovak corps should not attempt to reach the coast and instead remain in Western Siberia or the Urals. These differences in the Supreme War Council resulted in its passage of the Abbeville Resolution, a sort of compromise where British government was beholden to make a valid effort to secure the necessary tonnage to haul the legionaries to France. It also stated that pending the approval of the Soviet government, the Czecho-Slovak troops still west of Omsk were to evacuate Russia through the northern ports of Murmansk and Archangelsk. Those already in and east of that city were to continue on towards Vladi-vostok.[109]

The Bolsheviks, as expected, welcomed the project and Georgy Chicherin, Trotsky's successor as Commissar of Foreign Affairs, immediately wired orders to Omsk that all Czecho-Slovak troop trains west of the city were to be redirected towards the northern ports. In the absence of any Soviet objections to the project, the British and French govern-ments as well as the Supreme War Council assumed that their plan to divide the Legion between North Russia and Siberia was being carried out. Yet, while the Soviet government, along with British and French representatives in Russia, was kept abreast of the Supreme War Council's decision, apparently no one thought to alert those directly affected by the revision: the Czecho-Slovak officers and troops in Russia.[110] It was this oversight that would prove fatal to the project and perhaps fateful to the history of Russian and Central Europe.

The Czecho-Slovak commanders first heard of the decision to reroute the First Division, which comprised the main body of the corps still west of Omsk, from the order which Chicherin had cabled to the Omsk Soviet.[111] As might be expected, this seemingly sudden and radical change of plan ignited bewilderment among the legionaries, who were skeptical of Bolshevik explanations that the Allies were responsible for the revision.[112] Some were even convinced that the project was really a Bolshevik trap, perhaps originating with the Germans, to weaken the corps by splitting it and then detaining the troops.[113]

There are numerous reasons why the legionaries were inclined to suspect that the Soviet government was conspiring against their outfit. The constant obstruction of their trains throughout April, whether by Trotsky or the local soviets, was the most significant factor behind their distrust of the Bolsheviks. From their perspective, there were no good justifi-cations for their trains being stalled or for the Bolsheviks constantly demanding their com-plete disarmament. They had, or so they believed, faithfully observed the terms of the Penza Agreement. They constantly reminded the commissars they dealt with that they had no quarrel with the Soviet regime; their only aim was to reach France so they could fight the Central Powers.

Another cause for the Czecho-Slovaks' suspicions was the propaganda of the Czecho-Slovak Communists. In early April, the latter's press organs began running stories claiming that the Legion was to be redirected to the northern ports where it would break up due to exposure to the harsh climate, lack of food and the defection of its proletarian element. The purpose of these articles was to convince the legionaries to join the Czecho-Slovak Red Army rather than remain with a hopelessly doomed army corps. Hardly any legionaries took this propaganda seriously, but after they heard the First Division was to head for Archangelsk and Murmansk, they recalled these articles and were overcome with a sense of alarm at the new plan.[114]

A final reason why the Czecho-Slovaks were leery of Bolshevik intentions was that they, like many in the Allied camp, harbored an underlying fear that the Bolsheviks were working, either willingly or under duress, in the interests of Germany. Throughout the spring of 1918, as the movement of the corps along the Trans-Siberian Railway was delayed by one interruption after another, the troops tended to blame their disappointing progress on the hidden hand of the Kaiser and his newly-appointed ambassador to Moscow, Count Wilhelm von Mirbach.[115] Their suspicions of a Bolshevik-German conspiracy against them were only heightened by reports of German and Magyar POWs being armed in Internationalist battalions throughout Russia and Siberia. In reality, the Germans did not deliberately attempt to hinder the Czecho-Slovaks' evacuation although they did make demands on the Soviet government that were oblivious to their effect on the Legion's progress. In mid–April, Berlin, concerned about the possibility of a large-scale Japanese intervention in Eastern Siberia and eager to replenish its armies with its prisoners in Russia, demanded the Soviet government to immediately transport German POWs out of Siberia in order to bring them out of Japanese reach and to expedite their repatriation. Chicherin, who was devoted to Lenin's policy of preserving the costly peace with the Central Powers, complied with the request by ordering the soviets along the railway to facilitate the movement of German POWs westward, even if this meant delaying the Czecho-Slovaks' progress.[116] Maxa was indignant when he learned this order but his protests to Moscow were unable to reverse Chicherin's directions. Moreover, he concealed the contents of the order from the legionaries out of fear that it would fuel irrational or violent reactions among the Germanophobe legionaries.[117] Maxa's efforts to withhold information invariably bred speculation that was often far more sinister than the truth. Such rumor-mongering became a factor in the latest controversy over whether the First Czecho-Slovak Division should obey the orders to head for North Russia. Tales were soon leaping from one regiment to another that the Bolsheviks were plotting to deport them back to Austria-Hungary as traitors or that their transports would be torpedoed by German U-boats as soon as they set out into the Arctic Ocean.[118]

The Czecho-Slovak National Council in Russia did have some forewarning that the Allies were weighing the options of evacuating some of the corps through North Russia. Still, even it had not been officially informed of the Abbeville Resolution when they received word of Chicherin's telegram. Like the troops, the Czecho-Slovak leaders in Russia were also skeptical of Bolshevik explanations that the project was initiated by the Allies, and to verify this they dispatched two associates then in Omsk, Čermak and Augustin Štraka, to Moscow and Vologda to clear up confusion. Soon after his arrival in the Soviet capital, Čermak reported that the order to divide the corps between North Russia and Siberia did indeed originate with the Allies, and a couple days later Štraka corroborated this information after meeting with the French Ambassador, Joseph Noulens, in Vologda. After hearing from both men, Maxa decided to personally lead a Czecho-Slovak delegation to Moscow to discuss the scheme with the French Military Mission and the Soviet government. The delegation had a tense meeting with Trotsky on 15 May where the Commissar of War refused any possibility of returning to the original plan of allowing the entire corps to evacuate Russia from the Pacific coast. Feeling that they had little other choice, Maxa and his colleagues reluctantly agreed to send the First Czecho-Slovak Division to the northern ports while the Second Czecho-Slovak Division was to continue its concentration at Vladivostok. Shortly after their meeting with Trotsky, they began cabling instructions to this effect.[119]

If Maxa and his delegation had known just how unpopular the Abbeville Resolution would be with the legionaries, they might have applied greater pressure on the French Military Mission and Trotsky to adhere to the original evacuation plan. At least some members of the National Council were aware of the troops' aversion to the idea of splitting the corps between opposite ends of Russia. Lieutenant Jan Syrový, the commander of the 2nd Czecho-Slovak Regiment, reported that his troops "would rather desert and go to Vladivostok under their own steam" than set off for Archangelsk. Other regimental commanders in the First Division told of similar sentiments in their men.[120] To allay the troops' opposition to the scheme, some Czecho-Slovak leaders as well as one of the French attachés, General Vergé, published open letters supportive of the plan in the Legion's official newspaper.[121] Despite their efforts, graffiti in the form of Czech inscriptions and slogans denouncing the project continued to be scrawled on the sides of railcars. Unfortunately for the National Council, this strong indicator of the legionaries' mood could not be easily impressed upon Maxa's delegation in distant Moscow.[122]

The decision of the Czecho-Slovak leaders in Russia to agree to the unpopular revised evacuation destroyed, once and for all, their credibility among the legionaries. Even before this development, the troops and officers were losing faith in the judgment of the National Council. In mid–April, the entire officer corps of the First Division had gathered in the railway station at Kirsanov, just outside of Penza, and passed a resolution recommending the corps to resist disarmament and, if necessary, endeavor its passage to Vladivostok by way of force. When the Commander-in-Chief of the Czecho-Slovak Legion, General Shokhorov, learned of the Kirsanov Resolution, he suppressed it as insubordination against the authority of the National Council.[123] While the Kirsanov Resolution had no immediate ramifications, the fissure it revealed between the fighting men and their leaders continued to deepen as the latter yielded more arms to the soviets in the hope that Czecho-Slovak trains would be allowed to proceed to Vladivostok. In the meantime, the younger officers, echoing the Kirsanov Resolution, became more convinced that the Pacific port could be reached only through aggressive means. To prepare for such a contingency, those whose trains were idle passed the days by drilling their men and engaging in other training exercises. The positions of local Red garrisons were also mapped out and reconnaissance parties were formed to monitor these areas.[124] Perhaps the most thorough preparations were made in the area of Novonikolaevsk in Central Siberia, where the trains of Captain Eduard Kadlec and Captain Radola Gajda, the flamboyant commander of the 7th Czecho-Slovak Regiment, were shunted to sidings.[125]

Perhaps no two men better represent the spirit of adventurism that was overtaking the legionaries that spring than Kadlec and Gajda. While a penchant for the thrilling career of a soldier-of-fortune could already be seen in Kadlec's background, that trait was still maturing in Gajda. Born Rudolf Geidl in 1892, Gajda modified his Germanic name to a more Slavic version in his early adult life, during which he served in an Austro-Hungarian reserve artillery regiment in between his studies and work in the field of pharmaceuticals. When war broke out in 1914, Gajda was recently married and working in a drug store under his father-in-law. Initially, he showed little enthusiasm for entering the fight but he finally enlisted again with the Habsburg army when his call-up was inevitable. In late 1915, he was captured by the Montenegrins and, as a Slav POW, was allowed to serve in their army by passing himself off as a doctor. When the armies of the Central Powers overran the Balkans, he used his alias to obtain a placement aboard a medical ship to Russia where he entered the Serbian Volunteer Corps. As with the Montenegrins, in the Serbian unit Gajda displayed an uncanny ability to avoid service at the front by posing as a doctor while obtaining promotions up to the rank of captain. At the end of 1916, when the Serbian Volunteer Corps was crumbling apart after having been viciously mauled by the enemy on battlefields in southern Romania, Gajda was among the several hundred Czechs serving with it who transferred to the Czecho-Slovak Brigade. Eventually, he was named commanding officer of the 7th Tatra Regiment of the First Czecho-Slovak Army Corps.[126]

Radola Gajda, undated. He was one of several commanders in the Russian Civil War who were under thirty years of age.

With a narrow face, prominent nose and driven eyes, Gajda's appearance resembled that of a pet terrier and he undoubtedly possessed the indomitable spirit of one. Already during his journey from southern Russia to Central Siberia, his behavior was at times reckless. According to one account, he successfully resisted further disarmament demands from local commissars through the sheer abrasiveness of his personality.[127] He also made contact with underground anti–Bolshevik organizations, often filled with ex-tsarist officers, of which there was a significant group in Novonikolaevsk. In that Siberian town, on 10 May, Gajda had his first meeting with Colonel G. A. Grishin-Almazov, the military chief of an underground anti–Bolshevik network.[128] By then Kadlec, the only Czech officer with staff experience, had completed his blueprint for operations against the Bolsheviks, and it is possible that Gajda sought Grishin-Almazov's help in the coming fight against the Soviet regime.

It is impossible to know for certain whether Gajda or any other legionary deliberately sought to instigate a fight with the Bolsheviks or if they were simply preparing for any eventual outcome when he and Kadlec drafted their operational plans. Certainly hindsight into Gajda's later career, where he displayed a craving for conspiracy both in the Russian Civil War and in interwar Czechoslovakia, made him an easy target for historians seeking to pin the blame for the subsequent conflict on the legionaries.[129] Yet it was the course of events, more than a single human or organization, which would have the greatest impact on the Czecho-Slovak corps in the coming weeks. This process began with a small unfortunate act, not unlike the incident in Sarajevo that sparked the Great War, which eventually proved more monumental than its initial participants realized.

10

War Across an Iron Ribbon

The construction of the Trans-Siberian Railway, which began in the last decade of the nineteenth century, was a colossal undertaking that laid 5,000 miles of track across the wilderness of northern Asia. It was not only an ambitious but also an expensive endeavor; its costs even exceeded the amounts spent by France and the United States to excavate the Panama Canal.[1] Starting from the tree-covered Ural slopes at Chelyabinsk, the line crossed the mosquito-infested bogs and grass-plumed steppes of Western Siberia and then cut through the dark pine forests of Central Siberia. Its route to Irkutsk mostly paralleled the *trakt*, a rough dirt road built across the same expanse in the eighteenth century. Lake Baikal and the mountains along its southern rim presented a formidable obstacle which the railway's planners originally attempted to circumvent by ferrying entire trains on two massive icebreakers across the world's deepest freshwater lake. The inefficiency of this solution, however, quickly became apparent and as a result, the Circumbaikal route was eventually bored through the mountains south of the lake. Passing through thirty-nine tunnels, this section of the line was operational by late 1904, one year after the rest of the railway was opened to through traffic. From the east shore of Lake Baikal, the railway traversed the inhospitable highlands of Transbaikal Province to Chita and then turned eastward into Manchuria. This stretch of track, known as the Chinese Eastern Railway, was built and operated by the Russians under an agreement with the Chinese government. It offered a shorter, more direct route to the coast than the alternative route through the rough terrain along the Amur River to Khabarovsk. South of that city was the final leg of the railway, known as the Ussuri line for the river which it parallels. The eastern terminus of the Trans-Siberian Railway was the city of Vladivostok, which had been founded by the Russians in 1860 after annexing the surrounding territory from China.[2]

Since its addition to the tsars' dominions in the sixteenth and seventeenth centuries, Siberia was exploited as a colony from which the tsarist government extracted wealth in the form of furs, minerals and other resources; it was also famously used as a dumping ground for convicts and exiles from European Russia.[3] During and after the construction of the Trans-Siberian Railway, however, the migration of peasants from the overcrowded countryside of European Russia into the underdeveloped lands of Siberia accelerated considerably. Between 1897 and 1911, an estimated three and a half million immigrants arrived into the vast region and the towns of Omsk, Tomsk, Novonikolaevsk, Irkutsk, Chita and Vladivostok multiplied anywhere from two to eight times in size. Alongside this unprecedented growth in population occurred the rapid expansion of Siberia's timber, mining and cottage industries. The greatest boom was seen in agriculture, where the amount of Siberian land under cultivation more than doubled during this period.[4]

During the Great War, Siberian society was infused with POWs shipped east of the Urals by the hundreds of thousands. After the autumn of 1915, when the Russians began to utilize POWs on a large-scale to relieve labor shortages, many POWs in Siberia were assigned to small farms where they often worked without much supervision from authorities. In some cases the POWs were more than just an economic substitute for mobilized Russian males as some started families with Russian women. Others possessing an education or skills that were rare among the local populace provided services such as carpentry, engineering, doctoring, banking and teaching that were previously unavailable in the Siberian villages.[5] "Many of the prisoners like the life and opportunities in Siberia and they plan to stay there even after the peace comes," claimed one American YMCA secretary who worked with them in the region.[6, 7] Assuming that was true, then many prisoners had lost interest in the war and the cause they had served; nevertheless, in 1918 many Allied officials remained nervous about the presence of an estimated 800,000 enemy POWs in a nearly lawless Siberia.[8] The more imaginative among them feared that the unguarded POWs might act as a ready-made fifth column that would somehow place Siberia's immense resources at the disposal of the Central Powers. "The Germanic states are, in fact, aiming to establish exclusive control over the economic life of all Russia," warned French Ambassador Noulens in April 1918. "Furthermore, they are endeavoring through their prisoners of war to organize colonization centers in Siberia."[9] Hence, the reports of war prisoners being recruited into Internationalist battalions in early 1918 caused no shortage of consternation among the Allies and fueled demands for some form of intervention.

In the early months of Bolshevik rule, former POWs made up a larger portion of Red forces in Siberia than in European Russia.[10] A possible reason for this was due to the fact that Siberia, of all the regions of the former Russian Empire, was by all appearances the least conducive to Bolshevism. The urban proletariat, in whose name the Bolsheviks ruled, was a virtually nonexistent class east of the Urals. Even with the advent of the railroad and the expansion of towns and industry that came with it, over 97 percent of Siberia's population was considered rural as late as 1916.[11] Perhaps an even greater challenge for the Bolsheviks was the lack of extreme social polarization in the Siberian countryside in contrast to European Russia. In the early months of their reign, the Bolsheviks bought themselves valuable time to consolidate their seat of power by redirecting the peasantry's animosity away from themselves and towards the landed gentry and *kulaks*. Such class warfare, however, was harder to stir in the villages of Siberia, where the self-reliant pioneer spirit prevailed and no class of great landowners existed. The living conditions of the Siberian peasants were typically much better than the squalor familiar to their counterparts on the opposite side of the Urals, and they also tended larger herds of livestock and utilized more modern implements in their agricultural operations. More than a few of them could have fit any of the broad interpretations of the *kulak* label. Aside from their language and religion, about the only quality which the Siberian peasants shared with the peasantry of European Russia was their support of the Socialist Revolutionary Party.[12]

Although Siberia did not possess the extreme social stratification of European Russia, it would be wrong to suggest that its population lived in blissful harmony. The countryside was filled with disputes between new and established settlers, peasants and Cossacks, and Great Russian nationalists and Siberian autonomists. All of these festering troubles bubbled to the surface at one time or another during the revolutionary turmoil of 1917, especially the issue of Siberian separatism. This movement, known as Siberian regionalism, was similar in character to the nationalist movements among non–Russian peoples in the borderlands that sought autonomy or independence from the central government. Unlike the national minorities, however, the Siberian regionalists were mostly ethnic Russians who wanted to end the colonial exploitation of their adopted homeland and liberate themselves from often corrupt tsarist administrators. Even though their regionalism failed to attract the same level of broad devotion that nationalism attained in the borderlands, the Siberian separatists showed considerable determination to establish some sort of self-government. In early August 1917, a conference of Siberian regionalists resolved to convene an All-Siberian Regional Duma, or Sibobduma. The SRs polled extremely well among Siberian ballots later that year and it was they who held the majority on the Sibobduma when it was slated to meet in Tomsk in late January 1918. But by then that city, like others in Siberia, had fallen under control of Bolshevik-dominated soviets. Many Sibobduma delegates were arrested or forced to flee by Red Guards when they arrived in Tomsk though a few dozen delegates did manage to convene secretly on the night of 27–28 January. After forming a body called the Provisional Government of Autonomous Siberia, the members of this shadow government took the first train out of Tomsk for self-imposed exile in Manchuria. In their wake they left behind only a few figures to organize an underground resistance to Bolshevik rule in the region.

Despite the absence of a strong urban working class in Siberia, the Bolsheviks met little resistance when they took control of cities and towns there in the winter of 1917–18. The only exception was in Irkutsk, where the Red Guards had to seize the local institutions through violent street fighting.[13] By the time Czecho-Slovak trains began rolling into Siberia in April, the only significant areas of overt resistance in the vast region was in the southern Urals, where the Cossacks were waging a guerrilla war against the Red Guards, and along the border with Manchuria in Eastern Siberia. The Chinese Eastern Railway zone and its administrative seat, Harbin, had become a haven for anti–Bolshevik resistance after Chinese troops had disarmed and deported the Bolshevized Russian garrisons along the railway.[14] Located on foreign soil and known for its late-night cabarets, Harbin was an unlikely center for men seeking the regeneration of Holy Russia.[15] Indeed, upright Russian patriots, such as Admiral Aleksandr Kolchak, were disheartened when they converged on the city only to learn that the anti–Bolsheviks there were more interested in opium trafficking than orchestrating a military campaign against the Soviet Republic.[16] The anti–Bolsheviks there were also badly divided among their loyalties. Among the prominent figures who attracted various amounts of support was the Russian administrator of the Chinese Eastern Railway, General Dmitry Horvath; the head of the Provisional Government of Autonomous Siberia, Pyotr Derber; and a swashbuckling Cossack commander, Grigory Semenov, whose name was to become synonymous with terror in Eastern Siberia during the next two and a half years.

Although Semenov's detachment was only one of several private armies organized in the region by anti–Bolsheviks, it was virtually alone in its willingness to actually engage Soviet forces. His band was a heterogeneous mix of Transbaikal Cossacks, Mongols, Buryats and Serbian deserters, all amounting to less than 600 men. Semenov's operations, though failing in their objective to liberate the Transbaikal Province from Bolshevik rule, did succeed in attracting support in the form of funds and supplies from the British, French and Japanese. The bitter fighting between Semenov's troops and a much larger force of Red Guards under the command of a young ensign, Sergey Lazo, in the spring of 1918 rendered the Chinese Eastern Railway impassable after the latter, in order to stall the attacking *semenovtsy*, had blown up the railway bridge over the Onon River.[17] For the eastbound Czecho-Slovaks, these

A destroyed bridge over the Onon River, undated. The infrastructure of the Trans-Siberian Railway sustained heavy damage during the Russian Civil War.

operations forced their trains to take the long detour via the Amur line, adding 350 miles to their already protracted journey to reach Vladivostok.

While open resistance to Bolshevik rule in Siberia was confined to a few distant locales, underground anti–Bolshevik organizations were being organized in nearly all of the region's main centers by the spring of 1918. The SRs, by making common cause with ex-tsarist officers, led this conspiracy as they sought to form a resistance that would prepare for the eventual return of the Provisional Government of Autonomous Siberia. By the end of May, when the Czecho-Slovak trains were sitting paralyzed along the Trans-Siberian Railway, this organization may have possessed as many as 7,000 members installed in various Western and Central Siberian towns and cities. Colonel Grishin-Almazov, Gajda's host at Novonikolaevsk, was one of the leading conspirators in this resistance. Initially, the officers and their SR allies planned to stage an uprising against the Soviet regime at some point well in the future, but the arrival of the Czecho-Slovaks into the region during April and May, and the ensuing tensions between the legionaries and Bolsheviks, presented them with a unique opportunity that was too lucrative to pass up. As a result, representatives of the White underground immediately made contact with the Czecho-Slovak officers in the hope of enlisting their help in an insurrection against Bolshevik rule in Siberia.[18]

Although the diversion of the First Czecho-Slovak Division to the northern ports had been agreed to by the Allies, the Soviet government and most recently the National Council, not single train of legionaries headed northward. The National Council had given its consent to the plan on 15 May and the Legion's command quickly drafted a schedule for the first

Czecho-Slovak trains to embark on the new route a week later. In the meantime, news of the scuffle at Chelyabinsk became known in Moscow and other parts of Russia, causing the standoff between the Czecho-Slovaks and the Bolsheviks to intensify rather than diminish.[19]

The Chelyabinsk incident on 14 May, it will be recalled, pitted a group of Czecho-Slovak legionaries against Magyar POWs at the city's train station and left one man from the latter group dead. Three days later, the refusal of the Chelyabinsk Soviet to release eleven Czecho-Slovaks cooperating with the probe into the incident ignited outrage among the legionaries. That evening nearly 3,000 Czecho-Slovaks, many lacking rifles, marched on Chelyabinsk, seized the city armory, disarmed the stunned Red Guards and compelled the local soviet to free their wrongly-imprisoned comrades. Once these men were released, the legionaries evacuated the town and returned to their trains just a few miles away. In the meantime, the Chelyabinsk commissars were left dazed by the ease with which the Czecho-Slovaks had briefly seized the town. From that point on they sought to appease the legionaries and facilitate their travel eastward, but reports of the incident provoked quite a different response from the War Commissariat in Moscow.

News of the event first reached the Soviet capital on the same night the legionaries made their demonstration in Chelyabinsk and a more detailed report followed a day or two later. The latter was quite revealing of the new attitude prevailing in the Chelyabinsk Soviet towards the Czecho-Slovaks, as the local chairman stressed in his telegram the necessity of allowing the Legion to continue its evacuation to Vladivostok since anything else might

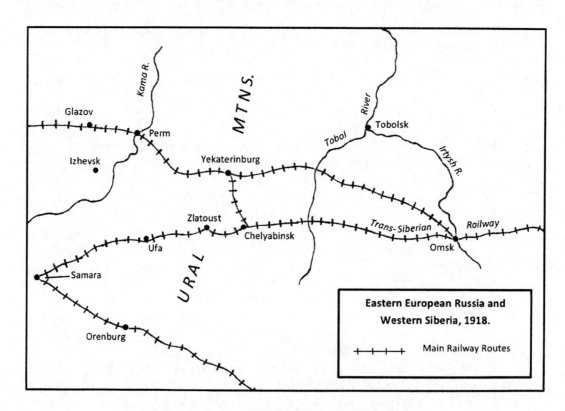

Eastern European Russia and Western Siberia in 1918.

"provoke a powerful rebellion."[20] The brazen Trotsky, however, was not so easily intimidated, nor was he inclined to let such a serious affront to the sovereignty of the Soviet regime go unpunished. Ignoring the advice in the report from Chelyabinsk, the Commissar of War undertook his own drastic measures on the night of 20–21 May by ordering the Cheka to round up and imprison all representatives and employees of the Czecho-Slovak National Council in Moscow. Among the detainees were Maxa and Čermak, who were told that their arrest was the result of hostile actions against the Soviet Republic committed by the legionaries at Chelyabinsk. They were promised their release only when the legionaries submitted to complete disarmament. Shortly after their imprisonment, the two leaders from the National Council were visited by a pair of Czecho-Slovak Communist commissars. The latter presented the captives with an order to the troops, to be issued in the name of the Czecho-Slovak National Council in Russia, instructing them to surrender their arms and accept the protection of the Soviet government. The commissars, of course, wanted Maxa and Čermak to sign the order so that it would appear to represent the authentic intentions of the National Council.[21]

Initially, Maxa refused to endorse the document and demanded to know the intentions of the Soviet leaders. His captors then proceeded to inform him of events at Chelyabinsk— exaggerating some details and omitting others to make the legionaries appear solely responsible for the provocation—and then threatened him with court-martial and possible execution. Maxa, not knowing the true version of the Chelyabinsk incident, quickly broke down under this threat and signed the order placed before him by the Czecho-Slovak Communists. Displaying no more personal courage than his colleague, Čermak followed by affixing his signature to the document.[22] This order, which might have had disastrous consequences for the Czecho-Slovak Legion if it were obeyed, was destined to fail in its objectives since a new set of occurrences that they had overlooked was taking place in Chelyabinsk.

On 20 May, just three days after the Czecho-Slovak troops had staged their dramatic march on Chelyabinsk, the Congress of the Czecho-Slovak Army Corps in Russia, consisting of 123 soldier delegates and a four-man deputation from the National Council, arrived into full plenary session inside the dining hall of the Chelyabinsk train station. It was comprised mainly of delegates from First Division but also included some from Second Division whose trains were still west of Irkutsk. Earlier, in their preliminary consultations, the delegates had discussed the project of sending the First Division to the northern ports. It was not much of a debate as the revision found no favor among the gathered representatives and it was quickly voted down.[23]

This decision represented a distinct challenge to the National Council deputation headed by Bohdan Pavlů, who had recently published a series of newspaper articles advocating the project to send the First Division to North Russia.[24] He and his three colleagues at the congress were supposed to ensure that the assembly agreed to the partial evacuation through Archangelsk, but they quickly perceived the impossibility of this task in light of the soldiers' mood. A Moravian of Slovak ethnicity and a one-time supporter of Kramář's Neo-Slavism, Pavlů was most concerned with preserving for himself some vestige of leadership in the movement.[25, 26] He understood that the National Council in Russia no longer held the confidence of the soldiers and that they were on the verge of forming a new committee that was to more aggressively open the route to Vladivostok by issuing ultimatums to the local soviets. Any soviets that resisted the demand were to be subject to armed action by the legionaries. Hence, when Pavlů spoke on the afternoon of 20 May, he did little to dissuade the congress from forming a new committee of leaders. Nor did he make any attempt to defend the project of diverting part of the corps to the northern ports. His only request was that the new council, which was to be known as the Provisional Executive Committee, would include himself and the three National Council representatives at the conference to give the organization a sense of political continuity.

· The soldier delegates, having expected the head of the National Council's delegation to condemn their defiance of that organization, were impressed by Pavlů's deference and cautiously accepted most of his proposals. They decided to allow the four National Council members present at the congress to join the Provisional Executive Committee, but for the time being they were to be denied voting privileges. Aside from them, the new committee was to include four elected congressional delegates and three regimental commanders. This latter group was to form a military council that would prepare operational plans in case large-scale military action was needed. The men elected into these three crucial posts were Lieutenant Colonel Voitsekhovsky, Lieutenant Čeček and Captain Gajda, commanders of the 3rd, 4th and 7th Regiments respectively. Through their repudiation of the authority of the Russian branch of the National Council in favor of their own Provisional Executive Committee, the Czecho-Slovak congress had effectively staged a revolution within a revolution. The delegates and the troops they represented, however, remained loyal to the Allied cause, Masaryk and even the National Council in Paris. Their mutiny, which is perhaps an excessively violent term to describe the orderly proceedings of the congress, was directed only against Maxa and his colleagues, who they felt were placing the corps at the mercy of Soviet and even German intrigues. Many legionaries still refused to believe that the order to split the corps between North Russia and Siberia originated with the Allies.

After the Provisional Executive Committee had been formed, commissars from the Chelyabinsk Soviet addressed the congress in an effort to resolve the impasse between the Czecho-Slovaks and the Bolsheviks. They subsequently wired a proposal to Moscow for peaceful resolution between the two sides, but any chance of success that their plan might have had was lost when on 23 May Pavlů revealed to the congress the receipt of the orders, signed by Maxa and Čermak, for the complete disarmament of the corps.[27]

With the National Council already stripped of its authority as far as the congress was concerned, the soldiers did not even consider obeying the telegram from Maxa. After a short debate, the Provisional Executive Committee was authorized to respond to the new orders with a telegram of its own that was sent all over Russia; the recipients included local soviets and Czecho-Slovak units scattered along the Trans-Siberian Railway, the Omsk headquarters of the Czecho-Slovak National Council in Russia, the Soviet government in Moscow and even the diplomatic community in faraway Vologda. It informed them of the congress's decision to yield no more arms, the formation of a new leadership in the form of a Provisional Executive Committee and its disavowal of the authority exercised by other Czecho-Slovak organizations, including the Russian branch of the National Council. After protesting the frequent obstructions of the Czecho-Slovak trains, the telegram closed with the ominous statement that "our hope for a peaceful settlement of this complicated situation is enhanced by the fact that any conflict would injure the position of local Soviet authorities in Siberia." In the upbeat atmosphere inside the dining hall at the Chelyabinsk train station, Pavlů noted that this daring proclamation was made even more stupendous by the fact that it was released on the tercentenary of the infamous Defenestration of Prague which had inaugurated the first Bohemian rebellion against the Habsburgs.[28]

While the congressional resolutions were being drafted, the three members of the military council of the Provisional Executive Committee busied themselves with formulating a plan in the event armed action was required to break through to Vladivostok. Their deliberations produced only a broad course of action and realistically this was all the three commanders could have hoped for. Čeček's group, centered on Penza, was separated from Voitsekhovsky's men in Chelyabinsk by 850 miles, and a slightly longer distance stood between the latter and Gajda's position at Novonikolaevsk. These distances meant that the three main groups could expect little support from each other, at least initially. They agreed that locally-based, largely improvised plans of action would be required if hostilities erupted along the railway. On the evening of the eventful 23 May, the commanders and delegates whose echelons were on the eastern and western flanks began boarding trains to return to their units. By the following afternoon, only Voitsekhovsky and a rump congress of delegates whose units were relatively nearby remained at the Chelyabinsk train station.[29]

While the Provisional Executive Committee debated its next course of action at Chelyabinsk, the Soviet government, as the legionaries suspected, was taking its own steps towards a final showdown against the Czecho-Slovaks. On 21 May, the same day that the fraudulent order from the incarcerated Maxa was released, the Commissariat of War cabled the soviets along the Trans-Siberian Railway from the Volga to Lake Baikal to approach the legionaries with invitations for "the men to organize themselves into labour battalions or else join the Red Army."[30] This telegram was issued under the expectation that the Czecho-Slovaks would voluntary disarm upon their receipt of the order signed by Maxa. It is compelling evidence that Trotsky was not inclined to allow the corps to complete an unmolested withdrawal to the ports even had legionaries laid down their rifles.

Two days later, the local soviets received another telegram from Moscow reiterating the previous orders in addition to instructions that the Czecho-Slovak formations "must be dissolved as a remnant of the old regular army."[31] It did not reveal why, after more than two months, the Bolsheviks were suddenly demanding that Article 5 of the Brest-Litovsk Treaty be rigidly observed.[32] Most likely, it was a convenient excuse for Trotsky to justify his orders to disarm the Legion. Regardless, the local soviets were much less eager than the War Commissar to confront the legionaries. The Chelyabinsk Soviet, in fact, did quite the opposite and began releasing Czecho-Slovak trains towards Omsk on the same day this order was issued.[33]

Not all soviets were as intimidated by the legionaries as was the Chelyabinsk Soviet. The district of the West Siberian Soviet, based in Omsk, was home to the largest concentration of POWs in all of Siberia and had assembled a force of Internationalists that by the end of April had an estimated strength of a few thousand. Confident of their strength, on 25 May the Omsk Bolsheviks sent a detachment of 300 men to intercept two approaching Czecho-Slovak trains at Kulomsino, a station just west of Omsk across the Irtysh River. At about midday, the lead legionary train, with the commander of the 6th Czecho-Slovak Regiment, Captain O. Hanuš, and his staff aboard, approached Kulomsino. From a distance, Hanuš noticed suspicious activity around the station, alerted his men and ordered his train personnel to leave the boilers in the locomotive running even while they were stopped. When the train ground to a halt before the station, the Bolshevik commander met Hanuš and demanded that he turn over the remainder of his arms—which amounted to only 120 rifles. When the Czecho-Slovak commander refused, the Red troops attempted to surround the train, but Hanuš thwarted their action by ordering the operators to throw the locomotive in reverse. In doing so, the Czecho-Slovak train escaped entrapment and managed to slip away.[34]

The lead train, after encountering the second train behind it, retreated about 25 miles to Marianovka, where the legionaries intended to wait for further trains from Chelyabinsk to reinforce their numbers and then resume their advance. However, even before the second train reached the station, lookouts spotted two westbound troop trains charging along the railway towards them. These trains, consisting of the Kulomsino expedition along with additional reinforcements from Omsk, pursued the legionaries to Marianovka. As the legionaries on the first train to return there were exiting their railcars, they watched as the other Czecho-Slovak train slowed down and then their cadres began leaping out of the sides of the moving boxcars. When they realized that they were being chased by a Bolshevik train, they joined their fellow legionaries on either side of the track. The rapid deployment of the Czecho-Slovaks forced the Bolsheviks to either fight from their railcars or face a hail of bullets upon leaving them. As one Bolshevik survivor later recounted, the Czecho-Slovaks did not allow "the Red Guardsmen a chance to fall in line" and instead "turned them into targets."[35] During the ensuing battle, the second Bolshevik train held cautiously back, its only contributions to the fight being two salvos fired from a railcar-mounted field gun before withdrawing completely. After exchanging gunfire for a little more than a half-hour, the surviving Red troops trapped in the first train finally gave themselves up. In this first engagement between Bolshevik armed forces and the Czecho-Slovak Legion, the latter emerged victorious at a cost of eighteen dead and fifteen wounded. They had inflicted 250 deaths on the enemy, and 130 Bolsheviks had surrendered. After reviewing the captives and the enemy dead, the Czecho-Slovaks learned that most were Internationalists of Magyar ethnicity.[36] This discovery reinforced their fear that a conspiracy between the Central Powers and the Bolsheviks was afoot.

Unaware of the shootout between legionaries and Red troops at Marianovka, the Provisional Executive Committee that same day made one last overture to Trotsky asking that the corps to be allowed to proceed to Vladivostok.[37] The Commissar of War, however, refused to yield in his demand for the Czecho-Slovaks' complete submission to the Soviet government. He became even brasher later that evening when he learned that the Chelyabinsk Soviet was still defying his previous orders by releasing Czecho-Slovak trains toward Omsk. Late that night, he fired off another telegram exhorting the local soviets to take aggressive action against the legionaries, noting that their failure to obey the new orders would constitute treason against the Soviet regime and warrant extreme penalties:

> All Soviets are hereby ordered to disarm the Czechoslovaks immediately. Every armed Czechoslovak found on the railway is to be shot on the spot; every troop train in which even one armed man is found shall be unloaded, and its soldiers shall be interned in a war prisoners' camp. Local commissars must proceed at once to carry out this order; every delay will be considered treason and will bring the offender severe punishment.[38]

By this telegram, which was sent in the final hours of 25 May, Trotsky made it apparent that, as far as Moscow was concerned, the Czecho-Slovaks were to be regarded as enemies of the Soviet regime. Given the weak state of the fledgling Red Army at the time, it was a daring if not reckless gamble that should have been taken only when all other options were exhausted. The Bolsheviks were still dependent on the Latvian Rifle Division for the toughest military assignments, but these troops were overstretched throughout Soviet Russia. The Internationalist battalions appear to have been fighters of mixed quality, perhaps depending on how dedicated they were to the world revolution, while the Red Guard volunteers were often next to useless outside their home districts. During the previous month the Soviet government had ordered compulsory military training for all male peasants, students and workers between the ages of eighteen and forty but by the end of May these conscripts would, at most, be only half finished with their intended eight weeks of training.[39]

Despite Trotsky's tough words to the local commissars along the legionaries' route, the situation remained eerily calm along most of the Trans-Siberian Railway into the following day. The Chelyabinsk Soviet adhered to its policy of cooperation with the Czecho-Slovaks while the Omsk Soviet, shaken by the loss of its armed expedition a day earlier, offered unmolested passage to Hanuš's trains, which the Czecho-Slovak commander cautiously accepted. While the peaceful intentions of the Chelyabinsk Soviet were apparently sincere, the Omsk Soviet was merely playing for time; its commissars embarked on a frenzied campaign to recruit as many soldiers from the local POW camps as possible in preparation for another showdown with the legionaries.[40]

Even as tranquility returned to the rails around Omsk, a new round of hostilities broke out far to the east of that city, and in this instance it was the Czecho-Slovaks who struck first. When Captain Gajda returned to Novonikolaevsk on 25 May, he immediately informed his officers of the resolutions adopted by the congress in Chelyabinsk and concluded that, in his opinion, hostilities with the Bolsheviks was the only viable means to open the route to Vladivostok. In other words, Gajda, who could not know of the fighting which took place that day at Marianovka, was not willing to wait to see whether or not the Provisional Executive Committee's plan to issue ultimatums would compel the soviets into compliance. At two o'clock that afternoon, Gajda sent a ciphered telegram to Captain Kadlec, at Mariinsk, to seize the station there. Kadlec obeyed and his men occupied the depot so quickly that the Bolshevik telegraph operators did not have enough time to send out a message of distress. Nearby Red garrisons had no idea that something out of the ordinary had occurred at Mariinsk.

While planning his own coup at Novonikolaevsk, Gajda ignored another stipulation

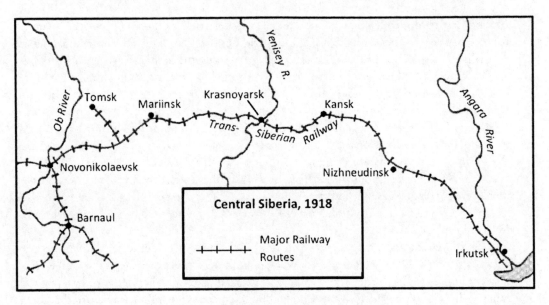

Central Siberia in 1918.

imposed by the Provisional Executive Committee. At the congress, the Czecho-Slovaks had agreed not to interfere in Russian domestic politics. If a shooting war occurred between them and the Bolsheviks, they would only attack the Red forces and stop short of over-throwing the soviets. At Novonikolaevsk, however, Gajda apparently had no intention of leaving even an emasculated Bolshevik authority in control of the city. It is true that a dis-armed soviet probably could not have survived the pressure from the local anti–Bolshevik underground for very long, but Gajda's actions put the Czecho-Slovaks squarely on the side of the Whites. After issuing his orders to Kadlec, he paid a visit to Colonel Grishin-Almazov, from which it seems reasonable to assume that he forewarned the resistance leader of his impending operation against the local Bolsheviks. Gajda's intentions were probably suspected by the local soviet, which remained in session unusually late into that night. If so, it was the start of a pattern that would turn up in the extroverted Czech captain's later political adven-tures in Russia and interwar Czechoslovakia: the utter inability to adequately conceal a plot from outsiders and even opponents.[41]

The Czecho-Slovak seizure of Novonikolaevsk, which began with a signal flare in the early morning hours of May 26, occurred almost effortlessly. The railroad station was the first building occupied followed by strategic points within the city itself. The local Red militia frequently laid down their arms without firing a shot while White volunteers, donning green and white armbands representing the forests and snows of Siberia, quickly occupied their posts. In less than an hour, soviet power in Novonikolaevsk was swept away and replaced by a city duma. By the next morning, Grishin-Almazov was preparing to set up a Siberian regional government in the anticipation that the events in Novonikolaevsk were a precursor to the overthrow of Bolshevism throughout all of Siberia. Four days later, the West Siberian Committee, an offshoot of the Provisional Government of Autonomous Siberia, was pro-claimed as the new authority at Novonikolaevsk.[42]

Within hours of dismantling soviet power from the city, Gajda issued a declaration to the citizens of Novonikolaevsk assuring them that the Czecho-Slovaks "do not wish to inter-fere in internal affairs of Russia," but many fielded doubts of his sincerity to uphold this vow, particularly his colleagues in Chelyabinsk.[43] When the Provisional Executive Commit-tee received reports indicating that Gajda's operations had delved into the political arena, it immediately dispatched instructions via courier to remind the firebrand officer that the Bol-sheviks were only to be neutralized as a military threat. The position of the Provisional Exec-utive Committee, though understandable, was quite unrealistic. They naively believed that they could battle Red forces without actually taking sides in the civil war, and this was perhaps one of the great miscalculations of the Czecho-Slovaks at Chelyabinsk. In only a matter of days, the Provisional Executive Committee would quickly realize this and reverse their own position to advocate alliances with anti–Bolshevik Russians. Although militarily weak, the White auxiliaries still managed to provide the legionaries with valuable services in espionage, reconnaissance and policing towns behind the new fronts. They were also assigned to guard German and Magyar POWs who were rounded up by the legionaries and returned to the camps.[44]

By 26 May, both Trotsky and Gajda had decided upon hostilities to break the stalemate between their two sides. Yet, despite the War Commissar's verbal prodding of the local soviets into detaining the legionaries and Gajda's operations in Central Siberia, the situation along most of the Trans-Siberian Railway, though tense, remained quiet. The soviets in the Volga region, including Penza, were preoccupied at the time with a series of mutinies that erupted among Red garrisons in Samara and Saratov; as a result they were in no way prepared to deal with the legionaries.[45] When the Penza Soviet cabled the War Commissar that it could not possibly carry out his instructions, Trotsky sent the following unbending reply later that day: "Comrades! Military orders ... should not be discussed but obeyed. Any representative of the War Commissariat who is so cowardly as to evade disarming the Czechoslovaks will be brought by me before the Military Tribunal. It is your duty to act immediately and energetically."[46]

Despite this sinister message, the Penza Bolsheviks continued to negotiate with the Czecho-Slovaks through 27 May in an effort to conclude a peaceful although localized agreement.[47] In Chelyabinsk, the Provisional Executive Committee and the city soviet remained on speaking terms as of 26 May even though the latter was being pressured by the Yekaterinburg and Omsk Soviets to attack the legionaries.[48] In distant Vladivostok, the tensions and suspicions which prevailed in the Siberian interior were completely absent. Some 14,000 legionaries were in the vicinity of the port, the first of them having arrived at the end of April, precisely a month after leaving Penza.[49] They were upbeat at having completed the transcontinental stretch of their journey, but they may also have been disappointed that there were no Allied transports waiting for them in the harbor.[50] The soviet in control of the port was dominated by Bolsheviks whose moderation was encouraged by the Allied cruisers tottering in the waters just off their shore.[51] Although the British and Japanese detachments that had landed in the city in early April were gone, the possibility of their return was never far away. Another important difference between the situation in Vladivostok and that in Western and Central Siberia was that in the former the local Czecho-Slovak National Council, headed by Václav Girsa, continued to exercise political authority over Czecho-Slovak affairs. Girsa had arrived in the port on the leading Czecho-Slovak train, and although that train had experienced difficulty in bargaining their passage with local soviets along the route, he and his colleagues remained confident that the entire corps could reach Vladivostok without resorting to arms.[52]

Despite Girsa's confidence in peace, during the day of 26 May fighting between the legionaries and Bolsheviks flared up in a new sector of the railway, this time just outside of Irkutsk. From its beginnings in 1652 as a small Cossack outpost along the Angara River some forty miles from Lake Baikal, Irkutsk had grown into the most important Siberian city between Omsk and Vladivostok by the early twentieth century.[53] It was also one of the most strategic points as far as the railway was concerned since it stood relatively close to the Circumbaikal sector, where the railway tunneled through the mountainous southern rim of the lake. The tunnels represented a fragile section of the railway that could be easily destroyed with explosives. The devastation of one or more of them could take months or even years to repair, of course snarling railway traffic in the meantime. Knowing this, the Bolsheviks made certain that an adequate inventory of dynamite was stocked in the arsenal at Irkutsk. If Japan or another foreign power invaded from the east, they would blow the tunnels and halt the enemy's progress into the heart of Siberia.[54]

The significance of Irkutsk and its nearby tunnels was far from the minds of the 600 legionaries from the First Czecho-Slovak Division, 2nd Artillery Brigade as their train steamed into Innokentievskaya station, west of Irkutsk. There they received permission from the stationmaster to proceed several miles to Glaskovo station which was directly across the Angara River from Irkutsk. When their train arrived to screeching halt at that station, they were greeted by a Bolshevik commissar who politely asked them to surrender whatever arms they had left. The Czech commander refused by explaining that his artillery troops had already turned over their field guns and that their remaining weaponry consisted of only sixteen rifles. After hearing this response, the commissar quietly disappeared into the dark station building adjacent to the train. Seconds later, witnesses claimed to have heard the command "*Fuerer!*" and machine guns inside the building began spewing bullets from the station's windows into the legionaries' train. The Czecho-Slovaks, lacking sufficient weapons to return fire, rushed into the structure and engaged the Bolshevik machine gunners in a hand-to-hand melee. Once again, the legionaries emerged victorious, though fifteen of their men were killed and twice as many wounded in the ambush. The Bolsheviks, with many Internationalists among them, suffered ten dead and the entire garrison was rounded up. This left Glaskovo station, the main railway terminal for Irkutsk, entirely in Czecho-Slovak hands.

After capturing Glaskovo, the artillery brigade sent a courier to Batternaya station, west of Innokentievskaya, to make contact with two legionary trains there and ask them to reinforce the Czecho-Slovak position outside Irkutsk. After receiving this message, the two trains totaling about 1,000 men disarmed the Red troops at Batternaya station and began chugging eastward. Along the way, they seized Innokentievskaya station, where they decided to stay the night before continuing onward to Glaskovo. Around midnight, a firefight broke out at Innokentievskaya between the Czecho-Slovaks and Austro-Hungarian and German POWs from a nearby camp. Accounts vary as to which side initiated the fighting; some claim the legionaries were ambushed while others accuse them of provoking hostilities by assaulting the POW camp. Regardless, all records agree that once again the legionaries prevailed in a brief battle.

At dawn, just as these legionaries were preparing to push onward to join the 2nd Artillery Brigade at Glaskovo, they spotted several men approaching from the east with a white flag fluttering above their heads. During the night, while the Czecho-Slovaks were exchanging fire with the POWs at Innokentievskaya, the Tsentrosibir, having had its confidence shaken by the loss at Glaskovo, began seeking a diplomatic solution to the predicament which it had largely foisted upon itself. It sent its chairman and another deputy to summon the American Consul General, Ernest L. Harris, and his French counterpart, Gaston Bourgeois. Though they were reluctant at first to entangle themselves in the unfolding skirmish, Harris and Bourgeois eventually agreed to help the Bolsheviks mediate a truce between them and the Czecho-Slovaks. Along with Harris's assistant, Consul David Macgowan, the five men set out that morning and made contact with the Czecho-Slovaks at Innokentievskaya, where they began discussing the situation in the railcar of the Czech commander, Captain Hoblík.

The American and French officials at Irkutsk, like their countries' ambassadors, attachés and other representatives in Russia, had virtually no idea what their governments' attitude was towards either party. While they understood that the Czecho-Slovaks were regarded as an Allied army, most also thought that their governments desired to maintain proper, if not friendly, relations with the Soviet regime in the hope that it might yet turn against Germany. Thus in their judgment and actions, which were largely intuitive, they sought to defuse the hostilities without showing too much preference to either side. This is what Harris and Bourgeois did at Innokentievskaya. As they listened to Captain Hoblík's version of events, they found his story plausible and verified that he had indeed been opposed by a mixed force of Austro-Hungarian POW and Russian combatants by viewing the uniforms of the dead and captured men. But since they believed that a continuation of the fighting would be counterproductive towards the goal of evacuating the Czecho-Slovaks from Russia, they dissuaded Hoblík from assisting the 2nd Artillery Brigade by marching on Irkutsk. Reluctantly, the Czech commander also agreed to turn over most of his men's arms in exchange from a new guarantee underwritten by the American, French and soviet officials in Irkutsk that would grant the three Czecho-Slovak trains unmolested passage to Vladivostok. That evening, with their arms reduced to thirty rifles per train, the Czecho-Slovak trains departed from Glaskovo with four additional passengers, three Bolshevik commissars and Consul Macgowan, who were to ensure their safe and unhindered transit to the coast. These trains did eventually complete the journey to Vladivostok without encountering any significant obstacles; however, they would be the last Czecho-Slovak trains to do so that summer.[55]

The local settlement between the Czecho-Slovaks and Bolsheviks at Irkutsk was more significant than either side, particularly the former, realized at the time. Had the 1,600 legionaries continued to proceed with their operations against the Irkutsk Bolsheviks, they probably would have succeeded in taking control of the city and might have neutralized the threat to the tunnels in the Circumbaikal sector of the railway. But because of the mediation conducted by the Harris and Bourgeois, the Tsentrosibir, like the Western Siberian Soviet in Omsk, obtained a new lease on life that it would use to recruit troops and prepare for another confrontation with the legionaries. Moreover, Bolshevik control of Irkutsk and the critical tunnels for the next several weeks would factor significantly in the U.S. and Allied decision to intervene in Siberia.[56]

Harris, at the encouragement of the Irkutsk Bolsheviks, soon proceeded along the railway west of Irkutsk to apply his mediation skills in other sectors contested between the legionaries and Red forces. Ignorant of the confrontational policies espoused by the War Commissariat in Moscow and the Provisional Executive Committee in Chelyabinsk, he and other Allied representatives who inserted themselves into the frays believed that the battles were the result of local misunderstandings and not a concerted effort by either to deny the other a presence along the Trans-Siberian Railway.[57] But even as he worked to maintain peace in Central Siberia, hostilities erupted at other points further to the west.

In the closing days of May, the commissars of the Chelyabinsk Soviet were facing an unavoidable dilemma. In their midst were a couple of thousand legionaries who a fortnight earlier had demonstrated the ease with which they could seize control of the town if they chose to do so. Their desire to appease the Czecho-Slovaks, however, was not acceptable to the less-grounded Bolsheviks in distant Moscow or even in neighboring Yekaterinburg or Omsk. Yekaterinburg, with an abundance of mines and foundries in its district, was known as a Red stronghold in the Urals. Its soviet was already actively trying to stiffen the resolve of its Chelyabinsk comrades through telegram exchanges, and on 26 May Czecho-Slovak intelligence operatives had intercepted a cable from the Yekaterinburg Soviet promising troops to Chelyabinsk for operations against the legionaries. A copy of this telegram was presented to the commander of the local Czecho-Slovak forces, Lieutenant Colonel Voitsekhovsky, who immediately decided to take military action before dawn on the following day. His plan proceeded without a hitch; the bulk of Red troops were caught dozing in their barracks while the few sentries readily gave themselves up. Indeed, most Chelyabinsk residents awoke the next morning without realizing anything significant had occurred until the Czecho-Slovaks began posting placards explaining their decision to disarm the local Red garrison.[58]

Although himself a Russian with strong anti–Bolshevik sympathies, as evidenced by his later career with the Siberian Whites, Voitsekhovsky was a responsible soldier who, unlike Gajda, obeyed the Provisional Executive Committee's original decision not to directly depose the local soviets. In Chelyabinsk, cooperation between the Czecho-Slovaks and the local soviet continued until the legionaries were unable to ignore their suspicions that the Bolsheviks were double-dealing with neighboring soviets behind their back. On 1 June the Chelyabinsk Soviet ceased to exist, three days after the Provisional Executive Committee announced its new policy to openly support the emerging anti–Bolshevik Russian organizations.[59]

The decision to openly coordinate the legionaries' campaign with White Russians was a significant development for the most westerly Czecho-Slovak units under the command of Lieutenant Čeček. Not only were these legionaries the most exposed owing to their position in the Russian heartland, they would also find themselves in the midst of one of the most progressive anti–Bolshevik groups to emerge in the course of the civil war. It was perhaps due to the difficulties of their position why the legionaries around Penza entered into hostilities less impulsively than Gajda at Novonikolaevsk and more methodically than Voitsekhovsky's troops at Chelyabinsk.[60]

Negotiations for a settlement between the Bolsheviks and Czecho-Slovaks in Penza continued into 27 May even though by then fighting was already underway between their cadres in the Urals and Central Siberia. Each side had their own reasons for carrying on the talks. The Penza Soviet had few troops available to use in operations against the Bolsheviks since earlier it had sent its militia into other districts to assist in the suppression of local anti–Bolshevik insurrections. The Czecho-Slovaks, meanwhile, hoped to exploit the Penza Soviet's vulnerability by attaining its permission for their departure to the east and thereby avoid military action altogether. Ultimately, the two sides succeeded in reaching only a temporary bargain whereby both sides would desist from escalating their forces in the vicinity of the city. Tensions remained high, however, and the Bolsheviks busied themselves by barricading streets and setting up machine gun nests during the uneasy truce.

This peace began to falter on the next morning when a train rolled into Penza station overflowing with Red soldiers and military equipment, including three armored cars. Before the passengers and materiel could be unloaded, alert legionaries from the 1st Czecho-Slovak Regiment quickly surrounded the train and seized its contents. Despite the outrage which this action sparked from the Penza commissars, Lieutenant Josef Švec, the local Czech commander in Čeček's absence, refused to back down. The soviet responded by calling all of the city's workers to arms while the legionaries put the train station firmly under their control and encircled Penza by mid-afternoon. For the next several hours, both sides waited to see what the other would do and hoped that they might receive reinforcements from elsewhere. The legionaries had about 2,300 men in the immediate outskirts of Penza when this operation began and they were expecting reinforcements from 4th Regiment, which was west of Penza and had not yet been disarmed. Against them was a collage of war prisoners and Russian nationals swept into the Red forces, including several hundred Internationalists, a few Latvian Riflemen, a mob of hastily-organized factory workers and about 800 Czecho-Slovak Communists, altogether totaling about 3,000 bayonets. For the time being, the Reds were content to hide in their defenses and wait in the hope that their own reinforcements en route to Penza would arrive in time to give them a commanding numerical superiority, but this was not to be. At midnight, the legionaries won the race for reinforcements when the 4th Regiment began arriving and brought their total strength outside of Penza to about 3,500.[61]

An improvised Czecho-Slovak armored train, undated. This train's "armor" includes sandbags and bales of hay.

At four in the morning on 29 May the Czecho-Slovaks launched a three-pronged attack on the city. The ensuing battle lasted for eight hours, costing the legionaries 30 dead and about 100 wounded, but in the end they had prevailed. The losses for the Bolsheviks were far more severe, with perhaps ten times as many dead and most of their fighters being captured. The outlook for these prisoners taken in this battle and others to follow was grim; neither side possessed adequate resources to guard, feed, and house large numbers of captives. Most, whether they were Russian, German, Magyar or even Bolshevized Czecho-Slovaks, were sent before firing squads. Those Reds whose lives were initially spared were sometimes imprisoned on trains and then sent eastward, but their fate was often worse than a quick death. Generally, the Czecho-Slovaks were more humane to the German and Austro-Hungarian POWs who were not serving in an armed capacity. They returned most of these POWs to nearby camps where they posted their own armed guards and restricted the prisoners' movement. Despite this pardon from execution, the POWs, who had grown accustomed to nearly uninhibited freedoms in the previous months, regarded the legionaries and their White Russian allies with considerable enmity.[62] "The severity of their new regime," complained Ferenc Imrey, a Hungarian POW who was forced to return to a camp, "made me feel that I had been treated as a gentleman by the Reds and that the rule of these White 'deliverers' of the country was more heavy handed than any Tsarist or other control that had preceded it."[63]

Within a day of seizing Penza, the Czecho-Slovak trains that had been west of the city passed through it and continued eastward. The legionaries, seeing no reason at this point why they should not continue their exodus towards Vladivostok, quietly abandoned the city. To guard their rear, the Czecho-Slovaks positioned an armored train, newly captured from the Bolsheviks, in the tail of their column and tore up the tracks every few miles behind this terrestrial battleship. Their voluntarily abandonment of a strategically important city so near the heart of Soviet Russia is powerful evidence that the Czecho-Slovak uprising was not, as Soviet historians later claimed, the product of an elaborate conspiracy concocted by the Allied governments and the anti-communist movement to topple the Bolshevik regime. If this were the case, it would have been in the interest of the legionaries and Allies to retain Penza for the anti–Bolshevik cause either through the indefinite occupation of the city or by holding it until the anti–Bolshevik elements there were strong enough to defend themselves.

Instead, on 2 June, two days after the Czecho-Slovaks had departed, Red troops retook control of Penza against little resistance.[64]

Further evidence that the Czecho-Slovak military operations were not instigated by the Allies exists in the reactions of various Allied representatives to the news of the conflict between the Czecho-Slovaks and the Soviet regime. We have already seen how the American and French consuls at Irkutsk negotiated ceasefires between the warring parties, and they were not alone. When the fighting began between the legionaries and the Bolsheviks, the initial response of nearly all Allied representatives was to restore peace.

In the days leading up to the fighting, the French Military Mission in Moscow actually took the Bolsheviks' side by deciding that the legionaries should submit to Soviet demands to disarm completely. The mission's chief, General Lavergne, apparently feared that fighting between the Czecho-Slovaks and the Bolsheviks would compromise French relations with Moscow and possibly induce to the latter to openly side with Germany. To bring the brash young Czecho-Slovak officers at the Chelyabinsk army congress into line, he dispatched two French officers, Major Guinet and Captain Pascal, to make their way to Chelyabinsk. Amid their journey, the team of officers made a detour through Omsk, where they arrived on 23 May to learn that the army congress had repudiated the authority of the Russian branch of the Czecho-Slovak National Council. Along with some leaders from the National Council, they had intended to proceed on towards Chelyabinsk but were realizing that their intervention was doomed to failure. Many delegates, including Čeček and Gajda, had by then left for their units and without a reliable and quick means to communicate with the distant commanders, the decisions made earlier by the Provisional Executive Committee could not be easily reversed.[65] Even into the first days of June, Guinet and the National Council members in Omsk desperately hoped that a peaceful settlement could still be concluded along the railway. As Czecho-Slovak trains released from Chelyabinsk began amassing on the railway just to the west of Omsk, Guinet fired off orders exhorting them to submit to disarmament.[66]

In distant Vologda, about 250 miles north of the Soviet capital, the Allied ambassadors were to have even less of an impact on the course of events long the Trans-Siberian Railway than the French Military Mission in Moscow. Like their less eminent colleagues in Irkutsk and other locales, the ambassadors had virtually no instructions from their governments on how to address the complications arising between the legionaries and the Soviet government. Subsequently, they relied mainly on their own judgment, and by late May 1918, their feelings towards the Bolsheviks were hardening amid persistent rumors that Lenin and Trotsky were German peons who had betrayed Russia in the Brest-Litovsk Treaty. After some indecision, they concluded that the Czecho-Slovaks should resist disarmament. They sent instructions to this effect by courier, but the message only reached the Volga theater after fighting between the two sides was already well underway.[67]

Harris, the American Consul General at Irkutsk, also continued his efforts to restore peace along the railway throughout the first week of June. While traveling west from Irkutsk, his train caught up with that of Colonel George Emerson, the chief American engineer of the Russian Railway Service Corps, who was likely horrified by the battles raging along the very tracks whose functions he and his commission were supposed to improve. Like Harris, Emerson had interjected himself into the brewing hostilities as a mediator. On 3 June he presided over a temporary truce between the Red troops and the Czecho-Slovaks east of Mariinsk. After his train crossed the front into the sector cleared by the legionaries, however,

he was stunned to discover anti–Bolshevik Russians setting up civil and military administrations in the towns freed from Red control. Realizing that the skirmishes along the Trans-
Siberian Railway were more than mere local misunderstandings, he and Harris, after meeting
each other on 8 June at Kargat, decided that the scope of the fighting was beyond their
ability to resolve.[68]

As it dawned on the Allied representatives in Russia that war between the Czecho-
Slovaks and Bolsheviks was inevitable, they, with few exceptions, quickly abandoned their
pacifist intentions. Major Guinet, who ardently opposed the legionaries' operations at first,
did an about-face and became one of their most enthusiastic supporters. Since he was soon
cut off from the French Military Mission in Moscow, he overstepped his authority and set
up his own French military mission in Chelyabinsk. Harris too became an ardent backer of
the Czecho-Slovak legionaries and an advocate of Allied intervention in Russia and Siberia.[69]

Surprisingly, the faction that seemed most naturally inclined to support the Czecho-
Slovak campaign along the railway, the senior Russian officers in the Legion, were actually
quite slow to lend it their approval. Like the Allies, the Legion's Russian officers were unfairly
blamed by Soviet historians for instigating the Czecho-Slovak uprising; such a suspicion is
understandable given the later careers of many of the officers in the White movement. Amazingly, though, many of these officers opposed military action against the Bolsheviks either
because they were committed to their mission of conveying the corps to Vladivostok or
because they were pessimistic regarding the prospects of a military campaign. General
Kolomensky, the Russian commander of the First Czecho-Slovak Division, was an outspoken
critic of any aggressive action, and for this reason he and his Russian chief of staff were
detained by their legionaries as the two sides slid towards open hostilities around Penza.
General Diterikhs, the Legion's Chief of Staff, also opposed fighting as did most of the units
who were waiting beside him in Vladivostok.[70] Having made it to their destination on the
Pacific coast without brandishing their weapons, they could not understand why their cadres
behind them could not do the same.

As the fighting spread along the railway and White Russians rallied to their side, the
Czecho-Slovak officers and their troops began to wonder if an evacuation to Vladivostok
should remain their objective. Any alteration of this plan would of course immediately affect
the rear of the Czecho-Slovak Army Corps, which was commanded by Čeček. After leaving
Penza, the next formidable obstacle in the path of Čeček's column was the Volga city of
Samara, about 220 miles to the east. The city had a population of about 200,000 and though
it was under Bolshevik control, it had been the scene of an anarchist uprising in mid–May.
Samara's industrial workers provided, as elsewhere, the core of Bolshevik support while the
peasants in the countryside favored the SRs. The local SR presence was enhanced by the
recent arrival of a number of Right SR leaders and deputies who, after the dissolution of the
Constituent Assembly in January, vowed to use their traditional stronghold in the Volga
region as a base from which they would resist the Bolsheviks. These plans, however, suffered
a setback when the deputies returned to the region to find their once-loyal constituents
increasingly radicalized by the violence that had engulfed the countryside.[71] The situation
appeared so unfavorable that one SR leader in Samara lamented that "unless there is a spur
from the outside in the near future, then we can give up all hopes of a *coup d'etat.*"[72]

Like other anti–Bolshevik groups, the Samara SRs latched onto the legionaries as that
longed-for "spur from the outside." During the Czecho-Slovaks' brief occupation of Penza,
a SR politician from Samara, I. M. Brushvit, traveled to the city and approached Čeček for

A Czecho-Slovak train, undated. Note the spacing of the sandbags in the foreground to allow rifles to poke between them.

help in overthrowing the Bolshevik regime in Samara. Unlike Gajda, Čeček was wary of making common cause with the Russian anti–Bolsheviks. Indeed, to get the Czech commander to consent to the operation, Brushvit had to tantalize him with a highly embellished account of the extent of the anti–Bolshevik conspiracy brewing in Samara.[73] Even then, Čeček committed his legionaries to only clearing the city of Red troops and warned that they would not stay any longer than was necessary to complete that task.

On the way to Samara, Brushvit rode in Čeček's armored train and the two men remained in steady contact.[74] As the Czecho-Slovak trains rolled eastward, a Soviet plane dumped leaflets on the column containing a message from Maxa, who was still being held captive by the Bolsheviks. In these fliers, the deposed leader of the National Council in Russia implored the legionaries to quit fighting "the brotherly Russian people."[75] His plea failed to induce the Czecho-Slovaks to pause even momentarily. Before long, Čeček's 8,000 men were concentrating outside of Samara, which was defended by a motley garrison of 2,000 Reds, including Latvians and Magyar Internationalists, some of whom had just arrived in the city and were forced to fight in unfamiliar surroundings. At dawn on 8 June, after having subdued the scattered enemy detachments in the outskirts of the city on the previous day, the Czecho-Slovaks charged into the city. The defenders' resistance immediately collapsed, not only from the intensity of the Czecho-Slovak assault, but also from an unexpected revolt by an underground organization of officers inside the city which caused considerable panic and disarray among the Red defenders.[76] Within a few hours, the fight for the city

Storm battalion of the Czecho-Slovak Legion in Russia, undated. Most soldiers are wearing French Adrian helmets but one in foreground, third from right, has a German helmet.

ended as quickly as it had begun; when Čeček later recalled the battle he wrote that his units "took Samara in the same way that one grabs hay with a pitchfork."[77]

For being such a considerable prize, Samara was taken rather cheaply by the Czecho-Slovaks as they lost only six men compared to an estimated 150 enemy dead and many more captured.[78] Once the fighting was over, the middle and upper classes—pariahs under the Bolshevik regime—danced in the streets while the city's church bells pealed in exultation.[79] The Right SR leaders, wasting no time to assert their authority, declared a new government for the region under the Committee of Members of the Constituent Assembly, known by its Russian acronym as the Komuch. Originally consisting of five Right SR members from the Constituent Assembly, nearly 100 members from that body eventually succeeded in joining the Komuch. Because of is multi-party composition and democratic lineage, it claimed to be the only legitimate all–Russian government. That title, not surprisingly, would be contested by more conservative White governments whose preferred parties, such as the Kadets or those further to the right, held only a few or even no seats in the original Constituent Assembly.[80] The Komuch's bold declaration in fact set the tone for the duration of the White movement in Siberia and the Volga basin. While in other theaters of the civil war politics were often subordinated to military objectives, in the eastern regions the reverse was true.

The Komuch leaders knew as well as anyone that the Bolsheviks would not be deterred by a claim to political supremacy, and therefore one of their earliest decrees was a call for volunteers into a People's Army.[81] The command of this new army was formed from the local officer underground as well as from several high-ranking officers who defected from the Red Army's Volga Military District headquarters. An early commander of the People's Army and certainly its most famous was Vladimir Kappel, who would distinguish himself as one of the most competent and energetic leaders among the White armies.

After a few days of existence, the People's Army managed to scratch together two companies of infantry, two cavalry squadrons and an artillery battery; but this small force could hardly expect to withstand a concerted attack by the much larger Red Army.[82] The Samara leaders understood that if their regime was to survive beyond a few weeks, they would need Czecho-Slovak protection. Fortunately for them, Ček was harboring doubts about whether the Allies wanted him to continue towards Vladivostok or hold his position on the Volga. Subsequently, he employed the offices of the U.S. Vice Consul in Samara, George Williams, as medium through which he could contact the diplomatic community in Vologda. Williams, who lacked direct communications with U.S. Ambassador Francis in Vologda, forwarded Ček's message to the American Consul in Moscow, DeWitt C. Poole. When he received the inquiry on 17 June, Poole became concerned that any further delay might sacrifice a unique opportunity in the Allied intervention which he and other representatives believed to be only a matter of time. Fearing that Ček's forces might move on unless he received explicit instructions to stay, Poole thought there was no time to consult the diplomats in Vologda. On the next day, after obtaining the agreement of the French Consul General in Moscow, Poole replied to Williams that he should inform the Czecho-Slovaks that "the Allies will be glad from a political point of view to have them hold their present positions." Neither Poole nor Ambassador Francis, who concurred with his subordinate's decision the following day, had any authority make such a far-reaching statement.[83] Ček, not knowing better at the time, accepted the instruction as an Allied commitment to support the legionaries and the anti–Bolshevik movement in Russia. This erroneous belief was soon fortified by a message sent from French Ambassador Noulens to Major Guinet in Chelyabinsk announcing that the Allies would intervene at the end of June and that the Czecho-Slovaks were to be the advance guard for the Allied expeditionary forces.[84] The legionaries, not having any way to verify these statements, accepted them at their face-value and were inspired by the prospect that they would soon be joined by other Allied forces. As a result, they threw themselves headlong into the civil war and, with the People's Army at their side, began expanding the Komuch's borders.

Further east along the Trans-Siberian Railway, local soviets fell in succession like a line of dominoes. Before May was out, Petropavlovsk and Tomsk joined Chelyabinsk and Novonikolaevsk as cities liberated from the Red yoke.[85, 86] On 7 June, legionaries from Voitsekhovsky's group who were advancing from the west put the soviet in Omsk to flight. Two days later, they joined hands with Czecho-Slovaks under Gajda who were approaching from the east.[87] Once the railway between Chelyabinsk and Novonikolaevsk was cleared of enemy troops, Gajda concentrated the forces under his command—about 2,800 men—on his eastern flank in order to break through Bolshevik lines near Mariinsk and link up with the 500 troops of the Second Czecho-Slovak Division's shock battalion. This small force, commanded by a Russian officer, Colonel Boris Ushakov, was the only Czecho-Slovak force between Krasnoyarsk and Irkutsk.[88] From 4–10 June, the forces facing each other on the Mariinsk front withheld their fire and observed the truce mediated by Colonel Emerson of the Russian Railway Service Corps. On 7 June the commanding officer of the Red troops at Mariinsk submitted a rather rosy report to the Krasnoyarsk Soviet of their military prospects on that front. "Morale among the Czechs is falling," he claimed, "They are beginning to realize the extent of the desperate situation into which their last venture thrust them."[89] He even promised that his Red soldiers were ready to take the offensive, yet neither side moved when the armistice expired three days later. Finally, on 16 June, the stalemate was broken on that front when the Czecho-Slovaks and their Russian allies attacked and rapidly overwhelmed the Red positions. When the Krasnoyarsk Soviet learned of this defeat, its leaders immediately began packing their bags. On 18 June they fled the city on a steamer headed northward on the Yenisey River, taking with them gold, silver and other valuables looted from the city's banks.[90] Gajda's troops entered Krasnoyarsk two days later and were finally able to reach Ushakov's small force near Kansk.[91] From there, the legionaries and their White auxiliaries began the long march towards Irkutsk.

While Gajda drove eastward, Čeček and Voitsekhovsky focused on clearing the railway between their groups while screening against possible Bolshevik attacks from other directions—a threat which Gajda, whose forces were operating primarily along a single route, did not have to worry about. From his headquarters in Chelyabinsk, Voitsekhovsky had to divert men from his east-west axis to counter enemy activity to the north, where Yekaterinburg, the capital of the Ural Regional Soviet, lay. His group did not make contact with Čeček's legionaries until 6 July; by then both groups had launched offensives in other directions. While Čeček's men were leading the People's Army in campaigns against other centers in the Volga region, Voitsekhovsky's troops advanced northward against Yekaterinburg, where the deposed tsar Nicholas II and his family were being held in captivity. The Bolsheviks were determined not to let the fallen monarch fall into the hands of the counterrevolutionaries even though none had declared themselves in favor of a Romanov restoration. With their enemies rampaging through the Urals, Volga, Siberia, the Kuban and even in Central Russia, where a spate of brief uprisings had occurred in Moscow and other nearby cities, it may have seemed to Soviet leaders that there was no secure place to hold the royals in captivity. Consequently, on the night of 16–17 July a Cheka execution squad murdered the ex-tsar and empress, their five children and the few servants who had resolved to share their master's fate. Eight days later, Yekaterinburg fell to the legionaries and the White Russians marching with them began piecing together clues on the Romanovs' demise.

During the first month of fighting between the Czecho-Slovaks and the Bolsheviks, the Russian Far East, which then held the most concentrated body of legionaries, remained quiet. For some time, the situation there had been anomalous to the rest of Siberia; the local soviet was supportive of the plan to evacuate the legionaries through its port while the Czecho-Slovaks leaders there had staunchly opposed any aggressive action to facilitate the movement of the rest of the corps along the railway.[92] Still, tension and suspicion between the two sides was an inevitable consequence of the bitter fighting taking place on the railway west of Lake Baikal. On 25 June, a conference between the Allied consuls at Vladivostok and two representatives of the National Council reached the conclusion that the 13,500 legionaries in the vicinity of the port needed to return to the west to clear the railways in Eastern Siberia of Red troops and link up with their cadres fighting in that direction.[93]

Before attacking westward along the railway, the Czecho-Slovaks needed to secure a base of operations. On 28 June, General Diterikhs, the commander of the legionaries in Vladivostok, notified the Allied representatives in the city of his plan to depose the local soviet on the grounds that it was smuggling military supplies out of the port. At ten o'clock the following day, a Czecho-Slovak detachment surrounded the headquarters of the Vladivostok Soviet and presented it with a thirty-minute ultimatum to surrender. When the deadline passed without any response from the commissars, the legionaries stormed the building. Throughout the remainder of the day, the Czecho-Slovaks seized public buildings and disarmed local Red troops. Their operations were aided by the Allies, who landed troops and

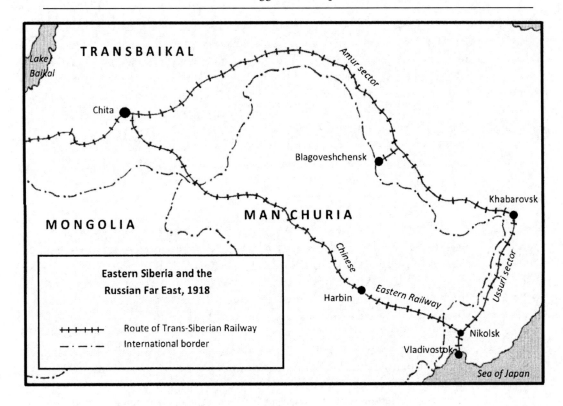

Eastern Siberia and the Russian Far East in 1918.

neutralized Bolshevized crews on Russian warships. By evening, order was being maintained in the city not only by the Czecho-Slovaks, but also through British, French, Japanese, Chinese and American soldiers and sailors who had disembarked earlier that day.[94]

Although the Czech-Slovaks were able to occupy Vladivostok with relative ease, they soon encountered stiff opposition as they advanced northwards along the railway towards Nikolsk, an important junction of about 30,000 residents some 70 miles from the port.[95] Adding to the legionaries' difficulties was the fact that they were inadequately armed; most had sacrificed their rifles in exchange for their passage to Vladivostok.[96] Nonetheless, after what one observer described as a "ghastly" battle, the legionaries succeeded in capturing Nikolsk on 5 July.[97] According to Admiral Austin M. Knight, the commander of the USS *Brooklyn* anchored in Vladivostok harbor, 43 legionaries were killed and 233 were wounded in the battle for the town. Bolshevik losses, by comparison, were estimated to be several times higher at about 250 dead and 1,000 captured.[98] On the same day they took Nikolsk, Czecho-Slovak representatives asked Knight's Japanese counterpart, Rear Admiral Katō Kanji, for additional arms and supplies. Their request was granted and one week later a Japanese naval transport arrived in Vladivostok bearing six mountain guns, 1,000 shells, twenty machine guns, 3,000,000 cartridges, seven instructors and a medical detachment of sixteen men to help the legionaries tend to their wounded.[99]

After their hard-fought victory at Nikolsk, Diterikhs hoped that his troops might be able to use the shortcut through Manchuria to more quickly reach their countrymen to the west. Before he could use that route, however, he had to enter into a series of complicated negotiations with anti–Bolshevik elements, such as General Horvath, who were unwilling to put politics and personal gain aside to make common cause with the legionaries against the Bolsheviks.[100] In the meantime, troops from the 5th and 8th Czecho-Slovak Regiments pursued the enemy northward along the Ussuri sector of the railway to Kraevsky. There, in the rolling valleys of pastureland and grain fields that reminded many U.S. travelers of the American Midwest, the Red forces, whose strength was estimated to have peaked over 10,000 bayonets, made a successful stand against their attackers.[101] The fighting soon lapsed into a stalemate, and both sides entrenched themselves next to the railway.[102]

In their first weeks of fighting, the legionaries from Vladivostok quickly learned, as Gajda's troops did when they pushed into the Circumbaikal sector, that the Red soldiers could be a stubborn adversary when not taken by surprise. Bolshevik forces in Eastern Siberia were strong since Red forces in the region had been built-up for operations against Semenov and other anti–Bolshevik threats from Manchuria.[103] Moreover, the local Red military commanders had over a month to prepare for hostilities with the Czecho-Slovaks after fighting broke out west of Lake Baikal. One of the more effective measures they undertook was a propaganda campaign aimed at the POWs from the Central Powers who were stranded in Eastern Siberia after fighting broke out to their west. In order to rally the POWs to the red flag, the Bolshevik recruiters portrayed the Czecho-Slovak Legion as a staunchly anti–German and anti–Magyar band of marauders.[104] Although it is difficult to say how effective these scare tactics were, Allied reports on the fighting along the Ussuri railway claimed that the majority of enemy soldiers fighting the legionaries were Austro-Hungarian and German POWs, not Russian Bolsheviks.[105, 106]

Despite Trotsky's determination to subdue them, their substantial disarmament and the widely scattered positions of their forces when hostilities broke out, the spirited Czecho-Slovak legionaries fought back with a ferocity and resourcefulness that stunned their enemies and amazed Allied observers in Russia. No Czecho-Slovak unit, despite several ambushes staged by Red detachments on unsuspecting Czecho-Slovak echelons, was completely overtaken by the enemy, though a few, such as a battalion of the 4th Regiment near Penza and another battalion at Zlatoust, were badly mauled by Bolshevik attacks.[107] Within a few weeks, new battlefronts, some hundreds and even thousands of miles east of those from the previous four years, had formed in Russia and Siberia. It was characteristic of the confusion prevalent in revolutionary Russia that the soldiers in those lines held differing views in regards to which war those new battlefronts belonged to. The indoctrinated Red troops understood the conflict to be a civil war, where the enemy was the bourgeoisie and their allies, the foreign capitalists. On the other hand, the Czecho-Slovaks and most Allied representatives in Russia deluded themselves and others into believing that the fighting was simply a new theater in the war against the Central Powers. The White Russians, though they clearly identified the Bolsheviks as their primary enemy, encouraged this view in the hope that it would gain them assistance in the form of Allied loans, supplies and troops.

Like their representatives in Russia, the Allied governments, with the exception of Washington, tended to agree that intervention in Russia and Siberia was necessary to halt the eastward expansion of the Central Powers. It must not be forgotten that they viewed events in Russia through the prism of the situation on the Western Front. In the spring of 1918, many British and French officials would have probably agreed with the bleak observation made several months earlier by General Macdonagh, Britain's Director of Military Intelligence. "It is difficult to imagine," the general wrote, "that the allies will be able to cross the

Rhine and dictate terms of peace on the enemy's own soil unless some miracle happens on the eastern front."[108] For many, the spectacular feats of the Czecho-Slovak Legion along the Trans-Siberian Railway, when they became known in the West, were to be that long-awaited miracle. Yet, although support for various schemes of intervention could be found in London, Paris and Tokyo, the willingness of these governments to put such plans into action depended on, for different reasons, the approval of the United States. By the middle of May 1918, the U.S. government had struck down no fewer than a half-dozen proposals from Britain and France for intervention in Russia. However, news of the legionaries' campaign against the Bolsheviks, combined with a new crisis on the Western Front and increasing pressure on the domestic scene, was gradually thawing Washington's opposition to such a venture.[109] Significantly, this change in policy would have a decisive effect on the Czecho-Slovaks' ultimate goal of establishing their own independent state, an objective that could be easily overlooked amid the fervor over the events taking place in Russia.

11

A New Eastern Front

While his legionaries in Russia were battling their way along the breadth of the Trans-Siberian Railway, Masaryk was engaged in a very different sort of campaign in the United States. His journey to America had begun in early March when he left Moscow and crossed Siberia to Vladivostok, well in advance of his troops. From there, he sailed to Tokyo and then boarded a steamer to cross the Pacific which landed in Vancouver, Canada, on 17 April 1918.

Masaryk's arrival in the U.S. was viewed with great anticipation by the Czech- and Slovak-American organizations. On the eve of the Great War at least 500,000 Czechs and 280,000 Slovaks were living in the U.S. as immigrants, with even more second-generation "immigrants" from both nationalities.[1] Many made their new homes in the Midwest, where they established various Czech and Slovak patriotic societies, including Sokol "nests," and had newspapers printed in their native languages.[2] Chicago was such a popular destination for Czech immigrants that it held the largest urban community of Czechs outside of Prague.[3] The city also became the headquarters of the Bohemian National Alliance, an umbrella organization for Czech-American societies that was formed after the outbreak of the war. The Slovak-Americans set up their own organization, the Slovak League, and like the SCSR in Russia, the Czecho-Slovak movement in the U.S. was wrought by internal rivalry among workers, devout Catholics and Slovak nationalists. After October 1915, however, the Bohemian National Alliance and the Slovak League reached a mutual understanding and worked together towards the common goal of Czecho-Slovak independence for the remainder of the war.[4]

Although the Czech- and Slovak-American organizations were enthusiastic supporters of the Entente cause, they had to exercise caution when planning their activities. Isolationism gripped a significant portion of the U.S. demographic. This view was favored by German-Americans who recoiled from the notion of their adopted country going to war against their fatherland. Irish-Americans also opposed any U.S. involvement in a conflict that might serve the interests of British imperialism.[5] Therefore, when Czech-Americans called for the dismemberment of Austria-Hungary and the liberation of their "oppressed" homeland, they had to avoid excessively belligerent tones that might give them the appearance of being warmongers. One of the most recognizable activities in which their organizations engaged was the fundraising they conducted on behalf of Masaryk and the Czecho-Slovak National Council in Paris.[6] Less known was the propaganda and intelligence-gathering operations which involved some Czech-Americans. It has already been mentioned how Emanuel Voska, who had been visiting Prague at the war's outbreak and acted as a courier between Masaryk and Steed in the early days of the conflict, returned to the U.S. to develop an impressive spy ring that eventually recruited contacts in allied, neutral and enemy lands across the globe.[7] Voska's organization coordinated its activities closely with two British intelligence officers in the U.S., Captain Guy Gaunt and Sir William Wiseman.[8] This cooperation provided mutual benefits to both sides: Wiseman eventually added Voska and his group to his payroll while in return the British officers received crucial information on the activities of Austrian and German agents and diplomats in the U.S. The feats credited to Voska's organization include identifying Austro-Hungarian and German reservists in the U.S. who attempted to return to Europe in the early weeks of the war, the exposure of an Austro-Hungarian ambassador's plot to instigate strikes among workers in U.S. armament factories and the uncovering of German dealings with Mexican and Hindu revolutionaries.[9] One of the most important assets to his successful spy ring was a Czech informant, František Kopecký, who was employed as a mail clerk in the Austro-Hungarian consulate in New York City. All letters which passed through Kopecký were copied and read by Voska and his operatives.[10]

Besides their accomplishments in fundraising and intelligence gathering, the Czech- and Slovak-Americans were also successful in lobbying politicians and other prominent Americans to build support for their cause. In this effort, they had little trouble securing the backing of Charles Crane, the aforementioned entrepreneur and philanthropist who was one of Masaryk's primary donors. Crane was also a generous donor to Woodrow Wilson's presidential campaigns and he became one of Wilson's advisors soon after the war began.[11] Besides Crane, the Czecho-Slovaks and their supporters eventually gained other advocates in Washington. In 1917, William Kenyon, a Republican senator from Iowa, introduced a Congressional resolution favoring Czecho-Slovak independence, but the proposal never made it to a vote.[12]

Despite the substantial achievements made by the Bohemian National Alliance and its affiliates by the spring of 1918, they had not succeeded in precipitating a radical shift in the attitude of President Wilson towards the Austro-Hungarian Empire. By then it was apparent that the United States and its prophetical head-of-state were destined to have a prominent role in shaping the postwar world should the Allies be victorious. Indeed, America's influence on the ideological and political aspects of the war was felt even before the country entered the conflict in April 1917. A year earlier, Wilson told an American-based peace organization that a lasting peace must be based on the principles of democracy, the rights of small states and freedom from aggression.[13] Since then, friend and foe alike perked their ears whenever the President spoke. On 22 January 1917 he struck a similar note in a speech to the Senate by declaring: "No Peace can last, or ought to last, which does not recognize and accept the principle that governments derive all their just powers from the consent of the governed, and that no right anywhere exists to hand peoples about from sovereignty to sovereignty as if they were property."[14] This statement and others spoken by the President brought much encouragement to nationalists from Austria-Hungary. At the same time, the leaders in Vienna were unnerved by this apparent condemnation of dynastic statecraft.[15] The ruling classes in the Habsburg and Hohenzollern monarchies were not the only ones rendered uncomfortable by the inspiring phrases being uttered on the other side of the Atlantic. Wilson's address to the Senate included a demand for "peace without victory," which was hardly compati- ble with the objectives of any belligerents—the Entente included. Although the Entente's "imperialist" war aims were kept mostly hidden until their publication by the Bolsheviks, Wilson sensed the existence of the secret pacts, such as the 1915 Treaty of London, among the Entente and vowed not to bind his country to such "selfish aims." For this reason, the

U.S. was officially not an Allied power but an "Associated Power" after it declared war against Germany.[16]

Based on his earlier statements on self-determination and the rights of small states, Wilson might have seemed predisposed to see the Habsburg Empire dismembered into smaller, democratic nation states. In fact, when the President spoke of the rights of small nations prior to the summer of 1918, he had in mind the restoration of established states such as Belgium, Serbia and Romania, not long-extinct ones such as Bohemia. Having no immediate argument with Vienna, he even abstained from declaring war on Austria-Hungary until the end of 1917 and in the meantime he enthusiastically backed Entente efforts to detach the Monarchy from her alliance with Germany by way of a separate peace. He believed that the subject nationalities of the Dual Monarchy would be content with mere autonomy for themselves; hence the nationalist leaders and exiles were to be sorely disappointed when he laid down his conditions for Austria-Hungary in Point Ten of his famous Fourteen Points address on 8 January 1918[17]: "The peoples of Austria-Hungary, whose place among nations we wish to see safeguarded and assured, should be accorded the freest opportunity of autonomous development."[18] As the Fourteen Points were published abroad, protests poured into Washington from various exile national committees and leaders in Western Europe and Russia.[19] The U.S. President, however, was unperturbed by the objections of stateless exiles. He believed that the Monarchy's faults lay not in Vienna but in Berlin, and if the Danubian Empire could be rescued from domination by its northern ally, it would be able to reform along genuinely democratic and federal lines. At the same time, his favorable attitude towards the Habsburg Monarchy was encouraged by his knowledge of clandestine talks that were taking place between Austrian and Allied agents in Switzerland. He and other statesmen were optimistic that these exchanges would open the path to formal negotiations leading to a separate peace.[20]

The Fourteen Points address was not simply a list of U.S. war aims; the President also hoped it would serve as a rallying point for all rational, morally-upstanding and benevolent peoples throughout the world. He thought its visions might not only encourage France and Italy to renounce the secret treaties, but also that it might draw Russia back into the war at the very moment the Bolsheviks were seeking peace with the Central Powers.[21] Although it failed to achieve these propagandistic objectives, the speech had definitely caught the attention of Masaryk.[22] He was in Kiev at the time of the famous address and was among those exiles who appealed to Washington for the dissolution of the Habsburg Empire and complete independence—not merely autonomy—for its peoples.[23] He recognized that he needed a lobbyist to win the President over to his cause, and he felt that that role could only be filled by someone of his stature.

While en route overland from Vancouver to Washington, Masaryk made a stop in Chicago, where he was given an enthusiastic reception by the large Czech community there. If he was expecting to receive a similar welcome in Washington, he was to be disappointed. Wilson, despite requests from Crane on Masaryk's behalf, was in no hurry to meet with the Czecho-Slovak leader.[24] Masaryk was not unknown to the senior officials in Washington since during his short stay in Tokyo he was solicited by the U.S. Ambassador, Roland Morris, for a written memorandum on his observations in revolutionary Russia. The document which the Czech professor submitted was a very accurate though unpopular assessment on everything from the durability of the Bolshevik regime to the weakness of their internal enemies. Indeed, his views on the Bolsheviks were so unconventional at the time that it may be

Masaryk, center, addresses a crowd in Chicago, 1918.

one of the reasons why Wilson and State Department officials were in no hurry to meet with him.[25]

The memorandum which Masaryk drafted in Japan foreshadowed that the ongoing controversy over Russia would provide him with the key he needed to open the doors to Washington officialdom. The question of intervention in Russia and Siberia, which had been a nagging matter in the administration's foreign policy for months, was becoming a dominant issue by the time Masaryk arrived in the capital on 9 May.[26] The question took on increased importance less than three weeks later when on 27 May the Germans achieved a stunning breakthrough on the Chemin des Dames in France. After pouring two million shells into French positions, the Kaiser's troops raced forward and in five days they succeeded in pushing the Allies back almost thirty miles, netting over 50,000 prisoners and initiating a mass exodus of civilians from Paris.[27] As the front bowed menacingly towards the French capital, the desperate British and French proposals to resurrect an eastern front to draw German reinforcements away from the battle in the West were viewed with a new urgency.[28] With Germany's exhaustion not yet evident, a panicked Supreme War Council convened in Versailles on 3 June and drafted yet another proposal to win Wilson's approval—by this time Moscow's consent was no longer considered—for military intervention in Russia with the aim of reestablishing an anti–German front. In addition to the crisis on the Western Front, the Supreme War Council was concerned by pessimistic reports of German activity in Russia. These dispatches from abroad fueled wild speculation in London as some British officials believed that intervention in Siberia was necessary to deter a German offensive against India. The French, in their moment of vulnerability, sent envoys to Washington to personally beg the President to drop his opposition to intervention in Russia.[29]

Most of the officials in Washington were leaning towards supporting an Allied intervention in Siberia, as were Wilson's political rivals in the Republican Party.[30] Against these pressures, Wilson's resistance to demands for action in Russia was eroding; only the warnings of his military advisors in the War Department prevented him from caving in altogether. The War Department, mindful of the great distances involved in Siberia, opposed the schemes for intervention in that region on the grounds that any military operation there would be a logistical nightmare and require the diversion of a substantial number of troops. In the opinions of the general staff, these men and resources could be more effectively deployed against Germany on the Western Front.[31] These logical voices, however, were soon drowned out by reports screaming of the Czecho-Slovak takeover of large portions of the Trans-Siberian Railway. This news sent Allied officials everywhere scrambling to formulate the proper response to exploit this unprecedented development to the utmost.[32] If the legionaries opened the railway into the Russian heartland, would it be possible to menace Germany's eastern frontier? And what should be done with the Bolsheviks? If the opportunity presented itself, should this upstart rabble which vilified capitalism, demonstrated nothing but contempt for traditional diplomatic protocol and made peace with the enemy be removed from the seat of Russian power?

Masaryk's primary motive for going to Washington, of course, was not to steer Wilson on the Siberian question but rather to urge him to recognize the right of the Czecho-Slovaks to establish their own independent state. Although most eyes in the capital were on the issue of intervention in Russia, the national question in Central Europe was by no means being ignored. On 29 May the State Department finally responded to the resolutions of the Rome Congress of Oppressed Nationalities of Austria-Hungary by stating that the aspirations of the Czecho-Slovaks and the Yugoslavs had "the earnest sympathy of this Government."[33] Still, it was the President's interest in the situation in Russia, and the role of the Czecho-Slovak legionaries there, which finally won Masaryk the audience he desired.

The Czech professor held his first meeting with President Wilson on the evening of 19 June 1918.[34] The meeting probably did not proceed as each man intended; indeed, their similar backgrounds were probably a mixed blessing. Both were close in age with Masaryk being six years older than the President, and although both could relate to each other as former university professors, each was supremely confident in his own judgment.[35] At that time, their views were not wholly different; Masaryk, like Wilson, still opposed intervention in Russia, despite the conflict there involving his troops. His primary interest was to discuss the need for Czecho-Slovak independence and the dissolution of the Habsburg Monarchy. On the other hand, Wilson, known for possessing a single-track mind on burning questions, preferred to keep the conversation on developments in Siberia.[36]

Although Washington continued to dig in its heels over the Siberian question, other countries acted as though intervention was simply a matter of when. On 20 June, Beneš approved a cable from Paris to the French Military Mission in Moscow instructing it to send word to the legionaries to hold their positions along the Trans-Siberian Railway. The Czecho-Slovaks were also authorized to rearm themselves from the military supplies stacked on the wharves at Vladivostok.[37] Although Beneš initially opposed intervention, he warmed up to the idea when he realized the opportunities which the legionaries in Russia had opened for the cause of Czecho-Slovak liberation.[38] The Czecho-Slovaks, who depended on Allied support to win their independence, were now needed by the Allies to renew military operations in the east. The Czecho-Slovak leader most favorable to intervention from the start was Štefánik, whose views on the subject tended to mirror those of the French military establishment to which he belonged. He was also an ardent anti–Bolshevik and was sometimes critical of Masaryk's non-confrontational policies regarding Soviet Russia.[39]

Like Wilson, Masaryk was coming under increasing pressure from his subordinates to commit his forces to intervention in Russia. When he realized that the large Red forces deployed between Lake Baikal and the Russian Far East threatened to cut off the legionaries still west of Irkutsk, he reversed his position. Six days after his meeting with Wilson, the Czech professor informed U.S. Secretary of State Robert Lansing that he felt Allied troops were now needed to rescue the legionaries in Central Siberia and further west. Despite this change of heart, Masaryk was slow to wrap his mind around the new situation. In the same interview with Lansing, he told the Secretary of State that he still desired the legionaries to be transported to France and that did not want them to be deployed in combat against the Bolsheviks. With Lansing's reluctant permission, he even wired a telegram to the Soviet Commissar of Foreign Affairs expressing his wish for the Czecho-Slovak corps and Soviet government to conclude a ceasefire at the earliest possible moment.[40]

Masaryk's call for intervention cemented Lansing's shift to the pro-interventionist camp, and thereafter it was only a matter of time before Wilson modified his own stance on the Siberian question.[41] In the afternoon heat of July 6, the President finally announced his new Siberian policy in a White House meeting attended by Lansing; Newton Baker, the Secretary of War; and General Peyton March, the Chief of Staff. Wilson informed his audience that while he continued to believe in the impossibility of reestablishing the eastern front with a large expeditionary force sent through Siberia, he was convinced that foreign involvement was needed to help the Czecho-Slovaks operating from Vladivostok to break through Bolshevik resistance in Eastern Siberia so they could link with their compatriots west of Lake Baikal. This operation, as he envisaged it, would not require any of the intervening powers to advance beyond Irkutsk. The number of Allied troops to Siberia was to be capped at 14,000; in other words only 7,000 soldiers each were to be sent there by the U.S. and Japan, which would be invited to participate in the operation. General March still opposed even this limited plan for intervention, but the decision was final and it was made public eleven days later in an *aide-mémoire* that became the foundation of U.S. policy in Siberia for almost the next two years.[42]

While Wilson would be able to keep a tight leash on his own country's activities in Siberia, he was to have less success in confining the actions of his nominal allies. Although London and Paris had for months been sounding the alarms to send an Allied expeditionary force into Russia, neither of these governments was consulted when the President made his plans for such an operation. His reasoning was somewhat ironic: there was no time to waste with such niceties; the legionaries were in danger and the critical Circumbaikal tunnels might be dynamited at any moment. The only nation that was consulted by Washington was Japan since it, according to Wilson's *aide-mémoire*, was to provide one-half of the Allied expeditionary force. While the Japanese gave their ostensible approval to the policies outlined in the *aide-mémoire*, they also refused to limit their expeditionary force to 7,000 troops. Even more troubling, they were unwilling to guarantee the territorial integrity of Russia. Likewise, when the British and French learned that the President was ready to go into Siberia, they took their own steps to make sure that they would not be left out of the loop.[43] The reaction of these countries to the *aide-mémoire* was foretelling of the lack of political unity that was to characterize the Allied intervention in Siberia, which in its worst moments would have the various intervening powers working toward cross-purposes.

With the stars and stripes unfurled above them, Americans show their support for the Czechoslovak cause in a parade, undated.

The news of the Czecho-Slovak campaign in Russia and Siberia fired Western peoples, especially Americans, with a sense of profound interest, if not outright enthusiasm, for these little-known peoples from Central Europe. In New York, an organization was formed to deliver aid to the legionaries fighting in Siberia, while former President Theodore Roosevelt personally donated $1,000 from his Nobel Peace Prize Fund to the legionaries.[44] Writing after the war, Masaryk noted that the Czecho-Slovak adventure along the Trans-Siberian Railway "had the glamour of a fairy tale, which stood out the more brightly against the dark background of German successes in France."[45] Beneš too observed that "the actual achievement of our troops was of such a character that no further propaganda of our cause was needed."[46] By mid-summer of 1918, both men set out to capitalize on this publicity and prestige won by their troops in Russia for a final push to secure Allied recognition for the Czecho-Slovak National Council.[47]

Of the two, Beneš's task in Western Europe was somewhat easier since by then independent Czecho-Slovak armies had been formally decreed by France in February and by Italy in June.[48] The British were the most careful of the Entente nations in avoiding postwar commitments in Central Europe even though their propaganda and intelligence bureaus were making the most extensive use of émigrés from that region. By the summer of 1918, however, the unsentimental official attitude of the British government towards the Czecho-Slovaks and other nationalities of Central Europe was thawing. On 3 June, Britain associated itself with a joint Allied declaration made through the Supreme War Council which echoed a U.S. statement made days earlier by expressing the "earnest sympathy for the nationalistic aspirations towards the freedom of the Czecho-Slovak and Yugo-Slav peoples."[49, 50] That same day, Beneš received a letter from Balfour granting the Czecho-Slovak National Council the same level of recognition it already enjoyed from France and Italy.[51]

Greater progress was made by Beneš after news of the Czecho-Slovak campaign in Russia trickled into the West. On 1 July, French President Raymond Poincaré granted the Czecho-Slovaks a "special diplomatic charter" and urged his allies to take similar action.[52] By then Beneš was again in London attempting to persuade the British government to recognize the Czecho-Slovak National Council as a provisional government. He argued, rather convincingly, that this recognition was necessary to ensure the National Council's maximum control and loyalty of the legionaries fighting on three fronts. At the time, Britain wanted to keep the Czecho-Slovak troops in Russia even though the National Council was still officially intent on observing the earlier agreements for their evacuation. The message which Beneš put forth indirectly to the Foreign Office was clear: the best way to guarantee that the Czecho-Slovak army in Russia would serve and obey Allied orders was to give their political leadership—the National Council in Paris—the authority of a governing body. This argument, though compelling, was not enough for Foreign Office to let its guard down. Britain did not go as far as to accord the National Council the status of a government, but it did recognize that organization "as the trustee of the future Czecho-Slovak Government" on 9 August. The same proclamation also recognized the Czecho-Slovak legions as an Allied army.[53] While this declaration was a considerable achievement for Beneš and the Czecho-Slovak National Council, it was carefully worded to avoid binding London to any commitment to a future independent Czecho-Slovak state.[54] Still, this proclamation along with the extensive employment of Bohemian émigrés throughout the war would have made it difficult for His Majesty's government to ignore the Czecho-Slovaks in any postwar settlement.

Meanwhile in the United States, Masaryk continued to lobby among American officials in the hope of extracting similar backing from Washington. Days after the *aide-mémoire* was made public, he drafted a memorandum to the State Department urging it to recognize the Czecho-Slovak National Council as a government. "I dispose of three armies," he stated, "I am, as a wit has said, the master of Siberia and half of Russia, and yet I am in the United States formally as a private man."[55] In spite of his efforts to draw attention to the Czecho-Slovak national cause, most of Masaryk's interactions with Washington officials centered on the Siberian intervention and the position of his troops there. At the end of July, the National Council representatives in Vladivostok sent a telegram to the Czecho-Slovak leader informing him of the critical position of the legionaries west of Lake Baikal and requesting his advice on what conditions, if any, the troops should remain in Russia. Masaryk had copies of this communication sent to the State Department and the British Ambassador in Washington, who forwarded it on to London. Although Wilson's *aide-mémoire* implied the evacuation of the Czecho-Slovaks from Vladivostok as soon as this was possible, the British urged the legionaries and their White Russian allies not to surrender a yard of the Trans-Siberian Railway. It was probably no coincidence that this recommendation was issued around the same time the British Foreign Office recognized the Czecho-Slovaks as co-belligerents in the war against the Central Powers.[56]

Not surprisingly, Wilson opposed British attempts to transform his rescue operation of the Czecho-Slovak army in their far-flung scheme for establishing a new anti–German front in Russia. While they set out to overcome the President's resistance to expanding the scope of the proposed intervention, British officials asked Beneš to impress upon his mentor the gravity of the situation faced by the legionaries in Siberia. The young Czech revolutionary obliged by forwarding Masaryk a copy of a telegram from General Diterikhs where the commander had given a very bleak assessment of the situation if the Czecho-Slovaks operating in the Russian Far East were unable to quickly break through enemy resistance in the Amur and Transbaikal provinces.[57] The telegram had its intended effect. Upon receiving it, Masaryk sent a copy to Lansing with an attached note pleading for the Allies to withhold no punches from the Bolsheviks, whose leaders he depicted as German stooges bent on "a holy war against the Allies and especially the Czecho-Slovak army."[58]

Lansing endorsed Masaryk's call for increasing U.S. support to the Czecho-Slovak Legion, but Wilson would have none of it. He successfully resisted British pressure for expanding Allied military operations in Russia and was irritated by Japan's obvious intention of using the intervention to aggrandize their country's position in Eastern Siberia. Moreover, he was by no means ready to commit the American Expeditionary Force to Siberia to the goal of eradicating Bolshevism from Russia. Nor was he prepared to officially acknowledge the Czecho-Slovak legionaries as an Allied army, unlike his European allies. The intervention in Siberia, as he saw it, was to be a humanitarian operation to help evacuate the Czecho-Slovaks and nothing more.[59]

Although Wilson initially avoided showing any support of Czecho-Slovak aspirations that summer, the U.S. recognition which Masaryk was lobbying for was not long in coming. Ever since the United States joined the war, there had been some support in the country for the dissolution of Austria-Hungary and liberation of her nationalities; among the more prestigious of these proponents was ex–President Theodore Roosevelt.[60] The cause for Czecho-Slovak national independence took on a life of its own, however, after the legionaries' feats in Russia were splashed in headlines across the U.S. The American press was quickly won over to the idea of an independent Czecho-Slovak state along with Secretary of State Lansing. In a letter to the President, Lansing advocated recognition of the Czecho-Slovak National Council based on the condition of Czecho-Slovak belligerency. In doing so, he argued, the U.S. would not be obliged to grant similar statuses to organizations like the Yugoslav Committee, which lacked an impressive military organization. Wilson eventually accepted his Secretary of State's argument and on 3 September Masaryk learned that the U.S. was preparing to recognize not only Czecho-Slovak belligerency but also his National Council as a *de facto* government. Through this announcement, along with statements of recognition from France, Italy, Great Britain and even Japan, the Czecho-Slovak National Council had acquired a status which neither the Polish nor Yugoslav organizations were to know during the war.

The significance of the legionaries' campaign in Russia cannot be understated in its effect on the Allied statements of recognition that were bestowed on the Czecho-Slovaks that summer. Most of these declarations were made at a time when the fortunes of the Czecho-Slovak Legion in Russia were soaring and subsequently, the Allied statesmen and publics were dazzled by the impressive victories of this small army in a vast land. On 11 September, just days after the U.S. announced its recognition of the Czecho-Slovak National Council as a *de facto* government, another meeting was held between Wilson and Masaryk. Amid their discussion, the U.S. President mentioned the importance of the Legion in his decision to support an independent Czecho-Slovak state.[61] That same day, British Prime Minister Lloyd George wired a cable to the Paris headquarters of the National Council praising the record of the Czecho-Slovak troops in Russia as "one of the greatest epics of history."

"Your nation," he added, "has rendered inestimable service to Russia and the Allies in their struggle to free the world from despotism; we shall never forget it."[62]

That struggle which so enamored the Western world and eased the exiles' navigations of the Allied foreign ministries continued in earnest during the hot summer months along the Trans-Siberian Railway. Although at times they were dogged by everything from swarms of mosquitoes in the marshy steppes to the exhaustion of continuous campaigning, the legionaries pursued their foes with relentless enthusiasm. Morale peaked not only in their ranks, but also in those of their White allies. Cossacks also aided the legionaries by providing some much needed cavalry support while Russian railroad personnel, by then thoroughly disillusioned with the soviet utopia, provided the Czecho-Slovaks with valuable assistance in shuttling their trains along the railways.[63]

Although the summer battles in the Urals and the Volga yielded new gains for the anti–Bolshevik coalition, their continued momentum and indeed the future of their entire campaign depended on clearing the railway supply-route to the Pacific coast. For Gajda, this meant continuing his eastward drive and taking the vital tunnels along the Circumbaikal route intact. As his forced rolled towards Irkutsk in late June, the Red forces resorted to destroying track and blowing up bridges to impede his progress. The ingenious Czecho-Slovak technicians and engineers, however, quickly repaired the damage so that by early July they were closing on the city. The Tsentrosibir, rather than make a desperate stand on the banks of the Angara River, relocated to Chita. On 12 July Gajda's troops entered Irkutsk against no resistance—nearly six weeks after legionaries had abandoned their foothold on the edge of the city following the intercession of the Allied consuls there. Despite their elation of taking one of the most important centers in Siberia, there was no time for the Czecho-Slovaks to celebrate. The Bolsheviks, during their evacuation of the city, had taken

Czecho-Slovak legionaries fend off Bolsheviks and mosquitoes, undated.

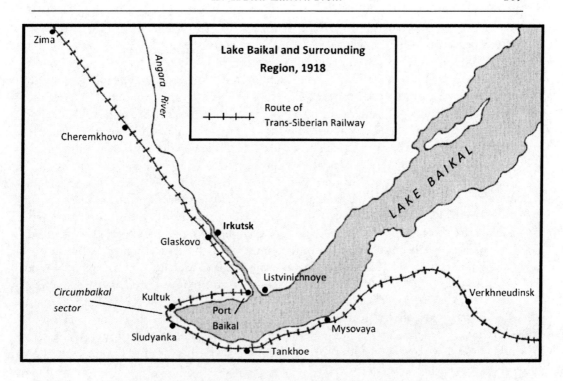

Southern Lake Baikal and surrounding area in 1918.

several carloads of high explosives with them.[64] This meant that the crucial tunnels south of Lake Baikal were still in grave danger.

To stall their erstwhile pursuers, the retreating Red troops had devastated the tracks east of Irkutsk. While his forces spent the next several days repairing the railway, Gajda sent a handful of White Russians to infiltrate the local Red forces in order to identify their positions. Through these spies, Gajda learned that most of the explosives were in a train parked at Port Baikal, near the lake. The Czech commander decided that as the repairs to the track continued, a surprise attack should be made against the Bolsheviks before they had time to prepare the tunnels for demolition. Subsequently, he employed Russian guides to lead 500 men from the ranks of the 7th Regiment and the shock battalion through the mountainous wilderness to engage the defenders at Kultuk. A smaller detachment was set to Baikal Station to surprise the Reds in their rear and, most importantly, destroy the trainload of explosives.[65]

After a several days' march across forty miles of rocky slopes and scrub oaks, the main Czecho-Slovak detachment encountered the Bolsheviks, as expected, at the town of Kultuk. The Reds quickly concentrated their local reinforcements there and unwittingly aided the task of the saboteur unit headed eastward along the north bank of the Angara River. After driving away the few defenders at the Baikal port of Listvinichnoye, the legionaries crossed the mouth of the Angara in watercraft they seized at the docks. Once they landed on the south bank, the Czecho-Slovaks raced for nearby Baikal station and easily overpowered the guards there. After locating the train laded with explosives, they set charges to it and a few seconds later a massive blast swallowed the train in flames, flattening nearby buildings and leaving only the skeletons of railcars once the smoke cleared. The detonation was so thunderous that it was audible in Irkutsk. It was also heard by the Red defenders at Kultuk, who realized they were being outflanked and beat a hasty retreat.[66]

With the main threat to the tunnel system apparently eliminated, the Czecho-Slovaks and their White Russian auxiliaries made a direct assault along the Circumbaikal sector, and one-by-one, they captured the tunnels. They took every tunnel intact until they reached the most easterly tunnel—Tunnel No. 39—which they found choked with rubble. Lieutenant Bečvar, who fought with Gajda's forces during the operation, described how the discovery that "the rails just ran into a mass of rock and huge stones" caused the hearts of his detachment to sink.[67] Gajda, however, was not to be stopped. He immediately ordered his men to wield shovels and pick axes to clear the tunnel—all 350 yards of it—of enough debris so that loco-motives and railcars could pass through it. Among the laborers drafted to help reopen the tunnel were 300 POWs brought in from a camp near Irkutsk. With little heavy machinery available, it was tedious work made hazardous by plunging rocks and periods of shelling from Bolshevik field guns mounted on either of the two icebreakers that prowled the nearby lake. To ward off these raids, the legionaries installed an artillery battery on the mountainside above Tunnel No. 39. One day, when the icebreaker *Angara* returned to harass the excavators, its crew was bewildered when firing from the shore sent geysers of water spurting up around their vessel. Before they were able to get out of range, the ship was struck by a shell on its stern. In the meantime, the mining of Tunnel No. 39 continued for three weeks, until the rubble was down low enough to provide just enough clearance for trains to travel through on tracks laid above the debris.

Legionaries patrol the tunnels along the southern rim of Lake Baikal, undated.

During that interval, the legionaries continued to pressure enemy positions on the other side of the mountain, but they made little headway until the tunnel was cleared. The fighting was bitter; a company of White Russian volunteers from Tomsk was decimated in one engagement while the Bolsheviks' control of the nearby lake enabled them to land raiding parties behind the Czecho-Slovaks' lines or on their flanks. The Bolsheviks used this period of stalemate to strengthen their defenses and augment their ranks with stranded war prisoners. However, their only major assault on the forces guarding the eastern side of the tunnel, which took place in early August, ended in disaster when the defenders poured fire into their ranks from the hills above and captured seven locomotives and an armored train.

After 10 August the legionaries' trains began passing through the reopened tunnel and the initiative of the struggle fell decisively with the Czecho-Slovaks and their White Russian allies. Using small vessels captured at the lake port of Listvinichnoye, eighty White Russians led by Colonel Ushakov landed behind Red lines just as Gajda's troops were poised to make a powerful frontal assault along the railway. Another detachment executed a flanking attack overland against Bolshevik positions. The fighting was difficult at first as the Bolsheviks outnumbered the attackers and fought resolutely against the frontal attack; they also discovered Ushakov's landing party and killed the colonel. Nonetheless, Ushakov's daring exploit succeeded when Bolshevik resistance along the railway crumbled after they learned that the White raiding party had sabotaged the tracks in their rear, leaving many of their trains with nowhere to go. Those that did manage to escape headed eastward in a disorderly rout. A Hungarian POW in a rail-side town along their path of retreat described the scene:

> Suddenly one day all was feverish activity. Trains began passing early in the morning, with locomotives running backward, showing that there had not been time or opportunity to turn them. Both tracks were being used for the constant stream of Red soldiers that were pouring through.[68]

As many as 6,000 Red troops were killed and 2,000 were captured in the series of battles around the lake, with most of these losses occurring in the days following the clearance of Tunnel No. 39. Czecho-Slovak and White casualties were much lighter although the death of heroes such as Colonel Ushakov made their victories bittersweet. But their success was decisive; the Red forces in Transbaikal Province never recovered from this crushing defeat. Their morale was completely dashed and a number of them retreated southward where they were pursued by detachments of legionaries to the Mongolian border. In the meantime Verkneudinsk, the next major town east of Irkutsk, fell to Gajda's forces on 20 August and the Czecho-Slovaks continued to advance virtually unopposed until they finally joined hands with their comrades from Vladivostok at Olovianaya, near the Manchurian border, only a week later.[69] The legionaries, at last, could claim mastery of the Trans-Siberian Railway from the Volga to the Pacific.

The American Expeditionary Force to Siberia (AEFS), whose main objective was to open the railway in Eastern Siberia for the Czecho-Slovaks, was landing at Vladivostok just as this goal was being realized. By the time the U.S. commander, General William S. Graves, arrived from San Francisco in early September, his orders, encapsulated in Wilson's *aide-mémoire*, were already obsolete.[70] One of the first American units to arrive in Siberia, the 27th Infantry Regiment, did arrive in time to join the Japanese Twelfth Division and a few hundred British troops in assisting the 5th Czecho-Slovak Regiment in breaking through the Ussuri front to advance on Khabarovsk.[71] On 18 September, the last major bastion of Bolshevism in Siberia, Blagoveshchensk, fell to a combined force of Czecho-Slovak, Japanese and Cossack troops.[72] By then, the AEFS was settling into an intervention whose official purposes had been rendered meaningless.

Other Allied nations were more deliberate in the aims they set for the Siberian intervention. The British and French continued their efforts to transform the Czecho-Slovak uprising along the Trans-Siberian Railway into an operation against Germany's eastern frontiers. On 11 July, after the legionaries in Vladivostok had begun marching back to the west, the British quietly ended their half-hearted attempts to find the necessary tonnage to transport the corps to Europe.[73] Once the divided Czecho-Slovak army reunited along the Chinese Eastern Railway, the British and French instructed them to retrace their journey westward and provide reinforcements for their comrades on the Volga and Ural fronts. According to Bečvar, these orders were received by his unit with trepidation. "To have fought and struggled to the east," he wrote, "merely to be sent back to the west in the very hour when we thought we had won our purpose, was hard, and few of us could prevent feeling an occasional twinge of resentment at our lots."[74]

Although Bečvar and his men disliked the thought of returning deep into Russia, they obeyed the orders because they were eager to serve the Allies and, more importantly, they believed that the expeditionary forces in the Russian Far East would soon be joining them in the Urals. While it may be wrong to say that the legionaries were deliberately misled about the intentions of the Allied expeditionary forces, it does seem that those who directed their redeployment did not draw the Czech commanders' attention to the fact that the main interventionists in Siberia, Japan and the U.S., had not committed themselves to operations west of Irkutsk. Wilson had thought it unnecessary for American "rescue forces" to proceed beyond Irkutsk since the Czecho-Slovaks were already approaching the city when he drafted his *aide-mémoire*. The Japanese, who before the year was out would have somewhere between 70,000 and 100,000 troops in Eastern Siberia and the Chinese Eastern Railway zone, turned down a plea from the British Ambassador in Tokyo asking them to reinforce the legionaries on the Volga front.[75] The Japanese cabinet was less concerned with the plight of the Czecho-Slovaks than they were with assuring their country a leading position in the Far East. Although they wanted to keep Eastern Siberia free of Bolshevik and German influence, they did not want a too centralized or nationalistic Russian government to take control. They may have even had their eye on an indefinite occupation of Eastern Siberia. In the meantime, they bullied Chinese and local Russian administrators in order to dominate the Chinese Eastern Railway, sought to increase their economic penetration of the region and threw their support behind petty Cossack atamans who established themselves along the railway in the wake of the Czecho-Slovak victories over the Bolsheviks. Among these Japanese tools was Semenov, who in June 1918 was hanging by his fingernails onto his last sliver of Russian territory in Transbaikal Province. His little army was saved from almost certain annihilation by the sudden uprising of the Czecho-Slovaks, which caused the Reds on his front to divert some of their troops towards Irkutsk. After the legionaries cleared the Transbaikal of Red forces in late summer into autumn of 1918, he established himself in Chita and began a two-year bloody reign of terror.[76]

The divergent Siberian policies pursued by the Allies led to friction among themselves from the moment their expeditionary forces arrived in the Russian Far East. Their commanders and soldiers regarded each other with such intense suspicions or prejudices that no petty insult was overlooked. For example, the British commander of the 25th Battalion of the Middlesex Regiment, Lieutenant Colonel John Ward, was frustrated by his inability to find proper carriages for his officers when his unit began their long trek towards Omsk in the autumn of 1918. Possession of first- and second-class carriages had become a sort of status symbol during the engagement along the railway, and as a result these were snapped up by whoever came across them first, often Czecho-Slovaks, White Russians and Cossacks. At the start of their journey, Ward's officers had to make do with rickety cattle cars. At Manchouli station, along the Chinese Eastern Railway, Ward discovered several unused second-class carriages, but the Japanese contingent occupying the station was unwilling to hand these over to even a nominal ally without a hefty payment. Only after a tense standoff in which troops on both sides raised their rifles did Ward secure the two carriages he needed.[77]

News of the arrival of Allied expeditionary forces in the Russian Far East bolstered the fighting spirit of the legionaries and White Russians fighting the Red Army some 5,000 miles to the west in the Volga region. By July this new eastern front, more accurately called the Volga front, had a definite chain of command led by Lieutenant Čeček; the positions directly beneath him were held by top officers from the People's Army. As a Czech, an automobile salesman by trade and a mere lieutenant, the thirty-two-year-old Čeček hardly seemed qualified to lead what was then the most important front in the Russian Civil War. As the commander of the local legionaries, however, he controlled the largest and most effective forces available to the Komuch in Samara; moreover, the anti–Bolshevik Russians hoped that Čeček's leadership would attract the Allied support they needed to defeat the Bolsheviks.

For such a relatively young, junior officer to hold such an important position was, in the circumstances of the Russian Civil War, not all that unusual. Operations in the civil war at this stage were very much unlike those in world war. Since relatively few combatants faced each other in vast theaters, the fronts were ill-defined and fluid. Fighting was often concentrated along railways and navigable rivers with little or no troops occupying the countryside between those arteries. Attaining victory in this new war required a different style of thinking than the old one. Because of the small size of the units engaged in the battles, talented commanders of lesser rank could distinguish themselves with greater ease than when their efforts were diluted in armies comprised of millions. This trend led to rapid promotion for certain individuals and was not restricted to the Czecho-Slovak Legion in Russia; it also appeared in the White armies and in the Red Army as well.[78]

Regardless of Čeček's abilities as a commander, the Komuch's long-term survival depended on attracting support from the local population for its administration and especially for its armed forces. At its peak in August, the Samara government could claim a population of 12,000,000 in its territory, but the population of the areas controlled by the Bolsheviks during the civil war rarely fell below five times that number.[79] It was imperative for the Komuch to introduce a political program that would secure the fanatical support of not only those people over which it directly ruled, but also those who remained within the confines of the Soviet Republic. For a time, this seemed within the realm of possibility. The Komuch deputies, having been elected to Russia's Constituent Assembly less than a year earlier, could and did claim legitimacy from that mandate. Most of them belong to the Social Revolutionary Party, the preferred party of Russia's peasant masses, and their open desire to govern by democratic principles should have at least gained them some traction among liberal, middle-class elements not traditionally bound to the SRs.[80]

In spite of its associations with the SRs, the Constituent Assembly and Russian democracy, the Komuch's bid to galvanize all of Russia, or even the Volga region, against the

Bolsheviks proved to be an abject failure. The reasons for its disappointing performance are numerous, and while some of these may be attributable to the conditions of the civil war, others lay in the very nature of the government itself. For instance, the committee's adherence to democratic politics, while admirable, was also disabling. Confidence in its ability to lead floundered as it often proved unable to act quickly or very decisively.[81] Also problematic was its moderate socialist outlook that failed to please any segment of society. For the region's peasants and industrial workers, the Komuch was too conservative while the middle and upper classes considered the committee to be nothing more than a watered-down version of Bolshevism.[82]

The least popular institution of the Komuch was the one the committee depended on most for its preservation: the People's Army.[83] Originally, it was be comprised of volunteers but these were lacking as the peasants in the Volga and elsewhere were tired of war and preferred to have nothing to do with the new conflict taking shape in their country. By the end of June 1918, conscription into the People's Army was ordered for all able-bodied men between the ages of 20 and 21. While these draftees may have brought the army's strength up to 30,000–40,000 men, they lacked any dedication, were often poorly trained and, like most peasant-soldiers, tended to desert when harvest approached.[84]

Despite this unpromising start for the People's Army, it and Čeček's legionaries formed a coalition force of fewer than 50,000 men spread out across a wide-arcing front that cruised to one victory after another in the summer of 1918. After carving out a territory stretching from Simbirsk to Ufa by late July, the Volga commanders faced the dilemma of deciding which direction they should attack next. Čeček and his staff at the Volga front headquarters in Samara believed that they should launch an offensive towards Saratov in the hope of eventually linking up with the Ural Cossacks and the Volunteer Army. Colonel Kappel of the People's Army and Captain Stepanov of the 1st Czecho-Slovak Regiment, however, were eager to move against the Volga city of Kazan from where they could continue the march towards Moscow or perhaps join hands with the Allied forces believed to be advancing southward out of North Russia. Their ambitions, against the orders of Čeček's headquarters, won out. On 5 August, the Czecho-Slovaks and White Russians, with an attacking force of just 2,500 troops, assaulted Kazan and took complete control of the ancient Tartar city two days later.[85] Their success was partially enabled by the deployment of a river flotilla operated by the legionaries and the defection of a Serbian battalion from the Red side at the height of the battle.[86] The victory yielded several unexpected laurels including the capture of a cache of heavy artillery, the forced evacuation of the Reds' Eastern Army Group headquarters and, the greatest prize of all, barges laded with 650,000,000 rubles' worth of gold, precious metals and jewels from Russia's treasury reserve that had been evacuated from Petrograd the previous year.[87] News of the Red debacle inspired an uprising among workers in Izhevsk, 150 miles north of Kazan, and for a time it seemed that nothing could stop the Czecho-Slovaks and their allies from carrying the anti–Bolshevik banner deep into the Soviet heartland.[88]

The Soviet government responded to the crisis on the Volga by summoning the workers and their loyal party stalwarts to defend the revolution against the "White Czechs," who they depicted as the hirelings of foreign imperialists, namely Britain and France. Officers from the tsarist army were called to the colors; many who otherwise opposed the Bolsheviks willingly served in the Red Army against what they perceived as a foreign threat to the Russian motherland.[89] Red Army garrisons posted as a screen against the Central Powers in western and central Russia were shuttled eastward to ward off the more imminent threat in

Volga and Urals. Four gunboats from the Baltic were hauled overland by rail and then launched in the Volga to wrest control of the river from the Czecho-Slovak flotilla. Altogether, the troop redeployments soon gave the Red Eastern Army Group a rapid and commanding numerical superiority over its enemies on the Volga and Ural fronts.[90] Just how serious the Bolsheviks regarded the situation on the Volga front became evident when Trotsky left Moscow to take personal charge there. Recalling his arrival at Svyazhsk, just west of Kazan, the War Commissar later wrote that "the soil itself seemed to be infected with panic."[91] In the following days and weeks he held the front by rallying the demoralized Red troops with speeches, stiffening sagging areas of the line with his leather-jacketed bodyguards and ordering "blocking units" to gun down deserters from his army.[92]

As Red resistance stiffened at the front during August, the Czecho-Slovaks were growing increasingly irritated with their White Russian allies. At this critical moment, the peasant conscripts in the People's Army began deserting to their villages so they could harvest their grain while soldiers had to be sent from the front to the rear to suppress anti–Komuch rebellions to the south and east of Samara.[93] Meanwhile, another major contender in the anti–Bolshevik movement, the Provisional Siberian Government in Omsk, put up a customs barrier against the Komuch and refused to send its army of nearly 40,000 troops to assist the People's Army. These actions appeared to validate recent complaints lodged by the Czecho-Slovaks' Provisional Executive Committee that their Russian allies seemed more interested in quarrelling with each other than uniting against the common Soviet enemy.[94] Nothing, it seemed, could compel the Whites to change their habits.

The Czecho-Slovaks, for their part, put their house in order at a follow-up army congress held from late July into early August in Chelyabinsk. This step was warranted due to the provisional nature attached to the leadership appointed by the May congress and the fact that a number of leading officers, mostly Russians, had been removed from their posts due to their opposition to operations against the Bolsheviks. Pavlů was rewarded for his faithfulness to the policies of the first congress by having his leadership confirmed at the latest assembly. It was then up to him to lead the search for a new commander-in-chief for the Czecho-Slovak army, and in this task he displayed a fixation for clenching as much power as possible. The most obvious candidates for commander-in-chief were either Čeček or Gajda, but they were too popular and ambitious for Pavlů's tastes. He wanted someone he believed he could control, and for this reason he also ruled out the Legion's Chief of Staff, the Russian General Diterikhs, who was probably the most qualified candidate. Eventually, he settled for Lieutenant Jan Syrový, the commander of the Czecho-Slovak 2nd Regiment who lost an eye in the Battle of Zborov and was said to bear a likeness to the legendary Hussite hero Jan Žižka. Though lacking the pomp and fame of Čeček and certainly Gajda, the thirty-three-year-old Syrový would prove to be a suitable if uninspiring pick. He was reliable for following orders and meshed well with superiors; perhaps one of his underrated qualities was his cool-headedness that would be invaluable in the crises ahead. In the meantime, Čeček and Gajda, as compensation for being passed over for the top post in the corps, were promoted to the commanding officers of the First and Second Divisions, respectively.[95]

As the young Czech commanders saw their careers attain new heights, they faced a worsening situation at the front. By the end of the summer, the advance of Voitsekhovsky's legionaries in the Urals had been checked by strong enemy resistance. They were under Allied orders to thrust westward along the railroad via Perm and Vyatka to Vologda, where they were told an Allied expeditionary force operating from Archangelsk would be waiting for them. Although a multinational Allied expeditionary force had indeed landed in the White Sea port in early August, its 1,500 troops, even after they were reinforced by 4,500 men from the U.S. 339th Regiment in September, remained too few to traverse the 400 miles of hostile

territory separating Archangelsk from Vologda. Nor would the Allied troops in North Russia come close to seizing another objective, the Dvina river port of Kotlas, from which they could have accessed a rail link to Vyatka.[96] At any rate, the Czecho-Slovak group in the Urals was in a desperate fight simply to hold its positions around Yekaterinburg, and the objectives they were given revealed the extent to which the Allies had overestimated the strength of the Czecho-Slovaks as well as their own expeditionary forces.[97]

Even more serious was the situation on the Volga, where the People's Army was hemorrhaging deserters as Trotsky was amassing three Red armies on the Komuch's borders. On 28 August, Colonel Kappel, commanding one of the most effective units in the People's Army, led a bold assault to sever the Reds' rail links with Moscow about twenty miles west of Kazan. This surprise attack nearly succeeded as Kappel's troops reached their objective and even threatened Trotsky's command train. The War Commissar, sensing the battle's critical moment, did not flinch and ordered his men to repel the Whites at any cost. After several hours of intense fighting,

Jan Syrový, undated. He wore a patch over his right eye after being wounded in the Battle of Zborov in July 1917.

Kappel's unit was worn down and forced to withdraw, leaving the initiative with the Red forces. As a result, the Fifth Red Army pressed forward and forced the legionaries and People's Army to evacuate Kazan on 10 September.[98] One Cossack soldier later recalled the ensuing flight:

> The main road out of Kazan was a dark river of people, in which we were caught, moving sluggishly like a piece of driftwood on a muddy river. Thousands of men, women, and children stumbled and cursed and wept along the night, their backs burdened with enormous sacks of household goods, the sound of rifle fire behind cracking them on like a whip.[99]

This scene was repeated two days later when the First Red Army, after having broken through the front to the south, captured Simbirsk. It was quickly becoming apparent that the anti–Bolshevik campaign in the Volga was threatened with total collapse unless the Whites could reinvigorate the effort through the State Conference then in session at Ufa.[100]

The Ufa State Conference was not the brainchild of the beleaguered Whites but rather of the Czecho-Slovaks and French attachés who warned them that their continued support of the anti–Bolshevik cause was contingent on the formation of a united movement. During the summer, nearly twenty anti–Bolshevik governments claimed some measure of authority between the Volga and Vladivostok; their political outlook ranged from socialist-pink to a closet-monarchist white. The two main contenders were the Komuch in Samara and the Provisional Siberian Government in Omsk, which had shed its initial socialist-regionalist program and mutated into a bastion of reaction.[101] The position of the Komuch, however, was undercut by the military crisis faced on its front. Its delegates were eager to work out a settlement that would establish a centralized anti–Bolshevik government east of the Volga that would be strong enough to turn back the Red tide. On the other hand, the Omsk delegation did not feel the hot breath of the enemy on the back of its neck and was in no hurry to compromise. The proceedings were frustrating for many. "While we are arguing," remarked one irritated Cossack delegate, "the Bolsheviks will capture Ufa together with the whole conference."[102] Once again, the Czecho-Slovaks and French observers had to coerce the recalcitrant delegates to come to terms by threatening to withdraw the Czecho-Slovak legionaries from the front. The resulting settlement created an All-Russian Provisional Government (ARPG) under the leadership of a five-man Directory that included SRs and Kadets. As with most compromises, the ARPG from its conception was ridiculed by all and cherished by no one.[103]

With three Red armies bearing down on the Volga front, the Directors of the ARPG reluctantly established their capital in distant Omsk. Their arrival in that city, which many travelers have likened to an overgrown steppe-village, was unceremonious. For a time, the Directors were forced to govern from their cramped carriages since the Omsk authorities refused to turn over any buildings to them. The city was especially dangerous for the socialist Directors as members of their party were terrorized and sometimes even murdered by reactionaries in the former Provisional Siberian Government and their Cossack allies. The only real deterrent that the eminent newcomers had against such brutes was a Czecho-Slovak garrison in the city who had already thwarted an earlier power-grab by the reactionaries. Indeed, the legionaries may have been the ARPG's only reliable supporters. Altogether, it was an auspicious start for the new government.[104]

While the ARPG struggled to put down roots in Omsk, the setbacks experienced by the anti–Bolshevik coalition on the Volga front reached their culmination on 7 October when Samara was captured by the Fourth Red Army. Desperate to forestall the onrushing enemy, the Czecho-Slovaks and the remnants of the People's Army dynamited railroad bridges and destroyed the tracks as they withdrew eastward. As with the retreat from Kazan, thousands of Russian refugees—bankers, lawyers, priests, merchants, shopkeepers and landowners who suffered grievously in their earlier encounters with Soviet rule—flowed eastward along the rails and roadways. With the loss of the Volga region, the Whites were deprived of one of the most populous and strategically significant regions they would ever possess in the course of the civil war. Moreover, the Bolsheviks' triumph there proved that the Soviet regime was weathering the crises it faced in the summer, when not only the frontiers but also the center of the Soviet republic were boiling over with rebellion. It was an opportunity that the Whites would never have again, and they had rather foolishly squandered it by engaging in rivalry among themselves instead of concentrating their resources on the Red enemy.[105]

Although their patience with the Whites was wearing thin by the mid-autumn of 1918, the Czecho-Slovaks still found it difficult to abandon the ARPG to a certain demise. They undoubtedly felt a personal responsibility to the anti–Bolsheviks who had befriended them and fought at their side throughout the summer. They were particularly fond of the Right SRs who tended to share their democratic principles, moderate socialist views and scorn for the Brest-Litovsk Treaty. The SRs also controlled the Siberian cooperatives who had kept the corps fed while it traveled and fought along the railway.[106] This bond, however, was breaking down as the anti–Bolshevik movement in Siberia veered further to the right and became more authoritarian in outlook. Although the SRs still had a presence in the ARPG, it was clearly delicate and was probably more dependent on the Czecho-Slovaks than even the SR Directors themselves would have liked to believe. As the legionaries were not unlimited in either their numbers or endurance, the SRs—and indeed all shades of anti–Bolsheviks—never seemed to comprehend that they could not rely on the Czecho-Slovaks indefinitely.

In the autumn of 1918, the exhausted legionaries fought on in the belief that they would soon be joined by the Allied expeditionary forces in Siberia and that by fighting the Bolsheviks they were opposing Germany. The mirages hiding the true state of affairs would soon dissipate, the first when no significant Allied force proceeded west of Irkutsk, and the second when the Central Powers collapsed later that autumn. Although this would be a painful realization for the legionaries, its depressing effect on their morale would be slightly tempered by the news that their homelands were at last free.

The Men of October 28

Despite the peace with Russia and the crushing victory over Italy at Caporetto, not all was well with the Austro-Hungarian Army in early 1918. Its pilots had lost control of the skies over the Italian Front after British and French air squadrons arrived there during the winter. From then on, Allied pilots were free to shower Austrian lines with bombs or propaganda leaflets as they pleased. Suddenly Habsburg troops were being snowed under by sheets containing promises of independence for the Slav ethnicities as well as reprints of Wilson's Fourteen Points. Although the propaganda offensive orchestrated by Steed was an ominous sign of things to come for the AOK, the most urgent trouble lay not with its soldiers' minds but rather with their stomachs. Long insulated from the severe hunger that had stricken Austria's cities, the army finally began to feel considerable materiel privations in early 1918.[1] The so-called "bread peace" with Ukraine drastically failed to meet its expectations for the delivery of grain, and as a result the general food situation in the empire worsened rather than improved.[2] To make things worse, the men's uniforms were threadbare and offered poor protection against the icy winds that swept across the Alpine battlefields.[3] Although cold and hungry, the frontline troops were not necessarily opposed to going over to the offensive. Some actually favored the idea in the hope that they could capture the enemy's abundant food stores to fill their bellies, as they had done during the previous November.[4]

The POWs from Russia, who began drifting into the Monarchy that spring, might have provided a significant source of reinforcements for the army. Of the approximately two million Austro-Hungarian POWs in Russia, just over 670,000 managed to return before the war's end. These returning prisoners, however, may have been more of a liability than an asset. The AOK, fearing that many had been indoctrinated by the Bolsheviks, quarantined the former POWs and subjected them to a screening process to weed out any revolutionaries hiding among them. Only after being deemed politically reliable were they allowed to visit their family homes, which, lacking food and fuel, were often not as inviting as they remembered. After a short leave, the "homecomers" were then expected to rejoin the army at the front. Once there, these men, despite the measures taken by the military authorities to cull out subversive elements, eventually played leading roles in many of the mutinies which broke out that summer and fall. It was not Bolshevism but rather their harsh treatment by the state, the lack of adequate food and their war-weariness that made them a source of decay that eventually spread to the rest of the army.[5]

The privations caused by the war and enemy blockade not only undermined the morale of the soldiers, but also the civilians. As in Russia a year earlier, social unrest increased as those in want of food grumbled against the activities of speculators, war profiteers and the upper classes. Nor was it unusual for people of one ethnicity to level accusations of hoarding against another ethnicity in the polyglot empire.[6] In reality, none of the nationalities were significantly better off than others; nevertheless, rumors circulated among hungry Czech workers than their suffering was, in part, caused by German areas of the Monarchy receiving a disproportionate share of food shipments.[7] The worst areas for insufficient food distribution were the large cities, including Prague.[8] More so than any street agitator or dissident party, the dire food shortages in the Monarchy by 1918 were a radicalizing force which the Austrian authorities never succeeded in mitigating.

The growing influence of the radical nationalists in the Bohemian lands became apparent to all after the parties in the Czech Union issued the biting Epiphany Declaration on 6 January 1918.[9] Shortly after sticking their necks out with this manifesto, however, the Prague politicians were stunned when they learned that Lloyd George and Wilson, during their recent speeches on war aims, stated their opposition to the dismemberment of Austria-Hungary. Subsequently, the Maffie conspirators, who may have thought that the achievements of Masaryk and his accomplices were more substantial than they actually were at this point, soon sent Beneš a long list of inquiries to clear up their confusion. Their most fundamental question was whether the Allies were supportive of Czecho-Slovak independence. This message never reached Beneš and it was just as well; he could have truthfully given them few comforting answers in January 1918. In a later communication with Prague, Beneš could only vaguely assure the underground that their cause enjoyed "real sympathies" from the Allies.[10]

Remarkably, the momentum of the Czecho-Slovak separatists in Bohemia continued to build despite the absence of Allied pledges to support their national aspirations. On 10 February several Czech political parties, including the Young Czechs, Realists and the Moravian People's Party, merged under a name that reflected its anti–Habsburg ideology: the Czech State Right Democracy Party. Although the two largest Czech political parties, the Agrarians and the Social Democrats, remained outside this union, the former worked closely with the State Right Democrats in the following months. An effort was made to bring the National Socialists on board, but they proved reluctant to temper their increasingly radical socialist program even in the name of national unity. Instead, the National Socialists drew closer to the Social Democrats and as a result two competing blocs emerged in the revolutionary movement in Bohemia.[11]

Competent Austrian authorities understood that the nationalist movement, rather than the socialist one, was the greater menace to their control of the Bohemian crownlands.[12] It was perhaps this knowledge that made the radical Czech nationalists an object of ridicule in a poignant speech delivered by Foreign Minister Czernin to Viennese municipal officials on 2 April. In a tirade against the domestic Czech politicians, he pointed out their failure to condemn the Czecho-Slovak legionaries as traitors and denounced their increasingly nationalistic outlook. "Poor, wretched Masaryk," declared Czernin, "is not the only one of his kind: there are many such Masaryks inside the Monarchy itself."[13] His statements were popular with few people; even loyal politicians in Vienna through it unwise to further antagonize the Czechs. Indeed, Czech reaction to the speech was swift and straightforward as demonstrators took to the streets of Prague in the following days to chant "Hail Masaryk!" and other slogans.[14]

The 2 April address soon precipitated Czernin's downfall, not because of what he said about the Czechs, but rather because of what he uttered about Austria's preliminary peace talks with the Allies. In his speech, Czernin mentioned the peace-feeling efforts between

Austria-Hungary and France in such a way as to imply that Paris doubted its side's ability to win the war. This assertion kicked off a duel of words between himself and Clemenceau in the Parisian and Viennese presses. The French Prime Minister ended this contest in his favor by publishing a letter that the French government received from Karl in the previous year through his Bourbon-Parma in-laws. The letter, which had been kept secret from Czernin and others, was damning since the young Emperor stated his acceptance of French claims to Alsace-Lorraine as a reasonable basis for a negotiated peace. This landed Karl in hot water with Berlin since earlier he had assured his brother monarch, Kaiser Wilhelm II, that he had no misgivings over German retention of the disputed provinces. As a result of this humiliation, Czernin was forced to resign while in the following month his former master made a pilgrimage to the German Army headquarters at Spa, Belgium, to beg for the Kaiser's forgiveness. Wilhelm granted his imperial colleague the pardon he was seeking, but it came at the cost of an agreement to strengthen the military, political and economic ties between the central empires.[15]

The Spa agreement provided further impetus to the liberation movements among the Slavs who viewed it as a step closer to the Greater Germany (*Grössdeutschland*) long promulgated by radical Pan-Germans.[16] This outcome, the Slavs feared, would cause the Germans to impose assimilation policies throughout the Austrian-half of the Monarchy. On the other hand, news of the Spa agreement was welcomed by the anti–Habsburg exiles abroad since it appeared to validate their long-standing allegations that Austria-Hungary had allowed itself to become a doorstep in a German-dominated Mitteleuropa.[17] Even before the agreement was reached, Beneš, in a dispatch to his Maffie accomplices in Prague, emphatically noted that the public spat between Clemenceau and Czernin had soured Allied attitudes towards Vienna.[18] The subsequent accord between the two emperors only exacerbated these feelings in the Allied camp to the point that the position of the pro–Habsburg element in Allied official circles was no longer tenable.[19] Up to that spring, many Allied statesmen still clung to the hope that a separate peace between them and Austria-Hungary was practical and desirable; hence Lloyd George and Wilson's moderate statements towards the Monarchy in their speeches on war aims in January. The Spa agreement, however, nixed those wistful desires for a separate peace with Vienna. The Habsburg and Hohenzollerns, it seemed, had resolved to stand or fall together; there was no longer any need for their enemies to distinguish between the two. Naturally, the Monarchy's loss was the exiles' gain. The Allies' hardened stance towards Austria-Hungary was another reason why the Czecho-Slovaks obtained official statements of support and recognition in the summer of 1918.

At the same time the Monarchy's foreign policy swung closer towards Germany, the Austrian government moved to settle the national question in Bohemia through the program espoused by the ethnic Germans. On 29 April, the Austrian Prime Minister, Ernst von Seidler, proposed dividing the Bohemian administration into twelve ethnic districts: seven Czech, four German and one representing both. This threatened imposition of the "German solution" in Bohemia merely reinforced the radical nationalism already prevalent among the Czechs and their South Slav allies in the Reichsrat. A few weeks after Seidler's announcement, on 15–17 May, Czech leaders staged a series of ceremonies ostensibly held to commemorate the fiftieth anniversary of the establishment of the Czech National Theater in Prague. Instead, the event, which attracted a multitude of representatives from other disaffected minorities in the Monarchy, was transformed into the equivalent of a congress of oppressed nationalities. In a show of solidarity, the visiting politicians readily joined their Czech hosts in condemning the Monarchy while championing the right of self-determination to its nationalities. The message was clear: the ethnicities would band together and resist Seidler's proposal at all costs. The Prime Minister's only other alternative to implement the "German solution" was to bypass the parliament via emergency decree, but the more liberal-minded Karl refused to consider this option.[20]

The Czech leaders, meanwhile, continued their separatist activities by reorganizing the Czecho-Slovak National Committee, a body that had existed in some form since late 1916. The make-up of the new committee, which was announced on 13 July 1918, included Czech Reichsrat deputies and other key politicians; Kramář was named its chairman while the roles of vice-chairmen were held by the leaders of the Agrarian and Socialist[21] parties, Antonín Švehla and Václáv Klofáč.[22] This work was encouraged by the Czecho-Slovak exiles, who by now were communicating regularly with Maffie. As the National Council tallied one success after another in the form of army agreements, diplomatic charters and statements of recognition, Beneš was eager to relay this news to Prague to steel the politicians' resolve and, perhaps most of all, keep them faithful to Masaryk's program for Czecho-Slovak liberation.[23]

The extent of the radicalization that had overtaken the Czech masses in the past months was not apparent to Beneš and his fellow émigrés living abroad, and as a result they were constantly unnerved by concerns that the Prague politicians might agree to a compromise with the Austrian government. Thus the young Czech exile was careful to remind the Prague politicians of the importance of following his directions. "It would be a catastrophe," he wrote in a July dispatch to Maffie, "if there were no unity now when we have achieved all our political aims."[24]

The Czech politicians did not disappoint Beneš that summer. On 16 July, the Reichsrat returned to session in Vienna and Seidler went before the deputies in a hopeless bid to secure their approval of his "German solution." His proposal floundered not only because of the expected resistance from the Czech and Yugoslav coalition, but also from the opposition it met from Poles, who were livid at the government's concessions to the Ukrainians in the "bread peace" concluded with the Rada. With the loss of his former Polish supporters, the Emperor finally accepted Seidler's resignation on 22 July.[25] His replacement, Baron Max von Hussarek, attempted to negotiate a compromise with the Czech leaders, but these efforts were futile since the latter would accept nothing less than their complete independence. Frustrated, Hussarek's government toyed with the idea of suppressing the Prague National Committee but was deterred by the Minister of the Interior who noted that similar organizations existed among other nationalities, including the German-Austrians.[26] Since it did not know where to draw the line for its repressive measures, the Austrian government simply never began them. In the meantime, the Reichsrat devolved into a shouting match between the Slav and German deputies that did nothing to alleviate the Monarchy's problems, least of all its national questions.[27]

While the Czech homeland was a significant pocket of national agitation in the polyglot empire, it was hardly the only one. The Croats, Serbs and Slovenes followed the Czech example by opposing the government at every turn. Even the leaders among the so-called master races, including the Poles and Magyars, were distancing themselves from the Habsburg dynasty as the war entered it final months. The Poles had been causing Vienna headaches since mid–1917, when Piłsudski and other Polish members of the Council of State in Warsaw grew less cooperative after they began to doubt the Central Powers' willingness to restore Polish independence as promised by their proclamation from the previous November.

Although the occupying powers soon replaced the Council of State with a more compliant Regency Council, their troubles with the Poles did not end there. Piłsudski continued to be a thorn in their side as he urged the troops serving with the Austrian-sponsored Polish Auxiliary Corps not to take an oath of allegiance to the Habsburg and Hohenzollern emperors. Two Polish brigades followed his advice and were subsequently disarmed. Piłsudski also dissuaded Polish volunteers from serving in Ludendorff's Polnische Wehrmacht and as a result of his activities he was arrested by the Germans and locked up in Magdeburg fortress. The final break between the Polish people and the central empires occurred when the latter signed the "bread peace" with the Ukrainian Rada on 9 February 1918. Polish patriots were enraged that the Central Powers, under the terms of the treaty, ceded ancestral lands of the Congress Kingdom to the Ukrainian republic. Poles in the Habsburg Monarchy also took issue with Vienna's promise to form a new Ukrainian crownland in eastern Galicia, a development that would almost certainly displace the Polish ruling class there. In protest of the "bread peace," the Polish Second Brigade deserted *en masse*, mobs of angry Poles filled the streets in Kraków and L'viv, and in Vienna the Polish Club in the Reichsrat sided with the opposition.[28] The Magyars, meanwhile, were looking ahead to defend the integrity of their historical frontiers amid any of the war's possible outcomes. If the Central Powers were victorious, they feared that a Greater Germany might encroach upon the frontiers of the Kingdom of Hungary. If Austria-Hungary was on the losing side, the Magyars expected their neighbors to stake claims on the regions of Upper Hungary, Transylvania and Croatia-Slovenia. The Magyars' solution to avert either of these catastrophes was to demand an exclusive national army of their own. Although AOK was adamant in its refusal to appease the Magyars, the issue severely corroded the spirit of cooperation between Vienna and Budapest.[29]

The only event which might have compelled the Czechs and other disaffected nationalities to lessen their intransigence and compromise with Austro-Hungarian leaders was a decisive military victory. On 15 June the Habsburg army attempted to win the war on the Italian Front by launching an offensive against Allied lines along the Piave River. The double-pronged attack initially made some respectable gains, particularly on the southern end of the front, against combined Italian, British and French forces roughly equal to their own strength. The army's advance soon stalled, however, when Allied air squadrons and unexpected flooding on the Piave knocked out the pontoon bridges the attackers needed to feed supplies and reinforcements onto the opposite bank. By the end of the month, the Austro-Hungarian troops were back at their starting lines after having incurred 142,550 casualties to the Allies' 84,830. As it became clear to the ragged troops that the army could not recover its former strength, defeatism set in among the units and soon thousands of soldiers shirked their duty through desertion or, less commonly, self-mutilation. With the Austro-Hungarian Army beginning to crack, the disgruntled nationalities saw even less reason to parlay with the government and the empire slid interminably towards its final dissolution.[30]

On the Western Front, Austria-Hungary's ally also found herself in an unenviable military position after Ludendorff's final offensive, launched on 15 July, was checked in two days. On 18 July, a counterattack consisting of nineteen French and four super-sized American divisions, supported by 2,100 guns, 750 tanks and over a thousand planes, crashed through the Marne salient and sent the German troops there reeling.[31] The U.S. contribution to the war effort was beginning to tell on the Western Front that summer, and by then fresh doughboys were arriving in France at the rate of 200,000–300,000 per month. Three weeks after the Marne counterattack, the reinvigorated Allies began a general offensive that continued throughout the rest of the summer and autumn, forcing even the stubborn Ludendorff to admit that his army was beaten.[32]

Although it was not yet apparent to all contemporary observers, the war in Europe, which many on the Allied side believed would last into 1919, was entering its final phase.[33] Masaryk was among those leaders who doubted that the fighting would cease before winter; nevertheless, while lobbying for Czecho-Slovak recognition in the U.S., he took other important steps to ensure that the transitions of the Czech and Slovak peoples from Habsburg subjects to citizens of an independent nation-state would be as smooth as possible when the now inevitable Allied victory arrived.

The lack of Slovak representation in the National Council continued to be problematic for a movement that claimed to represent the national aspirations of both Czechs and Slovaks. As noted earlier, two of the three top leaders in the National Council, Masaryk and Štefánik, could and did claim Slovak ethnicity, but many rightly doubted that a Czechified philosophy professor and a French officer could adequately speak in the name of the downtrodden peasants of Upper Hungary. The only indication during the war that native Slovaks might favor Masaryk's Czecho-Slovak program came on 1 May 1918 when Vavro Šrobár presided over a meeting of Slovak activists at Liptovsky Svätý Mikuláš that issued a resolution demanding self-determination for the "Hungarian branch of the Czechoslovak tribe."[34] The reason why so few Slovaks in Hungary voiced their national or political aspirations became evident when Šrobár was thrown in jail following the publication of the declaration. The lone Slovak deputy to the Hungarian Diet, Ferdis Juriga, dared not to call for Slovak independence until the closing weeks of the war. The populist Slovak leader, Andrej Hlinka, was bolder in his statements but held no official office during the war. A few other Slovak political figures, including Milan Hodža, worked for their national cause from the more tolerant environment of Vienna, where they were in frequent contact with Czechs in the Reichsrat and Maffie, but none ventured outside the Monarchy. By the summer of 1918, nearly all leading elements of Slovak political thought, including the fiery Hlinka, supported union with the Czechs in an independent state.[35] Still, it was difficult for them to convey their feelings abroad.

To compensate for this gaping weakness in his revolutionary movement, Masaryk looked to the sizeable communities of Slovak immigrants living in the United States to provide the mandate he wanted to govern their national homeland. Although most Slovak-Americans were not opposed to the political union of their national homeland with Bohemia, many were leery of the possibility that such a state might be dominated by the more numerous and better-educated Czechs. To address their concerns, Masaryk, shortly after his arrival in the U.S., called upon the various Czech- and Slovak-American groups to send delegates to Pittsburgh in order to define the Slovaks' position in the envisaged state. The convention produced the Pittsburgh Agreement, which was signed on 30 May 1918 and guaranteed the Slovaks an autonomous administration, including a parliament of their own.[36] If it were observed after the war, it would have created a Czecho-Slovak as opposed to a Czechoslovak state.[37]

Besides strengthening Czecho-Slovak unity, Masaryk was eager to create the image of solidarity among all Central European national movements. Part of his motivation for this undertaking were requests from less successful émigré groups, such as the Yugoslavs, for the Czech professor to lobby the U.S. government on their behalf.[38] Another consideration was his desire to dispel the fear of a "Balkanized" Central Europe in the U.S. and its allies. A number of overlapping claims existed among the Central European peoples; for the Czechs these included rival claims by Poland over the Silesian district of Těšín and by Romania over Ruthenia in northeastern Hungary.[39] Even before the war was over the dispute over Těšín threatened to undo the harmony between Czech and Polish exiles.[40] Masaryk understood that these ongoing disputes might be the ingredients for a new war; therefore he felt it was prudent for the national movements to take the initiative in settling these questions before they got out of hand and, equally important, so that the Allies would feel confident in the nationalities' commitment to peace.[41]

To put the friendships of the Central European peoples on display, Masaryk summoned the anti–Habsburg émigré leaders in the U.S. to Carnegie Hall in New York City in mid–September. There delegates claiming to represent irredentist Italians, Poles, Romanians, Ukrainians and Yugoslavs held a congress of oppressed peoples mirroring the one staged in Rome the previous spring. The assembly drafted a resolution expressing their appreciation of U.S. and Allied support for their causes and reiterated their aim to dismantle the Habsburg Empire. As a publicity stunt, the congress proved to be a homerun after President Wilson invited it to send a delegation to present the resolution at the White House. Afterwards, the delegation, led by Masaryk, decided to consecrate their fraternity in a permanent organization to be called the Mid-European Democratic Union. This group immediately launched a brief propaganda campaign that culminated in Philadelphia where Masaryk, while standing in front of Independence Hall, read a "declaration of common aims" on 26 October.[42]

The declaration which Masaryk, with some difficulty, persuaded the union to adopt was intended to reassure outside observers in the U.S. and elsewhere that the various nationalities could work together despite their outstanding differences. Yet, the image of solidarity which the union portrayed even at Philadelphia was mostly a façade. The inclusion of émigrés from previously unrepresented ethnicities of Central and Eastern Europe complicated the union's work. Its sessions were marred by bickering between those claiming to speak for Yugoslavs and irredentist Italians, Poles and Ukrainians as well as Albanians and irredentist Greeks. Masaryk's prestige provided much of the union's cohesion: at the time the delegates from lesser-known ethnic groups were eager to ride the professor's coattails in the hope that he would pull them along the path to success. The émigrés' willingness to compromise was also helped by the knowledge that they were an ocean away from the disputes which divided them. Although most were not quite free agents, their distance from the homelands and public opinion there gave them elbowroom which their domestic leaders did not enjoy. Even so, the Mid-European Democratic Union began breaking down before the guns fell silent in France as the Poles, unable to reconcile with Ukrainian aspirations in eastern Galicia, ceded from it.[43] In the mayhem that erupted in post-war Central and Eastern Europe, the Mid-Democratic European Union became, almost overnight, nothing more than an idealistic memory.

For Austro-Hungarian leaders, it was a troubling portent that by early autumn of 1918 the émigrés were shifting their focus from ridding the world of the Habsburg Empire to preparing for a world without it. The official recognition which the Allies bestowed on the Czecho-Slovaks, along with the deteriorating conditions inside the Monarchy and at the front, battered Vienna's confidence.[44] As their power slipped away, Austrian leaders resorted to drastic measures which they and their predecessors had previously been too timid to take. The first of these occurred on 14 September when Emperor Karl unilaterally announced his desire to commence talks to form a basis for a negotiated peace. This offer found no acceptance among the Allies, who knew they were winning the war and had previously published their terms for peace.[45] The young Emperor's peace efforts took on a new urgency after General Franchet d'Espérey's multinational Army of the Orient broke out of its dreary camp in Salonika in late September and forced Bulgaria to capitulate before the month was out. Suddenly, the link with Turkey was broken and the Habsburg Empire's southern frontier lay exposed to d'Espérey's army.[46] On 4 October, just four days after the Bulgarian armistice went into effect, both Austria-Hungary and Germany appealed to President Wilson to discuss peace on the basis of his Fourteen Points. Although a response was quickly sent to Germany, the Viennese statesmen heard nothing more than an eerie silence from Washington.[47]

With a crisis imminent, Karl was not idle while waiting for an American or Allied reply to his armistice offers, and soon he made a desperate gamble to defuse the threat of national revolution and demonstrate his sincere approval of Wilson's Fourteen Points. Twelve days after the joint appeal with Germany, he issued a manifesto that reorganized the Austrian half of the Monarchy into a federal state of autonomous administrations for the nationalities.[48] These administrations were to be based on the national committees already present among most ethnicities; those peoples who did not have a national committee were urged to form one quickly.[49]

This federalization decree, which resembled the schemes once touted by moderates as the ideal reform for the polyglot empire, was unable to inspire any of the ethnicities to maintain their allegiance to the dynasty in its final hours. Any positive effect the Emperor's manifesto might have had was frittered when Budapest succeeded in gaining exemption for the Kingdom of Hungary from its reforms. Even in this dire moment, the introspective Magyar ruling class believed that the privileges which it had guarded for itself in Hungary could somehow be maintained. While Karl gave into them, the Czechs, Croats and Serbs in Austria were unwilling to abandon their kin in Hungary to Magyar pretensions.[50] In fact, the manifesto had confirmed their long-standing suspicions that the dynasty, through its inability to restrain the Magyar oligarchy, was unable to refurbish the empire into a state that could truly guarantee equal rights and protection for all nationalities.

Despite its evident failings, the Emperor's manifesto stoked fears among the anti–Habsburg exiles abroad that the far-reaching concession might placate the dissident politicians and restore Habsburg prestige in the eyes of the Allies. Thus as Karl worked feverishly to save his inheritance, the exiles labored just as hard to destroy it. From the U.S., Masaryk hastily drafted a Czechoslovak declaration of independence which he published on 18 October.[51] On the other side of the Atlantic, Beneš and his staff formally upgraded the Czecho-Slovak National Council into a provisional government on 14 October. Its leadership was to consist of Masaryk as president, Beneš as acting foreign minister and Štefánik as acting minister of war. The prompt recognition which this government received from France only partially allayed the exiles' fears that the Allies might be negotiating with Vienna behind closed doors.[52]

To assure the Prague politicians' loyalty to the National Council, Beneš for some time had been clamoring for a group of them to meet him in Geneva. After the Emperor decreed that the Austrian government would accommodate the national committees, the Czech leaders finally mustered the nerve to ask the authorities for the passports they needed to leave the country. Remarkably, the Austrian government complied with the request and issued the needed documents to a seven-man delegation of Czech financial experts and politicians, the latter of which included Kramář and Klofáč.[53] The Czech delegation did not hide the nature of its business in Geneva, and both Kramář and Klofáč, while en route to Switzerland, made a stopover in Vienna. Kramář attended a conference with Austria's new Prime Minister, Heinrich Lammasch, who attempted to persuade various Slav leaders to preserve some links with the dynasty. The Czech leader politely rejected the suggestion by informing Lammasch that not even a politician of his imminence could convince the Czech people at this hour to accept anything less than complete independence. In the meantime, Klofáč met with the Emperor, whose only request of the Czech Socialist leader was for him to work towards a non-violent solution to events in Bohemia.[54]

The meeting between the Czecho-Slovak National Council delegation, led by Beneš, and the Prague politicians was held in Geneva from October 28 to 31 at the Hotel Beau Rivage, not far from where Beneš met Masaryk after his escape across the Austrian frontier only three years earlier. Back then, Beneš was obscure and hardly taken seriously by the politicians who remained back in Prague. In October 1918, Beneš and his three accompanying secretaries were still relatively unknown in the Bohemian lands, yet the more prominent figures who met them in Geneva knew by now that they could not ignore the young exiles sitting across from them.[55] The exiles completely dominated the conference by overawing the veteran politicians with a list of their accomplishments, from the establishment of Czecho-Slovak armies to various official recognitions of the National Council, all of which they had achieved under Masaryk's leadership. Against these impressive feats, the five Prague politicians, all of whom enjoyed far greater mandates than Masaryk prior to the war, could do nothing more than nod their heads when Beneš demanded that they approve the exiles' actions during the conflict and accept the National Council as an interim government. The form of government for the new state was also settled at the meeting as Beneš's argument for a democratic republic prevailed against the wishes of politicians like Kramář who preferred a constitutional monarchy. A final outcome of the meeting was that Masaryk, Štefánik and Beneš were all confirmed in the posts which the latter had designated for them in the provisional government. Kramář was named prime minister and entrusted with the task to lead the cabinet while Masaryk remained abroad.[56]

When the delegation to Geneva left Bohemia, Austrian authorities remained in control of the province despite a recent wave of strikes and working-class demonstrations fomented by the socialists throughout the empire.[57] With the government's authority growing weaker by the day, Kramář and his colleagues arranged for a group of mostly younger politicians to stand-in for them on the Czecho-Slovak National Committee during the delegation's absence from Prague. Moreover, if the opportunity presented itself, the men who remained behind, which included Švehla, Rašín, Jiří Stříbrný, a Czech Socialist, and František Soukup, a Social Democrat, were authorized to take charge of the administration of Bohemia. Late on October 27, just two days after the delegation left for Geneva, these interim leaders of the National Committee believed that the decisive moment was upon them.

Their assessment was mostly based on events outside of Bohemia. A week earlier, President Wilson had finally answered Karl's plea for peace negotiations on the basis of the Fourteen Points. By granting limited self-government to the nationalities of Austria, the Emperor believed he had fulfilled as best he could the President's call for the "autonomous development" of Austro-Hungarian peoples. Wilson, however, replied that that point had been modified due to new developments which arose since delivering that famous address ten months earlier. Among these developments was the United States' recognition of the Czecho-Slovak National Council as a *de facto* government.[58] In other words, the President refused to negotiate with Vienna until it acknowledged that it no longer spoke for the Czecho-Slovaks and possibly other nationalities as well. On 27 October Lammasch's cabinet accepted Wilson's condition as a basis for an immediate armistice.[59] For the first time in almost four centuries, the Habsburgs were surrendering their claim over the Bohemian crownlands.

Another development which encouraged the Czecho-Slovak National Committee to act was a message from Vlastimil Tusar, the organization's envoy to Vienna. On the evening of the 27 October, Tusar telephoned Prague to inform his colleagues of an astonishing request from AOK for the National Committee to dispatch representatives to the Italian Front in order to deter Czech and Slovak soldiers from deserting.[60] By then, Austria-Hungary's military situation had gone from worse to utterly hopeless. To the south, French and Serb units of d'Espérey's Army of the Orient were charging through occupied Serbia, where they were being welcomed as liberators.[61] Meanwhile, in late October, the Italian Army had finally gone on the offensive for the first time since its harrowing retreat from the Isonzo a year earlier. Unexpectedly, the starving and tattered frontline Habsburg troops managed to put up a stiff resistance for five days after the attack began. Indeed, the task of establishing a secure bridgehead on the east bank of the Piave was accomplished not by Italian troops but by British divisions in the line. Besides the British, the Italians also received valuable assistance from two French divisions and the Czecho-Slovak Legion's Sixth Division.[62] Amid the fighting, the initial resistance of the defenders unraveled when word spread throughout the Austro-Hungarian armies that the Emperor had released the officers from their sworn allegiance to him. Suddenly the front degenerated into a mass confusion as regiments from one nationality after another abandoned the front and struggled to get to the rear.[63] In their desperation, the AOK was reduced to pleading for help to defend the Habsburg Empire from the very organizations that more or less openly opposed it. Understandably, when this odd appeal reached Prague, the resolve of the National Committee to attain their highest goal was stiffened. It revealed to the revolutionary conspirators that the army, which had saved the empire during the uprisings of 1848, was now, seventy years later, a blunt instrument.

In the morning hours of 28 October, the National Committee decided to put the plan it had worked out the previous night into motion. Since the revolutionaries were eager to complete the regime change with as little bloodshed as possible, they first targeted the Office for the Distribution of Corn to safeguard the food supply and avoid riots. This task was completed almost effortlessly by Švehla and Soukup, and their success meant that not only could they dictate the civilians' rations, but also those of the Prague military garrison. The presence of these troops, whose ranks consisted mostly of Magyar and Romanian soldiers, caused some anxiety in the National Committee. Fortunately for them, nearly all Austrian officials, including the military commander in Prague, were uncertain as to how much power should be accorded to the national committees under the vague guidelines of the Emperor's manifesto. Subsequently, the Austro-Hungarian garrison made no effort to suppress the actions of the Czecho-Slovak National Committee in the Prague revolution's first critical hours.[64]

Around mid-day, representatives from the National Committee entered the offices of the Bohemian governor, Count Max von Coudenhove. Ironically, the governor was in Vienna at the time trying to learn to what extent he was to tolerate the activities of the National Committee. Since the staff he left behind was as clueless as the local military leaders were on how to address the present situation, the Czechs were able to assume the reins of the provincial administration with ease. That afternoon, Prague's streets filled with throngs of upbeat Czechs as the text and full implications of Vienna's note to Wilson from the days before became known. The largest crowd gathered in Wenceslas Square, where the demonstrators chanted anti–Habsburg slogans and waited impatiently for news of the events taking place in their midst. All around them the visible signs of Habsburg authority began to disappear as the imperial insignia were torn from soldiers' uniforms and the sides of buildings. That evening the National Committee held a general meeting where it unanimously approved the establishment of an independent Czechoslovak state.[65]

Whether or not the National Committee would manage to hold on to power in Bohemia in the coming days depended largely on the reactions of the Austro-Hungarian garrisons in Prague and other cities. On the first day of the revolution in Prague, the military commander there originally agreed to cooperate with the National Committee. By the following day, however, Austrian authorities were beginning to realize that the National Committee was not merely setting up an autonomous government but rather an independent state. As a result, the Ministry of War in Vienna ordered its garrisons throughout the empire not to support the national committees. In Prague, the officers ordered the Magyar and Romanian troops to retake key buildings inside the city, but the soldiers refused. Having lost their interest in serving the dynasty, the troops instead began agitating to return to their homelands in order to support the national causes there. The story was the same nearly everywhere: by the time the Austro-Hungarian military leaders decided to take action, they no longer had a reliable force at their command.

By 30 October the threat of an Austro-Hungarian counterattack against the National Committee dissipated as the latter and its affiliates had reached settlements with the military commands in Prague, Plzeň and other districts. That morning, Coudenhove returned to the Bohemian capital to make a futile demand for the Prague National Committee to share power with his office. His mission came to an abrupt end, however, when he was arrested by armed Sokol volunteers at the city's train station and then put under what amounted to house arrest for several days. Meanwhile, the Czechs in neighboring Moravia, stirred into action by events in Prague, had hastily formed a national committee in Brno and were in the process of assuming control of the administrative offices in that province. In Vienna, Tusar met with Prime Minister Lammasch who warmly greeted the National Committee representative as the Czechoslovak Ambassador.[66] Lammasch's attitude in that meeting was reflective of the stance adopted by virtually all Austrian leaders: having reconciled themselves to the empire's dissolution into nation-states, they strove to avoid unnecessary bloodshed and perhaps hoped to maintain some relevance through amicable relations with the successor governments.

The Czechs were not the first nationality in the Habsburg Empire to declare a new state for themselves. In L'viv, Ukrainian representatives from the Reichsrat and regional parliaments had formed a national committee on 18 October and then proclaimed the independence of eastern Galicia and Bukovina the next day. Unlike the Czech revolutionaries in Prague, the Ukrainians in L'viv failed to convince the Austrian authorities to turn over power to them; subsequently their West Ukrainian Republic held little actual authority in its first two weeks of existence. The next nationality to embark on a state-building exercise was not Slav but, surprisingly, the German-Austrians. In response the Emperor's manifesto, on 21 October the German-Austrian deputies withdrew from the Reichsrat and organized themselves into a national assembly for an independent German Austria.[67] Unlike most other ethnicities, however, the German-Austrians for a time left open the question of whether their new state was to be a republic or a constitutional monarchy under the House of Habsburg. Many of them desired their union (*Anschluss*) to Germany, which they believed would be compatible under the principle of self-determination espoused by President Wilson.[68]

After the Czecho-Slovak National Committee declared its independence on 28 October, other nationalities quickly followed. The next day, the Sabor in Zagreb and a large assembly of South Slavs in Ljubljana declared the independence of the Serbs, Croats and Slovenes in the Monarchy along with their willingness to join Serbia and Montenegro.[69] On 31 October the Galician Poles disarmed the Austro-Hungarian garrison in Kraków and installed their own committee as the new governing body. Meanwhile in L'viv, the Poles who comprised the majority of that city's inhabitants began fighting the Ukrainians who were trying to claim the city as the capital of their West Ukrainian Republic. For the next three weeks, the two ethnic groups engaged each other in fierce street battles until the West Ukrainian government withdrew to Ternopil. The entire spectacle was a sharp rebuke of the émigrés recent claims that their peoples would coexist peacefully.

The Galician Poles intended to join their homeland to Congress Poland, which was in the throes of considerable disarray during the last weeks of the war. As the occupying troops of Germany and Austria-Hungary deposed their officers and formed committees, the Regency Council which had depended on them for protection was left exposed to hostile political factions, some of which were backed by paramilitary forces. The German military leaders, not wanting to see Poland lapse into a civil war that might end with the establishment of yet another communist regime to their east, released Piłsudski from Magdeburg on 8 November and placed him on an express train to Warsaw. Piłsudski's prestige worked just as the Germans had hoped: most of the opposing parties rallied to his banner and the threat of a major civil war in Poland was averted. On 10 November, he was given dictatorial powers by the Regency Council before that body dissolved itself.[70] While Piłsudski's aura humbled his possible opponents in the Polish homeland, his rule was contested by Roman Dmowski's Polish National Committee in Paris, which had the sympathies of the Allies. Two months would pass before the rival Polish governments in Paris and Warsaw reconciled with each other.

The curdling of the Habsburg Empire into nation-states also induced the Magyars to make an endeavor to realize their dream of a truly independent Greater Hungary. Under the liberal Count Mihály Károlyi, they had formed a national committee of their own in Budapest to advance the principle of self-determination for Magyars while maintaining the tradition of Kossuth by denying similar rights to the minorities inside the historic Hungarian kingdom.[71] For this reason, the Slovaks' liberation from Magyar oppression came well after 28 October 1918, the date which was commemorated as the Czechoslovak Republic's independence day.

Because of the more oppressive conditions under the Hungarian regime, the liberation movement in the Slovak homelands had a much slower start. On 12 September Matúš Dula, the leader of the Slovak National Party, attempted to assemble Slovak politicians in Budapest to openly form a Slovak national committee, but for the following six weeks the Hungarian police made certain that such a meeting did not take place. In the meantime, on 20 October, Šrobár was released from his Hungarian prison cell and made a beeline for Prague, where he arrived in time to become the only Slovak to sign the National Committee's proclamation of an independent Czechoslovak state. The revolution in Bohemia remained unknown in

Upper Hungary when on 30 October, two days after the Czechoslovak state had been declared in Prague, Dula's efforts to form a Slovak national committee finally came to fruition in Turčansky Svätý Martin. The meeting was finally permitted by the Hungarian government in the hope that this concession might entice the Slovaks to remain within Greater Hungary. As a backup plan, Budapest also dispatched two companies of Magyar troops to the town to help ensure that the Slovak leaders adopted an "acceptable" resolution. The Slovaks were not so easily intimidated, however, especially after Milan Hodža arrived in Turčansky Svätý Martin that evening announcing the declaration of a Czechoslovak state in Prague. Amid their excitement over this news, the Slovak delegates hastily edited the resolution which they had passed earlier in the day in order to confirm their recognition of the Czechoslovak state.

After this declaration was made public, Magyar troops continued to advance into Upper Hungary and it became evident that the Slovak revolutionaries faced a much more resolute opponent in Budapest than the Czechs did in Vienna. In order to assert Czechoslovak claims over the Slovak homeland, on 2 November the National Committee ordered Šrobár, accompanied by three colleagues and about seventy armed Sokol volunteers for protection, to set up an administration for Slovakia. Although the party crossed the Hungarian frontier three days later, the threat of a Magyar attack forced them back into Moravia. Šrobár was recalled to Prague a few days later and the administration he was supposed to set up was discarded in favor of a centralized Czechoslovak government based in Prague.[72] Meanwhile, the Magyars continued to occupy the Slovak homeland with no intention of leaving.

By November 1918, Austria-Hungary had effectively ceased to exist, yet what remained of its army continued to fight regard actions in Italy and southern Hungary. Desperate to end hostilities in a struggle that had lost all meaning, the AOK eagerly concluded an armistice with the Allies at Padua on 3 November. Confusion over the precise time when the armistice took effect caused the Habsburg troops to lay down their arms prematurely, which enabled the Italians to advance against no resistance and take a trove of prisoners in their only convincing victory of the war.[73] The ethnic composition of the 350,000 soldiers they took captive in the battle is interesting in light of the Allied propaganda offensive on that front and the declaration of an independent Czechoslovak state several days earlier. Approximately 83,000 of the soldiers were of Czech and Slovak nationality; South Slavs, Poles and Ukrainians also entered Italian POW camps by the tens of thousands in those closing days of the war.[74] Although the Padua armistice ended military operations on the Italian Front, it did not apply to the front in Southern Hungary, where Allied troops continued to advance until the armistice went into effect on the Western Front on 11 November. Two days later, Count Károlyi, now leading the republican government in Budapest, agreed to a separate armistice with General d'Espérey which forced the Hungarians to pull out of Yugoslav territory but left them in control of Upper Hungary and Transylvania, regions that were respectively claimed by Czechoslovakia and Romania.[75]

Upper Hungary was not the only region claimed by the new Czechoslovak state that was initially off-limits to its authority. The German-Bohemians residing on the frontiers of Bohemia, Moravia and Silesia abhorred the prospect of becoming an ethnic minority in a Slavic state. They sought to be included in German-Austria and their deputies even joined the new German-Austrian National Assembly in Vienna. But due to the close economic integration of Bohemia and Moravia, they quickly learned that they could not easily divorce themselves from events in the rest of the provinces. After the Prague revolution, the regular food shipments which the industrialized borderlands depended upon quit arriving. In the first days of November, an elected representative for the German-Bohemians, Rudolf Lodgman von Auen, traveled to Prague to beg for the resumption of grain deliveries to feed the starving population in northern Bohemia. Czech leaders agreed to fulfill his request—but only if Lodgman and his fellow politicians joined the provisional National Assembly in Prague. Ominously for future Czech-German relations in the emerging state, Lodgman decided his malnourished constituents would rather starve than accept Czechoslovak rule. While turning their backs on the Czechs, the German population in the Bohemian and Moravian borderlands exercised their right to self-determination by organizing themselves into four provinces ostensibly belonging to German-Austria. Two of these provinces— Deutschböhmen and Sudetenland in northern Bohemia and northern Moravia—were completely isolated from German-Austria and all of the provinces were cut off from each other. Painfully aware of their weak geographical position, many German-Bohemian nationalists secretly pined for their union with Germany, not little German-Austria. This desire might have been realized if it were not for the utterly desperate straits the German Reich was in by November 1918. The leaders in Berlin, by then facing the twin disasters of military defeat abroad and revolution in the homeland, hardly had time to consider the welfare of their Bohemian brothers.[76]

Even though the authority of the new state was for the moment confined to the Czech areas of Bohemia and Moravia, the National Committee remained in high spirits as the war wound down in the first week of November. On 5 November, Kramář and the other politicians who went to Geneva returned to Prague praising the feats of the exiles who worked abroad during the war. The delegation, perhaps due to Beneš's own exaggerations, had an inflated sense of their nation's importance in the impending postwar settlement. Klofáč even proclaimed that "Wilson or anyone else would never say anything which Masaryk or Beneš did not underwrite."[77] Six days later, the armistice of Compiègne went to effect ending the fighting on the Western Front. In Vienna, Emperor Karl, by then possessing a "weary, careworn look" that contrasted sharply with the youthful vigor he displayed at the start of his two-year reign, abdicated his role in the Austrian government. That evening, he and his family slipped out of the city to avoid the wrath of the frenzied Viennese mobs.[78]

While Kramář and the Prague National Committee tried to preserve order in Bohemia amid the collapse of the Habsburg Monarchy, Beneš returned to Paris to push for Czechoslovakia's admission onto the Allied Supreme War Council. In his discussions with French officials with whom he had become rather well-acquainted, Beneš argued that the new Czechoslovak state was an island of stability in a Central Europe seething with revolution, border conflicts and the threat of communism. Although his claim was a stretch—not least because of Czechoslovakia's limited jurisdiction in the territory it claimed—it played successfully upon fears that viewed Bolshevism as the next great menace after the collapse of German militarism. The impressive record of the Czecho-Slovak corps in Russia, which was made possible by its successful resistance to Bolshevik subversion, strengthened Beneš claim of the Czechs and Slovaks' supposed immunity to communism. The French, and more reluctantly other Allied representatives, accepted this argument and permitted him to join the Supreme War Council. Although Beneš's acceptance came too late for him to have any input in the armistice terms with Germany, his new position would prove beneficial in the postwar peace conference. Czechoslovakia would remain alone among the successor states in having a representative on the Supreme War Council.[79]

From New York City, Masaryk watched events in Central Europe as closely as transatlantic communications at the time permitted. On 5 November, he received a telegram from the Czecho-Slovak National Council in Paris asking him to return to Prague as quickly as possible to begin serving as president of the new state.[80] Masaryk was eager to oblige. It would be four years in December since he left his wife and most of his children behind to work for Czecho-Slovak independence abroad. Since then, his eldest son, Herbert, had died after contracting typhus from Galician refugees. His daughter, Alice, had endured several months of imprisonment while his youngest son Jan was conscripted into the Austro-Hungarian Army. His wife, Charlotte, had been under police surveillance for most of the war, suffered a nervous breakdown and had to be placed in a nursing home.[81] The sixty-eight-year-old professor was also exhausted by his travels: his work had taken him to Prague, Geneva, Paris and London; later to Petrograd, Kiev, Moscow and Vladivostok; and finally to Tokyo, Vancouver, Chicago, Pittsburgh, New York City and Washington, D.C. He was not simply a tired man; he was also a changed man. As a philosophy professor prior to the war, he had always strove to defend truth, promote reform and place humanitarianism above all else, but since becoming a revolutionary he had violated many of the principles he once lectured others to uphold. He who once said that Czech nationalism must not be based on lies generated propaganda full of dubious assertions. He who had been critical of hyper-nationalism now advocated Czech independence on the basis of natural or historical rights while denying the same freedoms to German-Bohemians and others.[82] The practical solutions for the national cause had triumphed over the humanitarian ideal.

Before embarking on his return voyage to Europe, Masaryk paid a final visit to President Wilson to thank him on behalf of the Czechoslovak nation for making their independence possible. He also issued an army order to the Czecho-Slovak Legions in France and Italy announcing their imminent return to the homeland. He probably would have liked to make a similar promise to the legionaries in Russia, but instead he ordered them to continue faithfully serving Allied interests in that country. Masaryk left the U.S. on 20 November for Britain, where he was received at the docks by Henry Wickham Steed, Robert Seton-Watson, a hastily-assembled honor guard and a military band that, not knowing the Czechoslovak national anthem, welcomed him to the tune *See the Conquering Hero Comes.*[83]

These were heady times for Masaryk and his close supporters, like Steed and Seton-Watson, who against all odds had struggled to earn the Czechs and Slovaks their place among nations. Almost from the start, most other "oppressed peoples" of Central Europe had some sort of leverage in their effort to realize their national goals during the war. The aspirations of the South Slavs, for example, could count on at least some support from the Serbian government,[84] just as irredentist Italians and Romanians could rely on Rome and Bucharest for encouragement.[85] The Poles and Ukrainians, whose homelands were divided between the Central Powers and Russia, learned to play the belligerents against each other to obtain outside support.[86, 87] The Czechs and Slovaks, however, had neither a national homeland outside the Monarchy nor a natural ally they could depend on. In order to secure the foreign support they needed to win their independence, the Czech and Slovak exiles realized that this could not be obtained as a result of who they were but rather because of what they could do. In other words, they were imbued with a need for self-reliance that made their campaign the best organized, most effective and most successful of the national movements during World War I.

If there was a downside to the spectacular achievements of the Czecho-Slovak liberation movement, it was the high and sometimes unrealistic expectations shouldered by the new state and its leaders after the war. This was at least partially the fault of the exile propagandists who were more concerned with watchwords than accuracy in their works. Also to blame were the socialists, Czech chauvinists and Slovak autonomists who entertained their own dreams of how the new state organization should conform to their narrow ideologies. Foreigners too had their own preconceived notions of what an independent Czechoslovakia meant for Europe. France saw the new nation, along with Poland and Yugoslavia, as the centerpiece of a barrier against German *Drang nach Osten*. President Wilson expected Masaryk's state to become a pillar of a new democratic order in Central Europe. It was evident that Czechoslovakia, regardless of its long-term success, could not possibly fulfill all these hopes.

It did not take long for some of those who had placed Czecho-Slovak expectations so high during the war to realize the scope of the task that lay before them in the conflict's aftermath. The same day the armistice was signed at Compiègne, Masaryk's two main British accomplices, Steed and Seton-Watson, had a somber dinner in Paris with another journalist, Harold Williams. Although the Parisians around them were blissfully celebrating the end of over four years of uninterrupted slaughter, the stupor of having achieved their goals had already worn off these men who had devoted themselves to the destruction of Austria-Hungary. "They saw too clearly what disillusionments and difficulties awaited Europe," wrote Williams' wife. "They realized the moral responsibilities of victory only too clearly."[88] A month later, President Masaryk, amid his return journey to Prague, expressed similar anxiety in a speech to a detachment of Czecho-Slovak legionaries in France. "More than once I reminded you that you must hold out to the end," he told them. "All of us have done that, but now we must finish what we have begun. There is still work to do, in fact we are now faced by a more difficult task than before."[89] Those words were probably truer than even he had imagined.

13

The Siberian Vendée

The armistice in Compiègne did not usher peace into Russia. On the same day the guns fell silent on the Western Front, Allied expeditionary forces manning frontlines along the railway south of Archangelsk were fending off a determined Bolshevik attack.[1] Several hundreds of miles southeast of the North Russian theater, the Czecho-Slovak legionaries in the Urals found themselves up against an equally resilient enemy. For them the onset of the armistice in the West was anticlimactic. "The message carrying information concerning one of the greatest crises in world history," wrote Lieutenant Bečvar, "was then of no more interest to us than the weather forecast for tomorrow."[2] He and the other legionaries who had blazed their way through Central and Eastern Siberia earlier that year had now returned to the Urals to reinforce their cadres caught in the thickest of fighting. By then exhaustion and casualties were taking their toll on the Czecho-Slovaks, many of whom had been fighting for over five months with little respite.

Since the spring, the Czecho-Slovak Legion in Russia had recruited about 20,000 men, enough to form a third division. A smaller number of South Slav volunteers from the POW camps also enlisted to fight alongside the Czecho-Slovaks, but even with these additions the legionaries' strength was stretched to the limits.[3] In late August 1918, the National Council in Russia ended the practice of relying exclusively on volunteers by ordering all Czechs and Slovaks in Siberia to report for duty. This measure failed to satisfy the corps' manpower needs. Many POWs, because of the privations they suffered while in camps and not through any fault of their own, were unfit for service in the frontlines. Edward Heald, an American YMCA secretary, was especially sympathetic toward such POWs. "They are without uniforms," he observed, "their faces are sunken and haggard, they have seen the worst of prison camp life and are nothing more than wrecks of humanity."[4] Poor health was not the only factor which affected the pool of potential recruits; many were either apathetic to the Czechoslovak cause or were indoctrinated with pacifist or revolutionary propaganda. As the tide of the civil war turned in favor of the Red Army that autumn, these less-than-willing soldiers would be among the first to crack.[5]

Trouble first appeared in the Czecho-Slovak Legion in late September when the 1st and 4th Regiments refused to go into battle amid some of the worst fighting seen yet on the Volga front. Desertion was becoming a problem for all of the four regiments in the First Czecho-Slovak Division, and the situation did not improve during the following month.[6] On October 15, Čeček, the division's commander, was relieved of his duties as commander-in-chief on the Volga front and was sent to Vladivostok. Ten days later, Colonel Švec, Čeček's successor as commanding officer of the 4th Regiment, turned his revolver on himself when his men refused to leave their trains and fight.[7]

These legionaries used tree foliage to conceal the machine guns mounted on their railcar.

Lieutenant Colonel Voitsekhovsky, the Russian commander of the 3rd Czecho-Slovak Regiment, assumed Čeček's place as commander-in-chief on the Volga front. After being promoted to a general by the ARPG, Voitsekhovsky faced the daunting task of stemming the retreat of Czecho-Slovak and White forces west of Ufa. The railway in that sector was choked with legionaries and White soldiers competing for locomotives to pull their trains east, and the situation was little better on nearby roads as refugees fled eastward by carts or their feet. Most distressing of all was the position of the remnant of the People's Army, totaling about 15,000 troops, trapped behind enemy lines.

In order to salvage the situation, Voitsekhovsky's first step was to appeal for help from the legionaries. Since the general was a respected and popular former commander of their army, the shattered Czecho-Slovaks agreed to remain at the front until the beginning of December, by which time Voitsekhovsky hoped to have fresh Russian troops deployed a new defensive line in the Urals. Until then, his main task was to rescue the anti–Bolshevik units enveloped by the Reds and then evacuate the Ufa sector. On 10 November, Voitsekhovsky, with a crack force of legionaries, launched a counteroffensive just west of Ufa, near the town of Belebei. The attack succeeded in puncturing the Red front, allowing the encircled People's Army to break out from its pocket. The fighting around Belebei lasted a full week and was a tactical success for the Whites. Not only did it rescue the remnants of the People's Army, it also stalled the progress of the First and Fifth Red Armies long enough to prevent them from breeching the Urals before the arrival of heavy winter snows. The accomplishments of this counteroffensive, however, did not renew the enthusiasm of the legionaries for their continued participation in the Russian Civil War.[8]

Physical exhaustion and sheer attrition were some of the many reasons behind the legionaries' desire to quit the front. With the world war over in Europe and Czechoslovak statehood now a reality, the legionaries saw no use in their continuing to fight in Russia. They were homesick and eager to return to Central Europe to help consolidate their new state. Even Winston Churchill, who desperately wished for the Czecho-Slovaks to expend every last ounce of their strength in the campaign to quash Bolshevism, understood why they yearned to leave Siberia. "Home, which might have been forever barred and banned to them," he wrote, "now shone in the lights of freedom and honour. Very brightly did the beacon gleam to their eyes across the vast snows of Russia."[9] General Štefánik, however, was not about ready to let the legionaries begin the long march home. He had been designated Czechoslovak Minister of War while en route to Siberia with French General Janin. Both men had been caught unawares by the Czecho-Slovak uprising that summer and now that they were in a position to command the legionaries, they had ambitious goals in mind for them. Unfortunately for their plans, by the time Štefánik and Janin landed in Vladivostok on 16 November 1918 the fighting capabilities of the legionaries were rapidly waning.[10]

The situation of the civil war in Siberia when the two men arrived there was probably very different than they had expected. They were greeted on Vladivostok's quays by Czecho-Slovak and White Russian representatives who were eager to point fingers at each other for the worsening situation in the Volga and Urals. The Russians blamed the recent Bolshevik successes on the growing indiscipline and desertion among the Czecho-Slovaks, meanwhile the latter accused the anti–Bolshevik Russians of devoting more energy to political infighting than mounting a united resistance against the Soviet regime. Štefánik responded to this news by sending orders to the legionaries that they must continue serving Allied interests in Russia. In doing so, he believed that the troops would immeasurably strengthen Czechoslovakia's hand at the upcoming Paris Peace Conference, and he would never tire of reminding them of this when he inspected the Czecho-Slovak regiments in the following weeks.[11] Janin, meanwhile, thought he would reverse the crisis by taking command of all anti–Bolshevik forces, including Czecho-Slovaks and Russians, west of Lake Baikal. This post had been promised to him by Clemenceau—the anti–Bolshevik Russians had not even been consulted in the decision. The Whites, perhaps realizing that Janin's leadership might appear to validate communist propaganda that their movement was funded by Anglo-French imperialists, refused to confirm him as their commander-in-chief when he arrived in Omsk. The Frenchman, who was known for a bloated sense of his own self-importance,[12] had to settle for command of all non–Russian troops west of Lake Baikal and was, as a result, permanently embittered against the Siberian Whites.[13]

The Czecho-Slovaks' allegations that the White Russians were more interested in fighting each other than the Red Army gained further credence after a successful coup in Omsk overthrew the ARPG shortly after Štefánik and Janin arrived in Siberia. For months, rumors of an impending right-wing coup had long been floating around White Siberia, and many figures were not timid in expressing their desire to replace the impotent ARPG with a military dictatorship. These men included Russian Kadets, who were becoming increasingly less liberal in their political outlook; Major General Alfred Knox, the head of the British Military Mission to Siberia; and General Gajda, who rode his recent wave of popularity and promotions to be named Commander-in-Chief of the Siberian Army.[14] Unlike Gajda, most Czecho-Slovaks preferred to keep the ARPG in power, and when they caught wind of the conspiracies brewing against the ARPG, they offered their services to protect the Directory in Omsk.

Although the few Russians sympathetic to the ARPG urged their leaders to accept the offer, one of the SR Directors, A. V. Avksentev, refused to consider it. "I do not need your Latvians," he supposedly sneered.[15] This callous remark, which likened the legionaries to Lenin's Varangian Guard,[16] was indicative of the growing resentment which many Russians were feeling towards the Czecho-Slovaks' "interference."

Avksentev's refusal to accept Czecho-Slovak assistance left the ARPG at the mercy of its enemies. Shortly after midnight on 18 November, he and another SR Director were abruptly arrested by a dozen inebriated Siberian Cossack officers. Later that morning, in a raging snowstorm, the cabinet of the ARPG convened an emergency session at the Governor's Palace in Omsk. With two-fifths of the Directory behind bars, there was little doubt in anyone's mind that the authority of the ARPG was compromised. In its place, most of the ministers demanded the establishment of a military dictatorship under Vice-Admiral Aleksandr Vasilevich Kolchak. Their near-unanimous suggestion of Kolchak for the post was no coincidence, for the past month the admiral's advocates had been working behind the scenes to hoist the clean-shaven, dapper and seemingly un–Russian sailor to the helm of the White movement in Siberia.[17] Other candidates had been considered by the plotters, but either they were too far away from Siberia—as in the case of Generals Alekseev and Denikin—or they were suspected of being too close to the Japanese—such as Horvath or Semenov.[18] As a result, the little-known Kolchak was the preferred candidate and was elected military dictator by the ministers. Later that day, the admiral issued a proclamation announcing his appointment as Supreme Ruler and portrayed himself as an eventual harbinger of democracy even though the coup that brought him to power had just trampled on the last traces of representative government in Siberia.[19]

Why did the Omsk ministers elect a man about whom they knew very little to lead their new government? The answer appears to lie in the tiny bits of information they did have on the forty-four-year-old admiral, who was respected as a polar explorer and a heroic officer in the Russian Navy. Kolchak had graduated second in his class from the St. Petersburg Naval Academy in 1894 and a decade later he distinguished himself in the defense of Port Arthur during the war with Japan, for which he was awarded the St. George's Sword of Honor. During the world war, Kolchak served as a captain in the Baltic Fleet and then as a vice-admiral in the Black Sea Fleet. He excelled in naval defense and especially mine-laying operations, but the collapse of the established order in 1917 cut his promising career short. Although Kolchak did not mourn the demise of the incompetent tsarist regime, he found it difficult to share his authority with the sailor's committees and his tolerance of them expired in June 1917 when they demanded all naval officers to be disarmed. Rather than hand over his Sword of Honor to the revolutionary sailors, an enraged Kolchak, in front of the crew on his flagship *Georgey Pobedonosets*, instead hurled his prized saber into the sea. The dramatic scene was quickly memorialized in anti–Bolshevik folklore and cited as evidence of the admiral's courageous stand before the heathens of the revolution. In reality, the incident appears to fit a pattern of uncontrollable tantrums which Kolchak would display during his tenure as Supreme Ruler.[20]

Besides his record in the revolution, another quality which made Kolchak attractive for the post of military dictator was his familiarity to Allied officials. After leaving the Black Sea Fleet in the summer of 1917, Kolchak went to the U.S. in the service of the Provisional Government to consult with naval tacticians there on how to open the Black Sea Straits. He got along exceptionally well with the British and developed a close relationship with General

Admiral Kolchak exits the rear of an open automobile, undated. The covers around the engine compartment convey a sense of the inhospitable climate of the Supreme Ruler's realm.

Knox. The Whites, who now more than ever acknowledged their need of foreign aid to defeat the Red juggernaut, hoped that Kolchak's personal contacts with the Allies might assure their commitment to the anti–Bolshevik cause.[21]

Despite their effort to attract greater assistance from the Western Powers, the Siberian Whites made the serious folly of alienating their most valuable foreign allies thus far—the Czecho-Slovaks. The coup offended the democratic sensibilities of the legionaries not only because of the proto-monarchist title bestowed on Kolchak, but also because it had occurred at the expense of the Directory and the SRs, both of which the legionaries regarded favorably. The new rulers understood that their coup would probably not sit well with the legionaries and for this reason they feared the reaction of the strong Czecho-Slovak garrison in Omsk. To alleviate their anxieties, a British battalion from the Middlesex Regiment took up positions around the main buildings in Omsk in the days immediately following the coup to prevent any operation against the new government. This measure, along with the guard of honor and other services which the British Military Mission later availed to Kolchak, led many Allied representatives in Siberia, including Generals Janin and Graves, to claim that the Supreme Ruler was a British creature.[22, 23] If this was the case—and there is no conclusive evidence that it was—then the policy of Britain's military representatives in Siberia was badly out of synch with the Foreign Office in London, which was just about to grant *de facto* recognition to the ARPG.[24] Nonetheless, British paternalism of the Kolchak regime, whether real or imagined, was resented by the French, who suspected that Britain was trying to usurp their country in its pre-war role as Russia's principal partner.[25] As French indignations trickled down to their Czecho-Slovak protégés, the legionaries gained yet another reason to oppose the new regime and quit the front.

Czecho-Slovak representatives in Siberia were not shy about conveying the legionaries' repugnance for the government of the Supreme Ruler. From its headquarters in Chelyabinsk, Pavlů's committee, now subordinate to the Czechoslovak Foreign Ministry, summarized the views of the legionaries in a 21 November announcement by stating that "the Czech-Slovak Army, fighting for the ideals of freedom and democracy, cannot and will not either unite or cooperate with the makers of coups d'etat which run contrary to these principles."[26] The scathing manifesto not only demanded the restoration of the Directory, it also chided the White armies in Siberia for their failure to adequately assist the legionaries at the front who were making great sacrifices on their behalf.[27] By this time, the number of casualties in the Czecho-Slovak corps was approaching 9,000. Bolshevik bullets were only partly responsible for this tally as outbreaks of tuberculosis and influenza also took their toll. Along the front, the mercury plunged below -50° Fahrenheit and severe frostbite became another factor which disabled the men.[28] In these conditions, the most surprising aspect was not that the legionaries were mutinous by late autumn of 1918, but rather that they fought on the Ural slopes as long they did.

Foolishly, the Whites did nothing to mend their relations with the Czecho-Slovaks. As the legionaries met defeat on the battlefield, the ex-tsarist officers who now held a commission in the White armies became increasingly condescending of the Czech generals who had been mere lieutenants or captains a few months earlier. Many proud Russian patriots preferred to forget that it was the Czecho-Slovaks, and not themselves, who were instrumental in sweeping Bolshevik rule from Siberia. Kolchak stood out among this group when, amid his outrage over the National Council's protest against his regime, he admonished the Czecho-Slovaks for their interference in affairs which he declared to be "absolutely none of their concern."[29] To Sir Charles Eliot, the British High Commissioner to Siberia, he vented that the legionaries "were no good and the sooner they cleared out the better."[30] Mostly, the Whites wanted to have it both ways in regards to their relations with the Czecho-Slovaks: on one hand they desired the legionaries to continue fighting for their cause at the front but on the other they wanted the foreigners to have no input in the political direction of the anti–Bolshevik movement.

As the untested Siberian Army finally began arriving on the Ural front in late autumn, the Czecho-Slovak leaders and Allies searched for ways to keep the legionaries on the front-line as long as possible. Štefánik, while touring the Czecho-Slovak regiments, unsuccessfully appealed to the troops to remain at the front to enhance Czechoslovakia's position at the peace conference.[31] The British, knowing that the legionaries were disgruntled by the absence of any other Allied expeditionary forces in the Urals, tried to raise Czecho-Slovak morale by sending a battalion from the Middlesex Regiment to tour the rear of the frontlines. These troops, who were mostly invalids deemed unfit for service in France, had been stationed in Hong Kong before landing at Vladivostok on 3 August 1918. They and a battalion from the Hampshire Regiment which landed in Siberia in late November would be the only substantial contingent of Allied troops to venture west of Irkutsk.[32] Unfortunately, their appearance near the frontlines that winter was a source for more ridicule than inspiration to the legionaries. When thirty or so troops from the Middlesex Regiment marched in front of Lieutenant Bečvar and his fellow legionaries one frigid morning, the weary Czecho-Slovaks were not impressed when they noticed the Tommies were carrying trumpets and cymbals instead of rifles and grenades. The band soon began blasting Britain's national anthem, *God Save the King*, and when the notes penetrated the crisp air all the way to Bolshevik lines, Red artillery began lobbing shells into the area. The deafening explosions sent the Britons scurrying back to their train before they finished their tune, leaving the unlucky legionaries to sit out the rest of the bombardment.[33]

Most legionaries did not acknowledge that the Allied diplomats, consuls and attachés who promised their countries' unqualified support to them in the summer of 1918 had greatly overstepped their authority. Subsequently, many Czecho-Slovak soldiers felt they had been duped by the Allies who had left them "to die like rats in the Ural snows."[34] In the meantime, Bolshevik propagandists were quick to hone in on their disillusionment; one of their favorite themes suggested that the Allies—especially the Americans—would only spend money on the intervention while leaving the Czecho-Slovaks to do the grunt work.[35] Against such allegations, the traveling concerts of the Middlesex Regiment's band played into rather than refuted enemy propaganda.

It should not be surprising that the legionaries had little understanding of the real motivations and intrigues behind the clumsy foreign intervention in Russia. When the war in Western Europe ended in November, not even the Allies themselves knew what their next step should be in Russia. The officials with the clearest policy were the staunch anti-communists who wanted to transfer the troops, tanks and guns from France to Russia; even Lenin expected such a "capitalist crusade" to occur.[36] But this group, which included Churchill, Clemenceau and Marshal Foch, were soon faced with the reality that such a redeployment would not be so simple. Four long years of war left neither France nor Great Britain with the strength to launch a major campaign in Russia. Those Allied countries that were not as exhausted by the war, such as Japan and the United States, were reluctant to proceed beyond the limited aims of their intervention. Politically speaking, arguments for an all-out military effort in Russia were impossible to sell to constituents who had been repeatedly told that the war against Germany was the "war to end all war." Most Allied countries also had to contend with their own labor movements that were uncomfortable with supporting an assault on the world's first workers' state.[37] Moreover, few soldiers who survived the horror of the trenches on the Western Front were willing to risk their lives on the snowy plains of Russia. Discipline in most Allied armies broke down rapidly after the armistice was signed. During the winter of 1918–19, riots, mutinies and other demonstrations of indiscipline flared up among Allied troops in North Russia, in Britain and in the southern Ukraine, where a French and Greek expeditionary force consisting of 80,000 men, including tanks, were forced back to their ships by ragged partisan forces.[38] These incidents were obvious warning signals—and in some cases humiliations—which the Allied leaders could not ignore.

Unlike the anti-communists in their midst, some Allied statesmen never believed that the Bolsheviks should or could be removed from power in Russia by foreign intervention. At the Paris Peace Conference, President Wilson opined that he thought it was best to let the Russians "stew in their own juice."[39] British Prime Minister Lloyd George, citing the example of the French Revolution, doubted whether foreign intervention would be any more successful in twentieth-century Russia than it was in eighteenth-century France.[40] Even Clemenceau was forced to modify his views after France's operations in the southern Ukraine turned into a debacle by late spring of 1919. Thereafter, French leaders redirected their energies from intervention to containment of Bolshevism by supporting the friendly nation-states bordering Russia, such as Poland and Romania.[41] Thus Allied policies towards the civil war in Russia were disunited and erratic for most of 1919. Their intervention there was not halted, but nor were the quantities of troops and materiel sent to their expeditionary forces and White dependents expanded to levels deemed necessary by military advisors to defeat the Bolsheviks. The entire operation simply dragged on as a series of bungled half-measures in which the Czecho-Slovak legionaries found themselves inextricably intertwined.

Besides the lack of Allied commitment, another aspect of the fighting in Russia that fueled the legionaries' urge to leave the front was the brutal character of the fratricidal conflict. As veterans of the world war, most legionaries had seen their share of the horrors which machine guns, shellfire and gas wrought on men's bodies. Yet these ghastly scenes paled in comparison with the more personal tortures and atrocities that were recorded on all fronts of the Russian Civil War. For example, while fighting in the marshy steppes of western Siberia in the summer of 1918, a Czech officer in Lieutenant Bečvar's outfit was taken captive by the Reds. A few days later, the legionaries uncovered the unlucky man in a shallow grave; his corpse was naked, charred and covered with multiple stab wounds.[42] Similar mutilations were found on the body of Colonel Ushakov, the Russian officer who led a team of Whites behind Bolshevik lines along the shore of Lake Baikal in an ultimately successful, though deadly, operation. Each of these Bolshevik atrocities, it is worth noting, occurred before the Soviet government formally adopted terror as an official policy in August 1918.[43]

As menacing as the Red Terror was for the legionaries, in some ways the violence perpetrated by their White allies was more troublesome to them. White terror, though it was less systematic than that of the Reds, still managed to leave a trail of disfigured corpses that rivaled the handiwork of the Cheka executioners. The worst offenders in the White camp were the notorious Cossack warlords Grigory Semenov and Ivan Kalmykov. These two men respectively led the Transbaikal and Ussuri Cossacks—although their legitimacies as atamans are arguable—and operated from Chita and Khabarovsk after the Czecho-Slovaks cleared the nearby railways of Reds in the late summer and early autumn of 1918. Aged only in their mid to late twenties, each terrorized the peasants, war prisoners and travelers in their realms on the pretext of eradicating Bolshevism. Although they occasionally assisted the anti–Bolshevik cause by hunting partisans along the railways they controlled, their unruly bands more often preferred to torment helpless villagers, train passengers and workers in an unending spree of looting, bullying, raping, killing and pilfering.[44]

Militarily, the forces commanded by the Cossack bandits were weak and relied heavily on Japanese support. The Japanese bankrolled the rogue atamans for several reasons, a major one being that through them they could indirectly control the flow of traffic along the vital Trans-Siberian Railway. The atamans were also helpful in gaining their Japanese sponsors economic concessions in their areas of control, such as the waiver of custom fees on imported goods. Moreover, the Japanese encouraged their hirelings to oppose the Omsk regime at every turn, and by doing so they prevented the formation of a strong, centralized Russian government in Siberia.[45]

Even though Semenov and Kalmykov were no friends of Kolchak's dictatorship, their association with the anti–Bolshevik cause badly tarnished the image of the Supreme Ruler among observers in both Siberia and abroad. Despite having little direct interaction with the Omsk government, General Graves, the commander of the AEFS, condemned Kolchak and the Whites as a whole because of the bloody atrocities his men witnessed in Eastern Siberia.[46] Unlike murderous regimes of a later era, neither the Cossack atamans nor their charges were particularly secretive about their crimes. Some were downright boastful. Col-

***Semenovtsy*, undated. A close inspection of the soldiers' faces reveals their heterogeneous ethnic backgrounds.**

onel Sipailov, a former Okhrana agent employed by Semenov, bragged to an American railway engineer that he could not sleep at night without having killed someone earlier that day.[47] Another of Semenov's friends, Baron Nikolay Roman von Ungern-Sternberg, operated a well-known torture chamber at Dauria, just west of the border with Manchuria. A nobleman of Baltic German stock, Ungern-Sternberg immersed himself in militant Buddhism, opium and developing new methods for inflicting agony upon his prisoners. The baron's demented behavior quickly became fodder of gruesome legends; in one unverifiable story he was said to have responded to an outbreak of typhus among his troops by ordering all the ailing men to be shot.[48] Much further to the west in Omsk, the White terror was more subdued. Kolchak and other respectable leaders of the government did not condone the killings of political prisoners or suspected Bolsheviks but at the same time they did not seriously attempt to restrain or punish those who engaged in such activities. Much of the violence in the capital was perpetrated by reactionary officers and Siberian Cossacks who tortured, killed and then tossed their victims into "the Kingdom of the Irtysh," the Irtysh being the river adjacent to Omsk. The same elements were responsible for the murders, rapes and burnings committed by punitive expeditions in the countryside.[49] With rumors and confirmed reports of such terrible atrocities occurring from the Urals to the Pacific, it is perhaps not surprising that men like Graves and later many Czecho-Slovaks questioned whether the Russian population would really be better off under the Whites than the communists.

What role, if any, did the Czecho-Slovak legionaries have in this orgy of violence? In the early days of their campaign along the Trans-Siberian Railway, when the legionaries were vulnerable and felt themselves targeted by a Bolshevik-German conspiracy, the Czecho-Slovak leaders at Chelyabinsk authorized the execution of POWs, including Germans, Magyars and Communist Czechs.[50] Their hysteria against fighters in the Internationalist battalions probably led to instances where unarmed prisoners with no evident communist affiliation were dispatched by Czecho-Slovak firing squads. Non-Slavic prisoners were given the worst treatment by the legionaries, and gruesome tales of their mass-executions preceded the legionaries' advance. Their reputation had grown so fearsome that Ferenc Imrey, a Hungarian POW, went into hiding when the Czecho-Slovaks occupied the railside town where he was staying. After a few days, he was discovered by the legionaries and was sentenced to stand before a Czecho-Slovak firing squad for no reason other than he was of Magyar ethnicity. Fortunately for Imrey, the intervention of White Russian officers at the last moment saved his life, but several of his companions were not so lucky. Predictably, Imrey had an unfavorable opinion of the Czecho-Slovak Legion when he recounted his experiences as a POW in Siberia some years later. "Try as I may to put myself in their position during those days of their trek across Siberia," he wrote, "I cannot find, even in the polluted springs of hatred, justification for their wholesale murdering of our people, defenseless and at their mercy."[51]

Sadly, these victims of firing squads were probably more fortunate than their comrades who were imprisoned on freight trains. The destinations of many of these "death trains," if they had any, were the killing fields and torture chambers of Eastern Siberia. The inmates were provided very little food, water, sanitation or fuel to warm their mobile prison cells as the mercury plunged in the autumn of 1918, and the results were ghastly. Edward Heald encountered several of the trains while traveling the Trans-Siberian Railway from Vladivostok to Omsk that fall and left a chilling record of their occupants' plight. At Nikolsk, he met a train carrying Bolshevik prisoners from Samara, of which there were only 1,300 alive of the original cargo of 2,100 men. To the west, along the Chinese Eastern Railway, he saw two more trains carrying starving Bolshevik POWs guarded by Russian and Czecho-Slovak soldiers.[52] Imrey too wrote of encounters with death trains while traveling from Harbin to Nikolsk. In the latter town, the opening of a railcar for the first time in weeks revealed its occupants lying in a "frozen irrecognizable mass" after having succumbed to the cold and typhus.[53]

It is unclear whether the legionaries became intolerant of the atrocities against alleged Bolsheviks because their passions cooled as they lost interest in the civil war or if the White terror was simply a convenient excuse to use in their demands to evacuate Russia. Regardless, the Whites' murderous operations compelled the legionaries to protest when the reactionary officer-gangs began targeting all socialists indiscriminately in late 1918. One of the worst incidents occurred on the night of 21–22 December when an underground cell of Bolsheviks staged an abortive uprising in Omsk. The next day, while the Czecho-Slovak garrison in the city helped the Whites reduce the insurgents' stronghold in the suburb of Kulomsino, a contingent of Siberian Cossacks busied themselves with dispatching mostly unarmed political prisoners who had been released after the rebels briefly took control of the local prison. Although most of the freed prisoners made no serious attempt to escape, the White jailers still showed no mercy. Among the SRs and others whose mutilated remains washed up on the banks of the Irtysh were nine members from Russia's Constituent Assembly.[54]

This rash of killings laid bare the utter contempt of the Cossack and Siberian Army officers towards the leftists and moderate socialists, compelling some formerly anti–Bolshevik SRs to defect to the Reds. The incident also sparked an uproar in the Czecho-Slovak Legion since it seemed to confirm that the White leaders in Omsk were stuck in their old habit of purging their movement of democratic influences.[55, 56] Subsequently, it further deteriorated the troops' desire to fight at the front and agitation against the Kolchak regime from the disgusted Czecho-Slovaks reached such a pitch that the Whites themselves demanded the legionaries to be pulled from the front.[57]

The news of the massacre of political prisoners at Omsk might have stained the reputation of Kolchak's government more seriously if it had not been immediately followed by the Whites' impressive victory at Perm on Christmas Eve. The operation was led by Gajda, who had left the Czecho-Slovak Legion to pursue greater glory in Russian service. With the Siberian Army and a few units from the Second Czecho-Slovak Division still willing to take up arms, Gajda led his troops through the numbing cold to capture the northern industrial city from the Third Red Army. It was a costly defeat for the Bolsheviks, who abandoned nine armored trains, 260 locomotives, 120 field guns and 31,000 prisoners amid their retreat.[58] After months of giving ground to the Red Army on the southern end of the front, the Perm victory shimmered like a divine miracle for Omsk's new leaders. The Kolchak regime, it seemed, had delivered victory whereas the Directory had only brought defeat.

Confidence in the Omsk Stavka soared to such a height after Perm that some officers discounted their need of Allied and especially Czecho-Slovak support to win their contest against the Red Army.[59] Thus the legionaries were not as missed as they otherwise might have been when they began to withdraw from the Urals in January 1919. This movement was against the wishes of the Legion's Commander-in-Chief, General Syrový, and Štefánik, who tried to coax the legionaries back to the front by calling on them to fight their way home through Russia. When the two men finally realized that their troops were intent on leaving the front, they decided, along with other Allied representatives, to redeploy the Czecho-Slovaks along the Trans-Siberian Railway between Novonikolaevsk and Irkutsk in order to guard Kolchak's main supply route. Partisan activity there and in other regions had been a growing problem for Whites since September 1918, and the 5,000 miles of the Trans-Siberian Railway which Kolchak's forces needed to import munitions from abroad was a susceptible and inviting target for these insurgents. Some of these partisans were residual Red forces that had been chased from the railway in the summer of 1918 and had since established an operational base in the dense taiga and rugged wilderness along the route. Other detachments were truly homegrown movements that spawned in protest to the roving Cossack punitive expeditions or as a means to establish self-rule of the villages—a sort of peasant anarchy.[60] By watching over the railway they still needed to return home, the legionaries would be providing an invaluable service to the Kolchak government while avoiding the more intense fighting against the Red Armies.

While the Czecho-Slovak trains rolled towards Central Siberia that winter, Štefánik sought to put the Legion under a firm leadership that would restore its discipline so that the troops might again be useful at the front. The longer he stayed in Siberia pushing for his reforms, however, the more unpopular he became. His clear sympathies for conservative anti–Bolsheviks, including Kolchak, put him out of touch with most legionaries. His ban against further army congresses and soldier committees opened him up to the charge that he was an enemy of democracy and did not resonate well with the troops. Among his more inexplicable measures was the dismissal of the corps' Chief of Staff, General Diterikhs, who had served the Czecho-Slovaks faithfully and competently for the past year. This and other erratic decisions made by Štefánik have been attributed to his battle against a longtime illness that became more acute in early 1919.[61]

To the relief of Czecho-Slovak soldiers and officers alike, Štefánik soon departed from

Siberia to head back to Europe. The man he left in charge to whip the legionaries into an unquestionably obedient formation was Pavlů, who was now officially responsible to the Czechoslovak government rather than the legionaries who had elected him during the previous summer. Pavlů was a poor choice to lead the corps with the resolve that Štefánik wanted, a fact that should have been foreseeable given that his actions at the first army congress were those of an opportunist rather than a man with inflexible core values. He was eager to govern the troops through popular means, rather than authoritarian ones, and as a result he quickly moderated Štefánik's zero-tolerance stance towards army congresses almost as soon as the Slovak general set sail from Vladivostok. He only realized the error of his ways when preliminary consultations for a second army congress in April 1919 were laden with criticisms against his leadership. The legionaries, it turned out, did not want to even stay in Siberia guarding the railway; their only desire was to go home. They doubted Pavlů's ability to realize this goal anytime soon, and like Maxa a year earlier, he was being marginalized to the role of a lame-duck leader.[62]

Pavlů asserted his authority at the last possible moment when in early June 1919 legionary delegates began arriving in Irkutsk for the second army congress. By then the troops' agitation to return home reached feverish proportions as they learned news of Soviet Hungary's recent invasion of Slovakia.[63] As they watched the disgruntled delegates file into Irkutsk, both Pavlů and Syrový knew that their authority was at stake. The two men decided that the congress was fomenting insubordination in the corps and Syrový called in his military police to arrest the delegates as mutineers. Although all the detainees were soon released, the action sent a clear message to the troops that all further infractions would be taken seriously by the Czecho-Slovak Army Corps.[64]

While the Czecho-Slovak corps worked out the dilemmas of politics and redeployment in the early half of 1919, Siberia's Supreme Ruler addressed the problem of crushing the Bolsheviks. The solution he and his staff in the Omsk Stavka settled on was to attack as early as possible in order to keep the momentum that they felt was with them since the victory at Perm. Moreover, that achievement also dictated the main thrust of their offensive. Rather than push southward to link up with Denikin's Armed Forces of South Russia, the Omsk Stavka decided to invest most of their resources on the other end of the front, along the Perm-Vyatka railway, in order to advance into the desolate wilderness of North Russia. Somehow, they expected to reach the scanty Allied and White Russian forces operating several hundred miles away south of Archangelsk.[65]

As a naval technician, Kolchak understood his skills were not very applicable in a conflict being waged in the center of the world's largest continent. Therefore, he left the strategic and logistical considerations of the army to the top brass in Omsk Stavka. This arrangement might have sufficed if that headquarters was led by qualified officers from the tsarist army, but like nearly everything else in the White movement in Siberia, politics took precedence over military necessity. Subsequently, in these months the Omsk Stavka was staffed by mostly young, reactionary and relatively inexperienced officers imbued with a dangerous combination of vivid imaginations and overconfidence. Like rebellious teenagers, they went forward with their offensive plans despite the numerous warnings of wiser and more experienced army officers who pointed out that heavy snows could still impact the delivery of supplies, that the Whites needed to focus on the build up a strategic reserve of troops, or that it would make more sense to drive into the more hospitable lands on the southern end of the front.[66]

In the first week of March 1919 an estimated 110,000 White troops, many of them lacking boots or standard uniforms, surged westward out of the Urals against a slightly less numerous enemy. The unstoppable drive envisaged by the Omsk Stavka on the northern sector of the front soon came to nothing when Gajda's Siberian Army was stalled by stiff enemy resistance. On the opposite end of the front, the more neglected army built around the Ural and Orenburg Cossacks also made slow headway. The biggest surprise, however, occurred on in the center of Kolchak's army group, where the Western Army, formed around the remnants of the Komuch's People's Army, routed the Fifth Red Army. Its spectacular progress was aided by the sudden outbreak of anti–Bolshevik revolts in the Reds' rear, and in just two months it advanced to a depth of 250 miles. For a time, it appeared that the Reds were beaten; Gajda's officers were even promising their men that they would be in Moscow "in no more than six weeks."[67] But just when the Siberian Whites reached the pinnacle of their confidence, disaster struck. First came the spring thaw that liquefied roads and swelled the rivers, slowing the attackers' progress to a crawl. Then arrived fresh Red soldiers, party members and worker volunteers from all over Soviet Russia whom the Bolsheviks summoned to throw back the counterrevolutionaries from the east. On 28 April a newly-assembled Soviet force, led by Mikhail Frunze, a former millworker with no relevant military experience, tore into the left flank of the exhausted Western Army and sent it reeling throughout the month of May. This reverse soon affected Kolchak's entire front as the flanks of the northern and southern armies were exposed by the enemy advance in the center. By the end of June, Kolchak's fleeing troops were back at the Ural Mountains, their starting point for the spring offensive, and there was no sign that the enemy was ready to let up anytime soon.[68]

With his armies on the verge of losing the most formidable natural barrier standing between his capital and the Red armies, Kolchak began to lose faith in the young, cocksure military advisors he had surrounded himself with. In his search for proven talent, he appointed General Diterikhs to serve as commander-in-chief of his eastern army group. This infuriated Gajda, who may have coveted the position for himself, but by then his star was dimming. His Siberian Army was in shambles following the retreat back to the Urals, and on 1 July the Second Red Army retook Perm against little resistance. A week later, the Czech general quarreled with the Supreme Ruler, who summarily dismissed him.[69] In the meantime, the situation at the front continued to deteriorate. To the south, the Ural and Orenburg Cossacks were cut off from the rest of the Siberian Whites and were forced to retreat into Turkestan. In the center of the front, the rejuvenated Fifth Red Army seized Zlatoust and a crucial pass through the Urals by mid–July. Almost simultaneously, the remnants of the Siberian Army gave up Yekaterinburg.[70]

By now Diterikhs was convinced that the Urals were lost and urged the Supreme Ruler to withdraw his armies behind the River Tobol so they could rest and regroup. Instead, Kolchak decided on a risky counterattack at Chelyabinsk, which had been proposed to him by Major General Dmitri Lebedev, the mastermind at Omsk Stavka since the previous year. This operation, conducted with demoralized troops in difficult terrain, failed to meet its objective and cost the Siberian Whites dearly: they suffered perhaps 20,000 casualties, including many prisoners and others who deserted to the Reds. After this debacle, Lebedev was finally given his long over-due dismissal, but the damage his incompetent planning had wrought was by then largely irreparable. After their defeat at Chelyabinsk, Kolchak's forces were probably reduced to 60,000. The Red Eastern Army Group opposing them, despite having some of its divisions siphoned away after reaching the Urals, still enjoyed a vast numerical superiority with 200,000 men. To make matters worse, with the loss of the Urals, the supply-starved Siberian Whites lost one of the few mining and industrial regions that had been under their control.[71]

The pro-interventionists in the Allied camp were distraught over the sudden collapse of Kolchak's front since they had bet on his theater to be the most promising for a White victory. As they looked for a means to restore the Supreme Ruler's fortunes, their eyes fell upon the Czecho-Slovak legionaries. Clemenceau apparently hoped that the legionaries would return to the front as soon as they were rested. Churchill, serving as Britain's War Secretary, sensed that the legionaries were reluctant to voluntarily return to the front and devised a plan where the Czecho-Slovak corps could head for home *and* make a valuable contribution to the anti–Bolshevik cause. On 23 June, as the Red armies were approaching the Urals, Churchill informed Beneš of his scheme which called for some 30,000 Czecho-Slovaks, or about half of the corps' strength, to break through the Red Army's front and shoot their way to Archangelsk, from where they would board ships to Europe. Churchill hoped that the legionaries' drive would link up with the Allied expeditionary forces in North Russia who were planning to launch an attack toward Kotlas.[72] If such a connection were made, the Siberian Whites would have gained an alternative river-railroad supply route with Europe that was much shorter than their current supply line which ran along the Trans-Siberian Railway and the sea lanes to Vladivostok.

Beneš was cool to Churchill's scheme, which pretended that the Red Army of 1919 was not much stronger, better organized or ably-led than the Red forces of 1918. Although the Czechoslovak Foreign Minister did not want his country to be further entangled in Russia's civil wars, he heeded the War Secretary's request by communicating the details of the operation to General Syrový. Despite having just reasserted his authority by breaking up the second Czecho-Slovak army congress, Syrový knew his limitations and replied to Beneš that the legionaries would never agree to such a plan. This sober assessment did not please the anti-communist statesmen in Paris, including Kramář, who wanted Czechoslovakia and the Allies to hold nothing back in wiping his beloved Russia clean of Bolshevism. After learning of Syrový's initial rejection of Churchill's project, Kramář devised a new grand scheme for the legionaries to hack their way to South Russia, where Denikin's fortunes were soaring that summer. He quickly brought Pavlů on board with the plan and even General Janin gave it his approval. Clemenceau too liked the idea, but the final decision rested with Beneš. Unlike Kramář, Beneš was beginning to reconcile himself to the continuation of Soviet Russia, not because of any communist sympathies, but rather because he believed Czechoslovakia should look west, not east, for its security and political direction. An anti–Bolshevik Russia, as far as he was concerned, was not vital to his country's future as long as he enjoyed the backing of France. To Kramář's dismay, Beneš dropped the scheme and returned to the original plan of evacuating the Legion through Vladivostok. No one, not even he or Masaryk, knew when that date would come.[73]

By late summer of 1919, the defeat of White Siberia appeared inevitable and to the legionaries there seemed to be no reason why they should remain along the Trans-Siberian Railway on behalf of this lost cause. The questions surrounding Czechoslovakia's borders were mostly settled by then and the country had little to gain by keeping troops in Siberia. Yet as summer turned into autumn the Czecho-Slovaks' trains remained dispersed on the sidings along the railway between Novonikolaevsk and Irkutsk. As the winter season loomed, the legionaries were haunted by memories of their struggles against the extreme conditions they experienced the previous year: temperatures that sometimes plunged as low as –70°, icebound locomotives and blizzards that packed the snow into drifts as high as the roofs on the railcars. Added to that were the shortened spans of daylight which could be as demoralizing as the inhospitable weather. One YMCA nurse who traveled on a Czecho-Slovak train pitied the plight of the legionaries amid the long winter nights. "Often they have no light in the evenings," she wrote, "and having no place to go, [they] are compelled to sit in the dark and think—they have few pleasant things to think about."[74]

14

White Mountain Redressed

When the Czechoslovak Republic was born in the autumn of 1918, most of its leaders had an ambitious agenda to rectify what they perceived as centuries of injustices inflicted upon their people by the Habsburgs and their supposed allies. But before they could embark on any great national project, the Czechoslovak leaders needed to see their state's survival through the early months of turmoil, when potential enemies seemed to lurk everywhere. Plots to restore the fallen Habsburg monarchy were suspected—often without any foundation—among the Bohemian nobility and Catholic clergy.[1] On the opposite end of the political spectrum, Bolshevized street agitators, among them many former war prisoners returned from Russia, were attempting to whip their hungry audiences into a frenzy that would culminate in a communist revolution. By the time the armistice ended the fighting on the Western Front, the Czechoslovaks were already facing real challenges to their territorial claims from their ethnic rivals: the German-Bohemians in the borderlands, the Magyars in Upper Hungary and the Poles in Těšín were all contesting Prague's right to rule them. Against these threats, the Czechoslovak leaders initially had relatively few trustworthy soldiers at their disposal. In the early weeks of November, the main rail lines in Bohemia were choked with returning troops from the defunct Austro-Hungarian Army, but many of these men were demoralized, in poor health and politically unreliable. Armed volunteers recruited from the Sokols and other national societies may have been more dependable from a political standpoint, but their effectiveness was dubious due to their uneven or absence of military training. The legions, whose dedication and prowess were unquestionable, might have provided a valuable backbone to the republic's planned army. Unfortunately for the new Czechoslovak government, these units would remain abroad for several more weeks—and much longer for the corps in Russia.

Like the legionaries, the three top leaders of the Czecho-Slovak liberation movement were absent from the new state in its crucial early days. Masaryk, the designated President of the Republic, was in the U.S. when independence was declared in Prague, and it was not until late November when he finally began his transoceanic journey back to Europe. Meanwhile, the new state's designated Minister of War, Štefánik, was literally on the opposite side of the globe directing the operations of the Czecho-Slovak Legion in Siberia.[2] Of the revolutionary triumvirate, Beneš, now Minister of Foreign Affairs, was the closest to events in Central Europe during November 1918 since he remained in the Paris headquarters of the National Council. However, preoccupied as he was with consolidating Czechoslovakia's international position for the upcoming peace conference, he had little time to devote directly to the new state's domestic issues. In the days immediately following the Prague revolution of 28 October, the state's administration was entirely in the hands of the mostly junior politicians on the National Committee. On 5 November, when the Prague delegation returned from Geneva, the men who initially seized power politely stepped aside so Kramář and the cabinet approved by Beneš could begin exercising their authority.

The most pressing task faced by the Czechoslovak leaders was to establish their sovereignty over all the territories which they claimed for their new state. When a tentative constitution for Czechoslovakia was adopted on 13 November 1918, the authority of the Czechoslovak leaders in Prague was confined merely to Czech-speaking areas of Bohemia and Moravia. The obstacles standing in the way of their desire to rule the historical Bohemian crownlands were the German-speaking borderlands, where four provinces—Deutschböhmen, Sudetenland, Böhmerwaldgau and Deutschüdmähren—had sprung up and declared their allegiance to German-Austria.[3] The German-Bohemians were hoping that the principle of national self-determination, one of the catchphrases of the day, would spare them from being included in a Slav-dominated state. Along with their compatriots in the new Austrian Republic, the German-Bohemians had made their political goals clear by approving a provisional constitution that conveyed their desire to unite with Germany.[4] In the mayhem following the collapse of the central empires, however, such declarations were largely ignored. The appeals of the Allied representatives were also frequently shrugged off since Allied forces remained mostly outside of Central Europe. It was up to the new governments of Central and Eastern Europe then to restore some semblance of order. For them, it was an opportunity to secure their coveted borders to the point of using force in order to thwart the national pretensions of their neighbors and present the future peace conference with a *fait accompli*.

The Czechs were determined not to allow the German-speaking borderlands become part of the Austrian or especially the German realm. Against the wishes of Beneš, who was eager to maintain the Czecho-Slovaks' "moral prestige" in Paris, the Prague cabinet scratched together volunteer battalions from demobilized Czech soldiers and sent these units marching into the disputed borderlands.[5] The German-Bohemians also attempted to outfit their own armed detachments to defend their provinces, but this mobilization was less successful. The defeat of the Central Powers had sunk the morale of the German-Bohemians while the Czechs' spirits were soaring since they viewed themselves among the war's victors. Sheer numbers were also on the Czechs' side, as was the control of the critical food supplies. The intervention of neighboring Germany might have tipped the scales in favor of the German-Bohemians, but Berlin was preoccupied with its own revolutionary turmoil and unfolding civil war. As a result, the Czech battalions encountered hardly any resistance as they entered the German-speaking districts—much to Beneš's relief. Within a month of beginning their campaign against the separatist German provinces, the borderlands of Bohemia, Moravia and Lower Silesia were almost entirely under Czech occupation.[6]

Although the Czechs' seizure of the border territories was relatively bloodless, the campaign did not escape the notice of the Allied statesmen gathering in Paris in anticipation of the peace conference. The Austrian republican government protested the Czechoslovak action since the four provinces had been formally declared a part of German-Austria by the Austrian National Assembly. When these objections reached Paris, however, they fell on mostly unsympathetic ears. The French had unilaterally authorized the Czechs to complete the occupation of the historical Bohemian lands. They were opposed to recognizing the ethnic Germans' right to national self-determination since this might mean the addition of new territories to Germany. Other Allied representatives, such as those from Great Britain and the United States, were less prejudiced against the ethnic Germans but were not consulted about the fate of the Bohemian borderlands. When they finally learned of the Czechs' action, they could do nothing except acquiesce in the outcome while declaring that any permanent decision on Czechoslovakia's frontiers must await the peace conference.[7]

At the same time the Czechs were dueling with the ethnic Germans over the Bohemian borderlands, they were also vying with their Magyar neighbors for control over the Slovak-inhabited areas of Upper Hungary. Although the new Hungarian republican government led by Mihály Károlyi had a more liberal and democratic outlook than its royal predecessor, it was no less determined to preserve the integrity of Greater Hungary. Consequently, Budapest had no intention of allowing the Slovaks to join the Czechoslovak state. The Hungarians made this clear by sending troops into the region and subsequently disbanding the Slovak National Council that had formed at Turčiansky Svätý Martin in the closing days of the war.

The Prague government refused to accept the Hungarians' contention that Slovakia was to remain in their possession until a peace conference said otherwise. In an official statement, Prime Minister Kramář declared that Allied recognition of the "Czechoslovak" state precluded any debate over the Slovaks' future. When the Hungarians still refused to budge, the Prague government, rather than risk its limited forces in a possible shooting war over Slovakia, turned to its key ally, France, for a solution.[8]

From his office in Paris, Beneš watched the dispute unfold over Upper Hungary and appealed to the French government to formally demand that the Hungarians evacuate the Slovak-speaking districts. In the Belgrade armistice between the Károlyi government and General d'Espérey, Magyar troops were forced to withdraw behind a demarcation line on the southern and eastern parts of the Hungarian realm, allowing the Serbs and, to a lesser degree, the Romanians to occupy Hungarian territory they sought for themselves. Beneš coveted a similar arrangement for the benefit of Czechoslovakia. On 27 November the French Foreign Minister, Stéphane Pichon, heeded Beneš's request by ordering the chief of the French Military Mission in Budapest, Lieutenant Colonel Ferdinand Vyx, to instruct the Hungarian government to evacuate "Slovakia."[9]

This order led to much confusion since no definite administrative unit named Slovakia existed and because the ethnic frontier between the Slovak and Magyar populations was quite blurry. Naturally, the Hungarian leaders interpreted "Slovakia" to mean the purely Slovak areas in the mountainous regions of Upper Hungary; however, Beneš wanted Slovakia to include those districts plus the fertile plain south to the Danube where Slovaks were a minority. The tussle over Slovakia became even more muddled when an "East Slovak Republic" was declared in the eastern part of the contested region. The East Slovak Republic's founder, Victor Dvorčak, claimed that the eastern Slovaks were a separate nationality altogether and opposed union with the Czechs in a new state. His venture was patronized by Budapest, which was only too happy to exploit the misguided nationalism and anti–Czech sentiments among Slovaks against the Prague government.[10]

In the meantime, the indefatigable Beneš prevailed upon the French government to again order the Hungarians to withdraw from Slovakia, and this time they defined that area according to his wider interpretation. For a time, the Magyars contemplated resistance to the evacuation orders from Paris. But their confidence was eroding by 23 December, when they received the newest orders to withdraw to a demarcation line well to the south of Upper Hungary. The first battalions of Czechoslovak legionaries from Italy had returned to Prague a few days earlier and, after a showy parade in the capital, boarded trains headed for Slovakia.

Perhaps an even bigger consideration than the buildup of Czechoslovak forces was France's consistent support for the Prague government throughout the dispute. Károlyi's foreign policy was pro–Allied in the hope that Hungary might be spared a harsh punishment in the victors' peace, and risking open conflict with a recognized Allied belligerent was not conducive towards that goal.[11] After lodging a formal protest with the Allies, the Hungarians submitted to the French instructions by pulling their forces south of the new demarcation line. As the Magyar troops departed, the East Slovak Republic dissolved at the end of December and by 20 January 1919 the Prague government would occupy the entire area designated as Slovakia.

The third major border dispute that entangled the Czechoslovak government from its early days pitted them against their Slavic cousins to the north, the Poles. The quarrel, which was centered over possession of the Silesian duchy of Těšín, demonstrated that Masaryk's dream of democratic solidarity in Central Europe—encapsulated in the Mid-European Democratic Union—was as defunct as the ideal of Pan-Slavism. The émigrés and national leaders of both peoples who had willingly cooperated with each other to some extent against the central empires were now at each other's throats over a district that encompassed only 350 square miles. As the successor to Austrian Silesia within the Kingdom of Bohemia, Czechoslovakia's claims to the district initially appeared better founded. Since the fourteenth century, Těšín had been a duchy in the Bohemian crownlands, but prior to that time it had belonged to medieval Poland. While the Poles did not overlook that historical trivia, the real strength of their claim lay in the predominance of Poles in the district, which outnumbered Czechs by a ratio greater than three to one. The area was valued highly by both nations because of its coal resources, but it held additional importance to Czechoslovakia since one of the two railways linking the Bohemian lands with Slovakia ran through the district.

On 5 November 1918, the national councils of both peoples tried to ward off conflict by agreeing to a tentative division of Těšín that would leave the final decision to be made at the peace conference. This truce, however, did not last long. Under the temporary settlement, the Poles obtained control of the coal basin and railroad. The Czechs began to suspect that the Poles were seeking to make their possession of these vital points permanent, especially

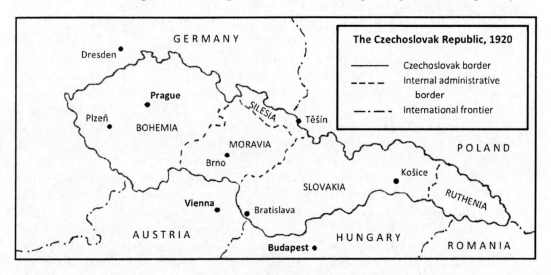

Map of the Czechoslovak Republic in 1920.

after Warsaw moved in troops and then scheduled elections for the district. Once again, the Czechoslovak government tried to win the dispute diplomatically by bringing the matter to the French government, which in a note to Vienna had backed Czechoslovak claims to all Bohemian, Moravian and Silesian territory held by the Habsburgs. Although these terms would include Těšín, Paris clearly did not have the duchy in mind when it drafted the note. While the French were prejudiced against the claims of the ethnic Germans, this was anything but the case regarding the Poles, whom they were eager to recruit as a future ally against Germany alongside Czechoslovakia. Therefore Paris, not wanting to poison future Franco-Polish relations, backed away from endorsing Czech claims to Těšín.[12]

Unable to secure the district diplomatically, the Czechoslovak cabinet decided to seize the duchy forcibly before the Polish elections were to be held. This decision was made despite the emphatic objections of President Masaryk, who was by then in Prague; nor would it have been popular with Beneš, who was working to uphold the pristine image of Czechoslovakia before the Paris Peace Conference. The Czechoslovak cabinet was convinced that no one would bat an eye at their takeover of Těšín if they gave their campaign the appearance of its having been authorized by the Allies. On 23 January 1919, as a delegation from an inter–Allied commission ordered the Polish commander in Těšín to withdraw his contingents from the district, Czechoslovak troops suddenly surged forward to occupy the areas that were to be evacuated by the Poles. The Czechoslovaks' elaborate ploy, however, began to unravel when the Polish troops rejected the Allied instructions and offered resistance to the Czechoslovak battalions. The result was a shooting war in Těšín that received much attention in Paris and placed Beneš in a very awkward position.[13]

The fighting, which lasted a week until the two sides agreed to a ceasefire, favored the Czechoslovaks since the Polish home army, as a result of Piłsudski's attempts to secure the far-flung borders of the sixteenth-century Polish-Lithuanian Commonwealth, already had its hands full with small conflicts or armed standoffs against German Freikorps[14] to the west, Lithuanians in the northeast, Bolsheviks to the east and Ukrainians to the southeast.[15] No battlefield success, however, could impress the statesmen and delegations gathered in Paris to construct a peace to end all wars. For U.S. Secretary of State Robert Lansing, the conflict in Těšín was analogous to the new political order in Central and Eastern Europe. "Just as the Russian, Austrian and German Empires have split into national groups," he commented in his diary, "so the great war seems to have split up into a lot of little wars."[16] At least one of the leading figures of the conference, British Prime Minister Lloyd George, never heard of the duchy that entered the spotlight only eleven days after the peace deliberations had begun.[17] On 29 January, the peacemakers summoned the leaders of the Polish and Czechoslovak delegations, Dmowski and Kramář respectively, to answer for their countries' actions in Těšín. Each tried to pin the blame on the other's country for violating the earlier agreement between them. The Allies succeeded in compelling the two nations to observe a new ceasefire while awaiting a final decision over the duchy's future. Under this agreement, the Czechoslovak detachments abandoned most of the territory they had just won to an Allied control commission. As a result, Czechoslovakia's Těšín campaign accomplished nothing beyond increasing Allied distrust of the successor states in Central and Eastern Europe.[18]

For the Czechoslovak Republic, Těšín remained an elusive prize but with that single exception, the new state had expanded its authority to its desired boundaries by late January 1919. That accomplishment helped to ensure that the Czechoslovak state would enter the Paris Peace Conference largely in the form which its founders intended.[19]

On 21 December 1918, a single round of artillery fire pierced the wintry air over Prague as President Masaryk stepped down from his train that had just arrived in the city's railway station. His homecoming in the Czechoslovak capital after four years abroad was an emotional event. He was reunited with two of his children, Jan and Alice, warmly greeted by old friends such as Šámal and embraced by his former political adversary, Kramář. From the station, he boarded an automobile that delivered him to his new residence in Prague Castle, the ancient seat of Bohemia's kings. The route to the castle was lined with throngs of people, and even though they were suffering through another winter of sparse food and fuel supplies, the crowds enthusiastically cheered the presidential motorcade and its legionary escorts as they paraded by. Later that day, Masaryk was officially sworn in as the first president of Czechoslovakia. Unfortunately, not every aspect of his return to Prague was as joyous as he might have hoped. His beloved wife, Charlotte, was in poor health and in a nursing home[20] while old friends who saw Masaryk for the first time in years were shocked by his exhausted appearance.[21] But if they thought that this seemingly tired old man would be content to sit at the head of the Czechoslovak state as a mere figurehead, as the cabinet expected him to do, they were wrong.

Under Czechoslovakia's provisional constitution, the presidency was to be mainly a ceremonial office and the real strings of power would be pulled by the cabinet and National Assembly. This arrangement satisfied a wide range of politicians, from conservatives such as Kramář to Social Democrats. Masaryk, however, criticized the constitution for the limited role in government it provided him, and the issue sparked new discord between him and Kramář. Masaryk eventually won this controversy when, in May 1919, the provisional constitution was amended to grant the president additional executive powers.[22] The growing rift between the two longtime rivals, however, did not end there.

Although the infant Czechoslovak government was faced with a barrage of domestic issues to settle; foreign policy, especially in regards to Russia, remained a hot-button topic due to the presence of the approximately 60,000 legionaries in Siberia. Masaryk was by now cool to his country's continuing involvement in Russia, though he and other Czechoslovak leaders saw the legionaries' presence there as a useful reminder to the Allied statesmen in Paris of Czech and Slovak sacrifices to win their independence. Like Lloyd George and other statesmen, he feared that strong opposition against the Bolsheviks might provoke the ire of his country's working classes and proletarian political parties.[23] Socialists, however, were not the only Czechoslovak citizens who increasingly disfavored the intervention. The troops' families wanted their fathers, husbands and sons back now that the world war was over, and the Legion's return was among the demands featured in mass demonstrations in Prague and other Bohemian cities during May 1919.[24]

Against the strong current of public opinion eager to end the intervention in Russia stood Kramář and a few Slavophiles. They had no faith in the collective security and democratic solidarity promised by Masaryk and the peacemakers in Paris. Kramář believed his little nation could only depend on a protector with whom it had blood-ties, in other words, Russia. Since he viewed Soviet Russia as neither Russian nor Slavic, he thought it essential to restore a nationalist Russia that would assume her inherent role as protector of the Slavs.[25] When he led the Czechoslovak delegation to the Paris Peace Conference in early 1919, he was ready to enlist his country behind the anti–Bolshevik crusade being urged by Marshal Foch.[26] He also integrated himself with Russian émigré leaders in the French capital as well as those who sought refuge in Prague. Amid his eagerness to assist them in their struggle against communism, he was ready back almost any proposal, including one scheme to enlist 100,000 volunteers from Russian POWs stuck in Central Europe into a new anti–Bolshevik corps that would march upon Soviet Russia from the west.[27, 28]

Kramář's efforts to rally a strong anti-communist effort in Paris, like those launched by Churchill or Foch, came to naught. Czechoslovakia, despite its formidable presence on Russian soil, was left out of the debate over the Russian question at the Paris Peace Conference. In any case, the five Allied powers (Great Britain, France, Italy, Japan and the United States) that did consider the matter were unable to reach a consensus among themselves. To the frustration of Kramář and other pro-interventionists, the civil war in Russia was left to play out with the ongoing limited Allied intervention.[29]

Kramář's influence in the Czechoslovak delegation was not as strong as it may have appeared. Although he was the nominal head of the delegation, the Allied statesmen and delegates looked to Beneš as a more authoritative voice, if for no other reason than the familiarity which had developed between them during the latter's exile.[30] Unlike Kramář, Beneš did not obsess over the Russian dilemma and instead focused on issues closer to his homeland. His efforts reached their culmination on 5 February when he put forward Czechoslovakia's territorial claims to the Council of Ten.[31] The three-and-a-half-hour-long presentation he gave was unremarkable except for the extent to which he bored his audience. He was fortunate that his task was made somewhat easier by his respectable reputation among Allied statesmen, the belligerent status accorded to Czechoslovakia during the war and the *de facto* recognition which his government had already achieved among some Allied states.[32] His cause was also helped by the fact that the territory most desired by Prague, except for Těšín, was already under Czechoslovak occupation and had been acquired at the expense of defeated "enemy" nations: Austria and Hungary. Compared to the exorbitant territorial demands made by other Central European delegations, particularly Poland and Romania, the minor border rectifications which Beneš asked for seemed quite modest. At Kramář's behest, he did mention the desirability of adding neighboring Slav populations, such as the nearly-extinct Sorbs of Lusatia and the Ukrainians of Ruthenia, to the Czechoslovak state, but he did not press these claims with vigor.[33] He also made a rather preposterous request for a 120 mile strip of land running north to south across western Hungary to function as a friendly link between Czechoslovakia and the Yugoslav kingdom to the south.

After Beneš finished his presentation, a Commission of Czechoslovak Affairs was set up by the conference to evaluate the Czechoslovak claims. Assignment to this commission and others like it appears to have been carried out haphazardly. Harold Nicolson, a young member of the British delegation to the conference and a specialist on the Balkans, was appointed to the Czechoslovak commission even though he was, by his own admission, "totally ill-equipped" for the subject.[34] The biases of the delegations also factored in the commission's decisions. Fortunately for the Czechoslovak government, the French delegation which tended to dominate the commission was intensely Czechophile and willing to approve almost any demand. This was slightly offset by the Italian delegation, which was strongly Slavophobe due to the clash of Italian and South Slav interests along the Adriatic coast. The Americans may have looked at the matter most objectively, but they were uncertain whether strategic considerations or the principle of self determination should take precedence in places like the German-speaking borderlands of Bohemia. Ultimately, they chose the former and sided with the French. While the Czechoslovak commission and others like it were not to have the final say over the new states' borders, the Council of Ten, which did have that responsibility, rarely challenged the commissions' decisions.[35]

As Beneš probably expected, the outlandish claims over the Lusatian Sorbs and the corridor to Yugoslavia was practically dismissed out of hand by the commission and the peacemakers. Aside from these rejections, Czechoslovakia was remarkably successful in realizing its territorial goals. If Lloyd George had his way, some of the German-speaking districts might have been pulled from Czechoslovak control and given to Germany as a conciliatory gesture. But his proposal was swept under a rug when Clemenceau pointed out that the defeated enemy might also be placated if the Germans were given back their naval fleet.[36] As a result, on 4 April the peacemakers confirmed Czechoslovak sovereignty over the historic lands of Bohemia without any major border rectifications.[37] The conference was also inclined to accept the Czechoslovak commission's recommendation of extending Slovakia's southern frontier to the Danube and Ipel' rivers, but the sudden emergence of an aggressive communist regime in Budapest complicated this issue. The Ukrainians of Ruthenia were also permitted to join the Czechoslovak state—largely because their emigrants to the United States voted for such a solution at a conference in Scranton, Pennsylvania, shortly after the world war.

Těšín, for the time being, remained an unsolved riddle. Further attempts to settle the dispute through an inter–Allied commission and plebiscite failed. The issue was resolved arbitrarily in July 1920, and the timing was fortuitous for Czechoslovakia since the two delegations most predisposed towards Poland, those of the U.S. and Italy, no longer held much clout with the Conference of Ambassadors that was deciding outstanding issues from the peace conference.[38] This left the decision to be largely settled by Britain and France, neither of which was happy with Polish provocations that led to a full-scale war with Soviet Russia that summer. Consequently, the arbiters declared an earlier proposed line as the border between Czechoslovakia and Poland in Těšín. The duchy was to remain somewhat divided but, most importantly for Prague, the Czechoslovaks obtained control of the coal basin and railway. Sadly, the dispute over Těšín was a lasting source of contention between Czechoslovakia and Poland throughout the interwar period.[39]

While Beneš had excellent results to show for his work on behalf of Czechoslovakia at the peace conference, the same could not be said for Kramář. His brand of Russophile politics failed to resonate with the hungry population of Bohemia and he appeared detached from more pertinent issues. These trends culminated into a crushing electoral defeat for his party during the parliamentary elections held in the Czech lands on 15–16 June 1919. Not surprisingly, the socialist parties made the largest gains in these lean times while the Agrarians were the only party right of center which managed to hold its own. These parties formed a new cabinet the following month from which Kramář and his party were excluded. He was incensed by this political setback, which he unfairly blamed on President Masaryk's meddling.[40] He was, in fact, unable to accept that his strong nationalist and Slavophile politics had lost their edge in a postwar world where Habsburg "tyranny" was extinct, the Czechoslovak dream had become a reality and communism was firmly embedded in Russia.

Kramář's replacement as prime minister was Vlastimil Tusar, a Social Democrat. Tusar and his colleagues had ambitious plans for social reform in the Czechoslovak state but most of these schemes were to remain unfulfilled despite their victories in the 1919 elections. The socialists were much weaker than they actually appeared: the united front formed by the Czech Social Democrat and (National) Socialist parties had barely outlasted the war. The former was further wrought by internal disagreement between a nationalistic right-wing and an increasingly radical left. By the time Tusar formed his government, Czechoslovakia's only major act of socialization in the interwar period, the land law reform, had already been passed by the provisional National Assembly. Its provisions disappointed most socialists as they wanted authorization for the state to confiscate all lands of the nobility over 100 hectares to provide the foundation for collective farms. Instead, the law set up a State Land Office that would delicately transfer noble lands over 250 hectares to small farmers and landless laborers. The land reform legislation most closely resembled the proposals of the Czech Agrarians, and it was their party which dominated the State Land Office that was responsible for breaking up the great estates and redistributing the properties. The State Land Office constructed a rural class of farm proprietors who were devoted to the Agrarian Party and helped to make it the most powerful party in Czechoslovak politics during most of the interwar period. Meanwhile, the Social Democrats suffered a final schism at the end of 1920 when its radical leftists, led by Bohumír Šmeral, broke away to form the Czechoslovak Communist Party that was subordinate to the Comintern in Moscow.[41, 42]

Despite the Slovak union with the Czechs early in the year, the challenges faced by the new government in Slovakia during much of 1919 bore little resemblance to the problems they encountered in the Bohemian lands. As Czechoslovak troops took control of the Slovak districts behind the withdrawing Hungarians at the end of 1918, Vavro Šrobár returned to his homeland to build a Czechoslovak administration there. The task before him was not an easy one. Since the discriminatory policies of Hungary's royal government had largely excluded the Slovaks from politics and the bureaucracy, the administration was bound to have many empty posts with few suitable candidates to fill them. Thus when it was time to select individuals to represent to Slovaks on the National Assembly in Prague, Šrobár simply nominated persons he was comfortable dealing with: in other words Czechophile, mostly Protestant Slovaks who shared his liberal views. Even though the majority of Slovaks were peasants, he did not appoint anyone from the peasantry despite finding room on the Slovak delegation for seven Czechs whom he held in high esteem. This was hardly a representative cross-section of Slovak society.[43]

Šrobár was likely as suspicious of the Slovak peasantry as they soon would be of him. Some of his concerns were justified in the highly-charged atmosphere following the Monarchy's collapse and the withdrawal of the Hungarians. Propaganda of all sorts was being distributed throughout the territory. There were pamphlets published by the Hungarian government containing irredentist messages for Slovakia's Magyar minority and anti–Czech content for the Slovaks. Propaganda printed by renegade Czech and Slovak communists, many of them former war prisoners returned from Russia, encouraged the peasants to seize more lands or called workers to arms.[44] Therefore Šrobár feared that the poorly educated Slovak masses, untested in politics and embittered by decades of oppression, might be easily led astray by such agitation. At the very least, he felt that he, and not the Slovak peasants, knew what was best for them.[45]

Šrobár's efforts to build an effective administration for Slovakia going into spring of 1919 were soon derailed by events completely outside his control. By March, the Magyars were becoming thoroughly disillusioned with Károlyi's government as his pro–Entente policy had failed to spare Hungary the cessation of large tracts of territory to Czechoslovakia, Romania and Yugoslavia.[46] The last straw came when Lieutenant Colonel Vyx presented the Hungarian government with yet another order from Paris to withdraw behind a new line of demarcation on their eastern boundary with Romania. On 20 March, amid rumors that the complete occupation of Hungary was imminent, the Károlyi government resigned in protest to this demand. In a desperate bid to save what was left of Greater Hungary, the socialists who remained in the cabinet cobbled a new government coalition with the communists in the hope that they would attract the military assistance of Soviet Russia. The man chosen to lead the Hungarian Soviet Republic was Béla Kun, a thirty-three-year-old Transylvanian Jew who had earned his communist credentials while being held as a POW in Russia.[47] It says a lot about the turbulence in Hungary at the time that Kun woke up as a lowly prison inmate on the same day he went to bed as the new head of state.[48]

The declaration of a soviet regime in Central Europe sent shockwaves throughout the continent, but it especially raised anxiety among Hungary's neighbors. Three days after the announcement of the Hungarian Soviet Republic, Šrobár's ministry in Slovakia declared martial law throughout the province.[49] In the meantime, the Allies attempted to negotiate milder terms for new demarcation lines with Budapest but Kun, still confident that help from Moscow would be forthcoming, was in no mood to compromise. With the failure of these talks, the French authorized the Czechoslovak and Romanian armies to cross into Hungary and secure strategic points near their borders. These forces advanced easily against the new Hungarian Red Army, which was undermanned and ill-trained. Tempted by their enemy's weakness, they soon pushed beyond the objectives set by Marshal Foch.[50]

By the end of April 1919, Soviet Hungary was in the throes of a military crisis as the Romanian Army approached within sixty miles of Budapest while Czechoslovak troops spilled over its borders to the north. Desperate to stave off their impending defeat, the Hungarian Communists replaced their Marxist internationalism with jingoist appeals for all Magyars to defend their sacred homeland. The ruse worked as within a fortnight 50,000 men flocked to the red banner, ten times the number that was recruited in the original call-up for the Hungarian Red Army. Magyar generals and officers from the old Austro-Hungarian Army also lent their expertise to the Red cause. Although the Hungarian Red Army remained heavily outnumbered by the ring of enemy armies on their frontiers, the threatening forces failed to act with a unified purpose. To the south, General d'Espérey's Army of the Orient, boasting an impressive strength of 72,000 troops, remained stationary. With no claims of Hungarian territory beyond what they already occupied, the Serbs serving with that army had no interest in advancing while d'Espérey was pessimistic about the reliability of his war-weary French soldiers.[51] Meanwhile, the Romanians halted their advance at the Tisza River to consolidate their recent gains, a process which took the better part of the next two months.[52] Hence, the lull in operations on its southern and eastern frontiers gave the expanding Hungarian Red Army an opportunity to throw the preponderance of its strength against the some 40,000 Czechoslovaks advancing from the north. Their counterattack quickly turned the tables on the Czechoslovaks and forced them back to their original demarcation line by the end of May.[53]

The Magyars did not halt at what was then designated by the Allies as the Czechoslovak-Hungarian frontier and instead they pressed onward deep into eastern Slovakia, achieving their objectives in only a matter of days.[54] This sudden reverse in military fortunes was a major embarrassment for the Czechoslovaks, but its causes went well beyond being simply outfought. One of the biggest problems for the Prague government was that its grip over many areas of Slovakia remained weak despite having occupied most of the province several months earlier. Since Šrobár's administration refused to employ civil servants who were Magyarized or "nationally unreliable," many areas went months without a functioning police force, school system or even a postal service. Unhappy with this state of affairs, angry Slovak peasants sabotaged the rear of the Czechoslovak Army by cutting telephone lines and tearing up railroads.[55] To combat this activity, Šrobár's administration resorted to ruthless measures; in some cases they took hostages to ensure the cooperation of the local population.[56]

Other factors behind the Czechoslovaks' rout in Slovakia were their numerical inferiority—the Hungarian Red Army swelled to 100,000 men according to conservative Allied estimates—and the enemy's better leadership.[57] The ex–Austro-Hungarian officers serving with the Hungarian Soviet Army performed brilliantly in a campaign which they viewed as an effort to reclaim the historical crownlands of St. Stephen.[58] The commanders of the Czechoslovak Army, on the other hand, had less clear motives. Originally, the Czechoslovak Army in Slovakia was led by the Italian General Luigi Piccione, who had been appointed to command the Czecho-Slovak Legion in Italy during the closing days of the war. Yet, as the Italians squared off against Yugoslavs over territory in the eastern Adriatic, they quickly lost their enthusiasm for Czechoslovak independence. Rome was courting Budapest as a possible ally against the Yugoslavs and even diverted a shipment of arms and munitions, originally destined for Bohemia, to Budapest.[59] Robert Seton-Watson, who was visiting Prague during the crisis with Soviet Hungary, even claimed that the Italian officers were deliberately undermining the morale of the Czechoslovak troops.[60] Although Seton-Watson's allegation is unproven, the Czechoslovak troops were highly dispirited since they were poorly armed and feared the enmity of the hostile Slovak population. During the Hungarian advance, the gendarmes and even the legionaries were known to take to their heels at the first setback; in some cases the armed bands of Sokol volunteers proved to be the most reliable units.[61] Eventually, Piccione was dismissed and replaced by a Frenchman, General Eugene Mittelhauser, who took over a demoralized army in an increasingly desperate position.[62]

The Czechoslovaks' fiasco in Slovakia was capped off on 16 June when Antonín Janoušek founded a Slovak Soviet Republic in the town of Prešov, the second autonomous Slovak government to be established under Hungarian patronage in the eight months since the world war ended.[63] This puppet regime was part of Kun's plan to fan the flames of social revolution throughout Central Europe; he and his collaborators hoped that the proletariat in unoccupied western Slovakia and even in Bohemia and Moravia would rally behind the Slovak Soviet Republic and depose the bourgeoisie government in Prague. They were also attempting to foment worker uprisings in Vienna, but the expected *putsches* there and elsewhere never materialized.[64]

In the meantime the Czechoslovak government, in order to retrieve control of Slovakia, resorted to its proven weapon of diplomacy. This time, however, the Allied statesmen in Paris were not as sympathetic to the Czechoslovak delegation's appeals since none of them had forgotten that the Czechoslovak Army had disregarded the limits set by Foch in their advance into Hungary. Indeed, the realization that the rational, upright Czechoslovaks were as seemingly prone to military adventurism as the Poles, Magyars and Romanians caused Lloyd George to complain, "They are all little brigand peoples who only want to steal territories."[65] Nevertheless, the Czechoslovak representatives in Paris spun their explanations of their predicament in a way that would evoke sympathy from the Allies. "I know nothing about a Czech offensive," Kramář cried at one point, "All I know relates to the advance of Hungarian Bolshevism, mixed and confused with Magyar chauvinism."[66] Although the Allies remained mistrustful of the Czechoslovaks, they were hardly enthusiastic about a Soviet Hungary spreading communism throughout Central Europe. Subsequently, they sent an ultimatum to Budapest offering the cessation of hostilities by the Entente's allies in exchange for the immediate withdrawal of the Hungarian Red Army from Slovakia.[67]

Kun, in contrast to his earlier contempt towards olive branches from Paris, was much more welcoming of this latest Allied proposal. Despite his military success in Slovakia, his hold on power was fragile as a well-organized counterrevolutionary underground took root in his capital. Even worse, the support from Soviet Russia which he promised his followers never arrived. In fact, Moscow was not capable of lending much aid in mid–1919 as the Red Army was engaged in simultaneous military operations against the Allies to the north, Kolchak to the east and the resurgent forces of Denikin to the south. With these realities in mind, the leaders of the Hungarian Soviet Republic accepted the Allied offer on 21 June by ordering their army to evacuate Slovakia by the end of the month.[68] Through this acceptance, Kun hoped that, like Lenin at Brest-Litovsk, he would obtain a valuable breathing spell for his regime to consolidate its domestic position.[69] Instead, the withdrawal of the Hungarian Red Army from Slovakia demonstrated that not even a soviet regime could preserve Greater Hungary, and as a result many Magyar nationalists deserted the red banner. In the meantime, the Slovak Soviet Republic collapsed and the disintegrating Hungarian Red Army was unable to hold its own in renewed fighting with the Romanians. Ignoring Allied orders to halt, the Romanian Army entered Budapest on 4 August. Two days earlier, Kun and his accomplices resigned their posts and fled abroad, ending the Hungarian Soviet Republic after a tumultuous 133 days of existence.[70]

The seesaw conflict between Czechoslovakia and Soviet Hungary had lasting repercussions on the development of the administration in Slovakia. The period of martial law, along with the Hungarian offensive that coincided with the Czechoslovak parliamentary elections in mid–June, deprived the Slovaks of the opportunity to express themselves at the polls.[71] Šrobár's administration, aware of their alienation from the bulk of the Slovak population, did not mourn the cancellation of elections in Slovakia. This gave time for this so-called "Lutheran aristocracy" to consolidate its position. Šrobár and his hirelings were perhaps most eager to deflect accountability away from themselves for difficulties in Slovakia. Their propaganda blamed the military reverses, the lack of certain commodities and the high unemployment which Slovakia was experiencing on Magyar-sympathizers and Bolsheviks. Intolerant of criticism, they rounded up dissidents and interned them in camps.[72] It is little wonder that many Slovaks felt that the revolution in their land had simply replaced one minority ruling class with another.

Milan Štefánik was the one man who might have been able to curtail Šrobár's dictatorship in Slovakia, but the young revolutionary who oversaw Slovak interests on the National Council never made it back to the nation he helped create. The Czechoslovak Minister of War had returned to Europe from Siberia in March 1919. Those who saw him in the following weeks were struck by his apparent physical and mental deterioration. Soon after arriving in Paris, he became bored with the proceedings of the peace conference, was disappointed with its indecision over Russia and, either because of disillusionment or sickness, sparred with Beneš. Specifically, he accused the Czechoslovak Foreign Minister of infringing upon his prerogative as Minister of War by concluding a military entente with France earlier that year. The convention clashed with the strong Italiophile views which Štefánik developed in the latter months of the war, and in a stormy meeting the two men laced their bitter arguments with stinging personal insults. Afterwards both men sent telegrams to Prague in an attempt to enlist other Czechoslovak leaders on their side, a contest which Štefánik was bound to lose as long as the Masaryk-Beneš partnership held firm. Even so, his ongoing grudge against Beneš might have caused a major rift in the Czechoslovak government if not for what occurred next. On 4 May, the plane carrying Štefánik from Rome to what would have been his first arrival into the postwar Czechoslovak state crashed while attempting to land at an airfield near Bratislava, killing all aboard.[73] This wreck was most likely fortuitous for the Slovak general's legacy since it prevented him from being publicly repudiated by either Masaryk or Beneš and it enhanced his wartime exploits with a heavy dose of tragic romanticism. Since most of his adult life was spent abroad, he was not widely known among the Slovaks during his lifetime, but in death this Lutheran French citizen was elevated to the status of a national hero by Slovaks of all confessions and political shades.[74, 75] Moreover, as details of the nasty quarrel between Štefánik and Beneš leaked out, anti–Czech Slovaks smelled a conspiracy and soon claimed that the plane was shot down by an anti-aircraft battery on orders from President Masaryk. Due to the hostilities that were then taking place with Soviet Hungary, there were indeed active batteries near the crash site but no evidence has ever surfaced to support this allegation.[76, 77]

Slovak nationalists found plenty of other grievances besides the seemingly oppressive Šrobár regime and the freak death of a national leader that they barely knew. One of the most pressing issues was the utter economic collapse which Slovakia experienced in the immediate postwar period. A great part of the disaster was due to the unfortunate reality that the economies of the Bohemian and Slovak lands could not be easily integrated. The rivers in Bohemia flowed north while those in Slovakia flowed south. Only two railways linked Slovakia with Moravia. Upon its separation from Hungary, Slovakia was cut off from its previous sources of coal and was unable to import sufficient quantities from its new partner to the west. Sugar refineries were forced to shutdown while the sugar beets they normally processed were left to rot in the fields since there was no available means to deliver them to the processors.[78] Factories which manufactured various wares also fell on hard economic times since they were ill-prepared to compete with the better-established and more efficient Bohemian firms that had once served as the industrial heart of the Habsburg Empire. These and other problems kept unemployment high in Slovakia for several years after the world war.[79]

The discontent brewing among Slovaks, though widespread by mid–1919, might have remained largely hidden to the world if it were not for the actions of Andrej Hlinka late that summer. Before the end of the world war, Hlinka, though traditionally wary of the secular Czechs, let his guard down long enough to sign the Turčiansky Svätý Martin declaration which endorsed the union of the Czech and Slovak peoples. He began to regret his decision when his old political adversary, Šrobár, was named as the senior administrator of Slovakia.[80] Even more troubling for the populist priest were the public acts of anticlericalism that were recorded in the Bohemian lands shortly after the war. The most famous incident occurred on 3 November 1918 in Prague when unruly crowds destroyed the Marian Column, a seventeenth-century monument adorned with a statue of the Blessed Virgin. There were numerous other attacks on religious statues, and this heretical activity rendered Hlinka and other pious Slovaks increasingly uncomfortable with their new compatriots.[81]

By mid-summer of 1919, after the Hungarian Red Army had been humbled and forced to withdraw from eastern Slovakia, Hlinka shifted decidedly into the opposition against the Czechoslovak state. Earlier he had learned of the Pittsburgh Agreement, which was supposed to guarantee the Slovaks their own autonomy and parliament in a future Czecho-Slovak state. He felt that neither Masaryk, who was a signatory to the agreement, nor Šrobár could be trusted to vouch for such an arrangement before the National Assembly.[82] Desperate to save the Slovak faith, culture and language from encroachment by the Czech infidels, he took his campaign for Slovak autonomy outside the country by appealing to the peacemakers in Paris. His journey to France was aided by the Polish government, which was only too happy to cause headaches for its Těšín rival. When Hlinka and his three companions arrived in Paris in early September, they presented the Allied delegations with a memorandum pleading for a guarantee of Slovak autonomy in the Czechoslovak state and tried to arrange interviews with Allied statesmen. In a meeting with one Allied official, Hlinka was said to have expressed nostalgia for the days when the Slovaks belonged to the Kingdom of Hungary.[83] These efforts, however, came to naught. The Treaty of St. Germain, which held the key clauses that placed the ethnic minorities in Central Europe under the protection of the League of Nations, was only days from being signed. None of the tired delegations were willing to revise the treaty on the eve of its approval to please a handful of discontented Slovaks.[84] France, in any case, had always opposed the idea of a federal Czecho-Slovak state and preferred a strong, centralized Czechoslovakia that would be a dependable military partner in Central Europe.

In Prague, news of Hlinka's actions in Paris outraged Czechoslovak politicians, especially Šrobár and his allies who labeled the renegade priest as a traitor.[85] Despite these denouncements, Hlinka returned to Czechoslovakia unrepentant and prepared to accept whatever punishment the state might have in store for him; on the other hand, his three assistants opted to remain abroad. Prime Minister Tusar recognized the undesirability of transforming populist leader into a martyr, but since he felt it was necessary to restrain this loose cannon, he had Hlinka arrested on 11 October.[86]

His imprisonment for the next several months effectively muzzled the most ardent and recognizable proponent of Slovak autonomy as the permanent constitution for Czechoslovakia was in the critical stages of being drafted. At the time, most Slovak political groups on the left consistently opposed Slovak autonomy while those on the right, such as the Agrarians, desired a gradual introduction of Slovak self-government. Most Czech politicians, however, felt blind-sided by Hlinka's actions in Paris and feared that autonomy might encourage the Slovaks to cause more complications for the Prague government. Moreover, Slovak autonomy did not receive any endorsement in parliament from President Masaryk even though this had been implicit in the Pittsburgh Agreement. The National Assembly voted against Slovak autonomy and in early February 1920 its Slovak members sent an official statement to Slovak groups in the U.S. politely declining the terms of the Pittsburgh Agreement on the basis that their national rights would be safeguarded with the impending adoption of the new Czechoslovak constitution.[87] It soon became evident that the debate might have gone another way if elections had been held as planned in the previous summer. On 18 April Hlinka was finally released from his Moravian prison cell and in elections held ten days later he easily won a seat to the National Assembly. Even more embarrassing to the government was the fact that Šrobár lost his seat.[88] The issue of Slovak autonomy in the state was destined to resurface throughout the interwar period, and Hlinka remained at the forefront of the separatist cause until his death in 1938.[89]

While Slovak disillusionment with the Czechoslovak republic may have been a surprise to the peacemakers in Paris, the same could not be said for the ethnic German and Magyar populations that would be minorities in the new state. Initially, some of the peacemakers may have been unaware of the considerable size of the ethnic German population in the Bohemian borderlands. When President Wilson was informed during his voyage to Europe that their number stood at over three million, he was said to have cried, "Why Masaryk never told me that!"[90] If indeed that was the first time that Wilson heard that figure, Masaryk was not to blame. The professor had always been candid about his intention to include the German-speaking areas of Bohemia in the future Czechoslovak state; he had even explained his reasoning for doing so in a memorandum to the U.S. State Department in August 1918.[91] The aspirations of the German-Bohemians were impossible to overlook by the start of the peace conference after their representatives joined the National Assembly in Vienna and protested Czech encroachments in the Bohemian borderlands.[92] These complaints met unsympathetic ears in Paris since ethnic Germans throughout Europe were stigmatized by the lingering effects of Allied wartime propaganda that depicted the German people as an aggressive and barbarian race.

Although nothing could surmount the injured national pride of the German and Magyar minorities who became Czechoslovak citizens, the new state did have some real benefits for them. For instance, Czechoslovakia's friendly status during the peace conference meant that its subjects received imports of food and other essential commodities sooner than their compatriots in neighboring Germany, Austria or Hungary. Moreover, if the Bohemian borderlands had been conjoined onto Germany, the industries in those districts would have had a hard time competing with the more efficient German firms.[93] Czechoslovak leaders also made some genuine efforts to win these minorities over, but too frequently they governed Czechoslovakia as a nation-state rather than as the multinational state that it truly was.[94] Rather than treat the ethnic Germans as fellow Bohemians, they were more likely to regard them as guests who had long overstayed their welcome.[95] The land reform in particular was counterproductive to mending relations among ethnicities. Even though nobles of Czech origin were subjected to the same expropriations as German and Magyar landowners, the rhetoric of "national revenge" commonly used to justify the legislation only rubbed salt in the wound.[96]

The rights of German-Bohemians and other ethnic and religious minorities in Czechoslovakia were guaranteed by the League of Nations under a minority treaty signed at St. Germain on 10 September 1919. The treaty's clauses, which essentially accorded the minorities the same equal treatment as Czechoslovak nationals in the new state, were incorporated into the permanent constitution passed by the National Assembly in 1920.[97] Still, the fact that the articles of the constitution were determined by a parliament consisting of Czech and mostly Czechified Slovak deputies left it open to criticism from many sides.

Masaryk's dream that the Czech and Slovak peoples would become one amalgamated identity was embodied in the constitution's Language Law that designated "Czechoslovak," instead of Czech and Slovak, as the official tongue.[98, 99] This program was intended to make the Slovaks the inseparable allies of the Czechs against the minorities whose numbers were imposing enough to hinder the democratic process.[100] While this arrangement appealed to Czechs, it quickly earned the resentment of the Slovaks, who felt that their culture was being submerged by the more advanced Czechs. The Czechoslovak idea, rather than unifying the two "peoples of the state," instead drove them further apart as it fueled the anti–Czech demagoguery of the Slovak separatists.[101]

The great irony of Czechoslovakia and other postwar successor states in Central Europe was that they were advocated by their proponents primarily as a solution to the ethnic problems in the region that were partly responsible for the outbreak of the First World War. Masaryk and many other nationalists envied the Western-model of the democratic nation-state but failed to appreciate the impracticality of adopting this system in Central and Eastern Europe, where the ethnicities were distributed unevenly and often intertwined.[102] Instead of carving neat, homogenous nation-states out of the polyglot Habsburg Empire, the postwar settlement gave rise to several smaller states with an ethnic makeup nearly as messy as the so-called monstrosity which they replaced.[103, 104] The establishment of Czechoslovakia did not resolve the Bohemian Question any more than the foundation of Yugoslavia settled ethnic strife in western Balkans. The new states, in fact, became heirs to the Gordian knot that had perplexed their Habsburg successors, and it was not long before this labyrinth of riddles again threatened the peace and stability of Europe.

15

Exodus from a White Hell

Although the operations of the Czechoslovak legionaries in Siberia after November 1918 were mostly inconsequential to the rise of their new state in Central Europe, the story of the Czechoslovak national liberation movement would seem incomplete without shedding some light on the final sacrifices made by the men who had assured its success.

While statesmen from all over the globe spent much of 1919 trying to repair a world devastated by four years of war, the legionaries guarding the Trans-Siberian Railway struggled to make their unpopular mission a little more tolerable. Since their evacuation of Ukraine in March 1918, the legionaries had lived out of trains. For most, home during this period was a *teplushka*, a boxcar outfitted with bunks, iron stoves and sometimes latrines which normally accommodated 20–30 men. In these tight living quarters, privacy was nonexistent. In the short but humid Siberian summers, the railcars felt like saunas; in the winter they were drafty. To make this rudimentary existence more tolerable, the legionaries added many creature comforts to their mobile barracks. To protect the occupants against the dreaded chill of winter, they installed interior walls and insulation. Other modifications had purely aesthetic purposes, such as the decorating of exterior panels with intricate paintings and artwork. Many of these expressed nostalgia for the landscapes and women back home that they one day hoped to see again.[1]

Throughout their time in Siberia, much of the legionaries' society was mounted on trains. Bakeries, tailor shops, doctor clinics, bank branches and printing presses were just a few of the services and outlets one might have encountered in Czecho-Slovak railcars. In a letter to his wife, Edward Heald, a YMCA secretary traveling with the legionaries, described the layout of his multifunctional railcar-dwelling. "One end of it has the appearance of a country grocery store," he wrote, "with its shelves filled with chocolate, candies, tobacco, cigarettes, soap, toilet articles of various kinds, candles, and various other things that are found in these parts only on Y.M.C.A. cars. An unpainted partition separates this part of the car from the other part which is used as a bedroom, living room, and dining room by the American secretaries."[2] The Czecho-Slovaks did not restrict the role of their trains to peaceful enterprises in the rear; they also fought from armored trains outfitted for war. Some of these steel-plated behemoths were industrial marvels which resembled battleships; others were improvised contraptions protected by sandbags and studded with machine guns and field artillery. Regardless of their precise construction, all types of armored trains proved to be effective weapons which enabled the legionaries to strike quickly and decisively wherever partisans threatened the railway zone.

The Czecho-Slovaks had plenty of company in the train yards and stations which they occupied. Untold masses of Russians whose lives were uprooted by the war and revolution

Many Czecho-Slovak *teplushkas* like this one were decorated with nostalgic paintings of home and the women they longed to see again, undated.

flocked to Siberia in search of something to eat or simply to escape the Red Terror. The population of Omsk, for example, ballooned from about 120,000 to at least 500,000 in a few short months.[3] Since not an empty room could be found in the city, many refugees lived out of idle railcars in the train yard. This spectacle amazed Carl Ackermann, a *New York Times* correspondent who visited Siberia in early 1919. "Judging by the crowds at every railroad depot," he observed, "and the millions of human beings who live, day in and week out, in passenger and freight cars, one would think the population of that vast country was housed entirely on wheels, or that it was the supreme desire of every one to travel, despite the discomforts and inconveniences."[4] Sadly, there were plenty of refugees even worse off than these railcar dwellers. Gustav Bečvar, serving with the Czecho-Slovak 6th Regiment that was garrisoned in Omsk for much of 1919, described the plight of the most unfortunate Russians:

> Near our trains hundreds of families settled down on the steppe. They dug deep holes in the ground, and covered these with improvised roofs....Queues of these pitable, destitute creatures formed near

Armored train *Orlík* of Czecho-Slovak Army Corps in Russia, undated. Imposing land battleships like these ruled the Russian railways during the civil war.

our trains at meal-times, waiting for whatever remains there might be from the field-kitchens. Our dogs did not like the refugees. They were quite sufficiently intelligent to notice that their food supply rapidly deteriorated as a result of the arrival of these newcomers.[5]

Such wretched living conditions merely exacerbated the problem of sanitation in Kolchak's capital, which was not particularly good to begin with, and soon the city's hospitals were overflowing with cases of influenza, typhus and cholera.[6]

Disease and hunger affected nearly all Siberian centers, not just Omsk, during Kolchak's reign as Supreme Ruler. The Trans-Siberian Railway, which was virtually the only artery available to the Whites to import goods or move commodities between the eastern and western ends of Siberia, was devoted to the needs of the army.[7] It could not even fulfill that task. Supplies arriving in Vladivostok took between four and six weeks to reach Omsk.[8] Even if the materiel made the journey to Omsk, there was no guarantee that it would be delivered to the front in the Urals. Officials in Kolchak's government and army regularly pilfered scarce imports, such as boots and uniforms, either to outfit their families or to make a quick profit on the black market. To explain how so much materiel vanished before reaching the soldiers, one quartermaster in Omsk concluded that, "There is a hole somewhere between us and the front."[9]

The culture of corruption seems to have penetrated every level of the Kolchak government except the Supreme Ruler himself. The admiral was aware of this defect in his administration. "The company is awful," he wrote to his wife in Paris, "I am surrounded by moral decay, cowardice, greed and treachery."[10] Yet he inexplicably did little to improve the discipline and conduct of the officials he was relying upon to defeat the Bolsheviks. Simply put, he was the wrong man for the job of dictator of Siberia. He was an honest, patriotic and well-meaning individual with a polished record of commanding sailors, but he was politically inept and incapable of inducing those around him to adopt the high ethical standards which he applied to himself. Part of this failure may be attributable to his own health troubles: he suffered long bouts of illness, especially early in his reign, which left his ministers with no oversight.[11] But even when he was well, he devoted too much time to military matters at the expense of civilian affairs. In both areas of administration, he had a tendency to depend on unqualified, conniving and self-serving individuals who led the economy, finances and most importantly the army of White Siberia to disaster.[12]

Kolchak's tolerance of such untrustworthy servants is all the more surprising in light of his ferocious temper. His legendary act of hurling his Sword of Honor into the Black Sea from the deck of his flagship in June 1917 may stand as one example of his uncontrollable rage.[13] In the summer of 1919, as he was receiving a steady stream of bad news from the front, contemporaries claimed that the Supreme Ruler lost all self-control. But instead of directing his wrath against the imbeciles and crooks responsible for the fiascos, he vented his anger on inanimate objects, such as pencils, inkpots or office furniture. In other instances he unleashed rambling tirades against those whose support for his regime he thought underwhelming, particularly the Czecho-Slovaks and the Allies.[14] His increasingly erratic behavior did nothing to restore the confidence of outsiders in his leadership. General Janin attributed the admiral's violent mood swings to a cocaine addiction, though in fairness it must be said that the Frenchman never had a high opinion of Kolchak after the two quarreled over the command of the anti–Bolshevik armies in December 1918. While some despairing White officials probably did turn to drugs and alcohol as their military prospects worsened, Kolchak's only confirmed vice during his reign in Omsk was an overt affair with the wife of one of his naval colleagues.[15]

The failure of the Kolchak regime to put Siberia on sound economic, much less military, footing fueled discontent among peasants that exploded into a mass insurgency across the Siberian wilderness. The partisans do not appear to have been dedicated to a single political ideology other than to rid their land of the ravaging armies and punitive expeditions which pressed their young men into service, requisitioned their horses and committed atrocities on a frightening scale. Often led by *frontoviki*, or demobilized world war veterans, the partisan detachments initially possessed few firearms. Nevertheless, these bands wielding pitchforks and scythes used the element of surprise to overtake Whites garrisons and plunder military trains. Before long, they greatly enhanced their firepower with everything from machine guns to grenade launchers.[16]

Even when they did not attack the Czecho-Slovak or White troops directly, the partisans could wreak havoc on anti–Bolshevik operations by sabotaging the railway. In Eastern Siberia, various sectors of the railway were guarded by the Americans, Japanese and the anti–Bolshevik forces of Semenov and Kalmykov. Between Irkutsk and Novonikolaevsk, the Czecho-Slovaks acted as watchmen over the vital supply route. To their west, that duty was taken up by a Polish division and White Russians. Even the most effective of these forces, however, could not be everywhere at once and there were inevitably plenty of unguarded stretches of track where the insurgents could tear up the rails or set fire to a bridge and then disappear into dark pine forests. According to one account, 826 bridges, 20 stations and 14 water-supply depots were destroyed along the Trans-Siberian Railway during the civil war, and partisan activity probably contributed greatly to this number.[17]

Although the Czecho-Slovaks did not relish in the anti-partisan operations, they were bound to energetically defend the railway knowing that someday they would need it for their long-awaited evacuation. They showed a disinterest in events outside the immediate railway zone and generally made only half-hearted attempts to pursue the insurgents deep into the taiga. Both sides gradually adopted a "live and let live" attitude as long as they stayed out of each other's way. This situation was very different from the savage struggle that took place along other sectors of the railway, particularly where White counter-insurgent detachments

Czecho-Slovak cavalrymen ford a Siberian river, undated. Cavalry units were deployed extensively in the Russian Civil War.

razed villages or executed every able-bodied male as a means to break the peasants' resistance.[18]

The Siberian peasants, it seems, still resented the presence of the Czecho-Slovaks even though the legionaries never terrorized local populations at the levels of the notorious White hangmen and Cossack warlords. After liberating the region from the Bolsheviks in the summer of 1918, the industrious Czecho-Slovaks reopened Siberian mines, factories and banks that had been paralyzed by the short experiment of nationalization. The industrial enterprises, though few in number, were of paramount importance to help make up for the deficit in manufactured wares at a time when Siberia was all but cut off from imports.[19] The Czecho-Slovaks' entrepreneurship, however, soon earned them the reputation of exploitative outsiders, not unlike how many Russians regarded Jews at the time.[20] The legionaries were no longer welcome in towns and villages as they had been in the summer of 1918, and many Russians insulted them as "Czech dogs," a reference to the heraldic lion patch on their uniforms which the peasants mistook for a rearing puppy.[21] Many Whites accused the Czecho-Slovaks of collecting an enormous cache of requisitioned property for themselves,[22] and others were probably jealous of their steady food rations, efficient supply service and success with local women.[23] Some 1,600 officers and men belonging to the corps married in Russia prior to their final evacuation, including Gajda who, despite already having a wife in Czechoslovakia, attached himself to the Supreme Ruler's dynasty by wedding Kolchak's niece.[24]

Despite the Russians' prevalent bitterness towards the Czecho-Slovaks in 1919, White leaders did make efforts to reach out to the legionaries, especially as their military fortunes sank during the summer. The officers of the Czecho-Slovak 6th Regiment stationed in Omsk, for example, were treated to banquets at which their Cossack and Russian hosts heaped praise upon the legionaries' past feats. The legionaries were astute enough to realize that the Whites desired their help at the front to stem the advance of the Red armies, but nothing could rekindle their enthusiasm for fighting.[25] The legionaries' only real desire by then was to go home.

Although the Allied powers had refrained from sending large forces into the depths of Siberia, they still provided Kolchak's armies with a vast array of arms and supplies. Before the shipments of war materiel ceased in the autumn of 1919, Britain alone had delivered 600,000 rifles, 346,000,000 cartridges, 6,831 machine guns, 192 field guns and 200,500 uniforms to Siberia. Additional war materiel was imported from France and the United States, and although the quantities were smaller than those furnished by the British, America's contribution of 250,000 rifles, nearly 2,000 machine guns and 400 field guns was nothing to scoff at.[26] The beginning of the end of this foreign support came after the White debacle at Chelyabinsk in late summer. Up to then General Knox, Kolchak's most ardent supporter among Allied officials in Siberia, was optimistic that the retreating Whites would recover their strength east of the Urals. However, the crushing Red victory at Chelyabinsk and the evident incompetence in the White military leadership compelled him to change his tune.[27] Around the same time that Knox wrote off the Whites as a lost cause in his reports to London, the U.S. State Department informed anti–Bolshevik plenipotentiaries in Washington that they would be sending no more supplies to the Whites.[28] During the remainder of the year, the bulk of Allied shipments to the Russian anti–Bolsheviks would be sent to Denikin's Armed Forces of South Russia.

With the Allies cutting their losses in Siberia, the Czecho-Slovaks were not unreasonable in thinking that their moment of departure was nigh as well. The peace deliberations at St. Germain were winding down by the end of the summer and the signing ceremony of that treaty would be held on 10 September, thus obliterating the political and diplomatic reasons for the intervention that were cited by Czechoslovak leaders earlier in the year. Moreover, other Allied units sent to Siberia, such as the 4,000 Canadians who arrived there the previous autumn, were pulled out that summer.[29] The legionaries had begun evacuating their sick and wounded at the end of July, and a few weeks later General Syrový asked his superior, General Janin, to give the order for the rest of the Czecho-Slovak Legion to depart from Siberia. From Paris, Beneš echoed Syrový's request in a telegram to Janin. The Frenchman, however, continued to vacillate. Apparently, he did not cherish the thought of pulling the rug out from beneath the feet of the Siberian Whites in their time of need.[30]

The pressure on Janin to issue evacuation orders continued to mount into the following month when a delegation from Prague arrived in Siberia. Led by František Krejči, a socialist deputy on the National Assembly, the delegation toured the Czecho-Slovak regiments along the railway between Irkutsk and Vladivostok; its members also paid their respects at eighteen cemeteries where fallen legionaries had been laid to rest.[31] When Krejči and his colleagues finally caught up with Janin's train in late September, they pleaded with the general to begin evacuating the Czecho-Slovak troops. The Frenchman heeded their wishes to the extent of sending Syrový and other Czecho-Slovak commanders the blueprints for the corps' impending withdrawal to Vladivostok, but no other action was taken. Throughout October 1919, the question of whether or not to pull the Czecho-Slovaks out of Siberia continued to be debated over telegrams between Janin and the Supreme War Council in Paris.[32]

At the time, some of the Allied reluctance to evacuate the legionaries out of Siberia was due to the Whites' successes elsewhere in Russia. Denikin's Armed Forces of South Russia proved to be the most threatening enemy to the Soviet regime as it repulsed Red counterattacks and approached within 250 miles of Moscow by mid–October. Meanwhile, General Nikolay Yudenich, commanding the small but strategically-positioned Northwestern Army, broke out of its pocket next to the Estonian frontier and menaced Petrograd, the cradle of the Revolution.[33] Even Kolchak's forces appeared to have achieved a miraculous recovery earlier that autumn. On 1 September the Siberian Whites launched a surprise counteroffensive against the Fifth and Third Red Armies that were pursuing them along the railways from Chelyabinsk and Yekaterinburg. The operation, which was the brainchild of General Diterikhs, was supposed to cut off the Fifth Red Army before it could withdraw safely behind the River Tobol. Although the Siberian Whites succeeded in clearing out the Reds between the Ishim and Tobol rivers, the Siberian Cossack cavalry failed to swoop behind the Fifth Red Army at the critical moment. As a result, both Red Armies retreated safely to the west bank of the Tobol, where they regrouped and added some 44,000 reinforcements to their ranks. The Whites would not be able to savor their victory for long.

On 14 October, the Red Eastern Army Group attacked across the Tobol River. Although they outnumbered the Whites by at least two to one, it took them three days of heavy losses to secure a bridgehead on the east bank. Once they gained a foothold across the river, however, the Red Armies carried everything before them. By 5 November, the Red spearheads were only 125 miles away from Omsk, which they were poised to reach in just a matter of days.

For weeks the more grounded minds in Omsk, including Diterikhs, had been urging the Supreme Ruler to relocate the seat of his government to Irkutsk, some 1,500 miles away and safely outside the immediate striking distance of the Red Armies. But Kolchak preferred to listen to the younger officers among his coterie who assured him that Omsk could be defended. If all was indeed lost, the admiral appeared ready to make a heroic if futile stand in his capital, like an honorable captain prepared to go down with his sinking ship. Realizing that his master was unwilling to listen to reason, an exasperated Diterikhs resigned as commander-in-chief of Kolchak's armies on 4 November and boarded the first available eastbound train. His replacement was the thirty-eight-year-old General Konstantin Sakharov, whose main qualification for the post was his conviction that Omsk could still be saved from the Red horde. A week later, with his remaining forces depleted by mutiny, desertion and the absence of reinforcements, Sakharov suddenly lost his nerve and ordered the evacuation of the capital with the intent of regrouping the tattered White armies in the vicinity of Tomsk and Taiga.[34]

Sakharov's belated admission that Omsk could not be defended turned what could have earlier been a relatively orderly evacuation into a jumbled rout that would cost the Whites dearly in the ensuing hours, days and weeks. When the general evacuation of the White capital was announced, panic set in among the hundreds of thousands of refugees who sought safety there. The legionaries of the Czecho-Slovak 6th Regiment were among those who watched delirious crowds swarm the train yard and station begging for space on an eastbound train. Bureaucrats, army officers and desperate aristocrats were among those who tried to bribe the Czecho-Slovaks with whatever valuables they possessed into taking them and their families. The legionaries were probably the best prepared of those fleeing Omsk in those hectic, gray November days. They had well-insulated *teplushkas* to travel in and their quartermasters had ensured that their trains were carrying sufficient stocks of food and fuel.[35] In contrast, the Kolchak government had made virtually no contingency plans to evacuate the city. Many of the refugee trains that left Omsk were undersupplied with coal and the stocks were woefully low at coaling stations further to the east. These trains would soon find themselves stranded in middle of nowhere, waiting for one of the few coal-supply trains that operated on the westbound track to loan them some coal so they could resume the journey. Often these trains would not move for days, while the Red Army behind them crept closer and closer.[36]

Thousands of others in Omsk did not bother attempting to squeeze onto a train and instead set out into the wintry steppe on foot or in sledges. Using the *trakt* which in most areas ran parallel to the railway, these refugees braved freezing weather, wolf packs, deep snow and partisans as they trudged eastward. Among this unfortunate lot were the remnants of Kolchak's armies. Clothed in tattered, irregular uniforms with their heads low, they appeared to one Czecho-Slovak officer who witnessed their sullen march more like beggars than soldiers.[37]

Among the last White trains to leave Omsk were those of the Supreme Ruler and the remaining stocks of the Russian gold reserve that had been captured at Kazan some fifteen months earlier. Even these echelons, with their high-ranking personnel and precious cargo, could not avoid the delays and complications which all eastbound trains experienced. Still, they had at least escaped. Hours after Kolchak's train slipped out of Omsk on the night of 13–14 November, the vanguard of the Fifth Red Army entered the city the next morning against no serious resistance. Although the Whites had managed to take the gold reserve with them, they left plenty of other trophies behind as the Reds claimed to have seized 200 locomotives, 3,000 railcars, 40,000 prisoners, three armored trains, 40 field guns, 900 machine guns and 5,000 artillery shells when they took Omsk.[38]

Kolchak had been reluctant to abandon his capital due to its symbolic importance. Its fall, he suspected, would have important ramifications for the White movement by discouraging its allies and emboldening its enemies.[39] He was right; the loss of his capital was the latest in a series of reverses for the enemies of the Soviet regime. Denikin's armies, which had seemed poise to march on Moscow, were suddenly thrown back to South Russia by overwhelming Red counteroffensives. In northwestern Russia, Yudenich's small army reached the outskirts of Petrograd and then was forced to retreat into Estonia, where the Whites were disarmed.[40] With a Red victory appearing more likely than ever, the Czecho-Slovaks sought to loosen their ties with the beleaguered Whites. Even as the Red Armies closed in on Omsk, the Czechoslovak government instructed the legionaries to withdraw from Siberia while remaining neutral in Russian affairs. As it shifted to a delicate non-interventionist policy, Prague also recalled Pavlů on 12 November and replaced him with the more socialist-leaning Václav Girsa.[41] One of Pavlů's last acts, which he carried out in unison with Girsa, was to sign a public disavowal of the Kolchak regime in the name of the Czecho-Slovak Legion. This manifesto, which alleged that "under the cover of Czechoslovak arms local Russian military authorities were allowed to commit acts which would horrify the world," was made public on 13 November and effectively left no doubt that the Czecho-Slovaks were attempting to distance themselves from the Whites both physically and diplomatically.[42]

Another group opposed to the Kolchak regime, the Social Revolutionaries, also took advantage of the Whites' disarray. After the earlier crackdowns on SRs and other socialists by White army officers and Cossacks, these dissidents went underground in Siberia but remained quite active. In Eastern Siberia, the moderate socialists there desired the creation of a regional democratic-socialist "buffer state" to save the population from the excesses of Soviet tyranny and White reaction. In late summer 1919, they recruited to their side General Radola Gajda, who was quite disgruntled after his break with the Supreme Ruler. In the early morning hours of 17 November, three days after the fall of Omsk, Gajda and his SR accomplices in Vladivostok proclaimed the formation of the Provisional People's Government of Siberia. The announced objective of its leaders was not to launch a military campaign against Soviet Russia but rather negotiate a truce with the Bolsheviks. But before the Provisional People's Government of Siberia dealt with its Red foes, it would first have to survive its much closer White enemies.

Gajda's plot for a *coup d'etat* in Vladivostok was not a carefully guarded secret. Local Allied representatives and Czecho-Slovak leaders had some inkling of the revolt, and the latter tried to dissuade the ambitious Czech general from carrying out his scheme. The Whites, led by the Kolchak-appointed governor-general Sergey Rozanov, were also aware of Gajda's plans and had prepared to act swiftly when the rebels struck. Rozanov's troops were quickly reinforced by Kalmykov's Ussuri Cossacks and Japanese troops were also on hand to provide the Whites valuable assistance. To offset the strength of this coalition, Gajda and his SR conspirators probably yearned for some aid from the 8,000 Czecho-Slovak troops in the vicinity of the port who were waiting to embark, but the legionaries were too homesick to follow their famous general on another adventure. Thus Gajda and the few hundred volunteers who joined his new People's Army were left to face the combined forces of Rozanov, Kalmykov and the Japanese alone. The latter quickly cordoned off the train yard where Gajda had his headquarters while searchlights from Japanese warships in the harbor sought out targets. After a five and a half hour bombardment of the area, the insurgents emerged from the devastated trains with their hands above their heads. Most of these prisoners were machine-gunned by the Whites a few hours later. A wounded Gajda was also captured, but his fate was more fortunate than that of his troops. After a brutal beating from his Russian captors, the Czech general was packed off to a British ship in the harbor and banned from Siberia.[43]

Although the SR bid for power in Vladivostok was quickly crushed, the party's groups continued to operate with more diligence and success in other Siberian centers. Among these was Irkutsk, which was designated as the new capital for the Supreme Ruler. Kolchak's ministers, who left Omsk just before the general evacuation was announced, arrived there in good time on 19 November. By then, however, a shadow government called the Political Center, a coalition of SRs and Mensheviks, had already taken root in the city. Rather than crush this potential opposition, the White cabinet instead tried to woo it into cooperating with them as they attempted to regain their footing in Central Siberia. Girsa, from his headquarters in Irkutsk, also sought to win the good graces of the Political Center.

Kolchak was less conciliatory than his ministers in coming to terms with even moderate dissidents of his regime. He and his entourage caught in the logjam of trains on the Trans-Siberian Railway were left seething by the condemnatory Czecho-Slovak manifesto. True to his temperamental character, the Supreme Ruler fired off his own reply to the Czecho-Slovaks, which was received in Irkutsk on 25 November. In his diatribe, Kolchak accused the legionaries of treacherous conduct by affiliating with "groups indistinguishable from the Bolsheviks." This telling passage of the admiral's true feelings towards the socialist parties did not aid the cabinet's efforts to reach a compromise with the Political Center. It also did not bode well for the ministers' hopes to draw the Czecho-Slovaks, who they thought were the only force in Siberia that could possibly fend off the Fifth Red Army, into the fighting. After receiving a storm of protests from his ministers, Kolchak reluctantly withdrew his statements but the damage was done since they were already known to the Czecho-Slovaks and socialists. In the meantime, the ministers sent one of their own, Viktor Pepeliaev, westward to rendezvous with the neurotic Supreme Ruler and restrain him from committing further diplomatic blunders. On 7 December, after a five day journey from Irkutsk, the Minister of the Interior boarded Kolchak's train at Taiga.[44]

As Kolchak's ministers struggled to stabilize their government after the disastrous abandonment of Omsk, the general disorder and slow progress along the eastbound track of the Trans-Siberian Railway only grew worse as the Czecho-Slovak units between Novonikolaevsk and Irkutsk began their withdrawal. Amazingly, the Allied Supreme War Council and General Janin continued to withhold the official orders for the Legion's evacuation even though the Whites' collapse should have been apparent to all by that time. When the mess of refugee trains from the west spilled into their sectors in early December and threatened to disrupt their own planned evacuation, the legionaries quickly took matters into their own hands. All along the sectors of railways which the legionaries guarded, the Russian stationmasters, conductors, telegraph operators and quartermasters were brushed aside and replaced by Czecho-Slovak technicians, engineers and officers who had been preparing for this moment during the past year. The Czecho-Slovaks effectively took control of every aspect of travel and communication along the railway between Novonikolaevsk and Irkutsk right down to each shovel-full of coal that was allotted to the trains. Naturally, this infuriated the White Russians whose dirty and cramped trains were delayed or shunted to a siding so that the legionaries could roll out of Siberia in their comparatively plush *teplushkas*.[45]

White officials quickly inundated General Syrový's headquarters in Irkutsk with protests and complaints over the Czecho-Slovaks' actions. Rather than try to turn his men around, Syrový instead urged Janin to formally sanction the evacuation that was already beginning to take place. The Frenchman finally relented and sent instructions for the evacuation to take place in the order previously agreed upon by the Allies: first the Czecho-Slovaks, then the Polish, Romanian and Serbian units. The Russian trains were to be last, and as a result the directive did nothing to improve the Whites' predicament. Not even the staff trains of White army generals or the trains bearing the Supreme Ruler himself were allowed to budge in front of the Czecho-Slovaks, whose echelons were the only ones allowed to proceed eastward along the rails normally used for westbound traffic. All other trains were left to operate on the crowded eastbound track, and their progress was rendered even more abysmal as the well-armed legionaries commandeered the short supply of operable locomotives to pull their wagons.[46]

Even prior to the legionaries' interference, the eastward flight was not going well for the Whites. The *ad hoc* evacuation from Omsk overburdened the railway and caused innumerable delays. Trains that had left the White capital before the government announced its intention to abandon it were able to reach Irkutsk in as little as nine days; by comparison, in their first ten days on the tracks the trains of the Czecho-Slovak 6th Regiment managed to cover just over a third of the distance to the city.[47] The limited availability of coal and operable locomotives were just a couple of the many factors working against the Whites. Finding sufficient quantities of unfrozen water for the engine boilers in the wintry landscape

An icebound locomotive, undated. Operational locomotives were in short supply throughout the Legion's stay in Russia.

was a major challenge, and deliberately thawing out snow for this purpose was inefficient and time-consuming. Typhus-bearing lice thrived in the packed quarters of the refugee trains, and spread of the disease was so feared that when just one or two passengers showed symptoms of infection, the entire carriage was unhitched and its occupants abandoned. The plight of the tens of thousands of soldiers and civilians retreating on foot on the nearby *trakt* was not any better. Day in and day out the wicked elements of the Siberian winter bore down upon them; icy winds sucked the warmth from their bodies while blowing snow blinded their path. Any stragglers who fell behind the winding columns were easy pickings for the wolves and partisans who lurked in the snow-blanketed forests. All along the *trakt* and the railway, blackened, frozen corpses of disease, cold or hunger victims became a common sight; their burial would have to wait until the ground thawed in late spring. In the meantime, shivering passers-by could not resist the temptation to supplement their layers of clothing with a hat, scarf or coat worn by the dead and, in doing so, they unwittingly exposed themselves to infected lice. Indeed, of all the enemies the Whites encountered during their retreat, the Red Army on their heels probably inflicted the fewest casualties on their ranks.[48]

Like his subjects, the Supreme Ruler and his cabal also had to endure the frustration of innumerable delays while the legionaries moved out ahead of them. On 10 December, Kolchak's seven trains were shunted aside at Mariinsk so the Czecho-Slovaks could use the echelon's locomotives to pull their own wagons forward. If this were not distressing enough, word soon spread among the Whites that the Fifth Red Army was capturing anywhere from ten to twenty trains of the most rearward echelons from Omsk with each passing day. Kolchak appealed to the Allied missions, then in Irkutsk, to compel the legionaries to facilitate the movement of the endangered echelons in the rear, but the Allied commissioners lacked any practical means of enforcing such a command. In the meantime, the Russians continued to fume at the Czecho-Slovaks and accused them of hauling railcars full of loot and prostitutes while the trains of helpless Russian civilians and wounded soldiers were left to the mercies of the Bolsheviks.[49] In all probability, such losses were unavoidable given the disorderly manner in which the Whites evacuated Omsk. The sudden deluge of refugee, military and supply trains on the Trans-Siberian Railway far exceeded the intended capacity of tracks that were already in a precarious condition due to the poor maintenance and the earlier fighting along it. When it became apparent that the lifeline that was the railway could not save the Czecho-Slovaks, other foreigners and Russians at the same time, the instinct of self-preservation set in among these groups. The Czecho-Slovaks, possessing martial and technical muscle that none of their rivals for the railway could match, won this contest.[50]

Throughout December, underground SR groups emerged into the open and staged one uprising after another in the towns and cities between Novonikolaevsk and Irkutsk. Rather than attempt to suppress these revolts, the Czecho-Slovak officers instead entered into negotiations with the rebels to preserve their neutrality, protect the railway zone and secure the unmolested passage of their troops through the area. The legionaries made similar arrangements with the rural partisans, who were now stronger than ever.[51] The legionaries' only objective, they made clear, was to leave Siberia with as few casualties as possible.

The Czecho-Slovaks' refusal to act against the insurgents caused the Whites, who could expect no mercy from the sniping guerrillas, to claim that they had been betrayed by the legionaries. General Kappel, the new commander-in-chief of Siberia's White armies, hoped that his troops could obtain a refuge from the weather and the partisans at Krasnoyarsk, but when he reached the outskirts of the city he found that it, along with its White garrison, had gone over to the SR rebels. His army, with its ranks thinned and exhausted from the grueling 900-mile march from Omsk, was too weak to retake Krasnoyarsk and continued to retreat eastward into the taiga. Rather than press on, many soldiers and refugees marching with Kappel simply gave up at this point. Thousands of soldiers and officers deserted to the insurgents while others allowed themselves to be run over by trains or shot themselves and their entire families.

Ataman Semenov, whose liar in Chita was insulated from the Red Army by formidable distances and Kolchak's shattered forces, was unfettered by the collapse of the Whites to his west.[52] Instead of drilling his forces in preparation for the inevitable showdown with the Red Army, he and his bands of marauders devoted most of their energies towards their incessant crime spree.[53] The only aid he extended to his beleaguered anti–Bolshevik allies was in the form of an ultimatum addressed to Syrový demanding that the Czecho-Slovaks halt their evacuation long enough for the refugee and hospital trains from Omsk to pass on to Irkutsk. Syrový was moved neither by the ataman's appeal to humanitarianism nor by his threat to attack the legionaries if they failed to comply with his demands. The Czech general simply warned Semenov that the legionaries would reciprocate any hostile actions against them.[54] At about the same time, on 23 December, Kolchak announced the promotion of Semenov to the new position of Commander-in-Chief of all Forces in the Far East. The admiral, who never liked the Cossack warlord, took this action only out of desperation. He knew that his own authority was weakening while he remained stranded at a siding along the Trans-Siberian Railway. Even worse, his cabinet's negotiations with the Political Center were proving fruitless while Irkutsk was on the verge of revolt. By granting the ataman the title which he coveted,

Kolchak hoped that Semenov would reinforce the White garrison in Irkutsk and keep that city firmly under White control.

From the perspective of the Czecho-Slovaks, Allied High Commissioners and Russian political moderates, the Supreme Ruler's promotion of a notorious brigand such as Semenov evaporated the last shred of respect they might have held for the admiral. Moreover, the legionaries were already suspicious that the Supreme Ruler and the Cossack warlord were plotting against them. In the closing days of December, Czecho-Slovak telegraph operators reportedly intercepted a coded telegram from Kolchak ordering the ataman to block the eastbound Czecho-Slovak trains at any cost—even if this meant dynamiting the crucial tunnels south of Lake Baikal. The existence of this order has never been confirmed by historians although contemporary Allied representatives in Siberia vouched for the tale. It is possible that it was nothing more than a concoction of Czecho-Slovak paranoia and rumors. Whatever the truth, the authenticity of the telegram gained wide acceptance among the Czecho-Slovaks and Allied missions in Siberia, not to mention later chroniclers of the Siberian fiasco—even those sympathetic to Kolchak. Clearly, the admiral's behavior at the end of 1919 appeared unhinged enough for observers to believe that he was capable of issuing an order that would have been detrimental not only to the Czecho-Slovaks but to the Whites as well since both groups were dependent on the railway.[55]

Shortly after Semenov assumed his new title as Commander-in-Chief of all Forces in the Far East, he loaded two cavalry and two infantry detachments onto a fleet of armored trains under Colonel Skipetrov and sent them barreling towards Irkutsk. By the time they reached the city on 30 December, Glaskovo and other suburbs in the vicinity of Irkutsk were already in rebel hands. In Irkutsk proper, a garrison of 3,500 White soldiers under General Sychev was holding out in the hope that Skipetrov's expedition would relieve them. Skipetrov and 200 *semenovtsy* managed to reach Irkutsk by crossing the Angara River on a steamer, but their attack failed to dislodge the SR rebels from Glaskovo and its train station. Caught in an increasingly hopeless position, the Whites and *semenovtsy* boarded an icebreaker and evacuated Irkutsk on the evening of 3 January 1920. The next morning, the Political Center assumed control of Irkutsk, but its weakness was evident from the start. To maintain order in the city, it had to rely on Japanese and Czecho-Slovak troops to police the streets.[56]

Despite the defeat of Skipetrov's expedition, Semenov's interferences with the railway and the Czecho-Slovak evacuation continued. Just days after the Whites evacuated Irkutsk, the ataman declared he would block the legionaries' passage through Transbaikal Province unless they handed over 300 railcars to him. When Colonel Skipetrov reemerged at Sludyanka on 9 January intent on enforcing Semenov's order, the legionaries there refused to surrender any of their railcars. Fighting broke out between the two sides and the resulting battle was disastrous for the *semenovtsy*: several were killed and wounded while about 600 were taken prisoner. Nor did the legionaries end their action against Semenov there. All along the Circumbaikal sector, the Czecho-Slovaks rounded up the *semenovtsy* and captured a number of their trains. Incidentally, the *semenovtsy* also picked a fight with troops from the U.S. 27th Infantry Regiment who were guarding the railway just east of the Circumbaikal sector. In a brief but sharp battle, a counterattack by the doughboys killed a number of *semenovtsy*, took others prisoner and captured an armored train. These firefights involving Czecho-Slovak and U.S. troops exposed the utter martial weakness of the Cossack warlords. In general, these irregular forces were badly led, poorly trained and lacked discipline. They also suffered from shortages of equipment and morale. Semenov's forces, for example, might have had a paper strength of 20,000 troops but of those perhaps less than a quarter were fully-armed *and* reliable. In any case, Semenov should have concentrated his meager strength on the partisan movement that was booming in Eastern Siberia. An ominous development for him occurred a few weeks later when his weaker partner to the east, Ataman Kalmykov, was chased out of Khabarovsk by a partisan army.[57]

The loss of Irkutsk ended Kolchak's fantasies of rebuilding his regime. It could be said, however, that real power had left him well before the Political Center secured the city. During the fighting in and around Irkutsk, the Supreme Ruler and his companions were marooned about 300 miles to the northwest at Nizhneudinsk. One day during his two-week stay in the train yard, the admiral peeked out of the curtains of his coach to see a new set of guards retracing their footsteps in the snow outside. Wrapped in greatcoats and wearing fleece hats for headgear, these soldiers might have been mistaken for Russians if it were not for the red and white cockades which the legionaries pinned to their outerwear.[58] It was then that the Supreme Ruler realized he was at the complete mercy of the Czecho-Slovak 6th Regiment. The legionaries, convinced that the hotheaded admiral had ordered Semenov to bar their route to the east, were taking no chances and monitored all messages and persons going to and from the Supreme Ruler's carriage. When Kolchak protested to Major Hašek, the local Czecho-Slovak commander, that the legionaries were making him feel a prisoner, Hašek assured him that the guards were posted around his train only to protect him from the rebels who controlled the nearby town. Understandably, the admiral and his inner circle were unconvinced by this explanation, especially after a Czecho-Slovak armored train parked next to their carriage with its gun turrets pointing at, rather than away, from them.[59]

On 1 January 1920, as demonstrators at the train station in Nizhneudinsk were demanding the Czecho-Slovaks to handover the admiral to them, the Allied High Commissioners in Glaskovo offered Kolchak and the state gold reserve in his echelon their guarantee of protection if he desired it. If he did not place himself under Allied—which really meant Czecho-Slovak—protection, then he would be responsible for his own fate. Kolchak, somewhat reluctantly, acknowledged his dire situation and accepted the Allied High Commissioners' guarantee of protection. Thus on 4 January the Czecho-Slovak 6th Regiment was given the formal responsibility to escort the Supreme Ruler and the gold reserve to Irkutsk. Before they could resume the journey, however, the legionaries demanded Kolchak to reduce his staff so its personnel could fit into a single coach. The admiral initially protested this stipulation, but the problem mostly resolved itself when the Supreme Ruler's bodyguard and private band defected to the insurgents at Nizhneudinsk. On 6 January Kolchak transferred his empty title of Supreme Ruler to General Denikin in South Russia, whose forces at that time were hardly better off. Later that day, the admiral and his remaining suite squeezed into a second-class passenger coach which, as a sign of Allied protection, was adorned with the flags of the intervening powers: Czechoslovakia, France, Great Britain, Japan and the United States. On the following day, the coach and the railcars laden with the state gold reserve lurched out of Nizhneudinsk with the trains of the 1st Battalion, 6th Regiment towards Irkutsk.[60]

The legionaries overseeing the admiral's safety did not relish their duty. Lieutenant Bečvar, who commanded the contingent responsible for guarding Kolchak, later recalled how the relatively benign attitude of the locals towards his legionaries changed as they escorted the fallen dictator along the Trans-Siberian Railway. "The fury of the Siberian people," he wrote, "which until now had been centered upon Kolchak, turned against ourselves."[61]

At the towns and stations along the route to Irkutsk, they met livid demonstrators demanding that the fallen dictator be handed over to them.[62] At Zima, the insurgents threatened to blow up the railway ahead unless the legionaries gave up Kolchak. To obtain their safe passage, the legionaries negotiated a compromise that permitted the partisans to attach one of their own men to the Czecho-Slovak guard on the admiral's train. A similar agreement had to be made further down the line when local miners refused to hand over their coal unless several more partisans could join the guards. As those inside the coach watched these events, they knew the noose around the admiral was tightening. One of Kolchak's officers attempted to bring General Janin's attention to their plight by sending a cable to Irkutsk, but by then the Frenchman and the Allied High Commissioners had already left the city for the Russian Far East.[63]

The first days of 1920 were not only ominous for Kolchak, they were also distressing for the tens of thousands of Czecho-Slovaks, Poles, Romanians, Serbs and White Russians attempting to retreat along the railway west of Irkutsk. On 8 January, a spearhead from the Fifth Red Army, advancing in sleighs to bypass the paralyzed traffic on the railway, reached Krasnoyarsk. Among those whose escape route was now blocked was the Polish division of about 5,000 men and officers. Although small groups of Poles managed to slip away either to continue the retreat with the Czecho-Slovaks or flee into Mongolia, most opted to lay down their arms when the Reds offered to repatriate them across Russia.[64] Four days later, the Red vanguard caught up to the Romanian trains. Desperate to get away, the Romanians abandoned their idle trains and retreated on foot to the Czecho-Slovak trains further to the east. To the Romanians' dismay, the legionaries refused to accommodate them and instead shooed them away. The Romanians took revenge of sorts on the inhospitable Czecho-Slovaks by destroying a bridge west of Kansk on which some Czecho-Slovak trains still needed to cross over. Around the same time, two battalions from a Yugoslav regiment gave up their evacuation attempt by joining the partisans. In the end, only 800 Poles, one Romanian train and three Yugoslav trains succeeded in completing the katabasis alongside the Czecho-Slovaks.[65]

On 13 January the first clash between the vanguard of the Fifth Red Army and the rear of the Czecho-Slovak Legion occurred around Kansk.[66] Unlike the Poles or Romanians, the troops from the Third Czecho-Slovak Division fought off the Bolsheviks but had to leave behind an armored train that was disabled in battle. This small prize whetted the appetite of the Red pursuers, who believed that the Czecho-Slovak corps was on the verge of disintegration just as the Polish and Romanian detachments had been. Their assessment may have originated with a group of Czechoslovak Communists attached to the Fifth Red Army's staff that was continuing their two-year-long campaign to undermine the legionaries' morale. Subsequently, the Fifth Red Army increased its pressure on the legionaries.[67] In an unexpected turn of events, however, the military position of the Czecho-Slovak rearguard was strengthened when, on 15 January, the skeletal formations of General Kappel's army emerged from the taiga at Kansk.[68] The Reds had lost contact with Kappel's force after the Whites bypassed Krasnoyarsk via a roundabout route through the wilderness. Thus the Bolsheviks were stunned when this army attacked their flank and plundered their stockpile of munitions and supplies. On 21 January, with Czecho-Slovak help, these hardened soldiers captured Nizhneudinsk from the rebels and earned themselves a brief respite from the bitter cold in the town's shelters. A few days later they were joined there by another band of White soldiers under General Voitsekhovsky, bringing their estimated strength to near 30,000. The reju-

Legionaries defend a snow-covered ridge, undated.

venation of this White Army amid the harrowing conditions impressed the legionaries from the Czecho-Slovak Third Division. For a few days, it seemed that the coalition between the Czecho-Slovaks and White Russian had been revived as the two armies traded supplies, held joint military conferences and together battled partisans and the Fifth Red Army.[69]

The renewed camaraderie between the legionaries and anti–Bolshevik Russians was limited only to the embattled units at the rear of the Czecho-Slovak column. The Czechoslovak political leaders, along with Generals Janin and Syrový, were more than ready to abandon the Whites. They were particularly disgusted by the reports of a crime spree which took place when Colonel Skipetrov and General Sychev evacuated Irkutsk with their men on the evening of 3 January. The fleeing Whites and *semenovtsy* took with them thirty-one political prisoners, mostly suspected SRs or Mensheviks, as hostages onboard the icebreaker *Angara* when they fled the city. As they steamed across the lightly-frozen surface of Lake Baikal, the *semenovtsy* began drinking heavily and stripped the thirty men and one woman of their valuables. The hostages were then summoned to the deck one by one, where they were attacked by an officer wielding a mallet normally used to knock ice off the ship deck. After a fierce bludgeoning, the victims were then cast overboard into the freezing waters of Baikal. News of the hostages' fate emerged only after the Czecho-Slovaks cleared the Circumbaikal tracks of *semenovtsy* and captured some of the perpetrators. The reports of the ghastly murders sparked outrage among foreigners and Russians alike in Irkutsk. Before long, the city's public opinion stepped up its demands on the Political Center, the legionaries and General Janin to turn over Kolchak, who was unfairly held responsible for the crime.[70]

It was into this highly-charged environment that the train bearing the former Supreme Ruler entered on 15 January, a week after departing from Nizhneudinsk. The Political Center, although too weak to police its own streets, managed to furnish a detachment of about 100 soldiers to take the admiral into its custody at Glaskovo station. Over the next several hours they, the guards installed on the train by the partisans, the legionaries and the Japanese troops at the station all eyed each other suspiciously, uncertain what would happen next. In the meantime, Lieutenant Bečvar and his commanding officer called upon Czechoslovak headquarters in Irkutsk to receive further instructions regarding the men and precious cargo that were under their guard. Those orders, which were ultimately decided by Janin, did not arrive until the following afternoon. It was then that the two Czech officers learned that Kolchak and the gold reserve were to be surrendered to the Political Center, and it was Bečvar who was burdened with the delicate task of informing the admiral of this decision.[71]

That evening, Bečvar made his way through the bitterly cold darkness and the cordon of guards to the idle coach with the flags of five nations flapping above it. According to his account, Kolchak took the news of his impending handover rather calmly and displayed none of the irrational behavior that had defined him in other low moments of his counter-revolutionary career. The admiral's only request was to speak personally with Janin, but when this could not be arranged, Kolchak graciously thanked Bečvar and saluted him off.[72] When the officers accompanying the admiral realized their hopeless situation, several of them dashed from the coach and, with Czecho-Slovak help, managed to evade the volley of gunfire from the rebel troops nearby. Shortly after midnight, the Czecho-Slovak sentries were ordered to stand down and the rebels moved in to claim their bag of prisoners. Kolchak, along with his mistress and Pepeliaev, were marched out of the train and across the icy surface of the Angara to a lorry waiting on the opposite bank. Surrounded by a cavalry escort, the prisoners were driven to Irkutsk prison to await their fate.[73]

The legionaries' surrender of Admiral Kolchak after being assigned to escort him safely out of Siberia was subjected to immediate criticism from all directions. White officers leading their bedraggled columns west of Irkutsk were livid at this latest perceived betrayal committed by the Czecho-Slovaks; so intense were these feelings that General Kappel, who was dying of severe frostbite to his legs, refused the legionaries' offer of quarters on one of their trains out of respect for Kolchak. On 26 January, this able commander, not yet forty, died on the windswept *trakt* surrounded by his devoted troops. The *semenovtsy*, seemingly unaware that their notorious crimes had sealed the admiral's doom, also cried foul at the handover. From Harbin, the Allied High Commissioners, none of whom bothered to remain in Irkutsk to oversee that their guarantee of protection to the ex-dictator was faithfully carried out, also protested and confronted Janin about his decision. The Frenchman, and to some extent Syrový, defended themselves by claiming that saving Kolchak would have forced the Czecho-Slovaks to engage the partisans who were demanding admiral's head. The legionaries could hardly be expected to risk more casualties on behalf of the man who harbored so much ill-will towards them. A less publicized reason for jettisoning Kolchak was that Czecho-Slovak political and military leaders hoped the action would facilitate a ceasefire between their forces and the pursuing Fifth Red Army.

Although the Political Center obtained its high-profile prisoner, this coalition government of moderate socialists remained only mildly popular. On the streets of Irkutsk, Bolshevik agitators were actively preaching their revolutionary gospel. The population still lived in fear of the Whites, who might return at any moment and begin meting out reprisals upon the city's inhabitants. Since the local Bolshevik groups had a much more efficient military organization than the feeble SRs, the Political Center liquidated itself on 21 January in favor of the Bolshevik Revolutionary Committee (Revkom) in order to better defend the city against the approaching White Army.

Although the Czecho-Slovaks had a long record of sympathy and cooperation with the moderate SRs, they did not lift a finger against the installation of the Revkom at Irkutsk. At this point they simply wanted order in the city and the unmolested passage of their troops to the east, and they were ready to come to terms with a Bolshevik authority that was ready to accept these conditions. Still, relations between the legionaries and the Revkom at Irkutsk were destined to be uneasy as long as fighting continued between the Czecho-Slovak rearguard and the Fifth Red Army. The battles along the railway were so intense that at one point a commissar with the Fifth Red Army demanded that his comrades in Irkutsk launch an attack against the Czecho-Slovaks there. The Revkom ignored the order and instead cooperated with the Czecho-Slovak leadership in Irkutsk to contact the Fifth Red Army's commanders and negotiate an armistice.

On 27 January a train carrying a delegation comprised of two Revkom members and a Czecho-Slovak staff officer, Lieutenant Gub, left Irkutsk on the westbound track of the Trans-Siberian Railway. They did not make contact with the Fifth Red Army until 2 February, and in that interval the fighting continued unabated.[74] At one point the vanguard of the Red Army fell on the rearmost Czecho-Slovak trains and although the human toll from this surprise attack was light—most of the ten injuries were from frostbite—the legionaries' losses were serious since they were forced to abandon twenty trains, including four armored ones. On the next day, however, the legionaries obtained a revenge of sorts when they lent their artillery and a cavalry regiment to support the White Army, now under General Voitsekhovsky, which was locked in battle with Red partisans from Irkutsk. The Czecho-Slovak intervention proved decisive and opened the way for the Whites to march on Irkutsk and attempt to rescue the imprisoned admiral. Moreover, the Third Czecho-Slovak Division appeared ready to assist them. This news alarmed General Syrový, who did not want to see his chances for an armistice with the Fifth Red Army ruined by the impetuous actions of the legionaries in the rearguard. Subsequently, he wired the Third Division's commander, General Přchala, to instruct his men to stand down and fight only in operations of self-defense. Despite this order, the sharp engagements continued. On the same day the delegation from Irkutsk was received by the Reds, the Czecho-Slovak 10th Regiment launched a successful counterattack against the Bolshevik vanguard, dispelling earlier hopes among the Fifth Red Army's command that the Czecho-Slovaks were a spent force.[75]

In Irkutsk, the imprisoned Kolchak had been appearing before a five-man panel dubbed the Extraordinary Investigation Commission since late January. Most of these proceedings were polite and orderly until the ninth and final session on 6 February, when the barks of gunfire from Voitsekhovsky's approaching army were audible from Irkutsk prison. The city was by then under a state of siege and all local Bolshevik party members were being mobilized. Although the determined efforts of the interrogators to corner Kolchak into admitting that he had committed any crime failed, the admiral's fate was already decided. Shortly after midnight on the following morning, Kolchak and his faithful minister, Pepeliaev, were placed before a Cheka firing squad. Illuminated by headlights from a nearby lorry, the admiral was upright and unflinching as he faced his executioners in the bitter cold; the same could not be said for his companion who was sharing his fate. Gunfire from the executioners' rifles ripped through the frosty air for a few seconds, after which both men fell into lifeless heaps in the snow. The Cheka squad then cut holes in the ice of the Ushakovka River, a tributary to the Angara, and cast the two corpses into the black waters. With that, Kolchak's remains were granted a burial style that had been accorded to countless victims of his regime.[76]

Revkom's announcement of the admiral's execution later that morning did not deter Voitsekhovsky and his troops from attempting to break into Glaskovo. The turning point was not Kolchak's demise but rather the news that the plenipotentiaries of the Czecho-Slovak Legion and Fifth Red Army had agreed to an armistice at Kutin. The settlement established a neutral zone between the rearmost Czecho-Slovak trains and the Bolshevik vanguard, thereby guaranteeing the legionaries unmolested passage to the east. In exchange, the Czecho-Slovaks were to leave the state gold reserve and Kolchak behind in Irkutsk while observing strict neutrality during the remainder of their evacuation.[77, 78] (The delegations would learn only later that the ex–Supreme Ruler had been shot the same day the armistice was signed.) The next day, on 8 February, the Czecho-Slovak leadership in Irkutsk received word of the armistice and promptly sent an ultimatum to Voitsekhovsky that the legionaries, in order to uphold the neutrality of the railway zone, would attack his forces if they continued their assault on Glaskovo. This threat compelled Voitsekhovsky to disengage and bypass Irkutsk with his little army. The grueling retreat which they had begun from the east-bank of the Tobol in mid–October ended only a few weeks later when about 16,000 White soldiers reached Chita—in all a distance of 2,500 miles.[79]

With the mayhem along the Trans-Siberian Railway settled at last, the legionary trains rolled past Irkutsk and on towards Vladivostok. East of Lake Baikal, the Czecho-Slovaks encountered American and Japanese troops who, like themselves, were supposed to protect the railway from partisans. Most of these soldiers, particularly those of the American Expeditionary Force to Siberia, were as homesick and disillusioned with their mission as were the Czecho-Slovaks.[80] In January 1920 the U.S. troops received their long-awaited orders to withdraw to Vladivostok. Another major development occurred that month when the Allies decided to lift their blockade of Soviet Russia.[81] Everywhere, it seemed, the interventionists were ready to cut their losses and abandon their undeclared war against the Bolsheviks.

The one exception among the interventionists was Japan, whose military leaders were not yet ready to quit Russia. Their objective all along had not been to topple the Soviet regime but rather to supplant Russian power in Eastern Asia with their own. In early 1920, this goal still appeared viable as the Red Army remained west of Lake Baikal and Semenov managed to hold onto power at Chita. Still, time was running out. The Czecho-Slovaks, the *raison d'être* for the intervention, were evacuating and behind them was the Fifth Red Army. Public opinion in Japan, like that of other Allied nations, was increasingly opposed to the intervention on the grounds that its rewards could not justify the blood and treasure which they were pouring into Siberia.[82] The Japanese Army leaders, therefore, were frantically searching for an excuse to continue to intervention that would be acceptable to both the world and their home islands. To buy themselves time, the Japanese officers hindered the Czecho-Slovak evacuation whenever possible. They exacerbated the shortage of locomotives along the railway by prohibiting engines arriving in Vladivostok from returning west. They bribed Semenov and Russian railway workers to stall Czecho-Slovak trains whenever possible. But nothing could hold the legionaries back indefinitely. When necessary, they used their own labor in the local workshops and mines to provide their outfit with the repairs and coal they needed to resume their journey.[83]

On 1 March the last Czecho-Slovak train departed from Irkutsk and one week later the Fifth Red Army held its first parade in the city.[84] By then White territory even east of Lake Baikal was rapidly shrinking. With Czecho-Slovak help, the SRs had relocated the Political Center from Irkutsk to Verkhneudinsk, where they continued to nurse fantasies that their Far Eastern Republic might be allowed to exist as a buffer state between Soviet Russia and the capitalist countries.[85] In Vladivostok, the Provisional Zemstvo Government of the Maritime Province, a Bolshevik government with an SR guise, had been allowed to function openly under the noses of American, Czecho-Slovak and Japanese troops since the end of January.[86] Only in Chita did the Whites, under Semenov, hold onto power. The Cossack warlord still had his armored trains and troops make boisterous demonstrations along the railway, but these charades fooled no one. His little army was so depleted by desertion and low morale that he relied on Japanese bayonets for protection. By April, Chita was virtually surrounded by partisan formations and the People's Revolutionary Army of the Far Eastern Republic.[87] But just when it appeared that Transbaikalia was about to turn Red, Eastern Siberia was shaken up by a new set of events.

The last units of the AEFS departed from Vladivostok on 1 April 1920 and the Japanese Army wasted no time in escalating its operations in Eastern Siberia. Three days after the doughboys left, the Japanese launched an offensive to seize control of Vladivostok and other towns and cities in the Maritime and Amur provinces. Telltale signs of the Japanese plans had been evident for some weeks: while U.S. and Czecho-Slovak troops were embarking from Vladivostok, thousands of Japanese troops were landing at the port.[88] In late March Tokyo, against international pressure to begin withdrawing its units from Russia, announced its intention to maintain its intervention in order to help the Czecho-Slovaks continue their evacuation—even though Girsa had openly stated that their help was no longer needed.[89] Indeed, the Japanese military operations in early April hindered rather than expedited the legionaries' evacuation. To avoid getting caught in the crossfire between the Japanese troops and the Russians, the legionaries were forced to stop their trains and sit tight while the firefights raged around them.[90]

As might be expected, the well-equipped and superbly-drilled Japanese troops easily crushed the few pockets of Russian resistance they encountered in their renewed takeover of Eastern Siberia. In a few days, after the fighting subsided, Japan was again the master of the main rail routes between Vladivostok and Chita.[91] It soon became evident to the legionaries, however, that the Japanese still had their further objectives in their sights.

On 9 April the Japanese fomented disorder at the railway station at Hailar, along the Chinese Eastern Railway, by arresting eleven railway workers and then firing wildly into the crowd of angry Russians who demanded the prisoners' release. Several trains of Czecho-Slovak troops from the Third Division were parked near the station during the ordeal, and although they avoided any involvement in the imbroglio, two legionaries were still killed by stray bullets. When Czecho-Slovak officers went to the local Japanese headquarters on April 12 to obtain a record of the incident, they found their host was not only unapologetic but also claiming that the legionaries, including their armored train *Orlík*, had fought on the side of the Russians. The Czecho-Slovak officers were perplexed why the Japanese commander had made such false allegations, and their confusion only increased the next day when they spotted Japanese platoons and gun crews taking up positions overlooking the town. It soon became known that the tracks east of town had been torn up and the telegraph wires were cut—the legionaries in Hailar were isolated. While the residents of Hailar took cover from the bombardment that was rumored to begin at any moment, a Czecho-Slovak major, with the help of two Chinese Army officers, made contact with the local Japanese commander. The latter demanded the Czecho-Slovaks to either surrender *Orlík* along with their hand grenades or face a Japanese assault. It was then that the major understood what the recent row with the Japanese was all about: they wanted *Orlík*, which was perhaps the most formidable armored train on that side of Siberia. Reluctantly, the major consented to the Japanese terms. After the legionaries surrendered their railborne-weapon and resumed their eastward journey, the Japanese excused their actions at Hailar as a misunderstanding.[92]

Prior to December 1919, the Czecho-Slovak evacuation from Siberia was restricted to those legionaries who were too disabled to return to active duty. Only after Janin issued his

Legionaries return to Prague, 1920. By then some Czecho-Slovak soldiers had not seen their homes or families in six years.

order for the general evacuation of all Allied troops under his command did the withdrawal of the Czecho-Slovak Legion begin in earnest.[93] When the last evacuees departed from Vladivostok in September 1920, a total of 67,750 persons had left on ships contracted by the Czechoslovak government. Of this number, 56,459 were legionaries; the rest were wives, children, hired war prisoners, anti–Bolshevik Russians and others who in some way had become affiliated with the Legion.[94] The Czecho-Slovaks left behind over 4,000 dead in addition to those who had deserted or went missing over the course of their campaign.[95] The sea routes taken by the transports bearing the legionaries varied considerably; some sailed to Europe by entering the Indian Ocean, crossing into the Mediterranean via the Suez Canal, and the arriving at Trieste, Naples or Marseilles, where the legionaries then boarded trains for the final stretch of the journey to their new state. Others reached Europe by way of the Panama Canal and landed at Hamburg. A few Czecho-Slovaks were even taken to the west coast of the United States and shuttled on yet another transcontinental journey by train to board ships that would take them across the Atlantic Ocean.[96] One group of invalid legionaries who crossed the U.S. by train during the summer of 1919 made a brief stop in Washington, D.C., where they were given a hero's welcome by President Wilson.[97] For most, the journey was less remarkable and at times downright uncomfortable as the transports were loaded beyond normal capacity in an effort to reduce shipping costs.[98] Regardless of the inconveniences or the length of their voyages, the Czecho-Slovak soldiers were undoubtedly relieved by the prospect of returning home.

The legionaries were not the only citizens of the new Czechoslovak state that had been stranded in Russia by the civil war. The violent chaos which engulfed that country in 1918 had paralyzed the repatriation of over 400,000 POWs from the Central Powers—including nearly 40,000 Czechs and Slovaks among them. Repatriation of these all but forgotten men to Czechoslovakia began only in June 1920. Not unlike those war prisoners who returned to their homelands during the Habsburg Monarchy's final months of existence, these soldiers were also treated suspiciously by the government.[99]

For these ex-prisoners and legionaries, the last of whom did not arrive within Czecho-slovakia's borders until November 1920, the return to "normalcy" which they and nearly all peoples strived towards after the trauma of the First World War was a long time in coming.[100] For many, that goal would never be realized. This was especially true for millions of Russians, whose lands and traditional institutions were utterly devastated by years of war and revolution. Even after the Czecho-Slovaks had left Siberia, the legacy of anti–Bolshevik resistance and intervention which they had fostered in that part of Russia persisted for another two years. The Japanese gradually scaled back their solo occupation of the region and Semenov was run out of Chita in October 1920 shortly after he was deprived of their protection.[101] For the next two years, the Japanese held onto the Maritime Province, where former officials from the Directory and Kolchak's cabinet intermingled with displaced *semenovtsy* and veterans of the Komuch's People's Army. All dreamt of the day they might rid Russia of communism, yet their cross-allegiances to leaders and regimes who were either dead, defunct or rendered impotent kept them as divided as ever. When the last Japanese troops embarked on transports from Vladivostok in late October 1922, these anti–Bolshevik Russians either left with them, crossed the border into Manchuria or Korea, or fled into the frozen wilderness of northeastern Siberia. During the following month, the Far Eastern Republic was absorbed into the Soviet Republic and, for the first time since the Czecho-Slovak uprising in May 1918, the entire span of the Trans-Siberian Railway was brought under control of a single, centralized authority.[102]

In the years following the close of the Russian Civil War, the White refugees dispersed across the globe as they waited for the Bolshevik regime to collapse. In a final service to the anti–Bolsheviks alongside whom they had once fought, the Czechoslovaks generously supported a sizable community of White Russians in their country, and their benefactors ranged from Czechoslovak Social Democrats up to President Masaryk.[103] Some Whites fared especially well in the anti-communist climate of interwar Czechoslovakia. General Voitsekhovsky, for example, had left Siberia in 1920 for Czechoslovakia, where he served as a general in the Czechoslovak Army until his retirement in 1939.[104] Still, resentment could be found among at least some White Russian émigrés regarding the Czechoslovaks' role in the civil war. The following passage by General Denikin captures this view:

> The Czechs were free to decide for themselves from alternatives, which to us were a tragic dilemma: either to shed their blood for Russia's salvation or to go away. They chose the latter. This gives us the right to regard the halo of "heroism" which envelops the Czecho-Slovak movement with scepticism, and exonerates us from every debt of gratitude towards them.[105]

Of course, Denikin and like-minded anti–Bolshevik émigrés were unable to satisfactorily explain why they thought the legionaries were obligated to shed blood for their cause in the first place.

16

The Legacy of Independence

While foreign intervention in revolutionary Russia was recorded as a controversial, blundering and embarrassing operation that was best forgotten in most Allied countries, it was more fondly remembered in Czechoslovakia. It was, after all, the superhuman efforts of the legionaries in the summer of 1918 which, along with the exiles' numerous books, pamphlets, speeches and proclamations outlining Austrian terror and the Czecho-Slovaks' "right" to self-determination, captured the hearts and minds of the Allied nations. In doing so, they had assured the Czecho-Slovak liberation movement and others a base of support among the First World War's victors and peacemakers.

For their contribution to Czechoslovakia's independence, the legionaries and their memory were handsomely rewarded. The anniversary of the Battle of Zborov on 2 July 1917 became a national holiday in the postwar Czechoslovak Republic second only to its Independence Day (28 October). On the fifth anniversary of the battle, the state set up its own monument to an unknown soldier by exhuming and transporting the remains of an unidentified Czecho-Slovak soldier from the battlefield to a final resting place in a Prague chapel.[1] The legionaries' uniforms became a familiar piece of the state's military regalia: the sentries who guarded Masaryk's residence at Prague Castle were attired in uniforms representing the Russian, French and Italian legions. Even the president himself made sure photos were snapped of him wearing a visored cap with a red, white and blue cockade pinned to the front in the style that had been favored by the legionaries.

The legionaries who returned home, whether they fought from a trench in France, a summit in Italy or an armored train in Russia, were granted numerous privileges from the state. For instance, they were given preference for openings in the country's civil service and were moved to the front of the list of recipients for expropriated lands. They would also dominate the leadership of the interwar Czechoslovak Army.[2] Heroes from the Czecho-Slovak Legion in Russia, including Stanislav Čeček, Radola Gajda and Jan Syrový, all held top army commands at various times even though they were relatively young men.[3] A number of veteran organizations for legionaries were formed in the 1920s and although the politics and economic interests of these groups differed widely, they were alike in that they formed a strong patriotic element which the nation could depend during the interwar years.[4]

Not all legionaries were content with their status as first citizens of the state. Among those who had difficulty adapting to Masaryk's concept of a stable, non-militaristic Czechoslovak state was Gajda. During the war years, Gajda had catapulted from an obscure pharmacist to a celebrated general in two armies. Although he was given an enthusiastic welcome and remained popular with legionaries when he returned to Bohemia, the war hero was quickly overcome with disillusionment. In order to retain the rank of general bestowed upon him in Russia, he was compelled to enroll in the French Army Staff College in Paris. Apparently, his proven capability as a warrior on the fluid battlefields of Siberia did not translate well in courses led by French officers who commanded troops on the static Western Front. His intractable personality and the cooling relations between officers of the French and Czechoslovak armies might also explain his instructors' low opinions of his military talent. Nevertheless, he returned to Czechoslovakia in 1922 to command an infantry division in eastern Slovakia and two years later was appointed to the Chief of Staff of the Czechoslovak Army, an impressive achievement for a man then only thirty-two years of age.

In Russia, Gajda's use of military force to attain political objectives had earned him praise from his troops and anti–Bolshevik allies, but in Czechoslovakia, that same combination was to prove mortal to his career as a soldier. His politics were widely suspect immediately after his banishment from Siberia; after all, in Russia he had at times backed political movements ranging from extreme conservatism to moderate socialism. Eventually, he ingratiated himself with budding Czech fascist organizations and this, along with his reputation as an impetuous soldier-of-fortune, made him a prime suspect when rumors began circulating in Prague of an impending coup from the right. While the threat was likely exaggerated, the government was nervous since militaristic, right-wing political leaders had recently assumed control in two other Central European states, Italy and Poland. As a result, Masaryk ordered Gajda to be dismissed as the army's chief of staff. An ensuing investigation by the Prague government led to almost certainly false allegations that the young general had leaked French military secrets to Soviet agents during his stint at the French Army Staff College. Despite French testimony that Gajda, as a student at the college, had no access to sensitive material, he was convicted in February 1928 of espionage, cooperating with the Czech fascist movement and plotting to overthrow the Czechoslovak government. Afterwards he was demoted to the rank of an army private. Disgruntled by his treatment, Gajda quit the Czechoslovak Army, squeezed into his old uniform from his days as a Siberian Army general and attempted to draw followers into the fascist movement primarily through recognition of his name and exploits in Siberia.[5]

It appears likely that the Czechoslovak government manipulated Gajda's trial in the hope that his conviction of spying for the Soviets would discredit not only this brash adventurer, but also the fascist movement as a whole. It hardly needed to resort to such measures since the Czech fascist movement never gained the wide following that fascism acquired in other Central European states. Nonetheless, two other high-profile figures—Karel Kramář and Jiří Stříbrný—moved towards Gajda's position on the extreme right in the postwar Czechoslovak state. Both of these men belonged to the so-called Men of October 28th, those who had led the resistance in Bohemia during the war and had declared Czechoslovak independence in Prague. They believed that contemporary historians of Czechoslovakia's liberation movement were placing too much emphasis on the exiles while overlooking the risks and accomplishments of the dissident politicians who stayed in Austria-Hungary. Kramář was the most prominent voice who declared that Czechoslovak independence was made at home and not abroad by either the exiles of the Allies.[6] Stříbrný, who was a member of the National Committee during the revolution in Prague, corroborated Kramář's argument.

Like Gajda, the importance of both of these men faded after the war and as a result they became disenchanted with the postwar Czechoslovak state. Kramář, as we have seen, served as the country's first prime minister but his National Democrat Party polled badly in the June 1919 elections, and his political fortunes never recovered.[7] In contrast, Stříbrný's decline was less dramatic: in September 1920 he was ousted from the cabinet, where he had served as the Minister of Postal and Telegraph Services and then as the Minister of Railroads, when his gambling problems had ignited a scandal. In the following years he and Kramář veered sharply to the right, opposing the Masaryk-Beneš partnership as stringent Czech nationalists and anti–German demagogues. Unlike Gajda, however, neither Kramář nor Stříbrný openly embraced fascism.[8]

The political achievements of the government's opponents on the far right were mild at best. In 1929, Gajda and Stříbrný managed to get themselves elected to the National Assembly. Two years later, Gajda's parliamentary career ended abruptly when he was convicted of slander against President Masaryk and of libel against a lesser government official. In 1932, he experienced further complications with the Prague government when his nephew led an abortive fascist coup in a Moravian army barracks and the ex-general was convicted of failing to report the plot.[9]

In their contests with the Czech far-right and other political rivals, Masaryk and Beneš did not rely on the inherent weakness of their opponents' message alone. In exile, they had learned how to hone and use the weapon of propaganda, which they wielded ruthlessly against the Habsburgs, Germans and even revolutionary rivals such as Dürich. After the war, they did not cease their propaganda activities but rather readjusted their message and its targets. Indeed, having witnessed firsthand how Britain's wartime propaganda reinforced morale at home while shielding her image abroad, Masaryk decided that a similar program was necessary for Czechoslovakia. His reasoning was understandable: the Czechs and especially the Slovaks were on the whole less politically-experienced than average British citizens, communist agitators abounded among former POWs from Russia, the civilian population was frustrated by the slow economic recovery following years of blockade and, finally, the country was surrounded by potentially hostile neighbors, especially Germany and Hungary, whose governments were known to engage in their own propaganda activities. Thus upon their return from exile, Masaryk and Beneš gathered their friends and trusted supporters into an informal clique known as the Hrad. This group functioned partly as a Czechoslovak-version of Britain's Wellington House; its members included influential writers and intellectuals who published articles and books to kindle Masaryk's image as a "philosopher-president" or "president-liberator." Meanwhile, the Ministry of Foreign Affairs, which was directed by Beneš for most of the interwar period, operated its own publishing house which churned out works to uphold the republic's image abroad.[10] For these two founders of the Czechoslovak state, propaganda was not just a means to an end; it became an end unto itself.

The postwar propaganda which Masaryk and Beneš aimed abroad was not nearly as successful as their wartime activities. These diminishing returns were caused, in part, by developments in Great Britain. At the end of World War I, the British shuttered most of their propaganda operations, including the Department of Propaganda in Enemy Countries, which dramatically reduced the influence of Masaryk's earnest backers, Henry Wickham Steed and Robert Seton-Watson.[11] In the following years, revelations that British wartime propaganda contained highly exaggerated or even outright false claims caused widespread dismay in the international community, especially in the U.S.[12, 13] As a result, the audience which all postwar propagandists catered to was increasingly skeptical; moreover, the absence of military crises deprived them of the opportunity to play upon raw emotions, a ploy that had been particularly useful to the Czecho-Slovaks during the war.

The President-Liberator on horseback, undated. Note that Masaryk is wearing a legionary uniform complete with a cockade on his cap.

Despite Masaryk and Beneš's ongoing propaganda campaign, Allied enthusiasm for an independent Czechoslovak state, and indeed the new order in Central Europe, subsided considerably in the postwar climate. The United States withdrew into isolationism while British foreign policy in Central Europe during the 1920s encouraged reconciliation among the successor states in the hope that they might one day reunite into a supranational federation that would ensure their security and prosperity.[14] This Habsburg-nostalgia, however, was not welcomed by Czechoslovakia and most other successor states who were determined to uphold their individual identities and, most of all, their independence. The British became frustrated by the intensely nationalistic policies of the successor states and displayed a growing indifference towards the future of the region by the end of the decade.[15]

France was more deeply involved in Central Europe since it regarded a number of the successor states as a bulwark against future German or Soviet expansion. French faith in this system, however, was shaken soon after Adolf Hitler became Germany's chancellor in 1933. In the following years, Poland signed a ten-year nonaggression pact with Germany and Hitler openly defied the military restrictions placed on his country by the Versailles Treaty. Faced with these ominous developments, Paris looked to Moscow for assurance against the Nazi threat, not to Prague, Belgrade or Bucharest.[16] Although Beneš would follow the French example by signing a mutual assistance pact with the Soviet Union, the myth that his nation was vital to France's security was irreparably shattered.[17]

Masaryk and Beneš's postwar propaganda was more successful inside the Czechoslovak Republic. Much of this campaign attempted to influence the postwar debate over which group—the exiles, the legionaries or the domestic resistance—had contributed the most to Czechoslovak independence. For most of Masaryk and Beneš's challengers, this was an uphill battle. The two men and their supporters were proficient and well-versed in the art of public opinion manipulation; in contrast their opponents were either too inexperienced or too chivalrous to succeed in that field. As a result, Masaryk and Beneš clenched and retained the coveted title of founders of the Czechoslovak state.

Propaganda, though important, was not the only means through which Masaryk endeared himself to the Czech and Slovak peoples. He possessed many qualities which people yearn for in a leader, being known as personable, refined and charismatic. Having not belonged to any major political party throughout most of his career, as president he was able to avoid the pitfalls of partisan politics.[18] A cult of personality developed around the president-liberator in postwar Czechoslovakia, and that aura was kindled by his closest associates in the Hrad. The extent to which he was deserving of this iconic status is debatable, but there can be no question that during the war Masaryk had carefully positioned his National Council as the pivot around which the entire Czecho-Slovak revolutionary movement revolved by the end of the war. This was a claim which neither the legionaries nor the dissident politicians could reasonably make.

For his work during the war, he was generously compensated. The presidency of Czechoslovakia was essentially his as long as he desired to hold that office. For his eightieth birthday in March 1930, the National Assembly awarded him twenty million crowns to spend on philanthropic causes dear to him.[19] By then he had served as the nation's president for a full decade and had led his people through the postwar unrest and the destabilizing effects of the global depression which struck in 1929. Although his command of Czechoslovak politics waned alongside his health during his final years in office, he continued to display an intense interest in maintaining a strong army and insisted on reviewing troops while on horseback even in his advanced age.[20] After suffering a serious stroke in 1934 which paralyzed his left side and left him temporarily blind, Masaryk was inclined not to seek reelection. Doubts over who might succeed him, however, compelled him to reconsider and subsequently the National Assembly elected him to the presidency for a fourth time.[21] He resigned at the end of the following year, since by then he was hardly capable of signing papers, and was succeeded by Beneš. In retirement, he continued to receive visits from his successor and longtime protégé each Friday evening until he finally died peacefully on 14 September 1937.[22]

Masaryk's determination to serve as Czechoslovakia's president until he was physically incapable of doing so was not intentional since he had always considered Beneš his logical successor. His younger colleague, however, lacked Masaryk's charm and venerability. As a result, Beneš's ability to win the necessary votes in the National Assembly to become president was in perpetual doubt. Not all of Beneš's unpopularity was his fault. Since Masaryk's virtual deitification rendered him beyond reproach, Beneš was a more accessible target and subsequently took flak for policies advocated by his superior.[23]

Throughout most of the interwar timeframe, Beneš served as Czechoslovakia's Minister of Foreign Affairs and his policy was directed at upholding the terms of the Versailles Treaty. For his nation's security, he turned to France, of course, and also sought allies in Central Europe. Shortly after the world war he concluded an alliance with Yugoslavia and Romania known as the Little Entente, and its primary aim was to prevent a Habsburg restoration and deter the truncated Kingdom of Hungary from attempting to regain its lost frontiers.[24] Both of these threats seemed real at the time. In early 1920, after having passed through Károlyi's liberal-democratic rule and Kun's Soviet regime during the previous year, Hungary had reverted back to a royal government with a former admiral of the Austro-Hungarian fleet, Miklós Horthy, serving as regent. Since Karl had only renounced his role in Hungary's government and never abdicated the Crown of St. Stephen, the return of a royal government in the Magyar homeland presented a strong attraction to the exiled monarch. On two separate occasions in 1921, Karl slipped into Hungary from Switzerland in an attempt to reclaim the Hungarian throne. Horthy showed no intention of subordinating himself to the returned king; nonetheless, the Little Entente nations used these opportunities to exhibit its unity and martial readiness by mobilizing against Hungary until the crises passed.[25]

Although the Little Entente passed this first test, the alliances brought little security to Czechoslovakia in the long term. The Little Entente's *bête noire*, a Habsburg restoration, dimmed considerably after 1922 when Karl died of pneumonia while in exile on the island of Madeira.[26] Still, the specter of a Habsburg restoration remained the linchpin of the Little Entente even though far more sinister threats were soon casting their shadows over Central Europe.

Much of the criticism against Beneš's foreign policy originated from parties on the right, particularly Kramář's National Democrats, who believed that Czechoslovakia's security depended on a non–Bolshevik Russia. They had little faith in France or the collective security offered by the League of Nations; in their view only a Slavic nation could be a reliable ally.[27] Ironically, these critics were horrified when Beneš sort of followed their advice by entering into a pact with Soviet Russia in 1935. This was done at the behest of France after Nazi Germany openly announced its rearmament. The pact had a significant caveat in that it was contingent on French support. In other words, if France refrained from backing Czechoslovakia amid a crisis, Soviet Russia was not obliged to come to Prague's aid.[28] This clause would soon have more importance than Beneš probably ever expected.

On 18 December 1935, Beneš defeated a National Democratic challenger[29] to become the second president of the Czechoslovak Republic.[30] His presidency coincided with troubling times for Europe and especially his nation. The dream of a league of democratic nations in Central Europe had long since passed; Czechoslovakia was by then the lone democracy east of the Rhine. Even more unsettling was Hitler's ongoing campaign to redress the terms of the Versailles Treaty and the unwillingness of Britain and France to obstruct his efforts. The Nazi threat to Czechoslovakia became more acute in March 1938 when Germany annexed Austria, leaving Bohemia surrounded on three sides by the Greater German Reich.[31] Just a few months later, the alliances which Beneš had cultivated in his more than fifteen years as Foreign Minister underwent their most crucial test when German troops began amassing on Czechoslovakia's borders. Hitler's pretext for his threatening moves was based on falsified claims of Czech terror against the "Sudeten" German minority in the Bohemian borderlands.[32] The Bohemian question, once a headache for the Habsburgs, had now become the curse of Europe.

Ironically, the leader of the fascist Sudeten German Party, Konrad Henlein, and his followers employed tactics against the Czechoslovak government which the Czechs themselves had perfected against Austria-Hungary during the First World War. The Sudeten Germans opposed the government at every turn, deliberately made excessive demands which the government could never accept, founded an armed legion in a foreign land and formed political alliances with radical nationalists among other ethnic minorities in the Czechoslovak state, including the Slovak followers of Hlinka. As one might expect, Henlein's campaign for Sudeten German autonomy was infused with covert moral and financial support from Nazi Germany. His cause also garnered sympathy in the Foreign Office in London. Hungary backed the Magyar minority in Slovakia while the Slovak autonomists discovered an unlikely ally in Berlin, which recognized their usefulness in dismantling the Czechoslovak state. Even Poland, which like Czechoslovakia possessed a German minority in its realms and was an offspring of the Versailles Treaty, failed to perceive the ominous implications that Hitler's revisionist aims might have for it and foolishly joined in the plunder.[33]

Effectively surrounded by hostile neighbors, Beneš's Czechoslovakia believed that its only salvation in the autumn of 1938 rested on its support from the West and perhaps Soviet Russia. The response of Britain and France was not encouraging when, in September, Beneš received recommendations from London and Paris to bow to Hitler's demands and cede the disputed borderlands. Britain's decision should not have been a shock to the Czechoslovak President given the Foreign Office's increasingly Czechophobe policy in the two decades since 1918, but the same could not be said of France's betrayal of her longtime ally.[34] "I remained faithful to her," Beneš fumed, "and now they throw us overboard."[35]

Czechoslovakia's military position against Nazi Germany may not have been as hopeless as it seemed in 1938. The Czechoslovak Army was well-equipped and would have possessed the advantage of fighting from the formidable border fortifications constructed in the interwar period. Many top German generals who inspected these defenses later testified that their army, which was frantically undergoing the process of rearmament, would have been unable to breach the fortifications.[36] But after being abandoned by France and listening to British Prime Minister Neville Chamberlain express incredulity that his countrymen were on the brink of war "because of a quarrel in a far away country between people of whom we know nothing," the Czechoslovak leaders were psychologically defeated.[37] Even most Czechoslovak generals, many of them veterans of the katabasis across Siberia, were pessimistic about their country's chances in the looming war. The only senior Czechoslovak officer to advocate defending every inch of Czechoslovakia was General Voitsekhovsky, the former White general who was no stranger to doomed military campaigns.[38] Surrounded by these mostly bleak assessments, it is perhaps not surprising that the tormented president decided not to risk war and accepted the agreement hammered out by the conference at Munich in late September

1938. This settlement, which Czechoslovakia was not a party to, recognized Hitler's claims to the predominantly German-speaking borderlands of Bohemia, Moravia and Silesia. Within days, Czechoslovakia ceded 11,000 square miles of territory and in the process was reduced to an indefensible and economically unviable rump state at the mercy of Berlin.

Under German pressure, Beneš quit the presidency on 5 October 1938 and the remainder of the Czechoslovak state continued to splinter further into its national components.[39] With Berlin's backing the Slovak populists, led by Josef Tiso since Hlinka's recent death, cowered the emergency government under General Syrový into recognizing Slovak autonomy.[40] The Ukrainians in Ruthenia were the next to follow although their period of self-government was to be brief when their land was returned to Horthy's Hungary the following spring. By that time, the Slovaks would possess nominal independence as a German client state while the remainder of the Czech homeland was occupied by German troops.[41]

For the next five years, the Czech-speaking areas of Bohemia and Moravia were administered as a protectorate of the German Reich. Although the German occupation was a humbling experience for Czech patriots, it was rather mild compared to the butchery which the Nazis practiced in nearby Poland and Eastern Europe.[42] A few leading Czechoslovak officials, including Beneš, escaped abroad before the rump Czecho-Slovak state succumbed to complete German control. Quite a few soldiers also chose to carry on the struggle against tyranny in foreign lands, among them General Čeček, who fled to Poland. When that country was overrun by the Nazi war machine in September 1939, he and other Czecho-Slovaks caught serving on behalf of the Poles were executed.[43] Unlike Čeček, other veterans of the Czecho-Slovak Legions from the First World War either incidentally or deliberately entered into the role of collaborators. Among the former category was General Syrový, who continued to serve as defense minister even after the Germans seized control of Bohemia and Moravia.[44] Meanwhile Gajda, who for a time made a political career of anti–German demagoguery, offered his services to the Nazis in the hope that his fascist party might at last achieve a nugget of the power that had eluded it since the early 1920s. His proposals failed to stir any enthusiasm among the Nazis, who had doubts about whether Gajda and his followers could keep the stability needed in the protectorate in order for its industries to maintain its high levels of output for the German war machine.[45, 46] After the war, both Syrový and Gajda were convicted of collaboration with the Nazis and sentenced to prison, where Gajda died in 1948 followed by Syrový in 1953.

While their Czech kin endured occupation and Germanization policies, the Slovaks initially reveled in the quasi-sovereignty which Hitler permitted them as he expanded the borders of his empire from the Pyrenees to the Volga River. Only when the war had turned decisively against the Nazis did the Slovaks attempt to wean themselves from German patronage. At the end of August 1944, the Slovaks staged a desperate uprising in an effort to realign their state with the Allies. Despite their brave resistance against superior forces, the Slovak rebellion was effectively crushed by the Germans after two months.[47] Thereafter, the Slovaks, like much of Eastern Europe, were forced to wait for the arrival of the Red Army to deliver them from Nazi occupation.

Throughout the Second World War, Beneš worked for Czechoslovak independence abroad just as he had during the First World War. In the earlier conflict, Beneš had made Paris his headquarters and won the confidence of France's highest statesmen. After France's perceived betrayal at Munich, however, he had no intention of returning to Paris. Instead, he made London the primary seat of his exile, a decision which proved wise after France's capitulation following the *blitzkrieg* of 1940.[48] Still, his latest campaign was faced with plenty of obstacles. Relations between the Czech leader and the British Foreign Office needed time to mend after the latter's predominantly Czechophobe policies of the interwar period.[49] Beneš also lacked the inside support which the he and Masaryk possessed through Henry Wickham Steed and Robert Seton-Watson in the previous war. Steed, for all practical purposes, was retired while Seton-Watson did return to the propaganda and intelligence departments reconstituted by the British government at the beginning of the war. However, the Scotsman chafed under the increased oversight of the new institutions that inhibited the relative freedom of action he had known during the First World War. Subsequently, he resigned from official duty in September 1942.[50] Another problem Beneš faced were the rivalries from other exiled Czechoslovak leaders, the most formidable being Milan Hodža's Czecho-Slovak National Council which sought to preserve the autonomy which the Slovaks achieved in 1938.[51]

Beneš gradually overcame each of these hurdles and in no small part due to his association with Masaryk, who continued to be regarded as a national hero by both Czechs and Slovaks. He was the obvious choice to head the Czechoslovak government-in-exile which received *de jure* recognition from Great Britain, the Soviet Union and the United States in 1941. He remained the recognized Czechoslovak leader throughout the war and returned to Prague on 16 May 1945, only a week after the Red Army cleared the city of residual German forces. By then, the experiences which he had weathered since the autumn of 1938 had significantly altered his outlook on everything from foreign policy to freedom of expression. To avoid a repetition of the nightmare at Munich, he negotiated a close alliance with Stalin's Soviet Russia. He was also less tolerant of political opposition after the war and persecuted many right-leaning party leaders on often unwarranted charges of collaboration with the Nazis.[52]

What Beneš's brief postwar government may be most remembered for is its radical solution to the Bohemian question. Before the war was over, Beneš had decided that a majority of the ethnic Germans must be expelled from the historic lands of Bohemia, Moravia and Lower Silesia. A large number of prewar Czechoslovakia's estimated 3,320,000 ethnic Germans had fled westward in the final stages of the conflict to escape the onslaught of the Red Army or Czech reprisals. Of those whom stayed behind, approximately two million were forcibly resettled outside Czechoslovakia between January and November 1946. Since additional tens of thousands of German-Bohemians opted to leave Czechoslovakia in the following years, by mid–1949 the Bohemian lands were home to fewer than 200,000 ethnic Germans.[53] Such dramatic reshufflings of peoples were not uncommon in Central and Eastern Europe after the Second World War. All across those lands, various ethnic groups were uprooted and herded or traded across frontiers in order to create homogenous nations and groupings from the centuries-old ethnic hodge-podge that the region was known for. In Slovakia, Magyars were driven from the southern border region into Hungary. Further to the east, Czechs and Slovaks living in Ruthenia and Volhynia were deported and resettled in the depopulated borderlands of Czechoslovakia.[54]

Beneš, it may be said, had a habit of concentrating too much on past enemies while overlooking future threats. In interwar Czechoslovakia, he orchestrated his foreign policy to prevent a Habsburg restoration when fascism was the real danger to the order established by the Versailles Treaty. After the Second World War, he focused his energies on eradicating the state's German minority and right-wing parties while disregarding the communist menace.[55] Beneš hoped to position Czechoslovakia as a bridge between the communist East and the capitalist West, but Stalin was intent on placing the Czechoslovak state firmly within Moscow's orbit. Since 1945, Czechoslovak Communists had been steadily subverting the country's institutions, particularly its police forces. By February 1948, the Communist control of the police was virtually complete. When the democratic ministers in the cabinet resigned in protest that month, the Communists simply formed a new government without them. Beneš, whose health was failing, lingered on as president until his abdication in June of that year.[56] In the following weeks, Prague was rife with rumors that the former president might flee into exile for the third time in his life to free his homeland from tyranny, but it was not to be. By the end of the summer Beneš suffered a serious stroke and died a few days later on 2 September 1948.[57]

With Beneš's abdication and death, Czechoslovakia lost its remaining links with the democratic republic established by Masaryk. The shell of the state remained more or less intact but gone was the government that was to promote the democratic and national development of the Czechs and Slovaks. In its place existed a regime which served the interests of Stalin and the Communist Party. Czechoslovakia would remain a Soviet fixture for forty years—except for a brief interlude in 1968 known as the Prague Spring. In 1989, Czechoslovakia regained her democratic liberties as the Soviet system collapsed throughout Central and Eastern Europe. This so-called Velvet Revolution, however, did not herald the return of Masaryk's amalgamated Czechoslovak nationalism. The old debate over whether the state should be a centralized Czechoslovak republic or a federated Czecho-Slovakia was resurrected, and in April 1990 the state was officially renamed the Czech and Slovak Federal Republic. The state completed its mitosis on 31 December 1992 when the "velvet divorce" left two independent countries, the Czech Republic and Slovakia, in its wake.[58]

Nearly a century has passed since the Czechs and Slovaks proclaimed their independence in an amalgamated nation-state. Although the three leading Czecho-Slovak revolutionaries—Masaryk, Beneš and Štefánik—are still remembered as national heroes in the Czech Republic and Slovakia, they, unlike earlier figures such as St. Wenceslas or Prince Pribina, have not been transformed into legends whose records seem more mythical than factual. The idols of the Czecho-Slovak liberation movement were indeed men and did err, but this does not diminish their remarkable accomplishments. After all, they fared better than many of their contemporaries; for both politicians and generals the First World War and its aftermath ruined more reputations than it made. When they had set out to win freedom for their homeland, the Czechoslovak revolutionaries were not first-rate politicians, experienced diplomats or vaunted commanders, yet they successfully synchronized a complex political, diplomatic and military campaign to achieve their goal. While the methods they employed and the outcome they engineered might be controversial, one indisputable truth is that their tale, which stands as a testament to their abilities, is an inspiring saga in the annals of humankind.

Chapter Notes

Preface

1. Examples of the more critical approach of Cold War-era historians surveying the revolutionary activities of Czecho-Slovaks and other groups include Zbyněk Zeman's following observation: "The men who had devoted their political skills and energies to the task of destroying the Habsburg monarchy had given but little thought to the hazards of the future in the area vacated by Habsburg power." Zbyněk Zeman, *The Break-Up of the Habsburg Empire 1914–1918* (London: Oxford University Press, 1961) x. Writing a few years later, historian Austro-Hungarian Arthur May commented that, "...in retrospect it is clear that the Danube Monarchy afforded a good deal that was admirable in terms of security, economic well-being, and cultural betterment, a prototype and forerunner of an integrated multinationality union toward which the nations of western Europe appear to be groping, slowly and hesitantly." Arthur May, *The Passing of the Habsburg Monarchy 1914–1918* (Philadelphia: University of Pennsylvania Press, 1966) 6. Regardless of the veracity of these statements, they demonstrate that the Habsburg Monarchy was viewed as a far lesser evil than the Communists who then controlled Czechoslovakia and much of Central Europe.

2. See John Bradley, *The Czechoslovak Legion in Russia, 1914–1920* (Boulder: East European Monographs, 1991) 24–27, 30–32. Bradley's book is based on a doctoral dissertation from 1963.

3. See Josef Kalvoda, *The Genesis of Czechoslovakia* (Boulder: East European Monographs, 1986) 17–32.

4. See Kalvoda, *Genesis*, 207–234. The phrase "to strangle the Bolshevik baby in its cradle" is famously attributed to Winston Churchill.

Introduction

1. William Henry Chamberlin, *The Russian Revolution 1917–1921*, Volume II (New York: Grosset & Dunlap, 1965), 106. According to Chamberlin, many cities of northern and central Russia lost over a third of their populations in the years from 1916 to 1920.

2. Quoted in Evan Mawdsley, *The Russian Civil War* (New York: Pegasus, 2007) 22.

3. Accounts of the Chelyabinsk incident disagree over whether the Czecho-Slovak legionnaire died or was simply wounded after been struck with the projectile.

4. Victor Fic, *The Bolsheviks and the Czechoslovak Legion* (New Delhi, Abhinav Publications, 1978), 230; Henry Baerlein, *The March of the Seventy Thousand* (London: Leonard Parsons, 1926) 133–134.

5. Fic, *Czechoslovak Legion*, 230–231; Joan McGuire Mohr, *The Czech and Slovak Legion in Siberia, 1917–1922* (Jefferson: McFarland & Company, 2012) 72.

6. Quoted in Fic, *Czechoslovak Legion*, 237.

7. Fic, Czechoslovak Legion, 6–13.

8. Fisher, H. A. L., *A History of Europe* (London: Edward Arnold & Company, 1936) 1155.

9. Orzoff, Andrea, *Battle for the Castle* (New York: Oxford University Press, 2009) 3–4.

10. Although the Yugoslavs attempted to form a "Yugoslav army" using volunteers from POW camps and neutral countries, the recruits ended up in formations subordinate to the Serbian Army. See Kenneth Calder, *Britain and the Origins of the New Europe, 1914–1918* (New York: Cambridge University Press, 1976), 203.

Chapter 1

1. Jaroslav Pánek, *A History of the Czech Lands* (Prague: Karolinum Press, 2009) 27.

2. *Ibid.* 56–66; Peter Toma and Dušan Kováč, *Slovakia* (Stanford: Hoover Institution Press, 2001) 4–6; Robert Seton-Watson, *A History of the Czechs and Slovaks* (London: Hutchinson & Company, 1943) 12–14.

3. Pánek, *Czech Lands*, 65–66.

4. Hans Kohn, *Pan-Slavism* (New York: Vintage Books, 1960) 15.

5. Pánek, *Czech Lands*, 71–72. The Magyars probably originated from an area around the Ural Mountains in present-day Russia. They are not Slavic. Their language belongs to the Ural-Altaic group and their closest linguistic cousins maybe found in northwestern Siberia and in the Baltic region, such as the Estonians and Finns.

6. *Ibid.* 74–75.

7. *Ibid.* 99–101.

8. *Ibid.* 194; Elizabeth Wiskemann, *Czechs and Germans* (London: Oxford University Press, 1938) 1–2.

9. Pánek, *Czech Lands*, 74–112.

10. *Ibid.* 121–143; Seton –Watson, *Czechs and Slovaks*, 27–28.

11. Seton-Watson, *Czechs and Slovaks*, 42–46.

12. *Ibid.* 53–55; Pánek, *Czech Lands*, 156.

13. Pánek, *Czech Lands*, 165–183, 192; Seton-Watson, *Czechs and Slovaks*, 87.

14. Pánek, *Czech Lands*, 194, 205; C. V. Wedgwood, *The Thirty Years War* (New York: Review Books, 1938) 70–81; Peter Wilson, *The Thirty Years War* (Cambridge: Harvard University Press, 2009), 278–282.

15. Wedgwood, *Thirty Years War*, 82–116.

16. Wilson, *Thirty Years War*, 287, 309.

17. *Ibid.* 303–307; Wedgwood, *Thirty Years War,* 124–127, 132.

18. Wiskemann, *Czechs and Germans*, 10.

19. Quoted in E. H. Gillett, *The Life and Times of John Huss*, Volume II (Boston: Gould and Lincoln, 1978) 611.

20. Wedgwood, *Thirty Years War*, 165–171; Wilson, *Thirty Years War.* 349–354.

21. Seton-Watson, *Czechs and Slovaks,* 124–129.

22. Pánek, *Czech Lands*, 204.

23. Wiskemann, *Czechs and Germans*, 10.

24. Toma and Kováč, *Slovakia*, 14–15.

25. Although the Crown of St. Wenceslas was officially elective until 1620, it was passed between generations as though it was hereditary since the days of the Přemyslid dynasty.

26. Wedgwood, *Thirty Years War*, 138; Wilson, *Thirty Years War* 349.

27. Wiskemann, *Czechs and Germans*, 11–12; Pánek, *Czech* Lands, 263–275.

28. Mike Rapport, *1848* (New York: Basic Books, 2009) 29.

29. Alan Sked, *The Decline and Fall of the Habsburg Empire* (New York: Dorset Press, 1989) 14, 29, 220; A. J. P. Taylor, *The Habsburg Monarchy 1809–1918* (Chicago: Chicago University Press, 1948) 39; Kohn, *Pan-Slavism*, 20; Eagle Glassheim, *Noble Nationalists* (Cambridge: Harvard University Press, 2005) 15–16.

30. Pánek, *Czech Lands*, 333; Taylor, *Habsburg Monarchy*, 49–50; Glassheim, *Noble Nationalists*, 15–16.

31. Pánek, *Czech Lands*, 298–301, 314; Wiskemann, *Czechs and Germans*, 14–15; Glassheim, *Noble Nationalists*, 27.

32. Rapport, *1848*, 69–72.

33. *Ibid.* pp. 130–134, 297–301.

34. Quoted in Rapport, *1848*, 132–133.

35. Kohn, *Pan-Slavism*, 75–76; Pánek, *Czech Lands*, 314–315.

36. Rapport, *1848*, 143, 235–236; Seton-Watson, *Czechs and Slovaks*, 261–264.

37. Kohn, *Pan-Slavism*, 80–87; Sked, *Habsburg Empire*, 91; Taylor, *Habsburg Monarchy*, 68–69, Rapport, *1848*, 233–237.

38. Taylor, *Habsburg Monarchy*, 14–16; Toma and Kováč, *Slovakia*, 21.

39. Taylor, Habsburg Monarchy, 27.

40. Kossuth's father was Magyar and his mother was Slovak.

41. Rapport, *1848*, 183, 239; Taylor, *Habsburg Monarchy*, 51–52; Seton-Watson, *Czechs and Slovaks*, 259; Toma and Kováč, *Slovakia*, 31.

42. Sked, *Habsburg Empire*, 90–91.

43. Toma and Kováč, *Slovakia*, 33–34; Seton-Watson, *Czechs and Slovaks*, 262.

44. Taylor, *Habsburg Monarchy*, 84–85.

45. *Ibid.* p. 83; Sked, *Habsburg Empire*, 92–98; Toma and Kováč, *Slovakia*, 34; Rapport, *1848*, 309–311.

46. Wiskemann, *Czechs and Germans*, 25–26.

47. Taylor, *Habsburg Monarchy*, 29; Pánek, *Czech Lands*, 296.

48. Taylor, *Habsburg Monarchy,* 94, 100–101, 133–136.

49. Mark Cornwall, ed., *The Last Years of Austria-Hungary* (Exeter, University of Exeter Press, 2002) p. 97.

50. Sked, *Habsburg Empire*, 188.

51. *Ibid.* 221–222; Taylor, *Habsburg* Monarchy, 141–143, 147–148; Cornwall, *Last Years*, 77.

52. Taylor, *Habsburg Monarchy*, 186; Seton-Watson, *Czechs and Slovaks*, 267–268.

53. Seton-Watson, *Czechs and Slovaks*, 279; Cornwall, *Last Years*, 103. The population numbers for each ethnicity in the Kingdom of Hungary, including Transylvania, may be found in A. J. P. Taylor, *The Habsburg Monarchy 1809–1918*, 268. This data is based on the 1910 census and also excludes the autonomous provinces of Croatia-Slavonia with its large population of Serbs and Croats.

54. Sked, *Habsburg Empire*, 210; Seton-Watson, *Czechs and* Slovaks, 273.

55. Paul Selver, *Masaryk* (Westport: Greenwood Press, 1975) 170–171; Victor Mamatey and Radomír Luža, ed., *A History of the Czechoslovak Republic 1918–1948* (Princeton: Princeton University Press, 1973) 8–9.

56. Mamatey and Luža, *Czechoslovak Republic*, 9; Hugh Seton-Watson and Christopher Seton-Watson, *The Making of a New Europe* (London: Methuen & Company, 1981), 44–48; Toma and Kováč, *Slovakia*, 43.

57. Sked, *Habsburg Empire*, 218.

58. Toma and Kováč, Slovakia, 43–45; Seton-Watson and Seton-Watson, *New Europe*, 48; Cornwall, *Last Years*, 104–105.

59. Seton-Watson and Seton-Watson, *New Europe*, 81–83.

60. Sked, *Habsburg Empire*, 210–212, 217–218; Taylor, *Habsburg Monarchy*, 187–188; Toma, *Slovakia*, 40.

61. Taylor, *Habsburg Monarchy*, 25–26, 31.

62. *Ibid.* 141–143, 160; Cornwall, *Last Years*, 77.

63. John Bradley, *Czech Nationalism in the Nineteenth Century* (Boulder: East European Monographs, 1984) 21; Pánek, *Czech Lands*, 366–369.

64. Bradley, *Czech Nationalism*, 35; Pánek, *Czech Lands*, 338; Taylor, *Habsburg Monarchy*, 156–157.

65. Cornwall, *Last Years*, 77–78. After the passage of these language ordinances, German was still to remain the official language between officials.

66. Taylor, *Habsburg Monarchy*, 157–160.

67. Cornwall, *Last Years*, 77–78.

68. Charles IV might be best described as having a cosmopolitan background. For example, he spoke French and Italian in addition to Czech and German. See Elizabeth Wiskemann, *Czechs and Germans*, 6–7; Robert Seton-Watson, *Czechs and* Slovaks, 27–28. As for Joseph II, he was definitely not a German nationalist. See Nancy Wingfield, *Flag Wars and Stone Saints* (Cambridge: Harvard University Press, 2007) 17–47.

69. Wingfield, *Flag Wars*, 39–40.

70. Taylor, *Habsburg Monarchy,* 163–164; Cornwall, *Last Years*, 79.

71. Taylor, *Habsburg Monarchy*, 203–204.

72. *Ibid.* pp. 181–182.

73. *Ibid.* p. 199; Wingfield, *Flag Wars*, 48–49.

74. Taylor, *Habsburg Monarchy*, 181–184; Alan Palmer, *Twilight of the Habsburgs* (New York: Atlantic Monthly Press, 1994) 282–283; Cornwall, *Last Years*, 81–83.

75. Wiskemann, *Czechs and Germans*, 51–52; Cornwall, *Last Years*, 86.

76. Wiskemann, *Czechs and Germans*, 109–110. While radical nationalists were generally absent among the nobilities of both Bohemia and Moravia, the latter province had a small but important party of anational aristocrats, the *Mittelpartei*, which was instrumental in brokering the Compromise of 1905. No equivalent party existed in Bohemia to bridge the differences between the two sides. See Eagle Glassheim, *Noble Nationalists*, 38–39.

77. Cornwall, *Last Years*, 64.

78. Sked, *Habsburg Empire*, 221–223; Taylor, *Habsburg Monarchy*, 116, 147–149.

79. Taylor, *Habsburg Monarchy*, 198–199; Palmer, *Twilight*, 270–271; Cornwall, *Last Years*, 50.

80. Taylor, *Habsburg Monarchy*, 165.

81. Bradley, *Czech Nationalism*, 33; Wiskemann, *Czechs and Germans*, 52–53. Universal male suffrage in Austria applied only to elections for the lower house of the Reichsrat. Aristocrats retained control of the upper chamber (*Herrenhaus*) and the curial system remained place for the provincial diets, including those of Bohemia and Moravia, into 1918.

82. Taylor, *Habsburg Monarchy*, 213.

83. H. Louis Rees, *The Czechs During World War I* (Boulder: East European Monographs, 1992) 5–7.

84. Andrea Orzoff, *Battle for the Castle* (New York: Oxford University Press, 2009) 35; Josef Kalvoda, Josef, *The Genesis of Czechoslovakia* (Boulder: East European Monographs, 1986) pp. 11–12. In the results of the 1911 parliamentary elections, the Czech Social Democratic Party received 357,234 votes while the Agrarian Party received 257,717 votes. However, the Agrarians occupied 37 seats in the Reichsrat compared to 26 for the Czech Social Democrats thanks to Austrian electoral laws which favored rural votes over urban votes. See Robert Kann, and Béla Király, Paula Fichtner (eds.), Victor Mamatey, "The Union of Czech Political Parties in the Reichsrat 1916–1918," *The Habsburg Empire in World War I* (New York, 1977) 3–4.

85. Zbyněk Zeman, *The Break-Up of the Habsburg Empire 1914–1918* (London: Oxford University Press, 1961) 14.

86. Kalvoda, *Genesis*, 10; Rees, *Czechs*, 7, 10; Kohn, *Pan-Slavism*, 30, 233–237; Sked, *Habsburg Empire*, 219; Taylor, *Habsburg Monarchy*, 224.

87. Kalvoda, *Genesis*, 11–12; Cornwall, *Last Years*, 58.

Chapter 2

1. Henry Wickham Steed, *Through Thirty Years 1892–1922*, Volume 1 (New York: Doubleday, Page & Company, 1924) 366–368; Arthur May, *The Passing of the Hapsburg Monarchy*, Volume 1 (Philadelphia: University of Pennsylvannia Press, 1966) 83.

2. Alan Palmer, *Twilight of the Habsburgs* (New York: Atlantic Monthly Press, 1994) 297–298; Hugh Seton-Watson and Christopher Seton-Watson, *The Making of a New Europe* (London: Methuen & Company, 1981) 52.

3. Palmer, *Twilight*, 295–296.

4. Mark Cornwall, ed., *The Last Years of Austria-Hungary* (Exeter: University of Exeter Press, 2002) 60–61; A. J. P. Taylor, *The Habsburg Monarchy 1809–1918* (Chicago: Chicago University Press, 1848), 196–197.

5. Seton-Watson and Seton-Watson, *New Europe*, 46, 51–52; Cornwall, *Last Years*, 109.

6. Elizabeth Wiskemann, *Czechs and Germans* (London: Oxford University Press, 1938) 45–50.

7. Hans Kohn, *Pan-Slavism* (New York: Vintage Books, 1960) 3–5, 14–15.

8. Congress Poland encompasses the Polish lands ruled by Russia from 1815–1915.

9. Kohn, *Pan-Slavism*, 175–179. For the origins of the Slavophile movement in Russia, see Richard Pipes, *Russia Under the Old Regime* (New York: Charles Scribner's Sons, 1974) 265–270.

10. Orlando Figes, *A People's Tragedy* (New York: Viking, 1997) 257–258.

11. Kohn, *Pan-Slavism*, 162, 173. Even the Russian Slavophiles, whose views were not opposed to the absolutist regime, aroused the suspicions of paranoid tsarist authorities. See Pipes, *Old Regime*, 266.

12. Figes, *People's Tragedy*, 69–83.

13. Kohn, *Pan-Slavism*, 157–158.

14. Figes, *People's* Tragedy, 102–115.

15. Kohn, *Pan-Slavism*, 241–244; Palmer, Twilight, 300–301; Cornwall, *Last Years*, 127–128.

16. Zbyněk Zeman *The Masaryks* (London: Weidenfeld and Nicolson, 1976) 49; Robert Seton-Watson, *A History of the Czechs and Slovaks* (London: Hutchinson & Company, 1943) 245.

17. Zbyněk Zeman, *The Break-Up of the Habsburg Empire* (London: Oxford University Press, 1961) 15; Wiskemann, *Czechs and Germans*, 47; Josef Kalvoda, *The Genesis of Czechoslovakia* (Boulder: East European Monographs, 1986) 13.

18. Cornwall, *Last Years*, 85.

19. John Bradley, *Czech Nationalism in the Nine-

teenth Century (Boulder: East European Monographs, 1984) 49–50.

20. Kohn, *Pan-Slavism*, 246–247; Zeman, *Break-Up*, 47; Wiktor Sukiennicki, *East Central Europe during World War I*, Volume 1 (Boulder: East European Monographs, 1984) 69–74.

21. Kohn, *Pan-Slavism*, 247, 252; Peter Toma and Dušan Kováč, *Slovakia* (Stanford: Hoover Institution Press, 2001) 44.

22. Kohn, *Pan*-Slavism, 252.

23. Figes, *People's Tragedy*, 200–202, 217–225; Robert Massie, *Nicholas and Alexandra* (London: Pan Books, 1969) 242–245.

24. Edmond Taylor, *The Fall of the Dynasties* (New York: Doubleday, 1963) 103–134; Palmer, *Twilight*, 301–304–305; David Stevenson, *Armaments and the Coming of War* (Oxford: Clarendon Press, 1996) 112–131; Taylor, *Habsburg Monarchy*, 217.

25. Kohn, *Pan-Slavism*, 350; Bradley, *Czech Nationalism*, 52; Palmer, *Twilight*, 303.

26. Cornwall, *Last Years*, 89; Bradley, *Czech Nationalism*, 22.

27. Kohn, *Pan-Slavism*, 252–253.

28. Karel Čapek, *President Masaryk Tells His Story* (New York: G.P. Putnam's Sons, 1935) 14–15; Paul Selver, *Masaryk* (Westport: Greenwood Press, 1975) 30, 36. The ethnic origins of Masaryk's mother, Terezie Kropáček, have been subject to dispute despite the obvious Czech spelling in her surname. (It was not unusual for persons who assimilated into another ethnic group to alter the spelling of their name to conform to their adopted language.) The professor, like Čapek and Selver, whose works are highly sympathetic towards Masaryk, contend that his mother was a full-blooded Czech who was German by culture. Other authors, however, have claimed that she was an ethnic German. See Peter Neville, *Eduard Beneš and Tomáš Masaryk: Czechoslovakia* (London: Haus Publishing, 2010) 7.

29. Zeman, *Masaryks*, 17; Selver, *Masaryk*, 30.

30. Henry Wickham Steed, introduction to *The Making of a State* by Tomáš Masaryk (New York: Frederick A. Stokes Company, 1927) xvi.

31. Gymnasium is the equivalent of high school in the United States.

32. Čapek, *President Masaryk*, 59, 65.

33. In the late nineteenth century, large numbers of Czechs migrated to Vienna either to study or for work. In 1910, about 100,000 Czechs were recorded as living in the imperial capital and the actual number may have been much higher. See Healy, Maureen, *Vienna and the Fall of the Habsburg Empire* (Cambridge, 2004) pp. 151–152.

34. Zeman, *Masaryks*, 18–22.

35. Čapek, *President Masaryk*, 114–117.

36. *Ibid.* 119, 124; Zeman, *Masaryks*, 14–34.

37. Zeman, *Masaryks*, 31–33.

38. The Uniate Church may be described as a hybrid of the Orthodox and Catholic confessions. The majority of its believers were Ukrainians living in Habsburg lands of Galicia, Bukovina and Ruthenia.

39. Selver, *Masaryk*, 59–60, 98–99. Masaryk's fascination with religion is evident in his discussions with Karel Čapek, recorded by the well-known Czech author in *Masaryk on Thought and Life* (New York: The Macmillan Company, 1938). Three out of eight chapters in that book are devoted to topics related to religion.

40. Kalvoda, *Genesis*, 19. Inferring broad political conclusions on a country's predominant faith, Masaryk believed that genuine democracy evolved much easier in predominantly Protestant countries than their Catholic (or Orthodox) counterparts, whom he considered more prone to backwardness or unable to reconcile with modern political trends. See Hanus Hajek, *T. G. Masaryk Revisited* (Boulder: East European Monographs, 1983) 124–126. As Czechoslovak president, he was only slightly less forthcoming about these views. See Čapek, *Masaryk on Thought and Life*, 186–189. Other examples of Masaryk's anti-Catholic bias may be found in his wartime propaganda which depicted the Vatican as having sided squarely with the Central Powers. See Tomáš Masaryk, *The New Europe* (Cranbury: Bucknell University Press, 1972) 47. For his ideas on a new Czech reformation, see Tomáš Masaryk, *The Meaning of Czech History* (Chapel Hill: The University of North Carolina Press, 1974) 13–14.

41. Bradley, *Czech Nationalism*, 74–85.

42. Quoted in Čapek, *President Masaryk*, 154.

43. Selver, *Masaryk*, 120–139; Zeman, *Masaryks*, 46–48.

44. Zeman, *Masaryks*, 51; Bradley, *Czech Nationalism*, 78; Selver, *Masaryk*, 175–177. Anti-Semitism was strong among some Czech nationalists since Jews often assimilated into German culture or were seen as German themselves.

45. The blood libel rumor accused Jews of sacrificing Christian children in order to use their blood in Passover meals. It seems to have originated in Western Europe in the twelfth century, spread eastward and was still widely accepted in Eastern Europe at the beginning of the twentieth century. See Ferguson, Niall, *The War of the World* (New York, 2006) pp. 60, 67.

46. Bradley, *Czech Nationalism*, 83; Zeman, *Masaryks*, 52–53, 167; Čapek, *President Masaryk*, 187–188; Selver, *Masaryk*, 174–188.

47. Sukiennicki, *East Central Europe*, 893–895; Kalvoda, *Genesis*, 23. In the summer of 1918, as Masaryk and the Czecho-Slovak liberation movement was on the cusp of its greatest successes, the Polish movement in the U.S. was experiencing considerable setbacks in part due to hostile propaganda generated by various Jewish-American organizations. Jewish enmity against the Polish liberation movement was cultivated by Roman Dmowski, the leader of the Polish National Committee who refused to abandon his well-known anti–Semitic convictions.

48. Zeman, *Masaryks*, 49–50; Selver, *Masaryk*, 160; Kalvoda, *Genesis*, 22.

49. In *T.G. Masaryk Revisited*, 160, Hanus Hajek writes that Masaryk's political philosophy was close to the English liberal-socialism tradition. Masaryk's writ-

ings consistently emphasize humanitarianism (which he refers to as "humanism") and democracy.

50. Masaryk, *Meaning*, 62–65.

51. Čapek, Masaryk on Thought and Life, 114.

52. Hajek, *Masaryk Revisited*, 106, 136–138. Chapter Seven (101–119) of Hajek's account offers a brief assessment of Masaryk's views on Marxism and his work, *Social Question*.

53. Zeman, *Masaryks*, 54.

54. Selver, *Masaryk*, 203–207; Kalvoda, *Genesis*, 20.

55. Selver, *Masaryk*, 108–109, 165–166, 170–171; Victor Mamatey and Radomír Luža, ed., *A History of the Czechoslovak Republic 1918–1948* (Princeton: Princeton University Press, 1973) 8–9.

56. George Kennan, *Russia Leaves the War* (Princeton, Princeton University Press, 1956) 176–177; Betty Miller Unterberger, *The United States, Revolutionary Russia and the Rise of Czechoslovakia* (Chapel Hill, The University of North Carolina Press, 1989) 26.

57. According to his memoir, Masaryk began to view the dynasty as morally and physically degenerate after 1907. See Tomáš Masaryk, *The Making of a State* (New York: Frederick A. Stokes Company, 1927) 29.

58. Selver, *Masaryk*, 210; Mamatey and Luža, *Czechoslovak Republic*, 8–9.

59. Taylor, *Habsburg Monarchy*, 265. Figures are from the 1910 census data.

60. Quoted in Alan Sked, *The Decline and Fall of the Habsburg Empire* (New York: Dorset Press, 1989) 223–224.

61. Ethnic Germans comprised almost forty percent of the inhabitants of Bohemia and thirty percent of the population of Moravia. In Lower Silesia, Germans outnumbered either the Czechs or Polish inhabitants.

62. Čapek, *President Masaryk*, 191; Taylor, *Habsburg Monarchy*, 265–267.

63. Selver, *Masaryk*, 216–238.

64. Kohn, *Pan-Slavism*, 254.

65. Cornwall, *Last Years*, 24–30, 128; Stevenson, *Armaments*, 275–276.

66. For examples of dire predictions for Austria-Hungary either before or at the start of the war see: May, *Passing of the Habsburg Monarchy*, 83; Henry Wickham Steed, *Through Thirty Years 1892–1922* Volume I (New York: Doubleday, Page & Company, 1924) 366–368; Kenneth Calder, *Britain and the Origins of the New Europe* (New York: Cambridge University Press, 1976) 14.

67. Cornwall, *Last Years*, 64–65; Taylor, *Habsburg Monarchy*, 221.

68. Norman Stone, *The Eastern Front 1914–1917* (New York: Charles Scribner's Sons, 1975) 34.

69. Gunther Rothenberg, *The Army of Francis Joseph* (West Lafayette: Purdue University Press, 1976) 151.

70. *Ibid.* pp, 83–108.

71. Bradley, *Czech Nationalism*, 36; Rothenberg, *Army of Francis Joseph*, 130, 148, 170.

72. *Ibid.* pp. 127–128, 151. According to the 1910 census, the Czech population in Austria-Hungary stood at 6,440,000, behind the Magyars (9,940,000) and Ger-

mans (9,950,000). See Taylor, *Habsburg Monarchy*, 265, 268.

73. John Bradley, *The Czechoslovak Legion in Russia* (Boulder: East European Monographs, 1991) 26–27.

74. Stone, *Eastern Front*, 126.

75. Zeman, *Break-Up*, 49–52.

76. Taylor, *Habsburg Monarchy*, 232; Stone, *Eastern Front*, 243; Edmund Glaise-Horstenau, *The Collapse of the Austro-Hungarian Empire* (London: J.M. Dent and Sons, 1930) 4. All of these sources generally agree that Slovene, Croat and Slovak regiments were reliable fighters for Austria-Hungary until the final months of the war.

77. Rothenberg, *Army of Francis Joseph*, 142–144, 152.

78. *Ibid.* pp. 178–179; Holger Herwig, *The First World War* (London, Arnold, 1997) 52–56.

79. For more on the deficiencies of the Austro-Hungarian Army, see: Rothenberg, *Army of Francis Joseph*, 84, 125, 174; Herwig, *First World War*, 12–14, 92; Stone, *Eastern Front*, 122–123; Cornwall, *Last Years*, 153–154.

80. For an account of the opening battles in Galicia, see Chapter 4 in Stone, *Eastern Front*, 70–91; Rothenberg, *Army of Francis Joseph*, 180; Cornwall, *Last Years*, 154–155; Herwig, *First World War*, 273. According to Maureen Healy, *Vienna and the Fall of the Habsburg Empire* (Cambridge: Cambridge University Press, 2004) 4–5, anywhere from 50,000 to 70,000 refugees from Galicia converged on Vienna alone in the autumn of 1914.

81. Bradley, *Czechoslovak Legion*, 27–28; Rothenberg, *Army of Francis Joseph*, 183–184; Alon Rachamimov, *POWs and the Great War* (Oxford: Berg, 2002) 31–34.

82. Zeman, *Break-up*, 49–50; Stone, *Eastern Front*, 126–127; Bradley, *Czechoslovak Legion*, 27–28.

83. Zeman, *Break-up*, 52–53; As Wiktor Sukiennicki points out in *East Central Europe*, 91–93, there was no significant change in Russian policy towards the Poles despite the promises made in the Polish manifesto. For more on Russia's proclamation to the "Peoples of Austria-Hungary," see C. Jay Smith, *The Russian Struggle for Power, 1914–1917* (New York: Greenwood Press, 1956) 18.

84. Bradley, *Czechoslovak Legion*, 28–29.

85. Cornwall, *Last Years*, 91.

Chapter 3

1. Tomáš Masaryk, *The Making of a State* (New York: Frederick A. Stokes Company, 1927) 1. For examples of other important figures on summer holiday in 1914, see: Holger Herwig, *The First World War* (London: Arnold, 1997) 6–7.

2. Masaryk, Making of a State, 1.

3. *Ibid.* pp. 3–4, 29.

4. Josef Kalvoda, *The Genesis of Czechoslovakia* (Boulder: East European Monographs, 1986) 43–44. According to Kalvoda (33), Masaryk's respectability

among Czech politicians was then at a low after he publicly defended the vice-chairman of the Czech National Socialist Party, Karel Šviha, from accusations of being a police informant. Conclusive evidence soon emerged that Šviha was indeed on the payroll of the Austrian police, badly marring the reputation of the National Socialists and Masaryk.

5. Henry Wickham Steed, *Through Thirty Years 1892–1922*, Volume II (New York: Doubleday, Page & Company, 1924) 42–43; Kalvoda, *Genesis*, 42–43.

6. *Ibid.* pp. 263, 306–314.

7. It is worth noting that Austrian police began their serious crackdown on dissident politicians only *after* Masaryk's letter arrived in London.

8. Masaryk, *Making of a State*, 5; H. Louis Rees, *The Czechs During World War I* (Boulder: East European Monographs, 1992) 14–15. In fact, Austrian police began their serious crackdown on dissident politicians *after* Masaryk's letter arrived in London.

9. For various predictions of the war's length by various figures see: Niall Ferguson, *The Pity of War* (New York: Basic Books, 1999) 319.

10. Steed, *Through Thirty* Years, Volume I, 43.

11. Masaryk, *Making of a State*, 6. Robert Seton-Watson wrote Kitchener's prediction "had a decisive effect upon his plans." See *Masaryk in England* (Cambridge: Cambridge University Press, 1943) 21.

12. Seton-Watson, *Masaryk in England*, 35–38.

13. Masaryk, Making of a State, 7.

14. Seton-Watson, *Masaryk in England*, 109–110.

15. Kalvoda, *Genesis*, 45–46.

16. Quoted in Victor Mamatey and Radomír Luža, ed., *A History of the Czechoslovak Republic 1918–1948* (Princeton, Princeton University Press, 1973) 168. Events a generation later seemed to validate Masaryk's contention. After seizing the Bohemian and Moravian borderlands following the Munich agreement in 1938, Hitler, over the course of several months, turned the remainder of Czecho-Slovakia into a protectorate-satellite of Nazi Germany.

17. Seton-Watson, *Masaryk in England*, 39–47. According to the memorandum, Masaryk opposed any suggestion that a Romanov should serve as a crowned head of an independent Czecho-Slovak state. Instead, he thought it would be wiser to seat a Western prince, specifically from either the Danish or Belgian dynasties, in Prague since this alternative would be more acceptable to Bohemia's significant German minority.

18. Hugh Seton-Watson and Christopher Seton-Watson, *The Making of a New Europe* (London: Methuen & Company, 1981) pp. 111.

19. John Keegan, *The First World War* (New York: Vintage Books, 2000) 217.

20. Masaryk, *Making of a State*, 13, 22–25; Seton-Watson, *Masaryk in England*, 40–41.

21. Kalvoda, *Genesis*. 48.

22. Masaryk, *Making of a State*, 4, 22.

23. *Ibid.* pp. 39–40.

24. Seton-Watson, *Masaryk in England*, 56.

25. Edvard Beneš, *My War Memoirs*, trans. Paul Selver (New York: Houghton Mifflin Company, 1928) 59, 73.

26. Kalvoda, *Genesis*, 49.

27. Zbyněk Zeman and Antonín Klimek, *The Life of Edvard Beneš 1884–1948* (Oxford: Clarendon Press, 1997) 12, 20. Masaryk, *Making of a State*, 27; Beneš, *War Memoirs*, 19–20, 25.

28. Zeman and Klimek, *Beneš*, 11–13.

29. Beneš, *War Memoirs*, 42.

30. Zeman, *Break-Up*, 82; Robert Kann, Béla Király and Paula Fichtner (eds.) *The Habsburg Empire in World War I* (Boulder: East European Monographs, 1977) Victor Mamatey, "The Union of Czech Political Parties in the Reichsrat 1916–1918," 6.

31. Kalvoda, *Genesis*, 49; Masaryk, *Making of a State*, 47

32. Kalvoda, *Genesis*, 39–40; D. Perman, *The Shaping of the Czechoslovak State* (Leiden: E. J. Brill, 1962) 17–19.

33. Kalvoda, *Genesis*, 43. After the publication of *Russland und Europa* in 1913, Masaryk's views of Russia's political climate were out in the open; Beneš, *War Memoirs*, 38–41.

34. Zeman, *Break-Up*, 76.

35. Masaryk, *Making of a* State, 32–33.

36. Ibid. 15.

37. Zbyněk Zeman, *The Masaryks* (London: Weidenfeld and Nicolson, 1976) 76–77.

38. Beneš, *War Memoirs*, 42–43.

39. Quotes from Beneš, *War Memoirs*, 32. See also Kann et al., *Habsburg Empire*, 7.

40. Zeman, *Break-Up*, pp. 45; Kann et al., *Habsburg Empire*, pp. 8–9.

41. Seton-Watson, *Masaryk in England*, 42.

42. Herwig, *First World War*, 137–139; Norman Stone, *The Eastern Front 1914–1917* (New York: Charles Scribner's Sons, 1975) 108–114; Ward Rutherford, *The Russian Army in World War I* (London: Gordon Cremonesi Publishers, 1975) 111–112.

43. Stone, *Eastern Fornt*, 119–121; Keegan, *First World War*, 171–174; W. Bruce Lincoln, *Passage Through Armageddon* (New York: Simon and Schuster, 1986) 123.

44. Beneš, *War Memoirs*, 62.

45. Zeman, *Break-Up*, 83–84.

46. Zeman, *Masaryks*, 77.

47. Zeman, *Break-Up*, 83–84.

48. Beneš, *War Memoirs*, 62–63; Masaryk, *Making of a State*, 51.

49. Kalvoda, *Genesis*, 70–71.

50. *Ibid.* p. 82.

51. *Ibid.* p. 11.

52. *Ibid.* pp. 69–70.

53. Masaryk, *Making of a State*, 58–59.

54. Beneš, *War Memoirs*, 50–53; Kalvoda, *Genesis*, 51; Masaryk, *Making of a State*, 27, 76. For more on the fundraising efforts of Czechs and Slovaks in America, see Nancy Gentile Ford, *Americans All!* (College Station: Texas A&M University Press, 2001) 28.

55. Beneš, *War Memoirs*, 70; Zeman and Klimek, *Beneš*, 19–20.

56. Kalvoda, *Genesis*, 78; Beneš, *War Memoirs*, 65–66.

57. Beneš, *War Memoirs*, 70–74.

58. Kalvoda, *Genesis*, 79.

59. Masaryk, *Making of a State*, 67–68.

60. Zeman and Kilmek, *Beneš*, 10; Beneš, *War Memoirs*, 72.

61. During the war Eisenmann was employed by the French Ministry of War as a consultant on Austria-Hungary.

62. Zeman and Klimek, *Beneš*, pp. 22; Beneš,*War Memoirs*, 74–76. Kalvoda, *Genesis*, 84.

63. Beneš, *War Memoirs*, 26.

64. Seton-Watson, *Masaryk in England*, 60.

65. Translation of the German phrase *Drang nach Osten* is "Drive toward the East." It was widely used by Slav nationalists amid their allegations that German policy was aimed at the subjugation and colonization of Central and Eastern Europe.

66. Robert Seton-Watson published the memorandum *Independent Bohemia* in *Masaryk in England*, 116–134.

67. Sir George Clerk of the Foreign Office wrote in response to Masaryk's memorandum: "The Allies have a long way to go before the points in this memo can come up for their practical consideration, but Prof. Masaryk is a recognized leader of Czech political thought and this paper should be borne in mind." Quoted in Kenneth Calder, *Britain and the Origins of the New Europe* (New York: Cambridge University Press, 1976) 81.

68. Kenneth Calder, *Britain and the Origins of the New Europe* (New York: Cambridge University Press, 1976) 20–21.

69. *Ibid.* pp. 8–17, 215.

70. *Ibid.* pp. 20–21, 28, 59.

71. *Ibid.* pp. 51–53, 56, 70; Kalvoda, *Genesis*, 51–56.

72. Calder, *Britain*, 49.

73. Kalvoda, *Genesis*, 44, 51–52.

74. Seton-Watson, *Masaryk in England*, 39, 68–71. The Principal of King's College, Ronald Burrows, was a good friend to Seton-Watson, who recommended Masaryk for the position. Burrows was one of the few men privy to the Scotsman's October 1914 memorandum and therefore had no doubt about the nature of the Czech professor's activities in Western Europe.

75. For the text of Masaryk's inaugural lecture see Robert Seton-Watson, *Masaryk in England*, 135–152. The professor's own comments on the event can be read in *The Making of a State*, 86–87.

76. Michael Sanders and Philip Taylor, *British Propaganda during the First World War 1914–18* (London: The Macmillan Press, 1982) 28.

77. Ibid. 1.

78. *Ibid.* 41–45, Gary Messinger, *British Propaganda and the State in the First World War* (New York: Manchester University Press, 1992) 34–39.

79. Calder, *Britain*, 15–16, 54–58.

80. Sanders, *British Propaganda*, 41–42; Andrea Orzoff, *Battle for the Castle* (New York: Oxford University Press, 2009) 44; Calder, *Britain*, 54.

81. Seton-Watson, *Masaryk in England*, 84–89. Arthur May, *The Passing of the Hapsburg Monarchy* (Philadelphia: Pennsylvania University Press, 1966) 243; Gábor Bátonyi, *Britain and Central Europe 1918–1933* (Oxford: Clarendon Press, 1999) 73; Zeman, *Masaryks*, 78.

82. Seton-Watson, *Masaryk in England*, 172, 179, 204; Masaryk, *Making of a State*, 82; May, *Passing*, 246–247; Zeman, *Break-Up*, 88.

83. Beneš, *War Memoirs*, 69.

84. Accounts and figures for the Gorlice –Tarnów offensive and Russian retreat in the summer 1915 can be found in Lincoln, *Passage*, 165; Keegan, *First World War*, 229–233; Herwig, *First World War*, 140–146.

85. Seton-Watson, *Masaryk in England*, 23.

86. Lincoln, *Pasaage*, 177–178.

87. Keegan, *First World War*, 250–254; Calder, *Britain*, 29–46.

88. Masaryk, *Making of a State*, 95; Beneš, *War Memoirs*, 82.

89. Zeman, *Break-Up*, 89–90; Kalvoda, *Genesis*, 86–87; Beneš, *War Memoirs*, 82.

90. May, *Passing*, 223–230; Calder, *Britain*, 97–98.

91. Calder, *Britain*, 99. In a letter addressed to a friend in November 1917, Permanent Under-Secretary of State of Foreign Office, Lord Robert Cecil, complained that nationalism had produced the modern ills of a united and militant Germany, instability in southeast Europe, far-flung imperialism in Italy and lamented that "it is a perfect curse to us in Ireland." Quoted in V. H. Rothwell, *British War Aims and Peace Diplomacy 1914–1918* (Oxford: Clarendon Press, 1971) 159.

92. May, *Passing*, 195–196.

93. Quoted in Rothwell, *British War Aims*, 159. Rothwell argues that the Steed, Seton-Watson and their coterie had no real leverage in Foreign Office until about February 1918. See Rothwell, *British War Aims*, 118–119.

94. The commission, led by Sir Ralph Paget and Sir William Tyrrell, was apparently confused on Czech aims since it believed that Bohemia's union with an independent Poland was a solution desired by both peoples.

95. Calder, *Britain*, 93–100; May, *Passing*, 230–239.

96. Calder, *Britain*, 207.

97. Zeman, *Break-Up*, 89.

98. Tomáš Masaryk, *The New Europe* (Cranbury: Bucknell University Press, 1972) 100. The argument that Austria-Hungary is an instrument of Pan-Germanism is one of several recurring themes throughout the book.

99. Cornwall, *Last Years*, 35–42.

100. May, *Passing*, 228–229; Victor Mamatey, *The United States and East Central Europe 1914–1918* (Princeton: Princeton University Press, 1957) 16–17; Kann et al., *The Habsburg Empire in World War I*, Paula Fichtner, "Americans and the Disintegration of the Habsburg Monarchy," 223. Foreign perceptions of Hungary and the Magyars may be found in the following:

May, *Passing*, 229; George Goldberg, *The Peace to End Peace* (New York: Harcourt, Brace & World, 1969) 124; Edvard Beneš, Bohemia's *Case for Independence* (New York: Arno Press, 1971) 41; Bátonyi, *Britain and Central Europe*, 71–72.

101. Beneš, *Bohemia's Case*, 43.

102. Cornwall, *Last Years*, 109; Herwig, *First World War*, 15–16.

103. Zeman, *Break-Up*, 16–19, 42; Bradley, *Czechoslovak Legion*, 12–13; Kalvoda, *Genesis*, 79–80; Unterberger, *Rise of Czechoslovakia*, 30–31; May, *Passing*, 360–361; Masaryk, *Making of a State*, 83.

104. Masaryk, *Making of a State*, 83. In a letter to Seton-Watson dated 9 June 1915, Masaryk wrote the following regarding the arrest of Kramář and Scheiner: "I hear the imprisonment of both leaders has stirred our political public. I wish it would." Quoted in Seton-Watson, *Masaryk in England*, 65.

105. Beneš, *War Memoirs*, 81, 83, 90.

106. Kalvoda, *Genesis*, 89–91; Masaryk, *Making of a State*, 78.

107. Selver, *Masaryk* 30.

108. Despite subsequent surgeries, Štefánik never completely recovered from the wounds he sustained in the Balkans and these ailments would plague him for the remainder of his life.

109. Unfortunately, Štefánik lacks a biographical account in the English language. For useful background information see Kalvoda, *Genesis*, 84–85; Toma and Kováč, *Slovakia*, 52; Zeman and Klimek, *Beneš*, pp. 24–25; Masaryk, *Making of a State*, 100–101; Joan McGuire Mohr, *The Czech and Slovak Legion in Siberia, 1917–1922* (Jefferson: McFarland & Company, 2012) 14–15.

110. Beneš, *War Memoirs*, 84; Kalvoda, *Genesis*, 85.

111. Zeman and Klimek, *Beneš*, 24; Toma and Kováč, *Slovakia*, 15.

112. Toma and Kováč, *Slovakia*, 24–26.

113. Margaret Macmillan, *Paris 1919* (New York: Random House, 2001) 43. As Macmillan and other historians have pointed out, Lloyd George sometimes demonstrated a poor grasp of geography and foreign subjects.

114. Masaryk, *Making of a State*, 95–97.

115. Beneš, *War Memoirs*, 123.

116. *Ibid.* 121.

117. Masaryk, *Making of a State*, 22.

Chapter 4

1. John Bradley, *Czech Nationalism in the Nineteenth Century* (Boulder: East European Monographs, 1984) 43.

2. Historians disagree on the precise number of Czechs and Slovaks living in Russia by 1914. Their combined population is put around 120,000 by John Bradley, *The Czechoslovak Legion in Russia 1914–1920* (Boulder: East European Monographs, 1990) 14. A much more conservative estimate of 60,000 is given by Victor M. Fic, *Revolutionary War for Independence and the Russian Question* (New Delhi: Abhinav Publications, 1977) 1–3.

3. Pastor, Peter and Samuel R. Williamson Jr., ed., Gerald Davis, "The Life of Prisoners of War in Russia 1914–1921," *Essays on World War I: Origins and Prisoners of War* (New York, 1983), 164.

4. Bradley, *Czechoslovak Legion*, 14–16.

5. Fic, Revolutionary War, 3–4.

6. C. Jay Smith, *The Russian Struggle for Power, 1914–1917* (New York: Greenwood Press, 1956) 16; Bradley, *Czechoslovak Legion*, 16.

7. Fic, Revolutionary War, 4–5.

8. Smith, *Russian Struggle*, 10; Robert Massie, *Nicholas and Alexandria* (London: Pan Books, 1969) 306; Orlando Figes, *A People's Tragedy* (New York: Viking, 1997) 81.

9. David Stefancic, *Armies in Exile* (Boulder: East European Monographs, 2005) 104–115; Wiktor Sukiennicki, *East Central Europe during World War I*, Volume 1 (Boulder: East European Monographs, 1984) 88–91.

10. Sukiennicki, *East Central Europe*, 114; Richard Luckett, *The White Generals* (London: Routledge, 1971) 131.

11. Smith, *Russian Struggle*, 8–10, 47–49. Apparently while developing the Twelve Points, the Russian Foreign Minister mistakenly believed that the Slovaks lived in Moravia and therefore would be included in an autonomous kingdom covering the historical lands of Bohemia. The Twelve Points were presented to the British and French Ambassadors in Petrograd in mid-September 1914.

12. Fic, *Revolutionary War*, 5; Henry Baerlein, *The March of the Seventy Thousand* (London: Leonard Parsons, 1926) 22, 25; Bradley, *Czechoslovak Legion*, 16–17.

13. Bradley, *Czechoslovak Legion*, 14, 39–40. Teachers and Sokol trainers were well-represented among the early Družina volunteers.

14. *Ibid.* 16–17.

15. Baerlein, *Seventy Thousand*, 25–27.

16. *Ibid.* 27; Josef Kalvoda, *The Genesis of Czechoslovakia* (Boulder: East European Monographs, 1986) 62–63.

17. Bradley, Czechoslovak Legion, 41.

18. For more on Vaněk's mission, see: Zbyněk Zeman, *The Break-Up of the Habsburg Empire 1914–1918* (London: Oxford University Press, 1961) 75–76; Bradley, *Czechoslovak Legion*, 41–42; Kalvoda, *Genesis*, 108.

19. Zeman, *Break-up*, 54–56.

20. Edvard Beneš, *Bohemia's Case for Independence* (New York: Arno Press, 1971) 57–59. Examples where wholesale defections of Czech regiments are presented as fact include: Baerlein, *Seventy Thousand*, 28; Holger Herwig, *The First World War* (London: Arnold, 1997) 139.

21. Bradley, *Czechoslovak Legion*, 30–32, 55; Zeman, *Break-up*, 55.

22. Bradley, *Czechoslovak Legion*, 18, 43; Baerlein, *Seventy Thousand*, 40.

23. Pastor, Peter, ed., Josef Kalvoda, "Czech and Slo-

vak Prisoners of War in Russia during the War and Revolution," *Essays on World War I*, 223.

24. Herwig, *First World War*, 119–120; Fic, *Revolutionary War*, 6–7; Alon Rachamimov, *POWs and the Great War* (Oxford: Berg, 2002) 93.

25. Rachamimov, *POWs*, 31–34, 37, 45, 59; Richard Pipes, *The Russian Revolution* (New York: Alfred A. Knopf, 1990) 418.

26. Beneš, *Bohemia's Case*, 54, 59.

27. Rachamimov, *POWs*, 43–44.

28. Ferenc Imrey, *Through Blood and Ice* (New York: E.P. Dutton & Company, 1930) 115–116. As Imrey's account shows, the Russians' dissimilar attitudes towards various ethnicities added to the tensions among the POWs.

29. Rachamimov, *POWs*, 57–59; 93–96.

30. Baerlein, *Seventy Thousand*, 40.

31. Bradley, *Czechoslovak Legion*, 19, 43; Rachamimov, *POWs*, 117, 130.

32. Smith, *Russian Struggle*, 47–48, 104–105, 116–119. In a private meeting with French Ambassador Maurice Paléologue on 21 November 1914, the Tsar first revealed the Russian government's desire to see the liberation of the Czecho-Slovaks, if not all Austro-Hungarian Slavs. At the end of the month, General Mikhail Alekseev, then Chief of Staff on Russia's Southwest Front, recommended the issuance of a proclamation promising independence to the Czech people in order to incite them to revolt and aid a planned Russian drive in Bohemia and Moravia.

33. Fic, Revolutionary War, 7–9.

34. Bradley, Czechoslovak Legion, 21.

35. For more on the background and execution of the Gorlice—Tarnów offensive, see Norman Stone, *The Eastern Front* (New York: Charles Scribner's Sons, 1975) 128–143.

36. W. Bruce Lincoln, *Passage Through Armageddon* (New York: Simon and Schuster, 1986) 124–137, 165; Keegan, John, *The First World War* (New York: Vintage Books, 1998) 229–233; Herwig, *First World War*, 140–146.

37. Baerlein, *Seventy Thousand*, 29–31.

38. Lincoln, *Passage*, 156; Stone, *Eastern Front*, 183; Ward Rutherford, *The Russian Army in World War I* (London: Gordon Cremonesi Publishers, 1975) 152. According to Lincoln, *Passage*, 179, the Russian Army's total casualties for 1915 was approximately 2,500,000 men.

39. Baerlein, *Seventy Thousand*, 38–39; Bradley, *Czechoslovak Legion*, 41.

40. Baerlein, *Seventy Thousand*, 43.

41. Bradley, *Czechoslovak Legion*, 23–24; Fic, *Revolutionary War*, 6; Luckett, *White Generals*, 7–8. For more on Russia's shell shortage problem, see Chapter 7 in Stone, *Eastern Front*, 144–164.

42. Rachamimov, *POWs*, 88–89; Fic, *Revolutionary War*, 10–13.

43. Peter Pastor, ed., Ivo Banac, "South Slav Prisoners of War in Revolutionary Russia, Essays on World War I," *Essays on World War I*, 124.

44. Fic, Revolutionary War, 12–14; Bradley, Czechoslovak Legion, 21.

45. Fic, *Revolutionary War*, 16–19.

46. Kalvoda, *Genesis*, 103, 114.

47. Robert Massie, *Nicholas and Alexandra* (London: Pan Books, 1969) 340–343, 370–375.

48. Fic, Revolutionary War, 31–33; Bradley, Czechoslovak Legion, 34; Pastor, Essays on World War I, 219.

49. Kalvoda, *Genesis*, 117–131.

50. Masaryk, *Making of a State*, 51.

51. Zeman, *Break-up*, 90.

52. Bradley, *Czechoslovak Legion*, 33–35.

53. Masaryk, *Making of a State*, 103.

54. Edvard Beneš, *My War Memoirs*, trans. Paul Selver (New York: Houghton Mifflin Company, 1928) 126–128. Beneš claims a number of French and Russian officials warned him against sending Dürich to Russia.

55. Kalvoda, *Genesis*, 98–99.

56. Beneš, *War Memoirs*, 126–129.

57. Bradley, *Czechoslovak Legion*, 33; Fic, *Revolutionary War*, 24–26; Kalvoda, *Genesis*, 101–105.

58. Herwig, *First World War*, 208–213; Stone, *Eastern Front*, 232–263; Lincoln, *Passage*, 240–259. The Brusilov Offensive cost the Central Powers 1,500,000 casualties, including 400,000 prisoners (mostly from the Austro-Hungarian Army). The Russians lost upwards of 500,000 in the operation; many of these were army's best troops.

59. Rutherford, *Russian Army*, 210–211.

60. Fic, Revolutionary War, 35; Bradley, Czechoslovak Legion, 37–38.

61. Fic, Revolutionary War, 36.

62. Fic, *Revolutionary War*, 37–39; Bradley, *Czechoslovak Legion*, 37; Kalvoda, *Genesis*, 106.

63. Bradley, *Czechoslovak Legion*, 36; Kalvoda, *Genesis*, 105–106.

64. Fic, *Revolutionary War*, 36–39.

65. *Ibid.* 41–43; Kalvoda, *Genesis*, 142.

66. Fic, Revolutionary War, 44–47.

67. Kalvoda, *Genesis*, 137, 145.

68. Bradley, *Czechoslovak Legion*, pp. 38; Kalvoda, *Genesis*, 148.

69. Kalvoda, *Genesis*, 145–146.

70. Lincoln, *Passage*, 296–297, 315–318.

71. Massie, *Nicholas and Alexandra*, 397, 412; Lincoln, *Passage*, 306–311.

72. Kenneth Calder, *Britain and the Origins of the New Europe 1914–1918* (New York: Cambridge University Press, 1976) 19–20, 80–92.

73. Fic, *Revolutionary War*, 43–44, 50; Bradley, *Czechoslovak Legion*, pp. 38.

74. Kalvoda, *Genesis*, 144–145.

75. Masaryk, *Making of a State*, 77.

76. Kalvoda, *Genesis*, 140–142.

77. Victor Mamatey, *The United States and East Central Europe* (Princeton: Princeton University Press, 1957) 42.

78. Keegan, *First World War*, 319.

79. Calder, *Britain*, 103.

80. Beneš, *War Memoirs*, 155.

81. Betty Miller Unterberger, *The United States, Revolutionary Russia and the Rise of Czechoslovakia* (Chapel Hill: The University of North Carolina Press, 1989) 32–36; Calder, *Britain*, 105–107.

82. Beneš, *War Memoirs*, 156–157.

83. Masaryk, *Making of a State*, 124–125.

84. H. Louis Rees, *The Czechs During World War I* (Boulder: East European Monographs, 1992) 24–25; Kann, Robert, Béla Király and Paula Fichtner, eds., *The Habsburg Empire in World War I*, Victor Mamatey, "The Union of Czech Political Parties in the Reichsrat 1916–1918," (Boulder: East European Monographs, 1977) 9–10.

85. Quoted in Beneš, *War Memoirs*, 228.

86. Masaryk, *Making of a State*, 128; Beneš, *War Memoirs*, pp. 227–228; Rees, *Czechs*, 26–27; Kann et al., *Habsburg Empire*, 12.

Chapter 5

1. The given date is according to the Gregorian calendar. At the time, Russia still used the Julian calendar which was thirteen days behind. For that reason the uprising in early 1917 is remembered as the February Revolution.

2. Orlando Figes, *A People's Tragedy* (New York: Viking, 1997) 300, 307–323; W. Bruce Lincoln, *Passage Through Armageddon* (New York: Simon and Schuster, 1986) 321–324, 336, 343–345; Richard Pipes, *The Russian Revolution* (New York: Alfred A. Knopf, 1990) 297–298.

3. Quoted in Zbyněk Zeman, *The Masaryks* (London: Weidenfeld and Nicolson, 1976) 93. Tomáš Masaryk's own comments on the immediate aftermath of the Russian Revolution may be found in *The Making of a State* (New York: Frederick A. Stokes Company, 1927) 130.

4. Josef Kalvoda, *The Genesis of Czechoslovakia* (Boulder: East European Monographs, 1986) 152.

5. Victor Fic, *Revolutionary War for Independence and the Russian Question* (New Delhi: Abhinav Publications, 1977) 52–55; Kalvoda, *Genesis*, 151–152.

6. Quoted in Pastor Peter, ed., Josef Kalvoda, "Czech and Slovak Prisoners of War in Russia during the War and Revolution," *Essays on World War I* (New York: Brooklyn College Press, 1983) 222.

7. *Ibid.* p. 223.

8. Edvard Beneš, *My War Memoirs*, trans. Paul Selver (New York: Houghton Mifflin Company, 1928) 181.

9. Masaryk, *Making of a State*, 132–133.

10. Kalvoda, *Genesis*, 158.

11. Lincoln, *Passage*, 356–371.

12. Masaryk, *Making of a State*, 133.

13. Figes, *People's Tragedy*, 412–413.

14. George Kennan, *Soviet-American Relations, 1917–1920: Russia Leaves the War*, Volume 1 (Princeton: Princeton University Press, 1956) 20–23.

15. Kalvoda, *Genesis*, 181–196; John Bradley, *The Czechoslovak Legion in Russia* (Boulder: East European Monographs, 1991) 51–52; Kenneth Calder, *Britain and the Origins of the New Europe* (New York: Cambridge University Press, 1976) 132–133.

16. Lincoln, *Passage*, 362–364.

17. *Ibid.* 362–365; Figes, *People's Tragedy*, 384–388.

18. Fic, *Revolutionary War*, 63–66.

19. Bradley, *Czechoslovak Legion*, 24; Fic, *Revolutionary War*, 55–57.

20. Bradley, *Czechoslovak Legion*, 43–44, 53.

21. Fic, *Revolutionary War*, 55–58.

22. Bradley, *Czechoslovak Legion*, 50–51; Pastor, *Essays on World War I*, 222.

23. Alon Rachamimov, *POWs and the Great War* (Oxford: Berg 2002) 58, 107–115; Pastor, *Essays on World War I*, 222; Fic, *Revolutionary War*, 71.

24. George Stewart, *The White Armies of Russia* (New York: Russell & Russell, 1970) 97; Rachamimov, *POWs*, 107–115; Pastor, *Essays on World War I*, 174–176, 222.

25. Figes, *People's Tragedy*, 383.

26. Fic, *Revolutionary War*, 63–66.

27. Allan Wildman, *The End of the Russian Imperial Army: The Old Army and the Soldiers' Revolt*, Volume I (Princeton: Princeton University Press, 1980) 103–104, 274; Anton Denikin, *The Russian Turmoil* (Westport: Hyperion Press, 1973) 251.

28. Fic, *Revolutionary War*, 65–66; Wiktor Sukiennicki, *East Central Europe during World War I*, Volume I (Boulder: East European Monographs, 1984) 320–321, 330.

29. Pastor, *Essays on World War I*, 224.

30. Bradley, *Czechoslovak Legion*, 54; Henry Baerlein, *The March of the Seventy Thousand* (London: Leonard Parsons, 1926) 70.

31. The army committees tended to be less radical than soviets and frequently included officers (at least initially) in addition to soldiers and NCOs.

32. Wildman, *Soldiers' Revolt*, 182–192, 228–232.

33. Ward Rutherford, *The Russian Army in World War I* (London: Gordon Cremonesi Publishers, 1975) 248; Wildman, *Soldiers' Revolt*, 362–371.

34. Wildman, *Soldiers' Revolt*, 346–362. In his memoirs Kerensky wrote that the German propaganda campaign "let loose a storm of proclamations more poisonous than the most poisonous gases." Alexander Kerensky, *The Catastrophe* (New York: D. Appleton and Company, 1927) 171.

35. Kerensky, *Catastrophe*, 193; Lincoln, *Passage*, 404–406; Nik Cornish, *The Russian Army and the First World War* (Gloucestershire: Spellmount, 2006) 171; Allan Wildman, *The End of the Russian Imperial Army: The Road to Soviet Power and Peace*, Volume II (Princeton: Princeton University Press, 1987) 24–31.

36. Wildman, *Soviet Power*, 78.

37. Figes, *People's Tragedy*, 418–419; Rutherford, *Russian Army*, 249–254.

38. Wildman, *Soviet Power*, 89; Figes, *People's Tragedy*,

418–419; Louise Erwin Heenan, *Russian Democracy's Fatal Blunder* (New York: Praeger, 1987) 109–110.

39. Bradley, *Czechoslovak Legion*, 55; Baerlein, *Seventy Thousand*, 70–72; Holger Herwig, *The First World War* (London: Arnold, 1997) 335. For the Russian viewpoint of the battle, see Wildman, *Soviet Power*, 89–95.

40. In the first days of the offensive, the breakthrough achieved by the Czecho-Slovaks at Zborov was only matched by a similar success on the front of the Russian Seventh Army near Brzezany. Several days later, a supporting attack by the Russian Eighth Army under General Kornilov sustained its advance for five days, penetrating up to 18 miles into enemy territory.

41. The consequences of the loose discipline in the revolutionary Russian Army became evident when soldiers from the Eleventh Army halted their progress to binge on a cache of wine and alcohol abandoned by the enemy.

42. Cornish, *Russian Army*, 163–164, 169; Wildman, *Soviet Power*, 92; Heenan, *Russian Democracy*, 115.

43. Wildman, *Soviet Power*, 171–174; Heenan, *Russian Democracy*, 120–121; Lincoln, *Passage*, 409–411; Rutherford, *Russian Army*, 251.

44. Wildman, *Soviet Power*, 114–119; Baerlein, *Seventy Thousand*, 75–76; Bradley, *Czechoslovak Legion*, 56.

45. Herwig, *First World War*, 335; Rutherford, *Russian Army*, 254.

46. Wildman, *Soviet Power*, 112–147.

47. The Root Commission, named after former U.S. Secretary of State Elihu Root, was one of several U.S. missions sent to Russia in 1917 to improve relations and cooperation between Russia and her new American ally.

48. Quoted in Edward Heald, *Witness to Revolution* (Kent: The Kent State University Press, 1972) 112. For more on the Root Commission, see Kennan, *Russia Leaves the War*, 22–23.

49. Herwig, *First World War*, 335.

50. Fic, *Revolutionary War*, 67–68; Baerlein, *Seventy Thousand*, 77–78; Rachamimov, *POWs*, 119.

51. Fic, *Revolutionary War*, 71; Pastor, *Essays on World War I*, 224.

52. Bradley, *Czechoslovak Legion*, 56–57.

53. Pastor, *Essays on World War I*, 227–228; Baerlein, *Seventy Thousand*, 78.

54. Pastor, *Essays on World War I*, 223–225.

55. Gustav Becvar, *The Lost Legion* (London: Stanley Paul & Company, 1939) 49; Rachamimov, *POWs*, 112–113.

56. For more on POW experiences in the Russian Revolution, see Rachamimov, *POWs*, 98–102; Stewart, *White Armies*, 326; Pastor, Peter, "Hungarian POWs in Russia During the Revolution and Civil War," *Essays on World War I*, 152; Ferenc Imrey, *Through Blood and Ice* (New York: E.P. Dutton & Company, 1930) 244–246.

57. Pastor, *Essays on World War I*, 225.

58. Masaryk, *Making of a State*, 160, 168; Fic, *Revolutionary War*, 157; Baerlein, *Seventy Thousand*, 27–28.

59. Fic, *Revolutionary War*, 69–70; Bradley, *Czechoslovak Legion*, 52, 57–60; Kalvoda, *Genesis*, 172.

60. Wildman, *Soviet Power*, 225–228.

61. Fic, *Revolutionary War* 73; Bradley, *Czechoslovak Legion*, 51–52.

62. For more on the disorders in the French Army in the spring of 1917, see John Keegan, *The First World War* (New York: Vintage Books, 2000) 327–330.

63. Fic, *Revolutionary War*, 73–74; Bradley, *Czechoslovak Legion*, 51–52; Pastor, *Essays on World War I*, 227.

64. Bradley, *Czechoslovak Legion*, 56.

65. Fic, *Revolutionary War*, 74–78; Bradley, *Czechoslovak Legion*, 70.

66. Lincoln, *Passage*, 361, 424–425; Figes, *People's Tragedy*, 152, 445–455.

67. Pipes, Russian Revolution, 347.

68. *Ibid.* 489; 499–500, 504; Figes, *People's Tragedy*, 483–484; Lincoln, *Passage*, 441–452, 464–468.

69. On the Julian calendar, the Bolshevik seizure of power in Petrograd began on 26 October 1917. The Bolsheviks switched Russia to the Gregorian calendar in February 1918.

70. Quoted in Victor Mamatey, *The United States and East Central Europe 1914–1918* (Princeton: Princeton University Press, 1957) 170–171.

71. Masaryk, *Making of a State*, 175; Lincoln, *Passage*, 468–471.

72. Lincoln, *Passage*, 460.

73. Bradley, *Czechoslovak Legion*, 61; Masaryk, *Maiking of a State*, 168–169; Kalvoda, *Genesis*, 215–216.

74. Lincoln, *Passage*, 484–485.

75. Baerlein, *Seventy Thousand*, 75, 92; David Bullock, *The Czech Legion 1914–20* (New York: Osprey Publishing, 2009) 42–47.

76. Baerlein, *Seventy Thousand*, 78, 92; Fic, *Revolutionary War*, 71–72, Pastor, *Essays on World War I*, 224–225.

Chapter 6

1. Laurence Moyer, *Victory Must Be Ours* (London: Leo Cooper, 1995) 122, 156–167, 265–266; Holger Herwig, *The First World War* (London: Arnold, 1997) 275; Arthur May, *The Passing of the Hapsburg Monarchy* (Philadelphia: Pennsylvannia University Press, 1966) 329–333; Mark Cornwall, *The Last Years of Austria-Hungary* (Exeter: University of Exeter Press, 2002) p. 186.

2. Hugh Seton-Watson and Christopher Seton-Watson, *The Making of a New Europe* (London: Methuen & Company, 1981) 114.

3. During their occupation of Romania, the Central Powers extracted over one million tons of oil, over two million tons of grain, 200,000 tons of timber, 100,000 cattle, 200,000 goats and pigs.

4. John Keegan, *The First World War* (New York: Vintage Books, 2002) 307–308; Norman Stone, *The Eastern Front* (New York: Charles Scribner's Sons, 1975) 264–281; Nik Cornish, *The Russian Army and the First World War* (Gloucestershire: Spellmount, 2006) 120, 128; Holger Herwig, *First World War*, 222;

W. Bruce Lincoln, *Passage Through Armageddon* (New York: Simon and Schuster, 1986) 258.

5. The German and Magyar ethnicities did incur proportionately higher wartime casualties than "subject nationalities" such as the Czechs, but none of the sacrifices made by any of the Monarchy's peoples could be labeled as slight.

6. Gunther Rothenberg, *The Army of Francis Joseph* (West Lafayette: Purdue University Press, 1976) 188; Alon Rachamimov, *POWs and the Great War* (Oxford: Berg, 2002) 31–34; May, *Passing*, 805.

7. Quoted in H. Louis Rees, *The Czechs During World War I* (Boulder: East European Monographs, 1992) 20–21.

8. *Ibid.* 19; Zbyněk Zeman, *The Break-Up of the Habsburg Empire* (London: Oxford University Press, 1961) 14–15, 44–45.

9. Rees, *Czechs*, 22.

10. Robert Kann, Béla Király, Paula Fichtner, eds., Victor Mamatey, "The Union of Czech Political Parties in the Reichsrat 1916–1918," *The Habsburg Empire in World War I* (Boulder: East European Monographs, 1977) 5, 7.

11. Moyer, *Victory*, 173; Herwig, *First World War*, 291–292.

12. May, *Passing*, 334–335; Rees, *Czechs*, 34–38.

13. Kann et al., 8.

14. Alan Palmer, *Twilight of the Habsburgs* (New York: Atlantic Monthly Press, 1994) 336; Rothenberg, *Army*, 200. During a period of the war, Austria-Hungary and Russia exchanged a small number of nurses to care for and comfort their POWs in enemy camps. While visiting a Siberian POW camp in early 1916, an Austrian nurse was surprised when Czech POWs—who were generally considered defectors by the AOK—were moved to tears when she offered them greetings in the name of his majesty, Franz Josef. See Rachamimov, *POWs*, 178.

15. Quoted in Palmer, *Twilight*, 339.

16. May, *Passing*, 335, 437.

17. James Bogle and Joanna Bogle, *A Heart for Europe* (Herefordshire: Gracewing, 2004 edition) 63–64. The Bogles' book is a highly sympathetic portrait of the last Emperor and Empress of Austria-Hungary. More balanced assessments of Karl can be found in: Edmond Taylor, *The Fall of the Dynasties* (New York: Doubleday, 1963) 272–273; Edmund von Glaise-Horstenau, *The Collapse of the Austro-Hungarian Empire* (London: J.M. Dent and Sons, 1930) 11–14.

18. Taylor, *Dynasties*, 273; A. J. P. Taylor, *The Habsburg Monarchy 1809–1918* (Chicago: Chicago University Press, 1948) 241; Rothenberg, *Army*, 204; Rees, *Czechs*, 27.

19. Although their lineages were Czech, both counts were captivated by German and feudal influences.

20. Glaise-Horstenau, *Collapse*, 14, Rees, *Czechs*, 27–29; Cornwall, *Last Years*, 186; Kann et al., *Habsburg Empire*, 11–12.

21. Taylor, *Habsburg Monarchy*, 234–235; Mark Cornwall, ed., Catherine Albrecht, "The Bohemian Question," *The Last Years of Austria-Hungary*, 91; Kann et al. *Habsburg Empire*, 14. The Austrian Social Democratic Party was the only major German-Austrian political party that did not endorse the "German solution."

22. Glaise-Horstenau, *Collapse*, 30; Zeman, *Break-up*, 119–120.

23. Rees, *Czechs*, 29.

24. Glaise-Horstenau, *Collapse*, 155.

25. Zeman, *Break-up*, 120–121.

26. Edvard Beneš, *My War Memoirs*, Translated by Paul Selver (New York: Houghton Mifflin Company, 1928) 229.

27. *Ibid.* 231–232; Elizabeth Wiskemann, *Czechs and Germans* (London: Oxford University Press, 1938) 52. The lower chamber of the Reichsrat consisted of 516 seats.

28. Rees, *Czechs*, 41; Kann et al. *Habsburg Empire*, 15.

29. Zeman, *Break-up*, 122–123.

30. *Ibid.* 123–126; Kann et al., *Habsburg Empire*, 16–18.

31. Wiktor Sukiennicki, *East Central Europe during World War I*, Volume I (Boulder: East European Monographs, 1984) 272–273; Mark Cornwall, ed., Janko Pleterski, "The Southern Slav Question," *The Last Years of Austria-Hungary* (Exeter, University of Exeter Press, 2002) 141–142; Zeman, *Break-up*, 127; Kann et al. *Habsburg Empire*, 17.

32. Quoted in Kann et al. *Habsburg Empire*, 17.

33. Cornwall, *Last Year*, 187–188.

34. Quoted in Bogle and Bogle, *Heart for Europe*, 42.

35. Bogle and Bogle, *Heart for Europe*, 66–71, Taylor, *Dynasties*, 342; Cornwall, *Last Years*, 170.

36. May, *Passing*, 398–403; Maureen Healy, *Vienna and the Fall of the Habsburg Empire* (Cambridge: Cambridge University Press, 2004) 47–52.

37. Bogle and Bogle, *Heart for Europe*, 58–60.

38. Rothenberg, *Army*, 204; May, *Passing*, 439.

39. Quoted in May, *Passing*, 434; Bogle and Bogle, *Heart for Europe*, 64.

40. The House of Bourbon-Parma was a cosmopolitan dynasty with French and, most recently, Italian ties.

41. Germany had seized Alsace-Lorraine during the Franco-Prussian War and the provinces had been a source of French *revanche* in the decades since.

42. May, *Passing*, 490; Taylor, *Dynasties*, 272–275. Karl's wife, Zita, was from the House of Bourbon-Parma, a cosmopolitan dynasty that had been in power in Italy until the Risorgimento. See Bogle and Bogle, *Heart for Europe*, 78. Germany had seized Alsace-Lorraine after the Franco-Prussian War and the provinces had been a source of French *revanche* in the decades since.

43. Quoted in Taylor, *Dynasties*, 274; Glaise-Horstenau, *Collapse*, 51–52.

44. Betty Miller Unterberger, *The United States, Revolutionary Russia and the Rise of Czechoslovakia* (Chapel Hill: The University of North Carolina Press, 1989) 45, 64–66.

45. Beneš, *War Memoirs*, 220–221, 258.

46. Gary Messinger, *British Propaganda and the State in the First World War* (New York: Manchester University Press, 1992) 106.

47. Beneš, *War Memoirs*, 220–221, 258.

48. V. H. Rothwell, *British War Aims and Peace Diplomacy 1914–1918* (Oxford: Clarendon Press, 1971) 81–82. The February 1917 memorandum authored by Eric Drummond in Foreign Office urged that any separate peace should guarantee the Czecho-Slovaks and Yugoslavs the same degree of autonomy in the Monarchy as the Magyars. This consideration for the Slavic ethnicities of the empire probably originated from a desire to resolve the national questions of Central and Southeastern Europe which were viewed as a partial cause of the war. The collaboration of Czech and South Slav émigrés with the British government during the war seems to have mattered little in these assessments since Drummond also made a convincing argument for the preservation of Austria-Hungary. If the empire could be induced into concluding a separate peace with the Entente, he predicted that relations between Vienna and Berlin would become strained and thus position the Monarchy as an effective barrier to *Drang nach Osten* that was more formidable than a collection of small nation-states. The exiles and their supporters would have vehemently disagreed with Drummond if they had known about this memorandum. Around the same time, General Robertson, Chief of the Imperial General Staff, warned the War Cabinet that victory was at least a year away; the Russian Revolution, mutinies in the French Army and rout of Italians at Caporetto— all of which occurred later in the year—would further shake the confidence of Entente leaders. See Rothwell, *British War Aims*, 96.

49. Beneš, *War Memoirs*, 187–188.

50. Taylor, *Dynasties*, 274–275.

51. In 1943, Italy would find itself in similar predicament and attempted to withdraw from the war after Mussolini fell from power. Nazi Germany responded by rapidly occupying the lands of its former ally.

52. Count Ottokar Czernin, *In the World War* (London: Cassell and Company, 1919) 21, 27.

53. Mark Thompson, *The White War* (New York: Basic Books, 2009) 23–31; May, *Passing*, 170–202.

54. Harold Nicolson, *Peacemaking 1919* (New York; Grosset & Dunlap, 1965) 159. Nicolson, who was an expert employed by the Foreign Office, labeled the Treaty of London as "the most encumbering" of Britain's wartime treaties. For more on Entente attitudes towards Italian demands, see Thompson, *White War*, 132.

55. Thompson, *White War*, 23–29.

56. *Ibid.* 56–62, 78, 261–276.

57. *Ibid.* 249; Keegan, *First World War*, 344–346.

58. Thompson, *White War*, 149, 248; Taylor, *Dynasties*, 275. Lloyd George was especially optimistic Austria-Hungary could be detached from the Central Powers through a separate peace. He hoped that Italy could be persuaded to abandon most of her claims on Habsburg lands by dangling before her prized territories which

she coveted in Asia Minor. Sonnino, however, refused to take the bait and was only prepared to do the opposite by abandoning the claims in Asia Minor which he knew were unlikely to be realized in any case. In the meantime, he stood firmly by his demands that Italy receive Habsburg territories promised to it by the Treaty of London. See Rothwell, *British War Aims*, 83, 133–134.

59. Bogle and Bogle, *Heart for Europe*, 86–87.

60. Beneš, *War Memoirs*, 163.

61. Mark Cornwall, *The Undermining of Austria-Hungary* (London: Macmillan Press, 2000) 113–114; Thompson, *White War*, 217.

62. Beneš, *War Memoirs*, 166.

63. Cornwall, *Undermining,* 117; Beneš, *War Memoirs*, 165–168.

64. Beneš, *War Memoirs*, 161; Cornwall, *Undermining*, 116–120.

65. *Ibid.* 117; Peter Pastor, Peter, ed., Rowan Williams, "The Czech Legion in Italy during World War I," *Essays on World War I* (New York: Brooklyn College Press, 1983) 200; Beneš, *War Memoirs*, 213.

66. Pastor, *Essays on World War I*, 201.

67. Thompson, *White War*, 6.

68. Pastor, *Essays on World War I*, 201–202.

69. Thompson, *White War*, 279–283.

70. Rothenberg, *Army*, 205–206; Thompson, *White War*, 294–327; Herwig, *First World War*, 336–346.

71. Taylor, *Dynasties*, 243–244.

72. Kann et al., *Habsburg Empire*, 17; Rees, *Czechs*, 70; May, *Passing*, 645.

73. Kann et al., *Habsburg Empire*, 20–21.

74. Rees, *Czechs*, 62–66.

75. Beneš, *War Memoirs*, 32.

76. Beneš, *War Memoirs*, 235; Tomáš Masaryk, *The Making of a State* (New York: Frederick A. Stokes Company, 1927) 213–214.

77. Kann et al., *Habsburg Empire*, 22; Zeman, *Break-up,* 171–172.

78. Glaise-Horstenau, *Collapse*, 36.

79. Rees, *Czechs,* 50–52, 76; Kann et al., *Habsburg Empire*, 19–17. Although Kramář was released in July 1917, he was prevented from returning to Prague for several months afterwards by Austrian authorities.

80. Rees, *Czechs*, 78–80; Kann et al., *Habsburg Empire*, 22–23.

81. Quoted in Rees, *Czechs*, 80.

82. Quoted in Zeman, *Break-up*, 175; Rees, *Czechs*, 80–81.

83. Zeman, *Break-up*, 174.

84. Glaise-Horstenau, *Collapse*, 13–14.

85. Alan Sked, *The Decline and Fall of the Habsburg Empire* (New York: Dorset Press, 1989) 263.

86. Kenneth Calder, *Britain and the Origins of the New Europe* (New York: Cambridge University Press, 1976) 111–117.

87. Robert Ferrell, *Woodrow Wilson and World War I 1917–1921* (New York: Harper & Row, 1985) 14, 108–112.

88. Keegan, *First World War*, 372–373.

Chapter 7

1. Edvard Beneš, *My War Memoirs* (New York: Houghton Mifflin Company, 1928) 91; Josef Kalvoda, *The Genesis of Czechoslovakia* (Boulder: East European Monographs, 1986) 70.

2. Kalvoda, *Genesis*, 137; David Bullock, *The Czech Legion 1914–20* (New York: Osprey Publishing, 2009) 11.

3. Austro-Hungarian troops were not deployed on the Western Front until August 1918.

4. Arthur May, *The Passing of the Hapsburg Monarchy* (Philadelphia: Pennsylvannia University Press, 1966) 719–720; Edmund Glaise-Horstenau, *The Collapse of the Austro-Hungarian Empire* (London: J.M. Dent and Sons, 1930) 170.

5. Alan Palmer, *The Gardeners of Salonika* (New York; Simon and Schuster, 1965) 41.

6. John Keegan, *The First World War* (New York: Vintage Books, 2000) 253–254.

7. Beneš, *War Memoirs*, 134.

8. *Ibid.* 137–138.

9. *Ibid.* 203–206, 216.

10. *Ibid.* 182–184; Nancy Gentile Ford, *Americans All!* (College Station: Texas A&M University Press, 2001) 31.

11. Beneš, *War Memoirs*, 101; Tomáš Masaryk, *The Making of a State* (New York: Frederick A. Stokes Company, 1927) 74.

12. Beneš, *War Memoirs*, 187–197.

13. *Ibid.* 268.

14. *Ibid.* 187–197.

15. Kalvoda, *Genesis*, 196–197.

16. John Keegan, *The First World War* (New York: Vintage Books, 2000) 350.

17. Gary Messinger, *British Propaganda and the State in the First World War* (New York: Manchester University Press, 1992) 153–154; Michael Sanders and Philip Taylor, *British Propaganda during the First World War 1914–1918* (London: The Macmillan Press, 1982) 89–90.

18. Messinger, British Propaganda, 154; J. Lee Thompson, Politicians, the Press & Propaganda: Lord Northcliffe & the Great War, 1914–1919 (Kent: The Kent State University Press, 1999) 4, 148–194.

19. Henry Wickham Steed, *Through Thirty Years*, Volume 2 (New York: Doubleday, Page & Company, 1924) 185–186.

20. *Ibid.* 187.

21. *Ibid.* 188; Sir Campbell Stuart, *Secrets of Crewe House* (London: Hodder and Stoughton, 1920) 28–33.

22. Stuart, *Crewe House*, 33–35; Steed, *Through Thirty Years*, 188–189. Steed's recommendations were close but not in complete agreement with those put forth by émigrés such as Masaryk. He differed from the émigrés by advocating the formation of "a non–German confederation of Central European and Danubian states" instead of "a number of small, disjointed states." He also supported the idea of union between German-Austria and the German Reich.

23. Steed, *Through Thirty Years*, 189–192; Stuart, *Crewe House*, 35–36; Sanders and Taylor, *British Propaganda*, 231.

24. Steed, *Through Thirty Years*, 192, 197.

25. Messinger, *British Propaganda*, 172.

26. Holger Herwig, *The First World War* (London: Arnold, 1997) 406; Keegan, *First World War*, 396–406.

27. Steed, *Through Thirty Years*, 168, 200–205.

28. Glaise-Horstenau, *Collapse*, 121; Mark Cornwall, *The Undermining of Austria-Hungary* (London: Macmillan Press, 2000) 188, 192–193; Stuart, *Crewe House*, 40.

29. Steed, *Through Thirty Years*, 208; Cornwall, *Undermining*, 197, 206–207.

30. Despite several subsequent requests to Lloyd George, Northcliffe never received any assurance that the government's policy towards Austria-Hungary was consistent with Crewe House propaganda. The press lord nonetheless remained the head of the Department of Enemy Propaganda until 12 November 1918.

31. Thompson, *Politicians*, 192–193, 196.

32. Messinger, *British Propaganda*, 176.

33. Steed, *Through Thirty Years*, 209, 213.

34. *Ibid.* 184–185; Zbyněk Zeman, *The Break-Up of the Habsburg Empire 1914–1918* (London: Oxford University Press, 1961), 192–193.

35. Zeman, *Break-Up*, 191. Steed, *Through Thirty Years*, 206, 211.

36. Beneš, *War Memoirs*, 197, 266.

37. Kalvoda, *Genesis*, 196–197, 258–259.

38. Beneš, *War Memoirs*, 276.

39. Cornwall, *Undermining*, 126, 127, 157–158.

40. *Ibid.* 142–144.

41. Pastor, Peter, *Essays in World War I*, 202; Cornwall, *Undermining*, 157; Beneš, *War Memoirs*, 288–289.

42. Beneš, *War Memoirs*, 290.

43. *Ibid.* 294; Cornwall, *Undermining*, 99, 158; Pastor, *Essays on World War I*, 203.

44. Kalvoda, *Genesis*, 261.

45. Beneš, *War Memoirs*, 295.

46. Cornwall, *Undermining*, 159.

47. This division was originally named the Czecho-Slovak First Division but was later renamed the Sixth Division to avoid confusion with the Czecho-Slovak First Division already existing in Russia. Eventually, the Czecho-Slovak formations in Russia, France and Italy were organized as though they were a single army.

48. Beneš, War Memoirs, 296; Pastor, Essays on World War I, 204.

49. Cornwall, *Undermining*, 228–230, 374; Pastor, *Essays on World War I*, 204, 208; Stuart, *Crewe House*, 38–39.

50. Mark Thompson, *The White War* (New York: Basic Books, 2008) 267–268.

51. *Ibid.* 6, 261–276.

52. Cornwall, *Undermining*, 385.

53. Pastor, Essays on World War I, 203.

54. *Ibid.* 210.

55. Cornwall, *Undermining*, 232–233.

56. *Ibid.* 382.

57. Pastor, Essays on World War I, 208.

58. *Ibid.* 207–208; Cornwall, *Undermining*, 374–375; Beneš, *War Memoirs*, 297.

59. Pastor, *Essays on World War I*, 208–209; Beneš, *War Memoirs*, 297.

60. Cornwall, *Undermining*, 378–386.

61. *Ibid.* 383.

62. Thompson, *White War*, 356.

63. Cornwall, *Undermining*, 328–335; Victor Matey, *The United States and East Central Europe 1914–1918* (Princeton: Princeton University Press, 1957) 274.

64. Cornwall, *Undermining*, 383; Kenneth Calder, *Britain and the Origins of the New Europe 1914–1918* (New York: Cambridge University Press, 1976) 191.

65. Wiktor Sukiennicki, *East Central Europe during World War I*, Volume I (Boulder: East European Monographs, 1984) 266–267; David Stefancic, *Armies in Exile* (Boulder: East European Monographs, 2005) 100, 123; Calder, *Britain*, 145–147.

66. George Goldberg, *The Peace to End Peace* (New York: Harcourt, Brace & World, 1969) 59–60; Calder, *Britain*, 105–106.

67. Calder, *Britain*, 156–164.

68. Calder, *Britain*, 71; Stefancic, *Armies in Exile*, 132–134. The Poles eventually enlisted over 20,000 men from the U.S. to serve in the Polish Legion in France, but most did not reach Europe until the final months of the war or after the armistice.

69. Beneš, *War Memoirs*, 295.

Chapter 8

1. James Bunyan, *Intervention, Civil War and Communism in Russia* (New York: Octagon Books, 1976) 78.

2. W. Bruce Lincoln, *Passage Through Armageddon* (New York: Simon and Schuster, 1986) 458–459; John Bradley, *The Czechoslovak Legion in Russia 1914–1920* (Boulder: East European Monographs, 1991) 72–74; Josef Kalvoda, *The Genesis of Czechoslovakia* (Boulder: East European Monographs, 1986) 244.

3. Victor Fic, *Revolutionary War for Independence and the Russian Question* (New Delhi: Abhinav Publications, 1977) 163; Nik Cornish, *The Russian Army and the First World War* (Gloucestershire: Spellmount, 2006) 159; 173.

4. Fic, *Revolutionary War*, 163–164; James Morley, *The Japanese Thrust into Siberia* (New York: Columbia University Press, 1957) 29–33.

5. Wiktor Sukiennicki, *East Central Europe during World War I*, Volume I (Boulder: East European Monographs, 1984) 506–507; George Kennan, *Soviet-American Relations 1917–1920: Russia Leaves the War* (Princeton: Princeton University Press, 1956) 178–179; John Silverlight, *The Victors' Dilemma* (New York: Weybright and Talley, 1970) 11.

6. Fic, *Revolutionary* War, 183–184; Bradley, *Czechoslovak Legion*, 66.

7. Louise Erwin Heenan, *Russian Democracy's Fatal Blunder* (New York: Praeger, 1987) 120; Victor Ma-

matey, *The United States and East Central Europe 1914–1918* (Princeton: Princeton University Press, 1957) 120–121; Cornish, *Russian Army*, 168–169.

8. Cornish, *Russian Army*, 198; Karel Čapek, *President Masaryk Tells His Story* (New York: G.P. Putnam's Sons, 1935) 274.

9. Tomáš Masaryk, *The Making of a State* (New York: Frederick A. Stokes Company, 1927) 186–187; Bradley, *Czechoslovak Legion*, 66–69.

10. Fic, *Revolutionary War,* 184–187; Kalvoda, *Genesis*, 205.

11. Masaryk, *Making of a State*, 188.

12. Anton Denikin, *The White Army*, trans. Catherine Zvegintzov (Gulf Breeze: Academic International Press, 1973) 39; Richard Luckett, *The White Generals* (London: Routledge, 1971) 98; Evan Mawdsley, *The Russian Civil War* (New York: Pegasus, 2007) 18–21.

13. Fic, *Revolutionary War*, 174–176.

14. Bradley, Czechoslovak Legion, 70.

15. Fic, *Revolutionary War*, 177–181; Bradley, *Czechoslovak Legion*, 58; Kalvoda, *Genesis*, 202, 215–218.

16. Henry Baerlein, *The March of the Seventy Thousand* (London: Leonard Parsons, 1926) 144; Zbyněk Zeman, *The Break-Up of the Habsburg Empire 1914–1918* (London: Oxford University Press, 1961) 204. By now Miliukov was writing that the Bolsheviks were a greater enemy to Russia than the Germans.

17. Bradley, Czechoslovak Legion, 70.

18. Kalvoda, *Genesis*, 215. Dürich's leadership over Král's movement was only nominal since he was in Ukraine at the time and would not each White-controlled areas of South Russia until several months later.

19. The western fringes of the Ukrainian population resided in eastern Galicia, Ruthenia and Bukovina, all of which were Habsburg dominions.

20. Sukiennicki, *East Central Europe*, 485–486, 496, 540; Bradley, *Czechoslovak Legion*, 63–64.

21. Sukiennicki, *East Central Europe*, 114; Zeman, *Break-Up*, 154.

22. Bradley, Czechoslovak Legion, 66.

23. Fic, *Revolutionary War*, 169–170; Masaryk, *Making of a State*, 184; Bradley, *Czechoslovak Legion*, 68. In its negotiations with the Ukrainian Rada, the Czecho-Slovak National Council in Russia closely followed the French policy. It would only recognize the Rada as an autonomous government within an abstract Russian federation.

24. Bradley, Czechoslovak Legion, 66.

25. *Ibid.* 14–18, 67–68; Fic, *Revolutionary War*, 194–197.

26. Bradley, *Czechoslovak Legion*, 63; Fic, *Revolutionary War,* 169. For Bolshevik attitudes towards self-determination, see Sukiennicki, *East Central Europe*, 455–460.

27. Sukiennicki, *East Central Europe*, 540–546, 552–565. Ukrainian demands from the Central Powers at Brest-Litovsk were not light, particularly as far as Austria-Hungary was concerned. In addition to the for-

merly Russian-controlled lands with Ukrainian populations, the Rada's delegation also demanded the inclusion of the eastern Galicia, Bukovina and Ruthenia into
their planned state; all which had substantial populations of Ukrainians and belonged to the Habsburg
Monarchy. With German mediation, a compromise was
eventually worked out between the Austrians and
Ukrainians where these disputed areas would form a
separate Ukrainian crownland in the Monarchy.
    28. Kennan, *Russia Leaves the War*, 185.
    29. Sukiennicki, *East Central Europe*, 485–497; 550;
Mawdsley, *Russian Civil War*, 24–26.
    30. Fic, *Revolutionary War*, 199; Bradley, *Czechoslo-
vak Legion*, 71–72.
    31. The Polish Council of State in Warsaw declared
its neutrality in the world war and demanded that Poles
abroad observe this policy. Dmowski's group defied
these instructions by forming the legion in Russia. See
Kenneth Calder, *Britain and the Origins of the New Europe 1914–1918* (New York: Cambridge University
Press, 1976) 160, 166. For the fate of the Polish Army
Corps in Russia, see David Stefancic, *Armies in Exile*
(Boulder: East European Monographs, 2005) 90–91;
Sukiennicki, *East Central Europe*, 463–470, 746–765;
and John Bradley, *Allied Intervention in Russia* (New
York: Basic Books, 1968), 18. For the consequences of
the Polish Army Corps' surrender on the Polish liberation movement abroad, see Calder, *Britain*, 182–186.
    32. Bradley, *Czechoslovak Legion*, 71.
    33. Mawdsley, *Russian Civil War*, 26.
    34. Masaryk, *Maiking of a State*, 177; Kalvoda, *Gen-
esis*, 233.
    35. Fic, *Revolutionary War*, 199–200.
    36. Masaryk, *Making of a State*, 177.
    37. Bradley, *Czechoslovak Legion*, 74.
    38. John Wheeler-Bennett, *Brest-Litovsk: The For-
gotten Peace* (New York: Norton, 1971) 72–73, 136, 142,
92, 116.
    39. *Ibid.* 115.
    40. Orlando Figes, A *People's Tragedy* (New York:
Viking, 1997) 540–541.
    41. Sukiennicki, *East Central Europe*, 481–497; Lin-
coln, *Passage*, 475–478.
    42. Mark Cornwall, ed., F.R. Bridge, "The Foreign
Policy of the Monarchy," *The Last Years of Austria-
Hungary* (Exeter: University of Exeter Press, 2002) 40–
41; Sukiennicki, *East Central Europe*, 538; Wheeler-
Bennett, *Forgotten Peace*, 175; Max Hoffmann, *War Di-
aries and Other Papers*, Volume 2 (London: Martin
Secker, 1929) 199.
    43. Wheeler-Bennett, *Forgotten Peace*, 125–127.
    44. Trotsky later wrote, "The delay in negotiations
was to our interest. That was my real object in going to
Brest-Litovsk." Leon Trotsky, *My Life* (New York:
Charles Scribner's Sons, 1930) 369.
    45. Wheeler-Bennett, *Forgotten Peace*, 156–165.
    46. Zeman, *Break-Up*, 134.
    47. H. Louis Rees, *The Czechs During World War I*
(Boulder: East European Monographs, 1992) 86–90;
Zeman, *Break-Up*, 134.

    48. Count Ottokar Czernin, *In the World War* (Lon-
don: Cassell and Company, 1919) 237.
    49. *Ibid.* 239.
    50. Quoted in Wheeler-Bennett, *Forgotten Peace*,
170.
    51. Hoffmann, *War Diaries*, Volume 2, 203–204,
211.
    52. Cornwall, *Last Years*, 41.
    53. Wheeler-Bennett, *Forgotten Peace*, 207.
    54. *Ibid.* 220; Cornwall, *Last Years*, 161.
    55. Quoted in Lincoln, *Passage*, 497–498.
    56. Trotsky, *My Life*, 386.
    57. Hoffmann, *War Diaries*, Volume 1, 206–207.
    58. Fic, *Revolutionary War*, 205–208; Baerlein, *Sev-
enty Thousand*, 99.
    59. Baerlein, *Seventy Thousand*, 99–100; Fic, *Revo-
lutionary War*, 212–213. For a revealing description of
Kiev after the series of battles fought there in late winter—early spring 1918, see Edward Heald, *Witness to
Revolution* (Kent: The Kent State University Press,
1972) 199–204.
    60. Gustav Becvar, *The Lost Legion* (London: Stan-
ley Paul & Company, 1939) 65–66.
    61. Baerlein, *Seventy Thousand*, 101; Bradley,
Czechoslovak Legion, 78–79.
    62. Becvar, *Lost Legion*, 67.
    63. *Ibid.* 68–69.
    64. Baerlein, *Seventy Thousand*, 128–129.
    65. *Ibid.* 101–102.
    66. Bradley, *Czechoslovak Legion*, 78–79; Peter Pas-
tor, ed., Josef Kalvoda, "Czech and Slovak Prisoners of
War in Russia during the War and Revolution," *Essays
on World War I* (New York: Brooklyn College Press,
1983) 228–229.
    67. Masaryk, *Making of a State*, 189.
    68. Wheeler-Bennett, *Forgotten Peace*, 327.
    69. Baerlein, *Seventy Thousand*, 102–103; Fic, *Rev-
olutionary War*, 214.
    70. Fic, *Revolutionary War*, 209.
    71. Kalvoda, *Genesis*, 61, 249.
    72. Wheeler-Bennett, *Forgotten Peace*, 245; Richard
Pipes, *The Russian Revolution* (New York: Alfred A.
Knopf, 1990) 593–594.
    73. Wheeler-Bennett, *Forgotten Peace*, 269.
    74. Pipes, *Russian Revolution*, 594.
    75. George Kennan, *Soviet-American Relations 1917–
1920: The Decision to Intervene* (Princeton: Princeton
University Press, 1958), 10.
    76. Victor Fic, *The Bolsheviks and the Czechoslovak
Legion* (New Delhi: Abhinav Publications, 1978) 5–7;
Kalvoda, Genesis, 250.
    77. The Latvian Rifle Division was founded in 1915
as one of the rare autonomous national units in the
tsarist army. Since then it was thoroughly Bolshevized
and coddled by Soviet leaders into serving as a guardians
in the early months of their regime.
    78. Pipes, *Russian Revolution*, 611; Mawdsley, *Rus-
sian Civil War*, 40.
    79. Pipes, *Russian Revolution*, 590–591, 613–614.
    80. Fic, *Revolutionary War*, 215; Bunyan, *Interven-*

tion, 80; Serge Petroff, *Remembering a Forgotten War* (Boulder: East European Monographs, 2000) 3.

81. Cornish, *Russian Army*, 194.

82. Peter Pastor, ed., Ivo Banac, "South Slav Prisoners of War in Revolutionary Russia," *Essays on World War I*, 130–132.

83. Kalvoda, *Genesis*, 308.

84. Stefancic, *Armies in Exile*, 90–91, Sukiennicki, *East Central Europe*, 463–470, 746–765; Bradley, *Allied Intervention*, 18.

85. Kalvoda, *Genesis*, 308.

Chapter 9

1. Richard Pipes, *The Russian Revolution* (New York: Alfred A. Knopf, 1990) 503–504, 512–515.

2. William Henry Chamberlin, *The Russian Revolution 1917–1921*, Volume 2 (New York: Grosset & Dunlap, 1965) 419.

3. R. Ernest Dupuy, *Perish by the Sword* (Harrisburg: The Military Publishing Company, 1939) 219.

4. Steven Marks, *Road to Power* (New York: Cornell University Press, 1991) 177–178.

5. *Ibid.* 196–200.

6. Richard Goldhurst, *The Midnight War* (New York: McGraw-Hill Book Company, 1978) 43; Edward Heald, *Witness to Revolution* (Kent: The Kent State University Press, 1972) 204.

7. For more on the Russian Railway Service Corps, see: Betty Miller Unterberger, *The United States, Revolutionary Russia and the Rise of Czechoslovakia* (Chapel Hill: The University of North Carolina Press, 1989) 77–80, 153–154; George Kennan, *Soviet-American Relations 1917–1920: Russia Leaves the War* (Princeton: Princeton University Press, 1956) 285–287, 297–298.

8. Pipes, *Russian Revolution*, 600–601.

9. Ibid. 588.

10. *Ibid.* 590, 597–603; Bruce Lockhart, *British Agent* (London: G.P. Putnam's Sons, 1933) 237, 245, 267.

11. Kennan, *Russia Leaves the War*, 286–287.

12. Lockhart, *British Agent*, 233.

13. Pipes, *Russian Revolution*, 589; Lockhart, *British Agent*, 222–223; Kennan, *Russia Leaves the War*, 382.

14. Lockhart, *British Agent*, 221, 237.

15. Pipes, *Russian Revolution*, 591; Lockhart, *British Agent*, 227.

16. Clifford Kinvig, *Churchill's Crusade* (London: Hambledon Continuum, 2006) 16–31; Kennan, *Russia Leaves the War*, 46–50.

17. See Chapter 5, 92–93.

18. Pipes, *Russian Revolution*, 609–612.

19. Isaac Deutscher, *The Prophet Armed* (New York: Oxford University Press, 1954) 5–8, 117–144.

20. *Ibid.* 151–173, 203, 215, 238–240.

21. Pipes, *Russian Revolution*, 611.

22. Victor Fic, *Bolsheviks*, 112.

23. Deutscher, *Prophet Armed*, 415.

24. Fic, *Bolsheviks*, 119–122.

25. In March 1918, the Bolsheviks formerly changed their name to the Communist Party, an example that was followed by their non-Russian comrades.

26. Victor Fic, *Revolutionary War for Independence and the Russian Question* (New Delhi: Abhinav Publications, 1977) 81–85; John Bradley, *The Czechoslovak Legion in Russia* (Boulder: East European Monographs, 1991) 59–60.

27. Fic, *Revolutionary War*, 86–88; Henry Baerlein, *The March of the Seventy Thousand* (London: Leonard Parsons, 1926) 93–94.

28. Bradley, *Czechoslovak Legion*, 60.

29. Fic, *Revolutionary War*, 90–92; Tomáš Masaryk, *The Making of a State* (New York: Frederick A. Stokes Company, 1927) 95–96; Josef Kalvoda, *The Genesis of Czechoslovakia* (Boulder: East European Monographs, 1986) 238.

30. Fic, *Bolsheviks*, 94–95.

31. Fic, Revolutionary War, 108.

32. *Ibid.* 96–97.

33. Masaryk, *Making of a State*, 176–177.

34. Fic, *Revolutionary War*, 99; Zbyněk Zeman, *The Break-up of the Habsburg Empire 1914–1918* (London: Oxford University Press, 1961) 205.

35. Fic, Revolutionary War, 109.

36. Fic, *Bolsheviks*, 18; Peter Pastor, ed., Josef Kalvoda, "Czech and Slovak Prisoners of War in Russia during the War and Revolution," *Essays on World War I* (New York, 1983) 225–226, 230.

37. Fic, *Bolsheviks*, 9–15.

38. *Ibid.* 13–14; Pipes, *Russian Revolution*, 613–615.

39. Pastor, *Essays on World War I*, 106–109.

40. Fic, *Bolsheviks*, 15.

41. Ibid. 78; Baerlein, *Seventy Thousand*, 109; Bradley, *Czechoslovak Legion*, 82.

42. Heald, *Witness to Revolution*, 173. Richard Goldhurst also offers some background information on Maxa in *The Midnight War*, 26.

43. Bradley, *Czechoslovak Legion*, 77.

44. *Ibid.* 81; Fic, *Bolsheviks*, 20–22; Kalvoda, *Genesis*, 313.

45. Fic, *Bolsheviks*, 22–23; Baerlein, *Seventy Thousand*, 109–110. The *hunghutze* continued their banditry throughout the duration of the Russian Civil War. See R. Ernest Dupuy, *Perish by the Sword* (Harrisburg: The Military Publishing Company, 1939) 219.

46. Fic, *Bolsheviks*, 34, 38.

47. *Ibid.* 109; James Bunyan, *Intervention, Civil War and Communism in Russia* (New York: Octagon Books, 1976) 81.

48. Bunyan, *Intervention*, 79.

49. Bradley, *Czechoslovak Legion*, 80–81.

50. Fic, *Bolsheviks*, 32–33.

51. In a letter to Robert Seton-Watson in the spring of 1918, Masaryk wrote on the Legion's disarmament: "This is good news: the corps going to France needs no weapons, as it will be armed again in France..." Robert Seton-Watson, *Masaryk in England* (Cambridge: Cambridge University Press, 1943) 111.

52. Gustav Becvar, *The Lost Legion* (London: Stanely Paul & Company, 1939) 79.

53. Baerlein, *Seventy Thousand*, 109–110.
54. Fic, *Bolsheviks*, 26–27, 38.
55. Kalvoda, *Genesis*, 313.
56. Fic, *Bolsheviks*, 40–42; Baerlein, *Seventy Thousand*, 114.
57. Fic, *Bolsheviks*, 42–43.
58. Kalvoda, *Genesis*, 318–319.
59. Fic, *Bolsheviks*, 43–44.
60. *Ibid.* 45–52.
61. *Ibid.* 53.
62. *Ibid.* 45, 56–57.
63. *Ibid.* 211; Bradley, *Czechoslovak Legion*, 79.
64. Fic, *Bolsheviks*, 187.
65. *Ibid.* 188–189; Fic, *Revolutionary War*, 141–145; Bradley, *Czechoslovak Legion*, 60. Masaryk, during his tour of the regiments in August 1917, made known his opposition to greater democratization of the corps, but not even he was able to settle the debate.
66. Fic, *Revolutionary War*, 149.
67. Pipes, *Russian Revolution*, 538.
68. Bradley, *Czechoslovak Legion*, p. 82.
69. Fic, *Bolsheviks*, 188, 192.
70. *Ibid.* 190–195; Bradley, *Czechoslovak Legion*, 82. On Rudolf Medek's later projects concerning the Legion, see Nancy Wingfield, *Flag Wars and Stone Saints* (Cambridge: Harvard University Press, 2007) 190–192.
71. Fic, *Bolshevik*, 196–197.
72. Orlando Figes, *A People's Tragedy* (New York: Viking, 1997) 156.
73. Fic, *Bolsheviks*, 199–200.
74. *Ibid.* 97.
75. *Ibid.* 199–200.
76. John Keegan, *The First World War* (New York: Vintage Books, 1998) 205–206; George Kennan, *Russia Leaves the War*, 276–278; John Albert White, *The Siberian Intervention* (Princeton: Princeton University Press, 1950) 6; James Morley, *The Japanese Thrust into Siberia 1918* (New York: Columbia University Press, 1957) 12.
77. Kennan, *Russia Leaves the War*, 277–281, Lockhart, *British Agent*, 228.
78. *Ibid.* 238.
79. *Ibid.* 222–223.
80. Alon Rachamimov, *POWs and the Great War* (Oxford: Berg, 2002) 39–40; Fic, *Bolsheviks*, 128; Peter Pastor, ed., Gerald Davis, "The Life of Prisoners of War in Russia 1914–1921," *Essays on World War I*, 165.
81. Peter Pastor, ed., Arnold Krammer, "Soviet Propaganda among German and Austro-Hungarian Prisoners of War in Russia 1917–1921," *Essays on World War I*, 244–246; Kennan, *Soviet-American Relations: The Decision to Intervene* (Princeton: Princeton University Press, 1958) 72.
82. Fic, *Bolsheviks*, 121–122.
83. According to one Hungarian prisoner, the Bolsheviks exploited the fact that practically no other group targeted the Magyar POWs in Russia with propaganda or favorable treatment. The reason for this seems to be that the tsarist government had few personnel able to translate or perform censor duties in the Magyar language. See Imrey, Ferenc, *Through Blood and Ice* (New York, 1930) pp. 259.
84. Peter Pastor, "Hungarian POWs in Russia during the Revolution and Civil War," *Essays on World War I* 149–159; Kennan, *Decision to Intervene*, 73; Rachamimov, *POWs*, 121.
85. When German and Austro-Hungarian repatriation commissions finally arrived into Russia in June 1918, they largely ended communist efforts to enlist POWs into Internationalist formations.
86. Fic, *Bolsheviks*, 125; Kennan, *Decision to Intervene*, 73; Rachamimov, *POWs*, 192.
87. Kennan, *Decision to Intervene*, 73.
88. Pastor, *Essays on World War I*, 254; Rachamimov, *POWs*, 121.
89. Seton-Watson, *Masaryk in England*, 103–112.
90. Quoted in Fic, *Bolsheviks*, 161, 157–163. For Allied attempts to investigate the existence of the International battalions, see Kennan, *Decision to Intervene*, 75–81; Lockhart, *British Agent*, 248–249.
91. As we shall see in Chapter 12, Masaryk's pessimistic but sober assessment on anti–Bolshevik movements in Russia in spring 1918 rendered him unpopular in certain Allied circles. Seton-Watson, *Masaryk in England*, 111.
92. Kennan, *Decision to Intervene*, 91–95; Morley, *Japanese Thrust*, 61–65; Clifford Kinvig, *Churchill's Crusade* (London: Hambledon Continuum, 2006) 53.
93. Kennan, *Russia Leaves the War*, 300–302, 316–328, 460–462, 474–475, 483; Kennan, *Decision to Intervene*, 84–86; Morley, *Japanese Thrust*, 48–56, 123–124. Britain and France, amid their desperation, even urged a solo Japanese intervention without the approval of the United States.
94. Morley, *Japanese Thrust*, 146–151; Bunyan, *Intervention*, 68–70.
95. Peter Fleming, *The Fate of Admiral Kolchak* (Edinburgh: Birlinn, 2001) 48–50.
96. The Allied landings at Vladivostok had little direct impact on the Czecho-Slovak Legion's progress since it occurred in one of the many periods when the legionaries' trains were stopped.
97. Fic, *Bolsheviks*, 66.
98. Pastor, ed., Ivo Banac, "South Slav Prisoners of War in Revolutionary Russia," *Essays on World War I*, 132.
99. Fic, *Bolsheviks*, 65.
100. Edvard Beneš, *My War Memoirs*, trans. Paul Selver (New York: Houghton Mifflin Company, 1928) 357–358.
101. Kalvoda, *Genesis*, 309.
102. For British and French deliberations over shipping the legionnaires from Vladivostok, see Kennan, *Decision to Intervene*, 146–148; Fic, *Bolsheviks*, 69–71. The scarcity of Pacific shipping is explained in Carol Wilcox Melton, *Between War and Peace* (Macon: Mercer University Press, 2001) 62; Bradley, *Allied Intervention*, 43, 79.
103. Beneš, *War Memoirs*, 357–358; Fic, *Bolsheviks*, 63–64.

104. Fic, *Bolsheviks*, 65–66; Kennan, *Decision to Intervene*, 19–20.

105. *Ibid.* 36–37.

106. Fic, *Bolsheviks*, 66.

107. Kinvig, *Churchill's Crusade*, 20, 25; Kennan, *Decision to Intervene*, 250–252, 261.

108. Quoted in John Silverlight, *The Victors' Dilemma* (New York: Weybright and Talley, 1970) 36.

109. Fic, *Bolsheviks*, 72–75; Kennan, *Decision to Intervene*, 145–148.

110. Kennan, *Decision to Intervene*, 148–149.

111. Fic, *Bolsheviks*, 76, 202.

112. *Ibid.* 203–204.

113. *Ibid.* 216.

114. Examples of the legionnaires' concerns and rumors regarding the Czech Communists can be found in Fic, *Bolsheviks*, 216; Bradley, *Czechoslovak Legion*, 83 and Carl Ackerman, *Trailing the Bolsheviki* (New York: Charles Scribner's Sons, 1919) 113–114.

115. Becvar, *Lost Legion*, 84; Joan McGuire Mohr, *The Czech and Slovak Legion in Siberia, 1917–1922* (Jefferson: McFarland & Company, 2012) 75–76.

116. Fic, *Bolsheviks*, 183–185; Bunyan, *Intervention*, 87.

117. Fic, *Bolsheviks*, 54–56.

118. *Ibid.* 217; Bradley, *Czechoslovak Legion*, 83.

119. Fic, *Bolsheviks*, 200–208.

120. Bradley, Czechoslovak Legion, 85.

121. This newspaper, *Československy deník* (*Czechoslovak Daily*), was published throughout the duration of the Legion's katabasis on a train-borne printing press.

122. Fic, *Bolsheviks*, 216–219.

123. Bunyan, *Intervention*, 83–85; Bradley, *Czechoslovak Legion*, 83; Fic, *Bolsheviks*, 8.

124. Fic, *Bolsheviks*, 212–213.

125. Bradley, *Czechoslovak Legion*, 83.

126. A sufficiently detailed biographical sketch of Gajda can be found in David Kelly, *The Czech Fascist Movement 1922–1942* (Boulder: East European Monographs, 1995) 26–28. The transfer of the Czech and Slovak soldiers and officers from the Serbian Volunteer Corps is mentioned in Pastor, ed., Josef Kalvoda, "Czech and Slovak Prisoners of War in Russia during the War and Revolution," *Essays on World War I*, 225.

127. Baerlein, *Seventy Thousand*, 132.

128. Fic, *Bolsheviks*, 317–318.

129. Zeman, *Break-up*, 208.

Chapter 10

1. Steven Marks, *Road to Power* (New York: Cornell University Press, 1991) 217.

2. W. Bruce Lincoln, *The Conquest of a Continent* (New York: Random House, 1994) 192–195, 227–248; John Albert White, *The Siberian Intervention* (Princeton: Princeton University Press, 1950) 47–48.

3. Alan Wood, ed., *The History of Siberia* (London: Routledge, 1991) 11–12; Benson Bobrick, *East of the Sun* (New York: Poseidon Press, 1992) 269–308.

4. Wood, *History of Siberia*, 144–150, 159–160; Lincoln, *Conquest*, 257–262, 270–271, 281; Bobrick, *East of the Sun*, 378–381.

5. Alon Rachamimov, *POWs and the Great War* (Oxford: Berg, 2002) 108–110; George Kennan, *Soviet-American Relations 1917–1920: The Decision to Intervene* (Princeton: Princeton University Press, 1958) 71; Edward Heald, *Witness to Revolution* (Kent: The Kent State University Press, 1972) 90–91; Peter Pastor, ed., Gerald Davis, "The Life of Prisoners of War in Russia 1914–1921," *Essays on World War I* (New York, 1983) 176, 179. Ferenc Imrey, a Hungarian POW, performed a variety of work during his years as a POW in Siberia, including gold mining, artistry, theater production, firefighting and teaching. For some of the diverse tasks which he and other POWs did see his memoir, *Through Blood and Ice* (New York: E.P. Dutton & Company, 1930) 134.

6. The Young Men's Christian Association (YMCA) undertook humanitarian work in World War I by sending volunteers, or "secretaries," into the belligerent countries to provide educational and recreational diversions for POWs. During the Czecho-Slovak katabasis across Russia, a YMCA secretary traveled with each regiment and lived among the legionaries as fighting erupted along the span of the Trans-Siberian Railway. Affectionately referred to as "uncles" by the legionaries, the YMCA secretaries provided comforts to the soldiers through stocks of chocolates and toiletries. A Hungarian prisoner, Ferenc Imrey, who later wrote of his experiences in Siberian prison camps, had considerable praise for the YMCA missions: "This Y. M. C. A. later proved a tremendous boon in our lives and was the only organization, other than the Red Cross, that wrought any appreciable amelioration in our lot." Imrey, Ferenc, *Through Blood and Ice* (New York, 1930) pp. 225.

7. Quoted in Heald, *Witness to Revolution*, 91.

8. Kennan, *The Decision to Intervene*, 71.

9. Quoted in James Bunyan, *Intervention, Civil War and Communism in Russia* (New York: Octagon Books, 1976) 71.

10. Victor Fic, *The Bolsheviks and the Czechoslovak Legion* (New Delhi: Abhinav Publications, 1978) 142–144.

11. Wood, *History of Siberia*, 160–161.

12. The economic and political development of Siberia is discussed in Wood, *History of Siberia*, 159–163. The term *kulak*, as Richard Pipes points out, had wide interpretations. See *The Russian Revolution* (New York: Alfred A. Knopf, 1990) 728–730.

13. Wood, *History of Siberia,* 161–164; Jonathon Smele, *Civil War in Siberia* (New York: Cambridge University Press, 1996) 14–21.

14. James Morley, *The Japanese Thrust into Siberia 1918* (New York: Columbia University Press, 1957) 110–113; George Kennan, *Soviet-American Relations 1917–1920: Russia Leaves the War* (Princeton: Princeton University Press, 1956) 303–305.

15. For a glimpse into Harbin's nightlife during Rus-

sia's revolutionary period, see Carl Ackerman, *Trailing the Bolsheviki* (New York: Charles Scribner's Sons, 1919) 64.

16. Peter Fleming, *The Fate of Admiral Kolchak* (Edinburgh: Birlinn, 2001) p. 68.

17. Jamie Bisher, *White Terror* (New York: Routledge, 2005) 35, 42–52, 60–61, 70–74; Morley, *Japanese Thrust*, 97–98, 193–201, 258; Fleming, *Fate of Admiral Kolchak*, 47–52.

18. Smele, *Civil War*, 21–27; Fic, *Bolsheviks*, 317–318; Kennan, *Decision to Intervene*, 162.

19. Fic, *Bolsheviks*, 209–210.

20. Quoted in Fic, *Bolsheviks*, 237.

21. Fic, *Bolsheviks*, 239–240; Kalvoda, *Genesis*, 328–329.

22. Fic, *Bolsheviks*, 240–241; Bunyan, *Intervention*, 88–89.

23. Fic, *Bolsheviks*, 220–221.

24. *Ibid.* 216–217.

25. Pavlů had been an editor for the Young Czech organ *Národní Listy* prior to 1914. At war's outbreak, he was mobilized as a reserve officer in the Austro-Hungarian Army, captured in Galicia in September 1914 and then was among the few Czecho-Slovak POWs freed later that year. After his liberation from the POW system, he served a liberal Czecho-Slovak organization in Petrograd until joining the National Council in Russia in 1917.

26. Kalvoda, *Genesis*, 73; John Bradley, *The Czechoslovak Legion in Russia* (Boulder: East European Monographs, 1991) 110.

27. Fic, *Bolsheviks*, 250–257.

28. *Ibid.* 257–258; Bunyan, *Intervention*, 89–90.

29. Fic, *Bolsheviks*, 260–261; Bradley, *Czechoslovak Legion*, 87.

30. Bunyan, *Intervention*, 88; Bradley, *Czechoslovak Legion*, 86, Fic, *Bolsheviks*, 242.

31. Fic, *Bolsheviks*, 268; Bunyan, *Intervention*, 89.

32. Fic, *Bolsheviks*, 7.

33. *Ibid.* 267–273.

34. *Ibid.* 277–280.

35. Quoted in Paul Dotsenko, *The Struggle for a Democracy in Siberia 1917–1920* (Stanford: Hoover Institution Press, 1983) 27.

36. Fic, *Bolsheviks*, 280–281.

37. *Ibid.* 243.

38. Quoted in Bunyan, *Intervention*, 91.

39. Pipes, *Russian Revolution*, 611–612.

40. Fic, *Bolsheviks*, 265–286; Dotsenko, *Struggle for a Democracy*, 28–29.

41. Fic, *Bolsheviks*, 315–320.

42. Fic, *Bolsheviks*, 320–321; Smele, *Civil War*, 27.

43. Quoted in Fic, *Bolsheviks*, 321–322.

44. Pastor, *Essays on World War I*, 185; Fic, *Bolsheviks*, 322–325.

45. Orlando Figes, *Peasant Russia, Civil War* (Oxford: Clarendon Press, 1989) 156, 161.

46. Quoted in Bunyan, *Intervention*, 92.

47. Fic, *Bolsheviks*, 288–296; Bradley, *Czechoslovak Legion*, 93.

48. Fic, *Bolsheviks*, 332–337.

49. Ibid. 56.

50. Henry Baerlein, *The March of the Seventy Thousand* (London: Leonard Parsons, 1926) 113.

51. Kennan, *Decision to Intervene*, 417.

52. Baerlein, *Seventy Thousand*, 113–114.

53. Wood, *History of Siberia*, 39; Fleming, *Fate of Admiral Kolchak*, 184.

54. Fic, *Bolsheviks*, 156. Fic claims that the scheme to destroy the tunnels along the Circumbaikal route in the event of a Japanese or Allied invasion was a joint project between the Bolsheviks and Germany. While it was certainly within Germany's interests to prevent an Allied threat from materializing to its east, the evidence for this cooperation is lacking.

55. *Ibid.* 326–329; Kennan, *Decision to Intervene*, 283–285; Betty Miller Unterberger, *The United States, Revolutionary Russia and the Rise of Czechoslovakia* (Chapel Hill: The University of North Carolina Press, 1989) 182–183. Other accounts also claim that legionaries heard commands in German in their early fire-fights with Red troops and militia. The implication, of course, is that a substantial portion of the enemy was comprised of German POWs or under the command of German officers. See also Joan McGuire Mohr, *The Czech and Slovak Legion in Siberia, 1917–1922* (Jefferson: McFarland & Company, 2012) 75–76.

56. Kennan, *Decision to Intervene*, 285–286.

57. *Ibid.* 289–290.

58. Fic, *Bolsheviks*, 332–338.

59. *Ibid.* 325, 341–342.

60. Bradley, *Czechoslovak Legion*, 93.

61. Fic, *Bolsheviks*, 288–290, 303–307, 310.

62. *Ibid.* 308–309; Richard Goldhurst, *The Midnight War* (New York: McGraw-Hill Book Company, 1978) 41.

63. Ferenc Imrey, *Through Blood and Ice* (New York: E.P. Dutton & Company, 1930) 309.

64. Bradley, *Czechoslovak Legion*, 93–94.

65. Fic, *Bolsheviks*, 263–266.

66. *Ibid.* 286–288; Kennan, *Decision to Intervene*, 158–159; Kalvoda, *Genesis*, 345.

67. Kennan, *Decision to Intervene*, 156–157, 212. U.S. Ambassador Francis, in a report sent on 2 May, cited the supposed dictatorial authority of the German Ambassador in Moscow, Count Wilhelm von Mirbach, as a reason for Allied intervention in Russia.

68. Kennan, *Decision to Intervene*, 286–290; Unterberger, *Rise of Czechoslovakia*, 187–188.

69. Bradley, *Czechoslovak Legion*, 96–101; Kennan, *Decision to Intervene*, pp. 382–383; Kalvoda, *Genesis*, 347.

70. Bradley, *Czechoslovak Legion*, 84; Fic, *Bolsheviks*, 243–244, 296–297.

71. Figes, *Peasant Russia*, 159–164.

72. Quoted in Figes, *Peasant Russia*, 162–163.

73. Brushvit may have persuaded Čeček into supporting the Right SR insurrection in Samara by falsely claiming that his fellow conspirators were in contact with and supported by the French government. Due to

the poor communications in Russia, Čeček lacked any means to verify Brushvit's claim.

74. Figes, *Peasant Russia*, 163–164; Serge Petroff, *Remembering a Forgotten War* (Boulder: East European Monographs, 2000) 12.

75. Quoted in Kalvoda, *Genesis*, 344.

76. Figes, *Peasant Russia*, 164; Petroff, *Forgotten War*, 8–9.

77. Quoted in Petroff, *Forgotten War*, 9.

78. Figes, *Peasant Russia*, 164; Petroff, *Forgotten War*, 9.

79. Bunyan, *Intervention*, 280.

80. Figes, *Peasant Russia*, 167.

81. *Ibid.* 172–173.

82. Petroff, *Forgotten War*, 13–16.

83. Poor communications and the general lack of understanding of events occurring in Russia were only partly responsible for the confusion in the diplomatic missions, especially where the Americans were concerned. President Wilson, rather impractically, preferred to micromanage the Department of State and his country's foreign policy. He entrusted his ambassadors with little information, leaving them only to guess what at what U.S. policy might be. (See George Kennan, *Soviet-American Relations 1917–1920*, Vol. I, *Russia Leaves the War*, Princeton, 1956, pp. 28–29.) Consul Poole and Ambassador Francis, for example, assumed that the U.S. government was ready to intervene in Russia at a time when Wilson still opposed sending an Allied military expedition to Russia.

84. Kennan, *Decision to Intervene*, 295–317, 388.

85. Tomsk was the only Siberian center where the Whites succeeded in deposing the local soviet without direct Czecho-Slovak aid.

86. Fleming, *Fate of Admiral Kolchak*, 23; Evan Mawdsley, *The Russian Civil War* (New York: Pegasus, 2005) 102.

87. Unterberger, *Rise of Czechoslovakia*, 208; Becvar, *Lost Legion*, 104–114; Fic, *Bolsheviks*, 344.

88. Fic, *Bolsheviks*, 343

89. Quoted in Dotsenko, *Struggle for a Democracy*, 31.

90. *Ibid.* 31–32.

91. Becvar, *Lost Legion*, 124.

92. Fic, *Bolsheviks*, 243–245.

93. Unterberger, *Rise of Czechoslovakia*, 213.

94. Morley, *Japanese Thrust*, 247–250.

95. Unterberger, *Rise of Czechoslovakia*, 238–239; Bisher, *White Terror*, 91.

96. Kalvoda, *Genesis*, 365.

97. Heald, *Witness to Revolution*, 217–218. Lieutenant Colonel John Ward, who led the British 25th Battalion of the Middlesex Regiment into Siberia about a month later, also wrote of Bolshevik atrocities against legionaries captured in the Nikolsk battle. John Ward, *With the "Die-Hards" in Siberia* (London: Cassell and Company, 1920) 8–9.

98. Carol Wilcox Melton, *Between War and Peace* (Macon: Mercer University Press, 2001) 25.

99. Morley, *Japanese Thrust*, 252.

100. *Ibid.* 254–257.

101. Reliable estimates of the number of men the Bolsheviks fielded on the Ussuri lines are difficult to come by. General Diterikhs, according to British Lieutenant Colonel John Ward, put the strength of enemy forces on that front as high as 20,000 men.

102. Ward, *With the "Die-Hards,"* 4–52; Heald, *Witness to Revolution*, 228–230 Baerlein, *Seventy Thousand*, 185.

103. Bisher, *White Terror*, 104.

104. Kennan, *Decision to Intervene*, 401–402; Peter Pastor, "Hungarian POWs in Russia during the Revolution and Civil War," *Essays on World War I*, 155–156; Fic, *Bolsheviks*, 144.

105. The Allied commanders on the Ussuri front claimed that their Red opponents were professionally led by German and Austro-Hungarian officers from the prison camps. Of course, many of them probably have exaggerated the German and Austro-Hungarian involvement to help justify the intervention.

106. Unterberger, *Rise of Czechoslovakia*, 238–239; Ward, *With the "Die-Hards,"* 5.

107. Fic, *Bolsheviks*, 310; Baerlein, *Seventy Thousand*, 136–137, 151–152.

108. Quoted in V. H. Rothwell, *British War Aims and Peace Diplomacy 1914–1918* (Oxford: Clarendon Press, 1971) 109.

109. Kennan, *Decision to Intervene*, 345, 353.

Chapter 11

1. The figure of 500,000 Czech and 280,000 Slovak immigrants living in the U.S. at the outbreak of World War I is conservative and is used by Zbyněk Zeman in *The Masaryks* (London: Weidenfeld and Nicolson, 1976) 109 and Josef Kalvoda in *The Genesis of Czechoslovakia* (Boulder: East European Monographs, 1986) 68. Others have given much higher estimates, such as the 1,500,000 Czech and Slovak immigrants used by Betty Miller Unterberger in *The United States, Revolutionary Russia and the Rise of Czechoslovakia* (Chapel Hill: The University of North Carolina Press, 1989) 7 and Nancy Gentile Ford in *Americans All!* (College Station: Texas A&M University Press, 2001) 27.

2. Unterberger, *Rise of Czechoslovakia*, 24; Ford, *Americans All!* 27–28.

3. Beneš, *My War Memoirs*, trans. Paul Selver (New York: Houghton Mifflin Company, 1928) 98–100; Unterberger, *Rise of Czechoslovakia*, 24.

4. Kalvoda, *Genesis*, 69–70; Ford, *Americans All!* 27–28.

5. Ford, *Americans All!* 17–21.

6. Beneš, *War Memoirs*, 50–53; Tomáš Masaryk, *The Making of a State* (New York: Frederick A. Stokes Company, 1927) 74–76; Ford, *Americans All!* 28.

7. Kalvoda, *Genesis*, 51.

8. Michael Sanders and Philip Taylor, *British Propaganda during the First World War 1914–18* (London: The Macmillan Press, 1982) 178–179; Kenneth

Calder, *Britain and the Origins of the New Europe* (New York: Cambridge University Press, 1976) 51.

9. Kalvoda, *Genesis*, 54–56; Calder, *Britain*, 51; Henry Baerlein, *The March of the Seventy Thousand* (London: Leonard Parsons, 1926) 3–16; Sanders and Taylor, *British Propaganda*, 182–183; Barbara Tuchman, *The Zimmerman Telegram* (New York: Bantam Books, 1958) 70–72, 81–84.

10. Kalvoda, *Genesis*, 51.

11. George Kennan, *Soviet-American Relations 1917–1920: Russia Leaves the War* (Princeton: Princeton University Press, 1956) 176–177; Unterberger, *Rise of Czechoslovakia*, 26; Kalvoda, *Genesis*, 51–52.

12. Unterberger, *Rise of Czechoslovakia*, 47–48; Beneš, *War Memoirs*, 119.

13. Victor Mamatey, *The United States and East Central Europe 1914–1918* (Princeton: Princeton University Press, 1957) 41–42.

14. Quoted in Mamatey, *The United States*, 49.

15. *Ibid.* 49–51.

16. George Goldberg, *The Peace to End Peace* (New York: Harcourt, Brace & World, 1969) 12.

17. Mamatey, *The United States*, 56–62, 213–215.

18. Quoted in Mamatey, *The United States*, 179–180.

19. Mamatey, *The United States*, 214–215.

20. Unterberger, *Rise of Czechoslovakia*, 93.

21. Kennan, *Russia Leaves the War*, 140.

22. Unterberger, *Rise of Czechoslovakia*, 67, 96–97.

23. Mamatey, *The United States*, 214–215.

24. George Kennan, *Soviet-American Relations: The Decision to Intervene* (Princeton: Princeton University Press, 1958) 361. Masaryk's cause was further aided by the fact that at this time Charles Crane's son, Richard, served as secretary to Secretary of State Robert Lansing. Later, Richard Crane served as the first U.S. minister to Czechoslovakia. See also: Mamatey, *The United States*, 281.

25. The precise reasons as to why Wilson continuously postponed meeting with Masaryk remain speculative. Both Josef Kalvoda and Victor Mamatey assert that Masaryk's "soft" attitude towards the Bolsheviks after leaving Russia in the spring 1918 made him suspect in official Washington. See Kalvoda, *Genesis*, 276–279, 289, 294 and Mamatey, *The United States*, 280–281. This thesis is supported by Robert Seton-Watson who reprinted Masaryk's assessments and concluded that at the time they "were too strong meat even for his friends in London, still more for the official world for which they were intended." Robert Seton-Watson, *Masaryk in England* (Cambridge: Cambridge University Press, 1943) 103–112.

26. Kennan, *Decision to Intervene*, 382, Unterberger, *Rise of Czechoslovakia*, 126.

27. Holger Herwig, *The First World War* (London: Arnold, 1997) 415.

28. Kennan, *Decision to Intervene*, 357–358.

29. V. H. Rothwell, *British War Aims and Peace Diplomacy 1914–1918* (Oxford: Clarendon Press, 1971) 185–190; Kennan, *Decision to Intervene*, 382–384.

30. Mamatey, *The United States*, 290.

31. Kennan, *Decision to Intervene*, 381–386. General March and most U.S. commanders were "Westerners," a label given to strategists who were convinced that the conflict would be decided on the Western Front and therefore all military resources must be concentrated there. During most of the war, the British Imperial General Staff agreed with this assessment. Opposing them were those who preferred a formula of achieving greater territorial gains with fewer casualties by attacking on other fronts, such as in Italy, the Balkans, the Middle East or Russia. The most prominent advocates for this strategy were Winston Churchill and David Lloyd George. See also Rothwell, *British War Aims*, 7; Mamatey, *The United States*, 73–74.

32. Kennan, *Decision to Intervene*, 292–293.

33. Unterberger, *Rise of Czechoslovakia*, 131.

34. *Ibid.* 222–224; Kennan, *Decision to Intervene*, 361, 388.

35. Zbyněk Zeman, *The Masaryks* (London: Weidenfeld and Nicolson, 1976) 111–112.

36. Unterberger, *Rise of Czechoslovakia*, 222–224; Kalvoda, *Genesis*, 298–300. Contact between Masaryk and Wilson remained limited to few more meetings, telegrams and memoranda exchanged between the men or their secretaries. Their relationship was never as close or collaborative as depicted by some chroniclers, principally Edmund von Glaise-Horstenau, who depicted the Czech professor as Wilson's advisor on Central European affairs. See Edmund von Glaise-Horstenau, trans. Ian F. D. Morrow, *The Collapse of the Austro-Hungarian Empire* (London: J.M. Dent and Sons, 1930) 219–221.

37. Beneš, *War Memoirs*, 393.

38. *Ibid.* 359, 368.

39. Zeman, *Masaryks*, 113.

40. Unterberger, *Rise of Czechoslovakia*, 224–228. Mamatey, *The United States*, 286–287; Kalvoda, *Genesis*, 372–374. Lansing thought this cable to the Soviet Commissar of Foreign Affairs, Georgey Chicherin, was ridiculous and only permitted Masaryk to send it using his own funds.

41. Kennan, *Decision to Intervene*, 391–392, 395. On 25 June 1918, the same day as the Lansing-Masaryk meeting, the State Department requested a military assessment of the Czecho-Slovak Legion from the U.S. Consul in Vladivostok.

42. *Ibid.* 395–398.

43. *Ibid.* 405–408; James Morley, *The Japanese Thrust into Siberia* (New York: Columbia University Press, 1957) 277–299; Unterberger, *Rise of Czechoslovakia*, 252.

44. Mamatey, *The United States*, 301.

45. Masaryk, *Making of a State*, 276.

46. Beneš, *War Memoirs*, 116.

47. Unterberger, *Rise of Czechoslovakia*, 251.

48. Beneš, *War Memoirs*, 266–267.

49. In this meeting, the French wanted the Supreme War Council go further by declaring its support for liberation of Czecho-Slovaks and Yugoslavs but the motion was blocked by Sonnino who continued to adhere

to his anti–Yugoslav policy. Although the British did not object to the proposed resolution, they were probably relieved by Sonnino's intransigence. Five days earlier, on 28 May 1918, Lloyd George and Lord Cecil both turned down a suggestion made by the French Foreign Minister, Stephane Pichon, to include the independence of the Poles and Czechs in official Allied war aims. The reason for British opposition, according to Lloyd George, was simply out of the consideration that "the allies must not give pledges that they could not realize." See Rothwell, V. H., *British War Aims and Peace Diplomacy 1914–1918* (Oxford, 1971), pp. 224–225.

50. Calder, *Britain*, 197.

51. Calder, *Britain*, 194; Beneš, *War Memoirs*, 372–376.

52. Beneš, *War Memoirs*, 385–389.

53. *Ibid*. 402–407; Calder, *Britain*, 204–210.

54. Calder, *Britain*, 210–211. In the words of Lord Robert Cecil, "Our recognition of the Czechs was carefully worded and though it would undoubtedly be consistent with the dismemberment of Austria it does not in fact bind us to that solution." Quoted in Rothwell, *British War Aims*, 228.

55. Quoted in Zeman, *Masaryks*, 110 and Kalvoda, *Genesis*, 370.

56. Unterberger, *Rise of Czechoslovakia*, 268–270.

57. *Ibid*. 272, 278–279.

58. Quoted in Kalvoda, *Genesis*, 396–400; Unterberger, *Rise of Czechoslovakia*, 279–280.

59. Unterberger, *Rise of Czechoslovakia*, 281–282.

60. Mamatey, *The United States*, 133–134; 162.

61. Kalvoda, *Genesis*, 389; 403–404; Unterberger, *Rise of Czechoslovakia*, 284–287; Beneš, *War Memoirs*, 414.

62. Quoted in Kalvoda, *Genesis*, 404.

63. Gustav Becvar, *The Lost Legion* (London: Stanley Paul & Company, 1939) 114, 117–130. The assistance which railway personnel provided to the legionnaires is mentioned in Baerlein, *Seventy Thousand*, 135. Other sources mention strikes initiated by the railway workers against the Soviet regime and deliberate sabotage of Soviet defensive measures along the railway: James Bunyan, *Intervention, Civil War and Communism in Russia* (New York: Octagon Books, 1976) 162–167; Paul Dotsenko, *The Struggle for Democracy in Siberia* (Stanford: Hoover Institution Press, 1983) 29, 32.

64. John Albert White, *The Siberian Intervention* (Princeton: Princeton University Press, 1950) 93; Becvar, *Lost Legion*, 133–134.

65. *Ibid*. 136–138; Baerlein, *Seventy Thousand*, 166–171.

66. Baerlein, *Seventy Thousand*, 166–171; Becvar, *Lost Legion*, 140–142; Richard Goldhurst, *The Midnight War* (New York: McGraw-Hill Book Company, 1978) 64–70; Jamie Bisher, *White Terror* (New York: Routledge, 2005) p. 82.

67. Becvar, *Lost Legion*, 146.

68. Ferenc Imrey, *Through Blood and Ice* (New York: E.P. Dutton & Company, 1930) 297–298.

69. Becvar, *Lost Legion*, 148–150, Baerlein, *Seventy Thousand*, 172–177; White, *Siberian Intervention*, 253; Bisher, *White Terror*, 82–84; Goldhurst, *Midnight War*, 68.

70. William Graves, *America's Siberian Adventure* (New York: Peter Smith, 1941) 55–56; Kennan, *Decision to Intervene*, 414.

71. Bisher, *White Terror*, 98–100; Baerlein, *Seventy Thousand*, 185–186; John Ward, *With the "Die-Hards" in Siberia* (London: Cassell and Company, 1920) 5–52.

72. White, *Siberian Intervention*, 93.

73. Kennan, *Decision to Intervene*, 414–415.

74. Becvar, *Lost Legion*, 158.

75. White, *Siberian Intervention*, 194–195, Goldhurst, *Midnight War*, 109, 118–119.

76. Bisher, *White Terror*, 85–90, White, *Siberian Intervention*, 195.

77. Ward, *With the "Die Hards,"* 7, 79–83.

78. Serge Petroff, *Remembering a Forgotten War* (Boulder: East European Monographs, 2000) 55; Baerlein, *Seventy Thousand*, 29.

79. Evan Mawdsley, *The Russian Civil War* (New York: Pegasus, 2007) 64, 70.

80. Orlando Figes, *Peasant Russia, Civil War* (Oxford: Clarendon Press, 1989) 167.

81. Petroff, *Forgotten War*, 13.

82. Orlando Figes, *A People's Tragedy* (New York: Viking, 1997) 579; Figes, *Peasant Russia*, 171–174; Mawdsley, *Russian Civil War*, 64–65.

83. Figes, *People's Tragedy*, 580.

84. Figes, *Peasant Russia*, 173–178; Mawdsley, *Russian Civil War*, 64–65; Petroff, *Forgotten War*, 57–59; Figes, *People's Tragedy*, 581–582.

85. Petroff, *Forgotten War*, 75–77; Mawdsley, *Russian Civil War*, 58–59.

86. Peter Pastor, Ivo Banac, "South Slav Prisoners of War in Revolutionary Russia," *Essays in World War I* (New York: Brooklyn College Press, 1983) 137.

87. Goldhurst, *Midnight War*, 62–63.

88. Figes, *People's Tragedy*, 580–581; Petroff, *Forgotten War*, 77; Mawdsley, *Russian Civil War*, 57–59.

89. Bunyan, *Intervention*, 271–272; Mawdsley, *Russian Civil War*, 47, 61; Petroff, *Forgotten War*, 55–56.

90. Mawdsley, *Russian Civil War*, 66–67.

91. Leon Trotsky, *My Life* (New York: Charles Scribner's Sons, 1930) 396.

92. *Ibid*. 397–407; Isaac Deutscher, *The Prophet Armed* (New York: Oxford University Press, 1954) 419–420; Bunyan, *Intervention*, 301.

93. Figes, *People's Tragedy*, 582; Figes, *Peasant Russia*, 178–181.

94. Jonathon Smele, *Civil War in Siberia* (New York: Cambridge University Press, 1996) 29–37; Bunyan, *Intervention*, 333–337.

95. Kalvoda, *Genesis*, 394; John Bradley, *The Czechoslovak Legion in Russia 1914–1920* (Boulder: East European Monographs, 1991) 103, 110–111; Baerlein, *Seventy Thousand*, 68–72.

96. Clifford Kinvig, *Churchill's Crusade* (London: Hambledon Continuum, 2006) 33–49; Goldhurst, *Midnight War*, 88.

97. Bunyan, *Intervention*, 111; Unterberger, *Rise of Czechoslovakia*, 267, 292; Kennan, *Decision to Intervene*, 425–427.

98. Trotsky, *My Life*, 402–403; Bunyan, *Intervention*, 301.

99. Marina Yurlova, *Cossack Girl* (New York: The Macaulay Company, 1934) 245.

100. Mawdsley, *Russian Civil War*, 67–68.

101. Smele, *Civil War*, 29–37; Bunyan, *Intervention*, 333–337.

102. Quoted in John Silverlight, *The Victor's Dilemma* (New York: Weybright and Talley, 1970) 80.

103. Smele, *Civil War*, 45–50; Mawdsley, *Russian Civil War*, 104–107, N. G. O. Pereira, *White Siberia* (London: McGill-Queen's University Press, 1996) 93–96.

104. Bunyan, *Intervention*, 338; Smele, *Civil War*, 42–44, 80–83; Pereira, *White Siberia*, 95, 100–101.

105. Figes, *Peasant Russia*, 182–184; Mawdsley, *Russian Civil War*, 68.

106. Goldhurst, *Midnight War*, 118–119.

Chapter 12

1. Mark Cornwall, *The Undermining of Austria-Hungary* (London: Macmillan Press, 2000) 153, 205, 258, 406–409; Zbyněk Zeman, *The Break-Up of the Habsburg Empire 1914–1918* (London: Oxford University Press, 1961) 139–143; Edmund von Glaise-Horstenau, *The Collapse of the Austro-Hungarian Empire*, trans. Ian F. D. Morrow (London: J.M. Dent and Sons, 1930) 162–163.

2. John Wheeler-Bennett, *Brest-Litovsk: The Forgotten Peace* (New York: Norton, 1971) 315–316; Arthur May, *The Passing of the Hapsburg Monarchy* (Philadelphia: University of Pennsylvania Press, 1966) 625–626; Mark Cornwall, ed., Rudolf Jeřábek, "The Eastern Front," *The Last Years of Austria-Hungary* (Exeter: University of Exeter Press, 2002) 161.

3. Glaise-Horstenau, *Collapse*, 234–235.

4. Holger Herwig, *The First World War* (London: Arnold, 1997) 365.

5. Alon Rachamimov, *POWs and the Great War* (Oxford: Berg 2002) 39–40, 192–194; Gunther Rothenberg, *The Army of Francis Joseph* (West Lafayette: Purdue University Press, 1976) 211; Zeman, *Break-up*, 142–143; Cornwall, *Undermining*, 269–270.

6. Maureen Healy, *Vienna and the Fall of the Habsburg Empire* (Cambridge: Cambridge University Press, 2004) 61–62.

7. H. Louis Rees, *The Czechs During World War I* (Boulder: East European Monographs, 1992) 86, 111; Zeman, *Break-up*, 142.

8. May, *Passing*, 664–669.

9. Rees, *Czechs*, 78–80.

10. *Ibid.* 91–94; Zeman, *Break-up*, 173–174, 179–181.

11. Rees, *Czechs*, 94–96.

12. Zeman, *Break-up*, 146; Rees, *Czechs*, 85–90.

13. Quoted in Rees, *Czechs*, 100.

14. Rees, *Czechs*, 101–103; Tomáš Masaryk, *The Making of a State*, trans. Henry Wickham Steed (New York: Frederick A. Stokes Company, 1927) 217, Josef Kalvoda, *The Genesis of Czechoslovakia* (Boulder: East European Monographs, 1986) p. 256.

15. Edmond Taylor, *The Fall of the Dynasties* (New York: Doubleday, 1963) 274, 343–344.

16. Zeman, *Break-up*, 161–162.

17. Taylor, *Dynasties*, 344.

18. Edvard Beneš, *My War Memoirs* trans. Paul Selver (New York: Houghton Mifflin Company, 1928) 338; Rees, *Czechs*, 104.

19. Taylor, *Dynasties*, 344; Kalvoda, *Genesis*, 267. In *British War Aims and Peace Diplomacy 1914–1918* (Oxford: Clarendon Press, 1971) 221–222, V. H. Rothwell offers a few reactions in Britain to news of the Spa agreement. For instance, at the end of May 1918 Foreign Secretary Balfour alerted his country's envoy to Washington that the "policy of trying to detach Austria from Germany *at present time* seems to us both inopportune and impracticable."

20. Rees, *Czechs*, 115–116; Victor Mamatey and Radomír Luža, ed., *A History of the Czechoslovak Republic 1918–1948* (Princeton: Princeton University Press, 1973) 22; Mark Cornwall, "Disintegration and Defeat: The Austro-Hungarian Revolution," *The Last Years of Austria-Hungary* (Exeter: University of Exeter Press, 2002) 188–189; Kalvoda, *Genesis*, 265.

21. Klofáč's Czech National Socialist Party had recently renamed itself the Czech Socialist Party.

22. Rees, *Czechs*, 25, 116–117; Robert Kann, Béla Király and Paula Fichtner, ed., Victor Mamatey, "The Union of Czech Political Parties in the Reichsrat 1916–1918," *The Habsburg Empire in World War I* (New York, 1977) 10, 23.

23. Zeman, *Break-up*, 180–181.

24. Beneš, *War Memoirs*, 387–389.

25. May, *Passing*, 661; Cornwall, *Last Years*, 190. Seidler had never wanted the job of Austria's prime minister and only agreed to serve as a stop-gap until a more permanent replacement was found.

26. Rees, *Czechs*, 119–121.

27. Kann, et al. *Habsburg Empire*, 22; Taylor, *Dynasties*, 344.

28. Wiktor Sukiennicki, *East Central Europe during World War I* (Boulder: East European Monographs, 1984) 284–301, 333–334, 397; David Stefancic, "Piłsudski's Polish Legions," Joseph Hapak, "The Polish Army in France," *Armies in Exile* (Boulder: East European Monographs, 2005) 104–115, 130–131; Cornwall, *Last Years*, 190.

29. Rothenberg, *Army*, 208–209.

30. Holger Herwig, *The First World War* (London: Arnold, 1997) 365, 370–373; Rothenberg, *Army*, 213–214; Jan Triska, *The Great War's Forgotten Front* (Boulder: East European Monographs, 1998) 82–92, 99.

31. Herwig, *First World War*, 416–417. One U.S. division contained 40,000 men, meaning that they were two to three times larger than European divisions at this

time. Robert Ferrell, *Woodrow Wilson and World War I, 1917–1921* (New York: Harper & Row, 1985) 52.

32. Ferrell, *Wilson and World War I*, 53; John Keegan, *The First World War* (New York: Vintage Books, 1998) 409–410.

33. On 2 July 1918 the Supreme War Council was handed a memorandum pressing for Allied intervention in Russia since without it there would be "the smallest chance of an Allied victory on the western front in 1919." Bunyan, James, *Intervention, Civil War and Communism in Russia* (New York: Octagon Books, 1976) p. 105. In his memoir, Masaryk indicates that the expectation that the war would persist into 1919 was prevalent. Masaryk, *Making of a State*, 289

34. Quoted in Peter Toma and Dušan Kováč, *Slovakia* (Stanford: Hoover Institution Press, 2001) 59–60.

35. *Ibid.* 57–61.

36. *Ibid.* 52–63.

37. Masaryk, *Making of a State*, 220–223.

38. *Ibid.* 245.

39. Zeman, *Break-up*, 197.

40. Masaryk, *Making of a State*, 251–252.

41. *Ibid.* 86–87.

42. *Ibid.* 250–251, 255; Victor Mamatey, *The United States and East Central Europe* (Princeton: Princeton University Press, 1957) 316–317.

43. Masaryk, *Making of a State*, 255; Mamatey, *The United States*, 341–343, 346.

44. Zeman, *Break-up*, 221.

45. Rees, *Czechs*, 122; Mamatey and Luža, *Czechoslovak Republic*, 23–24.

46. Alan Palmer, *The Gardeners of Salonika* (New York: Simon and Schuster, 1965) 199–230.

47. Taylor, *Dynasties*, 345; May, *Passing*, 764–766.

48. May, *Passing*, 769–772; Zeman, *Break-up*, 222.

49. Rees, *Czechs*, 123; Zeman, *Break-up*, 223.

50. May, *Passing* 769–772; Zeman, *Break-up*, 222.

51. Masaryk, *Making of a State*, 294; Kalvoda, *Genesis*, 424.

52. Kalvoda, *Genesis*, 421. Britain, unlike France, did not recognize the Czecho-Slovak provisional government and refused to commit any further to the Czecho-Slovak cause during the war. See Kenneth Calder, *Britain and the Origins of the New Europe* (New York: Cambridge University Press, 1976) 211. For Beneš, the continued postponement of a scheduled "congress of oppressed nationalities" in Paris may have added to his concerns that the Allies were in the process of negotiating a peace with Vienna, causing him to suddenly upgrade the National Council into a provisional government. The congress never met, not because the Allies were in talks with Austria-Hungary, but rather due to Italian efforts to halt the progress of the national movements, particularly that of the Yugoslavs. See Glaise-Horstenau, *Collapse*, 217; Cornwall, *Undermining*, 325–330.

53. The Czech delegation to Geneva comprised of seven men total; five politicians and two financial experts. Besides Kramář and Klofáč, the politicians included František Staněk (Agrarian), Gustav Habrman

(Czech Social Democrat) and Antonín Kalina (State's Right Democrat). See Zeman, Zbyněk, *The Break-Up of the Habsburg Empire 1914–1918* (London, 1961) p. 221.

54. Glaise-Horstenau, *Collapse*, 261–262; Kalvoda, *Genesis*, 427.

55. Zeman, Zbyněk Zeman and Antonín Klimek, *The Life of Edvard Beneš 1884–1948* (Oxford: Clarendon Press, 1997) 34–35.

56. Beneš, *War Memoirs*, 440–445; Mamatey, *Czechoslovak Republic*, 26–27.

57. Rees, *Czechs*, 123; Zeman, *Break-Up*, 223.

58. *Ibid.* 226.

59. May, *Passing*, 766–767, 795–796; Zeman, *Break-Up*, 226–227; Taylor, *Dynasties*, 346.

60. Zeman, *Break-Up*, 227; Peter Pastor, ed., *Márton Farkas, "The Military Collapse of the Austro-Hungarian Monarchy," War and Society in East Central Europe: Revolutions and Interventions in Hungary and Its Neighboring States 1918–1919* (Boulder: East European Monographs, 1988) Volume 20, 19.

61. Palmer, *Gardners of Salonika*, 230–235.

62. Rothenberg, *Army*, 217–218; Mark Thompson, *The White War* (New York: Basic Books, 2009) 354–360; May, *Passing*, 798–799.

63. Kann et al., Gunther Rothenberg, "The Habsburg Army in the First World War 1914–1918," *The Habsburg Empire in World War I*, 82.

64. Zeman, *Break-Up*, 227.

65. *Ibid.* 227–228; Taylor, *Dynasties*, 346–347; Glaise-Horstenau, *Collapse*, 264–266.

66. Glaise-Horstenau, *Collapse*, 267–268; Zeman, *Break-Up*, 228–230.

67. Sukiennicki, *East Central Europe*, 832–834; Taylor, *Dynasties*, 351–352; Mamatey and Luža, *Czechoslovak Republic*, 24.

68. May, *Passing*, 793–795; Glaise-Horstenau, *Collapse*, 325.

69. Zeman, *Break-Up*, 244–245; May, *Passing*, 781–784; Cornwall, *Last Years*, 145.

70. Sukiennicki, *East Central Europe*, 832–851.

71. May, *Passing*, 781–784; Timothy Snyder, *The Reconstruction of Nations* (New Haven: Yale University Press, 2003) 138; Taylor, *Dynasties*, 350–351; Mamateya and Luža, *Czechoslovak Republic*, 27.

72. Toma and Kováč, *Slovakia*, 62–66; Zeman, *Break-Up*, 230–231, Mamatey and Luža, *Czechoslovak Republic*, 30–31.

73. Rothenberg, *Army*, 217–218; Herwig, *First World War*, 437.

74. Alan Sked, *The Decline and Fall of the Habsburg Empire 1815–1918* (New York: Dorset Press, 1989) 260–261.

75. Mamatey, *Czechoslovak Republic*, 31.

76. *Ibid.* 22–23; Toma and Kováč, *Slovakia*, 60.

77. Quoted in Zeman and Klimek, *Beneš*, 35. See also Kalvoda, *Genesis*, 455.

78. Hoffmann, *War Diaries and Other Papers* (London: Martin Secker, 1929) 163; Taylor, *Dynasties*, 352–354.

79. Zeman and Klimek, *Beneš*, 35–36; Margaret MacMillan, *Paris 1919* (New York: Random House, 2001) 231.

80. Zbyněk Zeman, *The Masaryks* (London: Weidenfeld and Nicolson, 1976) 116.

81. *Ibid.* 73, 172; Masaryk, *Making of a State*, 48.

82. For Masaryk's comments on the Young Czechs, see Tomáš Masaryk, *The Meaning of Czech History*, trans. Peter Kussi (Chapel Hill: The University of North Carolina Press, 1974) pp. 88–89.

83. Masaryk, *Making of a State*, 311–313; Henry Wickham Steed, *Through Thirty Years 1892–1922* (New York: Doubleday, Page & Company, 1924) 260–261.

84. In December 1914, the Serbian Prime Minister Nikola Pašić, announced "the liberation and union of... Serbs, Croats and Slovenes" as one of his government's war aims. Of course, the centralized unity under Serbia that Pašić had in mind differed considerably from the federalized Yugoslavia envisaged by Ante Trumbić and other South Slav exiles.

85. Mamatey, *The United States*, 22–23, 34–37.

86. The plight of the Poles, who lost their independence at the end of the eighteenth century, had long attracted the sympathies of the West.

87. Sukiennicki, *East Central Europe*, 11; Mike Rapport, *1848* (New York: Basic Books, 2009) 125.

88. Quoted in Hugh Seton-Watson and Christopher Seton-Watson, *The Making of a New Europe* (London: Methuen & Company, 1981) 320.

89. Quoted in Paul Selver, *Masaryk* (Westport: Greenwood Press, 1975) 295.

Chapter 13

1. Richard Goldhurst, *The Midnight War* (New York: McGraw-Hill Book Company, 1978) 132–133.

2. Gustav Becvar, *The Lost Legion* (London: Stanley Paul & Company, 1939) 189.

3. Peter Pastor, ed., Josef Kalvoda, "Czech and Slovak Prisoners of War in Russia during the War and Revolution"; Ivo Banac, "South Slav Prisoners of War in Revolutionary Russia," *Essays on World War I* (Boulder: East European Monographs, 1983) 137, 225.

4. Quoted in Edward Heald, *Witness to Revolution* (Kent: The Kent State University Press, 1972) 211.

5. Josef Kalvoda, *The Genesis of Czechoslovakia* (Boulder: East European Monographs, 1986) 405.

6. Even though they were often thousands of miles away from Central Europe, many Czech and Slovak deserters nonetheless hoped to ultimately return to their homeland. The great distances involved were far from the only obstacle they faced. The Russian countryside was in upheaval and they had to dodge partisans, Red and White troops in contested areas. Remarkably, a few deserters, traveling either singly or in small bands, managed to reach their destinations in the new Czechoslovak state after hazardous journeys that took months or even years. It may be surmised, however, that many deserters never made it home. See Mohr, Joan McGuire, *The Czech and Slovak Legion in Siberia, 1917–1922* (Jefferson, 2012) p. 157.

7. Serge Petroff, *Remembering a Forgotten War* (Boulder: East European Monographs, 2000) 106; John Bradley, *The Czechoslovak Legion in Russia 1914–1920* (Boulder, East European Monographs, 1991) 104, Henry Baerlein, *The March of the Seventy Thousand* (London: Leonard Parsons, 1926) 192–195.

8. Petroff, *Forgotten War*, 106–109.

9. Winston Churchill, *The World Crisis 1918–1928: The Aftermath* (New York: Charles Scribner's Sons, 1929) 256.

10. Bradley, *Czechoslovak Legion*, 124–125.

11. Baerlein, *Seventy Thousand*, 197; Bradley, *Czechoslovak Legion*, 116.

12. General Janin may have been able to reach Siberia much sooner had he not insisted on meeting with heads of state in Washington and Tokyo amid his journey.

13. Bradley, *Czechoslovak Legion*, 124–125; Carol Wilcox Melton, *Between War and Peace* (Macon: Mercer University Press, 2001) 220.

14. Jonathon Smele, *Civil War in Siberia* (New York: Cambridge University Press, 1996) 50–60; N. G. O. Pereira, *White Siberia* (Montreal: McGill-Queen's University Press, 1996) 65–66; Paul Dotsenko, *The Struggle for a Democracy in Siberia 1917–1920* (Stanford: Hoover Institution Press, 1983) 52; Bradley, *Czechoslovak Legion*, 114–115.

15. Quoted in Dotsenko, *Struggle for Democracy*, 61.

16. The Varangian Guard was an elite group of Viking mercenaries employed as bodyguards to the Byzantine emperors during the Middle Ages.

17. Smele, *Civil War*, 102–109; Peter Fleming, *The Fate of Admiral Kolchak* (Edinburgh: Birlinn, 2001) 99, 109–111.

18. Smele, *Civil War*, 54, 60.

19. *Ibid.* 102–109; Fleming, *Admiral Kolchak*, 99, 109–111.

20. Smele, *Civil War*, 62–68; Fleming, *Admiral Kolchak*, 33–32.

21. Smele, *Civil War*, 72–75.

22. Ward's boastful account of the 25th Battalion's deployment in Omsk only fueled allegations that the Kolchak coup was engineered by the British. He wrote that at the conference held on the morning of 18 November 1918 "The Council of Ministers, and perhaps Koltchak himself, were unable to take the final plunge until they had a thorough understanding of the British attitude." Later, however, he assures the reader that the Council's decision to appoint Kolchak to the dictatorship "was entirely their own." See Ward, John, *With the "Die-Hards" in Siberia* (London, 1920) pp. 129–130.

23. John Ward, *With the "Die-Hards" in Siberia* (London: Cassell and Company, 1920) 128–145; Clifford Kinvig, *Churchill's Crusade* (London: Hambledon Continuum, 2006) 68–71.

24. John Silverlight, *The Victors' Dilemma* (New York: Weybright and Talley, 1970) 81–82.

25. Smele, *Civil War*, 120.

26. Quoted in Smele, *Civil War*, 195.

27. Smele, *Civil War*, 195–196.

28. Goldhurst, *Midnight War*, 119; Becvar, *Lost Legion*, 185, 190–191.

29. Quoted in Smele, *Civil War*, 197.

30. Quoted in Silverlight, *Victors' Dilemma*, 235.

31. Smele, *Civil War*, 197.

32. Ward, *With the "Die-Hards,"* 1–3; Kinvig, *Churchill's Crusade*, 56, 207–208.

33. Becvar, *Lost Legion*, 186–187. For the British point of view of this almost comical attempt to raise morale among frontline troops, see John Ward's *With the "Die-Hards" in Siberia*, 115–122.

34. Becvar, *Lost Legion*, 175, 186, 204.

35. Kalvoda, *Genesis*, 408.

36. Richard Pipes, *The Russian Revolution* (New York: Alfred A. Knopf, 1990) 65.

37. Pipes, *Russian Revolution*, 69–71; John Thompson, *Russia, Bolshevism and the Versailles Peace* (Princeton: Princeton University Press, 1966) 11–13; Silverlight, *Victors' Dilemma*, 86.

38. Thompson, *Russia, Bolshevism*, 12; Silverlight, *Victors' Dilemma*, 117, 148–149, 186–187, 199–207; Kinvig, *Churchill's Crusade*, 130–133; R. Ernest Dupuy, *Perish by the Sword* (Harrisburg: The Military Publishing Company, 1939) 171; Bradley, *Allied Intervention in Russia* (New York: Basic Books, 1968) 136, 150; Peter Pastor, ed., Theofanis Stavrou, "Greek Participation and the French Army Intervention in the Ukraine," Kim Munholland, "The French Army and Intervention in the Ukraine," *War and Society in East Central Europe: Revolutions and Interventions in Hungary and Its Neighbor States 1918–1919* (New York, 1988) Volume 20, 321–330, 335–353.

39. Quoted in Silverlight, *Victors' Dilemma*, 205.

40. Thompson, *Russia, Bolshevism,* 51–52.

41. Silverlight, *Victors' Dilemma*, 117, 199–207; Bradley, *Allied Intervention*, 136, 150; Pastor, *Revolutions and Interventions*, 321–330, 335–353.

42. Becvar, *Lost Legion*, 115.

43. Jamie Bisher, *White Terror* (New York: Routledge, 2005) 83; Pipes, *Russian Revolution*, 816–822.

44. Bisher, *White Terror*, 114, 163–166.

45. *Ibid.* 116, 123, 127–130. General Graves wrote that Semenov, the stronger of the two rogue atamans, "could not have existed one week in Siberia" without Japanese protection. See William Graves, *America's Siberian Adventure* (New York: Peter Smith, 1941) 86.

46. Graves, *Siberian Adventure*, 108, 144, 245.

47. Bisher, *White Terror*, 139, 160.

48. James Palmer, *The Bloody White Baron* (New York: Basic Books, 2009) 113–114; Graves, *Siberian Adventure*, 241–242; Bisher, *White Terror*, 186.

49. Smele, *Civil War*, 40–43, 83–84, 111–113.

50. Victor Fic, *The Bolsheviks and the Czechoslovak Legion* (New Delhi: Abhinav Publications, 1978) 308–309.

51. Ferenc Imrey, *Through Blood and Ice* (New York: E.P. Dutton & Company, 1930) 350–351. For more on Czecho-Slovak atrocities in Russia, see Imrey, *Blood and Ice*, 222, 304–305, 311–312; Bradley, *Czechoslovak Legion*, 94; Fic, *Bolsheviks*, 309.

52. Heald, *Witness to Revolution*, 248, 252–254.

53. Imrey, *Blood and Ice*, 323.

54. Smele, *Civil War*, 163–170; Bisher, *White Terror*, 131–132.

55. The killing of the political prisoners was ordered neither by Kolchak, who was convalescing at the time from a serious illness, nor any other minister. Yet they did little to bring the offenders to justice.

56. Smele, *Civil War*, 170–174; Pereira, *White Siberia*, 119.

57. Smele, *Civil War*, 197–198.

58. *Ibid.* 181, 196.

59. *Ibid.* 181–182.

60. Kalvoda, *Genesis*, 476; Bradley, *Czechoslovak Legion*, 117, 127; Smele, *Civil War*, 198–199; John Albert White, *The Siberian Intervention* (Princeton: Princeton University Press, 1950) 148–151; Pereira, *White Siberia*, 117; Dotsenko, *Struggle for a Democracy*, 90–94.

61. Tomáš Masaryk, *The Making of a State* (New York: Frederick A. Stokes, 1927) 100–104; Baerlein, *Seventy Thousand*, 197–200.

62. Bradley, *Czechoslovak Legion*, 116–118.

63. Becvar, *Lost Legion*, 207.

64. Bradley, *Czechoslovak Legion*, 119.

65. Smele, *Civil War*, 225–246; Silverlight, *Victors' Dilemma*, 247–253; Mawdsley, *Russian Civil War*, 141.

66. Smele, *Civil War*, 218–219, 242–243.

67. Quoted in Smele, *Civil War*, 311. For more on the offensive, see Orlando Figes, *Peasant Russia, Civil War* (Oxford: Clarendon Press, 1989) 325–332; Silverlight, *Victors' Dilemma*, 214–215. The estimated strength of the forces at the start of Kolchak's offensive was 110,000 for the Siberian Whites and about 100,000 for the Red Eastern Army Group. See Smele, *Civil War*, 312–314 and Mawdsley, *Russian Civil War*, 146. For the early gains of Kolchak's armies, see Mawdsley, *Russian Civil War*, 250.

68. Mawdsley, *Russian Civil War*, 134; Smele, *Civil War*, 315–317; Petroff, *Forgotten War*, 197–203.

69. Smele, *Civil War*, 318, 476–478.

70. *Ibid.* 318.

71. *Ibid.* 478–483; Petroff, *Forgotten War*, 212–219.

72. Bradley, *Czechoslovak Legion*, 130–131; Thompson, *Russia, Bolshevism*, 217–218.

73. Thompson, *Russia, Bolshevism*, 218; Bradley, *Czechoslovak Legion*, pp. 131–132; Mawdsley, *Russian Civil War*, 172.

74. Quoted in Mohr, *Czech and Slovak Legion*, 155.

Chapter 14

1. Eagle Glassheim, *Noble Nationalists* (Cambridge: Harvard University Press, 2005) 56–57.

2. Tomáš Masaryk, *The Making of a State*, trans. Henry Wickham Steed (New York: Frederick A. Stokes Company, 1927) 312; John Bradley, *The Czechoslovak Legion in Russia* (Boulder: East European Monographs, 1991) 124.

3. Victor Mamatey and Radomír Luža, ed., *A History of the Czechoslovak Republic 1918–1948* (Princeton: Princeton University Press, 1973) 27–28.

4. Arthur May, *The Passing of the Hapsburg Monarchy 1914–1918* (Philadelphia: University of Pennsylvania Press, 1966) 793–798.

5. Beneš implored Kramář to "avoid all struggles and bloody riots in the German parts of Bohemia." Quoted in D. Perman, *The Shaping of the Czechoslovak State* (Leiden: E. J. Brill, 1962) 76. Beneš's concern for Czechoslovakia's "moral prestige" may be found in the memoir of Harold Nicolson, *Peacemaking 1919* (New York: Grosset & Dunlap, 1965) 240.

6. Mamatey and Luža, 29.

7. *Ibid.* 29–30; Perman, *Shaping*, 82–88, 94–95.

8. Mamatey and Luža, *Czechoslovak Republic*, 30–32; András Siklós, *Revolution in Hungary and the Dissolution of the Multinational State* (Budapest: Akadémiai Kiadó, 1988) 103–105.

9. Siklós, *Revolution in Hungary*, 73, 107; Mamatey and Luža, *Czechoslovak Republic*, 30–32.

10. Siklós, *Revolution in Hungary*, 103–106; Mamatey and Luža, *Czechoslovak Republic*, 32; Perman, *Shaping*, 93–94.

11. Siklós, *Revolution in Hungary*, 74, 106–107.

12. Mamatey and Luža, *Czcehoslovak Republic*, 33–34; Perman, *Shaping*, 97–104.

13. Perman, *Shaping*, 108–111; Mamatey and Luža, *Czechoslovak Republic*, 33–34; Margaret Macmillan, *Paris 1919* (New York: Random House, 2001) 238–239.

14. The German Freikorps were irregular, mostly right-wing military units formed by officers and veterans of the German Army to battle communists and other perceived enemies following the collapse of Imperial Germany.

15. Timothy Snyder, *The Reconstruction of Nations* (New Haven: Yale University Press, 2003) 58–62.

16. Quoted in Perman, *Shaping*, 105.

17. In his 16 April 1919 address to the House of Commons, Lloyd George wondered, "How many members ever heard of Teschen? I do not mind saying that I had never heard of it." See Nicolson, Harold, *Peacemaking 1919* (New York, 1965) pp. 24–25. The name should not have been entirely obscure to the British Prime Minister since from 1914 to early 1917 the city of Těšín served as headquarters of the Austro-Hungarian Armee Oberkommando.

18. Perman, *Shaping*, 112–120; Mamatey and Luža, *Czechoslovak Republic*, 33–34; Macmillan, *Paris 1919*, 238–239.

19. Mamatey and Luža, *Czechoslovak Republic*, 34.

20. Charlotte Masarykova was later released to live with her husband but had to make frequent returns for treatment until her death on 13 May 1923.

21. Masaryk, *Making of a State*, 366; Zbyněk Zeman, *The Masaryks* (London: Weidenfeld and Nicolson, 1976) 121–122, 139.

22. Mamatey and Luža, *Czechoslovak Republic*, 54; Zeman, *Masaryks*, 123, 130.

23. Zeman, *Masaryks*, 134; Richard Pipes, *Russia Under the Bolshevik Regime* (New York: Alfred A. Knopf, 1993) 69.

24. Bradley, *Czechoslovak Legion*, 119.

25. Mamatey and Luža, *Czechoslovak Republic*, 64; Perman, *Shaping*, 17–19.

26. John Thompson, *Russia, Bolshevism and the Versailles Peace* (Princeton: Princeton University Press, 1966) 178–186, 366; Zeman, *Masaryks*, 133; Kalvoda, *Genesis*, 463.

27. Interest in the projected corps faded quickly after Russian recruiters were unable to convince any appreciable number of POWs to enlist as volunteers. The Russian peasant soldiers in Central Europe, like the majority of their brothers back home, had no desire to fight in their country's civil war.

28. Zeman, *Masaryks*, 133–134; Catherine Andreyev and Ivan Savický, *Russia Abroad: Prague and the Russian Diaspora 1918–1938* (New Haven: Yale University Press, 2004) 20–23.

29. George Goldberg, *The Peace to End Peace* (New York: Harcourt, Brace & World, 1969) 38–45.

30. Mamatey and Luža, *Czechoslovak Republic*, 35. Harold Nicolson, a member of the British delegation to the peace conference, thought Beneš was "an intelligent, young, plausible, little man with broad views." On the other hand, he developed a dislike for Kramář whom he blamed for being "behind everything nasty Beneš does." See Nicolson, *Peacemaking*, 240, 324.

31. The Council of Ten was comprised of two representatives from the five leading Allied powers (Great Britain, France, Italy, Japan and the United States) at the peace conference.

32. Both Lloyd George and Clemenceau were unimpressed by Beneš's presentation. Peter Neville, *Eduard Beneš and Tomáš Masaryk: Czechoslovakia* (London: Haus Publishing, 2010) 56–57. Harold Nicolson described it as "A lengthy and exacting performance. He dwelt too long on minor points, and after all, these viva voces are a pure farce." Quoted in Nicolson, *Peacemaking*, 257–258. The Czechoslovak Foreign Minister's garrulous nature was a common complaint at the peace conference with Nicolson later writing "never have I known so voluble a man." Quoted in Nicolson, *Peacemaking*, 276–277.

33. Masaryk, *Making of a State*, 257–258.

34. Nicolson, *Peacemaking*, 112–113.

35. Perman, *Shaping*, 122–147.

36. *Ibid.* 159–161; Goldberg, *The Peace*, 139.

37. Perman, *Shaping*, 169–176.

38. *Ibid.* 269.

39. Macmillan, *Paris 1919*, 235–240; Mamatey and Luža, *Czechoslovak Republic*, 35–36; Perman, *Shaping*, 228–257; 266–272.

40. Mamatey and Luža, *Czechoslovak Republic*, 62–65; Kalvoda, *Genesis*, 464.

41. Šmeral, it will be recalled, had led the Czech Social Democrats until he resigned in 1917 due to his opposition to the Czech nationalist program.

42. Mamatey and Luža, *Czechoslovak Republic*, 61, 63–64; Zeman, *Masaryks*, 136; Robert Kann and Béla

Király, Paula Fitchner, ed., Victor Mamatey, "The Union of Czech Political Parties in the Reichsrat 1916–1918," *The Habsburg Empire in World War I* (Boulder: East European Monographs, 1977) 7. For more on the Czechoslovak land reform, see Glassheim, *Noble Nationalists*, 62–76. Interestingly, the conservative parties supported land reform legislation as an act of national revenge against the Germanized nobility whose ancestors were accused of settling Czech estates confiscated by the Habsburgs after the Battle of White Mountain. Both Czech and German nobles were affected by the land redistributions, although some families were treated more lightly than others. In some cases these differences were due to their international connections or successful lobbying of officials; some nobles even dug into their genealogical records to prove that their ancestors patronized the Czech national revival or fought with the rebels at White Mountain.

43. Glassheim, *Noble Nationalists*, 57.

44. Siklós, *Revolution in Hungary*, 139; Peter Pastor, ed., Martin Vietor, "The Significance and Place of the Slovak Soviet Republic in the History of Czechoslovakia," *War and Society in East Central Europe: Revolutions and Interventions in Hungary and Its Neighbor States 1918–1919* (Boulder: East European Monographs, 1988) Volume 20, 432.

45. Mamatey and Luža, *Czechoslovak Republic*, 76.

46. Siklós, *Revolution in Hungary*, 134; May, Passing, 793.

47. Rudolf Tőkés, *Béla Kun and the Hungarian Soviet Republic* (Stanford: The Hoover Institution Press, 1967) 53–68; Peter Pastor, ed., György Borsányi, "Béla Kun and His Views on Strategy and Defense," *Revolutions and Interventions in Hungary and Its Neighbor States 1918–1919*, 61.

48. Tőkés, Hungarian Soviet Republic, 122–135; Pastor, *Interventions in Hungary*, 4.

49. Mamatey and Luža, *Czechoslovak Republic*, 76.

50. Tőkés, *Hungarian Soviet Republic*, 135, 157–162; Macmillan, *Paris 1919*, 265.

51. Peter Pastor, ed., Sándor Szakály, "The Officer Corps of the Hungarian Red Army," *Revolutions and Interventions in Hungary and Its Neighbor States*, 169–177. For Yugoslavia's reluctance to attack the Hungarian Soviet Republic see Pastor, *Interventions in Hungary*, 5. Another essay in the book, "The Hungarian Red Army as seen through British Eyes," Ferenc Tibor Zsuppan, 93, lists the troop strengths of the various forces in and around Soviet Hungary. Franchet d'Esperey's concern that his French troops might mutiny is mentioned in yet another essay, "General Henri Berthelot and the Army of the Danube 1918–1919," Glenn E. Torrey, 285.

52. Pastor, "The Romanian Intervention in Hungary, 1919," *Revolutions and Interventions in Hungary and Its Neighbor States 1918–1919*, 309.

53. Tőkés, *Hungarian Soviet Republic*, 162–163; Macmillan, *Paris 1919*, 265–266; Pastor, ed., László Fogarassy, "The Eastern Campaign of the Hungarian Red Army, April 1919," *Revolutions and Interventions in*

Hungary and Its Neighbor States 1918–1919, 36–37, 49–50, 93.

54. Tőkés, *Hungarian Soviet Republic*, 175, 191.

55. Pastor, *Interventions in Hungary*, 433, 438–440, 445; Jan Triska, *The Great War's Forgotten Front* (Boulder: East European Monographs, 1998) 136.

56. Pastor, *Interventions in Hungary*, 448.

57. Pastor, *Interventions in Hungary*, 97.

58. Peter Pastor, ed., Sándor Szakály, "The Officer Corps of the Hungarian Red Army," *Revolutions and Interventions in Hungary and Its Neighbor States*, 169–177.

59. Pastor, Peter, ed., Zsuzsa Nagy, "The Hungarian Democratic Republic and the Paris Peace Conference," *Revolutions and Interventions in Hungary and Its Neighbor States 19 18–1919*, 269–270, 444.

60. Pastor, *Interventions in Hungary*, 96.

61. Pastor, *Interventions in Hungary*, 447.

62. Triska, *Forgotten Front*, 136.

63. Tőkés, *Hungarian Soviet Republic*, 175, 184, 191.

64. Pastor, *Interventions in Hungary*, 453, Tőkés, *Hungarian Soviet Republic*, 184.

65. Quoted in Macmillan, *Paris 1919*, 265.

66. Quoted in Macmillan, *Paris 1919*, 238.

67. Macmillan, *Paris 1919*, 238; Pastor, *Interventions in Hungary*, 310.

68. Tőkés, *Hungarian Soviet Republic*, 181, 196–201.

69. *Ibid.* 189.

70. *Ibid.* 200–207; Mamatey and Luža, *Czechoslovak Republic*, 267; Pastor, *Interventions in Hungary*, 69–77, 174, 301–314; Macmillan, *Paris 1919*, 267.

71. Mamatey and Luža, *Czechoslovak Republic*, 62.

72. Pastor, *Interventions in Hungary*, 432, 456–458.

73. Kalvoda, *Genesis*, 477, 485–486; Neville, *Eduard Beneš*, 58–59; Nicolson, *Peacemaking*, 286, 326. Nicolson was impartial to the Czechoslovak exiled leaders, reserving both praise and criticism for them in his account, and had no reason to disparage Štefánik as a madman. In Paris, Nicolson recalled how Štefánik liked to spin tales of Bolshevik atrocities, including one where he was supposedly with the first men to reach Yekaterinburg just days after the murder of the Tsar and his family. In fact, the massacre of the imperial family and the liberation of Yekaterinburg by Czecho-Slovak and White forces both predated Štefánik's arrival in Siberia by several months.

74. Štefánik's mortal remains were consecrated in a mausoleum erected near his native village.

75. Mamatey and Luža, *Czechoslovak Republic*, 75.

76. Robert Seton-Watson, an ardent supporter of Masaryk, wrote that the allegation of the Czechoslovak president's complicity in Štefánik's death was an impudent story "to the disgust of all sane and decent people" (Seton-Watson, Robert, *A History of the Czechs and Slovaks* [London, 1943] p. 314).

77. Kalvoda, *Genesis*, 485–486.

78. Macmillan, *Paris 1919*, 241.

79. Mamatey and Luža, *Czechoslovak Republic*, 80, 114–117.

80. *Ibid.* 9, 82–83.

81. Zbyněk Zeman, *The Break-Up of the Habsburg*

Empire (London: Oxford University Press, 1961) 171–
172; Kann et al., *Habsburg Empire*, 22; Mamatey and
Luža, *Czechoslovak Republic*, 83. For an account of the
destruction of the Marian Column and other attacks on
religious symbols in postwar Czechoslovakia, see Nancy
Wingfield, *Flag Wars and Stone Saints* (Cambridge:
Harvard University Press, 2007) 144–148.

82. Mamatey and Luža, *Czechoslovak Republic*, 83–
85.

83. *Ibid*. 85; Perman, *Shaping*, 246; MacMillan,
Paris 1919, 241–242.

84. Mamatey and Luža, *Czechoslovak Republic*, 37,
41, 85.

85. Kalvoda, *Genesis*, 458.

86. Mamatey and Luža, *Czechoslovak Republic*, 85–
86.

87. *Ibid*. 93–94.

88. *Ibid*. 86, 99; Kalvoda, *Genesis*, 459.

89. Mamatey and Luža, *Czechoslovak Republic*, 160.

90. Quoted in Victor Mamatey, *The United States
and East Central Europe 1914–1918* (Princeton: Princeton University Press, 1957) 307.

91. Quoted in Mamatey, *The United States*, 306. In
the memorandum, Masaryk had bluntly asked whether
it should be considered "more just that ... ten million
Czechs and Slovaks be oppressed by Austria-Hungary,
or that the Germans in Bohemia and Slovakia, counting
only three millions, possess constitutionally guaranteed
national freedom?"

92. Perman, *Shaping*, 77–78.

93. Zeman, *Break-Up*, 236.

94. For instance, Masaryk made the conciliatory
gesture of attending a performance at the German theater in Prague just two days after his return from exile.
Zeman, *Masaryks*, 125.

95. Early in his presidency, Masaryk made the
mistake of referring to the German-Bohemians as
"colonists." Kramář became much more outspoken
against the Czechoslovakia's ethnic Germans and opposed any concessions to the republic's minorities as he
moved to the right and even flirted with fascism during
the interwar period. Mamatey and Luža, *Czechoslovak
Republic*, 65; Andrea Orzoff, *Battle for the Castle* (New
York: Oxford University Press, 2009) 91–92, 140.

96. Glassheim, *Noble Nationalists*, 71–75. According to this source, the State Land Office's discrimination
against ethnic Germans was real but done in a subtle
manner.

97. Mamatey and Luža, *Czechoslovak Republic*, 41;
Glassheim, *Noble Nationalists*, 59–62.

98. Under the constitution, the Czech and Slovak
languages were recognized as dialects of a common
"Czechoslovak" language.

99. A. J. P. Taylor, *The Habsburg Monarchy 1809–
1918* (Chicago: Chicago University Press, 1948) 251–
254; Mamatey and Luža, *Czechoslovak Republic*, 92–98.

100. Of the some 13 million inhabitants of the
postwar Czechoslovak state, 6,842,000 were Czechs,
1,977,000 were Slovaks, 3,123,000 were Germans and
745,000 were Magyars. The remaining 588,000 con-

sisted of smaller minority groups, including Poles and
Ukrainians. Jaroslav Pánek, *A History of the Czech Lands*
(Prague: Karolinum Press, 2009) 400. The "Czechoslo-
vak" idea had long appealed to Czechs for the purpose
of enhancing their numbers. In a meeting held on the
eve of World War I, Kramář supposedly told Robert
Seton-Watson that he wished to use the Slovaks to "re-
inforce his own race by two and a half million recruits!"
Hugh Seton-Watson and Christopher Seton-Watson,
The Making of a New Europe (London: Methuen &
Company, 1981) 100.

101. Mamatey and Luža, *Czechoslovak Republic*, 126.

102. Niall Ferguson has succinctly explained this
dilemma: "The more the model of the nation state was
applied to Central and Eastern Europe, then, the greater
the potential for conflict. The discrepancy between the
reality of mixed settlement—a complete patchwork of
pales and diasporas—and the ideal of homogenous political units was simply too great" (*The War of the World*
[New York: Allen Lane, 2006] lvii—lviii).

103. The exceptions were Austria and Hungary since
these states, which were regarded as former enemies by
the peacemakers, were truncated and denied the generous borders granted to most of their neighbors.

104. Taylor, *Habsburg Monarchy*, 251–254.

Chapter 15

1. Alon Rachamimov, *POWs and the Great War*
(Oxford: Berg, 2002) 52–53; Henry Baerlein, *The
March of the Seventy Thousand* (London: Leonard Parsons, 1926) 139; Gustav Becvar, *The Lost Legion* (London Stanley Paul & Company, 1939) 172.

2. Quoted in Edward Heald, *Witness to Revolution* (Kent: The Kent State University Press, 1972) 277–
278.

3. Baerlein, *Seventy Thousand*, 145–148, Richard
Pipes, *Russia Under the Bolshevik Regime* (New York:
Alfred A. Knopf, 1993) 114; Jonathon Smele, *Civil War
in Siberia* (New York: Cambridge University Press,
1996) 369 .

4. Carl Ackerman, *Trailing the Bolsheviki* (New
York: Charles Scribner's Sons, 1919) 37.

5. Becvar, *Lost Legion*, 214–215.

6. Smele, *Civil War*, 366.

7. *Ibid*. 374–375.

8. Evan Mawdsley, *The Russian Civil War* (New
York: Pegasus, 2007) 144.

9. Quoted in Baerlein, *Seventy Thousand*, 260.

10. Quoted in Peter Fleming, *The Fate of Admiral
Kolchak* (Edinburgh: Birlinn, 1963) 134.

11. Smele, *Civil War*, 131.

12. *Ibid*. 128.

13. *Ibid*. 68.

14. *Ibid*. 472–473.

15. Fleming, *Admiral Kolchak*, 141–144.

16. Pereira, *White Siberia*, 41, 145.

17. Richard Goldhurst, *The Midnight War* (New
York: McGraw-Hill Book Company, 1978) 189.

18. Stewart, George, *The White Armies of Russia*

(New York: Russell & Russell, 1970) 278; John Bradley, *The Czechoslovak Legion in Russia 1914–1920* (Boulder, East European Monographs, 1991) 138.

19. Baerlein, *Seventy Thousand*, 200–205; Smele, *Civil* War, 371 Peter Pastor, ed., Gerald Davis, "The Life of Prisoners of War in Russia 1914–1921," *Essays on World War I* (New York: Brooklyn College Press, 1983) 176.

20. Richard Luckett, *The White Generals* (London: Routledge, 1971) 294; Pereira, *White Siberia*, 63; David Footman, *Civil War in Russia* (London: Faber and Faber, 1961) 218.

21. Fleming, *Admiral Kolchak*, 78; Kalvoda, *Genesis*, 484.

22. General Denikin, whose own Armed Forces of South Russia had a reputation for walking away with anything that was not nailed down, wrote the following: "Trainloads of 'booty' were constant accompaniment to the Czech advance, with a demoralizing effect on the troops, crippling their fighting efficiency, and rousing the bitter and bewildered comments of the Russian population." Denikin was in South Russia throughout the civil war and therefore his observation is secondhand, but it is revealing of White émigrés views of the Czecho-Slovaks' behavior during the Russian Civil War. See Denikin, *The White Army* (Gulf Breeze, FL, 1973 ed.) pp. 140–141.

23. Pereira, *White Siberia*, 63; Fleming, *Admiral Kolchak*, 175.

24. Baerlein, *Seventy Thousand*, 141 David Kelly, *The Czech Fascist Movement 1922–1942* (Boulder: East European Monographs, 1995) 28; Bradley, *Czechoslovak Legion*, 115.

25. Becvar, *Lost Legion*, 205–206, 212.

26. Mawdsley, *Russian Civil War*, 144, W. Bruce Lincoln, *Red Victory* (New York: Da Capo Press, 1999) 198.

27. Footman, *Civil War in Russia*, 198–199.

28. Smele, *Civil War*, 485–487.

29. Clifford Kinvig, *Churchill's Crusade* (London: Hambledon Continuum, 2006) 63, 209–210.

30. Bradley, *Czechoslovak Legion*, 132.

31. *Ibid.* 132; Blanka Ševčík Glos and George Glos, *Czechoslovak Troops in Russia and Siberia during the First World War* (New York: Vantage Press, 2000) 68 – 71, Kalvoda, *Genesis*, 480.

32. Bradley, *Czechoslovak Legion*, 132.

33. Mawdsley, *Russian Civil War*, 194–199.

34. Smele, *Civil War*, 521–547; Serge Petroff, *Remembering a Forgotten War* (Boulder: East European Monographs, 2000) 223–230; Fleming, *Admiral Kolchak*, 161.

35. Becvar, *Lost Legion*, 220–222.

36. Smele, *Civil War*, 547.

37. Baerlein, *Seventy Thousand*, 234–235.

38. Lincoln, *Red Victory*, 266.

39. Smele, *Civil War*, 544–545.

40. Mawdsley, *Russian Civil War*, 200–203.

41. Bradley, *Czechoslovak Legion*, 142.

42. Quoted in Smele, *Civil War*, 551, 572.

43. Smele, *Civil War*, 552–569; James Morley, *The*

Japanese Thrust into Siberia (New York: Columbia University Press, 1957) 78; Goldhurst, *Midnight War*, 237–243; Baerlein, *Seventy Thousand*, 241–242.

44. Smele, *Civil War*, 572–584; Fleming, *AdmiralKolchak*, 170–172.

45. Smele, *Civil War*, 598–599.

46. *Ibid.* 599–600; John Albert White, *The Siberian Intervention* (Princeton: Princeton University Press, 1950) 351; Goldhurst, *Midnight War*, 248.

47. Fleming, *Admiral Kolchak*, 165; Becvar, *Lost Legion*, 222.

48. Francis McCullagh, *A Prisoner of the Reds* (New York: E.P. Dutton and Company, 1922) 3–5; Fleming, *Admiral Kolchak*, 165–170.

49. Smele, *Civil War*, 600–601; Pipes, *Bolshevik Regime*, 33.

50. Smele, *Civil War*, 544–545; Kalvoda, *Genesis*, 483. In a report to U.S. State Department, John Stevens, the commander of the Russian Railway Service Corps, defended the legionaries' actions during the evacuation. See Carol Wilcox Melton, *Between War and Peace* (Macon: Mercer University Press, 2001) 202.

51. Pereira, *White Siberia*, 117.

52. McCullagh, *Prisoner of the Reds*, 22; Smele, *Civil War*, 592–605; Jamie Bisher, *White Terror* (New York: Routledge, 2005) 207.

53. Bisher, *White Terror*, 197–198.

54. *Ibid.* 207; Smele, *Civil War*, 603, 605.

55. Smele, *Civil War*, 604–607. Peter Fleming's *The Fate of Admiral Kolchak* stands as an account that is sympathetic to the sailor yet unreservedly accepts the allegation that Kolchak ordered the Baikal tunnels to be destroyed.

56. Smele, *Civil War*, 605, 612–625; Bisher, *White Terror*, 208–213.

57. Bisher, *White Terror*, 215, 218, 230–231; R. Ernest Dupuy, *Perish by the Sword* (Harrisburg: The Military Publishing Company, 1939) 260–261.

58. For illustrations of the legionnaires' winter gear, see David Bullock, *The Czech Legion 1914–20* (New York: Osprey Publishing, 2009) 42–47, plate F.

59. Smele, *Civil War*, 627–628.

60. Smele, *Civil War*, 630– 635; Petroff, *Forgotten War*, 243; Fleming, *Admiral Kolchak*, 186–191.

61. Becvar, *Lost Legion*, 237.

62. Fleming, *Admiral Kolchak*, 196–197.

63. Smele, *Civil War*, 635–637.

64. Kinvig, *Churchill's Crusade*, 302–303; David Stefancic, ed., M.B. Biskupski, "The Militarization of the Discourse of Polish Politics and the Legion Movement of the First World War," *Armies in Exile* (Boulder: East European Monographs, 2005) 93–94. Among those cut off by the Bolsheviks at Krasnoyarsk was the British Army Captain Francis McCullagh who later described his experiences in his memoir, *A Prisoner of the Reds*, 23.

65. Bradley, *Czechoslovak Legion*, 148–153; Bisher, *White Terror*, 219; Smele, *Civil War*, 654–655; Peter Pastor, ed., Ivo Banac, "South Slav Prisoners of War in Revolutionary Russia," *Essays on World War I* (Boulder: East European Monographs, 1983) 137.

66. Smele, *Civil War*, 655.

67. Bradley, *Czechoslovak Legion*, 153; Kalvoda, *Genesis*, 474. Jaroslav Hašek, later a famous novelist, was among those Czechoslovak Communists who stayed in Russia to agitate against the Legion.

68. Interestingly, the most dependable soldiers under Kappel were former members of the Komuch's People's Army or anti–Bolshevik workers from Izhevsk and Votkinsk; in other words, they were moderate socialists who the Omsk reactionaries hated almost as much as Bolsheviks.

69. Bradley, *Czechoslovak Legion*, 153–154; Smele, *Civil War*, 655–659; Petroff, *Forgotten War*, 239–241, 248.

70. Smele, *Civil War*, 639–641.

71. *Ibid.* 635–637; Becvar, *Lost Legion*, 238–240.

72. Becvar, *Lost Legion*, 241–244.

73. Smele, *Civil War*, 638–639.

74. *Ibid.* 642–647, 656–659.

75. Bradley, *Czechoslovak Legion*, 154.

76. *Ibid.* 150; Smele, *Civil War*, 660–665.

77. When the Red Army took possession of the Russian gold reserve, it was unable to account for a portion of the missing treasure. This gave rise to allegations, especially among bitter White Russian émigrés, that the Czechoslovaks had helped themselves to the gold and even used it to fund the Legiobank, which continued to operate in postwar Czechoslovakia. Research into the subject, however, has turned up no hard evidence that the legionaries stole any part of the gold reserve. See Andreyev, Catherine and Ivan Savický, *Russia Abroad: Prague and the Russian Diaspora 1918–1938* (New Haven, 2004) p. 39.

78. Peter Pastor, ed., Josef Kalvoda, "Czech and Slovak Prisoners of War in Russia during the War and Revolution," *Essays on World War I*, 234.

79. Smele, *Civil War*, 666–667; White, *Siberian Intervention*, 386.

80. Bisher, *White Terror*, 149; Lincoln, *Red Victory*, 60.

81. White, *Siberian Intervention*, 312; John Thompson, *Russia, Bolshevism and the Versailles Peace* (Princeton: Princeton University Press, 1966) 359–360.

82. White, *Siberian Intervention*, 210; Canfield Smith, *Vladivostok Under Red and White Rule* (Seattle: University of Washington Press, 1975) 33; Bisher, *White Terror*, 240.

83. Bisher, *White Terror*, 233; White, *Siberian Intervention*, 351; Joan McGuire Mohr, *The Czech and Slovak Legion in Siberia, 1917–1922* (Jefferson: McFarland & Company, 2012) 192.

84. Smele, *Civil War*, 667.

85. White, *Siberian Intervention*, 367.

86. Smith, *Vladivostok*, 18.

87. Bisher, *White Terror*, 239, 250.

88. *Ibid.* 217.

89. Graves, *Siberian Adventure*, 303–304, 307; Bradley, *Czechoslovak Legion*, 155.

90. Bisher, *White Terror*, 246–248.

91. Smith, *Vladivostok*, 40–42.

92. Further details of the Hailar incident may be found in Bisher, *White Terror*, 251–255.

93. Baerlein, *Seventy Thousand*, 275–277.

94. Victor Mamatey, *The United States and East Central Europe* (Princeton: Princeton University Press, 1957) 295–295; Bradley, *Czechoslovak Legion*, 156.

95. John Bradley in *The Czechoslovak Legion in Russia 1914–1920*, 156, places the number of deaths incurred by the legionaries at 4,112. Other authors have given much higher figures using uncertain calculations or unnamed sources. For example, Richard Goldhurst in *The Midnight War*, 258, stated that 13,000 legionaries died in Siberia. He seems to have arrived to this figure by subtracting the approximate number of legionaries evacuated from Siberia (56,459) from the often-cited strength of the Czecho-Slovak Legion in Russia (70,000). These calculations are faulty since the maximum fighting strength of the Czecho-Slovak Legion in Russia was probably closer to 60,000. Moreover, Goldhurst's calculations do not account for those who deserted by leaving for home or joining the Communists. In *The Czech and Slovak Legion in Siberia, 1917–1922*, 212–213, Joan McGuire Mohr asserts that "over half of the original Legion soldiers had not survived" their ordeal without providing either a definite number, source or how she arrived to this estimate. Josef Kalvoda, in his essay "Czech and Slovak Prisoners of War in Russia during the War and Revolution" (in *Essays on World War I*, Peter Pastor, ed.), citing a Czechoslovak source, gives 61,450 as the total strength of the Czecho-Slovak Legion in Russia. Since 56,459 legionaries were evacuated from Siberia, that leaves approximately 5,000 men unaccounted for. Therefore, Bradley's figure of 4,112 dead seems more plausible than the higher figures.

96. Baerlein, *Seventy Thousand*, 276–277.

97. Betty Miller Unterberger, *The United States, Revolutionary Russia and the Rise of Czechoslovakia* (Chapel Hill: The University of North Carolina Press, 1989) 327; Mohr, *Czech and Slovak Legion*, 169–175.

98. Baerlein, *Seventy Thousand*, 277.

99. Zbyněk Zeman and Antonín Klimek, *The Life of Edvard Beneš* (Oxford: Clarendon Press, 1997) 67; Alon Rachamimov, *POWs and the Great War* (Oxford: Berg, 2002) 221.

100. Bradley, *Czechoslovak Legion*, 156.

101. Bisher, *White Terror*, 263–264.

102. Smith, *Vladivostok*, 147–184; Mawdsley, *Russian Civil War*, 235; Benson Bobrick, *East of the Sun* (New York: Poseidon Press, 1992) 413. According to Mawdsley, 235, between 2,000,000 and 3,500,000 émigrés fled Soviet Russia.

103. Catherine Andreyev and Ivan Savický, *Russia Abroad: Prague and the Russian Diaspora 1918–1938* (New Haven: Yale University Press, 2004). The Czechoslovak government's aid program for émigrés, Russian Action, was originally intended to foster Russian cultural, academic and economic endeavors among the émigrés until they could return to a non-communist or moderately-governed Russia; a transition which

many inaccurately forecasted to be imminent. See also Andrea Orzoff, *Battle for the Castle* (New York: Oxford University Press, 2009) 141; Paul Robinson, *The White Russian Army in Exile 1920–1941* (New York: Oxford University Press, 2002) 79. At one point, as many as 35,000 White Russian émigrés resided in interwar Prague.

104. Petroff, *Forgotten War*, 256–257, 279–280.

105. Anton Denikin, *The White Army*, trans. Catherine Zvegintzov (Gulf Breeze: Academic International Press, 1973) 145.

Chapter 16

1. Nancy Wingfield, *Flag War and Stone Saints* (Cambridge: Harvard University Press, 2007) 182–189.

2. For the Czechoslovak government's effort to reward the legionnaires and secure their loyalty, see Andrea Orzoff, *Battle for the Castle* (New York: Oxford University Press, 2009) 84–85 and Elizabeth Wiskemann, *Czechs and Germans* (London: Oxford University Press, 1938) 149. Masaryk's efforts to closely associate with the legacy of the legionnaires were resented by some veterans who thought the political exiles were depriving them of their credit for founding the Czechoslovak state. See David Kelly, *The Czech Fascist Movement 1922–1942* (Boulder: East European Monograhs, 1995) 31–32.

3. Kelly, *Czech Fascist Movement*, 32; Serge Petroff, *Remembering a Forgotten War* (Boulder: East European Monographs, 2000) 277.

4. Orzoff, *Battle for the Castle*, 85; Wingfield, *Flag Wars*, 185.

5. Kelly, *Czech Fascist Movement*, 51–60; Orzoff, *Battle for the Castle*, 102.

6. Josef Kalvoda, *The Genesis of Czechoslovakia* (Boulder: East European Monographs, 1986) 8.

7. Kelly, *Czech Fascist Movement*, 11–19.

8. *Ibid.* pp. 20–22; Orzoff, *Battle for the Castle*, 105–119.

9. For additional information on the activities of the Czechoslovak fascists and right extremists, see: Kelly, *Czech Fascist Movement*, 86–106; Wingfield, *Flag Wars*, 207–215; Victor Mamatey and Radomír Luža, *A History of the Czechoslovak Republic 1918–1948* (Princeton: Princeton University Press, 1973) 131–132, 145–148.

10. Orzoff, *Battle for the Castle*, 3–4, 7–9, 141–142.

11. Michael Sanders and Philip Taylor, *British Propaganda during the First World War* (London: The Macmillan Press, 1982) 246–248; Orzoff, *Battle for the Castle*, 143–145.

12. Even before the revelations of British wartime propaganda were fully exposed, there was suspicion in the U.S. that America had been duped not only into the war in Europe, but also the intervention in Siberia. In the summer of 1919, both the U.S. Secretary of War and Secretary of State agreed that the Czecho-Slovak Legion did not need U.S. intervention to withdraw from Siberia. The Allies and particularly France, they charged, had distorted events in Siberia to make intervention appear necessary to rescue the Czechs.

13. Orzoff, *Battle for the Castle*, 7–8; Carol Wilcox Melton, *Between War and Peace* (Macon: Mercer University Press, 2001) 160–161.

14. Gábor Bátonyi, *Britain and Central Europe 1918–1933* (Oxford: Clarendon Press, 1999) 10–12, 18–21.

15. *Ibid.* 55–56, 61–63, 210–217; Orzoff, *Battle for the Castle*, 143–145.

16. William Shirer, *The Rise and Fall of the Third Reich* (New York: Simon and Schuster, 1960) 284–285.

17. Orzoff, Battle for the Castle, 176.

18. An example of Masaryk's unusual charm comes from Edward Heald, a YMCA secretary attached to the Czecho-Slovak Legion in Russia. In a letter to his wife, Heald described meeting Masaryk in late 1917 and wrote, "I don't know when I have been more impressed with a man" (Edward Heald, *Witness to Revolution* [Kent: The Kent State University Press, 1972] 183).

19. Mamatey and Luža, *Czechoslovak Republic*, 142.

20. Zbyněk Zeman, *The Masaryks* (London: Weidenfeld and Nicolson, 1976) 152–153.

21. Mamatey and Luža, *Czechoslovak Republic*, 152; Zbyněk Zeman and Antonín Klimek, *The Life of Edvard Beneš* (Oxford: Clarendon Press, 1997) 95–96.

22. Zeman, *Masaryks*, 153–154; Mamatey and Luža, *Czechoslovak Republic*, 155.

23. Zeman and Klimek, *Beneš*, 47, 95.

24. Mamatey and Luža, *Czechoslovak Republic*, 220–221.

25. On Karl's ill-fated attempts to reclaim the Hungarian throne, see: Edmond Taylor, *The Fall of the Dynasties* (New York: Doubleday, 1963) 369–370; James Bogle and Joanna Bogle, *A Heart for Europe* (Herefordshire: Gracewing, 2004) 124–139.

26. Bogle and Bogle, *Heart for Europe*, 139–144. After Karl's death, his nine year-old son, Otto, was the rightful heir to the Habsburg titles.

27. Mamatey and Luža, *Czechoslovak Republic*, 131; Zeman and Klimek, *Beneš*, 77–78.

28. Mamatey and Luža, *Czechoslovak Republic*, 236–237.

29. Beneš's challenger for the presidency, Bohumíl Němec, was on record as an ardent Czech nationalist. This rendered him unacceptable to the minority parties and Slovak nationalists in the National Assembly, and it was the support of these groups which assured Beneš's victory.

30. *Ibid.* 155–156.

31. *Ibid.* 233.

32. Shirer, *Third Reich*, 363.

33. Mamatey and Luža, *Czechoslovak Republic*, 157–161; Peter Neville, *Eduard Beneš and Tomáš Masaryk: Czechoslovakia* (London: Haus Publishing, 2010) 107–110; Shirer, *Third Reich*, 420–421; Christopher Ailsby, *Hitler's Renegades: Foreign Nationals in the Service of the Third Reich* (Dulles: Brassey's Inc., 2004) 47–50.

34. Bátonyi, *East Central Europe*, 216–221.

35. Quoted in Mamatey and Luža, *Czechoslovak Republic*, 161.

36. Shirer, *Third Reich*, 423–424. It should be noted that the German annexation of Austria in March 1938 did leave Czechoslovakia exposed to the Nazi military threat on her southern frontier, where the fortifications were not nearly as formidable.

37. Quoted in Zeman, *Masaryks*, 164.

38. Zeman and Klimek, *Beneš*, 135–136.

39. *Ibid.* 137; Mamatey and Luža, *Czechoslovak Republic*, 163–165; Neville, *Eduard Beneš*, 124–125.

40. Mamatey and Luža, *Czechoslovak Republic*, 160.

41. *Ibid.* 260–261, 271–276.

42. *Ibid.* 297.

43. Richard Goldhurst, *The Midnight War* (New York: McGraw-Hill Book Company, 1978) 265.

44. Mamatey and Luža, *Czechoslovak Republic*, 298, 301.

45. The Czechs fared much better than most other Slavs under German occupation since the primary concern of Bohemia's Nazi administrators was to maintain the protectorate's high volume of industrial and agricultural production to supply their war effort. Subsequently, armed resistance to Nazi rule was considerably less intense among Czechs in comparison to many other conquered peoples; much to the distress of Beneš and other Czechoslovak leaders in exile.

46. Kelly, *Czech Fascist Movement*, 144–151; Zeman and Klimek, *Beneš*, 199; Neville, *Eduard Beneš*, 136.

47. Mamatey and Luža, *Czechoslovak Republic*, 278–294.

48. Zeman and Klimek, *Beneš*, p. 144.

49. Bátonyi, *East Central Europe*, 221.

50. Zeman and Klimek, *Beneš*, 145; Gary Messinger, *British Propaganda and the State in the First World War* (New York: Manchester University Press, 1992) 181. During the Second World War, Seton-Watson published two books sympathetic to the then defunct Czechoslovak state: *Masaryk in England* (Cambridge: Cambridge University Press, 1943) and *A History of the Czechs and Slovaks* (London: Hutchinson & Company, 1943).

51. Zeman and Klimek, *Beneš*, 166.

52. Mamatey and Luža, *Czechoslovak Republic*, 322–328; Zeman and Klimek, *Beneš*, 242–246.

53. Beginning in about April 1945 and continuing for several months afterward, as many as 600,000 Germans fled into Germany to escape reprisals. The official transfer of the German-Bohemians occurred from January through November 1946, when approximately two million were expelled to Germany. The only Germans allowed to remain behind were those with valuable skills or who could prove their active resistance to the Nazi occupation regime. In the years immediately following the transfer, ethnic Germans continued to leave Czechoslovakia by the tens of thousands and the few who stayed were not granted citizenship by the Czechoslovak state until 1953. See Wingfield, *Flag Wars*, 263–265; Jaroslav Pánek, *A History of the Czech Lands* (Prague: Karolinum Press, 2009) 472; Eagle Glassheim, *Noble Nationalists* (Cambridge: Harvard University Press, 2005) 208–210. Unlike the resettlement of the Germans from the Czech lands, the expulsion of Magyars from Slovakia was not authorized by the Allies. Ultimately, the Slovaks pressing for such measures had to settle for a population exchange where they received a Slovak from Hungary for every Magyar sent south from Slovakia. Mamatey and Luža, *Czechoslovak Republic*, 398.

54. Wingfield, *Flag Wars*, 263; Niall Ferguson, *The War of the World* (New York: Allen Lane, 2006) 583–584. According to Timothy Snyder, the population reshuffling during and after the Second World War forced an estimated twelve million ethnic Germans in Central and Eastern Europe from their homes. A similar number of non–Germans, mainly Ukrainians, Poles and Belarusians, were also displaced from their original homelands. See Timothy Snyder, *Bloodlands: Europe between Stalin and Hitler* (New York: 2010) 331–332. Interestingly, Masaryk had never considered such expulsions to be a practical solution since he believed that many "repatriated colonists," as long as they were resettled in a free society, would within a few years simply return to the lands from which they were expelled. Tomáš Masaryk, *The New Europe* (Cranbury: Bucknell University Press, 1972) 143.

55. Mamatey and Luža, *Czechoslovak Republic*, 328.

56. *Ibid.* 413–415.

57. Zeman and Klimek, *Beneš*, 281.

58. Pánek, *Czech Lands*, 589–615.

Bibliography

Ackerman, Carl. *Trailing the Bolsheviki*. New York: Charles Scribner's, 1919.

Ailsby, Christopher. *Hitler's Renegades: Foreign Nationals in the Service of the Third Reich*. Dulles, Va.: Brassey's, 2004.

Andreyev, Catherine, and Ivan Savický. *Russia Abroad: Prague and the Russian Diaspora 1918–1938*. New Haven: Yale University Press, 2004.

Baerlein, Henry. *The March of the Seventy Thousand*. London: Leonard Parsons, 1926.

Bátonyi, Gábor. *Britain and Central Europe 1918–1933*. Oxford: Clarendon Press, 1999.

Becvar, Gustav. *The Lost Legion*. London: Stanley Paul, 1939.

Beneš, Edvard. *Bohemia's Case for Independence*. New York: Arno Press, 1971.

_____. *My War Memoirs*. Translated by Paul Selver. New York: Houghton Mifflin, 1928.

Bisher, Jamie. *White Terror*. New York: Routledge, 2005.

Bobrick, Benson. *East of the Sun*. New York: Poseidon Press, 1992.

Bogle, James, and Joanna. *A Heart for Europe*. Herefordshire: Gracewing, 2004.

Bradley, John. *Allied Intervention in Russia*. New York: Basic Books, 1968.

_____. *Czech Nationalism in the Nineteenth Century*. Boulder: East European Monographs, 1984.

_____. *The Czechoslovak Legion in Russia 1914–1920*. Boulder: East European Monographs, 1991.

Bullock, David. *The Czech Legion 1914–20*. New York: Osprey, 2009.

Bunyan, James. *Intervention, Civil War and Communism in Russia*. New York: Octagon Books, 1976.

Calder, Kenneth. *Britain and the Origins of the New Europe, 1914–1918*. New York: Cambridge University Press, 1976.

Čapek, Karel. *Masaryk on Thought and Life*. New York: Macmillan, 1938.

_____. *President Masaryk Tells His Story*. New York: G.P. Putnam's, 1935.

Chamberlin, William Henry. *The Russian Revolution 1917–1921*. Volumes 1–2. New York: Grosset & Dunlap, 1965.

Churchill, Winston, *The World Crisis 1918–1928: The Aftermath*. New York: Charles Scribner's, 1929.

Cornish, Nik. *The Russian Army and the First World War*. Gloucestershire: Spellmount, 2006.

Cornwall, Mark, ed. *The Last Years of Austria-Hungary*. Exeter: University of Exeter Press, 2002.

_____. *The Undermining of Austria-Hungary*. London: Macmillan, 2000.

Czernin, Count Ottokar. *In the World War*. London: Cassell, 1919.

Denikin, General Anton. *The Russian Turmoil*. Westport: Hyperion Press, 1973.

_____. *The White Army*. Translated by Catherine Zvegintzov. Gulf Breeze: Academic International Press, 1973.

Deutscher, Isaac. *The Prophet Armed*. New York: Oxford University Press, 1954.

Dotsenko, Paul. *The Struggle for a Democracy in Siberia 1917–1920*. Stanford: Hoover Institution Press, 1983.

Dupuy, R. Ernest. *Perish by the Sword*. Harrisburg: Military, 1939.

Ferguson, Niall. *The Pity of War*. New York: Basic Books, 1999.

_____. *The War of the World*, New York: Allen Lane 2006.

Ferrell, Robert. *Woodrow Wilson and World War I 1917–1921*. New York: Harper & Row, 1985.

Fic, Victor. *The Bolsheviks and the Czechoslovak Legion*. New Delhi: Abhinav Publications, 1978.

_____. *Revolutionary War for Independence and the Russian Question*. New Delhi: Abhinav Publications, 1977.

Figes, Orlando. *A People's Tragedy*. New York: Viking, 1997.

_____. *Peasant Russia, Civil War*. Oxford: Clarendon Press, 1989.

Fisher, H. A. L. *A History of Europe*. London: Edward Arnold, 1936.

Fleming, Peter. *The Fate of Admiral Kolchak*. Edinburgh: Birlinn, 2001.

Footman, David. *Civil War in Russia*. London: Faber and Faber, 1961.

Ford, Nancy Gentile. *Americans All!* College Station: Texas A&M University Press, 2001.

Gillett, E. H. *The Life and Times of John Huss.* Volumes 1–2. Boston: Gould and Lincoln, 1978.

Glaise-Horstenau, Edmund. *The Collapse of the Austro-Hungarian Empire.* Translated by Ian F. D. Morrow. London: J.M. Dent, 1930.

Glassheim, Eagle. *Noble Nationalists.* Cambridge: Harvard University Press, 2005.

Glos, Blanka Ševčík, and George. *Czechoslovak Troops in Russia and Siberia During the First World War.* New York: Vantage, 2000.

Goldberg, George. *The Peace to End Peace.* New York: Harcourt, Brace & World, 1969.

Goldhurst, Richard. *The Midnight War.* New York: McGraw-Hill, 1978.

Graves, William. *America's Siberian Adventure.* New York: Peter Smith, 1941.

Hajek, Hanus. *T. G. Masaryk Revisited.* Boulder: Easter European Monographs, 1983.

Heald, Edward. *Witness to Revolution.* Kent: Kent State University Press, 1972.

Healy, Maureen. *Vienna and the Fall of the Habsburg Empire.* Cambridge: Cambridge University Press, 2004.

Heenan, Louise Erwin. *Russian Democracy's Fatal Blunder.* New York: Praeger, 1987.

Herwig, Holger. *The First World War.* London: Arnold, 1997.

Hoffmann, Max. *War Diaries and Other Papers.* Volumes 1–2. London: Martin Secker, 1929.

Imrey, Ferenc. *Through Blood and Ice.* New York: E.P Dutton, 1930.

Kalvoda, Josef. *The Genesis of Czechoslovakia.* Boulder: East European Monographs, 1986.

Kann, Robert, and Béla Király, Paula Fichtner, eds. *The Habsburg Empire in World War I.* Boulder: East European Monographs, 1977.

Keegan, John. *The First World War.* New York: Vintage, 2000.

Kelly, David. *The Czech Fascist Movement 1922–1942.* Boulder: East European Monographs, 1995.

Kennan, George. *Soviet-American Relations: Russia Leaves the War.* Princeton: Princeton University Press, 1956.

_____. *Soviet-American Relations: The Decision to Intervene.* Princeton: Princeton University Press, 1958.

Kerensky, Alexander. *The Catastrophe.* New York: D. Appleton, 1927.

Kinvig, Clifford. *Churchill's Crusade.* London: Hambledon Continuum, 2006.

Kohn, Hans. *Pan-Slavism.* New York: Vintage, 1960.

Lincoln, W. Bruce. *Passage Through Armageddon.* New York: Simon and Schuster, 1986.

_____. *Red Victory.* New York: Da Capo Press, 1999.

_____. *The Conquest of a Continent.* New York: Random House, 1994.

Lockhart, Bruce. *British Agent.* London: G.P. Putnam's Sons, 1933.

Luckett, Richard. *The White Generals.* London: Routledge, 1987.

Macmillan, Margaret. *Paris 1919.* New York: Random House, 2001.

Mamatey, Victor. *The United States and East Central Europe 1914–1918.* Princeton: Princeton University Press, 1957.

Mamatey, Victor, and Radomír Luža, eds. *A History of the Czechoslovak Republic 1918–1948.* Princeton: Princeton University Press, 1973.

Marks, Steven. *Road to Power.* Ithaca: Cornell University Press, 1991.

Masaryk, Tomáš. *The Making of a State.* Translated by Henry Wickham Steed. New York: Frederick A. Stokes, 1927.

_____. *The Meaning of Czech History.* Translated by Peter Kussi. Chapel Hill: University of North Carolina Press, 1974.

_____. *The New Europe.* Cranbury: Bucknell University Press, 1972.

Massie, Robert. *Nicholas and Alexandra.* London: Pan Books, 1969.

Mawdsley, Evan. *The Russian Civil War.* New York: Pegasus, 2007.

May, Arthur. *The Passing of the Hapsburg Monarchy.* Volumes 1–2. Philadelphia: University of Pennsylvania Press, 1966.

McCullagh, Francis. *A Prisoner of the Reds.* New York: E.P. Dutton, 1922.

Melton, Carol Wilcox. *Between War and Peace.* Macon: Mercer University Press, 2001.

Messinger, Gary. *British Propaganda and the State in the First World War.* New York: Manchester University Press, 1992.

Mohr, Joan McGuire. *The Czech and Slovak Legion in Siberia, 1917–1922.* Jefferson: McFarland, 2012.

Morley, James. *The Japanese Thrust into Siberia.* New York: Columbia University Press, 1957.

Moyer, Laurence. *Victory Must Be Ours.* London: Leo Cooper, 1995.

Neville, Peter. *Eduard Beneš and Tomáš Masaryk: Czechoslovakia.* London: Haus, 2010.

Nicolson, Harold. *Peacemaking 1919.* New York: Grosset & Dunlap, 1965.

Orzoff, Andrea. *Battle for the Castle.* New York: Oxford University Press, 2009.

Palmer, Alan. *The Gardeners of Salonika.* New York: Simon and Schuster, 1965.

_____. *Twilight of the Habsburgs.* New York: Atlantic Monthly Press, 1994.

Palmer, James. *The Bloody White Baron.* New York: Basic Books, 2009.

Pánek, Jaroslav. *A History of the Czech Lands.* Prague: Karolinum Press, 2009.

Pastor, Peter, ed. *War and Society in East Central Europe: Revolutions and Interventions in Hungary and Its Neighboring States 1918–1919.* Boulder: East European Monographs, 1988.

Pastor, Peter, and Samuel R. Williamson Jr., eds. *Essays on World War I: Origins and Prisoners of War*. New York: Brooklyn College Press, 1983.

Pereira, N.G.O. *White Siberia*. Montreal: McGill-Queen's University Press, 1996.

Perman, D. *The Shaping of the Czechoslovak State*. Leiden: E. J. Brill, 1962.

Petroff, Serge. *Remembering a Forgotten War*. Boulder: East European Monographs, 2000.

Pipes, Richard. *Russia Under the Bolshevik Regime*. New York: Alfred A. Knopf, 1993.

_____. *Russia Under the Old Regime*. New York: Charles Scribner's, 1974.

_____. *The Russian Revolution*. New York: Alfred A. Knopf, 1990.

Rachamimov, Alon. *POWs and the Great War*. Oxford: Berg, 2002.

Rapport, Mike. *1848: Year of Revolution*. New York: Basic Books, 2009.

Rees, H. Louis. *The Czechs During World War I*. Boulder: East European Monographs, 1992.

Robinson, Paul. *The White Russian Army in Exile 1920–1941*. New York: Oxford University Press, 2002.

Rothenberg, Gunther, *The Army of Francis Joseph*. West Lafayette: Purdue University Press, 1976.

Rothwell, V. H. *British War Aims and Peace Diplomacy 1914–1918*. Oxford: Clarendon Press, 1971.

Rutherford, Ward. *The Russian Army in World War I*. London: Gordon Cremonesi, 1975.

Sanders, Michael, and Philip Taylor. *British Propaganda During the First World War 1914–18*. London: Macmillan, 1982.

Selver, Paul. *Masaryk*. Westport: Greenwood Press, 1975.

Seton-Watson, Robert. *A History of the Czechs and Slovaks*. London: Hutchinson, 1943.

_____. *Masaryk in England*. Cambridge: Cambridge University Press, 1943.

Seton-Watson, Hugh, and Christopher Seton-Watson. *The Making of a New Europe*. London: Methuen, 1981.

Shirer, William. *The Rise and Fall of the Third Reich*. New York: Simon and Schuster, 1960.

Siklós, András. *Revolution in Hungary and the Dissolution of the Multinational State*. Budapest: Akadémiai Kiadó, 1988.

Silverlight, John. *The Victors' Dilemma*. New York: Weybright and Talley, 1970.

Sked, Alan. *The Decline and Fall of the Habsburg Empire*. New York: Dorset Press, 1989.

Smele, Jonathon. *Civil War in Siberia*. New York: Cambridge University Press, 1996.

Smith, C. Jay. *The Russian Struggle for Power, 1914–1917*. New York: Greenwood Press, 1956.

Smith, Canfield. *Vladivostok Under Red and White Rule*. Seattle: University of Washington Press, 1975.

Snyder, Timothy. *The Reconstruction of Nations*. New Haven: Yale University Press, 2003.

Steed, Henry Wickham. *Through Thirty Years 1892–1922*, Volumes 1–2. New York: Doubleday, Page, 1924.

Stefancic, David. *Armies in Exile*. Boulder: East European Monographs, 2005.

Stevenson, David. *Armaments and the Coming of War*. Oxford: Clarendon Press, 1996.

Stewart, George. *The White Armies of Russia*. New York: Russell & Russell, 1970.

Stone, Norman. *The Eastern Front 1914–1917*. New York: Charles Scribner's, 1975.

Stuart, Sir Campbell. *Secrets of Crewe House*. London: Hodder and Stoughton, 1920.

Sukiennicki, Wiktor. *East Central Europe during World War I*. Volumes 1–2. Boulder: East European Monographs, 1984.

Taylor, A. J. P. *The Habsburg Monarchy 1809–1918*. Chicago: Chicago University Press, 1948.

Taylor, Edmond. *The Fall of the Dynasties*. New York: Doubleday, 1963.

Thompson, J. Lee. *Politicians, the Press & Propaganda: Lord Northcliffe & the Great War, 1914–1919*. Kent: Kent State University Press, 1999.

Thompson, John. *Russia, Bolshevism and the Versailles Peace*. Princeton: Princeton University Press, 1966.

Thompson, Mark. *The White War*. New York: Basic Books, 2009.

Tőkés, Rudolf. *Béla Kun and the Hungarian Soviet Republic*. Stanford: Hoover Institution Press, 1967.

Toma, Peter, and Dušan Kováč. *Slovakia*. Stanford: Hoover Institution Press, 2001.

Triska, Jan. *The Great War's Forgotten Front*. Boulder: East European Monographs, 1998.

Trotsky, Leon. *My Life*. New York: Charles Scribner's, 1930.

Tuchman, Barbara. *The Zimmerman Telegram*. New York: Bantam Books, 1958.

Unterberger, Betty Miller. *The United States, Revolutionary Russia and the Rise of Czechoslovakia*. Chapel Hill: University of North Carolina Press, 1989.

Ward, John. *With the "Die-Hards" in Siberia*. London: Cassell, 1920.

Wedgwood, C. V. *The Thirty Years War*. New York: Review Books, 1938.

Wheeler-Bennett, John. *Brest-Litovsk: The Forgotten Peace*. New York: Norton, 1971.

White, John Albert. *The Siberian Intervention*. Princeton: Princeton University Press, 1950.

Wildman, Allan. *The End of the Russian Imperial Army: The Old Army and the Soldiers' Revolt*. Volume 1. Princeton: Princeton University Press, 1980.

_____. *The End of the Russian Imperial Army: The Road to Soviet Power and Peace*. Volume 2. Princeton: Princeton University Press, 1987.

Wilson, Peter. *The Thirty Years War: Europe's Tragedy*. Cambridge: Harvard University Press, 2009.

Wingfield Nancy. *Flag Wars and Stone Saints*. Cambridge: Harvard University Press, 2007.

Wiskemann, Elizabeth. *Czechs and Germans*. London: Oxford University Press, 1938.

Wood, Alan, ed. *The History of Siberia*. London: Routledge, 1991.

Yurlova, Marina. *Cossack Girl*. New York: The Macaulay, 1934.

Zeman, Zbyněk. *The Break-Up of the Habsburg Empire 1914–1918*. London: Oxford University Press, 1961.

_____. *The Masaryks*. London: Weidenfeld and Nicolson, 1976.

Zeman, Zbyněk, and Antonín Klimek. *The Life of Edvard Beneš 1884–1948*. Oxford: Clarendon Press, 1997.

Index

Page numbers in ***bold italics*** indicate pages with illustrations